The History of Economic Thought

The International Library of Critical Writings in Economics

Series Editor: Mark Blaug
Professor Emeritus, University of London
Consultant Professor, University of Buckingham
Visiting Professor, University of Exeter

1. Multinational Corporations
   Mark Casson

2. The Economics of Innovation
   Christopher Freeman

3. Entrepreneurship
   Mark Casson

4. International Investment
   Peter J. Buckley

5. Game Theory in Economics
   Ariel Rubinstein

6. The History of Economic Thought
   Mark Blaug

7. Monetary Theory
   Thomas Mayer

8. Joint Production of Commodities
   Neri Salvadori and Ian Steedman

9. Industrial Organization
   Oliver E. Williamson

10. Growth Theory (Volumes I, II and III)
    Edwin Burmeister and Robert Becker

11. Microeconomics: Theoretical and Applied (Volumes I, II and III)
    Robert E. Kuenne

The History of Economic Thought

Edited by

Mark Blaug
*Professor Emeritus,
University of London
Consultant Professor,
University of Buckingham*

An Elgar Reference Collection

© Mark Blaug 1990. For copyright of individual articles please refer to the Acknowledgements.

All rights reserved. No part of this publication may be reproduced, stored in a retrieval system, or transmitted in any form or by any means, electronic, mechanical, photocopying, recording, or otherwise without the prior permission of the publisher.

Published by
Edward Elgar Publishing Limited
Gower House
Croft Road
Aldershot
Hants GU11 3HR
England

Edward Elgar Publishing Company
Old Post Road
Brookfield
Vermont 05036
USA

British Library Cataloguing in Publication Data
The history of economic thought – (International library of
  critical writers in economics).
  1. Economics. Theories, history
  I. Blaug, Mark, *1927–* II. Series
  330.1

ISBN 1 85278 191 2

Printed in Great Britain by Galliard (Printers) Ltd, Great Yarmouth

Contents

Acknowledgements vii
Introduction ix

PART I   **CLASSICAL POLITICAL ECONOMY**
1. D. F. Gordon (1959), 'What was the Labour Theory of Value?', *American Economic Review*, **49** (2), May, 462–72   3
2. P. J. McNulty (1967), 'A Note on the History of Perfect Competition', *Journal of Political Economy*, Pt 1, **75** (4), August, 395–9   14
3. T. Peach (1984), 'David Ricardo's Early Treatment of Profitability: A New Interpretation', *Economic Journal*, **94**, December 733–51   19
4. N-P. Ong (1983), 'Ricardo's Invariable Measure of Value and Sraffa's "Standard Commodity"', *History of Political Economy*, **15** (2), Summer, 207–27   38
5. W. O. Thweatt (1976), 'James Mill and the Early Development of Comparative Advantage', *History of Political Economy*, **8** (2), Summer, 207–34   59
6. W. J. Baumol (1977), 'Say's (at Least) Eight Laws, or What Say and James Mill May Really Have Meant', *Economica*, **44** (174), May, 145–61.   87
7. W. D. Grampp (1979), 'The Economists and the Combination Laws', *Quarterly Journal of Economics*, **93** (4), November, 501–22   104
8. P. Van Parijs (1980), 'The Falling-Rate-of-Profit Theory of Crisis: A Rational Reconstruction by Way of Obituary', *Review of Radical Political Economics*, **12** (1), Spring, 1–16   126

PART II   **THE MARGINAL REVOLUTION AND ITS AFTERMATH**
9. P. Mirowski (1984), 'Physics and the "Marginalist Revolution"', *Cambridge Journal of Economics*, **8** (155), December, 361–79   145
10. T. W. Hutchison (1969), 'Economists and Economic Policy in Britain after 1870', *History of Political Economy*, **1** (2), Autumn, 231–55   164
11. R. B. Ekelund, Jr and R. F. Hebert (1969), 'Public Economics at the Ecole des Ponts et Chaussées: 1830–1850', *Journal of Public Economics*, **2** (3), July, 241–56   189

12.	Phil Gramm (1970), 'Giffen's Paradox and the Marshallian Demand Curve', *Manchester School of Economic and Social Studies,* **38** (1), March, 65–71	205
13.	D. A. Walker (1972), 'Competitive Tâtonnement Exchange Markets', *Kyklos*, **25** (2), 345–63	212
14.	D. A. Walker (1984), 'Is Walras's Theory of General Equilibrium a Normative Scheme?', *History of Political Economy*, **16** (3), Autumn, 445–69	231
15.	D. A. Collard (1973), 'Leon Walras and the Cambridge Caricature', *Economic Journal*, **83** (33), June, 465–76	256
16.	C. E. Ferguson and D. L. Hooks (1971), 'The Wicksell Effects in Wicksell and Modern Capital Theory', *History of Political Economy*, **3** (2), Autumn, 353–72	268

PART III   THE TWENTIETH CENTURY

17.	P. Murrell (1983), 'Did the Theory of Market Socialism Answer the Challenge of Ludwig von Mises?: A Reinterpretation of the Socialist Controversy', *History of Political Economy*, **15** (1), Spring, 92–105	291
18.	D. P. O'Brien (1985), 'Research Programmes in Competitive Structure', *Journal of Economic Studies*, **10** (4), 29–51	305
19.	L. S. Moss and K.I. Vaughn (1986), 'Hayek's Ricardo Effect: A Second Look', *History of Political Economy*, **18** (4), Winter, 545–65	328
20.	D. Patinkin (1972), 'Friedman on the Quantity Theory and Keynesian Economics', *Journal of Political Economy*, **80** (5), September–October, 883–905	349
21.	T. Mayer (1980), 'David Hume and Monetarism', *Quarterly Journal of Economics*, **95** (1), August, 89–101	372

Name Index   385

Acknowledgements

The editor and publishers wish to thank the following who have kindly given permission for the use of copyright material.

Academic Press Inc. (London) Ltd for article: Mirowski (1984), 'Physics and the "Marginalist Revolution"', *Cambridge Journal of Economics*, **8** (4), December, 361–79.

American Economic Association for article: D F. Gordon (1959), 'What Was the Labor Theory of Value?', *American Economic Review*, **49** (2), May, 462–72.

Basil Blackwell for articles: D. A. Collard (1973), 'Léon Walras and the Cambridge Caricature', *Economic Journal*, **83** (33), June, 465–76; T. Peach (1984), 'David Ricardo's Early Treatment of Profitability: A New Interpretation', *Economic Journal*, **94**, December, 733–51; W. J. Baumol (1977), 'Say's (at Least) Eight Laws, or What Say and James Mill May Really Have Meant', *Economica*, **44** (174), May, 145–61; Phil Gramm (1970), 'Giffen's Paradox and the Marshallian Demand Curve', *The Manchester School*, **38** (1), March, 65–71.

Duke University Press for articles: T. W. Hutchison (1969), 'Economists and Economic Policy in Britain After 1870', *History of Political Economy*, **1** (2), Autumn, 231–55; C. E. Ferguson and D. L. Hooks (1971), 'The Wicksell Effect in Wicksell and Modern Capital Theory', *History of Political Economy*, **3** (2), Autumn, 353–72; W. O. Thweatt (1976), 'James Mill and the Early Development of Comparative Advantage', *History of Political Economy*, **8** (2), summer, 207–34; P. Murrell (1983), 'Did the Theory of Market Socialism Answer the Challenge of Ludwig von Mises? A Reinterpretation of the Socialist Controversy', *History of Political Economy*, **15** (1), spring, 92–105; N–P. Ong (1983), 'Ricardo's Invariable Measure of Value and Sraffa's "Standard Commodity"', *History of Political Economy*, **15** (2), summer, 207–27; D. A. Walker (1984), 'Is Walras's Theory of General Equilibrium a Normative Scheme?', *History of Political Economy*, **16** (3), autumn, 445–69; L. S. Moss and K. I. Vaughn (1986), 'Hayek's Ricardo Effect: A Second Look', *History of Political Economy*, **18** (4), winter, 545–67.

Elsevier Science Publishers B. V. for article: R. B. Ekelund Jnr and R. F. Hébert (1973), 'Public Economics at the Ecole des Ponts et Chaussées: 1830–1850, *Journal of Public Economics*, **2** (3), July, 241–56.

Helbing & Lichtenhahn Verlag AG, Basel for article: D. A. Walker (1972), 'Competitive Tâtonnement Exchange Markets', *Kyklos*, **25** (2), 345–63.

John Wiley & Sons, Inc. for articles: W. D. Grampp (1979), 'The Economists and the

Combination Laws', *Quarterly Journal of Economics*, **93** (4), November, 501–22; T. Mayer (1980), 'David Hume and Monetarism', *Quarterly Journal of Economics*, **95** (1), August, 89–101.

MCB University Press for article: D.P. O'Brien (1985), 'Research Programmes in Competitive Structure', *Journal of Economic Studies*, **10** (4), 29–51.

Union for Radical Political Economics for article: P. van Parijs (1980), 'The Falling-Rate-of-Profit Theory of Crisis: A Rational Reconstruction By Way of Obituary', *Review of Radical Political Economics*, **12** (1), spring, 1–16.

University of Chicago Press for articles: P. J. McNulty (1967), 'A Note on the History of Perfect Competition', *Journal of Political Economy*, Pt 1, **75** (4), August, 395–9; D. Patinkin (1972), 'Friedman on the Quantity Theory and Keynesian Economics', *Journal of Political Economy*, **80** (5), September–October, 883–905.

Every effort has been made to trace all the copyright holders but if any have been inadvertently overlooked the publishers will be pleased to make the necessary arrangement at the first opportunity.

In addition the publishers wish to thank the Library of the London School of Economics and Political Science for their assistance in obtaining these articles.

Introduction

The history of economic thought has its own history and no more stands still as a field of study than does price theory or macroeconomics. It, too, grows typically by slow accretions and refinements but is subject to occasional outbursts of new interpretations and revised perspectives. The source of such outbursts is frequently a novel development in modern economics that brings about a backward glance at forerunners and precursors, as a result of which old words suddenly take on a new meaning: sometimes it is the publication of a complete edition of a great man's writings which likewise is capable of throwing new light on familiar texts once these are placed in the context of a lifetime's output; and occasionally it is simply the march of historical events which cause us to re-examine our fundamental beliefs, including the great economists of the past from whom we acquired those beliefs in the first place. The following collection of readings offers examples of each of these sources of the fresh currents that have been blowing through the history of economic thought in recent years. Indeed, the history of economic thought has undergone so much 'revisionism' in the last 20 years that even so masterful a text book of yesterday as Schumpeter's *History of Economic Analysis* (1954) now seems in many of its pages to be curiously old-fashioned.

The principal object of this collection is to give the reader a flavour of these sea-changes that have come over the subject since, say, 1966; in fact, only three essays out of our total of 21 date from the 1960s and these are included simply because they are neglected classics of their kind; the remainder date from the 1970s and as many as 10 were published after 1980. Another object is to convey the many types and modes of analysis that characterize the modern history of economic thought from exegetical Talmuddism piling quotations upon quotations to the theoretical rigours of mathematical reconstructions to the review of policy pronouncement against the background of changing economic institutions. In the final analysis, however, every anthology is the expression of the personal prejudices, predilections and preoccupations of the editor – and is sometimes read for that reason. Let me therefore confess that every essay in this book was chosen, not perhaps first of all but certainly second of all, because I learned much from reading them and in more than one case because my perception of a particular topic or question was totally altered by reading them. If they do even half as much for a reader of this volume as they did for me, their reprinting will be fully justified.

The 21 papers are conveniently divided into three parts, dealing respectively with the periods 1776–1870, 1870 to roughly 1914 and 1914 to the present day. We begin with a paper by Donald Gordon on the labour theory of value, that centre-stone of the arch that was classical political economy. I have always thought that this is the perfect test-case for the argument that great economists should be prevented from practicing the history of economic thought – they almost always get it wrong. Ricardo misinterpreted Smith on the labour theory of value and then Marx misinterpreted Ricardo as well as Smith and the misinterpretations of the very meaning of the labour theory of value have grown apace ever since then. Gordon's sorting out of this confusion is so decisive that almost nothing more remains to be said on the issue. That was in 1959 and so far that prediction has not been falsified.

Paul McNulty's brief but trenchant note of the history of perfect competition was the first of a number of essays that have taught us that the dynamic defence of competition in *The Wealth of Nations* or Marshall's *Principles of Economics* is radically different from the static defence of competition in the writings of Cournot, Walras or for that matter Samuelson and Hicks. This is a question which is intimately associated with the great debate of the 1930s on economic calculation under socialism as further considered by Paul Murrell in Chapter 17 (see below).

The next two papers by Terry Peach and Paul Ong, and indeed the paper by Collard (Chapter 15) and the one by Ferguson and Hooks (Chapter 16), reflect the so-called Cambridge controversies in capital theory that raged in the 1960s and early 1970s and which created, as a sort of backwash, a re-examination of the writings of David Ricardo. Piero Sraffa, a leading figure in the Cambridge controversies, was also the modern editor of the *Complete Works and Correspondence of David Ricardo* and he read Ricardo in the light of his own ideas, coming at last to regard him as a muddled forerunner of Sraffian economics. A key issue was that of the existence of a so-called 'corn model' in Ricardo's early writings by which he was said to have analysed the determinant of the rate of profit without the aid of any theory of value. Peach exhumes Ricardo's pamphlets and letters and comes to the guarded conclusion that Sraffa was wrong: Ricardo never did hold the 'corn model'. Similarly, Ong compares Ricardo's exposition of the requirements of a so-called 'invariable measure of value' with Sraffa's treatment of the equivalent concept in Sraffa's *Production of Commodities by Means of Commodities* (1960), finding that they are not actually equivalent. Ong's article is exceedingly difficult to read but the fault is not that of Ong's making: the topic itself is simply intrinsically difficult. Whether the effort required to understand it is worthwhile is a matter of opinion but suffice it to say that it troubled Ricardo all his life and that pages and pages of Sraffa's book are devoted to it – and both Ricardo and Sraffa were very clever men.

William Thweatt's essay on James Mill and comparative advantage must rank as one of the greatest surprise stories in the entire history of economic thought. Whatever one might have thought about Ricardo's tergiversations in the labour theory of value, everyone always agreed that his discovery of the 'law' of comparative advantage was one of the three or four great breakthroughs in the history of economic thought. Alas, as Thweatt demonstrates more or less conclusively, the breakthrough was due to James Mill and not to Ricardo and the famous pages in Ricardo's *Principles* expounding the law in terms of Portuguese wine and English cloth were almost certainly written by the elder Mill.

Baumol's article on Say's Law is another tribute to James Mill, that greatest of the many neglected minor economists of the past. For it was James Mill rather than Jean Baptiste Say that really invented what later came to be known as Say's Law of Markets. The infinite gradation of meanings that can be assigned to that proposition is beautifully displayed in Baumol's elegant essay.

We switch grounds in William Grampp's paper on the classical economists and the Combination Laws that illegalized trade unions in the opening decades of the nineteen century. We have always known that the classical economists favoured the repeal of the Combination Laws, not because they favoured trade unions but because they favoured freedom, including the workman's right to join any and all organizations. Grampp shows, however, that their attitude was more complex than that, thus exemplifying one of our earlier points that there is nothing so satisfying as to say something new on a question that everyone else thought was as old as the hills.

The next paper by Peter van Parrijs is concerned with Marx. Marx made many predictions about economic growth under capitalism culminating in capitalism's eventual collapse and all these predictions were based on one grand prediction, namely, that of the inexorable tendency of the rate of profit to decline. Now, virtually every great economist before him (and since) had his own theory of why the rate of profit tends to decline in the course of economic progress but in all these theories the forces that bring about the decline are capable of being offset by a sufficiently high rate of technical progress; in Marx, however, the rate of profit tends to decline because of technical progress. Ever since Marx's death over a century ago, Marxists and Marxologists have furiously debated the cogency of Marx's arguments for his theory of the declining rate of profit and that debate continues to this day. Van Parrijs is convinced that it is time to write an obituary of that theory but, no doubt his obituary will not be the last and will be followed by further re-assessments 10 or 20 years hence.

We turn now to one of the greater watersheds in the history of economic thought, the Marginal Revolution so-called of the 1870s. Much has been written on this topic over the years and yet it remains in some ways as mysterious as ever. There is less debate on the nature of the revolution than on the question of why it should have taken place in the 1870s rather than much earlier or much later. What was there about the 1870s that caused three men in three different countries independently but simultaneously to forge a new economics grounded on marginal utility and all that? This is a question that has never been satisfactorily answered by anyone. Paul Mirowski thinks he has found *the* answer: they sought to duplicate in economics what they had found in physics and in so doing willy-nilly invented 'neoclassical economics'; in short, neoclassical economics is the bastardized physics of the middle of the century illegitimately imported into economics. I include this paper not because I believe it, because I do not, but because it is highly provocative on a topic that has been too long dormant.

Terence Hutchinson explores the ramifications of the Marginal Revolution in an essay that neatly demonstrates that the marginalists or neoclassicals had more or less the same attitude to problems of economic policy as the classicals. In other words, the Marginal Revolution, whatever it was, was not a revolution in applied economics, which of course only deepens the puzzling nature of that intellectual revolution. For example, Robert Ekelund and Robert Hébert show that French engineer–economists teaching at the Ecole des Ponts et Chaussées had arrived as early as the 1830s and 1840s at many of the elements that we now associate with the marginalists of the 1870s. In short, the Marginal Revolution of the 1870s had already happened 30 years earlier but the economic mainstream simply had not noticed it.

Jevons, Menger and Walras, the triumvirate responsible for the Marginal Revolution, all placed the 'law' of diminishing marginal utility at the centre of their theories and all employed that law, more or less rigorously, to justify the notion of a 'universal' law of demand: the quantity demanded of any good is always inversely related to its price. But Alfred Marshall discovered the exception to this law, Giffen's Paradox, and so deprived economics of its only 'universal' law. Marshall's analysis of Giffen's Paradox was so peremptory and confused that his motives for doing so, not to mention the validity of the exception he had found, has been the subject of endless discussion ever since. Although with the aid of modern theory, we can now prove very elegantly just when demand curves will be positively rather than negatively inclined, the empirical significance of Giffen's Paradox still remains in doubt. That is surely why commentators keep going back to Marshall's writings on the question; for him Giffen's Paradox was an empirical fact and not a theoretical insight. Phil Gramm expertly clarifies the long-outstanding debate on Giffen goods and Marshallian demand curves.

The next three papers all deal with general equilbrium theory and the writings of Leon Walras. Donald Walker writes first of all on *tâtonnement* in Walras, that is, on his attempt to give a realistic account of the process whereby prices in a competitive market converge on equilibrium; in the same way that Ricardo was never satisfied with his own analysis of the 'invariable measure of value', so Walras was never satisfied with his discussion of *tâtonnement*, altering and adding to his treatment of it in every successive edition of this *Elements of Pure Economics*.

Walker's second paper on Walras is an extensive critique of one of the last papers of William Jaffé, that doyen of Walras scholars who died in 1980. Jaffé came to believe, towards the end of his life, that he had long been wrong about Walras: Walras presented general equilibrium theory as a substantive theory about the functioning of a capitalist economy when in fact he had designed that theory as a justification for a Utopian reconstruction of society; in short, Walras dishonestly tried to pass off a normative theory in the guise of a positive one. When I first read Jaffé I was convinced by his argument but when I first read Walker's devastating refutation of Jaffé, I realized that I had swallowed Jaffé's line too quickly. (I hate to admit how often I have had the same experience in other respects).

The next articles by David Collard on Walras and Charles Ferguson and Donald Hooks on Wicksell deal with the impact on the history of economics of the modern Cambridge controversies on capital theory. Collard shows that Walras never operated with an aggregate production function, that bugbear of the modern post-Keynesian critique of neoclassical economics. Ferguson and Hooks examine the writings of Knut Wicksell in which the phenomenon of 'reswitching' first made its appearance. Reswitching refers to the possibility that an investment project that is profitable at one rate of interest but unprofitable at a higher rate of interest can paradoxically become profitable once again at a still higher rate of interest. What this means – if one thinks about it – is that the demand curve for capital is not necessarily negatively inclined and, even worse, that it may be impossible to derive any demand curve for capital. This paradox of reswitching was first denied and then admitted to be one of the logical flaws in the analytical structure of neoclassical economics; what divides neoclassical economists from their critics is not whether there is such a thing as reswitching but whether it is empirically important or not. There are obvious parallels here with the destruction of the universal law of demand by Marshall, combined with Marshall's assiduous denial of its quantitative significance. Be that as it may, Ferguson and Hooks show why reswitching occurred to Wicksell and why it has loomed larger in modern capital theory than he ever imagined it would.

That brings us to five papers on twentieth century economics. In a paper written in 1920 and later in a book published in 1922, the Austrian economist, Ludwig von Mises argued that a socialist economy, having abolished the price system, would be unable to allocate resources efficiently. The gauntlet thus thrown down to socialists was firmly picked up and thrown back in the 1930s by a number of left-wing economists, most noticeably by Oskar Lange, a Polish–American economist. Employing Walrasian general equilibrium theory, Lange argued that a socialist economy could mimic a market economy: if the managers of socialist factories would maximize profits and minimize costs, and if the central planning bureau would raise prices in accordance with excess demand, 'market socialism' would function exactly as does market capitalism but without the unemployment and unequal income distribution endemic to capitalism.

Lange's demonstration that rational economic calculation was possible under socialism – possible, not necessarily desirable – swept the board in the 1930s. I remember reading Lange in the 1950s and being totally convinced by it. Poor von Mises. He had it all wrong. Or did he? Peter Murrell's essay, when I first read it, hit me like Walker's essay on Jaffé. How could I have missed seeing it for myself?

One of the great revolutions in modern economics was the Keynesian Revolution. But another, and almost equally important one, was the Monopolistic Competition Theory by which at long last orthodox economics came to terms with the patent failure of the model of perfect competition to accord with *any* market structure that can be observed in the modern world. This is the subject of Denis O'Brien's paper in which he examines the writings of Chamberlin and Robinson, two founders of the Monopolistic Competition Revolution.

Keynes's great competitor in Britain in the 1930s was not Pigou, as Keynes tried to make out, but Friedrich Hayek. Hayek's theory of business cycles turned on the question whether booms were normally associated with greater capital-intensity in the structure of production, and obversely for slumps, and that was related to what Hayek dubbed the 'Ricardo Effect', which held that a general rise in money wages leads to a substitution of machinery for labour. Hayek's theory was vigorously attacked by Sraffa and eventually and more fatally by Nicholas Kaldor. Hayek reformulated the argument again and again but he never succeeded in persuading the rest of the economics profession that he had a tenable theory of business cycles. It was for this reason that he lost the battle against Keynes and retired from the field, turning increasingly from economics to political philosophy after about 1940. Laurence Moss and Karen Vaughn reassess this now forgotten episode in the history of economic thought, which had, and may one day again, have great practical significance.

Keynesian economics was, throughout the 1940s, 1950s and early 1960s, the only macroeconomics that was imaginable; it was succeeded by Monetarism and monetarism à la Friedman was in turn succeeded by monetarism à la Lucas and Sargent or the New Classical Economics. The last two papers in the volume are concerned with monetarism in its Friedmanian version. Don Patinkin demonstrates that there is more Keynes in Friedman than Fisher, that Friedman presented monetarism as a modernized quantity theory of money but that in fact his exposition of monetarism was deeply and profoundly influenced by Keynes's monetary theory of interest. Contrariwise, Thomas Mayer argues that most of monetarism is in David Hume; monetarism, far from being a new brand of monetary economics, is over 200 years old.

Mark Blaug
March 1990

Part I
Classical Political Economy

[1]

STUDIES IN THE CLASSICAL ECONOMICS
WHAT WAS THE LABOR THEORY OF VALUE?

By DONALD F. GORDON
University of Washington

In a discipline that has long been rife with confused controversy, there is no concept, or perhaps I should say there is no word, which has borne a greater share of this confusion than has the notion of value; and around no set of doctrines concerning value have the problems been greater than around those that are normally called labor theories of value. This paper will attempt to establish, or at least affirm, two points; first—based mainly on accepted interpretations—that no major economist of the classical period held what would, by modern usage, be called a labor theory of value; second, that the three most eminent alleged labor theorists did nevertheless hold what could be accurately called a labor theory, but in a different and radically distinct sense of that term. Except for a few words on Marx, I will confine myself to the English literature.

By the modern meaning of the phrase "theory of value," the labor theory of value is presumably the proposition that commodities exchange at ratios that are reciprocals of the quantities of labor involved in their production, including, of course, that involved in the creation of capital goods, back to the Stone Age if necessary. Let us call this proposition "the labor theory of relative price." I will now turn to a brief survey of the classical period, looking for conclusive statements indicating that such a proposition was or was not a part of any leading system.

The case of Adam Smith presents little difficulty. In Chapter VII of Book I ("Of the Natural and Market Price of Commodities") he provided a classic account of how, in a competitive market, the prices of commodities—through shifts in the allocation of the factors—approach equality with their money costs of production, where the latter are estimated by the quantities of the three traditional factors remunerated at their natural or usual rates. Surely here there is no labor theory of relative prices.

Professor Stigler has recently[1] given us a convincing demonstration that Ricardo, likewise, did not subscribe to this proposition. Like Adam Smith, he accepted the theorem on the long-run equality of price

[1] George Stigler, "Ricardo and the 93% Labor Theory of Value," *A.E.R.*, June, 1958, pp. 357-367.

and cost. For all nonagricultural commodities, in which land is presumed not to enter, long-run average and marginal costs are presumed to be constant, but among these the proportions of capital to labor vary considerably. Thus fluctuations in the rates of wages and profits will cause fluctuations in the relative prices of these commodities, unconnected with any changes in their relative labor contents. This is the critical conclusion for our present purposes, and one which Ricardo demonstrated tirelessly, over and over again, in his *Principles* and other writings. It is also true, but not relevant to our purposes, that Ricardo believed that the influence of fluctuations in wages and interest rates on relative prices is not large enough to be empirically significant[2] On the basis of a comment of Ricardo's that this influence on relative prices "could not exceed 6 or 7 per cent,"[3] Stigler felicitously names this a "93 per cent labor theory of value" (or in our terms, a 93 per cent theory of relative price).

There is little question that, with two debatable exceptions, all the important participants in the post-Ricardian controversies of the 1820's and 1830's denied that commodities exchange in proportion to the quantity of labor embodied in their production. The two dubious cases were James Mill and McCulloch. Both claimed that Ricardo had gone too far in conceding to capital the capacity to influence exchange ratios, and that these were solely determined by labor. But a close reading suggests that they were both playing with words. They were concerned more with whether the words sounded as if everything was being attributed to labor rather than with the facts that the words described. They did not shrink from boldly changing the meaning of the word labor so that everything could be assigned to that word.[4] At

---

[2] Stigler distinguishes between the two positions by designating the cost-of-production theory as analytical and the labor theory as empirical. This may exaggerate, a little, the difference between them. If we ask the question of the cost-of-production theory that Stigler asks of the labor theory—did Ricardo believe that the relative values of commodities are governed exclusively by their cost of production?—we would have to answer in the negative for the analytical theory as well. For Ricardo believed that some commodities cannot be reproduced, some are monopolized, and so forth. On the other hand, he did not think these exceptions as significant, particularly for his purposes, as differences in labor-capital ratios. For most questions—but not all, as the foreign trade analysis shows—he used the cost-of-production model, and in this sense, he "believed" it.

[3] The reference is to a particular numerical example. Cf. *The Works and Correspondence of David Ricardo* (Sraffa ed.; Cambridge, England, 1951), Vol. 1, p. 36. Hereafter references to the *Works* will be by volume and page number only and included in the text. This 93% does not mean, of course, that at any point of time the relative price of commodities could not diverge from their relative labor contents by more than 7 per cent. Ricardo was only referring to changes in relative price caused by wage and profit fluctuations.

[4] Perhaps the most clear cut and flagrant is Mill's comment: "If the wine which is put in the cellar is increased in value one-tenth by being kept a year, one-tenth more of labor may be correctly considered as having been expended upon it." *Elements of Political Economy* (2nd ed.; London, 1824), pp. 97-98.

other points they were less concerned with the word labor, and turned their attention to the words regulate or determine. Mill, in particular, can normally be interpreted as arguing that if we hold interest rates, factor combinations, wages of different qualities of labor, and so forth, constant, then relative labor contents determine (but are not necessarily equal to the reciprocal of) exchange ratios. It is, of course, always true, and always trivial, that if we turn all variables but two in a system into constants, the one remaining exogenous variable can be said to determine the one remaining dependent variable.[5]

We have not the time here to follow McCulloch and James Mill through all their tedious and constantly shifting semantic arguments by which they strove to preserve the sound of their first principle, and fortunately it is not necessary. For nowhere, to my knowledge, did they clearly assert what I have termed the labor theory of relative price, and by their enthusiastic acceptance of Ricardo's theorem on the effects on relative values of fluctuations in wages and profits, they explicitly denied it. Moreover, from what we know of the close personal relationships among Mill, McCulloch, and Ricardo, we may reasonably infer that had a more than verbal difference existed among them, we would see more of it in their correspondence and in Ricardo's correspondence with Malthus. Certainly Ricardo did not believe his differences with either of his disciples were more than terminological. For he refers to McCulloch using "the word labor in a sense somewhat different to Political Economists in general" (Volume IX, page 377) and in the last letter of his life to Mill he writes: "*We all agree with respect to the facts*, but it is impossible to *say* that the value of commodities is proportioned to the quantity of labor employed upon them." (Volume IX, page 385; my italics.)

Having disposed of the two possibly controversial cases, we may quickly run through the remaining writers, largely by assertion. Ricardo's other followers accepted his nonlabor-theory position; some of his opponents, presuming, incorrectly, that he had a labor theory, criticized him on precisely that account.[6] I do not know of any interpretation of the classical period that has held Say, Senior, or Longfield to

---

[5] This I take to be the meaning of the passage: "The value of the first capital was regulated by quantity of labor; the value of that which was produced by the first capital was regulated by the value of the first; that, however, was valued by labor; the last, therefore, is valued by labor; and so on, without end, as often as successive productions may be supposed to be made. But, if the value of all capital must be determined by labor, it follows, upon suppositions, that the value of all commodities must be determined by labor." (*Ibid.*, p. 102.)

The case cited by Stigler, *op. cit.*, p. 363, may be interpreted, I think, in a similar manner. The same is true of the argument of the teenage John Stuart Mill. Cf. *The Measure of Value*, 1822 (Baltimore, 1936), pp. 19-20. Later, of course, Mill rejected even the verbal form of the labor theory of relative price.

[6] See Stigler, *op. cit.*

have had a labor theory of relative price. Mill, when he escaped from the surveillance of his father, added a variety of additional determinants to the Ricardian scheme. The so-called "Ricardian Socialists" are likewise no problem. Despite a great deal of discussion over the importance of labor and the significance of the laboring classes to society, I can find among them no clear (or even obscure) statement of the labor theory of relative price. Finally, Marx is now acknowledged by all commentators to have specifically rejected the notion that commodities exchange in proportion to their labor contents. While this was obscure in Volume I, it was made clear in Volume III and had, in fact, been indicated in the *Theories of Surplus Value* written before Volume I was published.[7]

Finally, we should recognize the fact that most of the writers in the classical period occasionally considered a model in which they either abstracted from the existence of capital or assumed that the ratio between capital and labor was the same in all industries. The best known example of the first was Smith's "early and rude state of society," a model which was briefly considered by a great number of later writers. Of a similar nature is Ricardo's treatment of international trade, where he rests his argument on his frequently expressed opinion that divergences from the labor theory of relative price are of little significance in practice. Finally, Marx's analysis of Volume I presumes that capital-labor ratios are the same in all industries. These cases do not disturb the general principle of the nonexistence of the labor theory of relative price, for in no case do they represent the complete model of th economist in question.

In this brief survey we have searched for statements clearly rejecting or accepting the labor theory of relative price. We have omitted from consideration a large number of statements by classical writers, stressing, in some manner or other, the importance of labor, but from which it is extremely difficult to derive any clear meaning. One of the best known examples is Smith's opening proposition: "The annual labor of every nation is the fund which originally supplies it with all the necessaries and conveniences of life."[8] Whatever he meant by this, it is this type of remark—of which, of course, there are a great many in Smith—that appears to have become the foundation of what was more or less standard fare among the Ricardian Socialists. (They would have been better named "Smithian Socialists.") Thompson, for example, asserts: "Labor is the sole universal measure, as well as the characteristic distinction of wealth. . . . Without labor there is no wealth. Labor is its distinguishing attribute . . . labor is the sole parent

---

[7] *Histoire des Doctrines Economiques* (Paris, 1925), Vol. VI, pp. 254, 256.
[8] *The Wealth of Nations* (Cannan ed.), p. lvii.

of wealth."⁹ And Hodgskin argued: "The *real price* of a coat or a pair of shoes or a loaf of bread, *all* which nature demands from man in order that he have either of these very useful articles is a certain quantity of labor."¹⁰ (Hodgskin's italics.)

With a little ingenuity and imagination we may attribute meanings to some of these obscurities, and to assert what the author "was trying to do" or "in effect was saying." But while these exercises may be good for the imagination, the results are very difficult to document. Fortunately for our present purposes they are unnecessary. The very obscurity of their typical proposition that "labor is the sole producer of value" suggests that those authors could not have intended it to have the same meaning as the proposition that "goods exchange in proportion to their labor contents." For being tolerably literate men, the probability of their using so many incorrect or ambiguous words in succession—which would be necessary for them to intend the second but state the first—must be close to zero. Thus while I would not want to suggest that I understand these propositions, I think we may reject, with great confidence, the idea that they contain a labor theory of relative price.[11]

I conclude that the main economists of the classical period did not hold what I have termed the labor theory of relative price, and that whatever may be the true import of many of the assertions about labor, they do not entail acceptance of that theory. Parenthetically we should note that while there never was a labor theory of value in that sense of the phrase, it could not be rejected today for demonstrated lack of scientific respectability. It is, of course, an unrealistic theory in its assumptions, but in this era one would not expect it to be dismissed on that account. Whether it predicts efficiently is largely unknown for it has rarely been tried. But when tested a few years ago on the problem for which Ricardo used it—the explanation of commodity movements in foreign trade—it performed at least as well in that field as do many currently more popular (and vastly more expensive) models do in their fields. Whether it predicts usefully may be more doubtful.

Nonetheless, I believe there were theories that could properly be called labor theories of value in quite a different sense, and I shall briefly outline what I take these theories to be, in the works of three pre-eminent alleged labor theorists: Smith, Ricardo, and Marx. The common element in labor theories is the notion that an absolute number

---

[9] *The Distribution of Wealth* (London, 1824), pp. 6-7.
[10] *Labor Defended Against the Claims of Capital* (London, 1831), p. 75.
[11] They may be the equivalent of what I shall later term the labor theory of absolute value, in either the Smithian or Ricardian form. The principle we use in this case may be termed the "principle of the nonequivalence of simplicity and confusion," or, for brevity and obscurity, the "principle of nonequivalence." It is frequently useful in exploring some of the darker recesses of the history of economics, if one is searching for merely negative conclusions.

may be attached to any economic good, independently of any other economic good, and that these absolute numbers are either the labor time that the commodity purchases or "contains." It is essential in interpreting what may be called labor theories of absolute value to distinguish between these numbers and the quite distinct, albeit related, set of numbers represented by exchange ratios. This is true even in the case, as in Smith, where the ratio between any two of the absolute numbers necessarily equals an exchange ratio. It is, perhaps, even more essential to recognize that all labor theories are normative proposals— they have that philosophical standing whether or not their authors were conscious of it. They are not normative in the simple sense of specifically advocating that all product should go to labor, but in the more general sense in which all proposals of units of social accounting are normative.

In the *Wealth of Nations* this notion of absolute value is developed in the chapter, "Of the Real and Nominal Price of Commodities, or of Their Price in Labor and Their Price in Money."[12] In that chapter, among other things, Smith proposes to assign an absolute number to every commodity, the amount of labor time required to purchase it, on the grounds that there is a certain constancy in the pain cost, or psychological disutility, of an hour's labor:

> Equal quantities of labor at all times and places, may be said to be of equal value to the laborer. In his ordinary state of health, strength and spirits; in the ordinary degree of his skill and dexterity, he must always lay down the same portion of his ease, his liberty and his happiness. The price which he pays must always be the same, whatever may be the quantity of goods which he receives in return for it. Of these, indeed, it may sometimes purchase a greater and sometimes a smaller quantity; but it is their value which varies, not that of the labor which purchases them.[13]

Smith usually calls the absolute value of a commodity "real price," sometimes "real value." It serves a somewhat similar function for Smith that modern welfare economics does. It enables him to estimate whether an individual or society is better off over changes in time and place.

For Ricardo, the absolute value of a commodity is the "difficulty or facility" involved in its production (Volume I, pages 273, 277, and Volume II, page 34). Most often he refers to it as "real value," sometimes as "absolute value" (Volume IV, pages 357 ff.) and occasionally as "positive value" (Volume IX, page 2). It is contrasted with "exchange value" or "relative value" which are terms for relative price. It is a cost theory of absolute value in the sense that it is a proposal to use the number of inputs in a commodity as a unit of social accounting. It is not a cost theory of relative price in either the sense that the long-

---

[12] I have found the best interpretation of this chapter to be that of Professor V. W. Bladen in "Adam Smith on Value," *Essays in Political Economy* (Toronto, 1938), pp. 27-43, and I have followed many of his suggestions.
[13] Smith, *op. cit.*, p. 33.

run price will equal money cost, conceived as constant with respect to output (which he also held); nor is it a cost theory in the sense that the relative values of commodities reflect Marshall's real (psychological) marginal disutilities.

The celebrated "measure of value" is a proposal to measure absolute value by observing exchange ratios. If among a class of commodities, all of which have a constant proportion of capital to labor, there is one single commodity whose inputs per unit of output never change through technological progress, that commodity is a perfect measure of the absolute value of all other commodities of that class. Why? Because for any one of them, observed exchange value (or relative price) in terms of the measure will change precisely in proportion to any changes in the inputs required to produce it; or, in other words, in proportion to its absolute value.[14] Further, changes in wages and inverse changes in profit rates will not produce any fluctuations in relative price between this measure and others of its class that would lead us to believe that a change in absolute value had occurred when in fact it had not.

Of course, commodities vary from one to another in the proportions of labor to capital involved in their production; so Ricardo had to choose as a measure of value a commodity with an average ratio of these factors. In terms of this commodity, some commodities would rise and some would fall when wages rose and profits fell. Relative values would change while absolute values stayed constant, and this would be an imperfection in the measure; nevertheless, it is the best available. The commodity with an average ratio of capital to labor is not chosen so as to create an index of general purchasing power among the mass of commodities; it is to minimize the fluctuations in exchange ratios with the measure when wages rise and profits fall. A perfect index of general purchasing power may, in fact, be a poor measure of value, for it overlooks the fact that the value of all commodities may fall (Volume IV, page 400).

The notion of a general fall in the value of all commodities would, of course, be nonsense if by value he meant relative price. The major part of Ricardo's writings on value, including the never ending discussion of the measure of value, would likewise be meaningless. Without absolute value there is nothing to measure.

But if we try to discover whether Ricardo meant by "difficulty or facility of production" the quantity of labor alone or the quantity of labor and "waiting," the answer is not obvious. He speaks occasionally of "capital and labor" as the determining items (Volume I, page 18 and 50) and he replies to Malthus' accusation that he confuses cost and

---

[14] For this problem Ricardo assumed no changes, autonomous or induced, in the ratio of capital to labor.

value, that Malthus is correct only if cost includes profits (Volume I, page 47; Volume II, pages 34, 101). Finally, on one occasion, at least, he refers to the quantity of labor and time as the determinants (Volume IX, page 304).

On the other hand, there is strong evidence that Ricardo regarded labor, with respect to absolute value, as not only quantitatively the most important, but qualitatively different—probably because of his view of its pain cost as opposed to mere "time." The problem, to repeat, is not one of determining empirical fact or logical deduction, but of normative definition. While in discussing relative price, he sometimes neglects to mention capital. When he turns to absolute value, it is in the overwhelming majority of cases, that he mentions labor alone, and in emotive language that he never applies to capital (e.g., Volume IX, page 397). Moreover, where he refers to capital and labor as determining absolute value, capital probably means, as it often does, merely accumulated labor rather than waiting. Even the proposition that "real value" includes profits and wages (Volume II, page 34) is not conclusive. For real value is estimated (but not defined) by the exchange rate between a commodity and the measure of value; and this relative price must include all costs, even if it were being used to estimate the quantity of one input alone.

Thus apart from the single (so far as I know) mention of time (quoted above) there is virtually no evidence that "difficulty or facility" of production is not defined in labor alone and convincing evidence that labor is qualitatively or normatively of special importance. In almost his last writing on the subject, and in the only place (so far as I know) that he refers to "what I *mean* by the word value" (Volume IX, page 397, my italics), he comes as close to a formal definition as he ever does; but he does not mention profits or waiting, and he dwells glowingly on the significance of labor. The theory of absolute value, if not of relative price, appears more than a 93 per cent labor theory.[15]

The function of absolute value in Ricardo's system is to enable him to discuss the shares of the factors in the total product. In his earlier essay on rent (Volume IV, pages 1-41) the shares had been conceived of as being distributed in a homogeneous product, corn. In his *Principles* he wanted to talk of wages and profits in terms of a homogeneous substance, and (absolute) value serves that purpose.

---

[15] Whatever the definition of the inputs that defines absolute value, it is estimated by the measure of value. In all cases it will be imperfect when wages rise and profits fall, but will be accurate when inputs fall. If we use the measure to estimate the aggregate value of a group of commodities at a point of time, then in both cases it will be a rather crude index (but with different weights in the two cases) of what it is designed to measure. But if we compare Ricardo's measure with the relationship between points on a social preference function (if one could be designed to satisfy our current values) and net national product, the superiority of the one or the other is not obvious.

When we turn to Marx the labor theory of (absolute) value is much more straightforward and distinct from relative price. Whatever the phrases such as the "substance of value" meant in Marx's mind—in particular, whether it referred to the social (moral?) relationship between men—his value is logically equivalent to calculating production by counting inputs of labor time. This means that by normative definition labor produces all value and is "exploited."

If the labor theory is one of absolute value, great confusion can arise from attempting to see in that theory an alternative to the modern theory of relative price. It was not concerned, as is the latter, with the logical derivation of solution values, in a rigorously defined model, possessing some empirical reference. In all three cases of the labor theory the assigning of absolute numbers to economic goods was for the purpose of making numerical comparisons that involved value judgments. It should be obvious that any unit of social accounting, such as the present-day national product, involves similar value judgments. Production even at its most "physical" only involves moving matter around, and when we propose rules for counting the total product of an economy, we are proposing value weights for the different components —components that had quite as much physical content before as after the alleged production. The current custom of using relative prices as weights is merely one, among a possibly large number of "reasonable" normative proposals, to add up to what we stubbornly, but misleadingly, call physical production. The labor theory is another.

Without going deeply into the fundamental philosophical standing of value or normative propositions, it is clear that they cannot be rigorously deduced from non-normative axioms, nor can empirical evidence be brought to bear on them in the usual sense. Modern critics, steeped in the logico-empirical tradition and approaching the labor theories with the empirical generalizations and clean theorems of the modern theory of relative price in mind, tend to dismiss them as hopeless jumbles of confusion. Even if more sympathetic they tend to suspect a large metaphysical component is included in the labor theory of value. This is true, but in somewhat the same sense that the index of industrial production has, likewise, a metaphysical element.[16]

The normative nature of the labor theory is clearly seen in the character of the defenses put forth by its proponents. Smith can only claim that labor time "may be said" to have always equal value to the laborer; he proceeds to appeal to our intuitive feeling of pain cost and

---

[16] A recent writer comments on Ricardo's concept of absolute value: "But there is nothing metaphysical in this: absolute value is simply a unit of social accounting." Marc Blaug, *Ricardian Economics* (New Haven, 1958), p. 36. I should say, rather, that there is something metaphysical in this because it is a unit of social accounting.

continues with more poetic assertion. Malthus adopted Smith's constant, but without apparently catching sight of the intuitive appeal to pain cost, and in his interminable discussions with Ricardo can only assert and reassert the constancy of the value of labor. But Ricardo in turn can only point to its fluctuations in relative price, which is irrelevant to the Smith-Malthus definition; he objects primarily to the "language" of his opponents; and he likewise can only iterate and reiterate—with occasional dramatic effects (e.g., Volume IX, page 397) —that value can only mean the toil and trouble of acquisition. This is not an argument of logic or of empirical evidence.

Marx, on the other hand, perhaps because of his background in Hegelian philosophy, attempts a proof of the labor theory[17]—a proof which is a travesty of logic. Of the various fallacies that make up this proof, the most egregious is the attempt to establish a fact (or a value proposition) from the definition of a term (the equality sign). But while Marx's proof of his labor theory of value is nonsensical, it is not because the labor theory is formally invalid or empirically false, and it would be quite as nonsensical to attempt a proof of its invalidity.

The failure to mark the essential difference between a logico-empirical theory of relative price and a normative theory of absolute value has been a rich source of confusion in the commentaries. Smith has been accused by the critics of having three theories of one phenomena: a labor cost theory, a labor command theory, and a cost-of-production theory. In fact, he has a definition of "better off," a primitive model of relative price, and a civilized cost-of-production model of relative price.

Ricardo's two closest disciples, McCulloch[18] and Mill,[19] clearly recognized his distinct theories. Beginning with Bailey,[20] however, what may be called the orthodox critics subjected Ricardo's discussion to analysis in terms of their own relative-price definition of the word value; and if critical, they found much to criticize in Ricardo's use of terms. These commentators, believing him to be analyzing relative price, have frequently mistaken his emphasis on labor, when speaking of absolute value, and have ascribed to him a labor theory of relative price.[21] The Marxist writers have on the whole been superior in recognizing in Ricardo a certain duality with respect to the term value, but

[17] *Capital* (Modern Library ed.), pp. 43-45.
[18] *Principles of Political Economy* (4th ed.; Edinburgh, 1849), pp. 315 ff.
[19] *Elements of Political Economy* (3rd ed.; London, 1826), pp. 73 ff., where the precise distinction is drawn that was blurred in the first edition (London, 1821), p. 59.
[20] Samuel Bailey, *A Critical Dissertation on the Nature, Measures and Causes of Value, . . .*, 1825 (London, 1931).
[21] To the methodological naïveté that Stigler credits with producing the misinterpretation of Ricardo's theory of relative price (cf. Stigler, *op. cit.*, p. 366) I would add, with perhaps equal weight, the confusion over relative price and absolute value and Ricardo's differential emphasis on labor between them.

they have generally looked upon absolute value and relative price as two aspects of, or two approaches to, the same phenomena.[22] They have, in interpreting both Ricardo and Marx, failed to mark the radical distinction between normative judgments and theorems derived from a model.

It should be unnecessary to add that we cannot discuss the "validity" of these labor theories in the usual sense; but we can compare them with our own intuitive judgments. The Smith version of the labor theory —that an hour's labor may be viewed as somehow possessing, via disutility or otherwise, a constant amount of moral weight—is broadly accepted by the unreflecting common sense of the contemporary world. If this were not true, we would not be exposed, as we now are, to brief tables showing the number of minutes required to earn a loaf of bread or a pair of shoes in the Soviet Union and the United States (and which, provided we are not too careless in choosing commodities, show us that we are better off). Even the sophisticated find it hard to resist the idea that there is some normative significance in the fact that for so many commodities an hour's labor buys so much more than it did in 1900.

On the other hand, the Ricardo-Marx labor index method of measuring total output does not have the same intuitive appeal. They were interested in distribution, and this was defined in terms of the shares of society's labor inputs that went to labor or profits out of a total that, by definition, could not increase. How neatly did Ricardo unwittingly provide the conceptual framework for Marx's class struggle! The modern mind cannot help but feel, with Smith, that the purchasing power of an hour's labor is a more significant variable.

[22] The same is true of the famous distinction that was originated by von Wieser (cf. *Natural Value* [New York, 1956], pp. xxvii-xxx) and used by Whitaker (cf. A. C. Whitaker, *History and Criticism of the Labor Theory of Value* [New York, 1904]) between "philosophical" and "empirical" approaches to value in Smith and Ricardo.

[2]

A NOTE ON THE HISTORY OF PERFECT COMPETITION

PAUL J. McNULTY[*]
Columbia University

PROFESSOR STIGLER opened his history of perfect competition with Adam Smith's treatment of the subject,[1] but noted that "Smith did not state how he was led to . . . [the] elements of a concept of competition." "We may reasonably infer," he added, "that the conditions of numerous rivals and of independence of action of these rivals were matters of direct observation" (Stigler, 1957, p. 2). The purpose of this note is to suggest (1) that Adam Smith was led to the concept of competition by his acquaintance with the economic literature of his time, and that the casualness with which he introduced and employed the term in the *Wealth of Nations* reflected the fact that competition was by then a familiar concept of economic reasoning, and (2) that the Smithian concept of competition was of a fundamentally different character than that which was later perfected by economic theorists.

Competition, as Stigler has pointed out, "entered economics from common discourse, and for long it connoted only the independent rivalry of two or more persons" (Stigler, 1957, p. 1). But any implication that its transition from an element of common discourse to a concept of economic analysis was a contribution of Adam Smith must be rejected. Neither the concept itself nor its analytical function was original with him. The idea that monopoly ("*monopolium*")

[*] I wish to thank my colleague, Maurice Wilkinson, for helpful discussion of some of the points dealt with herein, and to acknowledge the support of the faculty research fund of the Graduate School of Business, Columbia University.

[1] This is, of course, a not uncommon practice in economic literature. J. M. Clark, for example, in a chapter entitled "How Our Thinking about Competition Took Shape," also commences his historical survey of the subject with Adam Smith, whom he calls "a prophet of competition" (Clark, 1961, p. 24).

would result in high prices while competition in the form of many sellers ("*polypolium*") would drive prices down is found in the writings of the seventeenth-century German mercantilist, Johann Joachim Becher (Heckscher, 1962, p. 271). And Boisguillebert, according to Schumpeter, found in competition an "economic principle of order quite as clearly as did A. Smith more than half a century later. . . . His conception of competitive 'proportionate equilibrium' was as definite as A. Smith's" (Schumpeter, 1954, p. 216). Although Cantillon's was more explicitly a "bargaining" type of economic rivalry than was the concept of competition later employed by Smith, his discussion of market price foreshadowed Smith's treatment of the subject in several respects.

Suppose the Butchers on the one hand & the Buyers on the other. The price of meat will be determined after some altercation: & a pound of Beef will bear about the same ratio to a piece of money, that all the Beef offered for sale in the Market bears to all the money brought thither to buy Beef.

This proportion is settled by altercation; the Butcher holds out for a price according to the number of buyers he sees; the Buyers, on their part, offer less according as they believe that the Butcher will have less market: the price settled upon by some is ordinarily followed by the others. Some are more skillful in getting good prices for their merchandise, others more adroit in discrediting it. Though this method of fixing the prices of things in the Market has no just or geometrical basis, since it often depends upon the eagerness or the facility of a small number of Buyers or of Sellers; yet it does not seem possible to arrive at it in any other more suitable way. It remains true that the quantity of commodities or of merchandise offered for sale, compared with the demand or with the number of Buyers, is the basis upon which peo-

395

ple fix, or always think they fix, the prevailing market prices; & that in general these prices do not differ much from the intrinsic value [Monroe, 1948, pp. 261, 262].

A decade before the *Wealth of Nations* appeared, Turgot wrote:

> The competition of rich entrepreneurs engaged in agriculture establishes the current price of leases in proportion to the fertility of the land and the price at which its produce sells, always according to the estimates which the farmers make of all their expenses and the profit they should make on their advances; they can pay the proprietor only the surplus.
>
> But when the competition between them is very keen, they pay him all this surplus, the proprietor leasing his land only to the one who offers the highest rent [Monroe, 1948, p. 360].

Hume, in a letter to Turgot in 1766, foreshadowed not only Smith but also Jevons' law of indifference by noting that "the price of labour will always depend on the Quantity of Labour and the Quantity of Demand . . . there cannot be two prices for the same species of Labour . . . for the high price would tempt so many hands to go into that Species of Industry as must immediatly [*sic*] bring down the price" (Hume, 1955, pp. 208–9); and Turgot, in a reply, remarked that the wage rate (and presumably any other price) is "reduced by competition to its precise level." "In a country where trade and industry are free and active," he added, "competition sets . . . profit at the lowest rate possible" (Hume, 1955, pp. 210, 211).

Probably the most complete pre-Smithian analysis of competition was that of Sir James Steuart, who stressed that competition might exist among either buyers or sellers. When supply falls short of demand, he wrote, it "occasions a competition among the buyers, and raises the current, that is, the ordinary prices . . . [but] it is from the effects of competition among sellers that I apprehend prices are brought down" (Steuart, 1767, I, 174, 189). The ideal situation, according to Steuart, was that in which competition existed simultaneously among both buyers and sellers, which he termed "double competition."

Double competition is, when, in a certain degree, it takes place on both sides of the contract at once, or vibrates alternatively from one to the other. This is what restrains price to the adequate value of the merchandize. . . . *Double competition* is what is understood to take place in almost every operation of trade; it is this which prevents the excessive rise of prices; it is this which prevents their excessive fall. While *double competition* prevails, the balance is perfect, trade and industry flourish [Steuart, 1767, I, 196–97].

These examples suffice to show that by the time the *Wealth of Nations* appeared, competition was a familiar concept in economic writing and that its analytical function was its recognized tendency to bring market price to a level which would eliminate both excessive profits and unsatisfied demand, that is, to the lowest level sustainable over the long run. Adam Smith's employment of competition as the force tending to equate market and natural price was thus not original but was eminently in the tradition of the economic literature of his time. His contribution with respect to the concept of competition was the systematization of earlier thinking on the subject and, more importantly, the elevation of competition to the level of a general organizing principle of economic society—an achievement far greater, surely, than that of any of his predecessors.

Rather than considering Adam Smith as the progenitor of a concept whose refinement came at the hands of a group of successors, it is more accurate, as far as the history of competition is concerned, to think of Smith's work as marking the end of one era and the beginning of another. The pre-Smithian period saw the gradual emergence of a body of literature in which price determination through the principle of competition was coming to replace ethically and politically oriented price administration as the focus of economic analysis. The *Wealth of Nations* was in many ways the capstone of this work. After Smith's great achievement, the concept of competition became quite literally the *sine qua non* of economic reasoning. Ricardo limited his analysis, as Smith himself had not done, to those situations in "which competition operates without restraint" (Ricardo, 1955, p. 6); and John Stuart Mill went on to assert, without dissent from the profession, that "only through the principle of competition has political economy any pretension to the character of a science" (Mill, 1864, I, 306). The function of competition in late-nineteenth-century economics came to be more than simply the assurance of allocative efficiency in resource use; it also gave to economics itself an analytical rigor without which, it was felt, its claims to the status of science would be seriously weakened. If "There is no longer competition among men and among employers," Jevons could declare, then a problem "has little or nothing to do with economics. It is not a question of science" (Jevons, 1882, pp. 153–55). Economists came to believe that, unless competition could be postulated, their discipline, as even Edgeworth admitted, "would be indeed a dismal science" (Edgeworth, 1881, p. 50). But the concept of competition upon which nineteenth-century economists came to rely so heavily was not the concept which had earlier been employed by Adam Smith. On the contrary, the process of analytical refinement that began with Cournot and continued through the work of Jevons, Edgeworth, and J. B. Clark, reaching its fullest expression in Frank Knight's *Risk, Uncertainty and Profit* (Stigler, 1957), involved a basic conceptual change.

One aspect of this change was that price came to be a parameter rather than a variable from the standpoint of the individual firm (Schumpeter, 1950, p. 78). As Stigler has pointed out, the mathematical economists came "to define competition as that situation in which P does not vary with Q—in which the demand curve facing the firm is horizontal" (Stigler, 1957, p. 5). This was a quite drastic change from the concept employed by Smith, for whom competition meant nothing but the necessity for the individual seller or buyer to raise or lower his price or offer in response to market conditions. Smith's concept of competition was decidedly not one in which the firm was passive with respect to price but was, rather, one in which the market moved toward equilibrium through the active price responses of its various participants. When quantity supplied exceeded that demanded, he wrote, "some part must be sold to those who are willing to pay less . . . [and] the market price will sink more or less below the natural price, according as the greatness of the excess increases more or less the competition of the sellers, or according as it happens to be more or less important to them to get immediately rid of the commodity" (Smith, 1937, p. 57). Smith's concept of competition was competition "in the sense of rivalry in a race—a race to get limited supplies or a race to be rid of excess supplies" (Stigler, 1957, pp. 1–2). This is fundamentally different from the concept of perfect competition which, as Frank Knight has often stressed, implies "no presumption of psychological competition, emulation, or rivalry, and . . . [from which] 'bargaining' is also excluded" (Knight, 1946, p. 102). As far as the concept of competition is related to market structure, we should have to say that Smith, by suggesting that the individual seller could sell more by lowering price and less by raising it, presented a theory of *imperfect* competition. But, in fact, Smith's use of the term seems to have been largely independent of market structure. Of duopoly, he wrote: "If . . . capital [in the amount required to satisfy the demand for groceries] is divided between two different grocers, their competition will tend to make both of them sell cheaper" (Smith, 1937, p. 342). Although Smith specified that competition would be the more active, the greater was the number of competitors, the essence of competition in duopoly was evidently what it was in any other market structure, namely, the attempt to undersell one's rival in the market by lowering price.

The most fundamental difference between Smith and the mathematical economists who developed the concept of perfect competition does not, however, reside in the degree of individual control exerted over price but, rather, in the way in which competition is conceived. Not only did Smith fail to see competition as a "situation in which P does not vary with Q—in which the demand curve facing the firm is horizontal" (Stigler, 1957, p. 5); he did not conceive of competition as a "situation" at all but, rather, as an active process leading to a certain predicted result. The Smithian concept of competition is essentially one of business behavior which might reasonably be associated with the verb "to compete." The essence of that behavior was the active effort to undersell one's rival in the market, although, to be sure, Smith was not unaware of the organizational and technological elements in competition, as when he wrote that lowered prices and increased demand "encourages production, and thereby, increases the competition of producers who, in order to undersell one another, have recourse to new divisions of labour and new improvements of art, which might never otherwise have been thought of" (Smith, 1937, p. 706).

The concept of competition originating with Cournot, on the other hand, is totally devoid of behavioral content. This is because Cournot's focus was entirely on the effects, rather than the actual workings, of competition:

Everyone has a vague idea of the effects of competition. Theory should have attempted to render this idea more precise; and yet, for lack of regarding the question from the proper point of view, and for want of recourse to symbols (of which the use in this connection becomes indispensable), economic writers have not in the least improved on popular notions in this respect. These notions have remained as ill-defined and ill-applied in their works, as in popular language [Cournot, 1929, p. 79].

Cournot's attempt "to render more precise" the idea of the effects of competition resulted in what was perhaps the first formal definition of perfect competition—a definition, as Stigler has said, which was "enormously more precise and elegant than Smith's" (Stigler, 1957, p. 5). What must be stressed, however, is that it was not a definition of the *behavioral process* of competing but, rather, a definition of competition as a *state* in which that process had run its limits:

The effects of competition have reached their limit, when each of the partial productions D_k [the production of firm k] is *inappreciable*, not only with reference to the total production $D = F(p)$, but also with reference to the derivative $F'(p)$, so that the partial production D_k could be subtracted from D without any appreciable variation resulting in the price of the commodity [Cournot, 1929, p. 90].

For Smith, then, competition was a process through which a predicted result, the equation of price and cost, was achieved. With Cournot, it became the realized result itself. The two concepts are not only different; they are fundamentally incompatible. Competition came to mean, with the mathematical economists, a hypothetically realized situation in which business rivalry, or competition in the Smithian sense, was ruled out by definition. Perfect competition, as Hayek has cogently observed, "means indeed the absence of all competitive activities."

The reason for this ... [is that the idea of perfect competition] assumes throughout that state of affairs already to exist which, according to the truer view of the older theory, the process of competition tends to bring about (or to approximate) and that, if the state of affairs assumed by the theory of perfect competition ever existed, it would not only deprive of their scope all the activities which the verb "to compete" describes but would make them virtually impossible [Hayek, 1948, pp. 92, 96].

Frank Knight has said of competition that the "use of this word is one of our worst misfortunes of terminology" and has suggested that as far as perfect competition is concerned, " 'atomistic' is a better word for the idea" (Knight, 1946, p. 102). Although "atomistic" is indeed a good substitute for "competitive," as the latter term is used in the tradition from Cournot to Edgeworth, Jevons, Clark, and Knight, it is not a very good expression of the idea of competition advanced by Smith and his predecessors, for it fails to convey the sense of business rivalry and market activity which was the essence of the earlier meaning of the term.

Stigler has rightly pointed out that it was Knight's *Risk, Uncertainty and Profit* whose "meticulous discussion ... did most to drive home to economists generally the austere nature of the *rigorously defined concept* [of competition]" (Stigler, 1957, p. 11; emphasis added). Yet Knight has himself noted the lack of definition of the concept. "The critical reader of general economic literature must be struck," he has said, "by the *absence of any attempt accurately to define* that competition which is the principal subject under discussion" (Knight, 1935, p. 49; emphasis added). The resolution of this apparent contradiction must surely lie in the distinction between competition as a market structure and competition as behavioral activity. It is that distinction which must be made between the concept of perfect competition developed and refined by nineteenth- and twentieth-century theorists and the concept of competition earlier employed by Adam Smith and his predecessors.

REFERENCES

Clark, J. M. *Competition as a Dynamic Process.* Washington: Brookings Institution, 1961.

Cournot, Augustin. *Researches into the Mathematical Principles of the Theory of Wealth.* Translated by Nathaniel T. Bacon. New York: Macmillan Co., 1929.

Edgeworth, F. Y. *Mathematical Psychics.* London: E. Kegan Paul, 1881.

Hayek, F. A. *Individualism and Economic Order.* Chicago: Univ. of Chicago Press, 1948.

Heckscher, E. F. *Mercantilism.* 2 vols. New York: Macmillan Co., 1962.

Hume, David. *Writings on Economics.* Edited by Eugene Rotwein. Madison: Univ. of Wisconsin Press, 1955.

Jevons, W. S. *The State in Relation to Labour.* London: Macmillan Co., 1882.

Knight, Frank. *The Ethics of Competition.* New York: Harper & Bros., 1935.

———. "Immutable Law in Economics: Its Reality and Limitations," *A.E.R.,* XXXVI, No. 2 (May, 1946), 93–111.

Mill, J. S. *Principles of Political Economy.* 2 vols. New York: D. Appleton, 1864.

Monroe, A. E. *Early Economic Thought.* Cambridge, Mass.: Harvard Univ. Press, 1948.

Ricardo, David. *Principles of Political Economy and Taxation.* London: J. M. Dent & Sons, 1955.

Schumpeter, J. A. *Capitalism, Socialism and Democracy.* New York: Harper & Row, 1950.

———. *History of Economic Analysis.* New York: Oxford Univ. Press, 1954.

Smith, Adam. *The Wealth of Nations.* New York: Modern Library, 1937.

Steuart, Sir James. *An Inquiry into the Principles of Political Oeconomy.* 2 vols. London: A. Millar & T. Cadell, 1767.

Stigler, G. J. "Perfect Competition, Historically Contemplated," *J.P.E.,* LXV, No. 1 (February, 1957), 1–17.

THE ECONOMIC JOURNAL

DECEMBER 1984

DAVID RICARDO'S EARLY TREATMENT OF PROFITABILITY: A NEW INTERPRETATION*

Terry Peach

The nature of David Ricardo's early treatment of profitability has become a matter of dispute. For the participants in the recent controversy[1] two points are at issue: the substance of his approach, and the question of whether he is part of a 'neoclassical lineage' (Hollander) or an alternative 'surplus lineage' (Garegnani, Eatwell, Bharadwaj *et al.*). I will address the first of these points in the hope of casting some fresh interpretative light; establishing Ricardo's doctrinal home will not be my concern. Indeed, it is a major implication of this paper that the interest in assimilating his writings to a *type* of economics has been nugatory, at best.

The focus for the exegetical contest has been the validity of Piero Sraffa's 'corn model' interpretation. Prompted by discoveries made in the course of his own theoretical work,[2] Sraffa suggested in his introduction to the *Collected Works*[3] that at some time prior to 1815 Ricardo formulated a model in which the same commodity, corn, was the output and sole input for the agricultural sector of an abstract economy: the sole input by virtue of the assumption that production is effected by unassisted labour and seed corn, with corn as the only wage good. With the corn wage fixed, both for workers in agriculture and those in the manufacturing sector, and assuming a uniform rate of profit, the 'corn model' would enable distributive relations at the agricultural 'margin' to provide what Eatwell (1975) has called a "physical analogue" for the economy as a whole; (changes in) the general rate of profit could be calculated in physical terms, without recourse to 'values' and would be uniquely determined with reference to agricultural data.[4]

---

* Earlier versions of this paper, which grew out of my D.Phil. thesis, have been presented in Manchester, Cambridge and at the 1982 History of Economic Thought Conference, held in Nottingham. For helpful advice and criticism over a long gestation period I particularly want to than Paul Cammack, Walter Eltis, Andrew Glyn, Istvan Hont and Ian Steedman.

[1] Initiated by Hollander (1973) with contributions from Eatwell (1975) Garegnani (1982, 1983) and Bharadwaj (1983) to name only the principal contenders.

[2] "It should perhaps be stated that it was only when the Standard system and the distinction between basics and non-basics had emerged in the course of the present investigation that the ['corn model'] interpretation of Ricardo's theory suggested itself as a natural consequence" (Sraffa (1960), p. 93). For the relevant definitions see *ibid.* pp. 8 and 26.

[3] *The Works and Correspondence of David Ricardo*, edited by Piero Sraffa with the collaboration of M. H. Dobb. All references to the *Works* in this paper give the volume number in Roman numerals followed by the appropriate page number.

[4] In Sraffa's terminology, corn is the only basic commodity in the analysis, and the agricultural sector might be thought of as the simplest type of Standard system.

According to Sraffa, the 'corn model' was the "rational foundation of the principle of the determining role of the profits of agriculture" (I, p. xxxi) with this principle allegedly articulated by Ricardo in his statement that "it is the profits of the farmer which regulate the profits of all other trades". Sraffa disclosed, however, that the "rational foundation" was "never stated by Ricardo in any of his extant letters and papers" (*ibid.*); what he did was infer its explicit formulation, either in lost papers or conversation, on the basis of certain extant items of correspondence and the perceived method of analysis adopted by Ricardo in his *Essay on Profits*.

Although a theory of value is logically extraneous to a 'corn model' analysis, Sraffa argued that, at least until the *Essay*, Ricardo "had subscribed to the generally accepted [Smithian] view that a rise in corn prices, through its effect upon wages, would be followed by a rise of all other prices" (I, p. xxxiii). Had it not been for Ricardo's imputed adherence to the 'corn model', Sraffa suggested, this view of price behaviour would have "obscured the simple relation of the rise of wages to the fall of profits" (*ibid.*), which would be obvious if corn-wages rose relative to corn output but less so, we are told, if both increased in price terms.

The latter point has been vigorously emphasised by Garegnani and Bharadwaj, who claim that without the 'corn model', Ricardo's subscription to the 'adding up' approach to price would have precluded his articulated position on profitability. I dissent. I will argue that far from being an analytically extraneous leftover from a Smithian past, the 'adding up' approach was central to the treatment of profitability prior to the *Essay*.

Sraffa's interpretation of Ricardo's early writings on value and distribution attracted so much support, spanning over two decades, that it took on an air of final authority. But with the work of Samuel Hollander, a loud and discordant note was struck.

Hollander's view is that Ricardo's treatment of both the agricultural and manufacturing sectors must be characterised in terms of the manipulation of money variables; that is, in terms of the relationship between money wages (which may be influenced by changes in the price of corn, although this is only one possibility), prices and profits. All along, Ricardo is portrayed as striving to develop a general framework of analysis, using money variables, in terms of which the effects of a change in wages from whatever cause could be investigated. As for the assumption of a given commodity wage, this is relegated to the status of a mere 'simplifying device' on Ricardo's part: no issue of principle was allegedly involved.

In terms of my negative interpretative point – that the 'corn model' interpretation must be abandoned – I am in agreement with Professor Hollander. But I will argue that he fails to recognise the true nature of Ricardo's analytical method, that his views on Ricardo's use of 'fixwage' analysis are misconceived, and that he fails to give due place to Ricardo's object of analysis.

I now proceed to the interpretation of Ricardo's writings, beginning with his correspondence in 1813 and 1814.

I

Ricardo first alluded to his 'theory' of profits in August 1813, when discussing with Malthus the reason for an increased rate of profits in the period 1793–1813. According to Ricardo:

> My conclusion is that there has been a rapid increase of Capital which has been prevented from shewing itself in a low rate of interest by new facilities in the production of food.
>
> (17 August 1813; VI, p. 95)

An attempt was subsequently made to elaborate on this pronouncement in the inextant "papers on the profits of Capital".[1] With a view to clarifying the position therein Ricardo wrote to Hutches Trower (who was thought to "have not entirely made out the subject in dispute"):

> Interest rises only when the means of employment for Capital bears a greater proportion than before to the Capital itself, and falls when the Capital bears a greater proportion to the arena, as Mr. Malthus has called it, for its employment. On these points I believe we are all agreed, but I contend that the arena for the employment of new Capital cannot increase in any country in the same or greater proportion than the Capital itself, unless there be improvements in husbandry – or new facilities be offered for the introduction of food from foreign countries – that in short it is the profits of the farmer which regulate the profits of all other trades – and as the profits of the farmer must necessarily decrease with every augmentation of Capital employed on the land, provided no improvements be at the same time made in husbandry, all other profits must diminish and therefore the rate of interest must fall.
>
> (8 March 1814; VI, pp. 103–4)

The letter to Trower indicates Ricardo's belief that his views on profits were compatible with the 'competition of capitals' framework to the extent that it is within this framework that the 'regulatory' role of farmers' profits is enunciated:[2] the agricultural profit rate 'regulates' the "arena for the employment of new Capital" (i.e. the demand for capital) relative to the supply of capital, and hence it 'regulates' general profits on trade.

What did Ricardo intend by the notion of 'regulation'? In particular, did he have in mind the mathematically precise concept of 'unique determination'? Sraffa evidently believed that he did, hence the translation "the determining role" of agricultural profits for Ricardo's 'regulatory' role. Once this step is taken it is quite true, as opined by Garegnani (1982), that there is "a 'rational foundation' only in the ['corn model'] argument described by Sraffa". However, it must take a great deal of faith to conclude that Ricardo's somewhat vague pronouncement was therefore derivative of 'corn model' reasoning. We have to believe that the terminological translation is justified – although why it should be is unclear – and that the translated position was underpinned by a logically

---

[1] Mentioned by Trower in his letter to Ricardo of 2 March 1814; VI, p. 102.
[2] This point is taken up below.

consistent model: again, an heroic interpretative assumption. In view of these difficulties I suggest we press on, taking with us nothing more than Ricardo's imprecise assertion of a 'regulatory' function for farmers' profits.

Following the letter to Trower there was a lapse of over three months before the issue of profitability was again raised in correspondence, in the letter to Malthus which, for Sraffa, contained a "striking passage" (italicised below) which was the "nearest that Ricardo comes to an explicit statement on these ['corn model'] lines" (I, p. xxxii). Ricardo wrote:

> I cannot partake of your doubts respecting the effects of restrictions on the importation of corn, in tending to lower the rate of interest. The rise of the price or rather the value of corn without any augmentation of capital must necessarily diminish the demand for other things even if the prices of those commodities did not rise with the price of corn, which they would (tho' slowly) certainly do. With the same Capital there would be less production, and less demand. Demand has no other limits but the want of power of paying for the commodities demanded. Everything which tends to diminish production tends to diminish this power. *The rate of profits and of interest must depend on the proportion of production to the consumption necessary to such production* – this again essentially depends upon the cheapness of provisions, which is after all, whatever intervals we may be willing to allow, the great regulator of the wages of labour.
>
> (26 June 1814; VI, p. 108. My italics)

Three observations cast doubt on Sraffa's interpretation. First, it is contextually obvious that the "proportion of production..." expression does not specifically refer to events in the agricultural sector; Ricardo's prime analytical concern seems to have been with the production of "other things", the argument being that if their prices remain unchanged following a rise in the price (or exchangeable value) of corn – supposedly a counterfactual assumption – and if the amount of capital in existence was unchanged, the engendered rise in money wages (synonymously, the rise in the exchangeable value of commodity wages) would reduce manufacturers' profit margins and hence their rate of profit.

The second point has been anticipated. Whereas Sraffa's interpretation suggests that Ricardo was presenting a 'formula' for the rate of profit in the agricultural sector (and by 'corn model' extension, for the economy as a whole), what he appears to have been stressing, with no particular reference to agriculture, was the dependency of the rate of profit on the magnitude of the surplus which remains after defraying the cost of the direct labour input, with this cost "essentially" depending on the "cheapness of provisions". A statement of dependency should not be confused with one of identity.

Finally, consider two other 'striking passages' from Ricardo's earlier writings. Commenting on Bentham's *Sur Les Prix*[1] he wrote:

> There is but one way in which an increase of money no matter how it be introduced into the society, can augment riches, viz at the expence of the wages of labour; till the wages of labour have found their level with the

[1] Ricardo's notes were written between December 1810 and January 1811.

increased prices which the commodities will have experienced, there will be so much additional revenue to the manufacturer and farmer [because] they will obtain an increased price for their commodities, and can whilst wages do not increase employ an additional number of hands, so that the real riches of the country will be somewhat augmented. *A productive labourer will produce something more than before relatively to his consumption*, but this can be only of momentary duration.

(III, pp. 318–9. My italics)

It is clear both in this passage and in a letter to Mill of 1 January 1811 (where the argument is restated, with the labour producing "more relatively to that which he consumed"; VI, p. 16) that the expression in dispute was *not* used specifically in relation to the agricultural sector; and it is equally clear that valuation was to be effected in monetary terms. Of course, none of this rules out the possibility that Ricardo did, at some later stage, apply the expression to agriculture on the assumption that corn is both the output and sole input. But we have yet to encounter compelling evidence that he did so.

Superficially, this lacuna is filled by the following Malthusian criticism:

In no case of production, is the produce exactly of the same nature as the capital advanced. Consequently we can never properly refer to a material rate of produce, independent of demand, and of the abundance or scarcity of capital.

(5 August 1814; VI, p. 117)

For Sraffa, the point about produce not being "exactly of the same nature as the capital advanced" was "no doubt an echo of Ricardo's own formulation" (I, p. xxxi) made either in his lost manuscript or in conversation. If this had been so, we might expect Ricardo to have defended his 'corn model' assumptions when replying to Malthus. In fact, we find this:

Individuals do not estimate their profits by the material production, but nations invariably do. If we had precisely the same amount of commodities of all descriptions in the year 1815 that we now have in 1814 as a nation we should be no richer, but if money had sunk in value they would be represented by a greater quantity of money, and individuals would be apt to *think* themselves richer.

(11 August 1814; VI, p. 121. Ricardo's italics)

The estimation of profits "by the material production" had the advantage of abstracting from monetary disturbances which would mask the true magnitude of the materially specified profit share; moreover, this technique was not believed to be limited in application to the agricultural sector. I suggest, therefore, that any previous reference by Ricardo to a "material rate of produce" was based on the representation of the profit share in physical terms, but was not predicated on product–capital homogeneity.

This raises a conundrum: how would it have been possible to calculate the (material) profit:capital ratio unless by assuming homogeneity? The answer to this question is straightforward. But first it will help to review the analytical argument in Ricardo's *Essay on Profits*[1] and Sraffa's interpretation of it.

II

The *Essay* was published soon after Malthus's *An inquiry into the Nature of Progress of Rent* and *The Grounds of an Opinion on the Policy of Restricting the Importation of Foreign Corn*. As Sraffa remarked (IV, p. 4) it seems to have been only a few days after reading Malthus's pamphlets before Ricardo wrote his own, making use of Malthus's treatment of rent but questioning the wisdom of import restrictions.

As pointed out by Ronald Meek (1973, p. 93), Ricardo developed his analysis in two stages, with the first applied to agriculture. He began by focusing on "the first settling of a country rich in fertile land... which may be had by any one who chooses to take it", where there is "[no] deduction whatever for rent" (IV, p. 10). In this situation:

> if the capital employed... on such land were of the value of two hundred quarters of wheat, of which half consisted of fixed capital such as buildings, implements, &c. and the other half of circulating capital – if, after replacing the fixed and circulating capital, the value of the remaining produce were one hundred quarters of wheat, or of equal value with one hundred quarters of wheat, the neat profit to the owner of capital would be fifty per cent, or one hundred profit on two hundred capital.
> (*Ibid.*)

There is evidently capital on the land which is not of the same nature as agricultural output. Total capital is calculated as being "of the value of two hundred quarters of wheat", presumably on the basis of a (tacitly) assumed set of exchange relationships between wheat and other commodities. Wheat/corn is not the sole agricultural input, and this is quite explicitly the case for the fixed capital employed.

Still with reference to the "first settling", Ricardo continued:

> Profits might... increase, because the population increasing, at a more rapid rate than capital, wages might fall; and instead of the value of one hundred quarters of wheat being necessary for the circulating capital, ninety only might be required.
> (IV, 11)

The reference to circulating capital as being "of the value of one hundred quarters of wheat" may suggest that commodity wages do not consist solely of wheat/corn; at any rate, there is no explicit assumption *anywhere* in the *Essay* that wheat/corn is the only wage good, in which case Ricardo might well have adopted the same procedure for manufactured wage goods as he apparently did for fixed capital, calculating their wheat value on the basis of 'given' relative prices. Be this as it may, the assumption of product/capital homogeneity in agriculture was certainly not made.

[1] *An essay on the Influence of a low Price of Corn on the Profits of Stock.* Published 14 February 1815.

Apart from the possible influence of wage rate variation on profits, Ricardo drew attention to the impact on profitability of "improvements in agriculture or in the implements of husbandry" (again suggesting agriculture–manufacturing indecomposability). After remarking that "These are circumstances which are more or less at all times in operation" he assumed

> that no improvements take place in agriculture, and that capital and population advance in the proper proportion, so that the real wages of labour, continue uniformly the same; that we may know what peculiar effects are to be ascribed to the growth of capital, the increase of population, and the extension of cultivation, to the more remote, and less fertile land.
>
> (IV, p. 12)

The initial 'equilibrium' position is that of the "first settling", with the profit rate at 50%.[1] This is presumed to be disturbed by an increase in capital and population, calling forth a rise in the demand for food which has to be met "from land not so advantageously situated". The story unfolds thus:

> The necessity of employing more labourers, horses, &c. to carry the produce from the place where it was grown, to the place where it was to be consumed, although no alteration were to take place in the wages of labour, would make it necessary that more capital should be permanently employed to obtain the same produce. Suppose this addition to be of the value of ten quarters of wheat, the whole capital employed on the new land would be two hundred and ten, to obtain the same return as on the old; and, consequently the profits of stock would fall from fifty to forty-three per cent or ninety on two hundred and ten.
>
> (IV, p. 13)

But what happens to the rate of profit on the first land cultivated? Ricardo wrote:

> The return would be the same as before...but, the general profits of stock being regulated by the profits made on the least profitable employment of capital on agriculture, a division of the one hundred quarters would take place, forty-three per cent or eight-six quarters would constitute the profits of stock, and seven per cent or fourteen quarters, would constitute rent.
>
> (*Ibid.*)

It is important to recognise that the wheat value of the capital on the first land is unchanged even though conditions of production at the agricultural 'margin' have deteriorated. Since total capital was not assumed to consist wholly in commodities of the same nature as agricultural capital, the implication is that the exchangeable value of wheat vis-à-vis other commodities was treated as invariant to changed agricultural conditions of production.

---

[1] Ricardo wrote: "If the profits on capital employed in trade were more than fifty per cent, capital would be withdrawn from the land to be employed in trade. If they were less, capital would be taken from trade to agriculture" (IV, p. 12). I agree with Professor Hollander's comment that, "As [this] so-called 'proof' stands, it is in fact nothing more than an assertion...It would be quite inadequate if intended as justification for the proposition that the general rate is governed by the agricultural rate." (Hollander (1979), p. 139.)

In the continuation of the analysis, with "land of a worse quality, or less favourably situated" brought into cultivation in successive stages, or land already under cultivation worked more intensively, the extra capital employed is consistently referred to as being "of the value of" so many quarters of wheat, and the relative value of wheat continues to be taken as constant. The numerical examples are faithfully reproduced in the *Essay*'s table (IV, p. 17) with the first column heading making quite clear that "capital [is only] *estimated* in quarters of wheat" (my italics). It is shown that the agricultural profit rate, "being regulated by the least profitable employment of capital", will fall as conditions of production worsen and rent will increase.

To emphasise, this analysis of the agricultural sector is conducted on the basis of a constant relative price ratio between wheat and non-wheat agricultural inputs as conditions at the 'margin' deteriorate. What does this imply for absolute price movements? Logically, we have the two possibilities that either all prices move *pari passu* or remain unchanged. In the context of the *Essay* they remain unchanged, this following from the "rudimentary theory of exchange value" (Meek, 1973, p. 93), adumbrated by Ricardo in the second, manufacturing phase of his analysis. According to this new 'theory' – a rejection of the Smithian 'adding up' approach to price[1] –

> The exchangeable value of all commodities, rises as the difficulties of their production increase. If then new difficulties occur in the production of corn, from more labour being necessary, whilst no more labour is required to produce gold, silver, cloth, linen, &c. the exchangeable value of corn will necessarily rise, as compared with those things... Wherever competition can have its full effect, and the production of the commodity be not limited by nature, as in the case with some wines, the difficulty or facility of their production will ultimately regulate their exchangeable value.[2]
>
> (IV, pp. 19–20)

From which Ricardo deduced:

> The sole effect... of the progress of wealth on prices, independently of all improvements, either in agriculture or manufactures, appears to be to raise the price of raw produce and of labour, leaving all other commodities at their original prices, and to lower general profits in consequence of the general rise of wages.
>
> (IV, p. 20)

---

[1] From the inception of his economic writings, Ricardo subscribed to the 'adding up' approach concurrently with a belief that gold and silver should be treated as subject to the same 'laws' as all other commodities (explicitly articulated in the *High Price of Bullion*, published 1810, III, pp. 54 and 60; in a letter to Horner of 5 February 1810, VI, p. 5; and in a letter to Malthus of 18 June 1811, VI, p. 24). Ironically, his rejection of the approach seems to have resulted from a delayed realisation that the two positions were incompatible. Thus he wrote to Malthus soon after the *Essay* had been published: "If money be a commodity does not corn and labour enter into its price or value? and if they do, why should not money vary as compared with corn and labour by the same law as all other commodities do?" (27 March 1815; VI, p. 203). That Ricardo should have remained oblivious to this argument for so long serves to illustrate the important interpretative point that consistency cannot be presumed.

[2] It would be a mistake to think that this constitutes a labour theory of value. Letters written after the *Essay* indicate that Ricardo was at this stage thinking in terms of an absolute cost approach rather than the relative cost calculations which are analytically isomorphic to a 'pure' labour theory of value (cf. Hollander (1979), p. 161, and Bharadwaj (1983)). In Peach (1982) I argue that it was not until the beginning of March 1816 that the 'pure' labour theory of value was formulated.

If prices move as Ricardo indicates, the wheat value of non-wheat commodities would decline as conditions of production worsened. *Ergo*, the constant absolute prices interpretation of the agricultural analysis, confirmed by the following passage which, far from "an aside",[1] represents the 'conclusion' to that reasoning:

> If the money price of corn, and the wages of labour, did not vary in price in the least degree, during the progress of the country in wealth and population, still profits would fall and rents would rise; because *more* labourers would be employed on the more distant or less fertile land, in order to obtain the same supply of raw produce; and therefore the cost of production would have increased, whilst the value of the produce continued the same.
>
> (IV, p. 18. Ricardo's italics)

In the light of this interpretation, it was surely misleading for Sraffa to have said that, in the *Essay*, "the profit rate [was] calculated without *need* to mention price" (I, p. xxxii, my italics), in so far as one might erroneously infer that this lack of "need" was the logical consequence of 'corn model' assumptions. Truly, Ricardo's analysis does not mention price considerations, but this is only because of a tacit assumption about price behaviour; it has nothing to do with the assumption of a strict technical identity between product and capital.

The agricultural analysis of the *Essay*, as interpreted, provides an answer to the conundrum raised earlier, namely the means by which the (material) profit: capital ratio could be calculated without assuming homogeneity of input and output. But how might Ricardo have proceeded before the *Essay*?

III

Prior to the *Essay*, Ricardo thought that all prices would rise following a rise in the price of corn. Suppose he assumed, for the sake of analytical convenience, that prices varied *pari passu* with the price of corn.[2] In that case, together with the use of corn as *numéraire*, his formal analysis of the agricultural sector would have been identical to that presented in the first of the *Essay*, although based on a different view of price behaviour. This is my interpretative suggestion.

The first, indirect piece of supportive evidence comes from Malthus, who wrote to Ricardo:

> You seem to think that the state of production from the land, compared with the means necessary to make it produce, is almost the sole cause which regulates the profits of stock, and the means of advantageously employing capital... But unless it could be shewn that no improvements were ever to take place either in agriculture or manufactures, *and that upon a rise in the*

---

[1] Hollander (1979), p. 140, who also writes that "[this] extract leaves something to be desired..." (*ibid.*). These reactions seem to result from Professor Hollander's belief that Ricardo adopted an undifferentiated money variables approach to the analysis of both the agricultural and manufacturing sectors; since Ricardo's words do not fit the interpretation they are dismissed as either unimportant or out of phase with his true position.

[2] In doing so he would have been following Adam Smith: Smith [1776] (1976) Book IV, p. 15.

price of raw produce new leases would be immediately granted, new taxes levied, and that *the price of labour and of every other commodity both foreign and domestic would rise without delay exactly in proportion*, the doctrine is evidently not correct in practice. And as these contemporaneous effects are in my opinion not only improbable but impossible, *it would be quite useless to lay much stress upon it even as a theoretical framework.*

(9 October 1814; VI, pp. 139–40. My italics)

Malthus continued:

The profits of stock, or the means of employing capital advantageously may be said to be accurately equal to the price of produce, *minus* the expence of production. And consequently whenever the price of produce keeps a head of the price of production the profits of stock must rise... It is not the *quantity* of produce compared with the expence of production that determines profits (which I think is your proposition) but the exchangeable value or money price of that produce, compared with the money expence of production. And the exchangeable value of produce is not of course always proportioned to its quantity.

(VI, pp. 140–1. Malthus's italics)

If Ricardo assumed heterogeneous inputs to agriculture which varied in price *pari passu* with the price of corn, then as Malthus intimates, it would appear to be "the *quantity* of produce compared with the expense of production that determines profits", without any allowance for "the price of produce keep[ing] a head of the price of production". An attractive inference, therefore, is that "as a theoretical framework", Ricardo had assumed contemporaneous and proportional price rises.

The reply to Malthus was as follows:

You say "that I seem to think that the state of production from the land, compared with the means necessary to make it produce, is almost the sole cause which regulates the profits of stock, and the means of advantageously employing capital." This is a correct statement of my opinion, and not as you have said in another part of your letter, and which essentially differs from it, "that it is the *quantity* of produce compared with the expence of production, that determines profits."

(23 October 1814; VI, p. 144)

What was at stake here, I submit, was Ricardo's perception of the corn: corn measured expenses formulation. Thus, when he 'concluded' his agricultural analysis in the *Essay*, in which the formulation figured prominently, he characterised his result as being that "the cost of production would have increased, whilst the *value* of the produce continued the same" (my italics). What this means is that although the numerator in the profit expression was in physical terms it was given a value interpretation. If Ricardo viewed his analysis here in the same way he would naturally reject the Malthusian characterisation of his approach: it would not be that he was failing to allow for price considerations, rather that he was making a particular, strong assumption about price behaviour.

Further support for the interpretation that he went through a stage of assuming equi-proportional price changes between corn and other commodities is provided by his correspondence with Malthus after the *Essay* had been published. According to Malthus, Ricardo's failure in the *Essay* to allow for a reduced corn value of fixed capital and non-corn wage goods when calculating the impact of diminishing returns on agricultural profitability was a fatal flaw in his argument (VI, p. 185). Mischievously, Ricardo pointed out that this criticism was nullified if all commodities rose in price with the increased price of corn: a view which Malthus held:

> You, I think, agree with Mr. Torrens that a rise in the price of corn will be followed by a rise in the price of home commodities; but your theory requires that there should be no rise in the price of those commodities on which the wages of labour are expended, *for if they rose in the same proportion as corn, there could be no fall in the corn wages of labour.* Is it not however very improbable that all manufactures should rise at home and yet those on which [the wages of] labour are expended should not rise? Is not the price of soap, candles &c^a, though foreign commodities, necessarily affected by the rise in the price of those home goods which are given in exchange for them[?]
>
> (17 April 1815; VI, pp. 212–3. My italics)

And also:

> I will...suppose that you and Mr. Torrens are correct, and that commodities do rise in price with every increased price of corn. The value of fixed capital as well as circulating capital employed on the land will then rise also, and altho' the money value of the produce should be increased on the old land [when corn becomes more difficult to produce at the 'margin'] *it will still bear the same proportion to the money value of the capital employed.*
>
> (VI, p. 213. My italics)

For there to be an unchanged relationship between the money value of produce "on the old land" and the money value of capital when the price of corn increases, prices of agricultural inputs other than corn (including non-corn wage goods) would have to rise proportionately: something explicitly stated in the first of these two passages for wage goods. Since neither Malthus nor Torrens upheld the 'proportionality thesis',[1] I submit that Ricardo was making use of the analytically convenient assumption which he made in his analysis of agriculture during 1813 and 1814, when *he* maintained the positive relationship between movements in corn prices and movements in general prices.

---

[1] Malthus complained to Ricardo: "Surely I have always maintained that when corn rises, though other commodities would rise they would not rise in proportion" (23 April 1815; VI, p. 222). This is borne out in his two pamphlets *An Enquiry into the Nature and Progress of Rent* (1815*a*, pp. 24 and 49) and *Observations on the Corn Laws* (1815*b*, pp. 6 and 15). Similarly, numerical examples in Torrens's *Essay on the External Corn Trade* reveal that the 'proportionality' assumption was not made: Torrens (1815), pp. 83–4 and p. 190.

IV

The implications of this interpretation will now be explored, both for an understanding of the *Essay*'s composition and for further items of Ricardo's correspondence which have been cited in support of the 'corn model' reading. To round off the interpretation of Ricardo's analytical method, the section concludes with a brief outline of his treatment of the manufacturing sector.

The rapidity with which Ricardo was able to write his pamphlet has been remarked upon.[1] According to Sraffa, this celerity is to be explained by the first half of the *Essay* being "the revised version of a text prepared before the appearance of Malthus's pamphlets" (IV, p. 4, n. 3). Accepting this, and recalling that the detailed agricultural analysis of the *Essay* is formally compatible with two assumptions about price behaviour – that absolute prices are fixed or move *pari passu* with the price of corn – I suggest that Ricardo reproduced an analysis previously conducted on the latter assumption, tacitly swapping it for the former. Those revisions which needed to be made would have been annotation and the incorporation of the theory of differential rent. And to this portion of the manuscript would have been appended the remainder, containing a theory of exchange relationships which played no role in the agricultural analysis.

Turning to Ricardo's correspondence, first consider a letter to Malthus of 8 May 1815, which for Eatwell (1975) provides evidence that "the idea of the rate of profit as a purely material ratio lingers on in the letters of 1815":

> I have an account before me of the Capital actually employed on a farm of 200 Acres in Essex. It amounts to £3433 – or about £17 per Acre, of which not more than £1100, or £1200 is of that description which is not subject to the same variation of value as the produce of the land itself; for £2200 – consists of the value of the seeds in the ground, the advances for labour – the horses and livestock &c^a &c^a. If then the money value of the produce from the land should fall, *from facility of production*, it must ever continue to bear a greater ratio to the whole money value of the capital employed on the land, for there will be a great increase of average produce per acre, whilst the fall in money value will be common to both capital and produce and it cannot therefore be true that rent, profits, and wages, can all *really* fall at the same time.
>
> (VI, p. 226. Ricardo's italics)

Naturally for a defender of Sraffa's interpretation, Eatwell seizes upon the point that "the fall in money will be common to both capital and produce", which he reads as an echo of Ricardo's alleged 'corn model' formulation. But Ricardo's pre-*Essay* position regarding price behaviour would have ensured that price changes would be common to both produce and capital *irrespective of the composition of agricultural inputs*. For that reason, he had absolutely no need to make 'corn model' assumptions.

---

[1] Above, p. 738.

Next, an earlier letter of Ricardo's in which, surprisingly, it is Professor Hollander who divines a 'corn model':[1]

> The capitalist "who may find it necessary to employ a hundred days labour instead of fifty in order to produce a certain quantity of corn"[2] cannot retain the same share for himself unless the labourers who are employed for a hundred days will be satisfied with the same quantity of corn for their subsistence that the labourers for fifty had before. If you suppose the price of corn doubled, the capital to be employed estimated in money will probably be also nearly doubled – or at any rate will be greatly augmented; and if his money income is to arise from the sale of corn which remains to him after defraying the charges of production how is it possible to conceive that the rate of his profits will not be diminished?
>
> (25 July 1814; IV, pp. 114–5)

If, as Hollander has suggested, commodity wages were assumed to comprise solely corn, *with production effected by unassisted labour*, "the capital employed estimated in money" would be quadrupled, not doubled as Ricardo states, if the price of corn is doubled and the corn wage per labourer remains constant.[3] It seems possible, therefore, that the "nearly doubled"/"greatly augmented" capital excludes wage outlays,[4] with the monetary increase attributable, at least in part, to price rises of manufactured inputs consequent upon the rise in the price of corn.[5]

Taking this to be so, the fact that capital is not exactly doubled apparently conflicts with the interpretation that Ricardo assumed the prices of manufactures to vary *pari passu* with the price of corn. But my conjecture is that the assumption was only made for analytical convenience in formal analysis, although the "nearly doubled"/"at any rate...greatly augmented" expressions may suggest that Ricardo would not have thought it to be violently at odds with reality. However, he could not have taken strictly proportional price rises to be the end-point of an analytical scenario, for the simple reason that this would rule out a reduction in manufacturing profitability.

In the *Essay* and immediately after, the reduction in manufacturing profitability produced by an extension or intensification of the agricultural 'margin' was claimed as a result of rising money wages which, *per se*, did not generate price increases. Before the *Essay*, the argument seems to have been pure Adam Smith:

> It appears to me that the difficulty and expence of procuring corn will necessarily regulate the demand for the products of capital, for the demand

---

[1] Hollander (1979), p. 128.
[2] Ricardo is quoting from Malthus's letter of 6 July 1814; VI, p. 111.
[3] Professor Hollander corrects his mistake in Hollander (1983).
[4] Ricardo appears to have followed this procedure in the chapter "On Profits" in the *Principles*: I, pp. 115–8.
[5] Further casting doubt on the 'corn model' interpretation of Ricardo's letter is the ambiguity as to whether the corn which the labourers have to be "satisfied with" is the corn which they actually consume or the corn price for their labouring activity. It is the latter possibility which corresponds with the Malthusian scenario to which Ricardo was replying (Malthus alluded to a "diminution in the *real* wages of labour, or their price in corn", VI, p. 111, his italics); and further note Ricardo's willingness to use the "corn price of labour" and the "corn amount of wages" as synonyms when assuming a mixed commodity wage: VI, p. 189.

must essentially depend on the price at which they can be afforded, and the prices of all commodities must increase if the price of corn be increased.

(Letter to Malthus, 25 July 1814; VI, p. 114)

The mechanism for the reduction in manufacturing profitability is simple: the price of corn rises because its expenses of production increase; this raises the money wage and the cost of agriculturally produced inputs to the manufacturing sector; the prices of manufactured goods then rise because their expenses of production have increased; demand for manufactures falls off, prices reduce somewhat, and profitability declines.

To repeat, in the final 'equilibrium' position the prices of manufactured commodities have not risen to the same proportional extent as corn. What I have suggested is that Ricardo made life easier for himself, when analysing the agricultural sector, by assuming that they did.

V

In opposition to Sraffa's interpretation, it has been argued that the 'adding up' approach to price, articulated by Ricardo from the inception of his economic enquiries, was very much integral to the analysis of profitability from 1813 until the *Essay*. In this final section, I initially consider what the Ricardian 'theory' of profitability amounted to, and then the extent to which there really was any doctrinal or theoretical break in 1813.

First, it cannot be overstressed that Ricardo's dominant concern was always with 'permanent' movements in profitability.[1] Proximately, this may be understood as a concern with movements in the general rate of profit, with 'disequilibrium' profit rates for individual capitalists designated as 'temporary': they would be eradicated by way of inter/intra-sectoral capital flows.[2]

Secondly, it was a central plank of the Ricardian argument that capital accumulation would not, of itself, generate 'permanent' changes in the general rate of profit, this being grounded in an enthusiastic subscription to 'Mill's Law'. Thus he wrote to Malthus, somewhat ironically:

I go much further than you in ascribing effects to the wants and tastes of mankind – I believe them to be unlimited. Give men but the means of purchasing and their wants are insatiable. Mr. Mill's theory is built on this assumption. It does not attempt to say what the proportions will be to one another, of the commodities which will be produced in consequence of the accumulation of capital, but presumes that those commodities only will be produced which will be suited to the wants and tastes of mankind, because none other will be demanded.

(23 October 1814; VI, p. 148)[3]

---

[1] This is clear from the time he emphasised the link between conditions of production on the land and profitability. Thus in the letter to Trower of 8 March 1814 he wrote: "Nothing, I say, can increase the profits *permanently* on trade, with the same or an increased Capital, but a really cheaper mode of obtaining food" (VI, p. 104, my italics). See also his letters to Malthus of 30 August 1814 (VI, p. 128), 16 September 1814 (VI, p. 133), and 8 May 1815 (VI, pp. 228–9).

[2] A clear statement of this position is contained in the *Essay*: IV, pp. 24–5.

[3] Cf. sentiments expressed in Ricardo's letters to Malthus of 16 September 1814 (VI, p. 133) and 17 October (VI, p. 301).

Provided capitalists behaved rationally in the sense outlined and believed in by Ricardo, capital accumulation *could* proceed with only 'temporary' variations in individual profit rates.

The third feature of Ricardo's 'theory' is more contentious. *Pace* Samuel Hollander, 'permanent' alterations in profitability became (and possibly always were) defined relative to the 'subsistence' commodity wage: in this particular sense, Ricardo did have a 'fixwage' analysis.

Concentrating on the period from 1813 onwards, the first item of support for this interpretation is the following analytical cameo from Ricardo's letter to Malthus of 23 October 1814:

> An advanced price of raw produce may... proceed from a fall in the value of currency, which would raise the price of produce, for a time, more than it would wages, and would therefore raise profits. [But this] you will allow [is a] temporary cause.
>
> (VI, p. 146)

The fall in the value of currency produces a "temporary" impact on profitability because money wages do not rise concurrently and commensurately with the rise in the price of agriculturally produced wage-goods: but this is only a "temporary cause" of increased profitability because of the implicit 'fixwage' assumption: it was evidently Ricardo's view that the pre-disturbance commodity wage per labourer had to be re-established. By implication, 'permanent' changes in profitability were not associated with altered commodity wages.

This Ricardian analysis begs a question: what is it that defines the commodity wage serving as benchmark for 'permanent' movements in profitability? Only in the *Essay* do we find an answer, for after remarking that general profitability could be raised "by a fall in the wages of labour", Ricardo wrote:

> [This] cause is more or less *permanent*, according as the price from which wages fall, is more or less near that remuneration for labour, which is necessary to the actual subsistence of the labourer.
>
> (IV, p. 22. My italics)

Quite explicitly, 'permanent' changes in profitability were defined relative to the 'subsistence' wage.

Not long after the *Essay* had been published, we find yet more evidence of the 'temporary' status awarded by Ricardo to changes in profitability resulting from altered commodity wages:

> That profits may rise on the land if population increases faster than capital, I am not disposed to deny, but this will be a partial rise of profits on a particular trade, for a limited time, and is very different from a general rise of profits on trade in general.
>
> (Letter to Malthus, 17 October 1815; VI, p. 305)

Again, there is only a "limited" impact on profitability because, implicitly, the initial commodity wage must be restored; and taking into account the qualification made by Ricardo in the *Essay*, this commodity wage must presumably be set at the 'subsistence' level.

Further on this theme, there is the negative observation that, excepting the *Essay*'s qualification, Ricardo nowhere associates 'permanent' movements in profitability with variable commodity wages. However, this is not to say that he denied *de facto* commodity wage variability: a point emphasised with single-mindedness determination by Professor Hollander, and one scarcely worth labouring were it not for absurd statements to the contrary.[1] To stress, Ricardo did *not* suggest the 'fixwage' analysis as a literal description of reality, it should rather be viewed in the context of his 'theory' of 'permanent' movements in profitability.

The Ricardian 'theory' may now be stated: *ceteris paribus*,[2] 'permanent' changes in profitability will be the result of altered conditions of producing wage-goods. More particularly, Ricardo was concerned to disseminate a single proposition, that in the absence of free trade in corn, and in a given state of technology, capital accumulation would result in a 'permanent' reduction in profitability owing to worsened agricultural conditions of production. Above all, it was this that he struggled to give analytical representation; this was the 'regulatory' role of farmers' profits.

Having delineated the substance and form of Ricardo's approach to profitability in 1813 and after, I now assess the continuities and discontinuities with the earlier writings. At the outset, it should be stated that in the period 1809–12, Ricardo's attention was primarily directed towards the Bullion Controversy and only incidental concern was expressed in matters of distribution.[3] Even so, there is much in what he did have to say that forms the basis for his subsequent enquiries.

First, consider the following from the *Reply to Bosanquet*:

> [My] theory takes for granted, that whenever enormous profits can be made in any particular trade, a sufficient number of capitalists will be induced to engage in it, who will, by their competition, reduce the profits to the general rate of mercantile gains.
>
> (III, p. 165)

From the beginning, the presupposition of a general rate of profit was very much a 'primitive' in Ricardo's analytical vision.

As to the question of what produces movements in general profitability, the early Ricardo was concerned to argue that a change in the money supply would not be responsible. More precisely, and in the terminology which pervades the later writings:

---

[1] For example, that Ricardo treated wages as "necessarily at all times equal to the amount of the necessary cost of subsistence of the labourer" (Bohm-Bawerk [1921] (1959), p. 60). Cf. Cannan (1929) p. 299.

[2] In his letter to Malthus of 30 August 1814, Ricardo alluded to "bad government and the consequent insecurity of property, or...the little disposition to saving in the people" as factors producing a 'permanent' change in profitability (VI, p. 129). Mostly, however, he took the social propensity to save as given.

[3] Cf. Dobb (1973), p. 67; Hollander (1979), p. 103; Meek (1973), p. 86; and Sraffa, IV, p. 3.

> To suppose that any increased issues of the Bank can have the effect of *permanently* lowering the rate of interest...is to attribute a power to the circulating medium which it can never possess.
>
> (*High Price of Bullion*, III, p. 92. My italics)

All that could result from alterations in the money supply were 'temporary' variations in general profitability, "of momentary duration",[1] stemming from non-proportional changes between money wages and the prices of wage-goods.

As in Ricardo's later work, this analysis presumes that the initial level of commodity wages must be restored. In the Notes on Bentham's *Sur Les Prix*, the 'fixwage' assumption is rendered transparent:

> Labour is paid not by money but by money's worth[;] therefore if prices rise it will not occasion any increased production because more money must be given to the labourer to enable him to obtain the same amount of commodities.
>
> (III, p. 329)

By implication, 'permanent' movements in profitability were not from the inception associated with altered commodity wages.

Further taking into account Ricardo's early rejection of the possibility of general gluts (III, p. 108), his characterisation of capital accumulation as a labour-attracting process (III, p. 107), and the belief that "necessaries must... be augmented before any increased industry can be called forth" (III, p. 276), we have many ingredients for the 'theory' of profits enunciated in 1813. What we also find in the early writings is apparently unqualified support for a thesis on profitability which was later to be rejected: Adam Smith's 'competition of capital' doctrine. Thus:

> If Sir John [Sinclair] will take the trouble to consult the 4th chap. 2nd Book of Dr. A. Smith's celebrated work, he will there see it undeniably demonstrated, that the rate of interest for money is totally independent of the nominal amount of the circulating medium. *It is regulated solely by the competition of capital*, not consisting of money.
>
> (Letter to the *Morning Chronicle*, 18 September 1810, III, p. 143. My italics)

From this, it seems, 'permanent' movements in profitability would have been explained in terms of the variable intensity of competition.

In saying that the Smithian perspective was subsequently rejected by Ricardo, there is an important caveat which should be stated. Although the basis for 'permanent' changes in the general rate of profit was not sought in the 'competition of capitals' from 1813 onwards, it was 1816 before Ricardo ceased to express his 'theory' within 'orthodox' Smithian discourse.[2] For example, he wrote in a letter to Malthus of 16 September 1814:

---

[1] As Ricardo noted in relation to Bentham's *Sur Les Prix*, when advancing the same analysis. III, p. 319.

[2] By October 1816, Ricardo's perception of his approach to profitability had evolved to the point where he could write: 'I do not quite understand the expression that profits depend on the demand compared with the supply of capital.' Letter to Malthus, 11 October 1816: VII, p. 78.

[W]hen capital is scanty compared with the means of employing it, from whatever cause arising, profits will be high. Whether temporarily or permanently must of course depend of whether the cause be temporary or permanent. It is however very important to ascertain what the causes are which make capital scanty compared with the means of employing it, and how far when ascertained they may be considered temporary or permanent.

It is in this enquiry that I am led to believe that the state of the cultivation of the land is almost the only great permanent cause.

(VI, p. 133)

Here as in other cases,[1] Ricardo attempted to reconcile his 'theory' of profits with the received wisdom of Adam Smith, which continued to be championed by Malthus. But whereas Malthus ascribed to the 'competition of capitals' the aetiological role of "prime mover" (VI, p. 111) for Ricardo it had only a passive function: the 'permanent' reduction in profitability following worsened agricultural conditions of production was explained as an *ex post* fall in the demand for capital relative to the supply; the 'competition of capitals' was thereby displaced from its causal throne.

It emerges that 1813 was a watershed for Ricardo, although in a sense more subtle than that suggested by Sraffa's interpretation.[2] In important respects, the 'box of tools' with which profitability was analysed was essentially that of which Ricardo had been in possession from the beginning of his economic writings; notably, it included the concept of 'permanence', the 'fixwage' analysis and the 'adding up' approach to price. The major difference in analytical content was the role accorded to the 'competition of capitals'. What prompted this change was an altered object of analysis: a direct concern with changes in profitability in an attempt to understand recent and contemporary economic events, as opposed to the indirect concern exhibited during Ricardo's involvement with the 'Bullion Controversy'. With this shift in focus, a more critical treatment of previously accepted arguments was called for. Ricardo's quest for his own analytical system had begun.

VII

It is a tribute to Piero Sraffa's intellectual honesty that he should have revealed the manner in which the 'corn model' interpretation of Ricardo's writings suggested itself to him.[3] The interpretation was, in my view, a projection on to Ricardo's writings: a figment of Sraffa's imagination, rendered plausible by the illicit substitution of a precise twentieth-century notion – that of unique determination – for Ricardo's imprecise notion of 'regulation', together with a

---

[1] For example, letters to Trower of 8 March 1814 (quoted above, p. 735) and to Malthus of 8 May 1815, VI, pp. 228–9.

[2] The discontinuity implied by Sraffa's interpretation is made explicit in Garegnani (1982), where we find a reference to a "theory of profits which contrasted so sharply with the generally accepted one, running in terms of the 'competition' of capitals".

[3] See above, p. 733, n. 2.

belief, natural to economists today, that there must have been a logically coherent rationale for the interpreted position. Ricardo was thereby 'made sense of' in our terms, emerging as a 'theorist' we could all respect, if not endorse.

Hollander's achievement has been to challenge the consensus which grew around Sraffa's interpretation. But established interpretations are not easily displaced, especially one so attractive as Sraffa's, and particularly for those who wish to claim Ricardo for the school of thought to which they subscribe. Hence the contemporary debate, fuelled by Professor Hollander's unfortunate and equally distorting participation in the same unhelpful game: that of striving to establish lineages.

Understanding Ricardo is notoriously difficult. Let us not increase this difficulty by anachronistically cloaking him in the garb of more recent schools of thought.

University of Manchester

Date of receipt of final typescript: March 1984

REFERENCES

Bharadwaj, K. (1983). 'On a controversy over Ricardo's theory of distribution.' *Cambridge Journal of Economics*, vol. 7, pp. 11–36.
Böhm Bawerk, E. von. (1959). *Capital and Interest*, vol. 1, [1921], Illinois: Libertarian Press.
Cannan, E. (1929). *A Review of Economic Theory*. London: P. S. King.
Dobb, M. (1973). *Theories of Value and Distribution Since Adam Smith*. Cambridge: Cambridge University Press.
Eatwell, J. (1975). 'The interpretation of Ricardo's *Essay on Profits*.' *Economica*, vol. 62, pp. 181–7.
Garegnani, P. (1982). On Hollander's interpretation of Ricardo's early theory of profits.' *Cambridge Journal of Economics*, vol. 6, pp. 65–77.
—— (1983). 'Ricardo's early theory of profits and its "rational foundation": a reply to Professor Hollander.' *Cambridge Journal of Economics*, vol. 7, pp. 175–8.
Hollander, S. (1973). 'Ricardo's analysis of the profit rate, 1813–15.' *Economica*, vol. 60, pp. 260–82.
—— (1979). *The Economics of David Ricardo*. Toronto: Heinemann.
—— (1983). 'Professor Garegnani's defence of Sraffa on the material rate of profit.' *Cambridge Journal of Economics*, vol. 7, pp. 167–74.
Malthus, T. R. (1815a). *An inquiry into the Nature and Progress of Rent*. London: John Murray.
—— (1815b). *Observations on the Effects of the Corn Laws*, 3rd ed. London: John Murray.
Meek, R. L. (1973). *Studies in the Labour Theory of Value*, 2nd ed. London: Lawrence and Wishart.
Peach, T. (1982). *A Re-Interpretation of David Ricardo's Writings on Value and Distribution*. D.Phil. Oxford and Cambridge: Cambridge University Press. Forthcoming.
Ricardo, D. (1951–73). *Works and Correspondence* (ed. P. Sraffa) (10 vols.), Cambridge: Cambridge University Press.
Smith, A. (1976). *The Wealth of Nations* [1776]. Chicago: University of Chicago Press.
Sraffa, P. (1960). *Production of Commodities by Means of Commodities*, Cambridge: Cambridge University Press.
Torrens, R. (1815). *An Essay on the External Corn Trade*. London: J. Hatchard.

Ricardo's invariable measure of value and Sraffa's 'standard commodity'

Nai-Pew Ong

I. Introduction

It is our contention that Ricardo's invariable measure of value is conceived in order to salvage two of his earlier theoretical claims within the framework of his fully developed theory of prices of production. These are (i) his corn-model theory of income distribution which avers that the general rate of profit is inversely related to an abstractly conceived one-dimensional 'difficulty of production' of the real wage, and, consistently with this, (ii) his labor theory of value which purportedly substantiates his notion of the 'difficulty of production' of a commodity in general.[1] In the light of our exegesis, we examine whether Sraffa's 'standard commodity,' which is developed in his *Production of commodities by means of commodities*, is adequately a solution to the project underlying Ricardo's vain search for the invariable measure of value. We conclude that it is not.

II. Income Distribution and the 'Difficulty of Production' of the Wage

Ricardo's corn model of income distribution remained intact in its essential features up to the final edition of the *Principles*, where it stands as his proffered solution to "the principal problem in Political Economy."[2] In

---

Correspondence may be addressed to Dr. Nai-Pew Ong, Dept. of Economics, University of California—Riverside, Riverside CA 92521.

1. Ricardo's pre-labor-value conception of the 'difficulty of production' of the real wage and its relation to income distribution is first posited in his *Essay on the influence of a low price of corn on the profits of stock* (1815), in *The works and correspondence of David Ricardo*, ed. P. Sraffa (Cambridge, 1951–73), IV, 18–20, and in his letters in *Works*, VI, 233, 241, 247–48, 292–94. The identification of the uni-dimensional 'difficulty of production' with labor value, or more generally with 'natural value', 'absolute value', or 'real value', is developed from Smith's 'toil and trouble' notion and appears in *Principles of political economy and taxation* (1817, 1819, 1821) in *Works*, I, 12–13, 23, 48–49, 93, 112–13, and 273, and in his last pamphlet, 'Absolute value and exchangeable value,' in *Works*, IV, 375, 396–97. In his letter to Malthus of 11 Oct. 1821, Ricardo writes: "I say again that too much importance is attached to money—facility of production is the great and interesting point. How does that operate on the interests of mankind?" (*Works*, IX, 100). See David P. Levine, *Economic studies* (London, 1977), pp. 79–90. After chapter 1 of *Principles*, Ricardo in effect avoids the problem of the divergence of price of production from labor value and carries out his analysis in terms of the latter.

2. Preface to *Principles*, in *Works*, I, 5. The corn model of income distribution is repro-

the main, there are two distinct categories of changes in the 'value' of the real wage, which are held to lead to opposite changes in the general rate of profit.³ The first is the category of changes in the physical conditions of production or, for Ricardo, the 'difficulty of production' of the unit wage basket. The second is that of changes in the quantity of wage goods paid per unit labor. The recognition of the distinction between the two is crucial because it is the first category which is central to Ricardo's argument regarding how income distribution is determined over the long-term course of capital accumulation by the deteriorating marginal conditions of production of a constant real-wage basket, while the second category is important chiefly in buttressing one side of his theory of short-run equilibrating movements in the labor market under constant conditions of production.⁴

In his *Essay on profits*, Ricardo argues that the corn rate of profit varies inversely to the difficulty of producing the subsistence corn wage on the marginal piece of land, the degree of which is to be comprehended in terms of the simple ratio of labor or corn (as wage) input to corn output. Responding to criticisms by Malthus and others, Ricardo takes up Smith's notion of the labor (embodied) time of production as that which gives substance to his concept of value in general as being determined by the degree of difficulty or facility of producing the commodity. This position Ricardo is to consistently uphold from the first edition of his *Principles* up to his final pamphlet, 'Absolute value and exchangeable value,' written close to his death in 1823. "To me, it appears a contradiction to say a thing has increased in natural value while it continues to be produced under precisely the same circumstances as before."⁵ Not surprisingly, therefore, Ricardo summarizes his conclusion regarding the long-term distribution of income in his *Principles* in a sweeping statement: "in all countries, and all times, profits depend on the quantity of labour requisite to provide necessaries for the labourers, on that land or with that capital which yields no rent."⁶

---

duced in labor-value terms in the chapters of *Principles*, in *Works*, I, 'On rent,' pp. 69–83, 'On wages,' pp. 93–96, 'On profits,' pp. 112–13, and 'On foreign trade,' pp. 131–33.

3. For Ricardo, a nominal change in the wage "produces a general effect on price, and for that reason it produces no real effect whatever on profits," while a real change, which arises "from the circumstance of the labourer being more liberally rewarded, or from a [greater] difficulty of procuring the necessaries on which wages are expended, does not, except in some instances, produce the effect of raising price, but has a great effect in lowering profits" (ibid. 63–64). For other references regarding the two 'real' wage changes, see his *Notes on Malthus*, in *Works*, II, 252, 264–66.

4. The conception of a quantitative change in the wage bundle as being linked to the determination of the 'market price' as opposed to the long-run equilibrium 'natural price' of labor is elaborated in the chapter 'On wages' of *Principles*, in *Works*, I, 93–98. For a recent treatment of this, see Nai-Pew Ong, 'Marx's classical and post-classical conceptions of the wage,' *Australian Economic Papers*, Dec. 1980.

5. This is from the first draft of the paper in *Works*, IV, 375.

6. *Works*, I, 126.

By the third edition of the *Principles*, however, what appears alongside the above conclusion is Ricardo's "considerably modified" position on the circumstances of production which determine relative prices in the first chapter 'On value', where it is not merely the total quantity of labor necessarily expended in producing a commodity but also the time structure of that expenditure. The fully developed system of prices of production which takes into account the capitalist nature of production in the Ricardian sense of equalized profit rates, do not in general correspond to relative labor values, on account of the different durabilities of fixed capital and different ratios of fixed to circulating capitals. Furthermore, relative prices of production of commodities will be restructured not only as a result of changes in their particular conditions of production but even independently of such changes and merely in response to a shift in the general rate of profit (owing to either of the two categories of changes in the 'difficulty of production' of the real wage).[7] In order for Ricardo to sustain both (i) his long-term theory of income distribution and (ii) his labor theory of value,[8] in the framework of his mature prices-of-production system, he must provide a consistent notion of what he means when he speaks of an increase or decrease in the 'difficulty of production' of the commodity in general and real wage in particular, *in terms of how such changes manifest themselves as relative price changes of commodities*.

Given the nature of the divergence of relative price changes from actual changes in the conditions of production of the commodities in question, Ricardo's method of attacking this vexing problem is to posit the idea of a commodity as an invariable measure of value. This is to allow Ricardo unambiguously to separate out and quantify a change in the relative price of a commodity which is solely the result of a change in its physical conditions of production from that which is solely the result of a shift in the general rate of profit. The first type of change in the relative price of a commodity is what Ricardo specifically defines as a change in the 'real value' of the commodity.[9] This can then be shown to conform in direction and magnitude to the actual change in its 'difficulty of production'. Moreover, the use of the invariable measure of value, if successful, would be especially relevant to the type of change in 'real value' which Ricardo is most interested in, namely that of the real wage. For, if Ricardo's theory

---

7. Ibid. 30–43.

8. Sraffa has demonstrated that there is little evidence of a 'retreat' from the strict labor theory of value from the first to the third editions of *Principles*, in his introduction, *Works*, I, xxxviif. This is supported by Samuel Hollander, *The economics of David Ricardo* (Toronto, 1979), p. 217. Refer also to *Works*, I, 20. 25, 49–50, 73.

9. Ibid. 41–51. It is important to note that Ricardo introduces the term 'real value' in Sections V, VI, and VII, as soon as there arises the possible ambiguity about the origins of a change in the price of production of a commodity and when he is preoccupied with the problem of the invariable measure of value. "Wages are to be estimated by their real value, viz. by the quantity of labour and capital employed [i.e., not just necessary labor] in producing them" (ibid. 50). Refer also to the passage of n. 10 below.

of income distribution were truly correct, such a change of the 'real value' of the real wage would result in a shift in the general rate of profit, thereby altering the whole structure of relative prices, including that of the real wage itself. Thus if there were no invariable measure of value, the direction and magnitude of the actual change in the 'real value' of the real wage would be masked by the resulting round of price changes in general which is brought about as a direct consequence of the original change in the 'difficulty of production' of the real wage. Hence, to the extent of the consequential modification of the relative price of the real wage, the general rate of profit will not be accurately related in the inverse manner to the perceived change in the relative price of the real wage. This idea is presented sharply by Ricardo in the problem of a measure of value which will itself experience a change in its relative price in general owing to the change in the general rate of profit.

Clearly, Ricardo's search for the invariable measure is his peculiar way of reconciling his one-dimension notion of an absolute 'difficulty of production' of commodities in general, which underlies his theories of income distribution and 'natural value', with his discovery that the relative prices of production of commodities change with both the labor expended in their production and the time distribution of these expenditures, that is, according to *two dimensions* of changes in their conditions of production.

III. The Role and Nature of the Invariable Measure

The necessary property which the invariable measure of value must possess is its ability to separate out the change in the price of production of any commodity which is due strictly to a change in its 'difficulty of production', that is, the change in its 'real value'. Thus in the section 'On an invariable measure of value' of the first chapter of *Principles*, Ricardo begins his argument as follows:

> When commodities varied in relative value, it would be desirable to have the means to ascertaining which of them fell and which rose in real value, and this could be effected only by comparing them one after another with some invariable standard measure of value, which should itself be subject to none of the fluctuations to which other commodities are exposed.[10]

Changes in the relative prices of commodities which are due to shift in the general rate of profit are to be excluded by use of the invariable measure of value, for "every alteration in the permanent rate of profits would have some effect on the relative value of all these goods, independently of any alteration in the quantity of labour employed on their production."[11]

10. Ibid. 43. 11. Ibid. 45.

There are actually two distinct stages in Ricardo's arguments with regard to how the invariable measure of value is to perform the task desired of it. Firstly, there is the idea that the invariable measure of value should be an *invariable money medium*, that is, a commodity money with a relative price of production which does not vary with any shift in the general rate of profit. In spite of Ricardo's statement quoted above, however, it is not obvious that this idea will live up to the requirements of the second idea, which is that of the *divining rod* which Ricardo can use to separate out and measure the changes in relative prices which are due to changes in the 'difficulty of production' of commodities, independently of those which are due to a shift in the general rate of profit. It is this second idea that will make possible Ricardo's attempt to restate his earlier theories of income distribution and labor values *within* the system of prices of production, thereby eliminating the discrepancy between the first and subsequent chapters of the *Principles*. Furthermore, it is this second idea for which the term 'perfect measure of value' is reserved in his *Principles*.[12]

To substantiate our interpretation of Ricardo's need for an invariable measure of value, we now examine the only area in which he sketches out the implications of using such an invariable measure of value were he to possess one, that is, that of changes in income distribution stemming from changes in production conditions of commodities, especially the wage goods. This is from the last section of the first chapter of *Principles*:

> It is not by the absolute quantity of produce obtained by either class that we can correctly judge of the rate of profit, rent, and wages, but by the quantity of labour required to obtain that produce . . . [I]f we had an invariable standard by which to measure the value of this

---

12. Ibid. 43–46. The special task of the 'perfect measure of value' as that which divines the price effect of a change in the general rate of profit is spelt out in Section VI of ch. 1 of *Principles*, starting with "It would be a perfect measure . . ." and ending with "Neither gold then nor any other commodity . . . " (Ibid. 45). This peculiar idea reappears in his last letters, in *Works*, IX, 352, 361, 380, and in his last paper, 'Absolute value and exchangeable value,' in *Works*, IV, 390–97. In his Introduction, *Works*, I, xl–xlvii, Sraffa notes that Ricardo "ends [in his last paper] by bringing this criterion [of the invariable measure of 'absolute' value] to bear upon another problem, namely the distinction between two causes of change in exchangeable value" (ibid. xlvi). Sraffa fails to note, however, that such an application is already evident in the third edition of *Principles*, is central to the unification of Ricardo's theories of distribution, 'absolute value', and price, and is uniquely associated with the term 'perfect measure of value'. Mark Blaug in *Economic theory in retrospect* (Homewood, Ill., 1962), p. 91, merely remarks that the notion of an invariable money medium "seems . . . to have got mixed up in Ricardo's mind with the problem of locating the source of variations in the ratios of exchange between two goods." Maurice Dobb, in his *Theories of value and distribution since Adam Smith* (Cambridge, 1973), pp. 82–83, Ronald L. Meek, in his *Studies in the labor theory of value* (London, 1973), p. 111, and Samuel Hollander, in his *Economics of David Ricardo*, pp. 218–21, all fail to distinguish between the notions of the 'perfect measure of value' as divining rod for price changes and the invariable money medium.

produce, we *should* find that a less value has fallen to the class of labourers and landlords, and a greater to the class of capitalists, than had been given before. We *might* find, for example, that though the absolute quantity of commodities had been doubled, they were the produce of precisely the former quantity of labour. . . . If then in this medium, which had not varied in value, the wages of the labourer *should* be found to have fallen, it will not the less be a real fall, because they might furnish him with a greater quantity of cheap commodities than his former wages [*Works*, 1:49–50; emphasis added].[13]

The point of this discussion is that Ricardo wishes to investigate the change in income distribution as it appears in the system of prices of production, when measured by the invariable measure of value, and then to relate this to the changes in the labor values of commodities. Firstly, the change in the distribution of income among the three great classes is measured in terms of the quantities and altered prices of the commodities going to each class by the invariable measure of value. Secondly, such a change in income distribution, when held up to the special light of the invariable measure, "should" or "might" then be demonstrated to bear a systematic relationship to changes in the labor values of commodities, especially to those of the real wage. As indicated in the preceding paragraph, however, it is not obvious at all that an invariable money medium with a price which is invariable to shifts in income distribution will successfully fulfill the herculean task of locating certain price changes as owing strictly to changes in the 'natural value' of the commodities, and attributing the rest as owing strictly to changes in income distribution. Without this task of the divining rod, the second step which is revealed here cannot be taken.

The analysis of the possibility or impossibility of an invariable money medium additionally to be the divining rod or 'perfect measure of value' can only be fruitfully undertaken once the essential conditions and properties of the invariable money medium are revealed.

IV. The Theoretical Construction of the Invariable Money Medium

David Ricardo perceives that the first requirement of the invariable measure of value is that it must be an invariable money medium. This should be a commodity with a price of production which is indifferent to shifts in income distribution. It should also be a commodity with a labor value or

---

13. The use of the invariable measure of value to study changes in income distribution owing to the "increased difficulty of procuring an additional quantity of food" is also elaborated in the chapter 'On wages' in *Principles* (*Works* I, 102). Clearly, in this and other chapters, Ricardo simply assumes that a money "of an unvarying value" (ibid.) will be sufficient for him to reproduce his theory of the inverse relationship which supposedly exists between the general rate of profit and some one-dimensional 'difficulty of production' of the real wage.

'difficulty of production' which is held forever constant, so as to provide the constant unit of measure of income distribution at different points in time where the conditions of production of all other commodities, and especially those of the real wage, may have changed.

Since the invariable money medium is primarily a theoretical solution for a theoretical problem, Ricardo assumes that there is an ideal commodity with unchanging conditions of production, a highly peculiar idea in the capitalist economy, where technological change is an ongoing process (his identification of the invariable money medium with gold, etc., is of course problematic).[14] It is the second requirement of the invariable money medium which presents the main stumbling block for Ricardo's 'theoretically conceived' invariable measure of value. Without ever satisfactorily resolving this issue, Ricardo therefore fails to consider the theoretical problems involved in the *further* requirements of the invariable measure of value as the divining rod.

The logical possibility of a commodity which *may* satisfy the requirement of a commodity with a price of production which is invariable to shifts in the general rate of profit is already suggested by Ricardo's own examination of how prices of production diverge from labor values with the introduction of different durabilities of fixed capital and ratios of fixed to circulating capitals in particular lines of production of commodities. This emerges in Ricardo's criticism of Adam Smith's assertion that a rise of the general wage raises all prices: "only those commodities would rise which had less fixed capital employed upon them than the medium in which price was estimated, and that all those which had more, would positively fall in price when wages rose."[15] May not then the invariable money medium be "considered as a commodity produced with such proportions of the two kinds of capital [that is, fixed and circulating capitals, and ignoring the other factor of different durabilities of fixed capitals] as approach nearest to the average quantity employed in the production of most commodities?"[16]

As Sraffa has shown in his own construction of the 'standard commodity', this is not too misleading a description of an invariable money me-

---

14. "If we suppose this cause of variation [in the production conditions of gold] to be removed, and the same quantity of labour to be always required to obtain the same quantity of gold" (ibid. 44). It should be noted that Ricardo himself collapses the distinct notions of the invariable money medium and the 'perfect measure of value' into each other in this particular paragraph, even as he is only concerned with the former here.

15. Ibid. 45.

16. Ibid. It is clear that Ricardo recognizes that the problem lies with the time dimension of expenditure of labor, introduced through the notion of capital as embodying dated labor; so the invariable measure of value *as* invariable money medium must be produced by both 'capital' and direct labor. See his letters in *Works*, IX, 100, 298–305, 320. This also explains why Ricardo was wont to suppress the notion of changes in the time structure of production, as noted by Samuel Hollander, pp. 221–23.

dium which can be constructed in a technically static, non-developing situation.[17] A commodity can theoretically be conceived as being produced in a system of non-changing, physically specified conditions of production of a system of particular commodities, such that its relative price of production is held constant by the opposing impacts of the opposite movements of the rate of profit and the value of the real wage. Sraffa has shown that there has to be the requirement that all the conditions of production of the commodities which enter into the production of all commodities (his 'basic commodities') must remain unchanged because it is this which fixes the rate at which the real wage moves against the general rate of profit. The nature of the structural composition of the invariable money medium which is a specific weighted construction of the 'basic commodities' therefore requires that each invariable money medium be defined only in accordance with a constant set of production conditions, an issue which is further examined below.

V. The Theoretical Impossibility of the 'Perfect Measure of Value'

In the sixth section of the first chapter of *Principles*, 'On an invariable measure of value,' Ricardo begins by immediately conceding that it is next to impossible *in reality* to ever come across a commodity which is an invariable money medium, although he is close to correctly specifying the ideal conditions necessary for it to be possible *in theory*. Such is not simply the problem with the 'perfect measure of value' or the divining rod which can separate out and measure the change in any commodity's price of production owing strictly to only a change in its conditions of production and not to a shift in the general rate of profit; an invariable money medium, were Ricardo to possess one, "would be a perfect measure of value for all things produced under the same circumstances precisely as itself, but *for no others*" (*Works*, 1:45; emphasis added).[18] With this statement, Ricardo is in effect conceding that it is impossible in theory even to think out the ideal properties which a hypothetical invariable money medium must have in order to be the divining rod for sorting out the two types of price changes for all commodities in general.

Ricardo's recognition of the theoretical impossibility of the 'perfect

17. Sraffa, Piero, *Production of commodities by means of commodities* (Cambridge, 1960), chs. 3 and 4.
18. In his last letter to Malthus of 31 Aug. 1823, Ricardo notes: "You say of my measure, and say truly, that if all commodities were produced under the same circumstances of time &c as itself, it would be a perfect measure; and you say further that it is now a perfect measure for all commodities produced under such circumstances" (*Works* IX, 380). In his last letter to James Mill of 5 Sept. 1823, Ricardo concludes by saying that he is "more confirmed than ever that strictly speaking there is not in nature any correct measure of value nor can any ingenuity suggest one, for what constitutes a correct measure for some things is a reason why it cannot be a correct one for others" (ibid. 387).

measure of value' for any and all commodities strikes at the heart of his peculiar attempt at salvaging the central thesis of his grand theoretical scheme, that is, the notion of a one-dimensional absolute scale of the conditions of production of the commodity in general which grounds both his corn-model theory of income distribution and his labor theory of value. If there can be a theoretically conceivable 'perfect measure of value' which can be relied upon to isolate and measure the true impact on the price of production of a given change in the conditions of production of a commodity, then Ricardo can begin to demonstrate that such an absolute degree of 'difficulty of production' does indeed exist *and* manifest itself unambiguously and unvaryingly in his system of relative prices of production. Without such a 'perfect measure of value' in general, it appears that this peculiar route taken by Ricardo to establish the validity of his notion of some absolute scale for the conditions of production has run up against a dead end. However, as we shall see in the next section below, even if Ricardo can continue to imagine the aid afforded by such a divining rod, still he will not be able to sustain his notion of the absolute character of the conditions of production of the commodity within the system of prices of production.

VI. *The Impossibility of an Absolute 'Difficulty of Production'*

We have arrived at the juncture where we can investigate the true project underlying Ricardo's search for the invariable measure of value. Let us start by assuming that Ricardo can actually have the invariable measure of value which is both invariable money medium and 'perfect measure of value' or divining rod. Even if Ricardo can possess such an invariable measure of value, can he demonstrate that there is an unambiguous meaning to be attached to the notion of the degree of 'difficulty of production' of the commodity in general and of the real wage in particular? To achieve this, it must be shown that a given change in the conditions of production of any commodity, say, that owing to a change in its means of production, will always have the same, unambiguous impact on its price of production as measured by the invariable measure of value.

If a given change in the conditions of production of a commodity has, at all possible levels of the general rate of profit, either a positive or a negative effect on its price of production so measured, *but never one and then the other*, then it can be considered to have been a change which has either increased or decreased the degree of 'difficulty of production' of the commodity according to an absolute scale. However, if a given change in the conditions of production cannot ever be shown to have always the same impact on the price of production of the commodity, as measured by the invariable measure of value, then Ricardo's notion of the absolute scale of the 'difficulty of production' of commodities in general cannot be sustained in his fully developed theory of prices of production. Thus, for example, if a certain technically determinate change in the conditions of production of a commodity will generate *an increase* in its price of production at a certain range of the general rate of profit, but *a decrease* in its price of production outside that range of the general rate of profit, even when measured by the invariable measure of value, then there cannot be a substantive meaning to be attached to the notion of an absolute scale of the conditions of production of commodities in Ricardo's system of prices of production. The existence or non-existence of an absolute index of the conditions of production in the system of prices of production is the same as the existence or non-existence of a strict one-to-one relation between any given change in the technical conditions of production of a commodity and the resulting change in the price of production which can be attributed solely to it via the invariable measure of value.

We shall now argue that there cannot be such a strict one-to-one relation between a change in production conditions of any commodity and the resulting price change as measured by the invariable measure of value in general, which is independent of the prevailing general rate of profit. This can be seen as follows. In the system of interlocking production of commodities by means of other commodities, the conditions of production of a given commodity may be grasped in terms of a time distribution of labor expended at the various stages of production of all the means of production which enter into the commodity and that expended at the final stage of production of the commodity. This is elaborated by Sraffa in his idea of the "reduction to dated labor." These time-specific quantities of labor manifest themselves in the price of production of the commodity but only when compounded with the prevailing general rate of profit (see Appendix I below).

Even if there were an invariable measure of value as both invariable money medium and 'perfect measure of value', still there will be no change in this property of the price of production of the commodity in relation to its dated labor inputs. Each dated labor input from a specific stage of production of the commodity can only manifest itself bound up with the general rate of profit raised to some specific power. The presumed ability of the invariable measure of value to be the divining rod which separates out and measures the change in a commodity's price of production which owes to a change in its conditions of production and only to this, does not contradict this peculiar property of the price of production of Ricardo, since the change in its dated labor inputs still has to be valuated at the prevailing general rate of profit (see Appendix II, below). Hence, there cannot exist any strict one-to-one relation between any given change in the conditions of production of a commodity and the resulting change in its price of production as measured by the invariable measure of value, independently of the prevailing general rate of profit. By extension, there cannot exist any strict one-to-one relation between a given set of conditions of production of a commodity and its price of production as measured by the invariable measure of value, independently of the general rate of profit. There can be no absolute index of the conditions of production which manifests itself unambiguously and unvaryingly in the system of prices of production of commodities, since all labor inputs must be valuated at the general rate of profit which is itself variable.

To illustrate this, let us assume a certain change in the conditions of production of a commodity, involving both a change in the total quantity of necessary labor of production and a change in the distribution over past theoretical time of that quantity of labor. Let there be a small decrease in the necessary labor expended in a stage of production in the distant theoretical past, and a large increase in the necessary labor expended in the next-to-final stage of production, prior to the present. According to the labor theory of value, this represents a net increase in the labor value of the commodity. According to Ricardo's theory of price of production, this change would also effect a rise in the commodity's price as measured by the invariable measure of value, but only within a certain upper-bounded range of magnitudes of the general rate of profit. At progressively higher general rates of profit, this positive effect on the price would be smaller and smaller until at one critical general rate of profit it would disappear altogether. Above this critical level the same change in the conditions of production of the commodity would effect a *fall* and not a *rise* in its price of production. The dependence of the sign and magnitude of the impact of such a change on the general rate of profit is of course due to the requirement that in the system of prices of production, a change in necessary labor in the distant theoretical past is multiplied by a correspondingly higher *power* of the general rate of profit than another change in the more recent period (see Appendix III below).

The above difficulty with the notion of total labor time as the single absolute scale of the 'difficulty of production' of the commodity in the system of prices of production applies for the real wage as well. Ricardo has concluded in his corn model that an increase in the 'difficulty' of the conditions of production of the wage bundle must lead to a decline in the general rate of profit. If such a claim is not to be a mere tautology, that is, by defining the degree of 'difficulty' of production of the wage bundle according to the nature of its effect on the general rate of profit, there must be an independent specification of the notion of the absolute index of the 'difficulty of production'. This is supplied by the labor theory of value. The same type of change in the conditions of production as that given above, that is, a small decrease in the necessary labor in a theoretically distant past period and a large increase in the necessary labor in the theoretically recent period, when applied to the wage bundle of goods as a composite good, will not generate an unambiguous change in the general rate of profit. That is, the sign and magnitude of its impact on the general rate of profit are dependent on the initial level of the general rate of profit itself. Hence, what is taken to be a net increase in the total labor necessary to produce the real wage will not necessarily lead to a fall in the general rate of profit. If the above change in the conditions of production of the real wage occurs at an initial general rate of profit which is above a certain critical level, the resulting change in the general rate of profit will be positive, not negative (see Appendix IV below).

Equivalently, it can be shown that the general rate of profit in Ricardo's system of prices of production is determined *jointly* by the total quantity of labor necessary to produce the real wage *and* the distribution of this total quantity of necessary labor in theoretical time of all the stages of production leading up to and including the final stage of production of the real-wage basket of goods. Any unrestricted notion of a change in the actual conditions of production of the real-wage composite good will generally involve both aspects of the total quantity of necessary labor and its time distribution, as is represented by our example. Hence, whether the general rate of profit rises or falls, as a result of such a type of unrestricted change in the two-dimensional conditions of production of the composite real wage, depends on the initial size and time structure of the necessary labor expended in its production. There cannot in general be an absolute scale to which Ricardo can appeal to ascertain whether a given change in the total quantity *and* time structure of necessary labor of production of the real wage has increased or decreased its 'difficulty of production' independently of the initial level of the general rate of profit or, equivalently, of the initial conditions of production of the real wage itself.

From all these, the relativity to the initial general rate of profit of the impact of a change in the production conditions of the commodity in general and the real wage in particular, on their prices of production—and, in the case of the real wage, on the general rate of profit itself—is not eliminated by use of the hypothetical invariable measure of value. Such a relativity is due to the requirement in Ricardo's own theory of prices of production that there be an implicit cost in the very passage of time in the production process. Ricardo recognizes this and bases this notion of implicit cost of time on the fact that under capitalist production and reproduction, profits are continually accumulated as capital:

> It is hardly necessary to say, that commodities which have the same quantity of labour bestowed on their production, will differ in exchangeable value, if they cannot be brought to market in the same

time.... The difference in value arises in both cases from the profits being accumulated as capital, and is only a just compensation for the time that the profits were withheld.[19]

There cannot exist a single absolute index of the 'difficulty of production' in the system of prices of production because two aspects of the conditions of production of commodities are relevant to their price of production, namely, the total quantity of labor and the time which must pass before the capital advanced for the expenditure of labor can return to the capitalist. The mature theory of prices of production, unlike the simple labor theory of relative prices, has integrated the capitalist nature of production of commodities in its internal logic.

It is the peculiar manner in which Ricardo sees the ultimate appearance of the capitalist nature of commodity production, that is, as the uniformity of profit rates across all lines of production, which yields the strong image that the mere passage of time automatically enters in as a cost element at a uniform rate of valuation. This is incorrect—firstly, because the time dimension is theoretically specified according to the prevailing system of particular production processes and is valuated at the current general rate of profit; it has nothing to do with actual historical time. Secondly, the 'just compensation' of this theoretical passage of time is not that it is a reward to 'waiting',[20] but rather that it stems from the very nature of capitalist enterprise as the accumulation of capital through commodity production. Each individual capitalist 'valuates' time because his success as capitalist is made objective *as a social fact* according to the rate at which his profits are 'being accumulated as capital'.

What is central is the substantive character of capitalist commodity production. It is this which contradicts Ricardo's thesis that the conditions of production of commodities, which are themselves commodities, can be conceived of in a purely technical, one-dimensional manner independently of their capitalist character, when they impact on the prices of these commodities. Furthermore, it is this which contradicts Ricardo's claim that the conditions of production of the real wage, which are themselves commodities, can be conceived of in a purely technical, one-dimensional manner independently of their capitalist character, when they impact on the general rate of profit. Changes in relative prices and in income distri-

---

19. *Principles, Works*, I, 37.
20. Hollander, pp. 211, 214, suggests that Ricardo's 'just compensation' formulation of the rate of profit is the neoclassical idea of the reward to 'waiting' or postponement of present consumption. This is not supportable by Ricardo's observations in chapter 1 of *Principles*, as in note 19 above. Also, as early as 1810, Ricardo writes in his "Notes on Bentham's 'Sur les prix'" in *Works*, III, 284: "I like the distinction which Adam Smith makes between value in use and value in exchange. According to that opinion utility is not the measure [replacing 'source'] of value."

bution cannot be analyzed strictly on the basis of a knowledge of the changes in the technical conditions of production of the real wage without recourse to the prevailing set of relative prices and general rate of profit, because it is through these that the capitalist character of production and accumulation intrudes.

In Ricardo's mature model of prices of production, the incorporation of the capitalist nature of productive enterprise contradicts his own notion of some absolute scale of the degree of 'difficulty' or 'facility' of commodity production in general, to which the behavior of prices can ultimately and unambiguously be reduced. Hence, there cannot be, in this model of the capitalist economy, any theory which relates the nature of the change in the general rate of profit to the nature of the change in the production conditions of the real wage independently of the prevailing set of prices. As Ricardo himself had feared, his 'difficulty of production' theory of income distribution indeed is ultimately "stopped by the word price."[21]

VII. *The Sraffian 'Standard Commodity'*

What remains to be dealt with is the issue concerning whether the Sraffian 'standard commodity' can or cannot be taken to be the theoretical solution to the project of Ricardo's invariable measure of value.[22]

We have already pointed out that there are two distinct notions of income distribution in Ricardo's *Principles*. Firstly, there is the dynamic type of changes in income distribution which are brought about by changes in the conditions of production of the real wage, independently of any change in its magnitude or composition. It is this which frames Ricardo's theory of the long-term evolution of income distribution with the progress of capital accumulation. Secondly, there is the static type of income distribution of re-apportionment of a given net product between capital and labor without any change in the production conditions of the real wage. As noted above, the 'standard commodity' can only be an invariable measure of value which is by nature limited to an unchanged system of technical conditions of production of 'basic' commodities, which enter directly or indirectly into all commodities in the system. Clearly, the 'standard commodity' system cannot be used to study changes in the general rate of profit in the dynamic setting where there is unrestricted ongoing technical change in any and all lines of production. It is precisely such a situation, however, which Ricardo grounds his dynamic theory of income distribu-

---

21. Ricardo's letter to James Mill of 30 Dec. 1815, in *Works*, VI, 348.
22. The idea that the 'standard commodity' is the solution to Ricardo's invariable measure of value has its seed in Sraffa, *Production*, p. 94. Sraffa evidently takes the invariable measure of value narrowly as an invariable money medium and not as the divining rod of 'perfect measure' as well. See note 12 above. This idea has been accepted by Maurice Dobb, *Theories*, p. 263, by E. K. Hunt, *History of economic thought: a critical perspective* (New York, 1979), p. 414, by Alessandro Roncaglia, *Sraffa and the theory of prices* (New York, 1978), p. 72, and others.

tion in. The use of the 'standard commodity' is therefore restricted to the following rather artificial situation of changing production conditions of wage goods.

In Sraffa's system of production of commodities by means of commodities, the wage goods are taken to be 'non-basic' commodities. As such, changes in any of the conditions of production of the wage goods do not need to involve or affect the conditions of production of the 'basic' commodities, unless of course such changes themselves originate with the 'basic' commodities to begin with. Barring any change in the production conditions of these 'basic' commodities, the 'standard commodity' will remain the effective variable money medium even when the production conditions of the real wage are altered.

Such a restricted type of change in the production conditions of the real wage will usually, though not necessarily, alter the price of this fixed real wage in relation to the 'standard commodity'. In terms of the latter, the wage has changed, and this must generate a shift in the general rate of profit. With this shift in the general rate of profit, however, the price of the fixed real wage will *further* be altered in terms of the 'standard commodity'. This process continues until a new, final price of the real wage is reached in terms of the invariable 'standard commodity', and the general rate of profit stops shifting. Hence, in the Sraffian system, there still is no way to separate out the supposed direct price impact of a change in the production conditions of the given real wage from the supposed indirect price impact of the accompanying shift in the general rate of profit, even when the price is in terms of the 'standard commodity'. The only exception to this general conclusion is if, by the slightest of chances, the new production conditions of the real wage are exactly the same as those of the 'standard commodity', in which case there will be no subsequent price movements. Of course, as we have argued, even with this, the observed price change is determined in part by the original general rate of profit, so that it cannot be reducible to only the nature of the change in the production conditions of the real wage. With or without such a minute coincidence, then, the observed total price change of the real wage is an unresolved sum of both the direct and indirect price impacts, owing to *both* the change in its production conditions *and* the original general rate of profit, even in the 'standard commodity' money system.

Just as there is no way to divine the impact of a change in the conditions of production of a fixed real wage directly on its price separately from the impact of the resulting change in the general rate of profit in the 'standard' system, so too is there no way to relate this change in the general rate of profit to the total change in the 'price' of the fixed real-wage basket in such a way as to claim that there exists a strict one-to-one relationship between the general rate of profit and some one-dimensional 'difficulty of production' of the real wage. Ricardo's dilemma in his dynamic theory of the long-term evolution of income distribution involves the problem of ordering along an absolute scale all types of changes in the conditions of production of a fixed real wage and relating these to the changes in the general rate of profit. Sraffa's technically innovative 'standard commodity' system does not resolve this dilemma.[23]

If we leave aside the central issue of the nature of changes in income distribution in the dynamic setting, which constitutes the 'principal problem' in Ricardo's political economy, there remains the *static* notion of the distribution and redistribution of a given net product between capital and labor with unchanged production conditions in general. Sraffa's 'standard commodity' system is evidently better suited to dealing with this. The wage is specified and paid out in terms of the hypothetical 'standard commodity', and it can be easily shown that such a 'price' of labor must vary in an inverse, or more exactly *linearly* inverse, manner to the general rate of profit. What is of substantive importance here, however, is whether, the conception of the return to labor in terms of some non-existing, merely ideal 'commodity' is any progress at all over the old-fashioned Ricardian conception of a fixed basket of wage goods. Certainly, the 'standard commodity' is not meant to be an actual functioning money unit, except trivially as a unit of account.

VIII. *Conclusion*

To reproduce his theories of income distribution and labor value in his mature model of prices of production, Ricardo must reveal the existence of an absolute scale of the 'difficulty of production' which underlies and unambiguously manifests itself in this system of relative prices. He attempts to deal with this problem by arguing that if he were to possess an invariable measure of value, he could eliminate in essence the discrepancy between the price of production and the absolute 'difficulty of production' of the commodity. Our exegesis shows that the invariable measure of value

---

23. It is in this context that Samuel Hollander's remark that "[in] Sraffa's model there is no process analysis" (Hollander, p. 685) as opposed to Ricardo's, possesses some merit. We have argued that Ricardo's search for the invariable measure of value is his peculiar attempt to come up with a consistent notion of an absolute 'difficulty of production' of the commodity in general and of the real wage in particular to unify his earlier theories of income distribution and 'natural value' with his mature model of prices of production. This sheds some light on Sraffa's notion that there is in Ricardo the suggestion of a production of a composite commodity (or corn) by the productive consumption of only the same composite commodity (or corn). Once it is recognized that Ricardo is really searching for an absolute scale of the 'difficulty of production' of commodities, which constitute both the input and output of all capitalist productions, then Sraffa's formulation can be seen as a peculiarly simple but statical, and ultimately artificial, way to grasp the complex impact of complex changes in the conditions of capitalist commodity production. This is something which Samuel Hollander's critical appraisal of Sraffa's 'standard system' does not reveal (Hollander, pp. 684–89).

is meant to be not merely an invariable money medium, such as is Sraffa's 'standard commodity' under restricted conditions, but also a 'perfect measure of value' which can separate out and measure the price change which is due strictly to a change in the production conditions of the commodity, as opposed to that which is due strictly to an accompanying change in the general rate of profit. Close examination also reveals that while he does not discard the theoretical possibility of an invariable money medium, Ricardo recognizes the theoretical impossibility of a 'perfect measure of value' for all commodities in general. The project behind the search for an invariable measure of value appears therefore to be stalled.

We contend, however, that even if he were to possess in theory an invariable measure of value with both functions, still Ricardo could not have demonstrated the existence of an absolute scale of the conditions of commodity production in general insofar as there cannot be an unambiguous and definite relationship between a given change in production conditions and the resulting change in the price of the commodity, independently of the prevailing general rate of profit. Specifically, a given change in the production conditions of a commodity does not lead to the same price change even when measured by the invariable measure of value, at different general rates of profit. Furthermore, a given change in the production conditions of the real wage leads to different changes in both sign and magnitude of the general rate of profit itself, depending on its original level. All of this is due to the very nature of Ricardo's model of prices of production, in which are to be found two, not one, effective dimensions of the conditions of commodity production, that is, the total necessary labor of production and its distribution across past theoretical time. This results from the introduction of the *capitalist character* of commodity production into his conception of price determination.[24] Hence, Ricardo's earlier corn-model theory of income distribution and labor theory of value, which have been conceived on a substantively non-capitalist basis, cannot be sustained in his mature model of capitalist prices of production, even were he to possess the sought-for invariable measure of value.

Sraffa's *Production of commodities by means of commodities* is written as a prelude to, and it has successfully generated, a critique of the neoclassical conception of 'capital' as a physically determinate, scarce 'factor of

---

24. Karl Marx in essence does away with the problem of the invariable measure of value *à la* Ricardo, by postulating that there is an essential distinction between what appears to be the primordial 'essence' (i.e., labor values) and what is supposedly the phenomenal appearance of that 'essence' with a capitalist form (i.e., prices of production). This shifts the context of the problem of conceptualizing some absolute 'difficulty of production' (i.e., labor value) in the nature of capitalist production, but what then emerges is the so-called 'transformation problem' between labor values and prices of production, whose qualitative issues are yet to be dealt with, despite, or perhaps because of, all the quantitative 'solutions.'

production.' It does not, however, fulfil the double roles of Ricardo's invariable measure of value. As an invariable money medium, the 'standard commodity' is limited by the requirement of the constancy of the production conditions of 'basic' commodities. Even in the artificial situation where only the production conditions of 'non-basic' wage goods are changing (without affecting those of the 'basic' commodities), still the 'standard commodity' cannot live up to the role of the 'perfect measure of value', as Ricardo had already discovered.

I wish to acknowledge the assistance of two anonymous referees in sharpening the arguments presented here. They should not be held responsible for any errors remaining.

Appendices

Appendix I: Dated Labor and the Rate of Profit

Ricardo's conceptualization of the problem of the time distribution of labor necessary to the production of the commodity, for a given set of technical conditions of production of commodities by means of commodities, is evident in Sections III to V of chapter 1 of *Principles*. Let the distribution of necessary labor over past theoretical time of the production of commodity i be depicted by the row vector $[(L^i)]$ where

$$[(L^i)] = [L^i_0, L^i_{-1}, L^i_{-2}, L^i_{-3}, \ldots, L^i_{-T}] \qquad (A.1)$$

where each element L^i_{-t} is the quantity of necessary labor bestowed in period t prior to the final period (period 0) of production of the commodity i. For simplicity, we assume that the series is carried back far enough in theoretical time for the remaining, excluded quantities of dated labor to be in sum insignificant for a desired degree of approximation. See Sraffa, *Production of commodities by means of commodities*, p. 35. If the money wage rate is w, the price of production of the commodity i is

$$p^i = w \cdot (L^i_0 + L^i_{-1} \cdot (1 + r) + L^i_{-2} \cdot (1 + r)^2 + \cdots \\ + L^i_{-T} \cdot (1 + r)^T) \qquad (A.2)$$

where r is the general rate of profit, and where the wage is assumed to be paid out of revenue.

For simplicity, let the column vector of rising powers of $(1 + r)$ be given as

$$[(1 + r)] = [1, (1 + r), (1 + r)^2, (1 + r)^3, \ldots, (1 + r)^T] \qquad (A.3)$$

This and (A.1) allows us to rewrite the price of commodity i as

$$p^i = w \cdot [(L^i)] \cdot [(1 + r)] \qquad (A.4)$$

Let the row vector of the time distribution of necessary labor of production of the real wage be

$$[(L^w)] = [L^w{}_0, L^w{}_{-1}, L^w{}_{-2}, L^w{}_{-3}, \ldots, L^w{}_{-T}] \tag{A.5}$$

Then the money wage w which is necessary to buy this real wage must be

$$w = w \cdot [(L^w)] \cdot [(1 + r)] \tag{A.6}$$

Eliminating the money wage w from both sides of (A.6) yields the fundamental equation relating the time distribution of necessary labor to produce the real wage, $[(L^w)]$, and the general rate of profit r, viz.,

$$1 = [(L^w)] \cdot [(1 + r)] \tag{A.7}$$

Appendix II: The Pricing of a Change in Dated Labor

In general, a change in the production conditions of commodity i is given as

$$[(dL^i)] = [dL^i{}_0, dL^i{}_{-1}, dL^i{}_{-2}, dL^i{}_{-3}, \ldots, dL^i{}_{-T}] \tag{A.8}$$

This manifests itself as a change in the 'real value' of the commodity when it alters the price of production p^i. Such a price change is therefore

$$dp^i = w' \cdot [(L^i + dL^i)] \cdot [(1 + r')] - w^o \cdot [(L^i)] \cdot [(1 + r^o)] \tag{A.9}$$

where w^o, w', and r^o, r', are the original and new values of the money wage and the general rate of profit.

Assume, for simplicity, that the money wage w, which is merely the numéraire and does not affect relative prices at each given instant, remains the same. If the change in production conditions of commodity i does not disturb the time distribution of labor of production of the real wage, $[(L^w)]$, then the general rate of profit r is unchanged and the 'real' price change is

$$dp^i = w \cdot [(dL^i)] \cdot [(1 + r)] \tag{A.10}$$

With the unchanged $[(L^w)]$, r, and w, the specific task of a 'perfect measure of value' is not called for, and the invariable measure of value is simply the invariable money medium, that is, a commodity whose relative price of production has remained unchanged. In this simplest possible case, therefore, when measured with this invariable money medium, the change in the 'real value' of commodity i still remains inextricably tied to a definite level of the general rate of profit r and will be different for another level of r.

If the change in production conditions of commodity i does alter the time distribution of labor of production of the real wage, $[(L^w)]$, and therefore the general rate of profit r, then the total price change of i is:

$$dp^i = w \cdot [(dL^i)] \cdot [(1 + r')] + w \cdot [(L^i)] \cdot [(r' - r^o)] \tag{A.11}$$

From Ricardo's concept of the 'perfect measure of value', it is the first term of the right-hand side of (A.11) which is the change in the 'real value' of commodity i, while the second term is regarded as the price change due to the change in the general rate of profit from r^o to r'. Again, even when measured with the invariable measure as both invariable money medium *and* 'perfect measure of value', still the change in the 'real value' of commodity i must remain locked with a definite level of r, namely, the final r'.

Appendix III: The Ambiguity of a 'Real Value' Change

$$[(dL^j)] = [(0, dL^j_{-1}, 0, \ldots, 0, dL^j_{-T})] \tag{A.12}$$

where $|dL^j_{-1}| > |dL^j_{-T}|$, and $dL^j_{-1} > 0 > dL^j_{-T}$.

In the simplest situation as above, with a constant w and an unaltered $[(L^w)]$ and therefore unaltered r, the change in 'real value' of commodity j is:

$$dp^j = w \cdot (dL^j_{-1} \cdot (1 + r) + dL^j_{-T} \cdot (1 + r)^T) \tag{A.13}$$

The critical value of the general rate of profit r^*, is where

$$(1 + r^*)^{T-1} = (dL^j_{-1})/(-dL^j_{-T}) \tag{A.14}$$

The change in the 'real value' of commodity j will be positive, zero, or negative, depending on whether the prevailing general rate of profit r is less than, equal to, or greater than the critical value r^*. This example is suggested by Sraffa's case of the old wine and oak chest in his *Production of commodities by means of commodities*, pp. 37–39.

Appendix IV: The Ambiguous Impact of a Given Change in the Dated Labor of the Wage Bundle

Let $[(L^w)]$ be the original vector of labor of production of the real wage and r^o the corresponding general rate of profit. Let $[(dL^w)]$ be the change in the former, and dr the resulting change in the latter. Then from (A.7),

$$1 = [(L^w)] \cdot [(1 + r^o)] = [(L^w + dL^w)] \cdot [(1 + r^o + dr)] \tag{A.15}$$

In the column vector $[(1 + r^o + dr)]$, the term which only involves $(1 + r^o)$ and not dr can be separated from the remaining terms in each of its column elements. Furthermore, if we assume that we are considering only small changes in r, all terms involving the second and higher powers of dr can be safely ignored. With these, then, (A.15) becomes

$$[(L^w)] \cdot [(1 + r^o)] = [(L^w + dL^w)] \cdot [(1 + r^o)] + dr \cdot [(L^w + dL^w)] \cdot [(H(r^o))] \tag{A.16}$$

where $[(H(r^o))] = [0, 1, 2(1 + r^o), 3(1 + r^o)^2, \ldots, T(1 + r^o)^{T-1}]$.

Therefore, since the vector product of the second term on the right-hand side is positive, dr will be positive, zero, or negative, depending on whether $[(dL^w)] \cdot [(1 + r^o)]$ is negative, zero, or positive, respectively. If we assume that $[(dL^w)]$ takes the form given in (A.12) above, with $w = j$, then dr will be positive, zero, or negative, depending on whether r^o is greater than, equal to, or less than the critical value of r, r^*, given by

$$(1 + r^*)^{T-1} = (dL^w_{-1})/(-dL^w_{-T}) \tag{A.17}$$

[5]
James Mill and the early development of comparative advantage

William O. Thweatt

I

This essay explores anew the early development and subsequent incorporation into the main body of economic analysis of the law of comparative advantage. The main characters in this account are familiar—Torrens, Ricardo, McCulloch, and later, John Stuart Mill, but the hitherto unrecognized crucial role played by James Mill is shown and emphasized.

Modern texts in beginning economics and international trade credit David Ricardo with the formulation and development of the law of comparative advantage.[1] Specialized works in the history of economics do the same.[2] Frank Fetter's recent summary of "Ricardian economics" epitomizes the present consensus on Ricardo's supposed contribution to the theory of comparative advantage.[3]

WILLIAM THWEATT *is Professor of Economics at Vanderbilt University. A shortened version of this article was given as a paper at the Second Annual Conference of the History of Economics Society, at the University of North Carolina, June 1974.*

1. Cf. P. A. Samuelson, *Economics*, 9th ed. (New York, 1973), pp. 668, 670–71, and R. G. Lipsey and P. O. Steiner, *Economics*, 4th ed. (New York, 1975), pp. 737 and 740, for two popular beginning textbooks; Roy Harrod, *International Economics* (Cambridge, 1948), p. 20; S. Harris, *International and Interregional Economics* (New York, 1957), p. 15 and chap. 2, entitled "Ricardo and Comparative Advantage"; C. Kindleberger, *International Economics* (Homewood, Ill., 1968), p. 21; J. Viner, *Studies in the Theory of International Trade* (New York, 1937), p. 442; J. W. Angell, *The Theory of International Prices* (Cambridge, Mass., 1926), pp. 66, 82—to name but a few.

2. L. Rogin, *The Meaning and Validity of Economic Theory* (New York, 1956), p. 144; J. A. Schumpeter, *History of Economic Analysis* (New York, 1954), p. 607; M. Blaug, *Economic Theory in Retrospect*, rev. ed. (Homewood, Ill., 1968), pp. 126–30; H. W. Spiegel, *The Growth of Economic Thought* (Englewood Cliffs, N.J., 1971), p. 328.

3. F. W. Fetter, "The Rise and Decline of Ricardian Economics," *History of Political Economy* 1 (1969): 75–76. Fetter is not being novel, he is simply echoing long-held views such as: "The Law of Comparative Cost was a great, if not *the* great discovery made by Ricardo." E. D. K. Gonner, Introductory Essay to Ricardo's *Principles of Political Economy* (London, 1891), p. vii. "Ricardo's chapter is dominated by the new doctrine." J. H. Hollander, *David Ricardo: A Centenary Estimate* (Baltimore, 1910), p. 91. ". . . in April, 1817, appeared Ricardo's *Principles*, with the

Fetter tells us that Ricardo's theory of international trade, a contribution "peculiarly" his own, was a "magnificient intellectual tour de force." Although Robert Torrens had "expressed the general idea of comparative costs as early as 1808 . . . it was Ricardo who spelled out the argument in detail . . . made it his own . . . and drove home its practical application. . . . No idea of Ricardo's has stood up so well against critical attack, or has so powerfully influenced policy . . . culminating in the repeal of the Corn laws in 1846 . . . as did this analysis [which] by the 1840's permeated the thought of many [Britishers including the] scores who read the essence of his free trade ideas in the *Edinburgh Review* [and] in the *Westminster Review*."[4] Such is the state of the current myth.

Contrary to Fetter's caricature we hope to show that Ricardo's writings on the law of comparative advantage were not "peculiarly his own," nor that what Torrens wrote in 1808 should give him priority, any more than James Mill's simultaneous and equally valid statement. Furthermore, Ricardo did not spell out the argument in detail, did not make it his own, nor drive home its practical application. Also, Ricardo's analysis could hardly have "stood up so well against critical attack," since in the contemporary literature there was no criticism of what little Ricardo did write on the theory of comparative advantage—his theories of value and distribution were the chief targets of attack. And, interestingly, there was little anyone could have read in the *Edinburgh Review* or the *Westminster Review* about the law of comparative advantage. Indeed, so few of the arguments for free trade were based on comparative advantage, as distinct from a Smithian-derived "territorial division of labor" argument based squarely on absolute cost differences, that it is misleading to say the doctrine of comparative costs was influential in the discussion leading to the repeal of the Corn Laws in 1846.

Before examining the evidence for this position it may be helpful if first we briefly outline the concept of comparative costs. As Viner pointed out, as early as 1701 trade was seen as beneficial to a nation when it provided commodities "which could not be produced at home at all or could be produced at home only at costs absolutely greater than those at which they could be produced abroad."[5] Let us call this

---

theory of comparative cost set forth in classical detail." Idem, *Economic Journal* 21 (1911): 462. And Alfred Marshall, in his *Money, Credit and Commerce* (London, 1923), said Ricardo made comparative advantage into a "coherent doctrine," and "integrated it into an organic whole" (p. 41). Similar statements are contained in Seymour Harris, Schumpeter, and Viner cited supra nn. 1 and 2.

4. Fetter, pp. 75–76.
5. Viner, pp. 439–40.

notion, following Viner, the "eighteenth-century rule." In effect, the "rule" states that trade is beneficial whenever the resource cost of obtaining commodity A, in terms of commodity B, is lower when obtained through trade than when produced domestically. The "eighteenth-century rule," however, is compatible with explaining trade on both an absoute and on a comparative basis, and while not inconsistent with, does not necessarily imply, comparative costs.[6]

The further notion that, under these cost conditions, it still might be profitable to import commodity A even though it "could be produced at less cost at home than abroad" has to be considered "the essence" of the doctrine. Viner stressed that the explicit statement of "the essence" was the "sole addition of consequence which the doctrine of comparative costs made to the eighteenth-century rule."[7] Thus, "the essence" completes the explanation of the gains from trade in terms of comparative, as distinct from absolute, costs.

The full statement of the law of comparative advantage requires an explanation of the division of the gains from trade. There is, however, no dispute as to who first published a complete account of how the gains are divided in terms of reciprocal demands. John Stuart Mill first wrote it out sometime during 1829–30, but published it only in 1844 and later repeated it almost verbatim in his *Principles*. While there is still some unraveling to do with this part of the story, this will have to wait for another time, since there is enough to unravel with respect to the *early* development of the theory of the gains from trade. We therefore concentrate on the history of the "rule" and the "essence" components of the law of comparative advantage in attempting to ascertain the roles James Mill, Robert Torrens, and David Ricardo played in their development.

II

The occasion for the introduction of the eighteenth-century rule into what was to become the emerging orthodoxy of the British classical school was Napoleon's 1806 Berlin decree as he attempted to shut off England from trade with the Continent. Many an Englishman shuddered at the thought. It was in such an atmosphere of national concern that William Spence, who has been described as an English

---

6. The *locus classicus* of the "rule" is the remarkable pamphlet, *Considerations Upon the East-India Trade*, published anonymously in 1701. W. L. Barber, *British Economic Thought and India, 1600–1858* (Oxford, 1975), provides an excellent account of the role of this "remarkable document" in the history of trade theory in the eighteenth century, although he implies that the "eighteenth-century rule" is a "clear statement of the doctrine of comparative advantage" (p. 63), which it is not.

7. Viner, p. 441.

Physiocrat and an early underconsumptionist,[8] wrote his 1807 tract whose very title (*Britain Independent of Commerce or, Proofs Deduced from an Investigation into the True Causes of the Wealth of Nations, That Our Riches, Prosperity, and Power, are Derived from Sources Inherent in Ourselves, and Would Not be Affected even though Our Commerce Were Annihilated*) apparently was designed to assure his compatriots that they had no reason to fear Napoleon from this cause.

Spence's main contention was that since a nation's agriculture is the source of its wealth, a blockade of trade could not injure the national economy. He coupled this with the idea that it was essential for the landed proprietors of the country to spend all their incomes, lest prosperity be diminished through underconsumption. More than thirty books and pamphlets rapidly appeared in print—some, like Cobbett's *Political Register*, supporting Spence,[9] while most others attacked his ideas. One of the latter of particular importance was written by James Mill, who, for the first time in England, made use of the "law of markets" to dispose of the "dangerous doctrine" requiring landed proprietors to spend all their incomes "for the encouragement of agriculture."[10] Then making use of the eighteenth-century

---

8. Both B. Corry, *Money, Saving and Investment in English Economics, 1800-1850* (London, 1962), pp. 121-25, and B. Semmel, *The Rise of Free Trade Imperialism* (Cambridge, 1970), pp. 56-60, depict Spence as a follower of the French "Economistes"—an English Physiocrat. Spence did accept the Physiocratic "grand axiom" that agriculture creates all wealth, but their application of the axiom —government should favor agriculture at the expense of the "unproductive" manufacturing sector—he termed "erroneous," at least with respect to the great commercial states of Britain, France, and the Netherlands, wherein "agriculture has thriven only in consequence of the influence of manufactures." He insisted "agriculture *and* manufactures are the *two* chief wheels in the machine which creates national wealth. . . . of these two . . . it is the latter which communicates motion to the former." *Britain Independent of Commerce*, pp. 16 and 24; emphasis added. This, of course, was a very un-Physiocratic approach. In urging the necessity of an expanding landlord expediture of the social surplus for the continued prosperity of manufactures and thus the national economy, Spence was more in the long line of earlier British writers such as Cantillon, Sir James Steuart, and T. R. Malthus. Cf. R. Meek, *The Economics of Physiocracy* (London, 1962), pp. 322-28.

9. Cobbett devoted over fifty pages to Spence's tract in the November and December 1807 issues, and another twenty pages in the early months of 1808. That Cobbett's series of "Perish Commerce" articles popularized Spence's position has often been noted. Cf. L. Robbins, *Robert Torrens and the Evolution of Classical Economics* (London, 1958), p. 12; B. Semmel, p. 56; and D. Winch, *James Mill: Selected Economic Writings* (Edinburgh, 1966), p. 29. They fail to mention, however, that Spence felt compelled to reply to Cobbett's bitter charge of plagiarism. See Spence's letter in the *Political Register* (Dec. 1807), pp. 922-28.

10. "Spence's Britain Independent of Commerce," *Eclectic Review* 3 (Dec. 1807): 1056. James Mill's lifetime effort of establishing and defending a conservative politico-economic orthodoxy against "dangerous doctrine" probably makes him the

rule, he went on to show that a nation can benefit from "the trade of export and import." Mill's booklet was entitled *Commerce Defended*, and it appeared in early 1808, a few weeks after he had reviewed Spence's work.[11] The other important critique of Spence in terms of the emerging orthodoxy was Robert Torrens' *The Economists Refuted*, published almost at the same time as Mill's essay.

Torrens opened his work by attacking Spence's "idea of agriculture being the only source of wealth."[12] He then went on to refute the notion that foreign trade did not augment a country's wealth, using as proof an example also based on the eighteenth-century rule. It is interesting that most writers concerned with the origins of the "law of markets" concentrate on Mill's reply to Spence, while those concerned with the origins of the law of comparative advantage quote only what Torrens wrote, leaving the wrong impression that Mill had not written in this latter regard.[13] To show that this is not the case let

---

ideological founder of the British classical school. In a later study we hope to document this assertion.

11. Ibid. In his study on James Mill, D. Winch (p. 444) shows the date of Mill's *Commerce Defended* as 1807, but this surely is incorrect. Winch reproduces the 2d edition, of 1808, which is only slightly different from the A. M. Kelly photocopy reprint of the 1st edition (New York, 1965), the titlepage of which gives the correct date as 1808. A recent acquisition by the author, a copy of *The Economic Library of Jacob H. Hollander* (Baltimore, 1937), confirms on p. 193 the 1808 date for both the 1st and 2d editions.

12. *Economists Refuted*, p. 6. All references to this extremely rare pamphlet are to the 1857 reprint in R. Torrens, *The Principles and Practical Operation of Sir Robert Peel's Act of 1844 Explained and Defended* . . . 2d ed. (London, 1857). As Robbins, p. 260, and Corry, p. 158 n., have pointed out, this reprint omits a final chapter on making peace with France, but the main text contains only "numerous minor differences."

13. See, surprisingly perhaps, J. S. Mill, *Principles of Political Economy*, ed. Ashley (rpt. New York, 1965), p. 576 n., where he gives Torrens credit, along with Ricardo, for the doctrine of comparative costs based on what Torrens wrote in 1808, i.e., only the eighteenth-century rule. J. A. Schumpeter (p. 607) follows J. S. Mill in making this error, as indeed, does B. A. Corry (p. 122 n.). Even John Chipman's masterly "Survey of the Theory of International Trade: Part I, The Classical Theory," *Econometrica* 33 (1965): 479–83, the best account of the early development of the law of comparative advantage, completely overlooked Mill's *Commerce Defended*, by beginning: "Historians of economic doctrine have debated whether priority for the law of comparative advantage should go to Ricardo (1817) or to Torrens (1808, 1815)." Interestingly, William Spence himself never once mentioned Torrens, directing his reply to "Mr. Mill and the Edinburgh Reviewers." The review of Spence in the *Edinburgh Review* (Jan. 1808) most likely was by Henry Brougham, as noted by Semmel, (p. 56 n.), who, rightly, we think, takes issue with F. W. Fetter, "The Authorship of Economic Articles in the Edinburgh Review, 1802–47," *Journal of Political Economy* 61 (1953): 246, who ascribed the review to "T. R. Malthus (probably)." Semmel is exceptional in his treatment of James Mill, noting both his early formulation of the law of markets and his hint of the "principle of comparative cost," in *Commerce Defended*. Actually, Mill, like Torrens, in 1808 presented only the eighteenth-century rule.

us quote the eighteenth-century rule examples of both Mill and Torrens to establish Mill's equal priority along with Torrens.

In Mill's *Commerce Defended* (pp. 36–37), we read:

> On making a ton of iron in Great Britain, let us suppose, that the labourers, etc. employed in providing the ore and the coals, and in smelting and preparing the metal, have consumed ten quarters of corn. Every ton of iron therefore prepared in Great Britain costs ten quarters of corn. Let us suppose, that in the preparation of a certain quantity of British manufactures, nine quarters of corn have been consumed; and let us suppose, that this quantity of [manufactured] goods will purchase in the Baltic a ton of iron, and afford, besides, the expense requisite for importing the iron into Britain. Is there not an evident saving of a quarter of corn in the acquisition of this ton of iron? Is not the country one quarter of corn the richer, by means of its importation?

And, in Robert Torrens' *The Economists Refuted* (p. 53), we read:

> . . . if I wish to know the extent of the advantage which arises to England, from her giving France a hundred pounds' worth of broad cloth, in exchange for a hundred pounds' worth of lace, I take the quantity of lace which England has acquired by this transaction, and compare it with the quantity which she might, at the same expense of labour and capital, have acquired by manufacturing it at home. The lace that remains, beyond what the labour and capital employed on the cloth might have fabricated at home, is the amount of the advantage which England derives from the exchange.

Surely there is not much to choose between these two 1808 statements. Chipman's comment that what was being compared was the "cost ratio in one country with the international price ratio . . . but [that] the comparison of cost ratios (or rates of transformation) between two countries was lacking"[14] holds for both examples. If anything, Mill's presentation seems superior, particularly since he avoided Torrens' further ideas (i) that à la Adam Smith, trade by extending the division of labor increases productivity and creates a *surplus* above home requirements which foreign trade eliminates,[15] (ii) that an exchange of equivalents yields greater benefits to the nation receiving durables rather than perishables (hardwares as against

---

14. Chipman, p. 480.
15. *Economists Refuted*, pp. 15–26.

wine and fruit)[16] and necessaries rather than luxuries (woolen cloth as against lace),[17] (iii) that the advantages stemming from the home trade are more permanent than those of foreign trade, which are of "uncertain tenure" due to the "caprice of strangers and the hostility of rivals,"[18] and (iv) that "in every exchange of the home trade, the *whole* of the benefit remains in the country; in every exchange of the foreign trade a *part* of the benefit goes to enrich foreigners."[19]

Additionally, it surely distorts the story to proceed directly from 1808 to Torrens' February 1815 *Essay on the External Corn Trade*,[20] where, by adding the "essence" to the "rule," he stated for the first time the *complete* explanation of the gains from trade based on comparative advantage. To do so overlooks James Mill's important *Eclectic Review* article on the Corn Laws which appeared in July 1814. In this article Mill, again using the eighteenth-century rule, defended the orthodox position of free trade against Malthus' *Observations on the Effect of the Corn Laws*. Mill stressed the need for foreign trade in terms of efficiency, stating:

> If we import, we must pay for what we import, with the produce of a portion of our labour exported. But why not employ that labour in raising the same portion at home? The answer is, because it will procure more corn by going in the shape of commodities to purchase corn abroad, than if it had been employed in raising it at home. . . . A law, therefore, to prevent the importation of corn, can have only one effect,—to make a greater portion of the labour of the community necessary for the production of its food.[21]

Mill then goes on to take Malthus to task for his pro-Corn Law stance, making five main points in so doing: (i) a better regularity of food supply is secured via importation from various nations rather than from only the domestic economy, (ii) if a major exporter withholds supplies, the "world is wide" and another exporter will be forthcoming, (iii) the exporting nation which does restrict exports has more to lose than the importer because of its investment and specialization in corn production, (iv) the gain from trade can be measured by

---

16. Ibid., p. 50. Spence (pp. 47–48), also held this misconception, and Mill in his *Commerce Defended*, pp. 37 and 45, took him to task for it.
17. *Economists Refuted*, pp. 50–51.
18. Ibid., p. 31.
19. Ibid., pp. 30–31.
20. As does, for instance, Robbins, pp. 22–23, and Chipman, 480–81.
21. *Eclectic Review* N.S., 2 (July 1814): 4–5.

the difference between the domestic price of corn and the imported price (the eighteenth-century rule), and (v) in any event, historical facts show that Holland, with little domestic corn production, has attained opulence, relying upon imported corn for its food supply.

Interestingly, and hitherto unnoticed in the literature, all these arguments reappear, seven months later, in the replies of Torrens and Ricardo to Malthus' February 1815 pamphlet defending the Corn Laws.[22] Although Ricardo does not cite Mill explicitly, the last half of his *Essay on Profits* is so closely patterned on Mill's attack on Malthus' defense of the Corn Laws that we may take it that he had read Mill's article and discussed the issue with him in the Winter of 1814 while composing his own seminal essay.[23] As for Torrens, he *was* explicit. His Preface states: "one or two of [my] arguments . . . have been suggested by . . . an excellent article which appeared in the *Eclectic Review*."[24] This must be a reference to Mill's July 1814 article, since at that time Mill wrote all the articles on economic topics for the *Eclectic Review*.[25]

Notwithstanding the above remarks, it is true that up to February 1815 neither James Mill nor David Ricardo had gone beyond the eighteenth-century rule as an analytical argument in favor of repealing the Corn Laws. This Torrens did in his *External Corn Trade* essay

---

22. Cf. ibid., pp. 5–13, and Ricardo's *Essay on Profits*, pp. 27–32 and 39, as reprinted in *The Works and Correspondence of David Ricardo*, ed. P. Sraffa (Cambridge, 1951–1973), IV. In Torrens' "pamphlet" of over 360 pages, *An Essay on the External Corn Trade* (London, 1815), see "Part the First," chap. 2, esp. pp. 24, 35, 39–42, and 48.

23. Leaving open the question of the nature and extent of Mill's influence on Ricardo, the July 1814 Corn Law article shows clearly that both Stigler, "Sraffa's Ricardo," *American Economic Review* 43 (1953): 588, and T. W. Hutchison, "James Mill and the Political Education of Ricardo," *Cambridge Journal* 3, no. 2 (Nov. 1953): 81, are wrong when they maintain that "on matters of economics . . . Mill was inactive . . . during most of the period" (Stigler). Hutchison quotes a part of a sentence from a letter of Mill to Ricardo dated 9 Nov. 1815 in which he said, "for a good many years I have not been able to think of [political economy]." This of course, is belied by the Corn Law article, and furthermore, during this period, when Mill and Ricardo were both in London and much involved in matters economic, it was not quite cricket of Hutchison to omit the remaining portion of Mill's sentence, ". . . except when I was excited by your instructive conversation or by your writings." Sraffa, *Works*, VI, 320–21. This just might have been most of Mill's time!

24. *Essay on the External Corn Trade*, p. xiv. Torrens said, "one or two of the arguments contained in the Second Part," but much of the contents of chap. 2 of the First Part fall into this statement of indebtedness.

25. Although J. J. Spengler, "The Physiocrats and Say's Law of Markets, II," *Journal of Political Economy* 53, 4 (Dec. 1945), long ago said the article was written by "an anonymous reviewer," the more recent research of A. L. Lazenby, *James Mill: The Formation of a Scottish Emigré Writer* (D. Phil. diss., University of Sussex Library, Sept. 1972), p. 255, definitely attributes it to Mill. Donald Winch in a letter to the author dated 24 Aug. 1972 concurs in this.

published, Sraffa tells us, on the same day as Ricardo's *Essay on Profits*.[26] But he did not announce the "new doctrine" on the first page nor, for that matter, in the opening chapters. Not until after some 260 pages when, for the third time, he gave an explanation of the gains from trade based on the eighteenth-century rule,[27] did he finally add the further point, which we have called "the essence," enabling him to convert the long-known and often-used "rule" into the full statement of comparative costs:

> If England should have accquired such a degree of skill in manufactures, that, with any given portion of her capital, she could prepare a quantity of cloth, for which the Polish cultivator would give a greater quantity of corn, than she [England] could, with the same portion of capital, raise from her own soil, then, tracts of her territory, though they should be equal, nay, *even though they should be superior*, to the lands in Poland, will be neglected; and a part of her supply of corn will be imported from that country.[28]

So Robbins surely is right when, after quoting the above, he concluded Torrens was the "first in the field." He immediately added, however: "But as pure analysis it still lacks the final emphasis upon the comparison of ratios which is the ultimate essence of this principle."[29] It was to be 1827 before Torrens added this final touch, but by then both Ricardo in 1817 and, at greater length, James Mill in 1818 and 1821 had published complete statements embellished with the comparison of the cost ratios.[30] Nevertheless, by 1815 Torrens was on record. What about Ricardo?

Is it true, as Marshall was to put it in 1923, that "Ricardo took the fragmentary truth of his predecessors [Torrens and Mill?] and made them into a coherent doctrine," or as Schumpeter was to say, Tor-

---

26. Sraffa, Works, IV, 5.
27. *External Corn Trade*, pp. 48, 221–22, and 263–64. The initial use of the "rule" on p. 48 seems to have escaped the notice of E. R. A. Seligman and J. H. Hollander, "Ricardo and Torrens," *Economic Journal* 2 (1911): 448–68, and more recently that of Chipman, pp. 480–81. Lord Robbins (p. 23) cites only the example on pp. 263–64.
28. Ibid., pp. 263–64; emphasis added.
29. Robbins, p. 23.
30. For Torrens see the 4th edition of his *External Corn Trade*, and for Ricardo, Works, I, 135–36. For James Mill, see his Feb. 1818 article "Colonies" in the *Encyclopaedia Britannica*, Supplement to the 4th, 5th, and 6th eds. (Edinburgh, 1824), pp. 257–73, and his *Elements of Political Economy* (London, 1821), pp. 84–88. That Mill first published his "Colonies" article in early 1818 and not in 1824, the date of the reprint of the Supplement usually given as the date of publication of the article itself, I owe to the unpublished, meticulous study of A. L. Lazenby, pp. 301 and 42.

rens only "baptized the theorem," while Ricardo "elaborated it and fought for it victoriously"?[31]

In his *Essay on Profits* Ricardo too was urging freer trade, but on a completely different basis, as part of what has been called his "Corn Model" of economic growth.[32] Chipman, in his careful assessment of this period, concludes that the *Essay* "contains scarcely any recognition of the principle of comparative advantage."[33]

The reason why this is so becomes apparent once we determine the role foreign trade was to play in Ricardo's thinking. The hitch in Ricardo's growth theory was the shortage of land, setting a "limit upon the expansion of agriculture, and therefore, by implication . . . upon that of economy generally."[34] Foreign trade, acting as a substitute for the shortage of land, would convert diminishing returns in agriculture into constant returns. No need for *comparative* advantage here, and, as we shall see, no need for it later in his *Principles*.[35]

Ricardo, in this early period, was still groping, but despite the unfortunate loss of his "papers on the profits on Capital,"[36] we can see the direction of his thinking from what he wrote to Trower in March 1814:

> . . . in short it is the profits of the farmer which regulate the profits of all other trades,—and as the profits of the farmer must necessarily decrease with every augmentation of Capital employed on the land . . . all other profits must diminish.[37]

And, again in December of 1814, he insisted to Malthus:

> Accumulation of capital has a tendency to lower profits. Why? Because every accumulation is attended with increased difficulty in obtaining food. . . . If there were no increased difficulty, profits would never fall, because there are no other limits to the profitable production of manufactures but the rise of wages.[38]

---

31. Marshall, *Money, Credit and Commerce* (London, 1923), p. 41 n.; Schumpeter, p. 607. Cf. also Viner, p. 442, where he said: "Torrens clearly preceded Ricardo in publishing . . . the doctrine . . . however . . . Ricardo is entitled to the credit for first giving due emphasis to the doctrine, for first placing it in an appropriate setting, and for obtaining general acceptance of it by economists."

32. See Sraffa, *Works*, I, xxxi–xxxii. Cf., however, S. Hollander's critique of Sraffa in his "Ricardo's Analysis of the Profit Rate, 1813–15," *Economica* NS, 40, 159 (Aug. 1973): 260–82.

33. Chipman, p. 481.

34. Sir John Hicks, *Capital and Growth* (New York, 1965), p. 44.

35. Stigler sensed this, as can be seen in his remark, "the principle of comparative cost . . . had no special relevance to the politically strategic commodity, food." *Essays in the History of Economics* (Chicago, 1965), p. 274.

36. Sraffa, *Works*, IV, 3.

37. Ibid., VI, 104.

38. Ibid., p. 162.

This represents the essentials of Ricardo's analytic vision: profits are inversely related to wages, and wages are a function of the cost of producing food and necessaries. Because of diminishing returns, economic expansion, entailing an increase of capital and population on a fixed supply of land, caused these expenses to increase, driving wage costs higher and thus lowering agricultural profits. Since "it is the profits of the farmer which regulate the profits of all other trades," the limitation of land stops economic expansion as profits continue to fall.

What to do? In the very next sentence in this letter to Malthus, Ricardo supplied the answer: "If with every accumulation of capital we could tack a piece of fresh fertile land to our Island, profits would never fall."[39]

From this notion it was but a short step to the recommendation that the import duties of the Corn Laws be reduced so that low-cost, presumably constant-cost food could be imported from abroad, thereby averting diminishing returns, rising wage costs, and falling profits. Two months later, in February 1815, immediately after having finished reading Malthus' new pamphlet on rent, Ricardo incorporated the differential theory of rent into his own embryonic theory of profits and in a matter of three weeks published his *Essay of Profits*.[40]

With his theory of rent, profits, and wages now in place, Ricardo there concluded: "Profits of stock fall only, because land equally well adapted to produce food cannot be procured . . . . If, therefore, in the progress of countries in wealth and population, *new portions of fertile land could be added to such countries*, with every increase of capital, profits would never fall."[41] Additional portions of fertile land being impossible to come by, Ricardo, as a second-best alternative, recommended foreign trade as a device to overcome the land shortage so that through importation, corn could continue to be supplied "at a cheap price." The *Essay* concluded: "If by foreign commerce . . . the commodities consumed by the labourer should become much cheaper, wages would fall; and this . . . would raise the profits of the farmer, and therefore, all other profits."[42]

This straightforward analysis leading to a recommendation of free trade in commodities "consumed by the labourer" does not require

39. Ibid.
40. That it was Malthus' theory of differential rent and *not* Ricardo's, notwithstanding the note written by J. S. Mill for McCulloch's edition of the *Wealth of Nations*, is made clear in Sraffa, I, 6–7, as well as Ricardo's explicit acknowledgment in his *Essay*: "In all that I have said concerning the origin and progress of rent, I have briefly repeated, and endeavoured to elucidate the principles which Mr. Malthus has so ably laid down." (p. 15 n.).
41. Sraffa, *Works*, IV, 18; emphasis added.
42. Ibid., p. 26 n.

nor involve comparative advantage. Indeed, it is an argument which quite comfortably can be couched in terms of differences in absolute costs, with England specializing in manufactures, in which she had an absolute advantage, and her trading partners specializing in food and raw materials, their line of absolute advantage. What is surprising perhaps, and what we intend to demonstrate, is that Ricardo's view of foreign trade essentially never went beyond this conception—the three-paragraph illustration of comparative advantage in the *Principles* notwithstanding!

That free trade was needed primarily as an offset to diminishing returns in agriculture, Ricardo, in the *Essay*, made quite clear by restricting this "wise policy" to a nation "already wealthy"—a society "advanced in wealth and population." "It is *only* when a country is comparatively wealthy, when all its fertile land is in a state of high cultivation, and [it] is obliged to have recourse to its inferior lands to obtain the food necessary for its population . . . that it can become profitable to import corn."[43]

Ricardo, in early 1815, was urging a very restricted form of free trade—freer trade in food and necessaries for advanced, wealthy countries experiencing sharply diminishing returns, as progress forced the cultivation of wheat up the "bleak hillsides" of Ricardo's England.[44] But was his position any different when, after two years of Mill's constant badgering and tutoring, Ricardo completed his *Principles*? To see that the answer essentially is no, let us examine Ricardo's chapter on foreign trade; a chapter which J. Hollander, long ago, assured us was "dominated" by the principle of comparative costs as Ricardo set it out "in classical detail."[45]

After a few introductory paragraphs, Ricardo reasserted his basic theorem and the strategic role foreign trade played in averting diminishing returns:

> It has been my endeavour to shew throughout this work, that the rate of profits can never be increased but by a fall in wages, and that there can be no permanent fall of wages but in consequence of a fall [in the price] of the necessaries on which wages are expended. If, therefore, by the extension of foreign trade . . . the food and necessaries of the labourer can be brought to market at a reduced price, profits will rise . . . *but* if the commodities

43. Ibid., p. 27; emphasis added.
44. Cf. A. Marshall, *Principles of Economics*, variorum edition (London, 1961), I, 673.
45. See supra n. 3.

obtained at a cheaper rate, by the extension of foreign commerce
. . . be exclusively the commodities consumed by the rich, no
alteration will take place in the rate of profits. The rate of wages
would not be affected, although wine, velvets, silks, and other
expensive commodities should fall [in price] 50 per cent, and
consequently profits would continue unaltered.[46]

Ricardo, obviously, was advocating the repeal of the Corn Laws, not free trade in general. Freer trade was espoused only insofar as wage goods, needed to spur industrialization, could more readily be obtained. If England, the "richest country in Europe," could but obtain its food and raw produce "from abroad in exchange for manufactured goods" it would be difficult, Ricardo later maintained, "to say where the limit is at which you would cease to accumulate wealth."[47] This was so, providing, as he wrote in the *Principles*, the "commodites imported be of that description on which the wages of labour are expended."[48] Trade in such luxury goods as wine and velvets was irrelevant, since it left profits unaffected.

So, free or freer trade for Ricardo meant a policy appropriate to an advanced manufacturing nation in its relations with countries supplying it with food and raw materials. That Ricardo was still thinking of absolute cost differences based upon natural and human endowments peculiar to each country is clear from his description of the benefits to be derived from an international system where "each country naturally devotes its capital and labour to such employments as are most beneficial to each." Such a system "determines that wine shall be made in France and Portugal, that corn shall be grown in America and Poland, and that hardware and other goods shall be manufactured in England."[49]

Up to this point in the chapter on foreign trade Ricardo had, as it were, restored the original optimism of Adam Smith, notwithstanding the pessimism generated later by Malthus' introduction into the science of incessant population growth and diminishing returns in agriculture. And he had accomplished this on what was essentially the Smithian notion of absolute cost differences arising from the "peculiar powers bestowed by nature" upon the various regions of the globe. Had he stopped at this point, the doctrine of comparative advantage would have had to be passed along to subsequent genera-

46. Sraffa, *Works*, I, 132; emphasis added. Cf. also p. 118.
47. Ibid., IV, 179.
48. Ibid., I, 133.
49. Ibid., pp. 133–34.

tions by someone more interested in what is a piece of comparative statics, and not the rough dynamics, of Ricardo's classical trade-growth model.

But on the very next page, Ricardo, incongruously we think, inserted three paragraphs outlining the principle of comparative costs:

> England may be so circumstanced, that to produce the cloth may require the labour of 100 men for one year; and if she attempted to make the wine, it might require the labour of 120 men for the same time. England would therefore find it her interest to import wine, and to purchase it by the exportation of cloth.
>
> To produce the wine in Portugal, might require only the labour of 80 men for one year, and to produce the cloth in the same country, might require the labour of 90 men for the same time. It would therefore be advantageous for her to export wine in exchange for cloth. This exchange might even take place, notwithstanding that the commodity imported by Portugal could be produced there with less labour than in England. Though she could make the cloth with the labour of 90 men, she would import it from a country where it required the labour of 100 men to produce it, because it would be advantageous to her rather to employ her capital in the production of wine, for which she would obtain more cloth from England, than she could produce by diverting a portion of her capital from the cultivation of wines to the manufacture of cloth.
>
> Thus England would give the produce of the labour of 100 men, for the produce of the labour of 80. Such an exchange could not take place between the individuals of the same country. The labour of 100 Englishmen cannot be given for that of 80 Englishmen, but the produce of the labour of 100 Englishmen may be given for the produce of the labour of 80 Portuguese, 60 Russians, or 120 East Indians. The difference in this respect, between a single country and many, is easily accounted for, by considering the difficulty with which capital moves from one country to another, to seek a more profitable employment, and the activity with which it invariably passes from one province to another in the same country.[50]

Notice the brevity. The doctrine hardly "dominates the chapter," nor is it laid out in "classical detail," as J. Hollander would have it.[51] And from an analytic point of view, Chipman noted that the first

---

50. Ibid., pp. 135–36.
51. See supra n.3.

paragraph taken by itself is a "*non sequitur*, since nothing so far has been said about Portugal," and the second paragraph is "equally unsatisfactory, except when read in conjunction with the first."[52] Ricardo "saves himself," however, in the passages contained in the third paragraph, but at best his version of the doctrine is "carelessly worded." Indeed, it is Chipman's considered opinion that "Ricardo's . . . statement of the law is quite wanting, so much so as to cast some doubt as to whether he truly understood it."[53] How do we explain that Ricardo did not "truly understand" what Samuelson, in attributing the doctrine to him, called his "greatest tour de force"?[54]

Does it seem likely, in view of Ricardo's admitted analytic talents, that had he stumbled upon the new doctrine just prior to composing his *Principles*, as legend seems to have it, and having decided to develop and spell it out in detail by working it into a theoretic "organic whole," the end product of his labors—what he put into the chapter on foreign trade in his *opus magnum*—would have been wanting in the extreme? And, further, it is not the case that what he wrote in the *Principles* was not his *best* account of the doctrine. On the contrary, and this seems significant, it is the *only* account of it Ricardo ever wrote.[55]

In view of Ricardo's very brief and almost casual treatment of comparative costs, it seems doubtful whether his concern with the doctrine was serious. Certainly it did not fit in easily with the Ricardian theoretic structure of trade and development. Could it be that the idea for its inclusion in the chapter came from James Mill, being yet another, albeit more important, instance of his direct influence on Ricardo? The next section examines the likelihood of this possibility, and the concluding section explores how it was, in view of Ricardo's marginal relationship to the doctrine, that comparative advantage became a central plank in the core of classical political economy.

III

Is it so unlikely that Mill could have been responsible for the inclusion of the page-long account of the principle of comparative

---

52. Chipman, pp. 479–80.
53. Ibid., p. 480.
54. P. A. Samuelson, "Economists and the History of Ideas," *American Economic Review* 52 (1962): 9.
55. There is only one entry under "comparative costs and foreign trade" (to the three-paragraph example in the *Principles*), in the newly issued "General Index" of the Sraffa edition of Ricardo's *Works*. See, *Works*, XI, 19. Cf. also Carl Shoup, *Ricardo on Taxation* (New York, 1960), p. 169 n., where he stated: "it is in fact surprising how little use Ricardo makes of the doctrine of comparative costs in analyzing the effects of import and export duties and bounties."

costs in Ricardo's chapter on foreign trade? We know Ricardo already had used "Mill's words" in his *Economical and Secure Currency* pamphlet in dwelling upon the "*moral* part of the argument against the Bank," and Sraffa noted that the wording of the long final paragraph of that essay suggested "it was drafted or revised by Mill."[56] And Mill, it appears, may have played a similar role in the composition of the *Principles*.

Long ago, Simon Patten believed that "James Mill wrote or at least inspired the first three paragraphs of the Preface. They have his tone and style, and not Ricardo's."[57] And, of interest, Sraffa cites this approvingly,[58] before noting Mill's hand in the translations from J. B. Say and the "unmistakably characteristic" phrases of Mill in the three-page conclusion on the poor laws in the chapter "On Wages." That Mill's assistance to Ricardo often included the drafting and revising of various passages in the *Principles* we may take as established.

Furthermore, by referring to the Mill-Ricardo correspondence for the period between the *Essay on Profits* and the *Principles*, we can observe Mill's tactics as he went about attempting to "make of Ricardo the Quesnay of nineteenth century England."[59] This effort, by 1819, would culminate in Ricardo becoming, as Mill was to put it, the undisputed "head of Political Economy" in England.[60] In 1816 Mill, with this objective in mind, can be envisioned scanning the manuscript of the first seven chapters Ricardo had sent to him, making certain that all the original and sound doctrines of the emerging

---

56. Sraffa, *Works*, IV, 47 and 46 n. Mill's assistance here and, as noted above (see n.23) the similarity between Mill's (1814) and Ricardo's (1815) replies to Malthus' arguments in favor of the Corn Laws would seem to contradict Stigler's statement: "We must recall that Ricardo wrote the two pamphlets on the bullion controversy and the *Essay* (1815) without apparent intervention by Mill." See "Sraffa's Ricardo," p. 590.

57. "The Interpretation of Ricardo," *Quarterly Journal of Economics* 7 (1893): 338. For example, Ricardo opened his *Essay on Profits* with: "Mr. Malthus very correctly defines 'the rent of land,' " etc. The fourth paragraph of the Preface to the *Principles*, probably the first paragraph written by Ricardo begins: "In 1815, Mr. Malthus, in his 'Inquiry into the Nature and Progress of Rent,' " etc. In what probably are Mill's first three paragraphs we read of changes in income distribution during the "different stages of society," which Mill, as a student of the Scottish Historical School easily could have written, whereas it is doubtful if Ricardo would have begun in this fashion. There are other telltale traces of Mill's hand. For example the Mr. "Stuart" mentioned in the third paragraph. For an attempt to answer the minor, but intriguing, question of who "Stuart" was, see my "Will the Real Mr. Stuart Please Stand Up," *Annals Mid-South Academy of Economists* 3 (Nov. 1975).

58. Sraffa, *Works*, I, xxi–xxii.

59. E. Halévy, *The Growth of Philosophic Radicalism*, English ed. (1928, New York, 1965), p. 273.

60. Sraffa, *Works*, VIII, 10.

science were incorporated. Thus, in judging the seventh chapter on foreign trade, in addition to Ricardo's own trade-growth model making England the "workshop of the world," he would insist on having added the "four magic numbers that constitute the core of the doctrine of comparative advantage theory."[61] Otherwise the brief, but complete, statement of it by Torrens in February 1815 would analytically still have been superior. Mill would have been aware of this, in view of his long-time effort at spelling out (in 1808) and utilizing (in 1814) the gains-from-trade argument, and so most likely would have insisted on its being included in Ricardo's major work, which was soon to become the "Text Book" of the new school of political economy.[62]

This view imputes to Mill a considerable influence on Ricardo as he prepared the manuscript of the *Principles*. But the correspondence between the two, in 1815–16, gives support to this suggestion. For example, shortly after Ricardo published his *Essay on Profits* we find him writing to J. B. Say, telling him he understood from "Mr. Mill many able persons think . . . I have not been sufficiently diffuse. . . . Mr. Mill wishes me to write it over again more at large. I feel the undertaking exceeds my powers."[63] But Mill would not let Ricardo rest, being resolved he must write the primer for the new science "on which the progress of human happiness to a singular degree depends"; after which he must present its policy implications in Parliament![64]

Despite Mill's insistence that he persevere in composing the manuscript, Ricardo balked, and in October 1815 as the "affairs of the Bank are to be considered next session," he lost interest in the "great work," spending his time putting his "thoughts on paper respecting their [the Bank's] concerns."[65] Nevertheless Mill, in the role of persistent taskmaster, insisted that his plan—having Ricardo first write out a draft of his thoughts on each subject, and then send it to him for an analytical commentary, paragraph by paragraph, a procedure which Mill had earlier suggested Ricardo should use in composing his forthcoming book—now be the method Ricardo should use in preparing his currency essay. By the end of November Ricardo agreed he

---

61. P. A. Samuelson, "The Way of an Economist," reprinted in *The Collected Scientific Papers of Paul A. Samuelson*, ed. R. C. Merton (Cambridge, Mass., 1972), 3:678.
62. As it was described by Ricardo's stockbroker friend, Hutches Trower. See Sraffa *Works*, VII, 309.
63. Ibid., VI, 249.
64. Ibid., pp. 250–54 for Mill's letter of 23 Aug. 1815.
65. Ibid., p. 312.

would certainly practice "Mill's suggested procedure in any future performance."[66] In replying, Mill insisted "this is what you must do with the *opus magnum*."[67]

Even before the currency pamphlet was off the press, in late December, Mill again wrote Ricardo "in anticipation of the M.S. which I expect soon to receive as part of the great work."[68] But Ricardo, the following February, after having read his latest work on currency, lamented he had made "no progress in the very difficult art of composition," and a little later he told Malthus, "I have the greatest disinclination to commence work again. . . . I do not think I shall ever proceed further."[69]

Almost by way of apology Ricardo, in August 1816, explained to Mill that his "procrastination has not proceeded from not having you in my thoughts."[70] In an unusually sharp tone Mill retorted: "Why should a man that is not afraid to talk upon a subject before any body, be afraid to write . . . Another command of mine, is, that—as I know you have by this time, a pretty mass of papers, written first and last upon the subject—you put as much of them as possible . . . up in a parcel, and send them here . . . you should include those which you read to me in London."[71]

So we know that sometime between February and July (after which they both usually left London[72]), Ricardo had worked closely with Mill on an early draft-manuscript of the *Principles*. Presumably, Mill then had made suggestions requiring revisions, and so by August, hoping the revisions completed, Mill again wrote Ricardo to send him posthaste the "pretty mass of papers" for his further scrutiny and correction.

But it was to be October before Ricardo's parcel containing the first seven chapters of the manuscript was received by Mill. Ricardo's excuse was the "pretext that he must copy it out," but the real reason for the delay, Sraffa tells us, "was that he had been very much impeded by the question of price and value."[73] Ricardo asked Mill specifically to give him his "well considered opinion on this difficult point."[74] The papers were in such a "rough state" that Ricardo could only hope Mill would be able to make out what he had said, since he

66. Ibid., p. 324.
67. Ibid., p. 330.
68. Ibid., p. 338.
69. Ibid., VII, 19, 28.
70. Ibid., p. 53.
71. Ibid., p. 60.
72. Ibid., VI, p. xvi.
73. Ibid., I, p. xv.
74. Ibid., VII, 83.

was "desirous of ascertaining how far your opinion coincides with mine of the correctness of the views which I have taken. A hint or two of yours will enable me to make the next copy much more perfect."[75] Ricardo then waited "patiently for the further instructions which I am prepared to follow."[76]

Mill kept the manuscript for over three weeks, later making no apology to Ricardo, for he "wished to read it carefully, writing marginal contents for my own use, as I went along. . . . I now have got through the whole, and have the contents of each paragraph, regularly numbered, before me."[77] We can glean an idea of the impression Mill had of the work from the letter he sent to Ricardo after completing his study of the first seven chapters. Overall, Mill obviously was pleased, saying, "you have made out all your points."[78] He noted Ricardo's propositions on value, and his fundamental theorem on the inverse relationship between wages and profits, and was "very much struck" by Ricardo's paradoxical "curious effect."[79]

As to the analysis contained in the chapter on foreign trade, Mill said it was "original, and sound, and excellently demonstrated." He approved of Ricardo's opening—"no extension of foreign trade will immediately increase the amount of value in a country,"[80] and he continued almost triumphantly, "that it may be good for a country to import commodities from a country where the production of those same commodities costs more, than it would cost at home: that a change in manufacturing skill in one country, produces a new distribution of the precious metals, are new propositions of the highest importance, and which you fully prove."[81]

Mill was prescient in emphasizing the importance of Ricardo's now classic explanation of the way the "precious metals tend to be distributed so as to bring it about that trade takes place as if under conditions of barter." As Lord Robbins emphasized, Ricardo's contribution in this respect was "the basis of all further developments in

---

75. Ibid., p. 90.
76. Ibid. A perusal of this correspondence gives the definite impression that Ricardo held Mill's analytical powers in considerably higher regard than recent assessments of "Mill the economist." See, e.g., Sraffa, *Works*, I, p. xx; Stigler, "Sraffa's Ricardo," p. 588; D. Winch, p. 186; T. W. Hutchison, p. 81. Stigler does add, however: "Ricardo had a great respect for Mill, and so should we."
77. Ibid., p. 97.
78. Ibid., p. 98.
79. I.e., the *fall* in the exchange value (prices) of commodities produced by capital-intensive methods, due to a general *rise* in wage rates.
80. A statement the truth of which, Malthus would later claim, would stop commercial "intercourse between nations." See his *Principles of Political Economy* (London, 1820), p. 450 n. (390 n. in the 2d ed. of 1836).
81. Sraffa, *Works*, VII, 99.

this connection."[82] Indeed, if any theoretic analysis or concept which Ricardo developed on foreign trade can be said to have been integrated into an organic whole, or to have dominated the chapter, and if any could be looked upon as an intellectual *tour de force*, peculiarly Ricardo's own, then surely the last half of his chapter on foreign trade, containing the account of the relationship between prices, money incomes, and specie flows which underpins the *real* analysis of comparative costs, must be it. And that Mill had this lengthy analysis in mind when he credited Ricardo with "new propositions of the highest importance which you fully prove" is indicated by his laudatory reference to this part of Ricardo's chapter when shortly thereafter he wrote his article "Colonies"—an article written in late 1817 and published the following February. There Mill, after showing the benefits from trade on the basis of comparative advantage, using the "four magic numbers," said it "would take too many words" to describe how the "precious metals distribute themselves so as to leave the motives to this barter exactly the same as they would be," and referred the interested reader to Ricardo, "the first author of it."[83]

But it is significant that Mill also recognized the importance of including in the *Principles* a brief statement containing the "essence" of the doctrine of comparative advantage—of when it is profitable to import a commodity whose domestic labor costs are lower than those abroad. Apparently, in Mill's mind a complete account of the benefits stemming from trade required, at least, a brief mention of the comparative-cost ratios. Consequently, it appeared sandwiched in between Ricardo's interesting account of foreign trade averting growth-induced diminishing returns and his original and "excellently demonstrated" explanation of the movements in prices, incomes, and specie flows needed to obtain the mutual advantages of trade as if occurring under conditions of barter. According to Mill's lights, the chapter would then be fully consistent with the principles of the "new political economy."[84] And so Mill wrote approvingly to Ricardo, saying he had indeed "made great progress toward the production of a most admirable book."[85]

Of course, the above remarks are speculative. Perhaps the brief and poorly composed illustration of comparative advantage was all Ricardo's own doing. But if so, this makes it very difficult to account

---

82. *Robert Torrens*, p. 25.
83. "Colonies," p. 269.
84. S. G. Checkland, "The Propagation of Ricardian Economics in England," *Economica* n.s. 16, no. 61 (Feb. 1949): 40.
85. Sraffa, *Works*, VII, 99.

for two interesting and peculiar aspects of the particular example that appears in the *Principles*.

First, why the "odd geography" which had Portugal more efficient than England in producing both the cloth and the wine? Samuelson suggested[86] that Ricardo was trying to convince readers of mercantilist persuasion that England could gain from trade even if its labor costs all-round were higher than its trading partners'. And since Ricardo immediately added (in an attached footnote) that England possessed absolute advantages in machinery and skill and so could export manufactures at lower labor costs than obtained abroad, the argument for freer trade was just that much stronger. Perhaps so. On the other hand Ricardo could have gone along with Mill's suggestion to include the comparative-cost illustration, but chose this unrealistic example to intentionally belittle the importance of it. The reader, apparently, was not to take these three paragraphs too seriously.[87]

Further evidence that this may have been the case is the peculiar set of commodities Ricardo chose to illustrate the gains from trade under comparative advantage—cloth and *wine*! In all other places in the *Principles* when Ricardo discussed the gains from international trade, he did so in terms of being able to import "cheap" corn from America and Poland. And in his three major essays, written before and after the *Principles*, whenever Ricardo proposed freer trade, the reduced cost of corn was always emphasized.[88] In the comparative-advantage illustration, however, he selected not cloth and corn, "the commodities in common use" at the time,[89] but cloth and wine. In this famous example, therefore, on the basis of his "four magic numbers" England could export cloth and thereby import wine 20 percent cheaper than otherwise. But of what relevance was cheaper wine to Ricardo's trade-growth model, in which foreign trade was crucial because by averting diminishing returns it prevented wages from rising and profits from falling? None whatever, and he said so explicitly only three pages earlier when he declared that the rate of profits, the key variable deter-

---

86. *Collected Scientific Papers*, 3:679. For a similar view see Joan Robinson, *Reflections on the Theory of International Trade* (Manchester, 1974), p. 4.

87. Cf. Stigler's comment on this point, supra n. 35.

88. *Essay on Profits* (1815), *Funding System* (1820), *On Protection to Agriculture* (1822). See Sraffa, *Works*, IV, 22, 23, 179, 237.

89. J. Hollander, "Ricardo and Torrens," p. 461. It is strange that Seligman, in trying to establish Torrens' priority over Ricardo for the first statement of the theory of comparative advantage, should say that Ricardo employed the identical example utilized by Torrens, "namely, the corn trade between Poland and England." Ibid., p. 448. Equally strange is Hollander's reply, when he agrees with Seligman conceding only that this "can hardly be deemed evidence of plagiarism" (p. 461).

mining England's economic future, would not be affected even if the price of wine "should fall 50 per cent."[90] That the comparative-advantage example was irrelevant to the rest of the chapter can be seen from Ricardo limiting his recommendation for freer trade to the case where the commodities imported were "of that description on which the wages of labour are expended." And further, the recommendation was valid only for an economically advanced nation, such as the England of his day, where further economic expansion was threatened by the "scarcity, and consequently high value, of food and other raw produce."[91] Not the price of wine, but the problem of averting diminishing returns from the shortage of land was for Ricardo "a question of the utmost importance in political economy."[92]

That an analysis in terms of comparative costs had little to offer Ricardo in answering this important question he thus made clear in the one instance he had occasion to comment briefly on it. He did this by describing how it would result in a reduced cost of wine, a "nonbasic" good, changes in the price of which, like "velvets, silks, and other expensive commodities . . . consumed by the rich," in no way affected the level of profits.[93] So the famous example was, if nothing else, irrelevant to the general scheme of Ricardo's theories of trade, distribution, and economic growth. As Joan Robinson recently has stressed, there is "no need to argue against protection for a commodity [such as wine] which is useful and which cannot be produced at home . . . . What Ricardo was really concerned about was to abolish the corn laws so as to lower the real cost of *wage goods* and raise the rate of profit . . . . This was the desideratum of the whole argument."[94] The above remarks do seem to support the hypothesis that the idea for including the analysis in the *Principles* was not Ricardo's and therefore must have been James Mill's.

But Mill's idea or Ricardo's, the truth of the matter is that the statement of the law of comparative advantage as it appeared in Ricardo's *Principles* was very brief, poorly worded, the example unrealistic, and, more important, irrelevant and not part of Ricardo's general trade-growth model. Also Ricardo himself probably did not "fully understand" it. How then did the myth that it was Ricardo who "chanced upon," "developed," and "elaborated . . . and fought for" the doctrine of comparative advantage come about? To provide a

90. Sraffa, *Works*, I, 132.
91. Ibid. p. 133 and IV, 179.
92. Ibid., IV, 179.
93. Ibid., I, 132.
94. Joan Robinson, pp. 4 and 6; emphasis added.

possible answer to this intriguing question we examine the writings of James Mill and John Ramsey McCulloch—Ricardo's "two and only two genuine disciples," as Mill described himself and McCulloch just a week after Ricardo had passed away.[95]

IV

If it was not Ricardo who was responsible for incorporating the law of comparative advantage into mainstream political economy, it must have been one of his disciples—and so it turns out. But surprisingly (although not as surprisingly as it would have been prior to Denis O'Brien's definitive study on McCulloch, in which he shows that the notion McCulloch was "more Ricardian than Ricardo" is itself a complete myth[96]) it is not McCulloch, the popularizer of Ricardian doctrines and his most vociferous convert, but instead the lesser-known James Mill. In view of O'Brien's detailed study, we can be brief in commenting on McCulloch and comparative advantage.

O'Brien has made clear that "trade originated in McCulloch's view, as in Smith's, in a 'vent for surplus,' " and consequently, "McCulloch *never accepted the theory of comparative costs* as expounded by Torrens and Ricardo."[97] Apparently McCulloch, although accepting the Hume-Ricardo "theory of the distribution of the precious metals," nevertheless "clung firmly to *absolute* advantage as providing the basis for trade and indeed publicly rejected Ricardo's formulation."[98] In all of McCulloch's briefs for free trade in his many *Edinburgh Review* articles he relied upon absolute, not comparative, advantage. And in his influential review of Ricardo's *Principles*[99] there was barely any mention of Ricardo's chapter on foreign trade, still less of comparative advantage. Indeed, the subject of foreign trade, said McCulloch, formed a "subsidiary" part of the work! Explaining and defending Ricardo's value and distribution theories were the principal burdens of the review.

Furthermore, the absence of any mention of comparative advantage in McCulloch's review was of no concern to either Ricardo or Malthus, or, it appears, to anyone else. In another major review of Ricardo's *Principles* which appeared in the May 1817 issue of *Blackwood's Edinburgh Magazine*, the only reference to foreign trade was to Ricardo's 1815 *Essay on Profits*, in which he had shown the

---

95. Sraffa, *Works*, IX, 391.
96. D. P. O'Brien, *J. R. McCulloch: A Study in Classical Economics* (New York, 1970), p. 15.
97. Ibid., pp. 197, 191; emphasis added.
98. Ibid., pp. 192–93.
99. "Ricardo's Political Economy," *Edinburgh Review*, June, 1818, pp. 59–87.

"folly of restricting the corn trade."[100] Indeed, practically all the literature critical of Ricardo was confined to his labor theory of value and his "fundamental theorem of profits depending upon wages."[101] His views on foreign trade received scant attention, and the three-paragraph illustration of comparative advantage went completely unnoticed. Whether Ricardo intended it or not, his readers did not take the comparative-cost example seriously. In fact, it is amazing how very little comment it attracted.

Since McCulloch wrote so many of the articles on political economy in the *Edinburgh Review* during this long period of the Corn Law debate (78 of 133 articles between 1818 and 1837), it is not surprising that *no mention of the law of comparative advantage appeared in that prestigious journal*. What is surprising is how Fetter in his account of the "general idea of comparative costs" could write of the "scores" who read in the *Edinburgh* of Ricardo's "notion of a geographic division of labor based on different ratios of exchange."[102]

Indeed, other than Torrens' *Essay on the External Corn Trade*, and his verbatim quotation of Ricardo's comparative cost example in "Letter X" of *The Budget*, and two brief references to comparative advantage by Pennington and Longfield,[103] the only serious discus-

---

100. "Ricardo on the *Principles of Political Economy and Taxation*," p. 178.
101. M. Blaug, *Ricardian Economics* (New Haven, Conn., 1958), p. 209.
102. Fetter, pp. 75–76.
103. Pennington, *A Letter to Kirkman Finlay Esq.* (1840), reprinted in *Economic Writings of James Pennington* ed. R. S. Sayers (London, 1963), pp. 29–46; M. Longfield, *Three Lectures on Commerce* (Dublin, 1835) as reprinted (New York, 1971). Both Torrens and Pennington simply quoted the comparative advantage examples of Ricardo and James Mill. Longfield made up his own examples, but in one, in "Lecture III," p. 53, he had England twice as productive in one commodity and France twice as productive in the other—a special case of absolute advantage used by, among others, McCulloch, *Principles of Political Economy* (Edinburgh, 1825): 126, and William Ellis, "Exportation of Machinery," *Westminster Review*, 3 (April 1825): 388–89. Viner, *Studies*, p. 446 mistakenly cites these as examples of *comparative* advantage. O'Brien, pp. 192–93 has made it clear that McCulloch used only absolute advantage in explaining the gains from trade. Actually, in the example cited by both Viner and O'Brien, we find McCulloch in 1825 (*Principles*, p. 126) stating the example incorrectly by claiming that England could "manufacture 10,000 yards of cloth, *and* raise 1,000 quarters of wheat" (my emphasis), instead of 10,000 yards of cloth *or* 1,000 quarters of wheat, as he correctly wrote it in the 1843 edition of the *Principles* (p. 142). By the time of the 5th edition in 1864, the edition readily available to modern readers since it has been reprinted (New York 1965), McCulloch omits the numerical example, concluding that the gains from international trade arise from "enabling each country to obtain commodities which it could either not produce at all, or if at all, then only at a vast expense." (p. 94). This, as Viner long ago noted, does not go beyond the eighteenth-century rule, with all products being produced "where their real costs were lowest" (p. 440). Viner added that Adam Smith never advanced beyond this notion—neither did McCulloch! The abstract and mathematical account of

sions and use of the law of comparative costs, prior to the repeal of the Corn Laws in 1846, were by members of what might be called the Millian group. Besides Ricardo and James Mill, this would include William Ellis, George Grote, and James' son, John Stuart.

But first, what role did Torrens play in furthering the development and acceptance of the comparative-costs doctrine? He had, of course, contributed to the early development of the new doctrine, but in later years Torrens often merely repeated what Ricardo and Mill had already published. Lord Robbins in his commentary on Torrens' contribution to the development of classical international trade theory seems not always to have realized this.

For example, in giving priority to Torrens for the complete statement of the gains from trade on the basis of comparative advantage, Robbins admitted Torrens' 1815 analysis lacked the "final emphasis upon the comparison of ratios which is the ultimate essence of this principle."[104] This omission, Robbins assured us, "disappears completely in the extended version of the theory which is to be found in the fourth (1827) edition of the same essay. Here the exposition explicitly starts from the demonstration that if all cost differences are equal, then there is no incentive for trade." He then quoted: "No difference however great, in the cost of production universally in one country, and the cost of production universally in another can occasion an interchange of commodities between them . . . . On the contrary, a difference in the cost of production between two countries, affecting commodities in each, not universally but partially, gives immediate occasion to an interchange of commodities."[105] And Robbins concluded: "It is difficult to think of any passage in the whole literature of the subject before Taussig in which the essence of the doctrine is more forceably presented."[106]

With all deference to the scholarship of Lord Robbins, this statement does overlook the earlier expositions of the new doctrine in its "comparison of ratios" form in James Mill's *Encyclopaedia Britannica* article "Colonies" (1818) and in his 1821 *Elements*, as well as the unpublished and apparently completely unknown essay on comparative advantage of George Grote, a prominent member of the

---

comparative advantage contained in the anonymous *A Letter on the True Principles of Advantageous Exportation* (London, 1808) received no notice at the time of its publication and almost none since. Cf. *Economica*, no. 39 (Feb. 1933): 40–50. We owe this last reference to Barry J. Gordon.

104. Robbins, *Robert Torrens*, p. 23.
105. Ibid., pp. 23–24, quoting Torrens, *Essay on the External Corn Trade* (1827), as reprinted (Clifton, N.J., 1972), pp. 402–03.
106. Ibid., p. 24.

"Millian group."[107] Torrens probably was not aware of the Grote manuscript, but surely he knew of Mill's important publications.

Mill began with the obvious case of commodity interchange based on absolute advantage. He then considered, exactly as Torrens did later, the case in which Poland, though having the advantage over England in both cloth and corn, had the advantage in each commodity to the same degree. Under these conditions "Poland will have no motive to import either from England." But "if two countries can both of them produce two commodities, corn, for example, and cloth, but not both commodities with the same comparative facility, the two countries will find their advantage in confining themselves, each to one of the commodities, and bartering for the other."[108] As for describing the gains from trade on a comparative-cost basis, it would certainly appear that in 1827 Torrens simply was repeating the earlier analysis of James Mill. Torrens, a believer in the "great benefits of international division of labor" in his younger days, was later to break away from the orthodox trade policy of "unilateral lowering of obstacles," basing his own advocacy of freer trade upon reciprocity, colonization, and "the establishment of an imperial Zollverein."[109] There was no need for comparative costs in this approach. Viner sensed this when he concluded, "the doctrine was never an integral part of Torrens's thinking."[110]

If then we do not owe the early development of the doctrine of comparative advantage to Ricardo, Torrens, or McCulloch, then almost by elimination it must be due to the efforts of James Mill. And that this was indeed the case, the evidence presented above has attempted to demonstrate.

To summarize the case for Mill's crucial role in the early development of the doctrine, let us list his contributions. First, we had

---

107. The story of the discovery in 1930 of the Grote manuscript as part of what Sraffa refers to as the "Ricardo Papers," after having been lost for almost a century, is in Sraffa, *Works*, VI, p. xxxiv, where he also quotes from Grote's diary, which gives the exact date Grote sent the manuscript on foreign trade to Ricardo—Saturday, 27 March 1819. This was during a time when Grote often breakfasted with Ricardo and Mill and enjoyed, as he told his diary, "some most interesting and instructive discourse with them." See, Mrs. Grote, *The Personal Life of George Grote* (London, 1873), pp. 32–37. Grote's other manuscript papers on political economy, consisting of some 230 pages, are in the British Museum (Add. MSS. 29, 530). These essays, which form a fairly complete set of notes of a book on Political Economy, contain a further essay on foreign trade, somewhat shorter than the manuscript in the "Ricardo Papers." Both essays on trade are similar to Mill's 1821 presentation in the *Elements*. We are presently preparing the Grote manuscripts for publication.
108. *Elements of Political Economy* (London, 1821), pp. 84–85.
109. Robbins, *Robert Torrens*, pp. 255–56.
110. *Studies*, p. 443.

his *Commerce Defended*, published in 1808, in which he reintroduced into mainstream economic thought the "eighteenth-century rule," simultaneously with Torrens' *Economists Refuted*. Second, was Mill's use of "the rule" in his July 1814 *Eclectic Review* article to attack Malthus' views favoring the retention of the Corn Laws—an article which influenced both Ricardo's and Torrens' February 1815 contributions to the Corn Law debate, and yet an article the importance of which has gone virtually unnoticed since 1815.[111] Third, there was Mill's influence on Ricardo during the writing of the latter's *Principles*, culminating, we have maintained, in Ricardo inserting a brief mention of comparative costs into a chapter which would be complete without it in terms of Ricardo's dynamic model of trade and economic expansion. Finally, there was the publication of Mill's *Encyclopaedia Britannica* article "Colonies" in 1818 and the *Elements* in 1821, both of which contained the first extended discussions of the law based on a comparison of cost ratios—expositions which completely anticipated the 1827 "extended version" of the doctrine by Torrens. Mill's efforts were thus not inconsiderable, and surely outweigh those of Ricardo, Torrens, and McCulloch.

Ironically, Mill's last contribution to the development of the doctrine of comparative costs was to be of a negative kind. It will be recalled that Ricardo did not discuss the problem of how the gains from trade were distributed between the trading partners, assuming they were divided equally between them.[112] Mill, apparently intending to do the same, blundered into awarding the total gain to each of the trading bodies.[113] We now know the attempt to correct this blunder by J. S. Mill's group of "younger Utilitarians" led to J. S. Mill's eventual solution of the division of the gains on a basis of reciprocal demands. Published first in 1844 as Essay I in J. S. Mill's *Essays on Some Unsettled Questions in Political Economy*, it was reproduced almost verbatim in his "splendid edifice of theory" in the "great chapter" on international values in his 1848 *Principles*.[114]

So in a backhanded fashion James Mill also was instrumental in

---

111. Halévy, supra n. 59, p. 278, and Winch, *James Mill: Selected Economic Writings*, p. 199, refer very briefly to the *Eclectic Review* article without commenting on its importance.

112. Viner, pp. 444–45.

113. *Elements* (1821), pp. 85–87. Interestingly, Mill had *not* made this blunder three years earlier (February 1818) in his *Encyclopaedia Britannica* article on "Colonies" (p. 269), where he correctly, but arbitrarily, divided the gain according to the rule he later enunciated in the 3d edition of the *Elements* (1826), i.e., "the result of competition would be to divide the advantage equally" (p. 122).

114. F. Y. Edgeworth, *Papers Relating to Political Economy*, II (1925), pp. 22 and 9, as reprinted by B. Franklin (New York, n.d.).

the final elaboration of the comparative-cost doctrine by his son. And inasmuch as it was from John Stuart Mill, and not from McCulloch, Longfield, Torrens, or Pennington, "that later economists took over the doctrine,"[115] the modern theory of international trade is indebted to the "Millian group" in a way which up to now has not been recognized or appreciated.

When the ancestry of the doctrine becomes better known, the crucial role of James Mill in developing the concept, in recognizing its importance to orthodox theory and policy, and therefore in seeing that it was fully integrated into standard economics, will surely be better appreciated than it is at the present time.

115. Viner, p. 447. See also, C. F. Bastable, *Theory of International Trade* (Dublin, 1887), p. 22.

Say's (at Least) Eight Laws, or What Say and James Mill May Really Have Meant

By WILLIAM J. BAUMOL

Princeton and New York Universities

I. THE SAY'S LAW DISCUSSION AS A COMPLEX OF IDEAS

Revisionism usually supplies whatever excitement there is to be found in writings on *dogmengeschichte*. Here, achievement often consists in showing that a writer had been badly misinterpreted, or that his contribution is far greater than is generally supposed. This paper can, however, pretend to propose no more than a modest revision of our ideas on the early writings on Say's Law. It will be argued that J. B. Say and his contemporary James Mill, who is also sometimes credited with the notion that "supply creates its own demand", really seem to have had in mind a set of ideas rather more complex than that and, moreover, that the main policy implications they drew from their discussion went well beyond the comforting thought that fears of universal glut are baseless.

Certainly, their discussion was not Panglossian in spirit, for one of their main points was the superiority, from the point of view of growth in economic welfare, of investment outlays over idle consumption (either in the form of luxurious living by wealthy individuals or the military and other unproductive outlays of prodigal governments). Moreover, these authors maintained that only production can create real purchasing power, so that an impecunious community is in no position to provide effective demand in abundance. Restriction in output must necessarily limit effective demand and is certainly not a way to promote it, particularly in the long run.

These are ideas, it will be noted, that the modern literature does not reject, at least not with the universality with which it denies the notion that supply creates its own demand. Indeed, they are thoughts that may still be of some pertinence, particularly for development theory and policy. Moreover, for the time in which these authors were writing, these ideas can certainly not be considered a manifestation of conservatism. Rather, they can be interpreted as a reply to the defenders of the landed aristocracy and their consumption patterns, and as support for the expanding spirit of capitalist enterprise that accompanied the young industrial revolution.

Obviously, there is no limit to the extent to which one can subdivide the notions composing Say's discussion of markets or exchanges (*débouchés*), his related remarks on consumption, or the parallel materials in Mill. I will confine myself to those relationships that have played a substantial role in later discussions, particularly in recent literature, and to those observations that seem clearly to have been uppermost in the minds of the authors as indicated by the degree of emphasis devoted to them.

But before getting to that, it is appropriate first to recapitulate the contents of Say's Law, as it is understood nowadays, and as contrasted with the main proposition espoused by Say himself.

When discussing Say's Law, the literature since Ricardo seems generally to refer to one of two propositions—a strong assertion, which Becker and I have referred to elsewhere as "Say's Identity", and a weaker variant, which we labelled "Say's Equality".

The first of these, the identity, is the assertion that no one ever wants to hold money for any significant amount of time, so that, as a result, every offer (supply) of a quantity of goods automatically constitutes a demand for a bundle of some other items of equal market value. Thus, as in a barter economy, supply must automatically create its own demand and a general over-production of goods and services is logically impossible.

The second, equality, form of the law admits the possibility of (brief) periods of disequilibrium during which the total demand for goods may fall short of the total supply, but maintains that there exist reliable equilibrating forces that must soon bring the two together.

It should be noted that both of these propositions relate to the shorter run—the period relevant for the analysis of economic crises, recessions and unemployment. It is one of my main contentions that many of Say's central propositions are quite distinct either from the equality or the identity and that it is, in fact, not until the second edition of the *Traité* in 1814 that the full structure of either idea is spelled out in the book.

I believe that the related issues that Say *did* stress in his first edition give us some idea of the order of priorities in his mind, and this, as well as the amount of space and emphasis he accorded them, suggests to me that some of the associated propositions may have held even greater significance for him. To help the reader to judge these issues for himself, I have included in this article a translation of the pertinent sections of that book which I believe of interest in themselves, and which are fairly brief and quite easy to follow.

II. On Priority in Formulation of Say's Law

This paper may, incidentally shed some light on a more minor matter—the issue of priority in the formulation of Say's Law.

In the history of ideas, few things are more foolhardy than attribution of the parenthood of some proposition to a particular individual. The ascription is little more than a sporting act that will ultimately serve as a challenge to others, virtually certain in due course to come up with a predecessor who anticipated the idea with more or less exactitude.

As is well known, Say's Law is a notion whose lineage is older than its name suggests. Its roots in the writings of the Physiocrats have been investigated with great care by Spengler (1945). There are clear precursor statements in *The Wealth of Nations* (see Sowell, 1972, pp. 15-17, and Spengler, 1945, pp. 182-184). It has also been suggested that James Mill anticipated Say in the formulation of the principle. While the first edition of the *Traité* appeared in 1803, it has been argued that in 1807 Mill the elder, in his *Commerce Defended*, published something much closer to "Say's Law" as it is now generally understood. Spengler (1945) and Sowell (1972) show that this conclusion probably rests on a superficial reading of Say's first edition. Readers may have been misled because much of the pertinent discussion appears much later in the book than the chapter on *débouchés*, the chapter into which most of this material was collected in subsequent editions. Winch (1966, p. 34) disposes of the issue even more effectively. He reminds us, as Sowell did, that Mill was acquainted with the *Traité* when he wrote *Commerce Defended* and in fact cites it there. Moreover, he shows that Mill explicitly credited Say with the idea. I will, however, argue that the issue is a bit more convoluted. While it is true that Mill's version of the discussion did not differ all that much from Say's, I will suggest that neither of them offered an explicit exposition of Say's Law until some time later. Only the second edition of Say's *Traité* in 1814 describes explicitly the logic of Say's Law as we interpret it nowadays.

Let us now turn to the related issues that Say and Mill emphasized in their discussions.

III. Production as the Source of Disposable Income

The focal chapter's title, "Des Débouchés", is often translated as "on markets". However, it should be borne in mind that the term "market" is used as in "making a market", to denote the availability of effective demand, not as an institution (such as a marketplace) that facilitates the process of exchange. Perhaps a better translation of *des débouchés* is "on outlets for goods". I begin with the propositions which are the main subject of the extremely brief chapter on *débouchés* in the first edition of the *Traité*. These can be summarized as:

Say's First Proposition. A community's purchasing *power* (effective demand) is limited by and is equal to its output, because production provides *the means* by which outputs can be purchased. Furthermore,

Say's Second Proposition. Expenditure increases when output rises.

Note that the first proposition deals with purchasing *power*, not with actual purchases. It tells us, as Keynes did, that output is the source of effective demand—that output is purchasing power. But it does *not* say that all of that purchasing power will always be used to buy goods. Rather, these assertions state, in effect, that the marginal propensity to consume and invest is greater than zero and that the average propensity is (generally) not greater than unity. That is, they tell us that people who produce more are in a position to consume more and will generally do so. These points, which most of us would still accept, are made most emphatically in the very brief chapter on *débouchés* in the first edition, which I now present in its entirety:

Chapter 22 *On Markets*

> Every producer produces a quantity of a particular good that considerably exceeds his own consumption. The farmer harvests more grain than is required to feed him and his household; the hatter makes substantially more hats than he produces for his use; the wholesale grocer handles more sugar than he can consume. Each of them needs many other products to live comfortably. The exchanges they carry out of their own products for those of others, constitute what are called the *markets* for those products.
>
> In this operation money serves approximately the same role as the posters and the handbills in a large city which facilitate the intercourse of persons who

may want to do business with one another. During the course of the year each producer handles a very large quantity of money, but aside from small balances of little consequence, at the end of the year there ordinarily remains in his hands no more money than he had at the beginning. What matters is what he purchases with that money, that is, the products of others that he has exchanged against his own, a portion of which he has consumed, and a portion saved according to his needs, his saving habits and the state of this wealth.

I trust this shows that it is not the abundance of money but the abundance of other products in general that facilitates sales. This is one of the most important truths of political economy.

Imagine a very industrious individual having everything he needs to produce things: both ability and capital; if he were the only industrious person in a population which, aside from a few coarse foods, does not know how to make anything; what could he do with his products? He will purchase the quantity of rough food necessary to satisfy his needs. But what can he do with the residue? Nothing. But if the outputs of the country begin to multiply and grow more varied, then all of his produce can find a use, that is to say, it can be exchanged for things which he needs or for additional luxuries he can enjoy, or for the accumulation of the stocks that he considers appropriate.

What I have just said about a single industrious individual can be said equally of one hundred thousand. Their nation will offer them as much of a market as it can pay for additional objects; and it can pay for additional objects in proportion to the quantities it produces. Money performs no more than the role of a conduit in this double exchange. When the exchanges have been completed it will be found that one has paid for products with products.

Consequently, when a nation has too large a quantity of one particular type of product, the means of disposing of them is to create goods of another variety. It is when one can no longer produce any exchangeable object that exportation becomes advantageous. That is the case when it serves as a means to purchase products that cannot be furnished domestically, such as fruits from another climate. But the most profitable sales are those that a nation makes to itself; for they can take place only because of the two values produced: that which is sold and that which is purchased. Exportation should therefore be considered only as a supplement to and less advantageous than domestic consumption. [Say, 1803, Vol. I, Book 1, pp. 152-155]

Exactly the same point is emphasized by James Mill:

No proposition however in political economy seems to be more certain than this which I am going to announce, how paradoxical soever it may at first sight appear; and if it be true, none undoubtedly can be deemed of more importance. The production of commodities creates, and is the one and universal cause which creates a market for the commodities produced. Let us but consider what is meant by a market. Is any thing else understood by it than that something is ready to be exchanged for the commodity which we would dispose of? When goods are carried to market what is wanted is somebody to buy. But to buy, one must have wherewithal to pay. It is obviously therefore the collective means of payment which exist in the whole nation that constitute the entire market of the nation. But wherein consist the collective means of payment of the whole nation? Do they not consist in its annual produce, in the annual revenue of the general mass of its inhabitants? But if a nation's power of purchasing is exactly measured by its annual produce, as it undoubtedly is; the more you increase the annual produce, the more by that very act you extend the national market, the power of purchasing and the actual purchases of the nation. Whatever be the additional quantity of goods therefore which is at any time created in any country, an additional power of purchasing, exactly equivalent, is at the same instant created; so that a nation can never be naturally overstocked either with capital or with commodities; as the very operation of capital makes a vent for its produce. [Mill, 1807, pp. 81-82].

It is to be noted that both Mill and Say apparently misinterpreted the logic of their own propositions. From the valid assertion that a high income level *permits* a high level of demand, they seem to jump to the conclusion that demand will *necessarily* be high when output is high. This is an issue to which we will return later.

IV. INVESTMENT V. CONSUMPTION AS STIMULANTS TO WEALTH

There is a pair of related propositions which may have been even of more importance at least to Say, judging by the space he devoted to them and the vehemence with which he espoused them. Those observations, which deal with the relation between consumption and investment ("unproductive" and "reproductive" expenditures), can be described as:

Say's Third Proposition. A given investment expenditure is a far more effective stimulant to the wealth of an economy than an equal amount of consumption.

This proposition is the main substance of Say's chapter on consumption, whose translation now follows:

Chapter 3. *Is the Wealth of a State Increased by its Consumption?*

Reproductive consumption that ordinarily replaces with greater values those values that it destroys, is not ordinarily referred to as *consumption*, and I myself, when I happen to have used that word without explanation, have meant unproductive consumption, whose only purpose is to satisfy men's needs or to multiply their pleasures. It is only that sort of consumption that is referred to in the title of this chapter.

Many people, seeing that, overall, total production always equals consumption (because it is quite necessary for everything that is consumed to have been produced), imagined that the encouragement of consumption was favourable to production. The *Physiocrats* seized upon this idea and made it one of the fundamental principles of their doctrine. *Consumption is the measure of reproduction* they said;[1] that is, *the more there is consumed the more there is produced.* And since production brings wealth, they concluded that a state enriches itself through its consumption, that saving is in direct conflict with public prosperity, and that the most useful citizen is the one who expends most.[2]

This system is well designed to win the favour of the vulgar and so it has many partisans. The manufacturer and the merchant perceive general prosperity only in the sale of their wares, only in the greatest possible consumption of them. But when one considers this doctrine more attentively one finds that it leads to results quite different.

The consumption of each family can exceed, equal or fall short of its income. The consumption of all families together, that is, that of the nation, can follow the same course. That is, a nation, all things compensated for, can spend more or less than its income or exactly the amount of its income.

In the first of these cases the nation every year causes a dent in its capital; and, as a result, each year decreases its income; first, from the profits that would have corresponded to the capital that was eaten up and, second, from the profits from the industry w' ich this capital would have supported. Far from being the way to stimulate exchanges it is the way to reduce them. Each year production rises to the level of consumption; but it declines along with consumption, to the point where the entire nation with no more capital, no more cultivated land, no more industry, no more population, disappears entirely or pursues a sad and miserable existence. It is the situation into which many parts of Greece and Syria have fallen under Turkish rule.

If a country or the families that compose it consume no more than their income, since that country does not deplete any part of its capital, it will keep its income constant, and will offer every year the same market for the product of its industry.

Let us also note, in passing, that it is difficult for a nation encouraged to spend its entire income not to over-spend it quickly, and consequently to fall more or less rapidly into the same grievous extremes as those that consume a portion of their capital along with their income. Both individuals and a government that raise their regular expenses exactly to the level of their ordinary income take no account of accidents and unforeseen risks that never fail to take something away from income and to add something to expenses.

As for a nation that does not expend its entire income, and annually augments its capital, that is the one and the only one that provides the greatest annual markets for its product. In effect, each year it experiences growth in the profits from its capital and in the power of its industry and, consequently, in its income; that is to say, its means of consumption either direct or through exchange, in one word, its markets.

The public interest is consequently not served by consumption, but it is served and served prodigiously by saving, and though it seems extraordinary to many persons, not being any the less true as a consequence, the labouring class is served by it more than anyone else. These persons think, perhaps, that the values which the wealthy save out of outlays on their personal pleasures in order to add to their capitals are not consumed. They are consumed; they furnish markets for many producers; but they are consumed reproductively and furnish markets for the useful goods that are capable of engendering still others, instead of being evaporated in frivolous consumption.

I will explain this doctrine through an illustration expressed in terms of the most common of activities.

A wealthy individual who has an income of a hundred thousand francs, and who is in the habit of consuming them totally, decides one day to decrease his outlays. He gives up some of his domestic servants, and is better served, he purchases fewer jewels, and is not criticized quite so much; he gives less splendid dinners and makes better friends. In brief, instead of spending a hundred thousand francs per annum he expends no more than eighty thousand. From the first year on, he thereby adds twenty thousand francs to his productive capital. The hundred thousand francs that constitute his income are always spent in their entirety, but no more than eighty thousand of them are spent unproductively; the remaining twenty thousand are spent in a manner that reproduces them with profit. He lends them to a manufacturer of handkerchiefs whose enterprise was languishing for lack of funds. The class comprising the lackeys, jewellers, and merchants of fine foods do indeed experience a decrease in the demand for their services and their products; but the class that provides to handkerchief makers their clothes, their food, and their raw materials see theirs increase precisely by the same proportion. The encouragement given by reproductive consumption is thus the same as that which would have resulted from the satisfaction of the needs and pleasures of a single person. But it does not cease here.

In effect, there has been *in addition* an increase in income for the wealthy capitalist, and an increase in income for the manufacturer and his workers. On the basis of a very moderate evaluation based on experience,

the capitalist may find his income increased by	1,000 francs
the chief manufacturer may find his increased by the same amount	1,000 francs
and the class of workers may find their total salaries augmented by	3,000 francs
total	5,000

That year's consumption, consequently, will be 105 thousand francs rather than the 100 thousand to which they would have added up if the person with the large income has spent it all unproductively.[3] And what is even more, the same 20 thousand francs that increased that year's incomes by 5 thousand francs are reaccumulated and can yield the same service in all the years that follow for so long as one considers it appropriate to use them productively.

There are a thousand ways to invest savings. While the happy effects which we have just seen continue, the following year gives the same consumer the opportunity to carry out similar savings. He uses them for the construction of a steam engine, to irrigate a field; the effect on general wealth is the same: the yield of his lands is increased by a thousand francs, more or less, and the activity that is introduced into their cultivation yields an annual income to many workers.

Thus, many persons are in error when they imagine that the poor obtain resources only from the expenditures of the rich. The true resource of the poor man is his labour. To exercise his labour he has no need for the rich man's consumption; he needs only his capital. Similarly, a country or a district could be most fortunate if no rich men were to reside or consume there, so long as they were to invest their capital in it. The farmer would labour there for the manufacturer and the merchant, the merchant for the farmer and the manufacturer, and the latter for the other two. All would be well supplied with all the necessities of life. With frugality they could enrich themselves and they would also have the means to pay to the absentee capitalist the interest and the rents on the capital and the land which, so to speak, he would have lent to them.

I have insisted on carrying out this demonstration because the error it exposes is among those that are the most widespread. It is shared by those who advocate the mercantilist doctrine, and those who advocate the agriculturist doctrine, that is to say, the Physiocrats. They all consider consumption to be useful in relation to production, while it is in fact, useful only for the pleasure that it procures.[4] A consumer offers no advantages by *that which* he consumes, but by *that* which he provides as a replacement; now, he can give that much more in replacement as he undertakes less unrewarding consumption and more reproductive consumption. If an idle rich man who eats up an enormous income, does not ruin his country, at least he contributes nothing to its prosperity. A

---

[1] See Mercier de la Rivière, *Ordre essentiel des Sociétés polit*, Vol. 2, p. 138, and the other writings of the Physiocrats.

[2] A reviewer notes that the physiocratic concept of "consumption" was very different from Say's (or from ours) so that "Say's reading of his own definition into the physiocrat's words created a complete distortion of their doctrines." [W.B.]

[3] One may think there is double counting here, and that the profit of the entrepreneur and his employees merely are substitutes for those that would have been earned by the jeweller and the chef on the assumption of unproductive consumption. But there is really no double counting. The profits of the jeweller, the chef and all the suppliers of unproductive consumption are replaced by the suppliers of productive consumption. These suppliers have sold to the manufacturer or his workers 20 thousand francs in goods, in place of the same quantity of goods that would have been sold to the rich consumer. Besides, there have been 5 thousand francs in income by which the year's consumption can have risen. That is to say, with 20 thousand francs and labour, 25 thousand francs in handkerchiefs have been produced. One should not be astonished that I evaluate the gross product of a manufacturer at 25 per cent of his capital; the net product itself often reaches this proportion.

[4] I knew a young man who threw crystal flasks out of the window as soon as he had emptied them. *This is necessary, he said, to encourage workshops*. In this way, he diminished total social wealth, precisely by the amount the artisan had increased it in producing the flask. He should have given it to a household too poor to be able to procure one. In this way he would have provided its inhabitants one of the pleasures of wealth, and manufacture would have been given an advantage comparable to that which it would have received from an increase in general opulence.

wealthy man who does not expend his entire income does contribute to it; a wealthy man who increases his capital and, moreover, occupies himself usefully, contributes to it still more.

If there is any one habit that merits encouragement, in monarchies and republics alike, in large and small countries alike, it is saving. But does it need encouragement? Is it not enough to avoid honouring dissipation? Is it not enough to respect all savings and all of their uses, that is to say, the growth of all economic activity that is not criminal? For I am not speaking here of the vague and inadequate protection that is sometimes referred to as *respect for property*. It is not enough merely to protect individuals from being stripped by arbitrary acts, by injustice, by fraud and violence; it is also necessary to guarantee them from attack by chicanery, from increases in taxes even if freely consented to, because though a contribution may well be voted freely, it becomes obligatory the moment it is made into a requirement. Then, man's desire to accumulate goods, to prepare his resources for the future, will suffice to balance off his love of present enjoyment, and to provide for the general prosperity that is made up of the prosperity of individuals. [Say, 1803, Vol. II, Book 5, pp. 358–368]

While in this first edition of the *Traité* the issue of superiority of investment over consumption as a stimulus to growth is not referred to directly in the chapter on *débouchés*, it is explicitly incorporated into this chapter in later editions (see, e.g., p. 139 of the English translation of the third edition). To Mill, too, this is a central point: "The greatness of the produce of a country in any year, is altogether dependent upon the greatness of the quantity of the produce of the former year, which is set apart for the business of reproduction. The annual produce is therefore the greater, the less the portion is which is allotted for consumption". (Mill, 1807, p. 71).

Mill quotes approvingly Say's tale of the young man who threw crystal vases out of the window in order to encourage manufactures. He also points out that

> ... it is the maintenance of great fleets and armies, which is always the most formidable weight in the scale of consumption, and which has the most fatal tendency to turn the balance against reproduction and prosperity. It is by the lamentable contrivance of wars, almost always nourished by puerile prejudiced and blind passions, that the affairs of prosperous nations are first brought to the stationary condition, and from this plunged into the retrograde. [Mill, 1807, p. 74]

(This passage also reminds us of the circumstances in which Mill was writing. He was here involved in a debate on foreign trade, the hegemony of agriculture, war expenditure and under-consumption—issues arising out of Napoleon's attempted blockade of the British Isles.)

V. In the Very Long Run Demand Will Catch Up with Supply

Like all classical economists, Say was very much interested in the longer run. From the first edition on, Say never ceased to emphasize, as an empirical observation:

Say's Fourth Proposition. Over the centuries the community will always find demands for increased outputs, even for increases that are enormous.

In other words, there was in his opinion no basis for fear of secular stagnation. This view he based on the argument that production provides *the purchasing power* with which output can be acquired. Thus, from the first edition on, he recalled to the reader how much the output of his country had risen since the humiliating days of Henry V, and the end of the Hundred Years' War. He points out that the total income accruing to factors of production expands equally with the total output of the community. "Otherwise, by what means could one purchase nowadays in France at least to two or three times the quantity of things that were purchased in the miserable and unfortunate reign of Charles VI?" (Say, 1803, Vol. II, p. 180.) A translation of the full selection from which this quotation is taken is provided later in this paper. Charles VI (1368–1422) was the mentally unstable king of France who was forced by the English to adopt Henry V as his heir, disinheriting his son, later Charles VII (Jeanne d'Arc's Dauphin), and to give Henry his daughter, Catherine, in marriage.) Subsequent developments seem generally to have supported Say on this score. Real *per capita* GNP has no doubt risen at least tenfold since Say wrote, when the Industrial Revolution was only in its beginnings. Demand certainly seems to have risen comparably.

Now, it must be admitted that Say seems never to have devoted much space to a discussion of the very long-run correspondence of demand with supply, and I have not found any place where Mill dealt with it at all. Yet it seems to me to be implicit in their emphasis on production as the source of *growth* in the wealth of a nation. The fact that in his second edition Say moved his remark on Charles VI into the body of the chapter on *débouchés* and that he kept it there in the subsequent editions attests to the value he placed on the observation that demand in the long run is capable of keeping up with the most enormous increases in output.

Note that this proposition, which is clearly of some considerable importance for the analysis of economic development, is virtually irrelevant for stabilization policy. Say's observation that in the long run demand keeps up with rises in production is perfectly consistent with the existence of protracted periods of substantial unemployment. There is nothing in the principle that is inconsistent with a "general glut" whose possibility is denied by Say's identity. Note in this connection, Sowell's (1974, pp. 64ff) contention (against Patinkin and Blaug) that even Malthus' position in the glut controversy did *not* include a secular stagnation argument.

VI. MONEY NO MORE THAN A MEANS TO FACILITATE EXCHANGE

We come now to the first of the propositions that relate closely to "Say's Law". This is the emphasis that both Say and Mill place on the *un*importance of money as a contributor to effective demand. Say stresses the conclusion that money is no more than a conduit for, or a lubricant of, the exchange process but itself ultimately contributes nothing to effective demand. (Mill deals with the role of money only obliquely. He does say that his propositions are seen most clearly by considering "... the circumstances of a country in which all exchange should be in the way of barter, as the idea of money frequently tends to perplex" (p. 82). He also makes much of

Spence's observation, "Let it not be urged that what they might save would not be hoarded (for misers now-a-days are wiser than to keep their money in strong boxes at home) but would be lent on interest", emphasizing that these loans will finance effective demand in the form of reproductive consumption (p. 75).) We have already seen that two of the seven paragraphs that constitute the first edition chapter on *débouchés* are devoted to a description of the unimportance of money. Say makes this point by likening the role of money to that of advertising and stressing that producers generally add negligibly to their stock of money over the course of a year. Thus we may describe:

Say's Sixth Proposition. Production of goods rather than the supply of money is the primary determinant of demand. Money facilitates commerce but does not determine the amounts of goods that are exchanged.

This assertion gets closer to implying Say's identity than anything we have discussed up to this point. If in fact he had said that no one wants money for its own sake and that any cash accumulations will always and immediately be respent, Say's identity would indeed have been implied. However, to Say of the first edition, the irrelevance of money would seem to arise in quite another way—it is unimportant not because only goods are demanded, but because it is a poor means for the stimulation of demand. We are back at the Keynesian point that effective demand is a rising function of *real* output, and that money merely facilitates the working of that relationship. If that is what Say had in mind (and on this we can only guess from his inconclusive wording), then even his monetary discussion is still only distantly related to "Say's Law".

VII. GENERAL V. PARTICULAR GLUTS

So far as I have been able to judge, Say in his first edition and Mill in *Commerce Defended* make only one point that is really related directly to either the equality or identity form of Say's Law. This is an assertion which we may characterize as:

Say's Seventh Proposition. Any glut in the market for a good must involve relative underproduction of some other commodity, or commodities, and the mobility of capital out of the area with excess supply and into industries whose products are insufficient to meet demand will tend rapidly to eliminate the overproduction.

Certainly this argument suggests strongly that both authors believed in some form of Say's Law. However, this argument would appear to be a conclusion one draws from the Law rather than a bit of logic that argues its validity. It is a corollary rather than an underpinning of the Law.

Mill makes the point with characteristic force:

> It may be necessary, however, to remark, that a nation may easily have more than enough of any one commodity, though she can never have more than enough commodities in general. The quantity of any one commodity may easily be carried beyond its due proportion; but by that very circumstance is implied that some other commodity is not provided in sufficient proportion. What indeed is meant by a commodity's exceeding the market? Is it not that there is a portion

of it for which there is nothing that can be had in exchange. But of those other things then the proportion is too small. A part of the means of production which has been applied to the preparation of this superabundant commodity, should have been applied to the preparation of those other commodities till the balance between them had been established. Whenever this balance is properly preserved, there can be no superfluity of commodities, none for which a market will not be ready. This balance too the natural order of things has so powerful a tendency to produce, that it will always be very exactly preserved where the injudicious tampering of government does not prevent, or those disorders in the intercourse of the world, produced by the wars into which the inoffending part of mankind are plunged, by the folly much more frequently than by the wisdom of their rulers. [Mill, 1807, pp. 84–85]

Note that in this passage Mill not only emphasizes the possibility of a partial glut but also asserts explicitly the impossibility of an excess "of commodities in general". In other words, Mill does assert his adherence to Say's Law. Yet it seems to me that nowhere here or in Say's first edition does either author try to spell out the logical foundation for any variant of Say's Law. To make this point I shall now present a last passage from the *Traité*. This one is perhaps particularly significant because both Spengler (1945) and Sowell (1972) cite it as the passage containing the heart of Say's first discussion of the subject.

Chapter 5. *In What Proportions the Value of Products is Distributed Among the Three Factors of Production*

The magnitude of the demand for factors of production in general does not depend on *the magnitude of consumption* as all too many persons have imagined. Consumption is not at all a cause, it is an effect. In order to consume it is necessary to purchase; now, one can make purchases only with what one has produced. Is the quantity of outputs demanded consequently determined by the quantity of products created? Without any doubt. Everyone can, at his pleasure, consume what he has produced; or else he can buy another product with his own. The demand for products in general is therefore always equal to the sum of the products available.[1] A nation that produced annually no more than a value of two billion, would be able neither to purchase nor to consume three billion during the same period of time without drawing the billion deficit from its capitals every year. We see that the best way to provide markets for outputs is to produce more, not to destroy them. If this conclusion is obvious, as I believe it to be, what are we to think of the systems that encourage consumption in order to stimulate production?

It is not true that total output cannot exceed total consumption. Can one not accumulate a portion of the products created each year? Cannot everyone accumulate either some of his own products or some of those he acquires by exchange? Is not a market provided by this accumulation just as effectively as if that same value had been consumed?[2] Total output is consequently not limited by the magnitude of consumption. Limitation of consumption does not close off markets; rather the fostering of production will open new ones. A nation that enriches itself enjoys an advantage comparable to that acquired by one that extends its foreign commerce. It experiences the opening of new markets and the appearance of new customers. It extends its commerce, and does not wage wars to achieve this.

If production is not bounded by the magnitude of consumption,[3] if one can produce more than is consumed, what then are the bounds to production? They consist of the availability of the factors of production.

But, it may be said, *if there are goods that cannot be sold, there are necessarily more productive factors employed than there are opportunities for the consumption of their outputs*. Not at all. No glut ever occurs except when too large a quantity of factors of production is devoted to one type of production and not enough to another. In effect, what is the cause for the inability to carry out a sale? It is the difficulty of obtaining some other good (either an output or money) in exchange for the one that is offered. Means of production are consequently lacking for the former to the extent that they are superabundant for the latter. A region deep in the interior of a land finds no sale for its wheat, but if some factory is established there and part of the capital and the labour that formerly was devoted to the land is redirected to another type of production, the products of the one and the other can be exchanged without difficulty, even though these outputs have expanded rather than diminished. Inability to sell, therefore, arises not from overabundance but from the misallocation of the factors of production.

In the notes that Garnier has included in his excellent translation of Smith he states that in old nations like those of Europe, in which capital has been accumulated over several centuries, overabundance of the annual product would *obstruct trade, if it were not absorbed by proportionate amounts of consumption.* I realize that trade can be obstructed by the overabundance of particular products. It is an evil that can never be anything but temporary, for participation in the production of goods whose outputs exceed the need for them and whose value is debased will rapidly cease and it will instead be devoted to the production of the goods that are sought after. But I cannot conceive that the products of the labour of an entire nation can ever be overabundant since one good provides the means to purchase the other. The sum of its outputs composes the total wealth of a nation, and wealth is no more of an embarrassment to nations than it is to individuals.

This point having been thoroughly cleared up, it provides us an answer to the question with which we are concerned and which I repeat: *upon what elements does the demand for factors of production in general depend?* It depends on the volume of production, and since the volume of production depends on the quantity of factors of production, the demand for factors of production expands proportionately to the quantity of means of production themselves. That is to say, as a result, a nation always has the means to purchase everything it produces. Otherwise, by what means could one purchase nowadays in France at least to two or three times the quantity of things that were purchased in the miserable and unfortunate reign of Charles VI? [Say, 1803, Vol. II, Book 4, pp. 175–180]

This passage clearly summarizes all of the seven propositions we have listed so far. In particular it states emphatically that "... trade can be obstructed by the overabundance of particular products ... goods whose outputs exceed the need for them.... But ... the products of the labour of an entire nation can never be overabundant because one good provides the means to purchase the other".

VIII. Incompleteness of the Statement of the Law

What then, if anything, is lacking in this passage to qualify it as an explicit statement of Say's Law? The Law is surely enunciated in the latter

---

[1] A product consumed by its maker is a product that has been supplied and demanded by the same person. It constitutes part of the total supply of goods and of the total demand for them.

[2] Moreover, we will see later that the portion saved out of income and added to capitals is just as surely consumed every year, but in another manner; that is to say, in a reproductive manner.

[3] Here our subject is only unproductive consumption, not the use of capital for its reproduction with profit.

part of Mill's assertion "That a nation may easily have more than enough of any one commodity, *though she can never have more than enough of commodities in general*" (Mill, 1807, p. 84, my italics); and the same is obviously true of Say when he tells us that "The products of the labor of an entire nation can never be overabundant".

Thus the proclamation of Say's Law is found in both writings. As I have already suggested, all that is missing is its rationale. Thus, note that Say completes the preceding quotation by telling us that he "... cannot conceive that the products of the labor of an entire nation can ever be overabundant since one good provides the *means* to purchase the other" (my italics). In other words, the community can *afford to* purchase the goods *if it wishes to do so*. We are back at what we have labelled Say's first proposition, which asserts that production creates the *power* to purchase itself.

But this sidesteps the basic issue in the entire subsequent controversy over Say's Law. The issue is not whether the purchasing power needed to buy a nation's output is available, but whether it will in fact be used.

Mill treats the issue virtually as a tautology and, hence, as one whose logic requires no discussion: "What indeed is meant by a commodity's exceeding the market? Is it not that there is a portion of it for which there is nothing that can be had in exchange? But of those other things then the proportion is too small". (Mill, 1807, p. 85). In other words, every excess supply is, by definition, an excess demand for something else. But what is that something else? Must it necessarily be a commodity?

IX. Say's Second Edition: The Missing Ingredient Supplied

There are, it seems to me, two missing ingredients to the Say's Law discussion on the preceding paragraphs. For they fail to discuss the nature of the demand generated by the holders of the community's purchasing power, and they do not deal with the timing of that demand.

Other discussions both afterwards *and before* treated both these matters very explicitly. They asserted that people will always use their purchasing power to seek either consumers' or producers' goods in exchange; that is, they will demand goods rather than cash balances, because to do otherwise would be irrational. Moreover, it was (sometimes but not always) stated that this demand must accompany the acquisition of purchasive power through production *virtually without* delay. These statements clearly add up to Say's identity, with supply automatically and immediately creating an equivalent demand, or to a strong form of the equality, with fast acting and powerful equilibrating forces that either usually or always channel demands into commodities.

It is curious that Adam Smith had already discussed both these matters nearly thirty years before Say. (On the other side of the matter, Tucker (1960, pp. 92–99) points out that Ricardo was induced to emphasize his Say's Law discussion by his opposition to Smith's view that accumulation tends to *reduce* the rate of profit through a growing abundance of capital-seeking employment.) Concerned to support the idea that saving does not reduce the demand, he deals with the issues we have just raised in two well-known passages. The first examines the motivation of demand:

> In all countries where there is tolerable security, every man of common understanding will endeavour to employ whatever stock he can command, in procuring either present enjoyment or future profit.... A man must be perfectly crazy who, where there is tolerable security, does not employ all the stock which he commands, whether it be his own or borrowed of other people, in some one or other of those ... ways. [Smith, 1776, p. 268]

In the second passage he considers the timing of these expenditures:

> That portion of his revenue which a rich man annually spends, is in most cases consumed by idle guests, and menial servants, who leave nothing behind them in return for their consumption. That portion which he annually saves, as for the sake of profit it is *immediately* employed as a capital, is consumed in the same manner, *and nearly in the same time too*, but by a different set of people. [Smith, 1776, p. 321, my italics]

In other words, as has been pointed out before, Smith all but enunciated Say's Law and certainly spelled out its logic more completely than either Say or Mill in their first writings on the subject. The only lacunae in Smith's discussion are his stipulation that a state of "tolerable security" must prevail for (*ex ante*) investment always to equal saving (would he have considered a period of bad business prospects or great uncertainty to involve intolerable security?) and his failure to state explicitly the conclusion that total supply must, consequently, always be equal to the demand.

Say only gets around to these matters in his second edition where he tells us in his revised and expanded chapter on *débouchés* that:

> ... It is worthwhile to remark, that a product is no sooner *created* than it *from that instant* offers a market for other products to the full extent of its own value. For every product is created only to be consumed, whether productively or unproductively, and indeed to be consumed as quickly as possibly, since every value whose realization is delayed causes a loss to the individual who is currently its possessor of the interest earning corresponding to that delay.... A product is therefore, so far as everyone can arrange, destined to the most rapid consumption. From the moment it exists, it consequently seeks another product with which it can be exchanged. Gold and silver are no exception since no sooner has the merchant made a sale than he seeks to employ the product of his sale. [Say, 1814, pp. 147-148, his italics. A somewhat modified version of this passage is found in later editions. See, e.g., the 1821 English translation of the fourth edition, pp. 134-135. The translation here follows that one so far as possible.]

From the second edition on Say also deals far more directly with the role of money and its irrelevance as a determinant of demand. For example, in the English translation of the fourth edition of the *Traité* we are told

> Should a tradesman say, "I do not want other products for my woollens, I want money", ... You say, you only want money; I say, you want other commodities, and not money. For what, in point of fact, do you want the money? Is it not for the purchase of raw materials or stock for your trade, or victuals for your support? ... Thus, to say that sales are dull, owing to the scarcity of money is to mistake the means for the cause....
> There is always money enough to conduct the circulation and mutual interchange of other values, when those values really exist. Should the increase of traffic require more money to facilitate it, the want is easily supplied.... In such cases, merchants know well enough how to find substitutes for the product

serving as the medium of exchange or money:[1] and money itself soon pours in, for this reason, that all produce naturally gravitates to that place where it is most in demand.... [Say, 1821, pp. 133–134]

What is noteworthy in this comment is Say's implicit adherance in this passage to an equality rather than an identity form of the law. He admits that an excess demand for money can arise, but he tells us that it will only be temporary. If it is only local, supplies of money will soon flow in from elsewhere. And, in any event, the excess supply will be eliminated not by anything like the cash balance effect which trims demands down to the available (nominal) supply of cash, but by an increase in the supply of cash or substitutes for cash.

Thus the eighth (and for our purposes the last) of Say's eight propositions is Say's Law itself. Apparently this takes the form of a type of Say's equality, i.e., supply and demand are always equated by a rapid and powerful equilibration mechanism. However, we should be careful not to attribute to him thoughts on what he would have considered fine distinctions, such as that between the equality and the identity forms of the law. For very likely the subject was never explicitly considered by him.

Of course, one can go on indefinitely, listing observations that Say considered pertinent to his subject. My choice is consequently and unavoidably rather arbitrary. Note that I have not listed the rather curious tautological version of Say's Law that Say enunciated in his correspondence with Malthus. In a letter dated Paris, July 1827, Say wrote:...

> Our discussion on *débouchés* begins to be no more than a dispute on words. You wish me to accord the name products to goods that can satisfy a certain number of wants and which possess a certain value, even though that value is insufficient to repay the totality of their production costs. But the logic of my doctrine on production establishes clearly that there is no complete production unless all the inputs necessary for that piece of work are repayed by the value of the product ... everything that is truly produced that cannot be sold is an outlay made thoughtlessly and without producing anything; and my doctrine on *débouchés* remains intact. [*Cours Complet d'Économie Politique Pratique*, Brussels 1844, p. 649. See also Malthus's comment on p. 647.]

X. Concluding Comment

Several conclusions emerge from this discussion of Say's and Mill's discussion of Say's Law. First, on the relatively unimportant issue of priority matters are hazy, and the answer must depend on our definition of the Law itself. Obviously, it is at least hinted at from the first edition of the *Traité* onward. My own conclusion is that Spengler (1945), Winch (1966) and Sowell (1972) are right in awarding priority to Say. But they are right for the wrong reason. To me, the first statement of the Law as we understand it today appears complete with its logical underpinnings *neither* in the first edition of the *Traité* nor in *Commerce Defended* but in the second edition of Say's work. On that interpretation, Say's Law can be said to have achieved its first full codification in 1814, even though, as is always the case in the

---

[1] By bills at sight, or after date, bank-notes, running-credits, write-offs, & c. at London and Amsterdam.

history of ideas, any one who seeks to pinpoint its first origins must do so at his peril.

However, the major conclusion that emerges from our re-examination of Say's and Mill's texts is that the Say's Law discussion was, first and foremost, an examination of the influences that promote long-term economic growth, and not primarily a matter of short-term problems of unemployment and overproduction. The major emphasis of Say's and Mill's arguments was that investment (productive consumption), rather than consumption of luxuries, pyramid building or military expenditure (unproductive consumption), are the effective means to promote growth.

There is also a second observation, going beyond our textual examination, which also seems worth making. We tend to think today of the Malthusian side of the argument as Keynesian in spirit and consequently "progressive", while the Say–Mill–Ricardian position is interpreted to be the opposite. But viewed in terms of the circumstances of the early nineteenth century, when the debate was underway, this is the reverse of the truth. Malthus was the open defender of the role of the landed proprietors as against the rising capitalist class. (Marx characterizes those writings which "... regard *consumption* as a necessary spur to production" as "apologetics ... partly for the rich idlers and the 'unproductive labourers' whose *services* they consume, partly for 'strong governments' whose expenditure is heavy, for the increase of State debts, for holders of sinecures, etc". (1963, p. 281). It was on their behalf that he defended protective tariffs and it was their consumption of luxury goods and their employment of personal retainers that he was defending when he argued that they were necessary for the prevention of over-production. On the other hand, Say, Mill and Ricardo sought, against this position, to encourage the new industrial activity and, with it, the expansion of the output of the economy (See Blaug, 1958, pp. 94–97). It is always dangerous to interpret the political colour of earlier works in terms of the state of affairs of the reader's own era.

ACKNOWLEDGEMENTS

I am grateful to Elizabeth Bailey, Fritz Machlup and Donald Winch for their comments and suggestions, and to George de Menil and Arthur Laurie for their corrections of my translations.

REFERENCES

BLAUG, MARK (1958) *Ricardian Economics: A Historical Study*. New Haven: Yale University Press.

MARX, KARL (1963 edition). *Theories of Surplus Value*. Moscow: Progress Publishers, I.

MILL, JAMES (1807).*Commerce Defended*. London: C. and B. Baldwin.

SAY, J. B. (first ed. 1803). *Traité d'économie politique ou simple exposition de la manière dont se forment, se distribuent et se consomment les richesses* Paris: Deterville.

—— (2nd ed., 1914). *Traité d'économie politique ou simple exposition de la manière dont se forment, se distribuent et se consomment les richesses* Paris: A. A. Renouard.

—— (1821) *A Treatise on Political Economy; or the Production, Distribution and Consumption of Wealth*, Boston: Wells and Lilly.

—— (1844). *Cours complet d'économie politique pratique* Brussels: Société Typographique Belge.

SMITH, ADAM (1776). *An Inquiry into the Nature and Causes of the Wealth of Nations.* London: Methuen & Co. (Cannan ed. 1925).
SOWELL, THOMAS (1972). *Say's Law: An Historical Analysis.* Princeton: University Press.
—— (1974). *Classical Economics Reconsidered.* Princeton: University Press.
SPENGLER, J. J. (1945). The Physiocrats and Say's Law of Markets. *Journal of Political Economy,* 53, 193–211, 317–347. Reprinted in Spengler and Allen (1960).
—— and ALLEN, W. R. (1960). *Essays in Economic Thought: Aristotle to Marshall.* Chicago; Rand McNally.
TUCKER, G. S. L. (1960). *Progress and Profits in British Economic Thought, 1650–1850.* Cambridge: University Press.
WINCH, DONALD (1966). *James Mill: Selected Economic Writings.* Chicago: University Press.

[7]

THE ECONOMISTS AND THE COMBINATION LAWS

WILLIAM D. GRAMPP

The laws and the reasons for them, 502.—The economists and repeal, 503.—Why the laws were repealed, 515.

The Combination Laws of Great Britain prohibited workers from organizing to fix wages and imposed the same prohibition on employers. The repeal of the laws in 1824 was an important event—both curious and instructive.

It has been represented as a triumph of classical economics.[1] That is curious because the effect was to reduce competition in labor markets. Actually, the influence of the economists, although noticeable, was small. There were three other groups that influenced the event much more: One was the leadership of political parties, especially the Tory; another was the radical reformers; the third was the working class.

One finds that there was a similar grouping when other economic policies were enacted: a party leadership that was looking for the

---

1. The following are representative statements of almost all that has been written about why the laws were repealed:

"... Place's efforts would have failed had not the *laissez faire* ideas embodied in the *Wealth of Nations* gradually found acceptance by the governing class." A. Aspinall, *The Early English Trade Unions, Documents from the Home Office Papers in the Public Record Office* (London: 1949), p. xxv.

"Place's remarkable achievement carried through on the principles of *laissez faire*, with the help of M'Culloch and Joseph Hume...." Mary Dorothy George, "The Combination Laws," *Economic History Review*, VI (April, 1936), 178.

"But both Place and Hume were devotees of orthodox 'political economy,' and had given active assistance in the dismantling of *all* legislation restraining the 'freedom' of capital or of labour." E. P. Thompson, *The Making of the English Working Class* (New York: 1964), p. 517.

"A large body of opinion, which was in sympathy with the new economic theory of *laissez-faire*, realized that the right of combination could not be denied to the artisan classes while it was freely afforded in practice to employers, and was convinced, moreover, that some measure of combination should be allowed both to labour and to capital." R. Y. Hedges and Allen Winterbottom, *The Legal History of Trade Unionism* (London: 1930), p. 34.

"By 1824 reformers imbued with Benthamite philosophy campaigned for repeal of the Combination Laws on the ground that 'all artificial restraints should be lifted.'" K. W. Wedderburn, *The Worker and the Law* (London: 1965), p. 208.

The Combination Law of 1800 "was removed in the name of Laissez-faire in 1824." S. B. Clough and C. W. Cole, *Economic History of Europe*, rev. ed. (Boston: 1947), p. 522.

"As a result of the efforts of Benthamite reformers, such as Joseph Hume, Francis Place, and J. R. McCulloch, a Select Committee on Artisans and Machinery in 1824 recommended that employers and workmen should be free to make such agreements as they thought fit, ..." N. A. Citrine, *Trade Union Law* (London: 1950), pp. 6–7.

sensible thing to do; a reform movement that was driving the leadership to do it; and a group in the economy that believed it stood to gain if the thing were done. The Corn Laws were repealed by the Tory government under Peel in 1846, and he also was responsible for seeing the Resumption Act through the House of Commons in 1819. The repeal of the Corn Laws was preceded by a massive public campaign under middle-class leadership and was supported by the factory owners who believed they stood to gain.

The working class believed it would benefit by the repeal of the Combination Laws. That is not surprising except in one respect. Some of the workers would have preferred the laws to continue—and the right to organize denied—if in return the government would fix wages as by law it was directed to do but had not done. The repeal of the Combination Laws is in this respect instructive. It uncovers one of the origins of trade unionism: a second-best method of wage-fixing.

The repeal of the laws is instructive in other ways also. It shows that the reformers in getting what they wanted were not overly scrupulous in the way they went about getting it. Much of what has been written about the repeal is by historians and lawyers who have regarded it as enlarging the freedom of the working class and hence a good thing. They have not taken much notice of the questionable way the good thing was gotten. They probably would not change their opinion of it even if they did. But the record would be more accurate. This paper, while not a study of the event in its entirety but of the place of the economists in it, does contain information that belongs on the record.

THE LAWS AND THE REASONS FOR THEM

The act of repeal in 1824 expressly exempted combinations from indictment or prosecution for conspiracy under the common law and under thirty-five statutes that were repealed wholly or in part. They had been enacted over a period of 520 years. The common law prohibition was even older.

Under it, the restraint of trade was a conspiracy, and combinations were restraints of trade. Some of the statutes were directed solely at making combinations illegal. Those of 1799 and 1800 did that and also made them a summary offense; they were the first actually to be called "Combination Laws," the others thereafter being renamed. Some did not have as their main purpose the prohibiting of combinations but did so because combinations interfered with the main purpose. For example, the statutes that directed public authorities to fix wages could also include a prohibition against workers or employers combining to secure different wages.

An economist looking at the history of the laws would notice that four distinct arguments were made for them. (A lawyer might notice more.) (1) They prevented a particular combination from having a damaging effect, as the combination of London millwrights in 1799 was said to have. (2) Combinations, as a restraint of trade, enabled sellers to take advantage of buyers or vice versa, as workers were accused of doing when wages were rising and employers when wages were falling. (3) Combinations, as a restraint of trade, were inconsistent with competition. (4) Combinations interfered with the exercise of public authority, as in the fixing of wages.

The importance of each argument depended on the times. When markets were regulated, as in the sixteenth century, or when men said they should be, which was often, the second and the fourth were important. When labor was militant, as in 1799, the first was. How important at any time was the third, which is the reason a classical liberal could advance, I would like to know but do not. In 1824 there was much talk that men and masters should be free to make whatever bargains they pleased. The talkers, one would suppose, favored competition and opposed combinations. Actually, they favored both.

Why they opposed prohibiting combinations is explained below. Their claims will be seen to have met directly only the first of the arguments above. Much more was said, but it did not join issue squarely with the others.

The Economists and Repeal

The economists did not say much. Still, it should be described. One reason is to set the record straight. Another is to suggest how it got to be wrong. Another is to provide information about a topic that today is of particular interest: the relation of economists and their ideas to the making and unmaking of policy.

When the economists of the classical period (from Smith to John Mill) did have an effect on policy, the fact made itself known in particular ways. They usually had written something about the issue, not just a passing comment but a considered statement. Examples are what Smith wrote about the Corn Laws, what Ricardo wrote about them and what he wrote about the currency question, and what

Malthus wrote about poor relief.² This writing elicited a response from outside of economics, like the reply of Arthur Young to the *Essay on Profits* in which Ricardo made the theoretical case for reducing the tariff on grain.³ When the economists were influential, their authority was invoked, their opinions cited, and their names held up for all to see and to rally around. This was sometimes done by both sides to the debate.⁴ What was attributed to an economist might actually be an opinion he held or it might not, and he could be misrepresented by both sides of a controversy.⁵

When the economists were influential, they made their interest in the issue known in a clear and public way. They published their opinions in the newspapers and quarterlies; they sent letters to the great; they put their views before Parliament; they drafted legislation; and from 1821 onward they discussed the issue in the Political Economy Club. They did not always agree among themselves, and hence their influence could be felt on both sides of an issue as it was when Malthus supported the Corn Laws and the Ricardians opposed them.⁶

By this definition one may say that the economists had an influence on the Corn Laws, the resumption of gold payments, and the Poor Laws. One also may say they did not have an influence on the

---

2. Adam Smith, *The Wealth of Nations* (New York: 1937), Bk. III, Ch. 5.
David Ricardo, *An Essay on the Influence of a Low Price of Corn on the Profits of Stock; etc.*, Works, Vol. IV, Piero Sraffa, ed. (Cambridge: 1951), pp. 1–41; and *On Protection to Agriculture*, ibid., pp. 207–66.
Thomas R. Malthus, *An Essay on the Principle of Population, etc.*, 6th ed. [1826] (London: 1890), Bk. III, Chs. V–VII.

3. Arthur Young, *An Inquiry into the Rise of Prices in Europe, etc.* (London: 1815).

4. An early instance was the debate in 1796 over the bill to fix the wages of agricultural laborers. The Tories opposed the bill in the name of free labor markets, and the Whigs supported it, while insisting that they too favored free markets. *The Parliamentary History of England, etc.*, Vol. XXXII (London: 1818), pp. 703, 706 (Feb. 12, 1796).
The most important instance was the debate over the Corn Laws. See the present writer's, *The Manchester School of Economics* (Stanford: 1960), pp. 17–18.

5. An example of misrepresentation, and of ambiguity also, is the debate in 1824 over the usury laws. Serjeant Onslow for years had asked for their repeal because, among their effects, they restricted the economic freedom of the individual. But Alderman Heygate objected and said Smith favored some control of the rate of interest, which Smith did (*Wealth of Nations*, pp. 339–40). C. W. W. Wynn replied to Heygate and correctly said Bentham had objected to Smith's policy. John Calcraft followed and opposed repeal, citing figures of Ricardo showing the effective rate of interest paid on government securities to be much above the nominal rate. Hansard, Vol. X, pp. 559–63 (Feb. 16, 1824). No one that day troubled to refer to Ricardo's stated views. He had in 1818 testified against the usury laws before a Select committee and in 1821 had spoken against them in the House. Ricardo, *Works*, Vol. V, pp. 337–47, 109–10.

6. Thomas R. Malthus, *Observations on the Effects of the Corn Laws, etc.* (London: 1814); *The Grounds of an Opinion on the Policy of Restricting the Importation of Foreign Corn* (London: 1815); *An Inquiry into the Nature and Progress of Rent, etc.* (London: 1815).

Factory Acts before 1837 (when Senior wrote his celebrated letters). On the repeal of the Combination Laws they had a small influence.

M'Culloch

It was mainly that of M'Culloch. He made a substantial effort on behalf of repeal and is the only economist who did. But his interest seems to have been created by Francis Place and not to have come from M'Culloch's own ideas or those of other economists of the period. Of course, Place knew the economists well and subscribed to their doctrine as he understood it. But he was not one of them. He supplied M'Culloch with information about the Combination Laws, how they operated, and what their effect had been. Not all of the information was correct, but it convinced M'Culloch the laws were unjust and ineffective. He wrote on them extensively from 1818 to 1824; his major article was in the *Edinburgh Review* in 1824, a few months before the issue was put before Parliament.[7]

He made two arguments. One seems to have come from Place who had said the laws were unfair because they punished labor more severely than they punished employers. The inequity provoked the workers into combining out of resentment. They also combined to protect themselves against the combinations of masters. Because the unions were illegal, they were necessarily conspiratorial, and conspiracy bred violence.[8] All of this was repeated by M'Culloch, and he made an extension. It was a venture into criminal psychology. If a man wants to steal a lamb but knows he may be punished as much as if he stole a sheep, he will steal the sheep, not because the "return" is greater, but in order to "deserve" the punishment and to show his outrage over its injustice. The repeal of the laws, M'Culloch continued, would cause combinations to disappear and would bring about a "free and unrestrained competition" in labor markets.[9]

In this way did he connect repeal with competition, and in this sense are the historians correct when they say he did. But they fail to say his argument was made only at the urging of an outsider and that

---

7. [J. R. M'Culloch] "Art. III. 1., Draft of proposed Bill . . . Relating to Combinations of Workmen, etc.," *Edinburgh Review*, XXXIX, No. 77 (Jan. 1824), 315–45. This was enlarged and became *An Essay on the Circumstances Which Determine the Rate of Wages and the Condition of the Labouring Classes* (London: 1826; 2nd ed., 1854). For the complete bibliography of M'Culloch's writings on the Combination Laws, see D. P. O'Brien, *J. R. McCulloch A Study in Classical Economics* (New York: 1970), pp. 366–70.

8. See the testimony of Place, *First Report from Select Committee on Artisans and Machinery. British Sessional Papers, House of Commons*, Vol. V (Feb. 23, 1824), pp. 44, 45.

9. M'Culloch, *Edinburgh Review*, pp. 330–32.

the outsider seems to have supplied him with it. If we learned that Ricardo proposed a change in the Corn laws only after an outsider had suggested it to him and provided him with the idea of diminishing returns, we would attribute less influence to him in the ensuing debate.

M'Culloch did not rely entirely on Place. He used another and more substantial argument. It was that competition usually makes peaceable combinations ineffective. (He strongly opposed those that were violent and urged strong penalties against them.) If wages are below equilibrium, a union can raise them, thus doing what ought to be done and in time would be done by the market itself. A union, then, can do no harm and may do some good.[10]

What he said gratified the unions of the day (though ours would find it poor stuff). Two of them cited his opinion in their bylaws and used it to advance their cause. There was no other economist of the time whose authority they could invoke. M'Culloch was looked upon as their "champion" and "ardent defender." So Patrick O'Brien states in his valuable book on M'Culloch.[11] The statement does M'Culloch too much honor. He appears to have done so much for the unions because the other economists did so little.

Ricardo

The idea that combinations are powerless in a competitive market was stated by Ricardo in a letter to M'Culloch in 1820.[12] Ricardo said he had not studied the Combination Laws closely. His impression was that they were unjust to labor and yet did not protect employers from intimidation by it. "The true remedy for combinations," he wrote, "is perfect liberty on both sides, and adequate protection against violence and outrage. Wages should be the result of a free compact...." He wished M'Culloch well in his efforts but said he did not himself expect much from Parliament until it was reformed. This could mean that he believed M'Culloch should have been working for Parliamentary reform (which, incidentally, M'Culloch did not favor nearly as much as Ricardo did) or could mean that Ricardo himself did not care to spend his time on repeal. One has the impression Ricardo did not think there was much in the issue. Later he may have come to think otherwise. Joseph Hume has been understood to say that Ricardo did believe repeal was important. But

---

10. *Ibid.*, p. 323.
11. O'Brien, *op. cit.*, pp. 370, 369.
12. Ricardo, *Works*, Vol. VIII, p. 316.

we shall do well not to rely much on what Hume said or seemed to say.[13]

Malthus

Malthus was the only other economist who, to my knowledge, expressed an opinion during the campaign. He favored repeal but was reserved. He appeared before the Select Committee of the Commons named to inquire into the laws and also into those that prohibited the emigration of skilled workers and the export of machinery. Hume was the chairman. M'Culloch had appeared a few days earlier. His manner was different from that of Malthus, just as his economics was. M'Culloch came through clearly, categorically, and no doubt at full volume in the Scots for which he was noted. He rang out his answers with, "To be sure"—"Certainly"—"Unquestionably"—"Precisely so."[14]

The witnesses were asked rhetorical questions. Place said he prepared them for Hume and coached the working class witnesses in how to answer them.[15] Occasionally a witness would be difficult. He would be brought into line by being asked if he did not believe men and masters should be at "perfect liberty" to make whatever wage bargains they pleased.

Then Malthus appeared.[16] The rhetorical questions came forth in due course. The desired answers did not. He replied, "Not particularly"—"On the whole, perhaps"—"I have not data."[17]

He was asked if he had paid any attention of the Combination Laws. "No particular attention; a general one of course." The questioner imprudently drove on:

Is it your decided opinion, that masters and men, upon all occasions, should be left to make what bargains they please?

The question did not intimidate Malthus. Infirm of speech he was but not of mind or character. He answered:

I think so; but it is very important that any sort of force used on the part of the men, to prevent others taking lower wages, should be punished severely, such as acts of intimidation either towards the masters or other men.[18]

---

13. See below, pp. 513–14, 520.
14. *First Report, etc.*, pp. 592–98.
15. Graham Wallas, *The Life of Francis Place*, 4th ed. (London: 1925), pp. 212–13.
16. *First Report, etc.*, pp. 600–01.
17. He was sometimes mistaken as when he said masters could combine "without being liable to punishment." They could not. *Ibid.*, p. 601.
18. *Ibid.*, p. 601.

Now Hume and Place had been at pains to assure everyone that violence would not increase if the laws were repealed, that violence indeed could be expected to diminish, and that in any event there were other laws to prevent it. The last thing either man wanted was a witness to warn against it, especially a witness who was supposed to be friendly. After putting another question or two, the Select Committee dismissed Malthus, and he was heard from no more.

Smith

Neither Malthus nor his contemporaries, not even M'Culloch, had an important influence. Many years earlier, when the Combination Law of 1799 was before the Commons, the authority of Adam Smith was invoked. The ideas attributed to him appeared again in the hearings of Hume's committee. Smith had been dead thirty-four years. Even more curious is the fact that he really had not written anything about whether or not the laws should be repealed. One may infer he believed they should be. He was opposed in principle to interference by the government (though not always in practice) and he was sympathetic to labor and the common people. Yet these ideas were not used by the opponents of the laws, in 1799 or 1824, except possibly by Burdett. Three other ideas of Smith were used. One was that the property each man has in his own labor is the foundation of all property. Another was that workers have less bargaining power than masters. The third was that masters always are in a tacit combination not to raise wages.

Smith actually did say these things.[19] But none has much to do with the Combination Laws. The first was a reason he gave for opposing the law that regulated apprenticeship. The second and third he stated in the course of explaining that in the short run wages are determined by bargaining. He was represented, by those who cited him, as saying that masters always combine to lower wages. He did not really. What he did say was that they tacitly combine in order not to raise wages above their "actual rate"; that they sometimes combine to reduce wages "even below this rate"; but that they cannot do so "for any considerable time." What he meant, I suggest, is that employers keep an eye on each other so that none need pay more than the competitive or "actual" wage (an interpretation with which W. H. Hutt concurs[20]); that they sometimes combine to pay even less; but that

19. Smith, *op. cit.*, pp. 122, 66, 67.
20. W. H. Hutt, *The Theory of Collective Bargaining* (London: 1930), pp. 32–33.

they succeed only in the short run—this last, an idea that the advocates of repeal of course did not utilize.

The labor historian Aspinall was so impressed by what they did use that he reported Smith advocated the repeal of the Combination Laws.[21] Smith did not. The mistake of thinking he did may have come from the report of a speech Francis Burdett made in the Commons on the law of 1799. He is reported in Woodfall's *Debates* as saying he objected to the bill because he was in favor of "having all things of this kind, as well as articles of any marketable nature, to find their own level" and also because combinations of masters, being more numerous and dangerous than those of workers, ought to be the concern of Parliament. Woodfall adds, "For the support of this reasoning he quoted the authority of Dr. Adam Smith on the Wealth of Nations."[22] The report does not make clear how much of this was attributed to Smith by Burdett. He could not have correctly attributed all of it. While Smith did say combinations of employers were more effective than those of workers, he did not say that Parliament should be concerned only with the former. Or did he say it should ignore the latter?

Of course, he was inclined to "having all things of . . . any marketable nature, to find their own level." However, he also was inclined to make exceptions to the principle, which if it is to be used as a summary statement of his economic policy, must be used with care. Even more care is needed if it is to be taken as evidence that Smith influenced a particular person or policy. Pitt invoked the principle in 1796 when he opposed a bill to fix the wages of farm workers. The unwary will suppose he also must have opposed the Combination Law of 1799 and to have stood by the side of Burdett. Actually, Pitt supported it.

The Political Economy Club

So much use, and misuse, was made of the principle and of other ideas of Smith because (I suggest) there was so little else to use. The repeal of the Combination Laws simply did not interest most of the economists. Why it did not is puzzling. Certainly it was important in a practical sense, and it could have directed the economists to a valuable inquiry about the effect of organizations of workers and employers on the market for labor. This did not occur. The economists

---

21. Aspinall, *op. cit.*, p. ix.
22. William Woodfall *et al., Debates . . . in the Two Houses of Parliament, etc.* (London: 1799), Vol. III (June 10, 1799), p. 235.

had their minds on other things. What these other things were is suggested by the agenda of the Political Economy Club.[23] Nine years after the laws were repealed, combinations themselves were a topic, but not the laws affecting them, and it was put in an interesting form: "Have combinations which keep up the rate of Wages of Workmen the effect of distributing among the working classes a greater aggregate amount than if the competition were perfectly free?" The record does not say who proposed the topic but does say Malthus and M'Culloch were present when it was discussed.[24]

Torrens and Senior

After the laws were repealed, there were a few pamphlets and periodical articles about them. A writer in *Blackwoods* in 1825 said repeal had been a mistake and was responsible for the strikes and disorders that followed it. He singled out "the Political Economists" for particular blame. They had led Parliament astray.

There actually was considerable labor trouble, and it probably was greater than it would have been if the laws had not been repealed. But a part of it had a quite different cause: The cyclical increase in the demand for labor that occurred at the time of repeal and brought with it the familiar increase in labor militancy. The article is rich in invective, is not particularly informative, and is poor beside the writing of the thirties on the issue. There is no mention of M'Culloch by name, which is surprising because *Blackwoods* was then given to abusing him.[25]

A much better statement is in *The Law Magazine* of 1834. It is informative and judicious. It also is critical of the economists who, the writer said, had assured the public that once the laws were repealed, combinations would cease to be a problem. "On this subject the unanimity of the wise and liberal, such as Mr. Francis Place and others, was as wonderful, as it has since proved erroneous."[26] In the same year a pamphlet by E. E. Tunfell, *Character, Object, and Effects of Trades' Unions,* states the case against labor combinations in a

---

23. *The Political Economy Club, Minutes of Proceedings, 1821–1882, Rolls of Members, and Questions Discussed,* Vol. IV (London: 1882), pp. 41–70.

24. *Ibid.,* p. 114.

25. "The Combinations," *Blackwoods,* XVIII (Oct. 1825), 463–72. The magazine was the voice of the Edinburgh Tories, and they could not be expected to be as gentle with the editor of the Whig *Scotsman* as M'Culloch had been. He complained in 1821 of the "blackguard" behavior of Lockhart, the editor of *Blackwoods* and son-in-law of one of its new owners, Sir Walter Scott. "So," M'Culloch observed, "the libels of the son-in-law will be printed by the father-in-law." (A letter to John Scott in the Scottish National Library, MS 1706, f. 75.)

26. "Art. VII, Combinations and Combination Laws," *The Law Magazine,* XI (Feb. 1834), 155.

clear, cogent way. Three years earlier there had been another pamphlet, and it had made the same case. It was the anonymous *On Combinations of Trades*.

Neither is the work of an economist. *On Wages and Combinations* [1834] by Robert Torrens is. It is skillful but rather too intricate and is meant to show that only in special circumstances can unions raise wages permanently (if they can limit the supply of labor or if productivity increases). Usually they are powerless in the long run, Torrens wrote. The pamphlet is addressed to the electors of Bolton whom Torrens represented in the House. If they understood it, they were exceptional citizens. Torrens' conclusion was similar to that of Ricardo and M'Culloch. He reached it by a route different from that taken by M'Culloch. How Ricardo reached the same conclusion we do not know, since he did not explain himself.

The interest of Senior was engaged in 1830. Melbourne, then Home Secretary, asked him and a legal expert to report on union activity, which was considerable and militant. Senior and his colleague reported that if it was not stopped, Britain would lose its industrial superiority. They recommended legislation that would have drastically restricted the activities of unions and of employers, not as much as the Combination Laws had done but far more than the Whig Government cared to do. It was of the opinion (according to the Webbs) that what was recommended was a "serious infringement upon the constitutional liberties of the country."[27] The report was never published, which may be just as well for the memory of Senior, who has enough odium attached to his name for his part in the Poor law of 1834, his letters on the Factory Act of 1837, and his Report on the Handloom Weavers of 1839. Had his policy for unions been put into effect, they truly would have needed a champion and one stronger than M'Culloch.

Misreading the Evidence

The foregoing is meant to show that there is no evidence the economists had an important part in repeal or had any significant effect on the issue for the next decade. The belief they did have an important part is a mistake that comes, I believe, from a misunderstanding of our information about the period.

Francis Place managed the campaign for repeal. He is known to have been friendly with the Ricardians, to have professed their doc-

---

27. Sidney and Beatrice Webb, *The History of Trade Unionism* (New York: 1894), pp. 126–27.

trine, and to have been a familiar of James Mill and Bentham. How natural it is then to conclude that he was putting the doctrine into practice. The truth is nearer to the opposite, which is that an economist proposed to put an idea of Place into practice: the idea M'Culloch got from Place. Whether Place discussed the laws with any of the other economists, I do not know. I have found no evidence that he did but have found evidence of his having discussed other issues with them, such as a discussion with Ricardo about the repayment of the national debt.[28]

Place himself left behind misleading information. In 1826 in a labor newspaper, he wrote in praise of political economists, saying, "To them we owe the repeal of the manifold laws which constituted the obnoxious laws known by the name of the Combination Laws."[29] Now this statement is not borne out by the account Place wrote of the repeal campaign and which is given at length in the biography of him by Wallas.[30] Either the account is to be rejected, or the statement in the labor paper is to be rejected. There is nothing to corroborate the latter, and there is much to refute it. The issue is complicated slightly (but no more) by a statement in the account concerning the *Edinburgh Review* article of M'Culloch. Place said that several members of the House told him the article had persuaded them to support repeal and that one said he was going to make it the substance of a speech.[31] Hansard does not report such a speech, but this is not proof it was never made. Yet if it were, it would not be evidence of the economists' having had an important effect on the issue. Why Place should have given the economists more than their due is an interesting question. The answer is probably in the nature of the man. He had a high opinion of himself, but not being inclined to strut or swagger, he kept it to himself, one of the few opinions that he did. What he said of the economists was, as noted above, also said in *Blackwoods* and *The Law Magazine*. The writers of those articles may have gotten the idea from the speeches of Joseph Hume.

Those speeches are the most misleading of all of the information from the period. Hume addressed the House early in 1824 and moved the appointment of a Select Committee on the laws affecting combinations, the export of machinery, and the emigration of skilled

---

28. The letters that passed between Place and Ricardo on this issue in November, 1819, are in Ricardo's *Works*, Vol. VIII, pp. 118–25.
29. *Trades Newspaper and Mechanics Weekly Journal*, no. 52, June 18, 1826, quoted in Wallas, *op. cit.*, p. 161.
30. Wallas, *op. cit.*, Ch. viii.
31. *Ibid.*, p. 208.

workers. He opened by saying the House had suffered a great loss when his friend, Ricardo, had died five months before. ("Hear, hear," Hansard records.) He said Ricardo had advised him to propose an inquiry and he, Hume, had hoped Ricardo would assist him with it. He reminded the House that Ricardo had spoken against the Spitalfields Acts, and they were among the laws Hume now proposed to investigate and to repeal.[32]

When he finished speaking, William Huskisson rose.[33] He too paid his respects to Ricardo and referred to him as a friend. Huskisson declared himself in favor of repealing the laws concerning machinery and artisans. He was guarded about the Combination Laws. He said that when he had more information he might favor their repeal also. His declaration, although it was qualified, was important. As President of the Board of Trade, he spoke for the Tory Government. Later he did support the repeal of the Combination Laws.

What was said in the House that day seems to justify the conclusion that Ricardo had a particular interest in the Combination Laws and that his ideas and authority were a major reason why later they were repealed. Just such a conclusion has been drawn, but I have found no evidence to support it.

Hume began his speech by saying he was going to fulfill an "undertaking" of which he had given notice in the last session and that he was doing so "by the advice, and in the hopes of the assistance, of a distinguished individual, whose recent loss the kingdom had to deplore." Just what the undertaking was is not explicitly stated in the accounts of the speech in Hansard and the *Morning Chronicle* but is inferred to be the repeal of the laws against exporting machinery and the emigration of artisans. This is explicitly stated in the account in the *Times*.[34] What this suggests is that Ricardo had advised Hume to put before Parliament only the issues of machinery and artisans. Hume had been understood to say that Ricardo advised him to put before it the issue of combinations also. So we read in *The Law Magazine*.[35] So even do we read in Sraffa who in this instance does not follow his usual practice of giving us a telling citation.[36]

Early in 1824 Place wrote to Hume, "It was generally understood

32. Hansard, Vol. X (February 12, 1824), p. 141.
33. *Ibid.*, Vol. X, p. 150. *The Morning Chronicle* (February 13, 1824) reported that Huskisson also invoked the name of Smith and in doing so elicited cries of "hear, hear."
34. *The Morning Chronicle*, February 13, 1824; *The Times*, February 13, 1824.
35. "Art. VII, etc.," Vol. XI, p. 155.
36. Piero Sraffa, "Introduction to the Speeches in Parliament," *Works*, Vol. V, p. xx.

that you would move for a repeal of the Combination Laws in this session. . . . You and I had a similar understanding, and I acted upon it very extensively."[37] Was the understanding the same as the understanding to which Hume referred in his speech to Parliament? Probably not. Later in that speech Hume said he wished to add another issue to the undertaking he had pledged, and the additional issue was the repeal of the Combination Laws.

Of course, Ricardo conceivably could have advised Hume to seek the repeal of the Combination Laws, but that he may have done so is not proof that he did. Yet if he did not, the fact does not mean he was opposed to repeal. Quite the contrary. We know he had a good word for M'Culloch's efforts. He very likely would have had another for Hume's. The question is whether he believed the issue was important and whether he had any influence on the outcome. The answer, in my opinion, is no.

Yet what shall we make of Hume's connecting Ricardo with the Spitalfields Acts? They did, *inter alia,* prohibit combinations. Ricardo did speak against the acts and said they should have been repealed long ago.[38] However, what he objected to was their fixing of wages, and that was their more important provision. Some in the House agreed with Ricardo, but they did not want to repeal the laws until action first had been taken on the emigration of artisans. Such action was a part of what Hume now proposed. He then could say quite properly that by allowing emigration the House would prepare the way for doing what Ricardo had wanted done. The House indeed did repeal the laws against emigration. The decision, along with the repeal of the Combination Laws, suggests that Hume had two-thirds of a triumph (the other third being Parliament's declining to repeal the laws against the export of machinery). But in fact the decision was something less and was a rejection of a measure Ricardo had proposed. He had on occasion spoken against the truck system (the payment of wages in goods instead of in money). He believed (as Smith did not) that wages should be paid in whatever form the workers and employers agreed upon. Many of the Combination Laws prohibited the truck system because it was believed to provoke the workers into combining. When the laws were repealed, those prohibitions were in most instances allowed to remain.

The speech of Huskisson is not evidence that the economists were influential on this occasion. Although he held many of Ricardo's ideas

---

37. Letter of February 7, 1824, Wallas, *op. cit.*, pp. 210–11.
38. Ricardo spoke against the Spitalfields Acts on four occasions. *Works*, Vol. V, pp. 292, 295–97, 306–09.

of economic policy, they differed over when the ideas could be put into effect. Ricardo always believed more changes could be made than Huskisson and other political leaders were ready to propose. That Huskisson supported the repeal of the Combination Laws means only that he believed the time for it had come. Harriet Martineau said he "opened his hand one finger at a time, because the people or their rulers could not receive a whole handful of truth."[39] His support of repeal does not mean he did what Ricardo urged him to do even if we suppose (what is improbable) that Ricardo had urged him. In the last years of his life, Ricardo believed that his influence had declined, and there is reason to believe that he was right.[40]

Why the Laws Were Repealed

The Leadership of the Parties

An important reason why the laws were repealed is that the Tory Government, with the concurrence of the Whig leaders, wanted them to be. Some accounts suggest that the political leaders simply had no objection to repeal. That implies that they were indifferent or inactive. They were neither. While they did not initiate the proposal and did not take a large part in the debate or the hearings, they nevertheless approved of repeal. If they had not, it never would have carried.

In formulating economic policy, the parties were influenced by what was workable and what was fair. On neither point could the Combination Laws be defended. They had not prevented combinations from being formed, and after 1800 when the most comprehensive of all prohibitions was enacted, the combinations became more numerous than ever. Ricardo observed that the laws protected neither employers from being bullied by workers nor workers from being bullied by employers. By the standard of fairness the laws were objectionable because while they fell on employers, they fell more heavily on workers. Such, at any rate, was the leading opinion of the time.

In reaching their decision, the political leaders did not ignore economic doctrine but in this instance acted independently of it. They would be called "pragmatists" if that were not a word that too often is used when we fail to discover the principles on which men act. Here

---

39. Quoted by William Smart, *Economic Annals of the Nineteenth Century*, Vol. II (London: 1917), p. 290.
This is not, however, the view everyone has had of Huskisson. Some have made him out to be an opponent of classical economics, unconvincingly, in my opinion, but in a way that must be noticed. See William Atkinson, *Mr. Huskisson, Free Trade, and the Corn Laws; etc.* (London: 1840).
40. Ricardo, *Works*, Vol. VIII, p. 190.

they were influenced by the principles of workability and fairness more than by classical policy. They sometimes followed that policy and sometimes did not. Examples of the former are the following: the proposal of the Woollen Committee of 1806 to allow each weaver to use as many looms as he wished; the proposal of Viscount Sidmouth in 1813 to repeal the wage-fixing provisions of the Statute of Artificers; the repeal in 1813 of the apprenticeship provisions of that statute; the tireless efforts of Serjeant Onslow to get the usury laws repealed; the declaration of 1820 that commercial policy in the future should move toward free trade; the tariff reductions made by Huskisson in the following decade; and so on to the repeal of the Corn and Navigation Laws in 1846 and 1849.

On the other side, one can cite the recommendation of the same Woollen Committee to restrict the export of machinery and emigration of skilled workers; the Factory Acts, the first of which was an amendment to the Statute of Apprentices; the laws that regulated banking and currency, the safety of ships, the construction and operation of railroads, and the flotation of securities. Shall we add the laws that abolished the slave trade and then slavery? Desirable laws, surely, but they were just as surely restrictions on the market.

At times, the parties acted independently of classical policy. The repeal of the Combination Laws is an example. Some of the laws (as stated above) prohibited combinations in order to strengthen the wage fixing by the government. Some prohibited them in order to strengthen competition, that is, to strengthen wage fixing by the market. If Huskisson and his allies had acted on the principle of freedom of exchange, they would have repealed only the former. If they had acted to oppose that principle, they would have repealed only the latter. They repealed both, acting, as they did, on another principle, which was to do what was practical and what was fair. That they wanted to be practical, I may call on Jevons for support. Of all that was later written about repeal and the economists, his brief statement comes nearest the mark. Writing in 1882 about the state in relation to labor, he said he did not favor laws prohibiting unions because such laws do not work. "It was upon such grounds of distinct experience, rather than upon any theory of freedom of trade, that Parliament in 1824 . . . swept those mistaken laws away," he said.[41]

The party leadership did not always initiate a change in policy. At times, it responded to what others proposed or to necessity. It listened to those who believed their income would be affected by a

---

41. W. Stanley Jevons, *The State in Relation to Labour*, 4th ed. (London: 1910), p. 115.

change. It also listened to those who, acting not out of self-interest but in the public good as they saw it, marshalled the forces of opinion. They usually were the reformers.

The Labor Movement

Of those who believed their income would be affected by repeal, the most forthright were the workers. They, or those who spoke for them, believed that the laws held down wages and repeal would raise them. The employers might have believed just the opposite, and they too could have supported repeal out of self-interest. But they did not have a noticeable part in the campaign. Of some 150 petitions that were submitted to the Commons in 1824, almost all were from the working class and most claimed the laws held down wages. Only two were in favor of retaining the laws, and they came from employer groups.[42]

The ways in which labor saw its interest affected by repeal were not always what one would suppose. Labor did, as stated above, claim that the laws reduced its income. Also, there were groups in the working class that wanted the right to organize because the right was important in itself. But there were other groups that looked upon the right as a means to an end. That is, they believed that the workers by combining could do for themselves what the state was supposed to do for them but had not. That was to take the determination of wages away from the market.

The state had long tried to regulate the wages in particular employments. The laws by which this was done often (as stated above) prohibited combinations.[43] As late as 1823, the silk weavers petitioned

---

42. *Journals of the House of Commons* (London: n. d.), Vol. LXXIX, p. 19 *et passim*. The two petitions that favored retaining the Combination Laws also favored retaining the laws prohibiting the export of machinery and the emigration of artisans. A third petition favored retaining the law against exporting machinery.

The petitioning of Parliament in this way began in 1779 when groups assembled in different parts of the country and prepared a statement of the reforms they wanted made. In the nineteenth century large numbers of petitions were submitted to both Houses. (See M. F. Bond, *A Guide to House of Lords Papers and Petitions*, Record Office Memorandum No. 20, 1959.) The practice diminished late in the century, as the franchise was extended and possibly for that reason, and has been used very little in this century.

43. 1424, 3 Henry VI, cap. 1; 1542, 33 Henry VIII, cap. 9 (I); 1720, 7 Geo. I, cap. 13; 1756, 29 Geo. II, cap. 33; 1767, 8 Geo. III, cap. 17; 1771–72, 11 and 12 Geo. III, cap. 18 (I); 1771–72, 11 and 12 Geo. III, cap. 33 (I); 1773, 13 Geo. III, cap. 68; 1779–80, 19 and 20 Geo. III, cap. 24 (I); 1779–80, 19 and 20 Geo. III, cap. 36 (I); 1785, 25 Geo. III, cap. 48 (I); 1792, 32 Geo. III, cap. 44; 1807, 47 Geo. III, cap. 43.

The full text of the laws cited is in one of the following:

The Statutes of the United Kingdom of Great Britain and Ireland ["Statutes at Large"] (London: v. d.). The laws that applied only in Ireland are designated (I) and only in Scotland (S).

The Statutes at Large, Passed in the Parliaments Held in Ireland (Dublin: v. d.).

The Acts of the Parliaments of Scotland (London: v. d.).

Parliament to retain the laws by which their wages were fixed and also by which they were prohibited from combining. The petitions indicated that the workers were willing to forgo the right to organize in return for the government's fixing wages for them. The first of such petitions came from the weavers of Sudbury who were not actually covered by the law. It covered the Spitalfields workers, but they had not submitted a petition. Ricardo hinted that the workers of Sudbury were asking that wages be kept high in Spitalfields in order that employment would be maintained in Sudbury. However, a few days later a petition came from Middlesex where the law did apply.

There is additional evidence that workers wanted the state to intervene in the labor market. They themselves put forward a bill to repeal the Combination Laws. They did so before Hume took up the question, and their bill was much different from his. Theirs was drafted by a labor activist, Gravener Hensen, and was placed before Parliament in 1823 by Peter Moore, the Radical member for Coventry. The bill went far beyond repeal of the Combination Laws and specified in great detail the conditions of work and their enforcement. That was much too far for the Government but did convince it that the time had come to do something about the Combination Laws. Place believed the workers could be persuaded to support Hume's bill instead of Moore's. He also believed Moore would be no problem if Hume put him on the Select Committee where he would be outnumbered. Place was right on both points. The workers supported Hume, and Moore never attended the meetings of the committee.[44]

However, Place was wrong about something that was more important. He had told Hume, M'Culloch, and others that repeal would cause combinations to decline and in time to disappear. He had not said this to labor groups whose support he enlisted. He allowed them to believe that repeal would strengthen their organizations and on occasion encouraged the belief. He did not try to disabuse them of the belief that the Combination laws held wages down. One sees the belief expressed in many of the petitions he persuaded them to put before the House. But to the Select Committee, he said the idea was "absurd." Reformer that he was, he knew his cause was pure, and he was not fussy about his means. He also had the reformer's habit of thinking he was awfully clever with people. He sometimes was. But in the repeal

---

44. On Place see Wallas, *op. cit.*, pp. 209, 213.
Moore's bill was entitled "A Bill for Repealing Several Acts relating to Combinations of Workmen, and for more effectually protecting Trade and for settling Disputes between Masters and their Workpeople." It was ordered printed and appears in *Bills, Public: In Three Volumes: Volume the Second. Ireland continued, etc. Session 4 February-to-19 July 1823* (London: 1823), no continuous pagination.

campaign he did not use the labor movement as much as it used him. Once the laws were abolished, its power increased, and its activities multiplied. The act of repeal was a milestone in the development of modern trade unionism.[45]

The Reformers

Place was prominent among the radical reformers, and they took up the issue of the Combination Laws. The radicals did not constitute the entire reform movement, and not every part of it shared their views. It was an extensive and intricate collection of groups and people who meant to do good. One cannot help but respect them for their intentions and one also cannot help but notice that at times they were ridiculous. One thing about them is certain. They were influential. One part or another of the reform movement is associated with just about every important change made in the nineteenth century including every major change in economic policy and many minor changes.

In the repeal of the Combination Laws, the radicals could not have succeeded without the concurrence of the party leaders and the support of the working class. But the radicals were the first to act. They had made the Combination Laws an issue in 1799 when Burdett was their leader and spoke against the law of that year in the House. He was supported by another radical worthy, John Cam Hobhouse (later Lord Broughton).[46] The two were still in the House in 1824 and 1825. But the leadership of the group had passed to Hume. He, in turn, was prompted to act by Place, himself one of the principals of the movement. Place began to prepare the case for repeal in 1814. He persuaded M'Culloch to write against the laws, which M'Culloch did, beginning in 1818. Place prevailed on Hume to put the issue before the House in 1824 and kept Hume solidly for repeal when Place suspected the Tories of throwing sand in Hume's eyes. The two of them staged the hearings of the Select Committee, which went as planned except for the fiasco of Malthus' testimony. Place then advised Hume not to prepare a report, which was the customary thing to do, and instead to submit a set of resolutions, each of which was to contain a statement of fact so it could not easily be disputed. (Some of the "facts" had an opinion enclosed within them.) The act of repeal was written by a legislative expert, but Place managed to rewrite it. It went through the Commons without a vote, without any debate, and with

---

45. See the Webbs, *op. cit.*, p. 97; Thompson, *op. cit.*, p. 520; Aspinall, *op. cit.*, p. xxxi; Allen Hutt, *British Trade Unionism* (New York: 1953), p. 11.
46. Woodfall, *op. cit.*, Vol. III (June 10, 1799), p. 235.

remarkable speed. It was sent to the Lords where one of the members was Lauderdale, the economist. He favored repeal but believed it should be enacted properly. He believed the Lords should see the minutes of evidence collected by Hume's committee. If his request had been granted, the bill would have been opened to scrutiny and debate. Place feared that "sinister influences" might then prevail. He was furious with "the half-crazy Lauderdale," as he called him, and said later, "with almost incredible pains taken, Lauderdale was induced to hold his tongue. . . ." So it was that Place, after prevailing on one economist, M'Culloch, to speak out, prevailed on another to be quiet, about a law for which the economists are said to be responsible![47]

If Place was not overly scrupulous, neither was Hume. He led the House to believe that Ricardo when speaking against the Spitalfields Acts had expressly objected to the provisions that prohibited combinations when in fact Ricardo had not. He conceivably could have told Hume privately that he objected to those provisions. But that is not what Hume implied. It was that Ricardo had told the House that the prohibiting of combinations was wrong.[48] Hume also made questionable use of the testimony of the workers. When it supported repeal, he accepted it as a sincere statement of belief, as he did that of Richard Taylor before the Select Committee. When the testimony was unfavorable, he impugned it as he did the petition of the silk weavers for the retention of the Spitalfields Laws, which, the petition claimed, protected their wages. Hume insinuated that the weavers wanted the laws retained because the laws, while formally prohibiting combinations, actually promoted them.[49] To other workers, however, he represented himself as a defender of their right to combine. To employers, he was bullying if they opposed him, as he was to Thomas Osler of the Birmingham Chamber of Commerce who testified in favor of retaining the laws.[50] This occurred on March 26 (1824). On April 14 Lord Stanley put before the House a petition from Bolton in support of them. Hume rose to say that his committee had "received no evidence whatever. . . in favor of those laws."[51]

However Hume and Place may be judged, they cannot be said to have unduly protracted the proceedings in the House or to have burdened it with testimony against repeal. Liverpool and Eldon, the Tory Lords, said later they had not fully understood the law and would

47. Wallas, *op. cit.*, p. 216.
48. See above, p. 514.
49. *First Report, etc.*, p. 54; Hansard, Vol. X, p. 147.
50. *First Report, etc.*, pp. 324–25.
51. Hansard, Vol. XI, p. 409.

have voted against it if they had.⁵² Huskisson said that the Commons had not understood the bill as well as it might, that the bill had gone through in a questionable way, and he took some of the responsibility on himself.⁵³ Another contemporary comment was that the law was "hurried through with a rapidity almost suspicious."⁵⁴ It may in fact have set a speed record. It went through three readings in the Commons in one week and received the royal assent ten days later.

An examination shows it was not the product of a Parliament at its best.⁵⁵ Of the laws repealed entirely or in part, one was the Spitalfields Law of 1773⁵⁶—one to which Ricardo had objected. The provisions that fixed wages and prohibited combinations were repealed. This seems perfectly reasonable until one notices the act in its entirety had been repealed by the House four days earlier.⁵⁷ The law of 1799⁵⁸ was repealed in part but the clause that prohibited combinations among colliers in Scotland was retained. Actually, there was no need to repeal any of it because the entire act had been repealed in 1800 and was replaced by a general law against combinations.⁵⁹ It was repealed in 1824 (except for the arbitration provisions, which the 1824 act continued).

All in all, the law of 1824 was a muddle and had to be done over the next year. By then there was some opinion in favor of a return to prohibiting combinations, and a deputation of ship-builders worked hard to this end. The reformers no longer held the leading strings. Huskisson managed the bill in the Commons and now acted for the Government. Hume was on the new Select Committee but only as a member. Place was furious, again saw sinister influences at work, and predicted they would do their worst.⁶⁰ He was mistaken. The new bill, through the work of the Government, was much like that of 1824 but tidier. Its similarity to the earlier bill did not signify that the Government had succumbed to the reformers. The explanation is simply that the Government, and the Opposition, for some time had wanted the repeal of the laws and had allowed the reformers to make the case for it. Each side would have been amused if it had known that in the future repeal would be attributed to the classical economists, only one

---

52. S. Maccoby, *English Radicalism* (London: 1955), p. 525, n. 2.
53. Hansard, Vol. XII (March 29, 1825), pp. 1288–1301.
54. "Art. VII, etc.," *The Law Magazine*, XI, p. 160.
55. The formal designation of the act of repeal is 1824, 5 Geo. IV, cap. 95. See "Statutes at Large," Vol. LXIV, pp. 508–19.
56. 1773, 13 Geo. III, cap. 68.
57. 1824, 5 Geo. IV, cap. 66.
58. 1799, 39 Geo. III, cap. 56.
59. 1800, 39 and 40 Geo. III, cap. 106.
60. Wallas, *op. cit.*, p. 222.

of whom in fact had anything of consequence to say about it, and he was by no means the leading figure among them.

The law of 1825[61] contained all of the provisions of that of 1824, enlarged two of them, and added three others. In addition to prohibiting the use of coercion to influence wages, strikes, and other matters (as the 1824 act did), the later act also prohibited its being used in organizing combinations. The later act stated an action had to be brought within six months of an offense being committed and stated no Justice of the Peace could hear an action if he was a member of the trade where it originated. Neither limitation was in the act of 1824. The later act contained provisions (which the earlier act did not) that expressly stated it "shall not extend" to meetings of workmen or masters who assemble to consult and agree about wages and other conditions of work.

The act of 1825 in no sense withdrew the privileges that the act of 1824 had granted to combinations. On the contrary. The act of 1825 was, in the words of an observer of strong labor sympathies, "the starting point of a great new development in the history of English trade-unionism."[62] To one with sympathy for the grand principle of the market, the law was a great new development away from "having all things of ... any marketable nature to find their own level." That the classical economists should be made responsible for the development surely is a mistake and is unjust to them.

UNIVERSITY OF ILLINOIS AT CHICAGO CIRCLE

---

61. 6 Geo. IV, cap. 129. "Statutes at Large," Vol. LXV, pp. 1066–78.
62. Aspinall, *op. cit.*, p. xxxi.

The Falling-Rate-of-Profit Theory of Crisis: A Rational Reconstruction by Way of Obituary

Philippe Van Parijs

ABSTRACT: This paper traces the development of the falling-rate-of-profit theory of crisis from its original and traditional version to its modern variant and finally to A. Shaikh's recent defense based on the distinction between circulating and fixed capital. At each stage the major arguments in favor of and against the falling-rate-of-profit thesis are reviewed and criticized. On balance, the conclusions are almost universally negative: It cannot be shown in general that a rise in the organic composition of capital leads to a fall in the rate of profit; neither can it be shown that a fall in the general rate of profit necessarily induces a crisis of overproduction. Finally, Okishio's theorem is employed to show that profit-maximizing capitalists, under competitive conditions, would never adopt a technique which would lower the general rate of profit at a given level of wages. Thus, a falling-rate-of-profit crisis is not a theoretical *necessity*; indeed, it is not even a *possibility* under conditions of competitive capitalism. Shaikh's thesis is then discussed and it is seen that a falling rate of profit is a possibility when the assumptions of perfect competition are relaxed. The paper is concluded with a comment regarding the conflict between "scientific" and "extrascientific" considerations in the course of the discussions of the falling rate of profit.

* * * * *

For the purposes of this article[1], the *falling-rate-of-profit theory of crises* (theory) is defined as the theory which attempts to predict and explain the occurrence of economic crises under capitalism with the help of the following three propositions:

(i) The capitalist mode of production is such that the organic composition of capital (OCK) necessarily rises.
(ii) A rise in the OCK necessarily leads to a fall in the (general) rate of profit.
(iii) A fall in the (general) rate of profit necessarily leads to crises.

From the conjunction of these three propositions it obviously follows that

(iv) The capitalist mode of production is such that crises necessarily occur.

However familiar such a theory may now sound to radical economists and however uncontroversial its presence in Marx's writings from the *Grundrisse* to Volume III of *Capital*, it is not until the 1930s that it came to constitute the core of the Marxist interpretation of crises. Earlier Marxist approaches rather tended to locate the origin of crises either in disproportionality or in underconsumption. And it is only with Grossmann's [1929: ch. 2] and Dobb's [1937: ch. 4] influential presentations, that a prominent place was given, in the explanation of crises, to the theory of the falling rate of profit. At about the same time, however, severely critical treatments of the theory by Moszkowska [1935: ch. 4], Sweezy [1942: ch. 6] and Robinson [1942: ch. 5] opened the modern debate, which, as a result of a general revival of interest in Marxist economics, has attracted many contributions and aroused much passion throughout the 1970s.

The most recent discussion, especially the one arising from Shaikh's [1978b] cunning vindication of the theory, suggests that the time has now come to look back on the whole debate and write the theory's obituary. In this article, I shall try to do so by providing a *rational reconstruction* of the debate, i.e. by reconstructing it in such a way that unnecessary assumptions, irrelevant remarks, terminological inconsistencies, confusions and misunderstandings are, as far as possible, removed from the arguments actually put forward.

The justification for reconstructing the debate, rather than subjecting the issues it deals with to a straightforward discussion, is threefold. First of all, a rational reconstruction is likely to be more effective in convincing those who object to the conclusion to which it leads, that their arguments have been taken fully into account and that, nevertheless, the conclusion is what it is. Secondly, it may give some hints as to the way in which "bad news" (for example, the implications of Okishio's theorem) progressively spreads and is resisted in a scientific community which is more exposed than many others to the pressure of "extra-scientific" considerations. Thirdly and perhaps most importantly, by providing a systematic survey of the literature, it may help some students (and teachers) to find their way in this frequently confusing area of Marxist theory.

In order to keep the discussion as clear as possible, we shall assume the simplest possible universe in which the fundamental issues raised by the theory can be addressed. We shall be considering a society in which there are two classes: the capitalists, who own the means of production, and the workers, who own their labor-power. While the workers consume their means of subsistence, the capitalists are assumed not to consume anything. There is only one kind of means of production (commodity I), one kind of means of subsistence (commodity II) and one kind of labor-power (commodity LP).[2] The economy, therefore, has only two industries, one with a daily production of Y_I units of commodity I and one with a daily production of λ_{II} units of commodity II. And it uses daily, for the sake of this production, k units of commodity I and NT units of labor-power (i.e. NT labor hours of average intensity), with N the number of workers and T the length of the working day. Commodity I is assumed to consist of fixed capital, which means that the rate of turnover of the means of production (t_c) is smaller than 1, or that the stock (K) of good I is larger than its daily flow:[*]

(A1) $K = k/t_c > k$.

Workers, on the other hand, are assumed to be paid at the beginning of each day, which can be taken to mean that the rate of turnover of labor-power (t_V) is 1, or that the stock (L) of labor-power is equal to its daily flow:

(A2) $L = NT/t_V = NT$.

Further, it would be very convenient if we were able to formulate the equilibrium (or general) rate of profit, with whose behavior the theory is concerned, in simple value terms. Therefore, we shall boldly assume that the *law of value* holds in its simplest form[3], i.e. that

(A3) p_I^*, p_{II}^* and w^* are proportional to λ_I, λ_{II} and λ_{LP},

where p_I^* and p_{II}^* are the competitive equilibrium unit prices of commodities I and II, where w^* is the competitive equilibrium hourly money wage, where λ_I and λ_{II} are the unit values of commodities I and II (i.e. the

[*]In order to facilitate further reference, crucial propositions will be isolated and numbered. The letter which precedes the number indicates whether the proposition is a definition (D), an assumption (A) or a theorem (T). No proofs will be given for the theorems, but only the numbers of the propositions from which they follow.

amount of labor time directly or indirectly required to produce one unit of each) and where λ_{LP} is the (hourly) value of labor-power, equal to the daily subsistence bundle (B) divided by the length of the working day:

(D4) $\lambda_{LP} = \lambda_{II} B/T$.

Now, the (daily) rate of profit can be defined as

(D5) π = (daily receipts-daily costs)/capital advanced.

If the law of value holds, the competitive equilibrium rate of profit is then given by the familiar expression:

(T6) $\pi^* = s/(C+V)$,   (From A3, D5)

where

(D7) $s = y - (c+v)$,

i.e. the daily flow of *surplus-value* is given by the value of the daily gross product $(y = \lambda_I Y_I + \lambda_{II} Y_{II})$ minus the value of the means of production and labor-power used up (c+v);

(D8) $c = \lambda_I k$,

i.e. the (daily) flow of *constant capital* is given by the value of the (daily) flow of means of production used up;

(D9) $C = \lambda_I K = c/t_c$,

i.e. the *stock* of constant capital is given by the value of the stock of means of production, itself equal to the corresponding flow divided by the rate of turnover t_c (see A1 above); and

(D10) $V = v = \lambda_{LP} NT$,

i.e. the (daily) flow or stock of *variable capital* is given by the value of the amount of labor-power used daily, itself equal to the amount of labor-power "in stock" (see A2 above).

Within the framework of this elementary capitalist economy, I shall now try to review, as briefly and systematically as possible, the major arguments in favor of and against the FRP theory as defined above. In the next three sections, I consider what I shall call the "traditional" arguments, in spite of the fact that they are still to be found in the most recent literature. They basically concern the question of whether the tendencies asserted by the theory in its first two propositions are really *necessary* or just *contingent*. In the last two sections, I turn to the "fatal issues" which have recently gained prominence in the debate and which throw into irrelevance most of the traditional arguments. Roughly, these fatal issues are about the very *possibility* of technical change generating a fall in the rate of profit and of such a fall in the rate of profit (if it did occur) generating crises.

The Rise in the Organic Composition of Capital

Both proposition (i) and proposition (ii) of the theory make reference to the organic composition of capital. The OCK can be understood in at least two ways.[4] On the one hand, it can be understood as identical to the *value composition of capital* (VCK), defined as the ratio of the stock of constant capital to the stock of variable capital:

(D11)   VCK = C/V.

On the other hand, it can be understood as identical to the *ratio of dead to living labor* (RDL), defined as the ratio of the stock of constant capital to the flow (or stock) of labor-power:

(D12)   RDL = C/NT.

I shall call *textbook variant* of the FRP-theory the variant which adopts the first interpretation (OCK = VCK). And I shall call *modern variant* the one which adopts the second interpretation (OCK = RDL).[5]

Proposition (i) of the theory states that, under capitalism, the OCK necessarily rises. Whichever variant of the theory is adopted, it is crucial, in order to establish proposition (i), that one should be able to assert the necessity of a rise in the *technical composition of capital* (TCK), defined as the ratio of the stock of means of production to the flow (or stock) of labor-power:

(D13)   TCK = K/NT.

Now, *if* we can make it plausible that, under capitalism, technical progress necessarily tends to be *labor-saving*, i.e. that the mass of means of production necessarily grows faster (or falls less) than the amount of labor employed, or*

(A14) $\dot{K} > \dot{N} + \dot{T}$,

then it directly follows that, under capitalism, the TCK must rise.

(T15)   The TCK rises.   (From 13, 14)

However, why should individual profit-maximizing capitalists necessarily prefer to save labor rather than to save "capital"? The standard argument in support of this view is that, if the economy grows substantially faster than the potential labor force — a plausible assumption to make under capitalism — then labor-saving technology must be an intrinsic feature of the system (if it is to keep growing), whereas capital-saving technology is not.[6] However, it is a logical fallacy to infer from the fact that some feature x is necessary while another feature y is not, to the necessity of having more of x than of y. While there are good reasons why the capitalists should try to economize on labor, there are no good reasons (once K has ceased to be negligible) why they should economize on labor more than on (constant) capital. In the course of capitalist development, the balance of labor-saving and capital-saving innovations may be such that A14 holds and the TCK therefore rises. But this would be a contingent fact, not one stemming from the nature of the capitalist mode of production.[7]

Suppose, however, for the sake of the argument, that under capitalism the TCK necessarily rises. This still does not mean that the OCK must rise. For the *textbook variant*, which interprets OCK ≈ VCK, two additional steps are needed, as is indicated in the following relationship between the VCK and the TCK:

(T16)   VCK = (λ_I/λ_{II}) (T/B) TCK. (From 11,13,9,10,4)

The necessity of a rise in VCK could be safely inferred from the necessity of a rise in TCK[8] if one could assume that, necessarily,

(A17) λ_I/λ_{II} is constant or rises,

i.e. that productivity (as measured by $1/\lambda_I$ and $1/\lambda_{II}$) must increase at least as fast in industry II as in industry I, and also that, necessarily,

(A18)   B/T is constant or falls,

i.e. that the subsistence bundle per hour of labor does not increase, or, since under the law of value

(T19) $w^*/p_{II}^* = B/T$,   (From 2,4)

that the equilibrium real wage (w^*/p_{II}^*) does not rise. If these two assumptions are warranted, it is easy to conclude

(T20)   The VCK rises.   (From 16, 17, 18).

But it seems exceedingly hard to find any compelling argument which would rule out as impossible, under capitalist conditions, the two kinds of development which such a reasoning needs to exclude: technical change which substantially reduces the value of the means of production compared to that of the means of subsistence[9], and "cultural" change which substantially increases the amount of means of subsistence deemed "necessary" for the performance of one day's work.[10] Neither A17 nor A18, therefore, are given the solid foundation they need, and T20 remains contingent even if the necessity of a rise in the TCK is taken for granted (T15).

The step which the *modern variant* must take (beyond T15) is very different. As it interprets the OCK as RDL, the relevant connection between OCK and TCK is now given by:

(T21)   RDL = λ_I TCK   (From 12,13,9)

---

*Dotted variables are here used to represent rates of growth (*not* derivatives): for example, $\dot{K}$ is short for (dK/dt)/K, not for dK/dt. Incidentally, the growth rate of a product is the sum of the growth rates of its factors: for example, $(\dot{NT}) = \dot{N} + \dot{T}$.

Whether or not a rising TCK implies a rising OCK now depends on the trend in the unit value of the means of production, i.e. on the productivity trend in industry I.[11] If we can suppose that the level of productivity in industry I (represented by $1/\lambda_I$) is an increasing function of the TCK, i.e. that:

(A22) $1/\lambda_I = f(TCK)$, with $df/dTCK > 0$,

and if we can further suppose that the impact of the TCK on productivity decreases as both increase, i.e. that:

(A23) $df/dTCK < f/TCK$,

then it is correct to infer that the development of productivity in industry I cannot offset the rise in TCK, i.e.

(T24) $(1/\lambda_I)\dot{} < T\dot{C}K$,   (From 22,23)

which is clearly equivalent to

(T25)   The RDL rises.[12]   (From 21, 24)

Here again, however, and even more than in the case of the rise in TCK, the problem is to show the (capitalist) necessity of the assumptions. No argument can make the postulated technological fact (that the "marginal productivity" of TCK-increasing technical progress tends to fall) more than a contingent fact of capitalism — if it is a fact at all.

For the sake of the argument, however, let us suppose that, in addition to the necessity of a rising TCK (T15), we can take for granted the necessity of equal productivity increases in both industries and of a constant hourly real wage (textbook variant), as well as the necessity of a falling "marginal productivity" of TCK-increasing technical progress (modern variant). Let us suppose, in other words, that proposition (i) is established under both interpretations, i.e. that the capitalist mode of production is such that both the VCK and the RDL necessarily rise. If this is so, and even in the absence of any other downward pressure, proposition (ii) then claims, the equilibrium rate of profit will fall.

The Fall in the Equilibrium Rate of Profit

In order to examine critically this second proposition, we must start by ruling out the possibility of alternative downward pressures. This requires our reformulating, beforehand, in a more explicit way, the value rate of profit (T6). Given that the value of the (daily) net product (value of the gross product minus constant capital used up) is equal to the number of man-hours per day, i.e.

(T26) $y - c = NT$,   (From the definition of value)

the (daily) flow of surplus-value can be reformulated as

(T27) $s = NT - N\lambda_{II} B$ (From 7,10,4)

and the equilibrium rate of profit, therefore, as:

(T28) $\pi^* = (T - \lambda_{II}B)/(\lambda_I K/N + \lambda_{II}B)$
(From 6,27,9,10)

In order to make the influence of the OCK (in its two interpretations) more explicit, this expression can in turn be transformed into

(T29) $\pi^* = (T - \lambda_{II}B)/[\lambda_{II}B (VCK + 1)]$,   (From 28, 11)

(T30) $\pi^* = (T - \lambda_{II}B)/(RDL \cdot T + \lambda_{II}B)$.   (From 28, 12)

These two formulas make it clear that, apart from a rise in the OCK, there are three potential sources of downward pressure on the equilibrium rate of profit: a fall in the length of the working day (T), a rise in the real wage (B) and a rise in the unit value of the means of subsistence (λ_{II}).

The first two of these factors are typically stressed in a *profit-squeeze* approach to the falling rate of profit.[13] We want to discard them here because what the FRP-theory asserts, in its proposition (ii), is that: even if the length (as well as the intensity) of the working day is not pushed down nor the real wage pushed up by working class resistance, the rate of profit will still fall as a reflection of a rising organic composition of capital. We must therefore assume, for the sake of the argument:

(A31)   T is constant,

(A32)   B is constant.

The third factor (rising λ_{II}) is the one picked out in the Ricardian account of a falling rate of profit in terms of declining productivity for agricultural products.[14] Marx emphatically rejected this account on the grounds that, under capitalism, productivity keeps rising. His claim — the claim of proposition (ii) — is that, *although* productivity keeps increasing (i.e. values keep falling), the rate of profit must fall when the organic composition of capital rises. We can therefore suppose that:

(A33) λ_I and λ_{II} fall,

i.e. that productivity rises in both industries, as a reasonable assumption about what is bound to happen under capitalism.

After having thus ruled out all alternative sources of downward pressure on the equilibrium rate of profit, we can now turn to a critical examination of proposition (ii), i.e. to the question: why should a rise in the organic composition of capital necessarily lead to a fall in the equilibrium rate of profit? As in the case of proposition (i), let us take first the textbook variant and then the modern one.

The textbook variant can most conveniently be formulated in terms of the concept of *rate of exploitation* (e), defined by

(D34) $e = s/v$.

The equilibrium rate of profit can easily be formulated in terms of this rate and the VCK:

(T35) $\pi^* = e/(VCK + 1)$. (From 6,11,34)

Bearing in mind that the discussion of proposition (i), in its textbook variant, is supposed to have established that the VCK must rise (T20), it is obviously sufficient to assume that:

(A36) e is constant,

in order to be able to assert that the equilibrium rate of profit must fall:

(T37) π^* falls. (From 35,36,20)

Unfortunately, this additional assumption directly contradicts the three previous assumptions we have just made (A31-33), which jointly imply that the rate of exploitation must rise:

(T38) e rises. (From 34, 27, 10, 4, 31-33)

Therefore, if we want to show that a rising VCK leads to a falling rate of profit even if T and B are constant and productivity rises — which is the claim of proposition (ii) — then we cannot assume a constant rate of exploitation.[15]

This is not the end of the story for the textbook variant, for instead of A36 we can make a weaker assumption which would still enable us to derive a fall in the equilibrium rate of profit. We can assume that the ratio of the increase in the rate of exploitation (Δe) to the increase in the VCK (ΔVCK) is bound by an upper limit e/(VCK + 1):

(A39) $\Delta e/\Delta VCK < e/(VCK + 1)$,[16]

which is equivalent to

(T40) $\dot{e} < (VCK+1)$, (From 39)

and hence directly implies:

(T41) π^* falls. (From 40,35)

The new assumption (A39), unlike the old one (A36), is compatible with a rising rate of exploitation (T38). But this is not enough to make it plausible.

The most defensible attempt to establish the plausibility of assumption A39 runs along the following lines. Given our assumption on the rate of turnover of variable capital (A2), the only difference between e (=s/v) and VCK (=C/V) lies in their numerators (s and C). Now, whereas e's numerator has a finite upper limit — the daily flow of surplus value (s) cannot exceed the daily flow of value (v+s = NT, by T7 and T26) — VCK's numerator (C) can grow without limits. Clearly, this should tell us something about the (eventual) inability of increases in e to offset the negative influence of increases in VCK on the rate of profit. The trouble is that, however much VCK increases, it is always possible, in principle, for e to increase by an even larger amount: it may be true that s cannot tend towards infinity, but v can tend towards 0, and e (=s/v), therefore, can increase indefinitely. This crucial fact cannot but undermine any attempt to provide the weaker assumption A39, indispensable to establish the link between a rising VCK and a falling rate of profit, with more than a very shaky foundation.[17] What the previous argument was trying to get at, however, is a valid and important point. It is precisely the failure of the textbook variant to capture that point adequately, which led to the elaboration of the modern variant of the theory.

The modern variant of the theory tries to derive, from a rise in the ratio of dead to living labor (T25), the necessity of a fall in the equilibrium rate of profit. We shall see that it does not quite succeed in doing so. But it comes as close to it as is possible, by taking full account of the following trivial mathematical fact:[18]

(T42) $s/(C+V) \leq (v+s)/C$ (tautology)

i.e. whatever the (nonnegative) values taken by C, V, s and v, the ratio obtained by adding v to the numerator of s/C cannot possibly be smaller than the ratio obtained by adding V to its denominator. Using previous results, this tautology can immediately be transformed into the following inequality:

(T43) $\pi^* \leq 1/RDL$, (From 42,6,12,26,7)

i.e. the equilibrium rate of profit cannot possibly be larger than the ratio of living to dead labor, or the reciprocal of the RDL. Therefore, we can define the *maximum rate of profit* as

(T44) $\pi_{Max} = 1/RDL$.

And it could not be more obvious that, if the RDL rises, the maximum rate of profit must fall:

(T45) π_{Max} falls. (From 44,25)

However, the maximum rate of profit is not the equilibrium rate of profit, and a fall in the former does not have any straightforward implication as far as the latter is concerned. A fall in the maximum rate of profit does not even imply an eventual fall in the equilibrium rate[19]: the former can fall forever, while the latter keeps rising, as is clearly illustrated in the following diagram.

FIG. 1

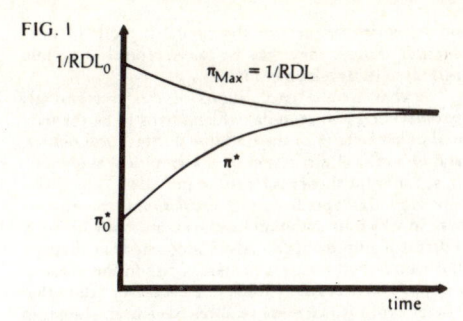

[Figure showing curves over time: $1/RDL_0$ at top left, $\pi_{Max} = 1/RDL$ curve, π^* curve, π_0^* at bottom left, with "time" as x-axis]

What we need is the stronger assumption that, necessarily,

(A46) The RDL rises sufficiently,

i.e. that at some future time x, the maximum rate of profit ($1/RDL_x$) will be lower than the current equilibrium rate (π_0^*).[20] Only then can we validly derive

(T47) π^* will eventually fall.   (From 43, 46)

In other words, the modern variant of the FRP-theory can only vindicate its proposition (ii) — which asserts that if the RDL rises the equilibrium rate of profit must fall — providing the latter's antecedent is strengthened (from a rise to a sufficient rise of the RDL) and its consequent weakened (from an actual to an eventual fall in the equilibrium rate of profit).[21] This means that even more is required from component (i) of the theory than what it has already proved unable to provide (the necessity of a rising RDL) and that component (iii) is provided with even less than what, as we shall soon see, is in any case insufficient to enable it to do its job (i.e. to prove the necessity of an actual fall in π^*).

The Potential Relevance of Empirical Considerations

Let us summarize the "traditional debate" reviewed by the previous two sections. In its first two propositions, the FRP-theory asserts that, under capitalism, the equilibrium rate of profit necessarily falls because the organic composition of capital necessarily rises. This could not be established in the textbook variant (in terms of value composition) because (1) no cogent reason could be given why the technical composition of capital should rise to such an extent as to overcompensate the effect on the value composition of possibly faster technical progress in industry I and/or of possible rises in the real wage rate, and because (2) no cogent reason could be given why the hypothetical rise in the value composition should necessarily overcompensate the effect on the equilibrium rate of profit of a rising rate of exploitation. The modern variant of the theory (in terms of the ratio of dead to living labor) was equally unsuccessful, since (1) it could not provide any cogent reason why the technical composition of capital should rise to such an extent as to overcompensate the effect, on the ratio of dead to living labor, of a fall in the value of the means of production, and since (2) it could not provide any cogent reason why the hypothetical rise in the ratio of dead to living labor should be such as to make its reciprocal (the maximum rate of profit) smaller than the current equilibrium rate.

If no compelling theoretical foundation can be given to the first two propositions of the theory, one may be tempted to turn to the facts. If it turns out that in all capitalist economies the organic composition of capital consistently rises and the equilibrium rate of profit consistently falls, it seems that this would constitute good evidence for the theory, even if it must be admitted that what happens *always* does not necessarily happen *out of necessity*. Since, on the other hand, what happens out of necessity must necessarily happen always, one must not overlook that turning to the facts also involves a serious risk for the theory. But it is at least worth a try, since coming up with favorable evidence, although it would not dispense us from looking for theoretical grounds, would give some credibility to the attempt to do so.

As is well known, however, the organic composition of capital, in capitalist economies, does not consistently rise, and the equilibrium rate of profit does not consistently fall.[22] Should this mean that the first two propositions of the theory are definitively refuted? This would be far too simple. If in a given (capitalist) economy, at a given time, the organic composition fails to rise and/or the rate of profit fails to fall, it may first be possible to claim that these facts are irrelevant to the theory as it is intended. If, as is the case here, the theory is intended to provide an explanation of *crises* (by showing their necessity under capitalist conditions), one need not be committed to the existence of secular trends in the organic composition and in the rate of profit. All one needs to claim is that in a period leading to a crisis, the organic composition rises and the rate of profit falls, however much these trends are offset by what happens during the crisis. On the other hand, if the theory is intended to provide a prediction of the *breakdown* of capitalism (by showing its eventual necessity), then there is no need to claim anything about the actual behavior of the rate of profit: a consistent rise in the organic composition will bring about its eventual fall, however long the period during which it keeps rising.

Suppose, however, that — as is actually the case — the available evidence shows that the organic composition does sometimes fail to rise and the rate of profit to fall in intercrisis periods and that the organic composition, at least in some capitalist economies, does not display a consistent upward secular trend. Does this mean that the theory, in the appropriate sense (i.e. either as a theory of crises or as a theory of breakdown), is refuted? Not yet. For at this stage various types of ad hoc strategies can be used.

First of all, it may be possible to claim that the embarrassing evidence does not really prove that (at a particular place, at a particular time) the organic composition actually falls or that the equilibrium rate of profit actually rises. This may be simply because of defects in the collection of the data, or because no distinction was made between a "productive" sector (the only one which must come into consideration for the estimation of constant and variable capital) and an "unproductive" sector (the public sector and, perhaps, the financial sector or the services, all of which "live off" surplus-value), or else because prices and wages can temporarily fall below or rise above their equilibrium positions.[23]

Secondly, it may be possible to concede that (at a given place, at a given time) the organic composition is actually shown to fall and/or the equilibrium rate of profit shown to rise, while claiming that the economies considered are *not purely capitalist*. The embarrassing behavior of the organic composition and/or of the equilibrium rate of profit could then be attributed to "precapitalist" or, possibly, to "socialist" elements in the economy.[24]

Finally, it may perhaps even be possible to accept both that the organic composition falls and/or that the equilibrium rate of profit rises, and that the economy in which this happens is purely capitalist, while still maintaining that rising organic composition and falling equilibrium rate of profit are necessary, intrinsic, fundamental features of the capitalist mode of production. The fact that these features do not reach the "level of appearances," not even in intercrisis periods nor in the long run, need not bother us too much. This can easily be explained by pointing out that the capitalist system can "make efforts," "*mobilize countertendencies*" (presumably of a more contingent, extrinsic, superficial nature) in order to prevent the "deeper" features from coming into the open.[25]

If one rejects this third type of strategy as empirically vacuous — there is no way, not even in principle, of testing its claims — one may well have to face the existence of genuine counterinstances, i.e. of adverse evidence which cannot be disposed of by an ad hoc strategy of the first ("not really falling/rising") or of the second ("not really capitalist") type. Most Marxist writings now seem to share the conviction that such genuine counterinstances actually exist. Their empirical claim is that there may well have been periods, in the history of capitalist economies, in which consistent rises in the organic compositions coincided with consistent falls in the rate of profit. But there were also periods in which this was not the case. Neither the rise in the organic composition nor the fall in the rate of profit, therefore, can be said to be fundamental, intrinsic, necessary features of the capitalist mode of production, though they may be fairly typical of certain periods in its development.[26]

What are the implications of this (increasingly popular) defeatist attitude, which seems to be the natural outcome both of the traditional theoretical debate and of a critical discussion of the empirical evidence? In so far as the theory is meant to provide a "scientifically grounded" prediction of *breakdown*, there is no way in which its ambition can be reconciled with such a defeatist attitude: if capitalism is doomed to collapse, this cannot be because a necessary rise in the organic composition necessarily leads to a necessary fall in the rate of profit, since these features have been shown to be contingent features of capitalism.

The theory's ambition to explain capitalist *crises*, on the other hand, is not completely destroyed by the adoption of a defeatist attitude. After all, one may argue, a rise in the organic composition of capital need not be "intrinsic to capitalism" in order to bring about a fall in the rate of profit, which in turn need not be "intrinsic to capitalism" in order to generate crises. Even those who adopt a defeatist position in the traditional debate (about necessity vs. contingency), therefore, usually leave open the possibility that the so-called "falling-rate-of-profit" approach may play a very significant role in the explanation of crises.

In the remaining two sections of this paper, I shall attempt to reconstruct other (non-"traditional") aspects of the debate which tend to show that the assumption on which such an "open-minded" attitude rests is doubly wrong. First, it will be argued that however much the rate of profit falls as a result of a rising organic composition, such a fall cannot, as such, generate capitalist crises. Secondly and more radically, it will be argued that, under capitalist conditions, a rise in the organic composition is, in any case, incapable of causing a fall in the general rate of profit. Open-mindedness, in other words, is not on: it is *impossible* (not just contingent) for the rate of profit to fall as a result of a rising organic composition, and impossible (not just contingent) for crises to be generated by such a fall. The theory of the falling rate of profit is not only unable to show that crises are a necessary feature of capitalism (the defeatist position): it is completely irrelevant to the explanation of them.

The Generation of Crises

The preceding sections have been discussing the merits of the first two propositions of our falling-rate-of-profit theory of crises. Let us now turn to its proposition (iii), which asserts that a fall in the equilibrium rate of profit induced by a rise in the organic composition of capital necessarily leads to crises. In conformity with standard usage, I shall take "crisis" to refer to a crisis of overproduction, i.e. to a situation in which production, employment and capacity utilization fall sharply as a result of commodities being unable to find buyers at the going prices. And the question we must ask is: what makes the occurrence of such a crisis necessary when the rate of profit falls for the reasons mentioned in propositions (i) — (ii)?

A first, rather devious, reply to this question is in terms of functional necessity. Roughly, the argument runs as follows.[27] By powerfully counteracting the tendency for the equilibrium rate of profit to fall, crises of overproduction perform a vital curative function for the capitalist mode of production. The way in which they do so, basically, is by decreasing the value of means of production and/or of labor-power, i.e. by increasing productivity in industries I and/or II. And this is achieved both through the elimination of the least efficient capitalists and through the pressure exerted on the remaining ones to introduce (labor- and capital-saving) technical innovations as well as to reorganize, concentrate and rationalize the production process.[28]

However, showing that crises have the "beneficial" effect of keeping in check the falling tendency of the equilibrium rate of profit does *not* amount to showing that crises are made necessary by such a tendency. Firstly, one may want to argue that crises, though possibly sufficient, are not necessary to prevent the equilibrium rate of profit from falling (i.e. that there are "functional equivalents", alternative ways of achieving the same result) and, furthermore, that such a fall is perfectly compatible with the survival of the capitalist system (i.e. that keeping it in check is not a "functional prerequisite", an "essential need" of the system). Secondly and more radically, *functional necessity* (for the survival of a system) should not be confused with *causal necessity* (within the structures of that system). Even if we discard the previous objection and take it for granted that crises of overproduction are functionally necessary to the survival of capitalism, this does not imply that they will necessarily occur, unless some omniscient, omnipotent agent makes whatever the system "needs" (i.e. whatever is functionally necessary to it) unavoidable (i.e. causally necessary). If such an assumption is implausible — and nobody seems to claim the contrary — considerations of "functional necessity" cannot help us to show that a fall in the rate of profit makes the occurrence of crises (causally) necessary.

A second kind of argument, the one most frequently used, does not confuse functional and causal necessity. It first proceeds to show that a fall in the equilibrium rate of profit implies a fall in the *rate of accumulation*, defined as the rate of increase of the capital advanced:

(D48) $\alpha = (\dot{C+V})$.

The second step in the argument must then try to show that a fall in the rate of accumulation must lead to crises of overproduction.

First then, why should the rate of accumulation fall when the equilibrium rate of profit falls? Since, by definition, surplus-value consists in what is left of the value of the gross product when one has taken away the amounts of value (c+v) required for the reproduction of the stock of capital (C+V), it also constitutes the upper limit to the amount by which the stock of capital can be increased (rather than just reproduced):

(T49) $\Delta C + \Delta V \leq s$ (From 7,9,10)

This obviously implies that:

(T50) $\alpha \leq \pi^*$,   (From 48,49,6)

i.e. that the equilibrium rate of profit is the upper limit of the rate of accumulation.

Of course, a fall in the maximum rate of accumulation (i.e. in the equilibrium rate of profit) need not mean a fall in the actual rate, if it is compensated by an increase in the proportion of surplus-value which is accumulated. But we have already assumed above (section 1) that capitalists do not consume. If we further assume — also in agreement with Marx's ideal-typic image of the capitalist — that

(A51) Whatever is not consumed is accumulated,

then it immediately follows that all the surplus-value produced is accumulated and, therefore, that the rate of accumulation is equal to its maximum value:

(T52) $\alpha = \pi^*$.   (From 50,51, section 1)

If the equilibrium rate of profit falls, then, clearly, the rate of accumulation must fall:

(T53) α falls.   (From 52,41)

So far so good. But how do we get from such a fall in the rate of accumulation to the emergence of "realization problems", i.e. of crises of overproduction? The standard view seems to be that at some point — the "definite point" at which the law of the falling rate of profit becomes a "barrier" to the capitalist mode of production — the amount of surplus-value produced becomes insufficient to purchase (for the sake of accumulation) all the commodities produced which are not consumed.[29] Exactly where this point lies is usually left vague. There are some suggestions, however, that it will be reached — crises of overproduction will break out — as soon as the amount of surplus-value begins to decline, not only in relation to capital advanced, but also in absolute terms.[30] The trouble is that, under the very assumptions of the theory, (1) such a point *cannot* possibly be reached, and (2) even if it were reached, this would not trigger off a crisis. Let us examine why this is so.

First, a rise in the amount of surplus-value produced is not only compatible with the theory of the falling rate of profit, as is often acknowledged. It is also implied by the very assumptions we have had to introduce in order to discard alternative sources of downward pressure on the equilibrium rate of profit. Providing we assume that, previous to the crisis, there is no fall in the overall level of employment, i.e.

(A54)   N does not fall,

it follows from the assumption of a constant real wage, of a constant working day and of a rising productivity, that:

(T55)   s rises.   (From 27, 31, 32, 33, 54)

In spite of a falling rate of profit (due to a rising organic composition), therefore, each period of production does not only make a positive amount of value available for accumulation (on top of what is required for simple reproduction), but the amount thus made available is larger than during the previous period.

In any case, however, whether the amount (s) available for accumulation increases or not is irrelevant to the question of whether overproduction crises must appear. Apart from interindustrial disproportionalities, assumed to be swiftly corrected under the law of value, overproduction can only arise from a lack of effective aggregate demand. But we have assumed (A51) that all the net value produced (v+s) which does not enter the workers' consumption (v) is accumulated by the capitalists. There is no discrepancy, therefore, between savings and investment, between the output produced and the (consumption and accumulation) demand for it. Say's law holds. There is no room for a lack of aggregate demand, no room for a crisis of overproduction.[31]

The failure of this second, standard argument does not mean that there is no way in which a fall in the equilibrium rate of profit (induced by a rise in the organic composition) can be understood as potentially relevant to the explanation of crises of overproduction. It only means that there is no way in which it can be so understood by appealing to its influence on the amount of surplus-value *available* for accumulation — in spite of the fact that this is often alleged to be a decisive advantage of the FRP-theory.[32] The only way in which such a fall in the equilibrium rate of profit can be conceived to enter the process by which crises are generated is by affecting the capitalists' subjective expectation of profitability and, thereby, their subjective propensity to invest. Within this "Keynesian", rather than "Marxian" perspective, it is at least possible to imagine that the rate of profit may become so low that capitalists lose any incentive to accumulate and, thereby, generate a lack of demand for means of production as well as (via a fall in the level of employment) for means of subsistence.

However, there remains a major difficulty. Technical change takes time. A rise in the organic composition of capital, therefore, must be a slow, long-run phenomenon. And so must be the resulting fall in the equilibrium rate of profit. In the long run, however, capitalists have plenty of time to adjust their level of expectation, i.e. their definition of what constitutes a "reasonable" rate of profit. If the fall in the rate of profit under consideration were a short-run one, it would be conceivable to explain the interruption of investment by the reaching of some threshold value — e.g. the rate of interest on bonds or the rate of profit abroad. But in a long-run perspective, such an interruption would only be part of the short-run adjustments which contribute to the formation of the equilibrium rate of profit. Showing that there is a long-run tendency for the equilibrium rate of profit to fall (as a result of a rising organic composition), therefore, is of no relevance to the explanation of crises of overproduction, even if one allows for the operation of a "Keynesian" mechanism.[33]

Let us sum up. It has been argued in this section that proposition (iii) of the theory is false, i.e. that a fall in the rate of profit induced by a rise in the organic composition does not make crises of overproduction necessary. This is so, firstly, because, even if we can show that it makes them functionally necessary to capitalism, this does not show them to be causally necessary under capitalism. This is so, secondly, because, even if we admit that a fall in the equilibrium rate of profit depresses the rate of accumulation, there is no way in which this can lead to realization problems unless the capitalists' propensity to invest is brought in. And this is so, finally, because a fall in the equilibrium rate of profit induced by a rising organic composition can only be a long-run phenomenon — in such a way that it will not generate an abrupt interruption of the accumulation process, even if the role of the propensity to invest is acknowledged.

This shows that it is impossible for a fall in the equilibrium rate of profit (due to a rise in the organic composition) to generate crises. But it still assumes that it is possible (though not necessary, as argued above) for a rise in the organic composition to generate a fall in the equilibrium rate of profit. The next section turns to an argument which shows that this too is impossible.

The "Choice of Technique" Argument

The "choice of technique" argument is the most serious of all objections formulated against the theory of the falling rate of profit. *It is so devastating that it deprives all the arguments (pro and contra) presented in the preceding sections of their relevance.* It applies whether the theory is meant as a theory of crises or as a theory of breakdown, whether it is formulated in terms of value composition (textbook variant) or in terms of the ratio of dead to living labor (modern variant), and whether the equilibrium rate of profit can be simply expressed in value terms or not. Although the argument first appeared — albeit in a sketchy formulation — only a few years after the publication of Volume III of *Capital*, it was not until the 1970s that it really entered the Marxist discussion.[34]

The central claim of the argument, sometimes referred to as Okishio's theorem, can be briefly formulated as follows. Under competitive capitalism, a profit-maximizing individual capitalist will only adopt a new technique of production (whether it increases the organic composition of capital or not) if it reduces the production cost per unit or increases profits per unit at going prices. A technical innovation which satisfies this condition — what we can call a *viable* innovation — enables the capitalist to get (temporarily) a transitional rate of profit higher than the initial general rate in the economy. Clearly, this does not, as such, say anything about the new *general*, "socially imposed" rate of profit, i.e. the rate which will prevail once the generalization of the technique within the industry and capital movements between industries will have equalized the rates of profit throughout the economy.[35] The point of Okishio's theorem, however, is precisely to assert that viable innovations necessarily increase the general rate of profit, if they affect it at all. Very roughly, this is due to the fact that the process by which prices are equalized involves a cheapening of the products of the innovating industry. And if the real wage remains constant, this can only increase the rate of profit in other industries — unless the innovation has taken place in a luxury-good industry (in which case capitalist consumers are the beneficiaries). Consequently, it is completely impossible for the general rate of profit to fall as a result of a viable technical innovation, if real wages are kept constant.[36]

A shrewd attempt at refuting this powerful objection has recently been made by Shaikh [1978b]. Okishio's version of the argument, he correctly points out, assumes the absence of fixed capital and, therefore, the identity of the rate of profit (π) and the profit margin (μ), defined respectively by

(D56) $\pi = \dfrac{\text{price per unit - cost per unit}}{\text{investment per unit}}$

$= \dfrac{\text{total profits (per period)}}{\text{total investment (at a given time)}}$

(D57) $\mu = \dfrac{\text{Price per unit - cost per unit}}{\text{cost per unit}}$

$= \dfrac{\text{total profits (per period)}}{\text{total costs (per period)}}$

As soon as fixed capital is allowed, however, the rate of profit and the profit margin are no longer identical, and they need not vary in the same direction as a result of technical change. Furthermore, the criterion of viability becomes ambiguous. If capitalists care about their profit margins, Okishio's theorem can still be used to conclude that the (average) profit margin in the economy cannot fall if real wages are constant. If they rather care about their rates of profit, a generalization of Okishio's theorem to the case of fixed capital shows that the (general) rate of profit in the economy can only rise, if it changes at all. However, if capitalists are *forced* (by competition) to care about their profit *margins* rather than their rates of profit, no Okishio theorem can prevent the general *rate* of profit from falling, as the result of a (capital-using, labor-saving) innovation.[37] The crucial question, therefore, is whether viable innovations, in a competitive capitalist economy with fixed capital, can be represented as moves into the northern area (above the initial general rate of profit π_0^*) or into the eastern area (above the initial profit margin μ_0) of the following diagram (Fig. 2), the two dimensions of which were merged in Okishio's version of the argument.

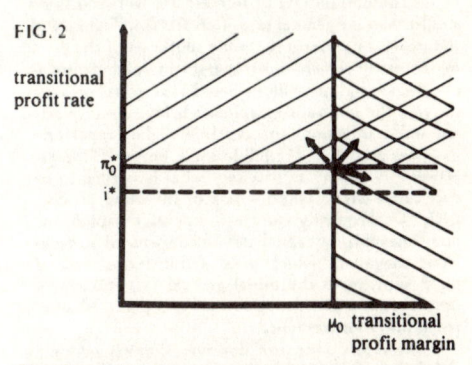

FIG. 2

transitional profit rate

π_0^*

i^*

μ_0 transitional profit margin

Moves from the initial position (μ_0, π_0^*) into the Northern area (above π_0^*) represent profit-rate-increasing technical changes. Moves into the Eastern area (on the right of μ_0) represent profit-margin-increasing technical changes. The success of Shaikh's rescue operation requires some moves into the South-eastern area to be viable.

In order to support the view that profit-margins are the crucial factor, Shaikh proposes a scenario of the following kind. Suppose that one capitalist attempts to increase his sales by introducing a (capital-intensive) technique which gives him a lower transitional π but a higher transitional μ. This would allow him to cut prices in such a way that his profit margin would remain positive, while his competitors (if they want to keep their prices competitive) would start making losses because the techniques they use imply higher unit costs. The whole industry would then be left with little option but to adopt the new technique and accept the rate of profit it yields.[38] In other words, distinguishing the rate of profit from the profit margin seems to make room for viable (because cost-reducing) innovations which lower the rate of profit. The "choice of technique" argument may not, after all, be as devastating as it seemed.

However, Shaikh's counterargument is not only incomplete (it stops before discussing the impact of profit-rate-reducing innovations on the *general* rate of profit).[39] It also fails to establish that, in a competitive economy, a capitalist conforming to the scenario sketched above behaves rationally. Why should a capitalist adopt a capital-intensive technique which will give him (at best) a rate of profit which is lower than the general rate? If he has extra capital at his disposal, he could instead expand his production with the old technique, or invest elsewhere in the economy at the general rate of profit, or at least buy safe financial assets which will give him the equilibrium rate of interest. If he has to borrow the capital he invests, it even becomes a matter of life and death (and not just a matter of opportunity cost) to avoid a transitional rate of profit which is lower than the interest rate. Admittedly, the equilibrium rate of interest (i*) will tend to be smaller than the general rate of profit (as in Fig. 2), and this leaves a narrow area (to the southeast of the starting point) in which profit-margin-increasing profit-rate-decreasing innovations could take place without carrying the innovating capitalist below the interest rate and so inflicting (unacceptable) real or opportunity losses on him. At "equilibrium", however, the gap between i* and π* is precisely what is needed to induce capitalists to take the risk of investing productively. Consequently, under competitive capitalism, profit-maximizing capitalists are condemned to technical innovations which yield a transitional rate of profit superior to the initial general rate. Okishio's (generalized) argument allows no exception. Shaikh's rescue operation has failed.

This is not quite true, however, if one is willing to shift from competitive to oligopolistic capitalism. Fair enough, one must then drop the notion of a general rate of profit (in terms of which the whole FRP-discussion has been conducted). But room can then be made for a fall in the (equilibrium) average rate of profit. This can be seen as follows. First of all, introducing a profit-margin-increasing profit-rate-decreasing innovation may here be preferable to expanding production with the current technique, because oligopolists have to face the constraint of a limited demand, and increasing their output may "spoil the market".[40] Secondly, one can also see that such technical change may be better than investing elsewhere in the economy, if one thinks of an oligopolistic economy as a hierarchy of industries with entrance barriers of different "heights" and, correspondingly, with different "equilibrium" rates of profit deviating upward from the equilibrium interest rate. In such a situation, a particular oligopolist may well be prevented (by the "barriers") from investing in an industry with a higher rate of profit. And the rate of profit which he can get by investing at a lower transitional rate (but a higher profit margin) in his own industry, may well be higher than the rate of return available in less well-protected industries or on financial markets, since the gap between the interest rate and the initial rate of profit in the industry is generally much wider here than in the competitive case (Fig. 2). In the oligopolistic case, therefore, a cost-reducing innovation which leads to a lower transitional rate of profit in one industry may well be viable. Furthermore, since the oligopolistic scenario does not require prices to be lowered in the innovating industry, a lower rate of profit in one industry will often unambiguously mean a lower average rate of profit. The shift to oligopoly not only makes Shaikh's argument more plausible; it also makes it complete.

The previous argument shows that, if one is prepared to move sufficiently far away from the ideal competitive world which is generally taken for granted in the discussion, some room can be made for the possibility (*just* the possibility) of a fall in the average (*not* the general) rate of profit, with a constant real wage and profit-maximization as the only criterion in the choice of techniques. One may also want to argue, on the other hand, that the capitalist choice of techniques need not be profit-maximizing, and that this opens up further possibilities for a fall in the (general or average) rate of profit, compatible with a constant real wage.

Firstly and most obviously, the capitalist choice of techniques may fail to be profit-maximizing because of the capitalists' mistakes. They adopt a new technique because they think it will enable them to make bigger profits, but for some reason it does not. If such mistakes are to be more than random events, there must be reasons why they should occur systematically. One such reason could be the acceleration of technical progress, which may shorten the economic life of new investment in a way which was not expected when the investment was decided upon. It seems unlikely, however, that capitalists would remain unable, for more than a short period, to anticipate the rate of technical progress and so to prevent such systematic mistakes.[4]

Secondly, one can imagine a competitive "capitalist" system in which profit-maximization governs the formation of prices and the allocation of factors, but not the choice of techniques, which is performed by some central authority according to a principle of productivity-maximization. Now, whereas all profit-increasing innovations are productivity-increasing, the reverse is not true: if the real wage is low, there may be productivity-increasing, or labor-time-reducing, innovations (of a capital-using, labor-saving kind) which are not profit-increasing, because the reduced *cost* in living labor they involve cannot compensate for the increased *cost* in dead labor (on which a rate of profit has to be paid). In such a "Lange-type" or "market-socialist" economy, therefore, technical change may clearly lead to a fall in the transitional and in the general rate of profit.[42]

Thirdly and most importantly, capitalists may knowingly (unlike case 1) and freely (unlike case 2) introduce a technology which lowers their profits at current prices, if they believe that such a technology makes them more immune to the threat of workers' resistance. A highly capital-intensive technology, which considerably reduces the level of skill required on the part of the labor involved, for instance, may well be introduced, even if, at current wages and prices, it yields lower profits. The promise that the heavy weight of the reserve army of unemployed will secure the compliance and moderate the wage claims of unskilled workers, may seem worth the sacrifice of higher profits in the short term.[43]

These three qualifications, like the previous remark about oligopoly, are meant to stress the dependence of Okishio-type objections on two of their crucial premises: profit maximization and perfect competition. When either of these assumptions is relaxed, a fall in the (general or average) rate of profit, without a rise in the real wage, can no longer be excluded on a priori grounds. But the claim that there is anything like a *systematic* tendency for such a fall to occur gains no support from this fact.

Conclusion

Let me conclude this sketchy rational reconstruction of a long debate, with three brief remarks. First of all, the discussion on the "*law* of the falling rate of profit" — our propositions (i) and (ii) — can very roughly be divided into three stages. What one could perhaps call the Grossmann stage of the discussion takes it for granted that a fall in the general rate of profit due to a rise in the organic composition is both possible and actually taking place, and focuses on the question of whether it constitutes a necessary feature of capitalism. What one could perhaps call the Mandel stage of the discussion admits that there may be no good grounds for asserting the necessity of a fall in the rate of profit due to a rising organic composition. However, it still takes the possibility of this fall for granted, and focuses on whether or not it has actually taken place. Finally, what one could call the Shaikh stage of the discussion admits that there may be no good grounds for asserting the necessity or the "actuality" of a fall in the rate of profit caused by a rise in the organic composition, and it concentrates on the question of whether or not such a fall is possible. Now, such a shift in the focus of the discussion is clearly of a degenerative kind. This does not mean that the quality of the discussion has fallen: on the contrary, arguments have rather tended to become increasingly subtle, rigorous and sophisticated. What makes the shift "degenerative" is rather that the discussion starts with a powerful claim (the capitalist necessity of a tendency for the rate of profit to fall because of a rising organic composition), which is potentially useful for explanatory, predictive and even practical purposes. But it ends up with a much weaker claim (the capitalist possibility of such a tendency), which, even if it can be successfully established, is of very little (and purely negative) interest in an attempt to explain or to predict, to shape or to smash, capitalist realities.

My second concluding remark concerns the importance of theoretical debate in forging the spectacles through which empirical reality is perceived. At the Grossmann stage of the discussion, it was the critics of the theory who came up with empirical data about profit rates and capital coefficients, while the proponents of the theory dismissed them as illusory appearances which could not shake their confidence in a theoretically grounded *necessity*. At the Shaikh stage of the discussion, the tables have turned. It is now the proponents of (whatever is left of) the theory who have to plead that empirical data are relevant, while its critics dismiss them as mere appearances which could not affect their confidence in a theoretically grounded impossibility. If profit-maximization and perfect competition can be safely assumed, then, they say, whatever the empirical evidence at the aggregate level, one can be certain that a fall in the equilibrium rate of profit must be attributed to a rise in the real wage.[44] Even if the equilibrium rate of profit falls regularly as the organic composition rises, for instance, while the rate of exploitation remains constant, one can be *sure* (under the microeconomic conditions mentioned) that the fall in the rate of profit is due to a rise in the real wage (which is reflected in the fact that the rate of exploitation failed to rise) and that it occurred *in spite of* the technical changes which took place (and whose impact is reflected in the rise of the organic composition and in the fact that the rate of exploitation failed to fall). However, in so far as the qualifications about oligopoly and non-profit-maximizing choice of technique are relevant, a somewhat more lenient look at the data is required.

Finally, the persistent favor which the falling-rate-of-profit theory of crises (and breakdown) has enjoyed in the Marxist scientific community also has "extrascientific" reasons: by asserting that crises (and breakdown) are objectively bound to occur even in the absence of any increase in the real wage, the theory unambiguously clears the working-class of the responsibility for generating the "fundamental problems" of the capitalist system. Therefore, as "bad news" accumulates about the soundness of the theory, the conflict between what one ought to believe and what one would like to believe, between "scientific" and "extrascientific" considerations, may become increasingly acute. The more vulnerable the community feels, the more likely "extrascientific" considerations are to prevail. The more self-confident it feels, on the other hand, the more able it becomes to give way to "scientific" considerations — and to stomach the truth. Because I believe contemporary Marxist ecnomics to be in the latter position, rather than in the former, I also believe that calling this rational reconstruction an *obituary* may turn out to be more than just wishful thinking.

Philippe Van Parijs
Centre de Philosophie des Sciences
1 Chemin d'Aristote
1348 Louvain-la-Neuve
Belgium

NOTES

1. Earlier versions of this paper were presented at the Economics Departments in Louvain-la-Neuve (Belgium) and Cambridge (England) and at the Philosophy Department in Ghent (Belgium). I am grateful to my audiences as well as to Phil Armstrong, Johannes Berger, Sue Black, J. Dean, Jim Devine, Michel De Vroey, Ernst Fahling, Heiner Ganssmann, Jacques Gouverneur, Bob Rowthorn, and particularly to Andrew Glyn and John Roemer, for useful comments.

2. The point of these oversimplifying assumptions is that we shall be able to speak in scalar terms, rather than in terms of vectors and matrices. The disadvantage is that we shall be forced to conceive of technological changes as just variations in the proportions of one kind of means of production and of one kind of labor-power needed for the production of the same commodities I and II. But the reasoning can easily be extended to more realistic situations.

3. For a discussion of the conditions under which the concept of value makes sense, see e.g. Morishima (1973: ch. 14), Steedman (1977: ch. 6-8, 10-13), Armstrong, et. al. (1978). And for a discussion of the conditions under which the (simplest) law of value holds, see e.g. Morishima (1973: ch. 6). The behavior of the equilibrium rate of profit under less restrictive conditions is discussed e.g. by Armstrong (1975: 8-10) and Steedman (1977: 129-132).

4. Marx's (1867:641) tricky definition of the OCK is familiar enough. For a recent discussion, see e.g. Fine & Harris (1979: 59-61). The VCK-interpretation is the textbook one (with sometimes a $V/(C+V)$ variant); see e.g. Sweezy (1942: 16), Mandel (1961: 19). The RDL-interpretation, (with sometimes a C/N or C/(N T) variant), already used by Moszkowska (1935: 52) or Okishio (1961: 87) has recently become increasingly popular: see e.g. Okishio (1972: 3-4), Cogoy (1973: 56-58), Hodgson (1974: 80-81), Wright (1975:13), Shaikh (1978a: 233), Robinson (1978:6).

5. The *textbook variant* is the one Marx clearly uses in his most explicit formulation of the theory (1894:221-224). In various formulations, it also appears e.g. in Sweezy (1942:96-97), Robinson (1942:35-36), Meek (1960: 129-130), Mandel (1962: I, 210-215), Salama & Valier (1973: 108-113), Bullock & Yaffe (1975: 19-20), Gamble & Walton (1976: 129-130), Gouverneur (1978: 168-170), etc. That Marx had the *modern variant* of the theory in mind is defended e.g. by Rosdolsky (1956: 209-215) and Bader et. al. (1975: 398-399). Passages particularly favorable to this interpretation are Marx (1858: 635-636, 643, 653) and Marx (1894: 223, 226). The underlying reasoning is present in Rosdolsky (1956), Dickinson (1957), Meek (1960), Okishio (1961). It received its definitive, most elegant formulation from Okishio (1972), and has since tended to become standard: see e.g. Glyn (1972: 100-101), Purdy (1973: 17-20), Hodgson (1974: 80-82), Himmelweit (1974: 2), Holländer (1974: 113-114), Itoh (1975: 6), Wright (1975: 13-16), Bader & al. (1975: 401-405), Shaikh (1978a: 233; 1978b: 239), etc.

6. This kind of argument is most explicitly defended by Yaffe (1972: 21). See also Sensat (1979: 143-144).

7. A similar view is adopted e.g. by Lange (1935: 84-85), Robinson (1942: 35-36; 1948: 114-115), Dobb (1973: 157) Sweezy (1973: 45-46, 49), Hodgson (1974: 60-62), Wright (1975: 17-18), etc.

8. However, there have been attempts at short-circuiting the argument by skipping the TCK intermediary and dealing straight away with the necessity of a rising VCK. For instance, Bullock & Yaffe (1975: 18-19) and, in a more sophisticated way, Bader et. al. (1975: 420-459) claim to derive the rise in the VCK from the concept of capital itself, defined as self-expanding value. Their argument runs roughly as follows. First, with a given labor force (N) and a given length of the working day (T), the amount of living labor employed is necessarily limited. As a consequence, with a fixed rate of turnover of variable capital (t_v), the value of the stock of variable capital can only decrease, as productivity improves and depresses its unit value (λ_{LP}). This implies that, if (constant plus variable) capital is to grow in value terms, there is only one way in which it can do so: through an increase in constant capital (dead labor) which more than offsets the fall in variable capital (the value of living labor). Hence the logical necessity of a rising VCK. This provides a good example of how heavy assumptions can be quietly smuggled in, in the guise of innocent-looking definitions.

9. This assumption is discussed e.g. by Glyn (1972: 95), Morishima (1973: 34-35), Shaikh (1978b: 250-251). It may gain some plausibility from the fact that any reduction in the value of the means of production also reduces the value of the means of subsistence (by reducing the amount of dead labor their production requires), not the other way round.

10. The possibility of such changes was clearly allowed for by Marx (1867: 185, 534-536).

11. This is the old "cheapening of the elements of constant capital" countertendency, mentioned by Marx (1867: 651-652, 1894: 243-246) and discussed e.g. by Mandel (1962: I, 213-214), Hodgson (1974: 64-65), Hussain (1977: 447-449), Shaikh (1978a: 234).

12. The above formulation is indirectly suggested by Lebowitz (1976: 252-253). Arguments of a similar type are presented by Glyn (1972: 95-98) and Stamatis (1976a: 80; 1976b: 106-107). Alternatively but (nearly) equivalently, the necessity of a rise in the RDL (or, as we shall see, of a fall in the maximum rate of profit) can also be derived from the necessity of mechanization, defined as technical progress which increases the amount of machinery per unit of output (not only per man), without decreasing the amount of other material inputs per unit (see e.g. Purdy 1973: 19; Shaikh 1978b: 239-240). Mechanization, which corresponds to a TCK growing faster than average productivity, is a slightly stronger condition than T24.

13. See e.g. Glyn & Sutcliffe (1972), Boddy & Crotty (1975) or Roemer (1978). The primary emphasis, both in a secular and in a cyclical perspective, is usually on the increase in the real wage, interpreted either as an increase in the "historical subsistence level" or as a deviation from it due to the growth of working-class power. Occasionally, the role of a decrease in the intensity of labor is also stressed: see e.g. Crotty & Rapping (1975: 463-464), Weisskopf (1978: 248).

14. See Ricardo (1817: 71-74). This type of account is occasionally revived, for instance with an emphasis on the growing costs of distribution and advertising (Shibata 1939: 55) or on the exhaustion of the world's natural resources (Steedman 1977: 129).

15. Put differently, a constant rate of exploitation can only be assumed if hourly real wages (B/T) *grow* at the same rate as productivity $(1/\lambda_{II})$. (See e.g. Sweezy 1942: 100-102, Robinson 1942: 36, Samuelson 1957: 892).

16. Variants of this condition are discussed by Sweezy (1942: 102)

and by Stamatis (1976a: 106-107, 1976b: 109-110).

17. This "most defensible" line of argument is repeatedly used (not always very clearly) by Marx himself (see e.g. 1858: 335-336, 340, 389; 1867: 444-445; 1894: 257-258). Attempts at rephrasing it more satisfactorily can be found e.g. in Meek (1960: 133-135), Mandel (1962: I, 212-213 & 1964: 49-50), Mattick (1969: 62-63), Bader et. al. (1975: 400-401), Bullock & Yaffe (1975: 20), Lebowitz (1976: 242-243). The decisive objection (that e can anyway rise without limits) is clearly stated e.g. by Robinson (1942: 38-40), Glyn (1972: 100) and Hodgson (1974: 60-61). It is quite true, as is sometimes retorted (e.g. by Mandel 1964: 50 or Mattick 1969:63), that the necessary labor time (v) will never be equal to 0 (nor, therefore, e equal to infinity). But will the value stock of constant capital (C) (and therefore, q) ever be equal to infinity?

18. The central role of this tautology (in the modern variant) is clearly emphasized e.g. by Okishio (1961: 89; 1972: 5), Glyn (1972: 100-101), Himmelweit (1974: 2), etc.

19. Contrary to what is often implicitly assumed (e.g. by Okishio 1961: 89; Hodgson 1974: 82; Itoh 1975: 6; Shaikh 1978a: 233, 1978b: 240). This point (that an actual fall in the maximum rate of profit does not imply an eventual fall in the equilibrium rate) is also made e.g. by Holländer (1974: 114), Stamatis (1976a: 107-109; 1976b: 113), Steedman (1977: 126-127), Roemer (1979: 6-8).

20. A particular specification of this condition corresponds to the assumption that, as time tends towards infinity, the RDL tends towards infinity. Under this stronger assumption, suggested e.g. by Steedman (1977: 127) or Sensat (1979: 130) and claimed by Armstrong & al. (1978: 25) to be generally assumed in the discussion, the eventual fall in the equilibrium rate of profit (T47) can be derived, *whatever* the initial rate of profit. One serious difficulty, with such an assumption, is that it can be shown (see e.g. Stamatis 1976a: 127-129) that, with NT constant, n_{Max} can only tend towards 0 if productivity in Industry I $(1/\lambda_1)$ stops growing. Otherwise, it has a strictly positive lower limit equal to λ_1.

21. Dissatisfaction is sometimes expressed with this reformulation, on the grounds that Marx meant more than an eventual fall (see e.g. Stamatis 1976b: 113; 1977: 8-9) and that claiming an eventual fall is empirically vacuous, as it is compatible with an actual rise for any finite length of time, however long (see e.g. Stamatis 1976a: 108-110). The answer, I suppose, is that it is better to be revisionist and vacuous than wrong.

22. A recent and sophisticated discussion of empirical data is provided by Weisskopf (1979).

23. Yaffe (1973: 50, 57) and Fine & Harris (1976a: 101) provide typical examples of this kind of strategy.

24. It may be argued, for instance, that the rate of profit is prevented from falling by the spreading of capitalism into non-capitalist areas or by an increase in state intervention.

25. See, typically, Mattick (1969: 61), Cogoy (1972: 407-408); 1973: 54-55, 61-62), Kay (1976: 73-74), Holloway & Picciotto (1977:91). Since it is unanimously recognized that the "countertendencies" cannot just be dismissed as exogenous with respect to the capitalist system (see e.g. Rosdolsky 1968: 209-213 & 1968: 467-472; Cogoy 1973: 56-59), it is hard to see how this third kind of strategy can avoid the following dilemma. Either a symmetric reasoning applies to the countertendencies, and then one ends up with a "law of the tendency for the rate of profit to fall and the tendency for counteracting influences to operate" (see e.g. Fine & Harris 1976a: 162-163; 1979: 63-64) — the remaining difference from the defeatist position being purely verbal. Or one is left with a stiff and strong but empirically vacuous claim about what is "fundamental" in capitalism — a nice example of how political economy can degenerate into full-time theory immunization.

26. This *defeatist* position has had a growing number of supporters since Moszkowska (1929: 71-72, 83-84, 118) and Sweezy (1942: 102). An "epistemological" rationalization for it — the "law of tendency"

is "just one possibility in the Discourse of Capital" — has recently been offered by Cutler et. al. (1977: 160-165). Attempts at periodizing capitalism in terms of whether the "tendency" is operative or not (e.g. Wright 1975: 5-6; Stamatis 1976a: 129-135 and 1977: 287-290) must presuppose a similar position.

27. See e.g. Marx (1894: 268) and, more explicitly, Cogoy (1973: 60), Fine & Harris (1976b: 94, 110-111). A critique of this "functionalist" type of argument is given by Itoh (1975: 10, 1978: 3).

28. See e.g. Mattick (1969: 70-71), Yaffe (1972: 30), Bullock & Yaffe (1975: 22), who also mention other ways in which crises perform a "curative function". But, as convincingly argued by Glyn (1972: 101-102), only those which will affect productivity are relevant to the fall in the equilibrium rate of profit.

29. This kind of argument seems to be put forward by Marx (1894: 251-252, 268), and also by Mattick (1969: 66-68, 75-79), Cogoy (1973: 64), Gamble & Walton (1976: 131-132), Shaikh (1978a: 231).

30. For instance, Shaikh (1978b: 237).

31. The point is clearly made e.g. by Robinson (1942: 85) and Berger (1979: 8).

32. It is often said that an emphasis on available (rather than expected) profits is the mark of a Marxian (rather than Keynesian) approach. See e.g. Robinson (1942: 29, 50-51, etc.), Mattick (1969: 21, 54-55), Yaffe (1972: 42), Itoh (1975: 10), Shaikh (1978a: 230), etc.

33. The connection between the theory of the falling rate of profit and crisis theory is challenged e.g. by Robinson (1948: 114), Itoh (1978a: 13) and, with a specific reference to the long-run character of the former, by Sweezy (1942: 148), Sowell (1967: 64), Sherman (1967: 492), Berger (1979: 8).

34. The first formulation of the argument (in the particular case in which there is only one kind of product) is due to Tugan-Baranowsky (1901: 212-215). A more general formulation is given by Bortkiewicz (1907: 454-470). The argument then sporadically reappears but is hardly noticed: see e.g. Moszkowska (1929: 77-80, 105-107, 1935: 46-49), Shibata (1934: 65-71, 1939: 50-52, 56-61), Samuelson (1957: 892-895, 1972: 54-56), Okishio (1961: 91-99). But it is only in the midseventies that it really entered the Marxist discussion, at least in Britain and in Germany: See e.g. Glyn (1973: 104-107), Holländer (1974: 123-124), Himmelweit (1974: 2-5), Nutzinger & Wolfstetter (1974: 171-172), etc. The most comprehensive and rigorous formulation of the essential mathematical results is Roemer (1977). See also Roemer (1979) for a further generalization.

35. This valid point is what misled many Marxists into believing that Okishio-type arguments were of no relevance to Marx's theory of the falling rate of profit. See especially Sweezy (1942: 104-105fn): had this footnote not been written, the last 35 years of Marxist crisis theory might have looked very different.

36. Formal proofs of this proposition can be found e.g. in Okishio (1961: 98-99), Glyn (1973: 106-107), Roemer (1977: 417-418).

37. See Shaikh (1978b: 242-245). Generalizations of Okishio's theorem to the case of fixed capital and joint production are presented and proved by Roemer (1979: 11-22).

38. See Shaikh (1978b: 245-246).

39. A fall in the *transitional* rate of profit of the innovating *industry* (which is where Shaikh stops) would only imply a fall in the *general* rate of profit if the price reductions required by Shaikh's scenario did not increase the rate of profit in other industries.

40. See Armstrong & Glyn (1979).

41. See Persky & Alberro (1978), discussed in Roemer (1979).

42. See e.g. Shibata (1939: 58-60), Roemer (1977: 411-414).

43. See e.g. Roemer (1978: 162-165), Sensat (1979: 152-153).

44. Similar formulations can be found, not always with the necessary emphasis on the "if", in Bortkiewicz (1907: 469), Shibata (1934: 71-74, 1939: 60-61), Okishio (1961: 96), Himmelweit (1974: 6), Nutzinger & Wolfstetter (1974: 171-172), Roemer (1977: 415).

REFERENCES

Armstrong, Philip. "Accumulation of Capital, the Rate of Profit, and Crisis." *CSE Bulletin* 11 (1975); 1-17.

─────── and Glyn, Andrew. "The Law of the Falling Rate of Profit and Oligopoly — a Comment on Shaikh." *Cambr. J. of Econ.* 3 (1979), forthcoming.

─────── Glyn, Andrew; and Harrison, John. "In Defence of Value." *Capital and Class* 5 (1978), 1-31.

Bader, Veit-Michael; Berger, Johannes; Ganssmann, Heiner; and others. *Krise und Kapitalismus bei Marx.* 2 Vols. Frankfurt: E.V.A., 1975.

Berger, Johannes. "Der Grundgedanke der Marxschen Krisentheorie." *Das Argument* 35 (1979), forthcoming.

Boddy, Raford; and Crotty, James. "Class Conflict and Macro-Policy: the Political Business Cycle." *Rev. of Rad. Pol. Econ.* 7.1 (1975), 1-19.

Bortkiewicz, Ladislaus von. "Wertrechnung und Preisrechnung im Marxschen System." *Archiv für Sozialwissenschaft und Sozialpolitik* 25 (1907), 445-488.

Bullock, Paul; and Yaffe, David. "Inflation, the Crisis and the Post-war Boom." *Revolutionary Communist* 3-4 (1975), 5-45.

Cogoy, Mario. "Les théories néo-marxistes, Marx et l'accumulation du capital." *Les Temps Modernes* (Sept. 1972), 396-427.

─────── "The Fall of the Rate of Profit and the Theory of Accumulation." *CSE Bulletin* 8 (1973), 52-67.

Crotty, James; and Rapping L.A. "Class Struggle, Macropolicy and the Business Cycle." *The Capitalist System* (R.C. Edwards, M. Reich and T.E. Weisskopf, eds), Englewood Cliffs: Prentice-Hall, 1978, 461-469.

Cutler, Antony; Hindess, Barry; Hirst, Paul; and Hussain, Athar. *Marx's Capital and Capitalism Today*, Vol. 1. London: Routledge, 1977.

Dickinson, H.D. "The Falling Rate of Profit in Marxian Economics." *Rev. of Econ. Studies* 24 (1957), 120-130.

Dobb, Maurice. (1937) *Political Economy and Capitalism*, London: Routledge, 1972.

─────── *Theories of Value and Distribution.* Cambridge: C.U.P., 1973.

Fine, Ben; and Harris, Laurence. "State Expenditure in Advanced Capitalism: A Reply." *New Left Review* 98 (1976a), 97-112.

─────── and Harris, Laurence. "Controversial Issues in Marxist Economic Theory." *Socialist Register* (R. Miliband and P. Saville eds), London: Merlin Press, 1976b, 141-178.

─────── and Harris, Laurence. *Rereading Capital* London: Macmillan, 1979.

Gamble, Andrew; and Walton, Paul. *Capitalism in Crisis.* Atlantic Highlands: Humanities Press, 1977.

Glyn, Andrew. "Capitalist Crisis and Organic Composition." *CSE Bulletin* 4 (1972), 93-103.

─────── "Productivity, Organic Composition and the Falling Rate of Profit." CSE Bulletin 6 (1973), 103-107.

─────── and Sutcliffe, Bob. *Capitalism in Crisis.* New York: Pantheon Books, 1972.

Gouverneur, Jacques. *Eléments d'Economie Politique Marxiste.* Brussels: Contradictions, 1978.

Grossmann, Henryk. (1929) *Das Akkumulantions- and Zusammenbruchsgesetz des kapitalistischen Systems.* Frankfurt, 1970.

Himmelweit, Susan. "The Continuing Saga of the Falling Rate of Profit. A Reply to Mario Cogoy." *CSE Bulletin* 9 (1974), 1-6.

Hodgson, Geoffrey. "The Theory of the Falling Rate of Profit." *New Left Review* 84 (1974), 55-82.

Holländer, Heinz. "Das Gesetz des tendenziellen Falls der Profitrate. Marxens Begrundung und ihre Implikationen." *Mehrwert* 6 (1974), 105-131.

Holloway, John; and Picciotto, Sol. "Capital, Crisis and the State." *Capital and Class* 2 (1977), 76-101.

Hussain, Athar. "Crises and Tendencies of Capitalism." *Economy and Society* 6 (1977), 436-460.

Itoh, Makoto. "The Formation of Marx's Theory of Crisis." *CSE Bulletin* 10 (1975), 1-19.

─────── "The Inflational Crisis of World Capitalism." *Capital and Class* 4 (1978), 1-10.

Kay, Geoffrey. "The Falling Rate of Profit, Unemployment and Crisis." *Critique* 6 (1976), 55-75.

Lange, Oscar. (1935) "Marxian Economics and Modern Economic Theory." *Marx and Modern Economics* (D. Horowitz ed.), New York: Monthly Review Press, 1968, 68-87.

Lebowitz, Michael A. "Marx's Falling Rate of Profit: a Dialectical View." *Canadian J. of Econ.* 9 (1976), 232-254.

Mandel, Ernest. *Traité d'Economie Marxiste.* 4 Vols. Paris: U.G.E., 1962.

─────── *An Introduction to Marxist Economic Theory.* New York: Pathfinder Press, 1964.

Marx, Karl. (1858) *Grundrisse der Kritik der politischen Oekonomie.* Berlin: Dietz, 1953.

─────── (1867) *Das Kapital.* Vol. 1. Berlin: Dietz, 1962.

─────── (1894) *Das Kapital.* Vol. 3. Berlin: Dietz, 1964.

Mattick, Paul. *Marx and Keynes.* Boston: Porter Sargent, 1969.

Meek, Ronald L. (1960) "The Falling Rate of Profit." *Economics and Ideology, and other Essays.* London: Chapman and Hall, 1967, 129-142.

Morishima, Michio. *Marx's Economics.* Cambridge: C.U.P., 1973.

Moszkowska, Nathalie. *Das Marxsche System. Ein Beitrag zu dessen Ausbau.* Berlin: Engelmann, 1929.

─────── *Zur Kritik moderner Krisentheorien.* Prag: Kacha, 1935.

Nutzinger, H.G.; and Wofstetter, E. (eds). *Die Marxsche Theorie und ihre Kritik.* 2 Vols. Frankfurt and New York, 1974.

Okishio, Nobuo. "Technical Change and the Rate of Profit." *Kobe Univ. Econ. Rev.* 7 (1961), 85-99.

─────── "A Formal Proof of Marx's Two Theorems." *Kobe Univ. Econ. Rev.* 18 (1973), 1 6.

Persky, Joseph; and Alberro. "Technical Innovation and the Dynamics of the Profit Rate.", Chicago: Univ. of Illinois, 1978.

Purdy, David. "The Theory of the Permanent Arms Economy — A Critique and an Alternative." *CSE Bulletin* 5 (1973), 12-33.

Ricardo, David. (1817) *On the Principles of Political Economy and Taxation.* London: Dent & Sons, 1977.

Robinson, Joan. (1942) *An Essay on Marxian Economics.* New York: St. Martin's Press, 1976.

─────── (1948) "Marx and Keynes." *Marx and Modern Economics* (D. Horowitz ed.), New York: Monthly Review Press, 1968, 103-116.

─────── "The Organic Composition of Capital." *Kyklos* 31 (1978), 5-20.

Roemer, John E. "Technical Change and the Tendency of the Rate of Profit to Fall", in *J. of Econ. Theory* 16 (1977), 403-424.

─────── "The Effect of Technological Change on the Real Wage and Marx's Falling Rate of Profit." *Australian Econ. Papers* (1978), 152-166.

─────── "Continuing Controversy on the Falling Rate of Profit: Fixed Capital and Other Issues.", *Cambr. J. of Econ.* 3 (1979), forthcoming.

Rosdolsky, Roman. "Zur neueren Kritik des Marxschen Gesetzes der fallenden Profitrate." *Kyklos* 9 (1956), 208-226.

─────── *Zur Entstehungsgeschichte des Marxschen "Kapital"*, Frankfurt: E.V.A., 1968.

Salama, Pierre; and Valier, Jacques. *Une Introduction à l'Economie Politique.* Paris: Maspero, 1973.

Samuelson, Paul A. "Wages and Interests: A Modern Dissection of Marxian Economic Models." *Amer. Econ. Rev.* 47 (1957), 884-912.

―――― "The Economics of Marx: An Ecumenical Reply." *J. of Econ. Lit.* 10 (1972), 51-57.

Sensat, Julius. *Habermas and Marxism.* Beverly Hills (Calif.): Sage Publications, 1979.

Shaikh, Anwar. "An Introduction to the History of Crisis Theories." *U.S. Capitalism in Crisis.* New York: URPE, 1978a, 219-241.

―――― "Political Economy and Capitalism: Notes on Dobb's Theory of Crises." *Cambr. J. of Econ.* 2 (1978b), 233-251.

Sherman, Howard J. "Marx and the Business Cycle." *Science and Society* 31 (1967), 486-504.

Shibata, Kei. "On the Law of Decline in the Rate of Profit." *Kyoto Univ. Econ. Rev.* 9.1 (1934), 61-75.

―――― "On the General Profit Rate." *Kyoto Univ. Econ. Rev.* 14:1 (1939), 31-66.

Sowell, Thomas. "Marx's *Capital* After One Hundred Years." *Canadian J. of Econ.* 33 (1967), 50-74.

Stamatis, Georgios. "Zum Marxschen Gesetz vom tendenziellen Fall der allgemeinen Profitrate." *Mehrwert* 10 (1976a), 70-138.

―――― "Zum Beweis der Konsistenz des Marxschen Gesetzes vom tendenziellen Fall der allgemeinen Profitrate." *Prokla* 25 (1976b), 105-116.

―――― *Die spezifisch kapitalistischen Produktionsmethoden und der tendenzielle Fall der allgemeinen Profitrate bei Karl Marx* Berlin: Mehrwert, 1977.

Steedman, Ian. *Marx after Sraffa.* London: New Left Books, 1977.

Sweezy, Paul M. (1942) *The Theory of Capitalist Development,* New York: Monthly Review Press, 1970.

Tugan-Baranowsky, Michael. *Theorie und Geschichte der Handelskrisen in England.* Jena: Fischer, 1901.

Weisskopf, Thomas E. "Marxist Perspectives on Cyclical Crises." *U.S. Capitalism in Crisis.* New York: URPE, 1978, 241-260.

―――― "Sources of Profit Rate Fluctuations in the Postwar U.S. Economy: an Empirical Test of Alternative Marxist Theories of Economic Crisis." *Cambr. J. of Econ.* 3 (1979), forthcoming.

Wright, Erik O. "Alternative Perspectives in Marxist Theory of Accumulation and Crisis." *Insurgent Sociologist* 6.1 (1975) 5-39.

Yaffe, David S. "The Marxian Theory of Crisis, Capital and the State." *CSE Bulletin* 4 (1972), 5-58.

―――― "The Crisis of Profitability: a Critique of the Glyn-Sutcliffe Thesis." *New Left Review* 80 (1973), 45-62.

Part II
The Marginal Revolution and its Aftermath

Physics and the 'marginalist revolution'

Philip Mirowski*

The mathematician is an inventor, not a discoverer (Wittgenstein, 1978, I, 168).

1. Internal *versus* external histories of science

Interest in the origins of neoclassical theory has a number of motivations. The first is antiquarian: it is concerned with tracing the intellectual antecedents of a given innovation. The second is epistemological: the methods of great discoverers are held to provide an exemplar for currently accepted methods of research. The third is ontological: the occurrence of independent simultaneous discovery is used to suggest the substantiality and reality of the phenomenon identified. William Stanley Jevons, for instance, wrote that, 'The theory in question has in fact been independently discovered three or four times over and must be true' (Jevons, 1972, IV, p. 278). The fourth is practical: it provides a reservoir of metaphors and theoretical suggestions which might serve to prompt novel contemporary lines of inquiry which are obscured or slighted by modern theory. Confusion or doubt over the origins of modern neoclassical economic theory would introduce the possibility of serious historical, epistemological, ontological and practical confusions in its exposition.

At present, the most popular textbook of the history of economic thought attempts to dispose of the issue by absolving itself of any responsibility for discussing origins:

Therefore, to try to explain the origin of the marginal utility revolution in the 1870s is doomed to failure: it was not a marginal utility revolution; it was not an abrupt change, but only a gradual transformation in which the old ideas were never definitively rejected; and it did not happen in the 1870s (Blaug, 1978, p. 322).

This text denies that there was any unified and self-conscious movement. In its stead, it portrays a haphazard and fragmented agglomeration of economic theorists, whose only common denominators were the twin notions of diminishing marginal utility and utility-determined prices. Since neither notion was particularly novel in the 1870s, it follows from this portrayal that there was no discontinuity in the economic thought of the period, and that economic theory has embodied one continuous discipline from Adam Smith until the present (see Bowley, 1973, ch. 4).

The thesis that innovations in economic theory in the 1870s and 1880s were unexcep-

---

*Tufts University and University of Massachusetts, Amherst. I should like to acknowledge helpful discussions with Larry Samuelson, Lawrence Boland and Don Katzner on the topic of this paper. None should be implicated in any errors or flights of fancy.

tional and merely a continuation of the unbroken threads of economic discourse in the preceding half century meets a number of difficulties. The first problem is that not all the major protagonists would have agreed with such an assessment. One cannot read the letters and published works of Stanley Jevons, Léon Walras, Francis Edgeworth, Irving Fisher, Vilfredo Pareto and others without repeatedly encountering assertions that their work represented a fundamental break with the economics of their time. Much of their professional lives was spent promoting the works of this small self-identified côterie. The second impediment to the gradualist view is the fact that the most discontinuous aspect of the 'marginalist revolution' was not the postulate of a utilitarian theory of value, but rather something no historian of economic thought has ever discussed in detail: the successful penetration of mathematical discourse into economic theory. In both their correspondence and in their published work, the early neoclassical economists recognised each other as *mathematical theorists* first and foremost; and when they proselytised for their works, it took the form of defending the 'mathematical method' in the context of economic theory. The third impediment to the gradualist view is the fact that all the major protagonists were concerned to differentiate their handiwork from previous political economy on the explicit ground that it was of a scientific character. While the claim that one's theory is 'scientific' (and therefore deserves respect) echoes throughout the last three centuries of social theory, in the case of Jevons *et al*. this claim assumes a very specific and narrow form, shared by all the principals. An understanding of these three points will lead inexorably to a re-evaluation of the significance of the rise of neoclassical economic theory.

The gradualist view of the genesis of neoclassical theory has generally been prefaced with some methodological remarks on the contrast between 'internalist' and 'externalist' intellectual histories (Blaug, 1978; Black, Coats and Goodwin, 1973). The internalist version, the one presently favoured by neoclassicals, assumes that all ideas are merely reactions to previous developments internal to the discipline under consideration. The job of an intellectual historian is to trace the descent of ideas from scientist to scientist through time, revealing how error was rooted out by the internal criticism of logical deduction and empirical testing, while scientific truths were preserved and nurtured. New insights and concepts are pioneered by key individuals, but the sources of those insights are not an important part of the historian's narrative (Popper, 1965). The historian may use sociological and other external considerations to explain adherence to superseded theories; but adherence to the successful theory is felt to need no other explanation other than its *prima facie* success (Bloor, 1976).

This view is in contrast to externalist intellectual history, which seeks the determinants of successful theories in the political, philosophical and/or social currents of the time. The externalist historian is satisfied to identify the link between an historical interlude and the construction and acceptance of a successful theory, without expending undue effort to trace the intellectual pedigree of its precursors within the science. Undoubtedly, much of the hostility of neoclassical economists to externalist explanations of the 'marginalist revolution' stems from the weak and unconvincing nature of the few attempts: Bukharin (1927) associated it with the rise of a new class of *rentiers* in *fin-de-siècle* Europe, whereas Stark (1944) saw it as a reflection of some general Kantian influences in conjunction with the assertion that the economy of mid-nineteenth century Europe was actually characterised by atomistic competition. It has been observed repeatedly that these portrayals are not historically accurate; nor do they describe correctly the milieu of the major protagonists (Blaug, 1978; Kauder, 1965).

The internalist/externalist dichotomy has itself impeded the understanding of the rise of neoclassical economic theory. It forces the student of history to choose between a tautology and a disdain for theory, which has rendered the history trivial for all present purposes. Further, recent philosophers of science have severely undermined the distinction (Bloor, 1976; Kuhn, 1970). It is particularly necessary for social theorists to be aware of both the social and intellectual parameters of their own practices.

2. An alternative thesis

Our first thesis may be stated simply and directly: there was a readily identifiable discontinuity in economic thought in the 1870s and 1880s which was the genesis of neoclassical theory; and both its timing and intellectual content can be explained by parallel developments in physics in the mid-nineteenth century. The evidence is drawn from (i) the published works of the first neoclassicists; (ii) an example from the physics of the time which reveals the parallels; and (iii), biographical information about the principals.

All the major protagonists of the 'marginalist revolution' explicitly stated in their *published* works the sources of the inspiration for their novel economic theories. Jevons (1970, pp. 144–147) wrote that his equation of exchange does '... not differ in general character from those which are really treated in many branches of physical science'. He then proceeds to compare the equality of the ratios of marginal utility of two goods and their inverted trading ratio to the law of the lever, where in equilibrium the point masses at each end are inversely proportional to the ratio of their respective distances from the fulcrum. Note at this stage that Jevons' exposition does not adequately support his statements in the text: since he does not derive the equilibrium of the lever from considerations of potential and kinetic energy, he fails to justify the parallel between the expression for physical equilibrium and his use of differential equations in his own equations of exchange (see further, Section 5).

Far from being an isolated and insignificant metaphor, this invocation of the physical realm is always present in Jevons' writings on price theory. For example, in his defence of the mathematical method before the Manchester Statistical Society, he insists that

Utility only exists when there is on the one side the person wanting, and on the other the thing wanted... Just as the gravitating force of a material body depends not alone on the mass of that body, but upon the masses and relative positions and distances of the surrounding material bodies, so utility is an attraction between a wanting being and what is wanted (Jevons, 1981, VII, p. 80).

When one observes that more than half of Jevons' published work concerns the logic and philosophy of science, one begins to see that the metaphor of physical science was the unifying principle, and not merely a rhetorical flourish. In his major book, *The Principles of Science*, he suggests that the notion of the hierarchy of the sciences justifies '... a calculus of moral effects, a kind of physical astronomy investigating the mutual perturbations of individuals' (1905, pp. 759–760). The reduction of social processes to simple utilitarian considerations is compared to the reduction of meteorology to chemistry and thence to physics, implying that there is only one scientific methodology and one mode of explanation—that of physics—in all human experience.

Léon Walras was equally explicit concerning the motivation behind his published work. In his *Elements of Pure Economics* he claims that, 'the pure theory of economics is a science which resembles the physico-mathematical sciences in every respect' (1969,

p. 71). Walras explains in great detail his occupation with 'pure economics' in Lessons One to Four of the *Elements*. In his opinion, a pure science is only concerned with the relationships among things, the 'play of the blind and ineluctable forces of nature' which are independent of all human will. Walras insists that there exists a limited subset of economic phenomena which could be the objects of a pure scientific inquiry: they are the configurations of prices in a regime of 'perfect competition' (for further elaboration see Mirowski, 1981). Such 'pure' relationships justify and indeed, for Walras, *demand* the application of the *same* mathematical techniques as those deployed in mid-nineteenth century physics; other social phenomena tainted by the influence of human will would be relegated to studies employing non-scientific rhetorical techniques.

The proposed unity of technique in physics and economics is fully revealed in Walras's article of 1909, 'Économique et Mécanique' (reprinted in Walras, 1960). In this article he develops the two favourite metaphors of the early neoclassical economists, the rational mechanics of the equilibrium of the lever and the mathematical relations between celestial bodies; he also asserts that the 'physico-mathematical science' of his *Elements* uses *precisely* the identical mathematical formulae. He then proceeds to scold physicists who had expressed scepticism about the application of mathematics to utilitarian social theories on the ground that utility is not a measurable quantum; Walras retorts that the physicists themselves have been vague in their quantification of such basic terms as 'mass' and 'force'. The proposed connections between the terms of the sciences could not have been made more manifest: 'Aussi a-t-on déjà signalé celles des *forces* et des *raretés* comme *vecteurs*, d'une part, et celles des *énergies* et des *utilités* comme *quantités scalaires*, d'autre part' (Walras, 1960, p. 7).

Francis Ysidro Edgeworth was a third partisan of 'mathematical psychics' who was quite explicit about the wellsprings of the neoclassical movement. If only because of his extravagant and florid writing style, he is worth quoting directly:

The application of mathematics to the world of the soul is countenanced by the hypothesis (agreeable to the general hypothesis that every psychical phenomenon is the concomitant, and in some sense the other side of a physical phenomenon), the particular hypothesis adopted in these pages, that Pleasure is the concomitant of Energy. *Energy* may be regarded as the central idea of Mathematical Psychics; *maximum energy* the object of the principal investigations in that science... 'Mecanique Sociale' may one day take her place along with 'Mecanique Celeste', throned each upon the double-sided height of one maximum principle, the supreme pinnacle of moral as of physical science. As the movements of each particle, constrained or loose, in a material cosmos are continually subordinated to one maximum sub-total of accumulated energy, so the movements of each soul whether selfishly isolated or linked sympathetically, may continually be realising the maximum of pleasure... (Edgeworth, 1881, pp. 9, 12).

Vilfredo Pareto, a fourth confederate of the marginalist cadre, adopted a much more pugnacious but essentially identical position:

Strange disputes about predestination, about the efficacy of grace, etc, and in our day incoherent ramblings on solidarity show that men have not freed themselves from these daydreams which people have gotten rid of in the physical sciences, but which still burden the social sciences... Thanks to the use of mathematics, this entire theory, as we develop it in the Appendix, rests on no more than a fact of experience, that is, on the determination of the quantities of goods which constitute combinations between which the individual is indifferent. The theory of economic science thus acquires the rigor of rational mechanics... (Pareto, 1971B, pp. 36, 113).

In some ways, Pareto was the most ruthless proponent of the physical metaphor, and because of this, found himself the first of the neoclassicals to have to defend himself from attacks by mathematicians and physicists (Volterra, 1971, pp. 365-396).

Once one recognises these passages for the manifestos that they are, one sees that they are ubiquitous in the writings of early neoclassical economists. They can be found in Fisher (1892), Antonelli (1886), Laundhardt (1885) and Auspitz and Lieben (1889). In fact, the explicit appropriation of this specific physical metaphor is present in every major innovator of the marginalist revolution, with the single exception (discussed later) of the Austrian school of Carl Menger. The adoption of the 'energetics' metaphor and framework of mid-nineteenth century physics is the birthmark of neoclassical economics, the Ariadne's thread which ties the protagonists, and which can lead us to the fundamental meaning of the neoclassical research programme.

3. Physics and economics

Historians of economic thought, and many other economists as well, have long been aware that there are some close familial resemblances between physical concepts and neoclassical economic theory (see Sebba, 1953; Lowe, 1951; Knight, 1956; Weisskopf, 1979; Samuelson, 1972; Thoben, 1982). The reason why these observations have passed without notice is that the extent and significance of the linkage has not been chronicled from the viewpoint of physics. For example, it has become a cliché to refer to neoclassical economics as being 'Newtonian', perhaps bolstered by some offhand assertions that both are atomistic, both have resort to the language of frictions and equilibrium, and, depending upon the disposition of the commentator, perhaps inclusion of a pejorative comment that both are 'mechanistic'. Indeed, if those observations exhausted the sum total of the analogy, then it would merit no further serious consideration. However, recourse to the history of mathematics and physics shows that the characterisation of neoclassical economics as 'Newtonian' is both inept and misleading.

Historians of science are increasingly sceptical of the conventional wisdom that the history of physics consists of two discrete periods: one, stretching from the sequence Galileo-Descartes-Newton to roughly 1895, called Classical Physics; and the second, a twentieth century phenomenon based on quantum mechanics and relativity. To quote a recent textbook:

The term 'Newtonian' as applied to 18th and 19th century physics implicitly conflates Newton's natural philosophy and the physics of this later period, and is hence a misleading description. The developments in theoretical mechanics in the 18th century show a significant departure from the mechanical and mathematical assumptions of Newton's natural philosophy; and the physics of imponderable 'fluids', active substances and the anomalous forms of matter current in the 18th century contrasts with Newton's theory of nature... Despite the dominance of the program of mechanical explanation ... the term 'Newtonian' is misleading when applied to physics in the 19th century. The conceptual innovations of 19th century physics—energy conservation, the theory of the physical field, the theory of light as vibrations of an electromagnetic ether, and the concept of entropy—cannot be meaningfully be described as 'Newtonian' (Harman, 1982, pp. 10-11).

In point of fact, the word 'physics' was not generally used in English until the middle of the nineteenth century to refer to the united study of mechanics, light, heat, etc., both because of its Aristotelian connections (Cannon, 1978, p. 113, *et seq*.) and because there was no consensus on a unified theory of these phenomena until the rise of energetics in the middle of the century. Problems with Newtonian concepts in the nineteenth century with respect to light, heat and electricity led to the proliferation of types of postulated matter and their associated separate attractions and repulsions, which in turn led to contradictions inherent in the idea of more than one Newtonian force (Agassi, 1971; Harman, 1982). Energetics as a unifying principle was created by Helmholtz's famous 1847 paper 'On the Conservation of Force' (Kahl, 1971), drawing upon earlier study of the conceptualisation of *vis viva* (or 'living force') and the interconvertability of heat and mechanical work. This innovation induced substantial revision of many previous physical doctrines, and created the discipline of physics as the unified study of phenomena linked by energetic principles.

This watershed in physics altered not only the subject matter but the techniques of research and methodological prescriptions as well. It was linked to the mathematical supersession by French analytical methods and Leibniz's notation for the calculus of the English use of the Newtonian calculus of fluxions and the English fondness for geometrical argument (Bos, 1980). It was accompanied by changes in the acceptable standards of theory formation: these included an increasing refusal to specify the underlying nature of phenomena described mathematically; fewer concessions made to intuitive plausibility; increasing imperatives to measure quantitatively without being precise as to what it was that was being measured; and a predisposition to accept the 'usefulness' of a model as a form of proof (Heidelberger, in Jahnke and Otte, 1981; Harman, 1982).

Crucial in this revolution in thought concerning physical processes was the transformation of vague 'forces' into a Protean, unique, and yet ontologically undefined 'energy', which could only be discussed cogently through the intermediary of its mathematical eidolon. In this guise, energy did not characterise Newtonian particles, but rather processes. It shifted the description of motion itself away from vectors such as momentum and towards scalars encompassing the new 'energy'. Its divergence from Newtonian concepts became apparent when the conservation law was enunciated, because the conservation law provided the only means by which to identify an energetic system as in some sense the 'same' as it underwent various changes and transformations (Theobald, 1966; Meyerson, 1962).

Some familiarity with the history of physics, even one as sketchy as that provided above, is necessary for an understanding of the fact that neoclassical economics was not prompted by a Newtonian analogy. Classical economists made reference to the Newtonian analogy in non-essential contexts (see Blaug, 1980, pp. 57–58); but they could not reconcile the inverse square law, the calculus of fluxions and other Newtonian techniques with their overall conception of social processes. The rise of energetics in physical theory induced the invention of neoclassical economic theory, by providing the metaphor, the mathematical techniques, and the new attitudes toward theory construction. Neoclassical economic theory was appropriated wholesale from mid-nineteenth century physics; utility was redefined so as to be identical with energy.

An example may make this clearer for the modern reader.

Consider a point-mass displaced a distance $q(=AB)$ in a two-dimensional plane, as in Fig. 1, by a force vector $\mathbf{F}$. The force vector can be decomposed into its perpendicular components, $\mathbf{F} = \mathbf{i}F_x + \mathbf{j}F_y$ (where $\mathbf{i}, \mathbf{j}$ are the unit vectors along the appropriate axes). Similarly, the vector of displacement can also be decomposed into its components, $d\mathbf{q} = \mathbf{i}dx + \mathbf{j}dy$. The work done (i.e. the product of the force and distance moved along the path of its action) in the instance of this displacement is defined as the summation of the forces times the displacements, or:

Physics and the marginalist revolution

[Fig. 1: vector from A at origin to B in the upper right of an xy-plane]

Fig. 1

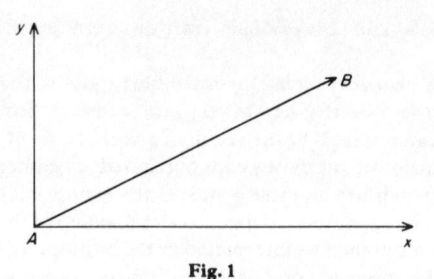

$$T = \int_A^B (F_x dx + F_y dy) = \tfrac{1}{2} m |\mathbf{v}|_B^2 - \tfrac{1}{2} m |\mathbf{v}|_A^2$$

Energetics redefined the change in mv^2 (i.e., the *vis viva* of the particle) to be the change in kinetic energy. The vector characterisation could then be translated into a single-valued scalar function, T. In the eighteenth century, there had been much controversy over whether the *vis viva* was conserved; this issue was clarified in energetics in the following manner. Suppose that the above expression in the parentheses were an exact differential; in other words, there existed a function U such that:

$$F_x = -\partial U/\partial x; \quad F_y = -\partial U/\partial y; \quad U = U(x,y).$$

This uniquely identified scalar function U was interpreted as the unobserved potential energy of the particle. Then it is the *total* energy of the particle, $T + U$, which is conserved through any motion of the particle. The postulate that total energy is conserved was significant, because it allows a rigorous specification of the 'principle of least action'. This principle, in its various forms, dated back to Maupertuis in the eighteenth century, who noted that the actual paths of motion traversed in many mechanical phenomena could be described mathematically as evincing the minimum of the particle's 'action'. William Hamilton in the 1830s pioneered 'the central conception of all modern theory in physics' (Schrödinger, quoted in Crowe, 1967, p. 17) by defining the action integral over time of the path of a particle as:

$$\int_{t_1,A}^{t_2,B} (T-U)\, dt.$$

The Hamiltonian principle of 'least action' asserts that the actual path of the particle from A to B will be the one which makes the action integral stationary. The path may be calculated by finding the constrained extrema, employing techniques of Lagrangean constrained maximisation/minimisation or, in more complicated cases, using directly the calculus of variations. In a conservative system, where $T + U = $ a constant, action is a function of position only, which implies that all motion is fully reversible, and exhibits no hysteresis (Kline, 1972, ch. 30).

To summarise: in the 1820s theoretical treatises in mechanics began to stress the work integral and its mathematical relationship to *vis viva* (Harman, 1982, p. 36). In the 1830s, Hamilton linked this framework to the mathematics of constrained extrema (Hankins, 1980). Starting in the 1840s, the interconvertability of mechanical energy and other energetic phenomena was postulated; by the 1860s, the mathematics of unobservable potentials and constrained extrema were extended to all physical phenomena.

Walras insisted that his *rareté* equations resembled those of the physical sciences in every respect. We may see now that he was very nearly correct. Simply redefine the variables of the earlier equations: let **F** be the vector of prices of a set of traded goods, and let q be the vector of the quantities of those goods purchased. The integral $\int \mathbf{F}.dq = T$ is then defined as the total expenditure on these goods. If the expression to be integrated is an exact differential, then it is possible to define a scalar function of the goods x and y of the form $U = U(x,y)$, which can then be interpreted as the 'utilities' of those goods. In exact parallel to the original concept of potential energy, these utilities are unobservable, and can only be inferred from theoretical linkage to other observable variables. Relative prices are equal to the ratios of the marginal utilities of the goods by construction: the 'potential field' of utility is defined as the locus of the set of constrained extrema, although the early marginalists reversed this logic in their expositions of the principle. Instead of treating utility as a derived phenomenon, they postulated the utility field as the fundamental exogenous data to which market transactions adjusted. The mathematics, however, are the same in both instances.

There *is* one major difference, however, between the mathematics of energetics and its transplanted version in neoclassical economics. The conservation principle in energetics does not translate directly into neoclassical theory: the sum of income and utility is not conserved, and is meaningless in the context of economic theory. Does this mean that neoclassical economics has managed to dispense with the artifice of a conservation principle? This may appear to be the case, because neither the progenitors of neoclassicism nor any of its modern adherents have ever seriously discussed this aspect of the physical metaphor (see Mirowski, 1984C). Yet to cast any problem in a constrained maximisation framework, the analyst *must* assume some sort of conservation principle. In physics, it is widely understood that the conservation principle is the means by which the system being considered retains its analytical identity.

In other words, the adoption of the energetics metaphor in economics has imposed an analytical regimen, the rigours of which have hitherto gone unnoticed. Neoclassical theorists, from the 1870s onwards, have surreptitiously assumed some form of conservation principle in their economic models. In the period of our present concern, the principle took two forms: (a) the income or endowment to be traded is given exogenously and, further, is assumed to be fully spent or traded; thus, for practical purposes, T is conserved; and/or (b) the transactors' estimation of the utility of the various goods is a datum not altered by the sequence of purchase, nor any other aspect of the trading or consuming process (or, as Marshall sheepishly admitted, desire was equated with satisfaction *by assumption*); so in effect the utility field U is conserved (see Mirowski, 1984C). In this case, the analogy between physics and economics would be as if physical theory had managed to preserve what has proved to be an anachronistic element: as if Hamilton had somehow managed to preserve the conservation of *vis viva* (kinetic energy) within the new mathematics of energetic extrema.

Once the parallels between mid-nineteenth century physics and neoclassical economic theory are outlined, and it is acknowledged that the progenitors themselves openly admitted them in their published writings, most would accept the thesis that the 'marginalist revolution' should be renamed the 'marginalist annexation'. Should doubts linger, however, the thesis should be clinched by an examination of the biographical particulars of the protagonists.

Physics and the marginalist revolution

The most obvious and straightforward case is that of the most respected of neoclassical progenitors, Léon Walras. In his first effort to mathematicise his father's concept of *rareté*, Walras attempted to implement a Newtonian model of market relations, postulating that 'the price of things is in inverse ratio to the quantity offered and in direct ratio to the quantity demanded' (Walras, 1965, I, pp. 216–217). Dissatisfied with this model, Walras tinkered with various formulations, but none involved the constrained maximisation of utility until the late autumn of 1872. At that time, a professor of mechanics at the Academy of Lausanne, Antoine Paul Piccard, wrote a memo to Walras sketching the mathematics of the optimisation of an unobserved *'quantité de besoin'* (Walras, 1965, I, pp. 308–311) along the lines outlined above. Although Walras trained originally as an engineer at the École des Mines, he did not possess a deep understanding of the new energetics: this can be opbserved in his reactions to the letters of Charles Émile Picard (Walras, 1965, III, pp. 417–420) correcting his errors of interpretation and mathematical representation. While these letters did prompt him to write 'Économique et Mécanique', they did not prompt him to revise his *Elements* significantly. This suggests that Walras did not comprehend the real thrust of these letters, which question the appropriateness of various aspects of the physical metaphor. It was left for his successors Antonelli and Pareto to explore some of the *social* implications of the mathematics of energetics.

It is significant that all the earliest members of the Lausanne school were trained as engineers. Giovanni Antonelli was an Italian civil engineer whose monograph *On the Mathematical Theory of Political Economy* explicitly discusses utility theory in the manner described above (pp. 366–368) (Antonelli, 1886). He is now considered a pioneer in the problem of integrability, which here we interpret as an acknowledgement and extrapolation of the implications of conservation principles. The significance of this problem did not receive widespread attention until well into the twentieth century (Samuelson, 1950). Vilfredo Pareto was also trained as an engineer, and this expertise enabled him to explore the implications of the path-independence of the realisation of utility, a direct extrapolation of the path-independence of equilibrium energy states in rational mechanics and thermodynamics (Pareto, 1971A). This work was consigned to oblivion partly because Pareto and Antonelli gave up economic theory in later life, and partly because no one outside a very limited circle of engineers who had a working knowledge of the new economic theory could read it. The English-speaking world had to wait until the 1930s when an influx of physicists—and engineers—manqués into economics led to the revival of their work.

The biographical evidence in the case of Jevons is not as direct, but is substantial. Prompted by his father to become an engineer, Jevons studied chemistry and mathematics in London. He attended some of Michael Faraday's renowned public lectures at the Royal Institution, at which Faraday claimed that magnetic forces did not obey the Newtonian force rule (Jevons, 1972, I, p. 82). This is significant because in the land of Newton in the 1850s Faraday was one of the very few partisans of field theories and energetics: indeed, Jevons' letters make clear his enormous respect for Faraday. We also have evidence that Jevons was familiar with the writings of Thomson and Joule on the interconvertability of heat and mechanical work, writings which led to the enunciation of the theory of the conservation of energy (Jevons, 1972, II, p. 66). Later in his life Jevons remained conversant with the field of energetics, and even wrote to James Clerk Maxwell arguing a point of controversy in Fourier's theory of heat (Jevons, 1972, IV, pp. 207–208).

If there was a difference between Jevons and Walras, it was this: Walras did not evince

370   P. Mirowski

any deep understanding of mid-nineteenth century physics, and applied the mathematical techniques and the metaphor in a mechanical and unimaginative manner, leaving it for others to draw out the logical and connotative implications of the physical metaphor. Jevons, on the other hand, was even less of a mathematician than Walras, but did dedicate his life's work to drawing out the meaning of the metaphor of energetics for the sphere of the economy. This point is not readily apparent, because Jevons' work is rarely considered as a whole. His major achievements were the *Theory of Political Economy*, *The Coal Question*, his work on sunspots and the business cycle, and *The Principles of Science*. The connection between the four can best be summarised in Jevons' own words, from his paper 'The Solar Influence on Commerce' (Jevons, 1972, VII, p. 97): 'Long ago George Stevenson acutely anticipated the results of subsequent scientific inquiry when he said that coal was sunshine bottled up; now it is among the mere commonplaces of science that all motions and energies of life ... are directly or indirectly derived from the sun.' The maximisation of utility, the prediction that England was rapidly exhausting energy stocks in the form of coal, and the lifelong theme that economic crises must be caused by energy fluctuations exogenous to the social operation of the economy, are all direct extrapolations from the energetic movement of the mid-nineteenth century (Mirowski, 1984A). The last point gains credibility when one notes that Jevons recorded in his journal that Faraday explicitly discussed the periodicity of sunspots in his lectures of 1853 (Jevons, 1972, I, p. 82). As for the *Principles of Science*, it can be read as a plea for the unity of methodology in all sciences, in the face of the serious upheavals and discontinuities which erupted both in subject matter and in research methods in mid-nineteenth century physics. The fact that his own conception of scientific endeavor was highly coloured by the rise of energetics can be observed in the *Principle's* definition of science: 'Science is the detection of identity, and classification is the placing together, either in thought or in the proximity of space, those objects between which identity has been detected' (Jevons, 1905, pp. 673–674).

4. The Austrians were not neoclassicals

Those familiar with conventional histories of neoclassical economic theory must, by this point, be impatient to object: what about Menger and the Austrians? Do they fit the thesis which links the rise of neoclassical theory to the rise of energetics in physics?

Although it has become conventional wisdom to cite the triumvirate of the marginal revolution as Jevons, Walras and Menger, these three actors themselves did not accept this regimentation. Jevons did not mention Menger once in all his writings: a curious reticence in one so determined in later life to uncover all predecessors and fellow revolutionaries. Walras did correspond with Menger, but only to discover to his amazement that Menger did not recognise his contribution on account of its mathematical nature. This was sufficient for Walras to deny Menger's role in the revolution, writing in a letter to Bortkiewicz in 1887 that Menger's and Bohm-Bawerk's efforts to describe the theory of 'Grenznuten' in 'ordinary language' was unsuccessful, and even painful (Walras, 1965, II, p. 232). Walras viewed Menger's 1871 *Principles* as merely an attempt at *translation* of marginalist ideas into ordinary language, and a failed one at that: there was nothing novel or original there; he thus denied Menger any status as an equal. (Interestingly enough, this opinion seems to be shared by many modern neoclassical economists. In this regard, see Samuelson, 1952, p. 61.) Menger did not conform to

Walras's main criteria for a neoclassical theorist: he was not mathematical, he did not adhere to the norms of physical science, and therefore he was not 'scientific'.

In contrast, historians of economic thought are persistently perplexed by Menger's recalcitrance at being elevated to membership in the triumvirate. Howey, the most careful of these writers, notes:

> ...although Menger talked about the Austrian school, no one would gather from his words in any of his publications after 1871 down to his death that the Austrian School had the slightest connection with the Marginal Utility School. He either did not admit the connection, or wished to minimise it, or took it for granted. Menger never publicly admitted any kinship with Walras or with Jevons (Howey, 1960, p. 142).

There is much more here than petty squabbles over precedence or methodology, or personality clashes, or nationalistic insularity. There is the possibility that the Austrians, or at the very least Menger, were not part of the fledgling movement of neoclassical economic theory. This possibility has already been suggested by some Austrian economists, notably by Erich Streissler in a centenary collection of essays on the marginalist revolution (Black, Coats and Goodwin, 1973, pp. 160–175). Streissler points out that Menger's scales of successive marginal satisfaction, introduced in the middle of his *Grundsätze* (Menger, 1981, p. 127), were not at all central to his conception of economic theory. This contention is indirectly supported by Kauder (1965, p. 76), who reports that Menger crossed out this table in his author's copy of the book. Howey (1960, p. 40) notes that Menger's 'importance of satisfactions' cannot easily be translated into the language of utility because it did not vary in *quantity*. 'Satisfaction' never varied, but its subjective importance could be altered in a regular manner. Streissler maintains that Menger's major concerns—uncertainty, changes in the quality of goods, the absence of a notion of equilibrium, and hostility to the 'law of one price'—were motivated so fundamentally by his radical subjectivism that he could not be considered as promoting the same theory as Jevons and Walras. From our present perspective, we can find support for Streissler's thesis by examining Menger's relationship to physical theory.

After a personal visit, Bortkiewicz wrote to Walras that Menger did not have the least idea of mathematical analysis (Walras, 1965, II, p. 519). Perusal of his major works indicates that he was also unfamiliar with the physics of his time. Yet despite these inadequacies, Menger launched a scathing attack upon the German historicist school in his *Untersuchungen über die Methode*, mainly consisting of the contention that his opponents did not understand the nature of 'exact science' (Menger, 1963). In sharp contrast with Jevons' *Principles of Science,* Menger's weak and unconvincing claims that he was promoting the methods of 'exact research of a Newton, Lavoisier or Helmholtz' reveal an ignorance hastily camouflaged by bombast. He attempted to extend his radical subjectivism to physics without giving a single example from the physical sciences. He denigrated empiricism without being specific about the practices to which he objected. His conception of science was severely Aristotelian and he never addressed the fact that the scientists of his day had rejected this. He rather appropriated their names for credibility.

Menger cannot be considered a neoclassical economist because he rejected two basic pillars of that theory: the law of one price, which states that all generic goods in a market (however defined) must trade at the same price in equilibrium (see Dennis, 1982); and the concept that traded goods in some sense are related as equivalents in equilibrium (Menger, 1981, pp. 191–194). Absence of the first subverts any deterministic notion of equilibrium. Absence of the second explains Menger's hostility towards quantification. Absence of both effectively prevented the introduction of the physics analogy into economic theory. The mere postulation of a diminishing marginal utility is not sufficient to generate a neoclassical theory of price. In this respect Menger is no different from Dupuit (1952), who also recognised diminishing marginal utility, but also repudiated a single equilibrium price. Were it not for three historical accidents—first, the *Grundsätze* was first published in 1871; second, Menger's illustrious student Wieser promoted his claim to be a founder of neoclassical theory (and himself *did* adopt the new marginalist techniques from Laundhardt and Auspitz and Lieben); and third, Menger's works were largely unavailable outside the German-speaking world—Menger would not today be considered as one of the marginalist revolutionaries.

There has been much disagreement as to what constitutes the 'hard core' of neoclassical economic theory: the fundamental basis of the research programme which, if altered, would signal the substantive development of a non-neoclassical economic theory (Latsis, 1976; Boland, 1982). The core is not simply methodological individualism, nor is it utilitarianism, because both were active research strategies in social theory well before the rise of neoclassical theory, and because the Austrian and certain sociological research programmes also hold them as tenets. It is the second thesis of this paper that the hard core of neoclassical economic theory is the adoption of mid-nineteenth century physics as a rigid paradigm, a hard core it has preserved and nourished throughout the twentieth century, even after physics has moved onwards to new metaphors and new techniques. This thesis explains a number of issues which have eluded other attempts at locating the hard core of neoclassical theory.

First, it explains why neoclassical theory and mathematical formalism have been indissolubly wedded since the 1870s, even though a cogent defence of the necessity of the link has been notable by its absence. Second, it explains the success of neoclassicism in pre-empting other research programmes in economics by means of the forceful claim that it is scientific, even though standards of scientific discourse in the larger culture have changed periodically during the last hundred years. Third, it explains the preference for techniques of constrained maximisation over any other analytical techniques, which include input–output matrices, game theory, Markov chains, and a myriad of other techniques proposed over the last century (Samuelson, 1972). Fourth, it explains the persistent use of an unobservable and unmeasurable value determinant—utility—in textbooks and in applied research, despite protestations that utility is not 'needed' for neoclassical results (Wong, 1978). Fifth, it explains the modern controversy over the necessity for a 'microfoundation for macroeconomics', which can be interpreted as a complaint that Keynesian economics has not conformed to the hard core research strategy, and is therefore somehow illegitimate (Weintraub, 1979; Lucas, 1981). Sixth, it explains why neoclassicism links certain economic variables to particular exogenous variables, which are themselves 'naturally' determined and therefore analytically immutable and outside of the scope of economic theory. All these characteristics are borrowed from nineteenth century energetics.

5. Physical metaphors, organic metaphors and the role of Marshall

It is not unusual for a science to adopt the metaphors and/or analytical techniques of another discipline. The story of Darwin's appropriation of the concept of population pressure on resources from Malthus's *Essay on Population* is but one example of a pervasive phenomenon. Indeed, some historians of science attempt to explain the rise of energetics by the influence of German *Naturphilosophie* in mid-nineteenth century culture (Kuhn, 1977). What is unusual and noteworthy about the rise to preeminence of neoclassical economic theory is the lack of consciousness, and therefore the concomitant lack of any assessment or critique, of the sources of its analytical and technical inspiration. Newtonian action-at-a-distance came under severe scrutiny and criticism from philosophical perspectives in the eighteenth and nineteenth centuries. Darwinian natural selection has repeatedly been reconsidered at the level of the fundamental organising metaphor. The list could be extended indefinitely: many of the basic organising principles of physics have undergone criticism and revision over the past two hundred years. All these episodes reveal a willingness to reconsider theory at the level of the 'hard core', as opposed to revision of the 'protective belt'. In effect, the strength of physics lies in its openness to fundamental revision, and not, as the naïve conception has it, in its unwavering preservation of eternal verities.

Neoclassical economists, on the other hand, have often appealed to the dignity of the scientific endeavour, without understanding what it entails, or why they felt justified in claiming privileged scientific status for their paradigm. Until Georgescu-Roegen (1971), the extent of the dependence of modern neoclassical theory upon the physical metaphor had not even been surveyed seriously. What is still missing is a preliminary balance sheet of the gains and losses from adherence to this research strategy.

For early neoclassical theory, one can compile a condensed set of accounts. On the credit side, the main object of the early marginalists has been achieved: the abolition of the *anomie* and the lack of systematic theory of mid-nineteenth century political economy, and the creation in its place of a shared research programme with shared goals, as well as a well-defined set of research techniques. Attention moved away from broad and ill-defined growth and development issues to a much narrower set of concerns tethered to the notion of short-period equilibrium price (Garegnani, 1976). Systematic empiricism was encouraged by a shift in focus to certain easily quantifiable variables. The discipline of economics was divided up into a set of subfields, both theoretical and applied, which could provide researchers with a clearly defined expertise and thus identity. This played an important part in the growing professionalisation of economics in the later nineteenth century, guaranteeing it a secure place in the academic environment (Checkland, 1951). In other words, the appropriation of the physical metaphor effectively appropriated credibility for economics as a respected science.

The debit side of the account is more subtle, and so more contentious. Perhaps the major debit entry is the fact that the early neoclassicals themselves did not adequately understand the physical metaphor and the constraints which it imposed upon social theory. For example, Jevons did not explicitly derive the equilibrium of the lever from energetics principles in his *Theory of Political Economy*, thus leaving him open to ridicule by Marshall, who jeeringly suggested in a book review that he try to integrate his equation of exchange (Jevons, 1981, VII, p. 145). With the single exception of Marshall, all the early neoclassicals used the energetics metaphor; no other economists understood enough physics to discuss its implications and flaws.

Yet consider a short impressionistic list of these flaws. First, all energetics before the second law of thermodynamics (the entropy law) presumed that all phenomena were perfectly reversible, and thus equilibrium could not be time-dependent. In pre-entropy physics, history does not matter. The conservation principle is crucial in this respect, because it defines identity through time. When this metaphor is imported into the social sphere, it implies that in equilibrium byegones are byegones; thus one could practically ignore how a market actually functions in real time, paying attention only to putative 'eventual' outcomes. Hicks (1979) and Shackle (1967) are the latest in a long line of illustrious figures to complain about this issue; but their complaints have not made any substantive headway because they have not seen how deeply rooted this principle is in neoclassical techniques. Second, something must be conserved in order to apply the techniques of constrained extrema, the 'maximum principle'. When the physical metaphor is imported into the social sphere, neoclassicists were not at all precise about what the conserved entity was, and they have not yet been able to settle this issue (Mirowski, 1984C). If utility is conserved, then surprise and regret as psychological phenomena have analytically been ruled out of court. If income or endowments are conserved, then Say's Law is implicitly invoked, and there is no theory of output other than a psychological notion of 'virtual' production (Clower, 1970). Third, in energetics, all physical phenomena are fully and reversibly transformable into any other phenomena. When this idea is transported into the context of the economy, then all goods become fully and reversibly transformable into all other goods through trades. There is no requirement for a specific money commodity or set of financial institutions, because they would be redundant. The analogue of energetics is the barter economy. Fourth, equilibrium is identified with extremum principles in physics because they provide a concise method of summarising the actual path of particles in empirical experience. When the metaphor is imported into economics, the use of extremum principles is claimed to 'prove' the superior efficacy of a particular kind of economic organisation. Physics long ago renounced this teleological interpretation; economics has come to embrace it.

If contemporaries had understood what kind of economy the energetics metaphor described, then neoclassicism would have met substantial logical opposition. We may infer this from the fact that when the physics metaphor was explicitly introduced into the social sphere in other contexts, it met with strenuous opposition (Sorokin, 1956, ch. 1). But this is where economics is the anomaly in the history of social theory: because the 'inventors' did not understand energetics or the social metaphor with any great depth or subtlety, they rarely discussed the merits or demerits of the application of physical techniques and metaphors to social theory. No other economists understood enough physics to see its implications; nor were they induced to study physics by any of the writings of the early marginalists. Effectively, neoclassical economic theory was a *fait accompli* whose origins and fundamental bases were buried by historical accident, to the extent that the sources of inspiration of Jevons, Walras, Pareto, *et al*. could appear as a puzzle to their posterity.

It should not appear from my summary that the entire economics profession were sleepwalkers, stumbling unwittingly into a maze of energetics. Alfred Marshall, for one, certainly discussed some aspects of the adoption of physical metaphors (Marshall, 1898); and he clearly had some reservations. However, the case of Marshall is actually illuminated by an understanding of energetics.

Marshall's place in the history of economic thought has always been a curious one. He hinted, both privately and in print, that many of Jevons' ideas had been 'familiar truths' to him when they were published, thus intimating that somehow he also deserved 'discoverer' status. Since much of what appears in introductory and intermediate microeconomics texts as the theory of supply and demand is, in fact, the handiwork of Marshall, there is a grain of truth in his claim. However, once the actual sequence of events is uncovered, it appears that Marshall's major service in the marginalist revolution was as a populariser; and, like other populariers, he altered the material which he promoted.

Recent study of Marshall's early unpublished writings, especially by Bharadwaj (1978), reveals that his early work was on the equilibrium of a supply curve with a phenomenological demand curve: he did not much care what lay behind his demand schedule. Implicitly, movements along the demand curve came from variations in the number of buyers, rather than a posited constrained maximisation by an individual buyer. 'The word "utility" itself was used only once in relation to Adam Smith, and not approvingly' (Bharadwaj, 1978, p. 367).

The saga of the journey between Marshall's early *Essay* and his *Principles* is the story of a decision to incorporate the innovations of the marginalist revolutionaries in order to shore up the foundations of the demand blade of the 'scissors', while preserving his original concerns with the underlying theories of the supply schedule. Unhappily, the superficial parallels between diminishing returns and diminishing marginal utility could not obscure the fact that the result was more like paper and stone rather than scissors. For example, much of Marshall's typology of markets involved altering of the timeframe of analysis and deriving its resulting effects upon the supply schedule. This method produced some embarrassment when applied to the demand side, either because the underlying demand determinants remained constant over time, revealing that the fundamental cause of price was an exogenous posited psychology, as Jevons had maintained, or because the demand curve would also be shifted in relatively arbitrary ways, undermining any claim that an equilibrium of demand and supply had been identified. Perhaps it was predictable that the attack would be pressed against the part of the system which Marshall originated (Sraffa, 1926), and that the ensuing retreat would vindicate Jevon's position.

Marshall sensed that his concerns could be overwhelmed by the zeal of his marginalist allies, and this partly explains why he does not conform in style to the characteristics of the marginalist cadre identified above. His defence of Ricardo *vis-à-vis* Jevons; his softpedalling of the mathematical method; his insistence on the basic continuity of economics from Adam Smith to his time; his persistent praise of organic metaphors: all these activities are attempts to incorporate energetics into economics while controlling or perhaps altering some of its more objectionable aspects. Many wave as a banner Marshall's claim that, 'The Mecca of the economist lies in economic biology', but few bother to quote the next sentence: 'But biological conceptions are more complex than those of mechanics; a volume on Foundations must therefore give a relatively large place to mechanical analogies . . .' (Marshall, 1920, p. xiv). However much he might protest, the fact remains that Marshall did render the energetics metaphor palatable for an English audience which would probably have resisted the brash revolution of a Jevons. Further, he fostered the illusion that 'The new doctrines have supplanted the older . . . but very seldom have subverted them' (Marshall, 1920, p. v).

It is important to appreciate that Marshall thought that the physical interpretation could be separated from the mathematical technique, and that his reservations lay in the interpretation rather than the technique. Those who happily quote Marshall's dictum to 'burn the mathematics' should read carefully the preface to the eighth edition of the *Principles*:

The new analysis is endeavouring gradually and tentatively to bring over into economics, as far as the widely different nature of the material will allow, those methods of the science of small increments (commonly called the differential calculus) to which man owes directly or indirectly the greater part of the control that he has obtained in recent times over physical nature. It is still in its infancy; it has no dogmas, and no standard of orthodoxy ... there is a remarkable harmony and agreement on essentials among those who are working constructively by the new method; and especially among such of them as have served an apprenticeship in the simpler and more definite, and therefore more advanced, problems of physics (Marshall, 1920, pp. xvi–xvii).

But of course there was dogma and a standard of orthodoxy: that was why agreement had been achieved relatively quickly by the mathematical workers; the standards and ideas had been appropriated during their apprenticeship in physics. The *Principles* is a book that touts the mathematical method while attempting to deny that the method could influence the content of what was being expressed. The clearest manifestation of this tension occurs in the Appendix to the *Principles*, where, in the midst of a series of abstruse notes concerning the application of constrained maximisation to utility, there is an incongruous discussion of the applications of Taylor's Theorem to the webbing between a duck's appendages (Marshall, 1920, pp. 841–842). The purpose of the digression is to suggest that the calculus was being borrowed from an organic evolutionary metaphor. Not only did Taylor's Theorem have nothing to do with the duck's webbing in Marshall's actual example; but the calculus of constrained maximisation was not employed by evolutionary theorists in Marshall's day.

6. The history of economic thought as an active generator of research programmes

The energetics metaphor can be found in every major neoclassical theorist of the nineteenth century and can be used to explain some controversies in the history of economic thought. It is a very neat pattern; perhaps too neat. Is it being too wise after the event in defining neoclassicism tautologically as coextensive with the introduction of the physics metaphor into social theory, and then brushing other authors aside? I do not think so. This article merely points out what has been there for all to see in published writings, biographies, and the history of science.

This paper has *not* specified why the energetics metaphor was so attractive to nineteenth century economic theorists, or discussed why the economics tail still is or is not wagged by the physics dog. Such omissions are due in part to prosaic reasons of space limitation, but also to the fact that such a discussion requires a much larger original content and a grounding in the philosophies of science and theory choice. The philosophy of science is so important because it indicates where to begin searching for acceptable explanations of the adoption of the physics metaphor. Should we look to the level of personal motivation or structural tendencies? Should we look to empirical inadequacies or logical flaws, or some less rigid intellectual influences? These questions give rise to a research project, which could be carried out at many different levels: the level of individual desires (e.g., Jevons' personal motivations (Mirowski, 1984A), that of individual influences (e.g. Edgeworth's family were friends of Hamilton), that of class interests, that of the sociology of professions (here the location of economists in universities), that of the cannons of empiricism (the rise of quantification as a preferred empirical technique), that of the status of alternative competing research programmes (say, the dilution of the Ricardian programme by Mill and the retreat of the labour theory of value), and that of metaphysical predispositions in the larger culture [e.g., the western tendency to see social relations as rooted in 'natural' processes (Levine, 1977)].

Physics and the marginalist revolution

Another reason why modern philosophy of science is important is that it has highlighted the significance of the history of science. Discussion of the above issue can be cogently prosecuted only in conjunction with the study of the actual (as opposed to mythical) history of mathematics, physics, etc. Only then would we be able to extend the inquiries into the twentieth century with questions like: what is the relation between the penetration of input–output methods into economics and the preceding rise of matrix methods in quantum mechanics? What is the link between Niels Bohr's 'Correspondence Principle' and that of Paul Samuelson? Another question of interest concerns the relation of mathematical technique to model content. Did mathematical economic theorists before 1870 'fail' because they were inept, or for other more profound reasons (Mirowski, 1984B)?

Finally, we can clarify the issues broached at the outset. The antiquarian question has been settled: neoclassical economic theory is bowdlerised nineteenth century physics. The epistemological issue has been illuminated: present research techniques may be favoured *because* they were appropriated from physics. The ontological issue has been reinterpreted: neoclassicism was not 'simultaneously discovered' because it was 'true', as Jevons and others would have it; instead, the timing of its genesis is explained by the timing of the energetics revolution in physics, and by the fact that scientifically trained individuals in different Western European countries at that time had access to the same body of knowledge and techniques. The practical issue, however, has scarcely been addressed. One cannot predict where new theories will come from, but one can venture a broad inductive generalisation from past patterns: that a substantial non-neoclassical economic theory will distinguish itself by consciously repudiating the energetics metaphor.

Bibliography

Agassi, J. 1971. *Faraday as a Natural Philosopher*, Chicago, University of Chicago Press
Agassi, J. 1981. *Science and Society*, Boston, Reidel
Antonelli, G. B. 1886. *Sulla theoria mathematica della economia politica*, trans. in Chipman, J., Hurwicz, L., Richter, M. and Sonnenschein, H. (eds) 1971, *Preferences, Utility and Demand*, New York, Harcourt Brace Jovanovich
Auspitz, R. and Lieben, R. 1889. *Untersuchungen über die Theorie des Preises*, Leipzig, Duncker and Humblot
Bharadwaj, K. 1978. The subversion of classical analysis: Alfred Marshall's early writing on value, *Cambridge Journal of Economics*, vol. 2, no. 3, September
Black, R., Coats, A. and Goodwin, C. (eds) 1973. *The Marginal Revolution in Economics*, Durham, N.C., Duke University Press
Blaug, M. 1978. *Economic Theory in Retrospect*, 3rd edn, Cambridge, CUP
Blaug, M. 1980. *The Methodology of Economics*, Cambridge, CUP
Bloor, D. 1976. *Knowledge and Social Imagery*, Boston, Routledge and Kegan Paul
Boland, L. 1982. *The Foundations of Economic Method*, Boston, Allen and Unwin
Bos, H. 1980. Mathematics and rational mechanics, in Rousseau, G. and Porter, R. (eds), *The Ferment of Knowledge*, Cambridge, CUP
Bowley, M. 1973. *Studies in the History of Economic Thought Before 1870*, London, Macmillan
Brannigan, A. 1981. *The Social Basis of Scientific Discoveries*, Cambridge, CUP
Bukharin, N. 1927. *Economic Theory of the Leisure Class*, New York, International
Cannon, S. 1978. *Science in Culture*, New York, Dawson
Checkland, S. 1951. The advent of academic economics in England, *Manchester School*, January
Clower, R. 1970. The Keynesian counterrevolution, in Clower, R. (ed.), *Monetary Theory*, Baltimore, Penguin

378 P. Mirowski

Crowe, M. 1967. *A History of Vector Analysis*, Notre Dame University Press
Dennis, K. 1982. Economic theory and mathematical translation, *Journal of Economic Issues*, September
Dupuit, J. 1952. On the measurement of utility of public works, Barbach (trans.), *International Economic Papers*, no. 2
Edgeworth, F. Y. 1881. *Mathematical Psychics*, London, Kegan Paul
Farmer, M. 1983. Some thoughts on the past, present and future of the rational actor in economics, paper presented to History of Thought Conference, University of Manchester, September
Fisher, I. 1892. *Mathematical Investigations into the Theory of Value and Prices*, Transactions of the Connecticut Academy, vol. 9
Garegnani, P. 1976. On a change in the Notion of Equilibrium, in Brown, M. *et al*. (eds), *Essays in Modern Capital Theory*, Amsterdam, North Holland
Georgescu-Roegen, N. 1971. *The Entropy Law and the Economic Process*, Harvard University Press
Hankins, T. 1980. *Sir William Rowan Hamilton*, Baltimore, Johns Hopkins University Press
Harding, S. (ed.) 1976. *Can Theories be Refuted?* Boston, Reidel
Harman, P. M. 1982. *Energy, Force and Matter*, Cambridge, CUP
Hicks, J. R. 1979. *Causality in Economics*, New York, Basic Books
Howey, R. S. 1960. *The Rise of the Marginal Utility School*, Lawrence, University of Kansas Press
Jahnke, H. and Otte, M. (eds) 1981, *Epistemological and Social Problems of the Sciences in the Early 19th Century*, Boston, Reidel
Jevons, W. S. 1905. *The Principles of Science*, 2nd edn, London, Macmillan
Jevons, W. S. 1970. *The Theory of Political Economy*, Black, R. (ed.) Baltimore, Penguin
Jevons, W. S. 1972–81. *The Papers and Correspondence of W. S. Jevons*, 7 vols, Black, R. (ed.), London, Macmillan
Kahl, R. (ed.) 1971. *Selected Writings of Hermann von Helmholtz*, Middletown, Connecticut, Wesleyan University Press
Kauder, E. 1965. *A History of Marginal Utility Theory*, Princeton University Press
Kline, M. 1972. *Mathematical Thought from Ancient to Modern Times*, Oxford, OUP
Knight, F. 1956. Statics and dynamics, in *On the History and Methodology of Economics*, University of Chicago Press
Knorr-Cetina, K. and Mulkay, M. 1983. *Science Observed: Perspectives on the Social Study of Science*, London, Sage
Kuhn, T. 1977. *The Essential Tension*, University of Chicago Press
Latsis, S. 1976. *Method and Appraisal in Economics*, Cambridge, CUP
Laundhardt, W. 1885. *Mathematische Begrundung der Volkswirtschaftslehre*, Leipzig, Engelmann
Levine, D. 1977. *Economic Studies: Contribution to the Critique of Economic Theory*, Boston, Routledge and Kegan Paul
Lisman, J. H. C. 1949. Economics and thermodynamics, *Econometrica*, January
Lowe, A. 1951. On the mechanistic approach in economics, *Social Research*, vol. 18
Lucas, R. 1981. *Essays in Business Cycle Theory*, London, MIT Press
Marshall, A. 1898, Mechanical and biological analogies in economics, reprinted in Pigou, A. C. (ed.), *Memorials of Alfred Marshall*, London, Macmillan
Marshall, A. 1920. *Principles of Economics*, 8th edn, London, Macmillan
McCloskey, D. 1983. The rhetoric of economics, *Journal of Economic Literature*
Menard, C. 1980. Three forms of resistance to statistics: Say, Cournot, Walras, *History of Political Economy*, Winter
Menger, C. 1963. *Problems of Economics and Sociology*, Nock, (trans.), Urbana, University Illinois Press
Menger, C. 1981. *Principles of Economics*, Dingwell and Hoselitz (trans.), New York University Press
Meyerson, E. 1962. *Identity and Reality*, New York, Dover
Mirowski, P. 1981. Is there a mathematical neoinstitutional economics?, *Journal of Economic Issues*, September
Mirowski, P. 1983. Review of Nelson and Winter's evolutionary theory of economic change, *Journal of Economic Issues*, September
Mirowski, P. 1984A. Macroeconomic fluctuations and 'natural' processes in early neoclassical economics, *Journal of Economic History*, June

Physics and the marginalist revolution 379

Mirowski, P. 1984B. Whewell, Cournot, and the abortive penetration of mathematics into political economy, Tufts University Discussion Paper
Mirowski, P. 1984C. The role of conservation principles in 20th century economic theory, *Philosophy of the Social Sciences*, December
Nelson, R. and Winter, S. 1982. *An Evolutionary Theory of Economic Change*, Harvard University Press
O'Hear, A. 1980. *Karl Popper*, London, Routledge and Kegan Paul
Pareto, V. 1953. On the economic principle, *International Economic Papers*, no. 3
Pareto, V. 1971A. Ophelimity in nonclosed cycles, in Chipman, J., Hurwicz, L., Richter, M. and Sonnenschein, H. (eds), *Preferences, Utility and Demand*, New York, Harcourt Brace Jovanovich
Pareto, V. 1971B. *Manual of Political Economy*, Schwier, A. (trans.), New York, Kelley
Popper, K. 1957. *The Poverty of Historicism*, London, Routledge and Kegan Paul
Popper, K. 1965. *Conjectures and Refutations*, New York, Harper and Row
Samuelson, P. 1950. On the problem of integrability in utility theory, *Economica*, November
Samuelson, P. 1952. Economic theory and mathematics—an appraisal, *American Economic Review*, May
Samuelson, P. (ed.) 1954. Symposium on mathematics in economics, *Review of Economics and Statistics*, November
Samuelson, P. 1972. Maximum principles in analytical economics, *American Economic Review*, June
Sebba, G. 1953. The development of the concepts of mechanism and model in physical science and economic thought, *American Economic Review*, March
Shackle, G. L. S. 1967. *Time in Economics*, Amsterdam, North Holland
Sorokin, P. 1956. *Contemporary Sociological Theories*, New York, Harper and Row
Sraffa, P. 1926. The laws of returns under competitive conditions, *Economic Journal*, December
Stark, W. 1944. *The History of Economics in Relation to its Social Development*, London, Routledge and Kegan Paul
Sussmann, M. 1972. *Elementary General Thermodynamics*, Reading, Addison-Wesley
Theobald, D. W. 1966. *The Concept of Energy*, London, Spon
Thoben, H. 1982. Mechanistic and organistic analogies in Economics reconsidered, *Kyklos*, vol. 35
Volterra, V. 1971. in Chipman, J., Hurwicz, L., Richter, M. and Sonnenschein, H. (eds), *Preferences, Utility and Demand*, New York, Harcourt Brace Jovanovich
Walras, L. 1960. Économique et Mécanique, *Metroeconomica*, pp. 1–13
Walras, L. 1965. *Collected Papers and Correspondence*, Jaffee, W. (ed.), 3 vols, Amsterdam, North Holland
Walras, L. 1969. *Elements of Pure Economics*, Jaffee, W. (trans.), New York, Kelley
Weinberger, O. 1931. Rudolf Auspitz und Richard Lieben: Ein Beitrag zur Geschichte der Mathematischen Methode in der Volkswirtschaftlehre, *Zeitschrift für die gesamte Staatwissenschaft*, vol. 91, pp. 457–492
Weintraub, E. R. 1979. *Microfoundations*, Cambridge, CUP
Weisskopf, W. 1979. The method is the ideology, *Journal of Economic Issues*, September
Westfall, R. S. 1980. *Never at Rest: a Biography of Issac Newton*, Cambridge, CUP
Wittgenstein, L. 1978. *Remarks on the Foundations of Mathematics*, rev. edn, London, MIT Press
Wong, S. 1978. *The Foundation of Paul Samuelson's Revealed Preference Theory*, Boston, Routledge and Kegan Paul
Wright, C. 1980. *Wittgenstein on the Foundations of Mathematics*, Harvard University Press
Zowadzki, W. 1914. *Les Mathématiques Appliquées à L'Économie Politique*, Paris, Marcel Rivière

[10]
Economists and Economic Policy in Britain After 1870

T. W. Hutchison

I

THE LONG re- or e-volution in the economic role of government in Great Britain has continued through succeeding waves, on one sector or another of the front, since the high tide of the "classical," individualist, competitive market economy began perceptibly to recede, just about, or perhaps just over, 100 years ago. In round figures 1870 seems to be the most generally suitable starting date from which this long, vast, continuing process may be traced. A few years either side of our round figure we have such variously significant events as these:

1. In 1867 came the Second Reform Act—the most basic change from the preceding decades for the ultimate shaping of policy.
2. In 1869, with a very different kind of significance, there was Mill's retraction regarding the wages-fund theory. The decline in credibility of the more rigorous forms of the classical distribution doctrines was perhaps more significant, in terms of policy developments, than the new departures in the theory of value.
3. In 1871 there was the appearance of Jevons's theory which is usually taken as significant for these departures.

In favor of a later starting point than 1870, it could be argued that it is not until the 1880s that the new trend in policies really becomes unmistakable, with a marked rise in public expenditure. Still, as we shall see, a definite shift in the current of ideas is perceptible in the 1870s.

On the other hand, with regard to economic doctrines, one could argue that a considerably earlier date might be taken, which would bring in J. S. Mill and Book V of his *Principles*—since Jevons, Sidgwick, and Marshall on some points hardly go beyond Mill, and on one or

MR. HUTCHISON *is Mitsui Professor of Economics in the University of Birmingham.*

two points perhaps not as far, regarding possible developments in economic policy. But it can be countered, first, that though in several respects the post-1870 economists do not go beyond Mill, in more important ways they do; and furthermore, that Mill can be regarded as concerned much more with prophetic hopes than with operational policies. It may be putting it rather strongly to say, as Clapham did, that "Mill remained to his death in 1873 only the philosopher who raises a standard"[1] but two major fundamental conditions put all Mill's discussion of economic policies in a different mood from the proposals which gathered force after 1870: (1) Before 1867 there was no feasible electoral basis for the sort of proposals Mill was discussing, especially with regard to redistribution in general and progressive inheritance duties in particular. (2) As Mill himself believed and assumed when writing his *Principles*, "the great Malthusian difficulty," as Cairnes called it, continued to inhibit proposals aimed at general improvement in the condition of the people.

It is the combination of the new electoral base and the lifting, or what was believed or realized to be the lifting, of "the great Malthusian difficulty," that made for a new epoch in policy, transforming prophetic aspirations and speculations into feasible policy proposals.

A further development, coincidentally almost simultaneous with these, was the first premonitory forebodings regarding Britain's relative economic position in the world which was at its peak in the mid-1860s, and which later, towards the end of the century, was to give rise to much debate regarding economic policy, and in particular regarding the principles of commercial policy.

There is one further preliminary. This is a word regarding the relations of economists' policy proposals and criticisms with, on the one hand, their own "theories" or analyses and, on the other hand, with the actual historical changes in economic policies. With regard to neither of these relationships am I assuming that any particular simple thesis can be sustained.

(1) Regarding the relation between economists' theorizing and such policy proposals or criticisms as they undertake, I would simply venture the impressionist judgment or guess that although I am sure that there are some important exceptions to this generalization, perhaps

1. J. H. Clapham, *An Economic History of Modern Britain*, vol. 2, *Free Trade and Steel* (1932), p. 391.

increasingly from this period onwards, economists' policy proposals, much more often than they may usually admit, have only a fairly tenuous base, if any firm base at all, in any kind of systematic or empirically tested theory. I do not mean this with regard simply to the positive predictions implied in specific policy proposals or criticisms.

(2) With regard to their influence or noninfluence on actual policy developments, economists may either provide the basis of positive predictions relevant for new kinds of policies, or they may act persuasively on the public's or the politicians' attitudes and values, or choice of new objectives or of much higher levels of old objectives. Whichever sort of influence they may have, all one seems able to say is that for better or for worse sometimes economists have roughly kept in step with changes in public or political opinions or aspirations; sometimes they have been a step or two behind; and sometimes they have been a leading force.

All the same, though no simple general thesis about economists will probably stand up for long, in studying their policy proposals it does seem to me that we *are* concerned with the proof of the whole intellectual pudding of economics, in that, according to what I would guess to be economists' own tenets, this lies in the improved prescience or heightened success of economic policies which may result from what economists do.

II

Though he enters as something of a revolutionary, or at any rate claiming to be a revolutionary, on a central point of theory, on the subject of the role of government Jevons was a transitional figure both chronologically and doctrinally. Chronologically he is almost too neatly so. His writing career covered exactly the quarter of a century from 1857 to 1882, pretty precisely bisected by our year 1870. I am not suggesting that in or about that year Jevons underwent a sudden Pauline conversion from his earlier adherence to the strictest individualist principles, to his later position, for which he is better known, as, in Clapham's description, "a cautious empirical innovator" who "watched with critical impartiality the inroads of the state on individual liberty in the early '80s."[2] In fact, I don't think it can be documented that anything in the way of a change of view by Jevons

2. Clapham, 2:390 and 439.

took place on any important *specific point* of economic policy or the role of government. It is simply that, as the 1870s wore on, more cases occurred to him which seemed to call for governmental action, or at least for detailed empirical examination, and which were not to be disposed of by a sweeping application of laissez-faire principles.

In his first publication in Australia in 1857, the 22-year-old Jevons had begun by proclaiming comprehensively that "freedom for *all* commercial transactions is the spirit of improved legislation."[3] In particular, the earlier Jevons was a strong champion of Malthus and of the more rigorous interpretation of his doctrines in terms of self-help. Jevons considered it worth repeating in 1869 that "the British Poor Law of 1834 is one of the wisest measures ever concerted by any government."[4] (Twenty-three years later Marshall, though agreeing that the poor law was justifiable in its own day, was to reject the whole basis of that law for *his* day.) Though he supported the Education Act of 1870, Jevons was not only opposed to any extension of state action with regard to health services for the poor but was against *private* medical charities in that they discouraged self-help. At times he expressed a strenuously moralistic interpretation of social and economic "science" redolent of the female fringe-operators and popularizers of classical political economy about half a century previously: "The social sciences," Jevons wrote, "are the necessary complement to the physical sciences, for by their aid alone can the main body of the population be rendered honest, temperate, provident, and intelligent."[5]

As regards external commercial policy, for Jevons in 1869 free trade was an unquestioned and almost unquestionable article of faith:

> Freedom of trade may be regarded as a fundamental axiom of political economy; and though even axioms *may* be mistaken, and any different views concerning them must not be *prohibited*, yet we need not be frightened into questioning our own axioms. We may welcome *bona fide* investigation into the state of trade, and the causes of the present depression, but we can no more expect to have our opinions on free trade altered by such an investigation than the Mathematical Society would expect to

---

3. W. S. Jevons, *Empire* (Sydney) April 8, 1857.
4. W. S. Jevons, *Methods of Social Reform* (1883) p. 192.
5. Ibid., p. 196.

have the axioms of Euclid disproved during the investigation of a complex problem.⁶

The earlier and more severely individualistic strain in Jevons comes out especially in his treatment of taxation. He expressed concern in 1870 that

> the working classes so long as they make a temperate use of spirituous liquors and tobacco pay a distinctly less proportion of their income to the state, and even intemperance does not make their contribution proportionally greater than those of more wealthy persons.⁷

In his main work on taxation, his pamphlet *The Match Tax* (1871)' Jevons expressed some regret at the repeal of the tax because he wanted to retain taxes on articles of wide popular consumption, rejecting the classical argument about the effects on wages of taxing "necessaries." Jevons figured out statistically that the burden of taxation was then very roughly proportional, but that—as he had complained the previous year—half the taxes paid by the poor were from alcohol and tobacco; these were not only avoidable but ought to be avoided. The great exponent of the utility approach to the problems of value and price came down very firmly in favor of proportional taxation on all except paupers:

> The more carefully and maturely I ponder over this question of taxation from various points of view, the more convinced I always return to the principle, that all classes of persons above the rank of actual paupers, should contribute to the state in the proportion of their incomes. I will not say this is a theoretically perfect rule. From feelings of humanity we might desire to graduate the rate of contribution and relieve persons who are comparatively poorer at the expense of those who are comparatively richer. But we must beware of obeying the dictates of ill-considered humanity. If we once professedly enter upon the course of exempting the poor, there will be no stopping.⁸

It is in his Introductory Lecture at University College in 1876 that a shift in Jevons's attitudes seems to become prominent. Even here he

---

6. Ibid., p. 182.
7. W. S. Jevons, *Essays in Economic Method*, ed. R. L. Smyth (1962) p. 34.
8. W. S. Jevons, *The Principles of Economics and Other Papers*, ed. H. Higgs (1905), p. 235.

began by duly noting that "it is impossible to doubt that the *laissez-faire* principle properly applied is the wholesome and true one." But the spread of urban industrialism and its all-pervasive "externalities," or neighborhood effects, led Jevons to predict:

> It seems to me, while population grows more numerous and dense, while industry becomes more complex and interdependent, as we travel faster and make use of more intense forces, we shall necessarily need more legislative supervision.[9]

He called for a new empirical branch of economics:

> If such a thing is possible, we need a new branch of political and statistical science which shall carefully investigate the limits to the *laissez-faire* principle, and show where we want greater freedom and where less. . . . I am quite satisfied if we have pointed out the need and the probable rise of one new branch, which is only to be found briefly and imperfectly represented in the works of Mill and other economists.[10]

Jevons then proceeds to give an example, representing a blend of paternalism and externalities, with regard to slum clearance and public housing:

> I am quite convinced, for instance, that the great mass of the people will not have healthy houses by the ordinary action of self-interest. The only chance of securing good sanitary arrangements is to pull down the houses which are hopelessly bad, as provided by an Act of the present ministry, and most carefully to superintend under legislative regulations *all* new houses that are built.[11]

Jevons went on a year or two later to suggest increased public expenditure over a wide range of elementary paternalist or public goods and services, such as libraries, museums, parks, municipal orchestras, and meteorological services.[12] He claimed that these were

9. Ibid., p. 204.
10. Ibid., pp. 204-6.
11. Ibid., p. 205.
12. Ibid.: "Community of consumption . . . is often most economical. . . . On reasonable suppositions I have calculated that a private watch costs people on the average about one-fifteenth part of a penny for each look at the time of day; but a great public clock is none the worse, however many people may look at it. As a general rule, I should say that the average cost of public clocks is not more than one-hundred and fiftieth of a penny

"unsanctified by the *laissez-faire* principle," though it would seem that they could be accommodated in the capacious and elastic third heading of Adam Smith regarding public works.

More widely, following up his remarks on public housing, Jevons suggested a further move into the field of town and country planning, by laying a heavy emphasis on what he called "the general interests of the public" as against those of private individuals:

> Our idea of happiness in this country at present seems to consist in buying a piece of land if possible, and building a high wall round it. If a man can only secure, for instance, a beautiful view from his own garden and windows, he cares not how many thousands of other persons he cuts off from the daily enjoyment of that view. The rights of private property and private action are pushed so far that the general interests of the public are made of no account whatever.[13]

On nationalized or state enterprise Jevons had written as early as 1867 a sentence anticipatory of his later empirical and experimental attitude:

> My own strong opinion is that no abstract principle, and no absolute rule, can guide us in determining what kinds of industrial enterprise, the State should undertake and what not.[14]

After praising the Post Office, he called for the taking over of telegraph services, though when this was done in 1870 he condemned the financial arrangements. Later Jevons advocated a state-run parcel post (1879), but, unlike Walter Bagehot, he was opposed to nationalization of the railways (1874).[15]

In his final and admirable book, *The State in Relation to Labour*, published in the year of his death, Jevons dealt with consumer protection and government inspection, factory legislation and hours of work, and trade union legislation.

He returned again, long before the days of mass motoring and air travel, to the mounting importance of externalities and neighborhood

---

for each look, securing an economy of ten times." See also Jevons's papers "Amusements of the People," "The Rationale of Free Public Libraries," and "The Use and Abuse of Museums," in *Methods of Social Reform* (1883).

13. Jevons, *Principles*, p. 206.
14. Ibid., p. 278.
15. See his paper "The Railways and the State" (1874) in *Methods of Social Reform*.

effects with the development of urban industrialism and with the threats to freedom deriving from the complex technology of affluence:

> So intricate are the ways, industrial, sanitary, or political, in which one class or section of the people affect other classes or sections, that there is hardly any limit to the interference of the legislator. . . . It is impossible in short that we can have the constant multiplication of institutions and instruments of civilisation which evolution is producing, without a growing complication of relations, and a consequent growth of social regulations.[16]

Regarding hours of work, Jevons argued that legislators up till then had "in fact, always abstained from interfering with the liberty of adult men to work as long or as short a time as they like." But he went on:

> I see nothing to forbid the state interfering in the matter . . . neither principle, experience, nor precedent, in other cases of legislation, prevents us from contemplating the idea of State interference in such circumstances.[17]

In fact, ten years later (1892) in the House of Commons, championing an eight-hour bill for miners, Joseph Chamberlain, in his radical socialistic or at any rate interventionist phase, quoted Jevons in support of his case, though in terms of very general utilitarian principle:

> The State is justified in passing any law, or even in doing any single act, which in its ulterior consequences adds to the sum of human happiness.

Chamberlain drew a contrast, as he put it, with

> the strict doctrine of *laissez-faire* which perhaps 20 years ago [i.e., c.1870] was accepted as preferable.[18]

It is in its magnificently eloquent, often quoted statements of an empirical experimental, anti-a-priori approach to policy questions that Jevons's *The State in Relation to Labour* is famous. Jevons indeed

---

16. W. S. Jevons, *The State in Relation to Labour* (1882), p. 14.
17. Ibid., pp. 64-65.
18. See J. L. Garvin, *Life of Joseph Chamberlain* (1933) 2:534; and J. H. Clapham, *An Economic History of Modern Britain*, vol. 3 (1938), p. 397. I have not so far been able to discover in Jevons's writings the actual Benthamistic words ascribed to him by Chamberlain, but I don't think they amount to a distortion of Jevons's later views.

is a forerunner of Sir Karl Popper both in his conception of scientific method in his *Principles of Science* and consequentially also in his advocacy of empirical, piecemeal social experimentation.

Jevons's proposals for increasing governmental action are almost entirely confined to the heading describable as Inadequacies of Individual Choice with its subheadings (*a*) paternalism, (*b*) ignorance, (*c*) "externalities" or "neighborhood effects," and (*d*) public goods and services.

Under the heading Monopoly and Restrictive Practices there is only a little in Jevons, including, for example, his treatment already mentioned, of nationalization. But there is also his discussion of trade union monopolies, which he regarded with serious forebodings. He did not, however, propose to undo the favorable legislation of 1871 and 1875, and is curiously optimistic about the future of trade unions. He asks whether "the lawgiver ought not simply to prohibit societies which tend toward such monopoly." But he concludes in the negative.[19]

Under the other main headings for state intervention there is almost nothing to be found in Jevons. As we have seen, with regard to distribution and redistribution, one of the main fields opened up in the last quarter of the nineteenth century, Jevons seems to have remained strictly, even severely, classical, especially regarding proportionality in taxation.

On the great twentieth-century subject of the Monetary Framework and Macroeconomic Policy, on which before 1900 there were only some anticipatory rumblings, there is hardly an inkling in Jevons, in spite of the fact that he was a pioneer of research into business cycles and price index-numbers. With regard to the then orthodoxy, Professor Fetter has pointed out that "in his philosophic approach to the limitations of any metallic standard Jevons soared on a high speculative level." Fetter goes on to quote Jevons:

> But in itself gold-digging has ever seemed to me almost a dead loss of labour as regards the world in general—a wrong against the human race, just such as is that of a government against a people in over-issuing and depreciating its own currency.

Yet, Fetter concludes, Jevons, "either because he was the pure scientist unconcerned with policy-making, or because as a child of an era he was not prepared to fight its myths and its idols, made no public sug-

19. Jevons, *The State in Relation to Labour*, p. 101.

gestion for a better standard, although he wrote but did not publish a proposal for a tabular standard of value."[20] Jevons does indeed proclaim at one point:

> The only method of regulating the *amount* of the currency is to leave it at perfect freedom to regulate itself...to attempt to regulate its quantity is the last thing which a statesman should do.[21]

Finally, under the heading of commercial policy, external economic relations, or Britain and her Relative Position in the World Economy, Jevons, in his first and brilliant book, *The Coal Question* (1865), had uttered, at the very high peak of Britain's relative economic standing in the world, a prescient warning, if rather overanxious in the shorter term, that our occupation of this supreme position as the workshop of the world might prove highly transient.[22] Before the end of the century the problem of the weakening of Britain's relative economic position was to give rise to much policy debate. But Jevons reasserted in his last work, as Marshall was to do later, his firm adherence to free trade principles.

III

The historical and institutional critics of classical political economy in the 1870s and early 1880s, who come next, were mostly more concerned with theories and methods than with policy. There seems to be little on policy questions in Cliff Leslie, for example. But Arnold Toynbee (d. 1883), a figure of some influence in Oxford, "one of the noblest of the rising generation" as Marshall called him,[23] perceived the politico-economic disequilibrium that had come about with the extension of the suffrage:

> Wealth is in the hands of the few rich, the suffrage in the hands of the many poor; in the concentration of wealth and the diffusion of political power lies a great danger of modern society.

---

20. F. W. Fetter, *The Development of British Monetary Orthodoxy, 1797-1875* (1965), p. 248.
21. W. S. Jevons, *Money and the Mechanism of Exchange*, 23d ed. (1910), p. 340.
22. See also Jevons's warning of 1869: "I shudder to think what might be the effect of any serious impediment to our future progress, such as a long-continued war, the competition of other nations, or a comparative failure of our own material resources." *Methods of Social Reform*, p. 193.
23. A. C. Pigou, ed., *Memorials of Alfred Marshall* (1925), p. 152.

Toynbee saw the importance of this politico-economic conjuncture for the problem of distribution, which, he affirmed, "is the true problem of political economy at the present time."[24]

Toynbee laid down the principles for state action in the following two propositions:

> *First*, that where individual rights conflict with the interests of the community, there the State ought to interfere; and *second* that where the people are unable to provide a thing for themselves, and that thing is of *primary social importance*, then again the State should interfere and provide it for them.[25]

In this connection, almost simultaneously with Jevons, Toynbee raised the question of public housing, or "the dwellings of the people," a subject

> upon which it is difficult to understand why so little is said. . . . I do not hesitate to say a community must step in and give the necessary aid. These labourers cannot obtain dwellings for themselves; the municipalities, or the State in some form, should have power to buy up land and let it below the market value for the erection of decent dwellings.[26]

Toynbee was arguing from the point of view of a Tory or even imperialist socialist:

> We demand that the material conditions of those who labour should be bettered, in order that, every source of weakness being removed at home, we, this English nation, may bring to the tasks which God has assigned us, the irresistible strength of a prosperous and united people.[27]

As regards Walter Bagehot there is not much to say here. I have noted his support for railway nationalization (1865).[28] In his major field of the monetary framework Bagehot seems to have provided or buttressed the orthodoxy of the day which was to survive until 1914 or 1931. Regarding the position of the Bank of England, as Professor Fetter puts it:

24. A. Toynbee, *Lectures on the Industrial Revolution* (1894), pp. 212 and 250.
25. Ibid., p. 216.
26. Ibid., pp. 217-18.
27. Ibid., p. 221.
28. In *The Economist*, Jan. 7, 1865, under the title "The Advantages That Would Accrue from an Ownership of the Railways by the State." See Clapham, 2:189.

In the eyes of Bagehot banking statesmanship and the profit motive were to be happily married, and his great service to the next half century of central banking was that he convinced his countrymen that this was an honourable union blessed by the laws of free trade.[29]

One year after Jevons's death appeared Sidgwick's *Principles of Political Economy*. These principles run very much on the general lines of Mill, but are more precise and penetrating at some important points. First Sidgwick brings more precision regarding externalities and public goods:

> There is a large and varied class of cases in which private interest cannot be relied upon as a sufficient stimulus to the performance of the most socially useful services because such services are incapable of being appropriated by those who produce them or who would otherwise be willing to purchase them.

He then mentions the lighthouse example, as had Mill. Sidgwick goes on to note, however: "It does not follow, of course, that wherever *laissez-faire* falls short governmental interference is expedient."[30]

On the subject of distribution, Sidgwick certainly regards a "right" distribution of wealth as a second main objective of policy alongside increasing production. He takes equality of sacrifice to imply proportionality in taxation and holds this to be "the obviously equitable principle," going on to oppose progression and the redressing of inequalities of income by taxation:

> Most economists hold that any such communistic tendency should be rigidly excluded in the adjustment of taxation; and that whatever Government may legitimately do to remedy the inequalities of distribution resulting from natural liberty should be done otherwise than by unequal imposition of financial burdens. And this is, in the main, the conclusion which I am myself disposed to adopt; but I must interpret or limit it by one important proviso which seems to me necessitated by the acceptance of the principle that the community ought to protect its members from starvation—a degree of communism which, as we have seen, is legally established in England.[31]

---

29. Fetter, p. 271.
30. H. Sidgwick, *Principles of Political Economy* (1883), pp. 412 and 419.
31. Ibid., p. 562.

As regards the monetary framework, Sidgwick, in a chapter entitled "Cases of Governmental Interference to Promote Production," raises some fundamental questions regarding what he calls "currency." He holds that the state "ought to guard so far as it can against fluctuations in the value of the medium of exchange. It can only do this, however, to a very limited extent."[32] Regarding the position of the Bank of England, Sidgwick questioned the orthodox acceptance of the happy marriage of private profit and social interest advocated by Bagehot:

> When we consider merely from an abstract point of view the proposal to give a particular joint-stock company an exclusive privilege of issuing notes, the value of which will, in the last resort be sustained by the authority of Government, without subjecting its exercise of this privilege to any governmental control whatsoever; it certainly appears a very hazardous measure.[33]

Finally, at this point mention should be made of Foxwell's monograph of 1886, *Irregularity of Employment and Fluctuations of Prices*. This was the outstanding anticipation at this time of what was to be the overriding problem and concern—between wars—of much of the first half of the twentieth century. Foxwell starts from the "conviction, continually increasing in strength, that uncertainty of employment is the root evil of the present industrial system." He foresaw and emphasized the growing popular concern for "social security": "I cannot venture to say what would be the general opinion of the working class upon the point; but my own feeling would be that when a certain necessary limit had been reached, regularity of income was far more important than amount of income."[34] Certainly Foxwell's lecture is more notable for its attempt to shatter complacency about a major problem for policy, and to establish the reduction of the irregularity of employment as an objective, than for the particular remedial measures he proposes. But after analyzing the effects of changes in the value of money, Foxwell concludes in favor of stability of the price level, or rather a slightly and steadily rising level.

32. Ibid., p. 453.
33. Ibid., p. 462.
34. H. S. Foxwell, *Irregularity of Employment and Fluctuations of Prices* (1886), pp. 7 and 17.

IV

In considering Alfred Marshall's ideas on policy one might, as with Jevons, try to discover and apply some pattern of development; though in Marshall's case the pattern would presumably be the different though very familiar one of a transition from an earlier, youthful, reformist enthusiasm to a much more cautious and sceptical attitude later on. There is quite a lot of evidence for this sort of pattern with regard to Marshall, though there do seem to be one or two important exceptions or irregularities. There are also, in any case, due to his delays of many decades in publishing his ideas, considerable chronological difficulties in trying to trace out at all definitely or precisely *any* simple lines for Marshall's intellectual development.

However, we may suitably start with his early paper (of 1873), "The Future of the Working Classes," which provides a glowing statement of early aspirations and which begins, incidentally, with an enthusiastic tribute to Mrs. Harriet Taylor Mill for her contribution to the chapter of the same title in her second husband's *Principles*.

Marshall warms up in the manner of Marx, by citing contemporary blue books on such mid-Victorian industrial phenomena as "lads and maidens, not 8 years old, toiling in the brickfields under monstrous loads from 5 o'clock in the morning till 8 o'clock at night." He goes on:

> Our thoughts from youth upwards are dominated by a Pagan belief . . . that it is an ordinance of Nature that multitudes of men must toil a weary toil, which may give to others the means of refinement and luxury, but which can afford to themselves scarce any opportunity of mental growth. May not the world outgrow this belief, as it has outgrown others? It may and it will.[35]

It certainly has, nearly a hundred years later, in some privileged parts of the world; though whether the parallel cultural accompaniments would have met with Marshall's approval seems highly doubtful. Economically, in fact, Marshall was never at all unrealistic or revolutionary. He denounced the socialists "who attributed to every man an unlimited capacity for those self-forgetting virtues that they found in their own breasts" and whose schemes "involve a submersion of existing arrangements according to which the work of every man is

---

35. Pigou, *Memorials*, pp. 107-9.

chosen by himself, and the remuneration he obtains for it is decided by free competition."³⁶

It was in his social, cultural, and educational hopes that Marshall seems to have been, and for some time to have remained, rather overoptimistic. He saw that education and technological progress could and would raise the earning powers of the masses and reduce hours and physical toil. It was with regard to what would be done with the time and energy left over that Marshall may seem to have been unrealistic. He envisaged a country which

> is to have a fair share of wealth, and not an abnormally large population. Everyone is to have in youth an education which is thorough while it lasts, and which lasts long. No one is to do in the day so much manual work as will leave him little time or little aptitude for intellectual or artistic enjoyment in the evening. Since there will be nothing tending to render the individual coarse and unrefined, there will be nothing tending to render society coarse and unrefined. Exceptional morbid growths must exist in every society; but otherwise every man will be surrounded from birth upwards by almost all the influences which we have seen to be at present characteristic of the occupations of gentlemen; everyone who is not a gentleman will have himself alone to blame for it.³⁷

Marshall claimed with regard to the working population that "their moral stength is gaining new life." As regards the "artisan" class:

> Some are, in the true sense of the word, becoming gentlemen. Some few of them may, indeed, interpret this to mean little more than becoming at times dandyfied perambulating machines, for the display of the cheaper triumphs of the haberdasher and the tailor, but many artisans are becoming artists, who take a proud interest in the glories of their art, are truly citizens, or courteous, gentle, throughtful, able, and independent men.³⁸

After this early statement of Marshall's social visions, it seems more convenient to continue by subject headings than entirely chronologically, partly for the reason previously mentioned of Marshall's delays in publication, and also because Marshall, unlike Jevons, con-

36. Ibid., p. 109.
37. Ibid., p. 110.
38. Ibid., p. 116.

tributed at different times to most or all of the main sectors of possible governmental action in the economy.

First, let us take the four-part heading, Inadequacies of Individual Choice, under which all or most of Jevons's contributions were made.

On grounds both of paternalism and externalities Marshall strongly advocated, from his paper of 1873 onwards through the decades, increased public spending on education: "The difference between the value of the labour of the educated man and that of the uneducated, is, as a rule, many times greater than the difference between the costs of their education. . . . No individual reaps the full gains derived from educating a child."[39] Subsequently Marshall was to emphasize the economic dangers to Britain of lagging behind Germany in technical and scientific education.

As regards housing, though not recommending subsidies in the same way as Jevons or Toynbee, Marshall in 1884 advocates government controls on movement into slum areas: "To hinder people from going where their presence helps to lower the average standard of human life, is no more contrary to economic principle than the rule that when a steamer is full, admission should be refused to any more even though they themselves are willing to take the risk of being drowned."[40] Later (1902), as contrasted with Toynbee and Jevons, Marshall was to proclaim that "municipal housing seems to me scarcely ever right and generally very wrong. Municipal free baths seem to me nearly always right."[41]

In his paper "Economic Chivalry" (1907) Marshall suggests with regard to town planning:

> The State could so care for the amenities of life outside of the house that fresh air and variety of colour and of scene might await the citizen and his children very soon after they start on a holiday walk. Everyone in health and strength can order his house well; the State alone can bring the beauties of nature and art within the reach of the ordinary citizen.[42]

In this essay, in which he proclaims "Let the State be up and doing," Marshall emphasizes especially "the imperative duty to inspect and arbitrate," taking as an illustration "the careless treatment of milk":

39. Ibid., p. 118.
40. Ibid., p. 148.
41. Ibid., p. 445.
42. Ibid., p. 345.

Let the government arouse itself to do energetically its proper work of educating British farmers up to the Danish standard, if not beyond; and of enforcing sanitary regulations in critical matters such as this.[43]

It is under this broad general heading also that we might mention Marshall's abstract criticisms in the *Principles* of the doctrine of maximum satisfaction (bk. 5, chap. 13), where he seems to suggest taxing goods the production of which is subject to diminishing returns and subsidizing increasing return industries out of the proceeds. But though Marshall emphasizes that his conclusions "do not by themselves afford a valid ground for government interference," these rather excessively abstract propositions may have produced more confusion than enlightenment.

Our next main heading, Poverty, Distribution, and Redistribution, certainly was of major concern to Marshall. As he told the Royal Commission on the Aged Poor (1893): "I have devoted myself for the last 25 years to the problem of poverty, and . . . very little of my work has been devoted to any enquiry which does not bear on that."[44]

Marshall emphasized to the Commission the lifting of "the great Malthusian difficulty" and the change in the nature of the problem compared with the beginning of the century:

You can trace the economic dogmas of present Poor Law literature direct from those times; and the doctrines which they laid down I think were fairly true in their time. The doctrine is that if you tax the rich, and give money to the working classes, the result will be that the working classes will increase in number and the result will be you will have lowered wages in the next generation; and the grant will not have improved the position of the working classes on the whole. As regards this a change has come, which separates the economics of this generation from the economics of the past; but it seems to me not to have penetrated the Poor Law literature yet; and this is the main thing that I desire to urge. That change insists upon the fact that if the money is so spent as to increase the earning power of the next generation it may not lower wages.[45]

43. Ibid., p. 337.
44. Marshall, *Official Papers by Alfred Marshall* (1926), p. 205.
45. Ibid., p. 225.

On the question of progressive taxation we have seen that Jevons and Sidgwick were opposed, as was the Irish public finance expert C. F. Bastable. Mr. Shehab in his valuable book states that in the 1890s and before, Marshall also "was preaching against it," though especially later, and as late as 1917, aged seventy-five, he was to come out strongly in favor. But Mr. Shehab's evidence for Marshall's earlier opposition to progression is based simply on a footnote in Clapham, which recalls that "in his lectures in the 1890s Marshall used to tell his pupils that graduated income taxation would weaken the chief pillar of the tax's yield, collection at source."[46] This does not seem to amount to outright opposition to progression in principle. Admittedly also—though Mr. Shehab does not cite this—Marshall himself wrote in 1909 that he had for fifteen years "somewhat eagerly" opposed death duties, because they checked the growth of capital, but that now he considers them "a good method of raising a large part of the national revenue." On the other hand, though admittedly his later statements are much more explicit, Marshall had proclaimed as early as 1889 for example: "I myself certainly think that the rich ought to be taxed much more heavily than they are, in order to provide for their poorer brethren the material means for a healthy physical and mental development."[47]

Subsequently Marshall was certainly moving more explicitly, though still cautiously, towards progression in his Memorandum (1897) to the Royal Commission on Local Taxes. However, for the theoretical case in favor of progressive taxation, such as it was, one would have to go to Edgeworth's paper of the same year.[48] By 1907 Marshall is praising his contemporaries in that "our age has reversed the old rules that the poor paid a larger percentage of their income in rates and taxes than the well-to-do." But he seems to ascribe this change to the growth of sheer British chivalry rather than to the extension of the franchise.[49] His 1917 paper, one of his last, is much his most forthright statement on progression, expressing the hope that "the various advances towards graduation made before the war will be sustained and developed after it."[50]

46. F. Shehab, *Progressive Taxation* (1953), p. 199; and Clapham, 3:403.
47. Pigou, *Memorials*, p. 229.
48. F. Y. Edgeworth, "The Pure Theory of Taxation," *Papers Relating to Political Economy*, vol. 2 (1925), pp. 63 ff.
49. Pigou, *Memorials*, p. 327.
50. Ibid., p. 350. In a letter to *The Times* (Nov. 16, 1909) Marshall had given his blessing to Lloyd George's Budget of 1909 with its proposals for supertax and for taxing

It may be of some interest also to note that insofar as Mr. Shehab's view is justified that Marshall only moved more explicitly in his later years towards advocating progression, it would mean that he made this move in spite of the fact that through the various editions of his *Principles* he seemed to put less and less weight and trust in the concept of utility or any possibility of its measurement. Marshall, at any rate, seems to have moved with the times, though there is not necessarily anything virtuous in doing that. But generally it may be said that economists, for better or for worse, were rather "behind" than in advance of public opinion in the move towards progression rather than proportionality in taxation.

I shall deal very briefly with the next main heading, Monopolies and Restrictive Practices. This again was a major concern of Marshall. It is one of the main themes of *Industry and Trade*. (Incidentally, it really is ludicrous to suggest that economists only got interested in monopolistic problems in the 1930s.) In his paper of 1890, "Some Aspects of Competition," Marshall wrote:

> It is clear that combinations and partial monopolies will play a great part in future economic history; that their effects contain much good as well as much evil, and that to denounce them without discrimination would be to repeat the error which our forefathers made with regard to protection. . . . It is a matter of pressing urgency that public opinion should accustom itself to deal with such questions.[51]

But Marshall has little to suggest in the way of remedies and countermeasures, most of his discussion being concerned with state regulation and nationalization, to the second of which he was usually vigorously opposed. This is no criticism of Marshall. In the nearly eighty years that have passed since Marshall was examining the subject, it has hardly proved possible to propose systematic policies, based on

---

land values: "In so far as the Budget proposes to check the appropriation of what is really public property by private persons, and in so far as it proposes to bring under taxation some income, which has escaped taxation merely because it does not appear above the surface in a money form, I regard it as sound finance. In so far as its proceeds are to be applied to social problems where a little money may do much towards raising the level of life of the people and increasing their happiness it seems to me a Social Welfare Budget. I do not profess to have mastered all its details; but on the whole I incline to think it merits that name."

51. Ibid., p. 289.

tested coherent theories, for this large problem. Nor has price theory, including the analysis of imperfect and monopolistic competition developed in the 1930s, shown itself to be of great assistance in propounding answers to this problem.

I would have liked to be able to devote more attention to the next major sector, though it really came to a head in the second quarter of this century, that is, the Monetary Framework, Stabilization, Employment, or "Macroeconomic" Policy, or the comprehensive process recently described by Sir John Hicks as the Nationalization of Money. Not that Marshall's proposals from the vantage, or disadvantage, point of 1969 seem very extensive or relevant. Generally, for reasons recently examined by Professor Matthews, Marshall in about 1900, unlike Foxwell and other contemporaries, did not consider that the problem of unemployment was growing more serious.[52] Marshall's various suggestions regarding these problems are scattered through half a century of papers and memoranda. But perhaps the single most compact or systematic treatment, on very simple lines, is in his short paper to the Industrial Remuneration Conference of 1885, not collected in the *Memorials*, though some sentences from it were eventually quoted in *Money, Credit and Commerce* (1922).

Marshall posed the question: "How far do remediable causes influence prejudicially (*a*) the continuity of employment, (*b*) the rates of wages?" He sees the main remediable causes as "chiefly connected in some way or other with the want of knowledge" and proceeds to discuss nine remedies, some of which today certainly seem of rather marginal relevance—such as avoiding vagaries of fashion in dress, especially female dress, countering excessive secrecy in traders by publishing income-tax returns in local newspapers, treating fraud more severely, and encouraging the growth of moral feeling against gambling, especially among the young. More significant seem his proposals for further research by economists on short-term fluctuations and for the development of economic forecasting:

> I see no reason why a body of able disinterested men, with a wide range of business knowledge, should not be able to issue predictions of trade storms and of trade weather generally, that would have an appreciable effect in rendering the employment

[52]. *Economic Journal* 78 (Sept. 1968): 566-67.

of industry more steady and continuous . . . though the time has not yet come for putting it [this proposal] into practice.[53]

Undoubtedly Marshall's main suggestions were in the monetary field, though they did not go far. First he proposed that

> arrangements must be made with the Bank of England, *or otherwise,* for raising the normal limit of the ultimate cash reserve of the nation. . . . It would not do much, but it would do a little towards steadying the money market directly and industry indirectly.[54]

Elsewhere, however, Marshall (1899) laid it down that "the function of a legislator as regards currency is to do as little as possible."[55]

Finally, Marshall made his proposal, which he elaborated on a number of other occasions, that the government "should publish tables showing as closely as may be the changes in the purchasing power of gold; and should facilitate contracts for payments to be made in terms of units of fixed purchasing power." He considered (1887) that this would do something to reduce price fluctuations and therefore fluctuations in employment:

> The only effective remedy for them is to be sought in relieving the currency of the duty, which it is not fitted to perform, of acting as a standard of value; and by establishing, in accordance with a plan that has long been familiar to economists an authoritative standard of purchasing power independent of the currency.[56]

However, in reviewing this list of Marshall's remedies for aggregate fluctuations, or his proposals for macroeconomic policy either through rules or authorities, we have perhaps merely made it plain how completely different a world Marshall was living in, as regards the objectives and techniques of economic policy, from the world that we live in.[57]

53. *Industrial Remuneration Conference, Report of the Proceedings and Papers* (1885), p. 181.
54. Ibid., p. 179.
55. "Evidence to the Committee on Indian Currency (1898)," *Official Papers by Alfred Marshall*, p. 292.
56. Pigou, *Memorials*, p. 188.
57. In a letter to *The Times* (Feb. 15, 1886) Marshall expressed some very limited support for relief works: "It is often said that political economy has proved that outdoor relief must do more harm than good: I venture to question this. . . . Works that are not in themselves necessary, but are undertaken in order to give employment, should be

When we come to our last heading, Britain's External Commercial Policy and Her Relative Economic Position in the World, quite often in perusing Marshall's writings of about three-quarters of a century ago we may feel how little has changed, and how similar are the problems, the warnings, and the admonitions which Marshall handed out to those we in Britain have been listening to most days, and especially most weekends, in the 1950s and 60s. Certainly Britain's economic position in the world and her slower rate of growth relative to other countries were of major concern to Marshall and an important theme in *Industry and Trade*.

Perhaps the most significant illustrations of this point are in two letters written at the end of 1897 to the Master of Balliol, concerning a strike in the engineering industry. The contrast with other optimistic expressions of Marshall about the rapidly increasing economic chivalry of unions and management in Britain is rather remarkable. Marshall writes of the strike:

> If the men should win, and I were an engineering employer, I would sell my works for anything I could get and emigrate to America. If I were a working man, I would wish for no better or more hopeful conditions of life than those which I understand to prevail at the Carnegie works now.

In his next letter (December 5, 1897) Marshall summarizes his views in the following paragraphs:

> (i) This is the crisis of our industry. For the last twenty years we have indeed been still progressing; but we have been retrograding relatively to the Americans and to the nations of central Europe (not France, I think) and to Eastern lands.
>
> (ii) The causes are partly natural, inevitable, and some are, from a cosmopolitan point of view, matters for satisfaction.
>
> (iii) But one is unmixed evil for all, and a threat to national well-being. It is the dominance in some unions of the desire to "make work" and an increase in their power to do so.
>
> (iv) And there is another like it. It is the apathy of many employers and their contentment with inferior methods, until

such as can be suspended at any time. The pay should be enough to afford the necessaries of life, but so far below the ordinary wages of unskilled labour in ordinary trades that people will not be contented to take it for long, but will always be on the look-out for work elsewhere. I for one can see no economic objection to letting public money flow freely for relief works on this plan."

driven out of the field or threatened severely, at least, by more enterprising foreigners.

He goes on to speak of "the laborious laziness" in many British workshops.[58]

Later Marshall makes the suggestion, as had Jevons in his *Coal Question* a generation before, of time running out for Britain:

> There is an urgent duty upon us to make even more rapid advance during this age of economic grace, for it may run out before the end of the century.[59]

With the aid of two world wars it of course ran out before the end of the half-century.

Marshall returned to the theme, in quite vehement terms, in a letter of January 20, 1901:

> The Christian Socialists did, I believe, a great deal more good than harm: but they did harm. Their authority has been used with great effect by those mean, lazy and selfish men who since 1860 have done so much to undermine the vigour and honest work of English industry, and have removed her from the honourable leadership which she used to hold among the nations. . . .
>
> Fifty years ago nine-tenths of those changes, which have enabled the working classes to have healthy homes and food, originated in England. America had a few specialities, and so had France. But, speaking generally, anything which was not English was really dearer than the English, though bought at a lower price. We owed our leadership partly to accidental advantages, most of which have now passed away. But we owed it mainly to the fact that we worked much harder than any continental nation. Now, on the average, we work less long and not more vigorously than our fathers did: and, meanwhile, the average amount of thoughtful work done by the German has nearly doubled; and a similar though less marked improvement is to be seen in other countries. Americans and Germans jeer at the way in which many of our businessmen give their energies to pleasure, and play with their work; and they say, truly as I believe, "unless you completely shake off the habits that have grown on you in

58. Pigou, *Memorials*, pp. 398-400.
59. Ibid., p. 326.

the last thirty years, you will go to join Spain." . . . It is, I believe, a fact that there is scarcely any industry, which has changed its form during the last ten years, in which we are not behind several countries; and that every Teutonic country, whether behind us or in front of us, is on the average growing in vigour of body and mind faster than we; and that, because there is none of them that is not less self-complacent than we are, less afraid to meet frankly and generously a new idea that is "competing" for the field. . . .

Our real danger is that we shall be undersold in the product of high class industries, and have to turn more and more to low class industries. There is no fear of our going backwards absolutely, but only relatively. The danger is that our industries will become of a lower grade relatively to other countries: that those which are in front of us will run farther away from us, and those which are behind us will catch us up. This might be tolerable if peace were assured; but I fear it is not. Here I am very sad and anxious. . . .

I think therefore that the first step towards a right use of wealth within the country is the taking an unaggressive position among nations.[60]

Marshall considered the remedy of protective tariffs, then being energetically canvassed, in his "Memorandum on Fiscal Policy" of 1903, surely one of the finest policy documents—mainly nonquantitative of course—ever written by an academic economist, the publication of which apparently was only dragged out of him five years after it was written. Marshall regards "the future of England with grave anxiety." Though he had recognized the force of the infant industries argument for protection for less developed countries, Marshall comes out firmly and categorically against the senile industries argument for protection for Britain; nor is he enthusiastic about the imperialist element in the tariff program, which might turn out to be too favorable to (what were to become) the white dominions. He emphasizes the dangers of retaliation in view of the urgency of Britain's demands for imports, and the possibilities of political mismanagement. Free trade, Marshall says, "diminishes the money value of political power." Finally, he notes that Britain is falling behind in certain new industries such as electrical engineering and chemicals.[61]

60. Ibid., pp. 392-94.
61. *Official Papers by Alfred Marshall*, pp. 365 ff.

Thus, though Marshall was keenly aware of the looming problem of the changing relative economic position of Britain, he had no major policy changes to propose. His influence and that of other economists in the opening years of this century probably helped to retain Britain's mainly free trade policy for another two or three decades. In fact, though Marshall's interests extended across the whole range of feasible extensions of government intervention in the economy, for the most part he had no far-reaching proposals to make. Certainly that was the case with regard to The Monetary Framework, or Macro-Economic Policy, the problems of Monopoly and Restrictive Practices, and Britain's External Commercial Policy, with the two latter of which he was especially profoundly preoccupied. It was under the headings of Poverty and Redistribution, and Inadequacies of Individual Choice, with its various subheadings of paternalism, ignorance, "externalities" and public goods and services, that Marshall's most definite proposals fall for extending state action.

It seems, therefore, in some ways rather strange for Keynes (and especially Keynes) to have complained that "Marshall was too anxious to do good." It is not very apparent that the good was very extensive that Marshall was too anxious to do. Certainly Marshall, like some of the classical economists, was prone to moralizing or preaching.[62] But moralizing and preaching are not so much *oneself doing* good or even necessarily being "anxious" *oneself to do good*. They rather consist in *urging other people to be good*—which may often be vain and presumptuous, but is apt to be rather less dangerous.

In fact, Marshall had strictly limited and disciplined ideas about the role of the academic economist as well as a conscientious grasp of that vital kind of knowledge which consists in an awareness and acceptance of the extent of one's own ignorance. "Why should I be ashamed to say that I know of no simple remedy?"[63] Marshall once exclaimed. Here again we have a notable contrast in attitude with many economists today.[64]

---

62. However, Marshall himself maintained that "when the academic student takes on himself the role of a preacher, he is generally less effective than when he treats the problems of life objectively." Pigou, *Memorials*, p. 397.

63. Ibid., p. 387.

64. The preceding article was delivered at the Nottingham Conference on the History of Economic Thought in January 1969. Footnotes and some paragraphs at the end have been added. It is intended as part of a much more extensive survey down to more recent times.

PUBLIC ECONOMICS AT THE ECOLE DES PONTS ET CHAUSSEES: 1830–1850

Robert B. EKELUND, Jr.

Texas A&M University

and

Robert F. HEBERT*

Clemson University

First version received November 1972, final version received February 1973

If economics is no longer the Dismal Science, good news still does not always travel fast amongst economists. Delay is especially likely if the good news happens to appear first in a journal for highway engineers; and delay is yet more likely, as far as English-speaking economists are concerned, if the engineering journal happens to be the *Annales des Ponts et Chaussées*.

J.R. Nelson (1964, p. vii)

1. Introduction

The problem of measuring the benefits of public goods[1] and the costs of providing them was first systematically broached by engineers of the Ecole des Ponts et Chaussées in the nineteenth century. Although no formal course of instruction in political economy was offered there until 1847, the Ecole produced a long and rich tradition of

---

* We wish to express our appreciation of assistance rendered by the interlibrary loan staffs of Clemson University and Texas A&M University, and for extensive comments on earlier drafts of this paper by Raymond Battalio, Alfred Chalk, and two anonymous referees of this journal. The usual caveat obtains, however. This research was sponsored by the Texas A&M University Fund for Organized Research and the J.E. Sirrine Foundation.

[1] Throughout this paper we give the term "public good" a broader definition than Paul Samuelson, who defines a public good in such a way that when supplied to one consumer it can also be supplied to additional consumers at zero marginal cost. Our definition includes highways, canals, and railroads, which have been termed "public goods" in the modern sense by J.G. Head (cf. Samuelson 1958, Head 1962).

economic studies beginning with the works of Vauban in the eighteenth century.

This paper seeks to identify only one part of the Ecole's tentacular tradition in applied economics and empirical research. It attempts to evaluate the major contributions to public economics which appeared during the first two decades of the *Annales des Ponts et Chaussées*, official journal of the Ecole, which began publication in 1831. Our investigation reveals that individual French performances, such as those of Henri Navier, Joseph Minard, and the better-known Jules Dupuit, constitute an impressive and early advance in the analysis of public sector economics.

2. Henri Navier and early cost–benefit analysis

In the 1832 lead article in the *Annales*, a French engineer named Henri Navier (1785–1836) presented what may well be the first systematic discussion of public goods provision based on cost–benefit analysis (Navier 1832). [2] He began by reminding his readers of Smith's dictum, that social wealth is increased by the division of labor and the extent of the market. Navier focused on the latter as the subject of his inquiry. He maintained that transport provision is the chief means of extending the market, insofar as it renders transportation costs as low as possible, and thus increases the benefit to society.

2.1. Transport costs and public welfare

In attempting to establish a relationship between freight rates and public welfare, Navier divided transport costs into two parts: (1) construction and maintenance costs, which in his day were often borne by the state or locality; and (2) direct costs of carriage, which were ultimately paid by the shipper. Navier insisted that from a welfare standpoint reduction of the latter is the more important:

> ... although every saving is advantageous to society insofar as it permits greater consumption or favors the accumulation of capital, the particular saving realized by reducing business' share of transportation costs seems to be more important than any other, since it immediately influences the price of merchandise, and thus the extent of the market (Navier 1832, p. 2). [3]

---

[2] Translations, except where noted, were made by the authors.

[3] Navier added that "... the extent of the market itself is determined by the condition that production costs plus transport costs not exceed the current (demand) price of the merchandise".

The main objective of public works administration, then, should be to improve social welfare, which in the case of transport enterprises, means reducing as much as possible the freight costs borne by the shipper. Thus, Navier clearly identified transport cost reductions as the crucial source of saving, or benefit, to society, and he related these savings to increased consumption of transported goods.

Institutional practices of Navier's time plainly constrained the benefit of public goods, however. State provision was the most common means of providing public works in France, and had been since long before the French Revolution. Navier clearly preferred this means of public goods provision, but he attacked the prevailing opinion of French administrators that such projects should generally be self-liquidating. With respect to public works, Navier proclaimed: "The establishment of tolls sometimes appears ... to be the most convenient way to produce the necessary funds; but it is certainly not the most equitable way" (Navier 1832, p. 7).[4] He argued further:

> Consider what happens today when a canal is built. The substitution of a water route for a land route reduces transport costs by a ratio of 8 to 1. This results in a great saving for commerce. But because of the duties imposed on canals, the cost advantage is reduced to 3 to 1, or 2 to 1; and thus, because of the added inconvenience of reaching the canal and the slower movement of goods by water, most businesses continue to ship by land. Consequently, the canal is practically useless to commerce. In general, the utility of French canals is not nearly as great as it could be. A considerable amount of capital has been spent in order to create a new element of prosperity, but because of the tolls imposed, this goal has never been reached (Navier 1832, p. 8).

To Navier, at least, it was apparent that public administrators often did not understand the welfare aspects of toll reductions on public thoroughfares.

Navier never solved the problem of an optimum tariff, although he offered several insights into the pricing of public goods. He maintained, for example, that capital costs of construction should not be recouped through either general or selective tolls, but instead should be imputed to "l'ensemble des impôts", since the progress in goods production and

---

[4] Navier's position was avant-garde even by the standards of a later century. For example, Pigou (1947, p. 29) argued that "when public authorities provide commodities and services for the specific use of particular individuals, gratis supply to the users is but rarely desirable. The broad general rule should be to finance these public enterprises by charging fees to the users of the commodities and services concerned proportioned to the amount of their use, *and adequate in the aggregate to cover all costs*". Although he was willing to admit an exception in the case of highways because of the "great inconvenience and ... heavy expenses of collection", he did not think the same was true of either canals or railroads.

circulation occasioned by new transport facilities will increase the public revenue through indirect taxes. He recognized that: "consideration of the state's interest provides no absolute criterion for setting tolls, which are both paid and received by the state itself. It is clear, however, that the toll cannot exceed the saving in the cost of transport ..." without damaging the public welfare. Navier suggested, therefore, that the state experiment with tolls between the limits of zero and the average benefit of new constructions, while attempting to keep the toll as low as possible in relation to maintenance and interest costs. His argument for low tolls was emphatic: "De plus l'établissement même du péage ... en diminue beaucoup l'utilité" (Navier 1832, pp. 18–19).

2.2. Navier's Rule for the provision of public goods

Despite his argument against tolls to recoup capital and maintenance expenses on public works, Navier recognized that the "free" provision of public goods (i.e., zero toll) provided no standard on which to base public investment decisions. Indeed, he argued that political pressures and costly miscalculations had saddled taxpayers with heavy and unnecessary burdens in the past. He therefore sought a decision rule to guide the state in the execution of public works.

Navier provided such a rule in the form of a statement of minimum demand for public works, below which the undertaking would be against the interests of the state. In his words, "... in order for the operation not be onerous to taxpayers, the annual saving obtained by it must be at least equal to the interest on capital plus maintenance costs" (Navier 1832, p. 16). For transport enterprises this meant establishing a minimum tonnage which, unless met, would not justify the provision of the public good.

Navier's principle, which he illustrated in a numerical example drawn from commercial statistics gathered by a fellow engineer, is set forth algebraically here in the interest of space. What we shall call "Navier's Rule" may be expressed as $A \leq Q_t \, P^*$, where Q_t is the annual quantity shipped per league, and $P^* = (P_r - P_c)$ is the "cost savings" on canal over highway transport. Since $Q_t = f(P^*)$, Navier's Rule means that there must be some P^* and Q_t such that $P^* Q_t \geq A$. The expression, $P^* Q_t$, may be regarded as the total "savings", or "benefit", from instituting the project, and A represents annual recurring costs. If $P^* Q_t > A$, Navier alleged that the state will annually gain a net amount equal to P^* multiplied by the quantity carried above Q_t. In effect, Navier set up a cost-benefit criterion: public works such as transport enterprises should only be provided if the total benefit (in the form of cost savings) exceeds the total (recurring) costs.

Navier modified this rule slightly in the case of the provision of public goods by private enterprise (i.e., regulated monopoly). The modification allows a suitable return to risk and uncertainty to be counted as part of the costs against which the social benefits of public works are to be measured. In Navier's words, the return "... should be at least equivalent to the return earned by other enterprises of a similar nature", which comes remarkably close to the "capital attraction" standard utilized by modern regulatory commissions. But his argument was even more sophisticated because it was based squarely on sound principles of resource allocation. Navier repudiated the conventional wisdom that since the holders of public goods franchises bear all costs, they can be hurt without the state suffering as a consequence. On the contrary, he maintained that economic losses signal resource misallocation, and that "... un travail mal appliqué cause nécessairement a la societé une perte véritable" (Navier 1832, pp. 24–25n).[5]

By modern standards, there are several deficiencies in Navier's rule for public goods provision: (1) benefits are not expressed in present value terms; (2) the current benefit rate is (incorrectly) assumed to continue indefinitely;[6] (3) the concept of diminishing marginal utility is noticeably absent. Before the third problem was broached by Dupuit, Navier's contemporary, Joseph Minard (1781–1870), made significant progress toward overcoming the first two deficiencies.

3. Joseph Minard and the subjective evaluation of social welfare

Joseph Minard's ideas on the subject of public economics were formalized for a proposed course of instruction at the Ecole in 1831, but

---

[5] Regulation of private suppliers of public goods was considered essential to protect "l'intérêt publique", which Navier defined as the harmony between three separate interests; the interest of the state, as far as the existence of the enterprise itself is concerned; the interst of commerce, as far as the determination of suitable tolls is concerned; and the interest of the firm's stockholders. In safeguarding the public interest, government should, for the most part, determine whether the enterprise will be completed; and test new and existing tariffs for "suitability" in conjunction with Navier's Rule.

[6] Cf. Marglin (1963, pp. 22–24). Navier's Rule may be viewed as a less sophisticated version of Marglin's "myopic rule".

did not appear in print until 1850 (Minard 1850).[7] The delay was unfortunate, since J.B. Say read Minard's manuscript as early as 1832 and rated it very highly. He urged Minard to publish his researches for the benefit of both engineers and economists (Say 1832).

3.1. Minard on demand, value and utility

Minard's "elementary notions" of political economy begin with the familiar distinction between "use value" and "exchange value". Accordingly, public works offer examples of both: lighthouses and most roads, bridges, and ports in France have only use value according to Minard; whereas, canals, bridges and railroads on which tolls are charged have both use value and exchange value, since they offer services which can be purchased. Exchange value is reflected in market prices, and prices, according to Minard, vary both with the quantity of money available and with changes in supply and demand. On the effects of changes in demand and "offer", Minard charged:

> In general, the price of anything rises when it is demanded more or offered less; but the increase is not exactly in direct proportion to the demand, or in inverse proportion to the offer since on the one hand, demands are dependent upon price and need, which has limits, whereas offers are not determined by need (Minard 1850, p. 5).

The concept of a demand schedule, thought not yet explicit in economic literature, appears to have been grasped by Minard and extended to public goods. In discussing the "correlation between tariffs and revenues" on selected British and Belgian railroads, Minard noted:

> ... the future consumption (of railway services) ... depends on the schedule of charges; traffic will diminish when the charges are increased, and, up to a limit, will increase when they are lowered, so that there is a tariff somewhere in between which yields the greatest profit (Minard 1850, p. 107).

In the case of public goods, Minard pointed out that "production" usually results in a "service flow" rather than a "goods flow". This recognition led him to include elements of form, place, and time utility in his configuration of value. Thus, he observed: "If stones must be crushed for the upkeep of a road which is a considerable distance from the quarry, the breakage and the transport of the stones add to their value". Likewise, vegetables and other produce hauled to Paris "... re-

---

[7] In his "Notions élémentaires ..." Minard wrote: "L'ouvrage, écrit en entier en 1831, a réçu depuis plusiers additions". The additions referred to appear, however, to be a mere updating of the manuscript, especially in regard to the use of numerous statistical examples of events subsequent to the first writing of the treatise.

ceive, acordingly, an increase in value resulting from their transport" (Minard 1850, pp. 6–7).

Another unique element in Minard's treatise is his explicit treatment of time in economic analysis. Time entered Minard's discussion of value in at least three ways: (1) length of time involved in production (including transport); (2) the durability of goods; and (3) the effects of compound interest on the present value of capital. This last observation played a major role in Minard's cost–benefit calculations of public works, and as such, marked major improvement of Navier's earlier analysis.

3.2. Income distribution and public utility

Minard held that the source of increased real wealth available to society through public goods construction is an unequal distribution of income. It is a fact of common experience, he argued, that a price reduction which increases consumption does so in two quarters: (1) in the increased purchases of former customers, and (2) in additional purchases by new consumers.

Thus he argued that if the price of coal is reduced by one franc after the opening of a canal, the following increase in coal consumption consists not only of more purchases by existing customers, "but also by those who could not afford it before the canal" (Minard 1850, p. 14). Therefore, the utility derived from this canal cannot ordinarily be measured simply by multiplying the change in price (of one franc) by the increased traffic, as Navier had suggested. Minard maintained that Navier's method would apply only in the improbable case where all consumers at the new price were former consumers as well. His criticism of Navier's measure of public utility was, however, weakened by an apparent inability to separate income and substitution effects from each other and from changes in consumer preferences or product quality. Still, the size of the "externality" involved in providing certain public works impressed him, and he assumed unequivocally that this externality depended upon inequality of income distribution. Indeed, "public utility" did not make much sense to Minard if income distribution was not skewed. In the following lengthy passage he underlined the classic premises upon which public finance rests:

> ... most questions of political economy are connected with the unequal distribution of wealth, and solutions to them would be puzzling if this inequality did not exist. The

R.B. Ekelund, Jr. and R.F. Hebert, The Ecole des Ponts et Chaussées: 1830–1850

> material needs of most people are very great, so that anything which tends to satisfy or frustrate those needs assumes the first importance.
>
> If all were equally wealthy, it would be extremely difficult to determine whether it would be better for the country to dig a canal or to build a theatre, or an *Arc de Triomphe*; the asnwer would depend on the preference of the greatest number. But we would all undoubtedly admit that satisfaction of the basic, physical needs of life is preferable to the pleasure of seeing a comedy or gazing at an *Arc de Triomphe*. In the real world, moreover, there are many cold, ill-housed unfortunates who would be somewhat better off by the fact that a canal lowered the price of fuel and construction materials. The public interest would be better served, therefore, by the construction of a canal instead of a theatre, or an *Arc de Triomphe* (Minard 1850, p. 16).

Clearly, Minard did not flinch from the grand, interpersonal judgments necessary to make decisions on the desirability of alternative public expenditures. Unlike Navier, he set priorities on expenditures according to whether they produced "community utility" (e.g., public fountains), "departmental utility" (e.g., a road or canal crossing several departments), or "national utility" (e.g., military installations or quarantine stations). None of these practices, however, are very far from modern conventions in public finance.

3.3. The welfare evaluation of public goods: theory and practice

Whereas Navier measured the benefits of a public good in terms of actual dollar costs saved, Minard introduced more subjective elements into his "benefit" measure. His general statements concerning the utility of public works, though less exact than Navier's, are more comprehensive, and contain clear directions for calculations of social welfare. Most public expenditures, in Minard's view, are undertaken to finance improvements of existing facilities. Thus, "it is the improvement which one seeks to express in terms of economies, and these economies represent utility created". Essentially, Minard suggested that the "benefit" of a public good be measured on the basis of opportunity costs. Thus:

> A bridge is built in order to avoid crossing another bridge farther away, or to avoid a long, slow, or dangerous route; in the final analysis, to save time. A road, canal, or railroad is constructed if it can transport goods more cheaply or more rapidly than existing means of transport. A port, wharf, or station is built in order to avoid risks, the value of which can be estimated by losses incurred or by the actual amount paid for insurance (Minard 1850, pp. 54–55).

Specifically, "the expenses entailed in a given consumption in the old order of things, less those incurred by the new means employed for the same service, gives the economy gained by society". The costs must account for capital and interest, upkeep and renovation, and depreciation. Most importantly, however, Minard added a conceptual adjustment to the social economies realized, in the form of time saved. Time must be given a value, he insisted, "... because a service rendered more promptly is almost always a better buy; 'time is money', as the English proverb says" (Minard 1850, p. 55). Minard applied this principle in a number of benefit—cost studies in which he subjectively assigned a monetary value to the time saved by public improvements.

Evaluating the utility of new constructions was more difficult, Minard felt. He warned that some benefits are more apparent than real. For example, the increase in property values surrounding a new bridge is usually offset, he thought, by a decrease in property values near the old bridge. On the other hand, failure to consider gains in temporal utility results in the underestimation of social benefits. Thus, Minard argued that, disregarding time factors, it cannot be demonstrated that a railway — as a means of carrying goods only — increases public welfare more than a canal. In fact, transport rates may be higher on the railroad. But all things considered (including time saved), Minard maintained that the railroad appeared superior to the canal from the standpoint of social utility (Minard 1850, p. 48).

In short, Minard was keenly aware of the difficulties of determining the full benefits of public goods, since these benefits consist of both those which existed before and those which are added by improvements or new construction. He expressed the hope that statistical information would help to identify the former, but insofar as the latter are concerned, only an approximation could be attained, and then, only with luck. Minard himself was not overwhelmed by his own caveats, however. He boldly declared that it was the job of the engineer to "evaluate, in money terms, the utility of the (proposed) construction, and to compare it ... with the costs" (Minard 1850, pp. 106–107). He put these theoretical ideas to use, moreover, in copious examples of public goods, both hypothetical and empirical.

On the cost side of project evaluation, Minard contributed a formal description of the analytical relationship between total production costs and the life of a public project. He was concerned with identifying the real costs of maintaining a public construction in perpetuity, and correctly represented this sum as the discounted present value of a stream of replacement and maintenance costs, including an allowance for inflation, which, for convenience, he assumed to progress at a geometric rate. According to Minard, the sum which be paid in order to construct, maintain, and rebuild a public work is expressed by the formula:

$$C\left(\frac{n^p}{m^p - n^p}\right) + E\left(\frac{m}{m-n}\right), \qquad (1)$$

where C is the nominal cost of the project, E is the annual upkeep expense, m is the interest (discount) rate, n is a price deflator (inflator), and p is the useful life of the project. Pressing the argument further, Minard termed the above formulation incomplete, "since to reconstruct a work requires a length of time during which its use cannot be enjoyed, and in this case there is a loss of capital". Minard let q stand for this "capital loss", and rewrote his complete formula for the real costs of a public work as:

$$(C+q)\left(\frac{n^p}{m^p - n^p}\right) + E\left(\frac{m}{m-n}\right), \text{(Minard 1850, p. 68)}. \qquad (2)$$

Against this idea of the cost of a public good in perpetuity, Minard examined the nature of the reasoning behind the construction of most public works. Although the benefit was assumed perpetual, according to Minard, "the truth is that the utility and value of public constructions change with time" (Minard 1850, p. 71).[8] This variability was affirmed by Minard in numerous examples reaching back to the Roman aqueducts.

All of Minard's examples suggest calculations of benefit based on the real costs of projects. These benefits were, without exception, identified with the savings realized by instituting the project. His measures were not totally objective in that they assigned a hypothetical value to some of the benefits, e.g., the subjective treatment of the evaluation of time. In other words, "non-objective" and difficult-to-calculate benefits were not summarily excluded on those grounds, and Minard consistently sought a pecuniary measure of "utility" or the real-wealth change from public improvements.

---

[8] Jevons (1879, p. 240) paid tribute to Minard when he noted' "Minard fully understood this point in finance and showed that in the case of some public works ... the real cost is incomparably greater than it is represented to be merely stating the sums of money expended". However, Jevons failed to make use of Minard's mathematical formulation explaining the analytical relation between expenses and the duration of constructions of public works.

3.4. Welfare aspects in the pricing of public goods

Minard gave considerable space in his treatise to a discussion of the principles involved in pricing the services of public works. Since most public works in France were financed by the state, the central question was whether or not the state should impose tolls on public works constructed from general funds. And if so, what level of tolls was an optimum? The answer, as Minard clearly recognized, involved considerations of social welfare and income redistribution. He observed:

> Where a toll is charged, those who consume the service, whether directly or indirectly, pay for it entirely; on the other hand (where consumption is gratuitous), everyone is charged for the service, indiscriminately, through taxes. Therefore, consumers of the service pay only a part of the cost, while non-users pay the other part. The latter bear a non-compensatory loss which is exactly equal to the gain of the consumers, provided the number of consumers remains unchanged. But the number increases *when there is no toll* (Minard 1850, p. 27, emphasis supplied).

Despite the import of this passage, Minard did not seek to establish a prima facie case for zero tolls. Instead, he pointed out that increased consumption of public works may affect maintenance and administrative costs. Thus he wrote:

> If the increased usage does not occasion any increase in costs, as in the case of a bridge on which maintenance remains the same regardless of traffic, then there is an increase in utility and social welfare; if the costs are increased slightly, as for a canal, the advantage is less; finally, if the costs increase considerably due to increased traction, as on a highway or railroad, the advantage is almost nothing, since it becomes necessary to raise taxes to the level of expenses. Thus, the free use of constructions can, depending on their nature, offer great or small advantages; and in every case it involves the necessity of levying an unjust tax on those who gain nothing from the constructions (Minard 1850, pp. 27–28).

Finally, Minard added that where tolls are removed, taxpayers should contribute to the general fund in proportion to the utility they receive; that is, taxes should be allocated according to whether the public good provides "community", "departmental", or "national" utility.

Conceptually, tolls themselves were not considered taxes by Minard, but payments for services rendered. He argued:

> When the proceeds of the toll do not exceed maintenance and interst costs it does no harm to the social welfare, since ... the toll is a fair means of reimbursing these expenses which must be incurred in the project (Minard 1850, pp. 81–82).

But if tolls are higher, Minard recognized that part of the social return was destroyed. His argument thus appears more tractable than Navier's. Whereas Navier argued emphatically that "the higher the toll, the greater the decrease in utility", Minard countered that "the toll has a great advantage in yielding a revenue proportional to the principal cause of deterioration of highways" (Minard 1850, p. 84).

As always, Minard supported his position by observation. He noted that the greatest degree of commercial prosperity existed in countries such as England, Holland, Belgium, and Prussia, which levied tolls on highways and canals. He even went so far to suggest that where public works are financed through general funds, toll receipts above maintenance costs might be used to construct public works in other regions of the country whose inhabitants could not benefit from the first ones.

In examining the tariff structure of Belgian railways, moreover, Minard made an important and timely discovery, namely, that there is a minimum price for public goods consistent with social welfare. He showed, for example, that passenger fares on Belgian railroads were too low, since they produced disproportionate benefits. Five-sixths of the net benefits from the railway went to travelers, whereas the state earned less than three percent on the capital it advanced for railway construction. Thus, Minard argued: "The division of the economy obtained on passenger transport appears to favor excessively the traveling public, and prejudice those who travel little, yet pay taxes all the same". In raising tariffs, however, Minard insisted that "gross revenue should not be allowed to fall below operation costs, in which case it would be even less possible to meet the interest on borrowed capital" (Minard 1850, p. 112).

In retrospect, Minard's principles of public goods provision appear to be much more than the "elementary notions" to which his treatise referred. In addition to his statements on demand, subjective assessments of "utility" and the concept of opportunity costs were marshalled to the "benefit" side of public works evaluation. Costs (as Jevons discovered) were to be capitalized in calculating the present value of public investments, and Minard devised a rigorous mathematical formula for this purpose. Benefits were not easily handled, of course, although the analytical equipment Minard commanded was more than sufficient to give minimal and approximate guides to the analysis of important public goods issues.

Minard's essay also raised questions on the role of income distribution in the production of public goods. Interpersonal welfare judgments and suppositions of a specific social welfare function characterized his statements,[9] but Minard consistently sought a "scientific method" of evaluating the practical effects of public goods provision.

---

[9] Minard recognized two polar cases in public goods provision: (a) those where the recipients of the service was identifiable and could be made to pay the entire cost of provision,

4. Dupuit and the culmination of the early tradition in public economics

The position of Jules Dupuit in the history of economic analysis is fairly well established. Nevertheless, his important work takes on new perspective when viewed against the background of the earlier performances of Navier and Minard; it emerges as the crowning glory of two especially fruitful decades in a long tradition of interest in and concern with public sector problems. Moreover, in the decision rules put forward by the writers reviewed here we find optimality criteria which have been rediscovered only recently.

4.1. Dupuit's rule

Dupuit's attack on earlier measures of public utility, including, specifically Navier's, has been detailed by himself (1844) and more recently, by Ekelund (1968). His objections to earlier methods of utility measurement were twofold: (1) measurement of the utility of any quantity of a good consumed is not based on differences in cost of transportation but on differences in costs of production, assuming a competitive market; and (2) the increases in quantity taken at the lower cost (price) do not all take the same value, but are valued discretely according to the law of diminishing marginal utility.

Utilizing this last principle, Dupuit devised his own analytical apparatus for the evaluation of public goods. This apparatus is illustrated in fig. 1, where the curve PZ represents the demand curve for the use of a public good and AA' represents the constant unit costs of production (maintenance and interest costs) assumed by Dupuit. If we let q be the use of the good (i.e., crossings of a bridge), X be the quantity of the good, $F(q,X)$ the demand curve (PZ) for q, c the user's cost per unit of q, which Dupuit assumed to be zero, and $C(X)$ the cost of producing X, then we may set forth Dupuit's rule as follows: an incremental unit of X is justified if

---

and (b) those where consumers were made to pay only a part of total cost, with the balance being paid from tax revenues. He would adhere to the "benefit" principle whenever possible, but in the latter case he believed that the welfare effects of distribution were positive. In addition, he was aware of the great advantages of making public goods free, where possible.

R.B. Ekelund, Jr. and R.F. Hebert, The Ecole des Ponts et Chaussées: 1830–1850

Price

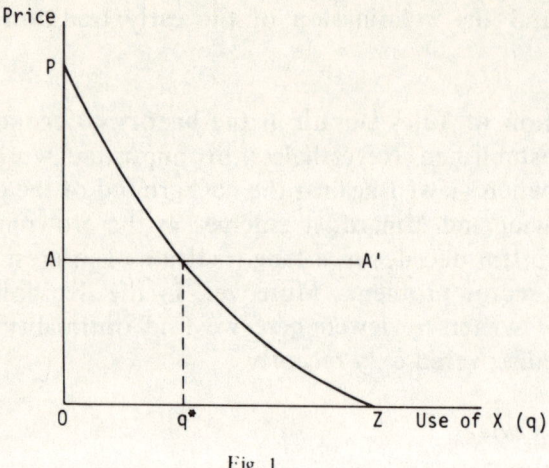

Fig. 1.

$$\int_0^{q^*} \frac{\partial F(q,X)}{\partial X} dq - cq^* > C'(X), \qquad (3)$$

where q^* is such that $\partial F(q^*,X)/\partial X = c$.

Thus, for the optimum quantity (X^*) and the optimum use (q^{**}) we have

$$\int_0^{q^{**}} \frac{\partial F(q,X^*)}{\partial X} dq - cq^{**} = C'(X^*) \qquad (4)$$

which is the Bowen (1943) – Samuelson (1954) optimality condition for public goods. Dupuit's (1844) famous bridge example is a special case of the Bowen–Samuelson formulation in two respects: (1) q is a number of users, and (2) $c = 0$.[10]

An incredibly complete demonstration of the welfare conclusions of competitive equilibrium, which was the sine qua non of neoclassical economics, followed Dupuit's theoretical footing in utility analysis. In more than one work, Dupuit asserted the efficacy of competition in establishing a welfare maximum. He affirmed the desirability of reducing international trade barriers which, he believed, had effects upon

---

[10] We are indebted to an anonymous referee of this journal for calling our attention to this point.

welfare which were analogous to reduced costs of production (Dupuit 1861, pp. 63; 140–41). Moreover, he condemned all private or governmental interferences in markets where competition existed, and some monopolies arbitrarily granted by governments, as in agriculture and mail carriage (Dupuit 1859, 1851). Exceptions were made in the case of discriminating monopolists since, to his credit, Dupuit showed how price discrimination, judiciously applied, could increase social welfare (Dupuit 1844) (Ekelund 1970). In sum, Dupuit utilized his complete set of tools to analyze the welfare effects of all manner of public goods provision.

5. Conclusion

An examination of the thought of three members of the Ecole in the 1830–50 period reveals remarkable progress in the theory of public economics. Navier provided a frame for welfare ideas with a transport–opportunity cost measure of benefit and with detailed procedures for measuring costs. Minard extended the welfare theory of public finance in many directions, but most especially in the inclusion of non-objective "psychic" benefits (time savings, etc.) into the calculation and in an understanding of how time (here with a strong suggestion of long and short run analysis) affects the computation of costs. More fundamentally, Minard may have been the first writer to recognize that the mere existence of a public sector affects welfare distribution. On the other hand, Navier's explicit attempt to reach a framework within which an empirical measure of public utility might be obtained, and specifically, his overestimate of the utility of a canal, led Dupuit to develop an alternative means of evaluating public goods.

The tradition at the Ecole des Ponts et Chaussées, nurtured by the early works of the 1830–50 period, produced nothing less than an entirely new branch of economic inquiry, and the analysis of the welfare aspects of public finance was well on its way by 1850. An essential feature of the tradition, as demonstrated in the writing of this period, was a refusal to separate empirical research from theory. For example, a clear rapport exists between the concepts "public utility" (in Navier, Minard and Dupuit) and "theoretical utility" (in Dupuit). As such the Ecole's tradition provides an excellent case study of the impact of empirical pursuits in an "allied field" upon economic theory. Developments in public economics by the writers considered in the present paper constitute incremental evidence on the point, although additional evidence is needed for a detailed assessment.

Finally, French engineers of the Ecole des Ponts et Chaussées, of which Navier, Minard and Dupuit were only representative, attacked economic questions with the boldness and assurance of intelligent children, unaware of many of the complexities and assumptions of their arguments. Most fortuitously, they were not jaded into a familiar habit of thought which makes the complexity of many important economic and social problems an acceptable excuse for ignoring them. As such their approach to economic inquiry was as unique as their very sizeable contributions.

References

Bowen, H.R., 1943, The interpretation of voting in the allocation of economic resources, Quarterly Journal of Economics LVIII, 27–49.
Dupuit, Jules, 1844, On the measurement of utility of public works. Translated by Barback, R.H., 1952, International Economic Papers, No. 2. (Macmillan, London) pp. 83–110.
Dupuit, Jules, 1851, De l'impôt payé aux maîtres de poste par les entrepreneurs de voitures publiques, Journal des Economistes, 1st Ser., XXVII, 131–151.
Dupuit, Jules, 1859, Des crises alimentaires et des moyens employés pour y remediés, Journal des Economistes, 2nd Ser., XXII, 161–176.
Dupuit, Jules, 1861, La liberté commerciale, son principe et ses conséquences. (Guillaumin, Paris).
Ekelund, R.B., Jr., 1968, Jules Dupuit and the early theory of marginal cost pricing, Journal of Political Economy LXXVI, 462–471.
Ekelund, R.B., Jr. 1970, Price discrimination and product differentiation in economic theory: an early analysis, Quarterly Journal of Economics, 268–278.
Head, J.G., 1962, Public goods and public policy, Public Finance XVII, 197–219.
Jevons, W.S., 1879, Theory of political economy, 2nd ed. (Kelley and Millman reprint) 1957.
Marglin, S.A., 1963, Approaches to dynamic investment planning. (North-Holland Publishing Company, Amsterdam).
Minard, Joseph, 1850, Notions élémentaires d'économie politique appliquées aux travaux publique. Annales des Ponts et Chaussées, Memoirs et Documents, 2nd Ser., XIX, 1–125.
Navier, Henri, 1832, De l'exécution des travaux publique, et particulierement des concessions, Annales des Ponts et Chaussées, Memoirs et Documents, 1st Ser., III, 1–31.
Nelson, J.R., ed., 1964, Marginal cost pricing in practice. (Prentice-Hall, Englewood Cliffs, N.J.).
Pigou, A.C., 1947, A study in public finance, 3rd ed. (Macmillan, London).
Samuelson, P.A., 1954, The pure theory of public expenditures, Review of Economics and Statistics XXXVI, 387–389.
Samuelson, P.A., 1958, Aspects of public expenditure theories, Review of Economics and Statistics XL, 332–338.
Say, J.B., 1832, Letter to Joseph Minard. Reprinted in Minard, op. cit., p. 2 n.

[12]

Giffen's Paradox and the Marshallian Demand Curve

The purpose of this paper is to reassess the meaning of Giffen's Paradox in Marshallian demand analysis. When viewed in methodological and textual context Giffen's Paradox becomes compatible with Friedman's constant real-income interpretation of the Marshallian demand curve. An apparent inconsistency in the *Principles*, which had rendered impossible a wholly acceptable and conclusive interpretation of Marshall's demand curve, is thus removed.

I. The Methodology of the Marshallian Demand Curve

Throughout the *Principles* Marshall gives insights into his general methodological framework. Perhaps the clearest statement of his methodology is found in the Preface to the Fifth Edition where he states:

> ... we reduce to inaction all other forces by the phrase "other things being equal." We do not suppose that they are inert: but for the time we ignore their activity. This scientific device is a great deal older than science: it is the method by which, consciously or unconsciously, sensible men have dealt from time immemorial with every difficult problem of ordinary life [12, p. 44].

Marshall's assumption of a constant purchasing power of money in the formulation of the demand curve is a clear example of this methodology.[1] As is true of much of Marshallian demand theory, the constant purchasing power of money assumption is not without precedent. David Ricardo [15, p. 46], Augustin Cournot [2, p. 26], Jules Dupuit [3, pp. 83–110], John Stuart Mill [13, p. 439], and numerous others had used the assumption before Marshall.

---

[1]Marshall's constant purchasing power of money assumption is stated explicitly several times in the exposition of his theory. In outlining the general premises of his analysis Marshall stated:
> ... we may throughout this volume *neglect possible changes in the general purchasing power of money*. Thus the price of anything will be taken as representative of its exchange value *relatively* to things in general (emphasis added) [11, p. 62].

In his statement of marginal diminishing price Marshall restated the assumed constancy of the purchasing power of money as follows:
> The larger the amount of a thing that a person has, the less, other things being equal (i.e., the *purchasing power of money, and the amount of money at his command being equal*), will be the price which he will pay for a little more of it: or in other words his marginal demand price for it diminishes (emphasis added) [11, p. 95].

The logical necessity for the constant purchasing power assumption is deeply woven into the fabric of the Classical System. It is not an assumed parameter used solely to limit the domain of the demand curve, though this is the result of its application. Its logic is more basic. The constant purchasing power assumption is the product of the classical dichotomy. The theoretical division of economic analysis into a study of the value of money on the one hand and a study of relative values on the other forced its inclusion as a parameter in the study of demand. The constant purchasing power assumption was a simplification that dichotomized the economic system and made partial equilibrium analysis accessible. But the convenience it afforded was purchased by the imposition of a limited domain of applicability.[2] Giffen's Paradox is an example of this limitation.

II. Giffen's Paradox and the Marshallian Demand Curve

Marshall states Giffen's Paradox as follows:

> There are, however, some exceptions. For instance, as Sir R. Giffen has pointed out, a rise in the price of bread makes so large a drain on the resources of the poorer labouring families and raises so much the marginal utility of money to them, that they are forced to curtail their consumption of meat and the more expensive farinaceous foods : and, bread being still the cheapest food which they can get and will take, they consume more, and not less of it [11, p. 132].

George Stigler's interpretation of Giffen's Paradox is that : "One suspects that the paradox was a last minute addition to the *Principles*, for it stands in bold conflict with the law of demand" [18, p. 152]. Friedman follows the same line of reasoning in stating :

> The possibility of interpreting Marshall in these two quite different ways arises in part from the vagueness of Marshall's exposition, from his failure to give precise and rigorous definitions. A more fundamental reason, however, is the existence of inconsistency in the third and later editions of the *Principles*. In that edition Marshall introduced the celebrated passage bearing on the Giffen phenomenon [5, p. 56].[3]

[2] For a similar assessment of Marshall's methodology, as it applied to the theory of the firm and the process of adjustment, see Hicks [9, pp. 49–57].

[3] There may be some significance in the fact that Giffen's Paradox first appeared in the Third Edition, for as Guillebaud has pointed out :
> ... it was in this Third Edition that Marshall had the opportunity of justifying and defending his position in the light of the criticism which it had encountered [7, p. 332].

Contrary to these interpretations, Giffen's Paradox is neither a contradiction to the law of demand nor an inconsistency in Marshall's theory if it is viewed in the methodological and textual context from which it has been so untimely ripped. It occurs in a section of Chapter VI that discusses the fact that in practical application it is seldom necessary to take account of changes in the purchasing power of money, "for there are very few practical problems, in which the corrections to be made under this head would be of any importance" [11, p. 132]. This point is clarified in a footnote with the statement that "In mathematical language the neglected elements would generally belong to the second order of small quantities" [11, p. 132]. Giffen's Paradox is not, therefore, as Stigler implies, an exception to the law of demand but an exception to the general case in which the neglect of the income effect results in an error of the second order of smallness.

Marshall's law of demand states:
> There is then one general *law of demand* : The greater the amount to be sold, the smaller must be the price at which it is offered in order that it may find purchasers ; or, in other words, the amount demanded increases with a fall in price, and diminishes with a rise in price [11, p. 99].

Giffen's Paradox is not a contradiction to this law because in Marshall's theoretical formulation of the demand curve the marginal utility of money, total money income, and thus real income are assumed constant.[4] Giffen's Paradox exists only because the good under empirical observation, bread, makes up such a large part of the subject's budget that a change in its price greatly affects the marginal utility of money to him and thus his real income. This change in real income is abstracted from throughout the theoretical formulation of Marshall's demand curve [II, Note II pp. 838–839] [5, pp. 93–94]. The inclusion of Giffen's Paradox shows clearly that Marshall was aware that *in reality* real income changes with price changes.[5] Its inclusion, far from being a source of inconsistency, is a key to Marshall's framework of analysis.

[4] As Friedman has shown, the only way the purchasing power of money can remain constant as the price of the good under analysis changes is for the subject to be compensated by changes in money income or counter movements in the prices of other goods he consumes, in order that his level of real income remain constant [5, p. 53–56].

[5] Alford attributes the presence of Giffen's Paradox in the Third Edition of *Principles* to a change in the factual material available to Marshall [1, p. 42]. Marshall's additional factual material appears to have been Giffen's *Final Report of the Royal Commission on Agricultural Depression* [14, p. 58].

In general Marshall developed tools to deal with actual market situations [6, p. 181]. In most practical problems the income effect is of the "second order of small quantities" and his theoretical formulation of the demand curve is directly applicable to actual market situations.[6] Only in the extreme case, Giffen's Paradox, is the income effect present in a perceivable magnitude and thus warrants formal recognition as an exception to the general case where Marshall's formulation was a workable approximation of reality. In general formulations Marshall made weak assumptions concerning his income parameter, and second order movements in variables were permitted in order to make the demand curve more operational. Yet, in the formulation of his theoretical statement of the demand curve, Marshall rigidly adhered to the exclusion of changes in the purchasing power of money. Errors in interpretation seem to have resulted from his failure to distinguish explicitly at what point on his continuum of levels of abstraction between operational approximations and rigorous formulations he was operating in various facets of his analysis.[7]

With the presentation of Giffen's Paradox, Marshall had reached the limit beyond which the classical dichotomy was not an acceptable approximation of reality. He had reached the boundary of the classical methodological framework. While the income effect was outside the analysis of relative prices and was excluded by the classical dichotomy, the possible exception had to be acknowledged as to the applicability of the theory. This did not mean, however, that the parameters of the Marshallian demand curve were inconsistent but only that the formulation had a limited domain.[8]

---

[6]Marshall, in general, dealt with examples in which the proportion of the subject's budget used in the purchase of a good was small and the income effect of a price change was negligible. As Marshall stated :
> ... the assumption, which underlies our whole reasoning [is] that his expenditure on any one thing, as, for example, tea, is only a small part of his whole expenditure [11, p. 842].

[7]For a similar assessment of the continuum nature of Marshall's *ceteris paribus* approach see Alford [1, p. 40].

[8]A modern vestige of this methodology is evident in Frank Knight's analysis of demand. Examining the Slutsky-Hicks demand curve he concludes : "The 'income effect' of Slutsky *et al.* is merely a particular case or mode of change in the purchasing power of money, or the price level ; and it is this problem as a whole that should be isolated and reserved for separate treatment" [10, p. 299].

III. THE LAW OF DEMAND

Marshall's statement of the universal law of demand has been one of the most criticized parts of his theory [11, p. 99].[9] This criticism seems largely the result of a failure to recognize Marshall's general disbelief in "universal laws" except as *ceteris paribus* constructs. As Marshall stated :

> Some parts of economics are relatively abstract or *pure*, because they are concerned mainly with broad general propositions : for, in order that a proposition may be of broad application it must necessarily contain few details : it cannot adopt itself to particular cases ; and if it points to any prediction, that must be governed by a strong conditioning clause in which a very large meaning is given to the phrase "other things being equal" [11, p. 37, N. 2].

The law of demand began as an empirical generalization of the inverse relation between price and quantity purchased. This idea is evident in the statement of "Gregory King's Law" and early writings on demand theory [4]. Cournot stated the law of demand as follows : "The cheaper an article is, the greater ordinarily is the demand for it" [2, p. 46]. J. S. Mill followed the same line of analysis in stating : " . . . if the thing is cheap, there is usually a demand for more of it than when it is dear" [13, p. 446]. While J. S. Mill and Cournot expressed the law of demand as being "ordinarily" or "usually" true, Marshall stated it as a "general law" and "the one universal rule to which the demand curve conforms" [11, p. 99, N. 2]. As pointed out above, to Marshall the demand schedule was a theoretical construction that was valid only if its *ceteris paribus* assumptions were met. The law of demand was the result of limitations placed on the formulation of the demand schedule due to the exclusion of the income effect which was beyond the domain of the analysis of relative prices in the classical system. As Marshall stated :

[9]Henry Schultz expressed the current assessment of the law of demand when he stated :
> It is clear, therefore, that there is nothing "universal" about this law. But its extreme simplicity and the ease with which it can be manipulated, coupled with the good approximate description which it provides in many instances of actual economic behavior, have earned for it a secure place among the fundamental laws of economics. This is another illustration of the fact that in science it is often more important that a law be simple than it be true [17, pp. 53–54].

The rejection of the law of demand has become a part of most expositions on demand theory [8, pp. 24–37] [16, pp. 90–122]. This rejection is predicated on the mathematical possibility of the positive income effect being larger in absolute magnitude than the negative substitution effect of the constant money-income formulation.

> ... it follows that such a discussion of demand as is possible at this stage of our work, must be confined to an elementary analysis of an almost purely formal kind. The higher study of consumption must come after, and not before, the main body of economic analysis [11, p. 90].

Thus while the law of demand may have been an approximation or simplification prior to Marshall's analysis, to him it was a rigorous formulation resulting from *ceteris paribus* assumptions. Marshall's formal statement of the law of demand as a "universal rule" is further evidence that he viewed the demand curve as an abstract or pure construct.

IV. Conclusion

The inconsistency in Friedman's paper over Giffen's Paradox is the result of the integration of his interpretation of Marshall's demand curve and his own work on the theoretical aspects of the constant real-income demand curve [5, pp. 47-99]. In this facet of his analysis, Friedman imputes to Marshall the rigorous formulation of the constant real-income demand curve which is, in reality, his own. In doing so he weakens his case for the real-income interpretation. To Marshall the constant purchasing power parameter was not a formulation that was maintained on an empirical basis. It was a theoretical assumption and one of "those simplifications of genius, of which there are several instances in Marshall" [8, p. 32]. Viewing Giffen's Paradox in methodological and textual context not only removes the inconsistency in current interpretations, but it also produces an interpretation that is compatible with Marshall's general methodological approach. It allows us to derive a single interpretation while recognizing that each part of the theory is there because Marshall felt it was needed to form a logical whole.

WILLIAM P. GRAMM*

Texas A. & M. University.

---

*The author wishes to acknowledge a great debt owed to Alfred Chalk, Robert Ekelund, Charles Maurice, Thomas Saving and the editors of this journal for helpful comments on earlier drafts of this paper.

REFERENCES

1. Alford, R. F. G., "Marshall's Demand Curve," *Ec.*, XXIII (February 1956), 23–48.

2. Cournot, A. *Researches into the Mathematical Principles of the Theory of Wealth.* Trans. by Bacon. New York : Augustus M. Kelly, 1960.

3. Dupuit, J. "On the Measurement of the Utility of Public Works," *Annales des Ponts et Chausseés*, 8, 1844 as translated in *International Economic Papers.* London : Macmillan and Company, 1952, 83–110.

4. Evans, G. H., Jr. "The Law of Demand—The Role of Gregory King and Charles Davenant," *Q. J. E.*, LXXI (August, 1967), 483–492.

5. Friedman, M. "The Marshallian Demand Curve," *J. P. E.*, (December, 1949), 463–495 ; reprinted in *Essays in Positive Economics.* Chicago : University of Chicago Press, 1953, 47–99.

6. Georgescu-Roegen, N. "Revisiting Marshall's Constancy of Marginal Utility of Money," *S. E. J.*, XXXV (October, 1968), 176–181.

7. Guillebaud, C. W. "The Evolution of Marshall's Principles of Economics," *E. J.*, LII (December, 1942), 330–349.

8. Hicks, J. R. *Value and Capital.* 2nd ed., Oxford : Oxford University Press, 1946.

9. ———. *Capital and Growth.* Oxford : Oxford University Press, 1965.

10. Knight, F. H. "Realism and Relevance in the Theory of Demand," *J. P. E.*, LII (December, 1944), 289–318.

11. Marshall, A. *Principles of Economics.* 8th ed. London : Macmillan and Company, 1920.

12. ———. *Principles of Economics.* 9th (variorum) ed. Guillebaud, editor. London : Macmillan and Company, 1961.

13. Mill, J. S. *Principles of Political Economy.* Ashley ed. New York : Augustus M. Kelley, 1965.

14. Prest, A. R. "Notes on the History of the Giffen Paradox : Comment," *J. P. E.*, LVI (February, 1948), 58–60.

15. Ricardo, D. *Principles of Political Economy and Taxation.* Sraffa, ed. Cambridge : Cambridge University Press, 1951.

16. Samuelson, P. A. *Foundations of Economic Analysis.* Cambridge : Harvard University Press, 1947.

17. Schultz, H. *The Theory and Measurement of Demand.* Chicago : University of Chicago Press, 1938.

18. Stigler, G. J. "Notes on the History of the Giffen Paradox," *J. P. E.*, LV (April, 1947), 152–156.

[13]
COMPETITIVE TÂTONNEMENT EXCHANGE MARKETS*

This study has three objectives: (1) to analyze the types of competitive *tâtonnement* exchange models that have been developed, in order to clarify their essential characteristics; (2) to show the necessity for further modifications in the models; and (3) to draw the implications of these modifications for the direction which a future revision of the analysis of the stability of competitive *tâtonnement* markets should take.

The following characteristics, which define a competitive *tâtonnement* exchange market, will be called the *tâtonnement* properties. There must be only one price at any moment, for otherwise there can be neither market quantities demanded and supplied $[D(p)$ and $S(p)]$ simultaneously at a given price, nor a market excess demand quantity $[E(p)]$, nor, consequently, a *tâtonnement* equilibrium price. There must be an information-dissemination procedure by which the price is made known to the participants. There must also be a way of collecting and aggregating the individual demand and supply quantities at any quoted price in order to discover the sign of $E(p)$, which implies that its magnitude must also be known. That magnitude must also be known if the rate of price change is to be proportional to $E(p)$ (Negishi 1962, pp. 646–7), or if the proportional change in the price is to be equal to the ratio of $E(p)$ to $D(p)$ (HAHN 1961, p. 63), or any sign-preserving function of $E(p)$ (SAMUELSON 1955, pp. 263, 270; ARROW, BLOCK, and HURWICZ 1959 p. 85; UZAWA 1961, p. 622). Transactions at disequilibrium prices must be excluded (KALDOR 1934, pp. 126–7)[1]. Trade is allowed to occur only at a value at which

---

* The author wishes to acknowledge the helpful observations and criticisms of ROBERT MUNDELL, WILLIAM JAFFÉ, and THEODORE SCHULTZ.

1. REDER (1947, pp. 126–7) has suggested that there are many different simultaneous prices in disequilibrium states of a competitive market. Similarly, ARROW (1959) has argued that disequilibrium transactions occur simultaneously at different prices during the equilibrating process, and that monopolistic competition describes the disequilibrium behavior of the firms. These are useful observations about the character of some markets in which disequilibrium rates of production and consumption occur, but the type of behavior that the writers suggest could not result in the equilibrium of a *tâtonnement* exchange market, for in such a market disequilibrium transactions are not allowed (JAFFÉ 1967, p. 3;

DONALD A. WALKER

$D(p) = S(p)$. It will be shown, through a brief survey of the development of the theory of competitive exchange, that these *tâtonnement* properties cannot be the outcome of impersonal competitive forces, but must be secured by market institutions and rules specifically designed for the purpose of attaining them. It will be shown that the conclusion to be drawn regarding models that are provided with the necessary institutions and conventions is that they cannot reasonably be supposed to follow the Walrasian pricing rule in all circumstances regardless of its consequences, and that many of the conclusions about stability which result from a mechanical application of that rule are therefore inappropriate.

There have been a variety of types of *tâtonnement* exchange models. These deal, more or less successfully, with the problems that arise in an effort to ensure the *tâtonnement* properties. First, WALRAS developed a model which was subsequently adopted by many economists (WICKSELL 1934, p. 55 ff.; KOOPMANS 1951, p. 95; LANGE and TAYLOR 1938, pp. 70–90), in which he did not provide any explicit structural framework to generate them. He gave the impression that in a purely competitive market the equilibrating process works itself out through the action of impersonal forces. In JAFFÉ's (1967, p. 2) words:

> It is the impersonal mechanism of pure competition in a perfect market, 'ever unconscious, an automatic sense, unweeting why or whence', which imposes, as Walras saw it, the selfsame solution which only a computer-like *intellectus angelicus* knowing all the parameters could arrive at algebraically[2].

It was in WALRAS's type of model that the existing treatment of stability had its origin. WALRAS, and all subsequent economists, said that a point of intersection of the D and S curves in an exchange market is a point of unstable equilibrium if $D'(p) - S'(p) > 0$ in the

---

WALKER 1970, p. 691). Their perceptive remarks should be viewed as an injunction to develop a more realistic model of a type of normal market, and as suggestions about the course that development should take.

2. Professor JAFFÉ has pointed out to me that WALRAS (1874; 1883, p. 16) did mention, very briefly, the possibility of having a central broker or 'calculateur' examine the order books of traders in order to find a price at which $D(p) = S(p)$. He would then declare that trade may occur at that price. However, these observations did not appear in WALRAS's *Eléments d'économie politique pure*, and the impression given by the latter work is the one which influenced other economists, and which became a central part of doctrine regarding the character of purely competitive markets.

neighborhood of that point, and is a point of stable equilibrium if $D'(p) - S'(p) < 0$. WALRAS arrived at this conclusion because he assumed that competitive markets follow the Walrasian pricing rule (WALRAS 1900, pp. 64, 69–70, 129–33, 472; and see HICKS 1939, pp. 62–66; SAMUELSON 1955, p. 263), whereby dp/dt, the rate of change of the price with respect to time, has the same sign as $E(p)$. The result is that if the initial price is on either side of an unstable solution price, the quoted price will be changed away from that solution value. If it is on either side of a stable solution price, it will be changed so that it moves towards that solution value.

In this analysis WALRAS simply assumed that there is only one price at any moment in an organized market, without providing his model with any rules to ensure the existence of that condition or its preservation when the price is changed. He did not state explicitly how or by whom the price is 'cried', nor did he describe the procedure by which it is changed. In his treatment of exchange-market behavior in the *Eléments* WALRAS only says (1900, p. 46), regarding the pricing process, that unsatisfied buyers 'vont à l'enchère', and that unsatisfied sellers 'vont au rabais'. He said even less in an article on the operation of the stock market. Without identifying the economic actors or the details of the process in question, he wrote that if $D(p) \neq S(p)$, 'on va à l'enchère' or 'on va au rabais' (1880; 1936, p. 408). These incomplete statements cannot ensure the *tâtonnement* properties. They do not make clear whether a frustrated trader shouts a new price loudly, or whether he reports his new offer to a central market authority who then cries the price. In the *Eléments* and elsewhere WALRAS simply asserted that disequilibrium transactions do not occur in exchange markets (WALRAS 1900, pp. 44–47 and *passim*; JAFFÉ 1967, pp. 2, 5), whereas he should have introduced a rule to the effect that such transactions are not allowed[3]. He tacitly assumed that in some way the

3. See WALKER (1970, pp. 692–4) where much of the most recent evidence regarding WALRAS's state of mind on this matter is examined. In his theory of production, WALRAS introduced the use of tickets (WALRAS 1900, pp. VII, 214–15; JAFFÉ 1967, p. 12–13; WALRAS 1954, *Translator's Note* [6] to Lesson 20, pp. 528–9). This recontracting mechanism was employed for the purpose of excluding disequilibrium rates of production, but WALRAS's treatment of the procedure is incomplete. As in his theory of exchange in the *Eléments*, he did not deal with the problems of how information is collected and disseminated, and how the price is changed. He mentions the tickets, without explaining how they are used.

347

criers of the price learn the state of the market excess demand, but he provided no procedure of information collection and dissemination to achieve that knowledge. That WALRAS's model is incomplete is recognized by JAFFÉ when he says that for a Walrasian system to operate it needs an *intellectus angelicus*, or 'a battery of totalizators, as it were' (JAFFÉ 1967, p. 12), to add up individual supply and demand quantities in all markets, and to solve the equations of Walrasian equilibrium. Much of the time WALRAS appears to have thought that the *tâtonnement* properties are ensured by stating that there is 'libre concurrence' (JAFFÉ 1956, Letters 928, 999, 1200 enclosure, 1775 enclosure; WALRAS 1900, pp. 129–30; WALKER 1970, pp. 693–4)[4]. In fact, it was pointed out to him that the invocation of that phrase is not enough, for in 1904 he acknowledged the receipt of an offprint of an article from CHARLES RIST in which RIST wrote that a

purely competitive market, defined as a market in which there are no obstacles to commerce between buyers and sellers, in which there is no collusion, and in which there is full knowledge of bids and offers, has never existed 'naturally' and has always required the intervention of an authority to enforce 'the rules of the game'[5].

Although WALRAS himself had argued that the intervention of the state is necessary to preserve the structure of a competitive market, he had been thinking of the necessity of anti-trust laws to prevent a process which, he believed, would begin with some firms taking over others, and end with the formation of a monopoly (WALRAS 1900, pp. 475–6, n; JAFFÉ 1965, Letters 1027 [7], 1042). RIST's original and perceptive remarks did not affect his work, which in most respects had taken its final form many years before 1904, and did not change in any significant respect after 1900.

In a second type of model the extreme assumption is made that the traders have knowledge of the entire initial D and S functions [MARSHALL 1920, pp. 333–4; WICKSTEED 1933, vol. 1, p. 219][6], that

4. STIGLER (1957, p. 9) has remarked on this matter, observing that 'Walras gave no adequate definition of competition'.

5. This quotation is taken from JAFFÉ's summary (1965, *Letter* 1577 [2]).

6. WICKSTEED assumed that only the sellers have perfect knowledge of the D and S curves. MARSHALL's model is clearly described in the 1st through the 4th editions of his *Principles* (1920, Book V, chapter 2). However, it appears that his dislike of it led him to blur its outlines in the 5th and subsequent editions. Other aspects of MARSHALL's perfect-knowledge model are discussed by WALKER (1969, pp. 591–2).

is, knowledge of the D and S functions associated with the asset distribution that exists when the market day opens, before any trade has taken place. This will be called the assumption of perfect knowledge. Since the traders know the D and S functions, they also know the initial solution price. They select it as the trading price, because demanders would refuse to pay a higher value, and suppliers would refuse to accept a lower one (MARSHALL, 1920, pp. 333–4). This model is not interesting, because it assumes away the problems of the theory of exchange. It eliminates any consideration of the action of economic forces, the existence of a path of quoted prices, the possibility of disequilibrium demand and supply quantities, and everything else that is of interest about exchange behavior. Also, the model is incomplete in two respects. First, it does not explain how the trading price is determined if there are multiple initial solutions. Second, the degree of knowledge possessed by the traders is introduced on the analytical level of an assumption, whereas it should be the derivative outcome of more fundamental market properties. Reasonable assumptions that would result in a *perfect* degree of knowledge are hard to find, which is precisely why perfect knowledge was introduced as a postulate by MARSHALL and WICKSTEED, and also why MARSHALL went on to drop the postulate and to develop another model in preference to the perfect-knowledge one (WALKER 1969). As an illustration of the difficulty of the problem, EDGEWORTH (1881, p. 18) says that 'free communication' could be attained by traders collected at the same point in space. In the light of the tenor of the section of his book in which this comment appears, his meaning was probably that perfect knowledge could be attained by dimensionless traders occupying a single point. By contrast, it will be shown below that a reasonable complete formulation which enables perfect knowledge to be a derivative characteristic requires the introduction of a central market authority and its enforcement of special rules.

In a sub-variety of perfect-knowledge model, E. SCHNEIDER (1962, pp. 240–41) assumes that the demand side of the market is 'transparent to the sellers'. This model is incomplete, and its conclusions therefore cannot be shown to follow from its fragmentary assumptions. Why there is only one price at any moment, how the sellers achieve knowledge of the D curve, how they know the initial solution price without knowledge of the S curve as well as the D curve, are

349

unexplained. In fact, while commenting on his model, SCHNEIDER neglects what he assumed about the sellers' knowledge, and says (p. 242) that '...we assumed complete "transparency", or perfect knowledge, for all parties in our partial system'. Furthermore, no explanation is given of why the sellers should have any interest in setting only the initial solution price even if they know its value. It would be more to their advantage to charge a succession of different prices, and trade at each of them (SMITH 1962, pp. 124–5, 134; SMITH 1964, p. 182). Instead of establishing the results that he asserts flow from the condition of the sellers' perfect knowledge of the D function, SCHNEIDER in actuality shows the necessity of a central authority and special rules to secure the *tâtonnement* properties. This occurs when he tries to demonstrate the realism of his knowledgeable-sellers model by reference to what he describes as the behavior of a real market in which a broker operates. Clearly, his example (1962, p. 242) of a broker to whom both D and S functions are reported by the traders, and who follows the rule of setting the initial solution price, is not illustrative of the behavior of sellers to whom only the D curve is known. Similarly, BOULDING (1966, p. 109) has an incomplete perfect-knowledge model. He assumes, as an unexplained postulate, that his traders have knowledge '...of the prices at which transactions are being carried on, and of the prices at which other buyers and sellers are willing to buy or sell'. The latter clause appears to be the assumption that the traders know the unrealized points on the D and S schedules, i.e., that they have perfect knowledge. However, BOULDING does not follow the implications of this assumption, since his traders engage in disequilibrium transactions, with consequences that have been explored elsewhere (WALKER 1969, pp. 593–4).

In a third type of model, economists have taken the course of trying to postulate basic conditions that are necessary to generate the properties of a *tâtonnement* market as derivative outcomes (KNIGHT 1921, pp. 76–88; STIGLER 1957, pp. 11–15), without assuming the existence of a central authority and its enforcement of the rules of a *tâtonnement* market. This course results in a multiplication of 'ideal' conditions: an indefinitely large number of traders, perfect divisibility of the commodity, complete absence of frictions, etc. A crucial ideal condition is that the traders have *statistical* knowledge, that is, they all simultaneously know the quoted price and all offers to buy and sell at that price (BÖHM-BAWERK 1959, pp. 220ff., 434, n. 12; KNIGHT 1921, pp. 76–9; STIGLER 1957, pp. 12, 15)[7]. Thus, statistical knowledge is the awareness by all traders of the particular realized points on the D and S curves that are determined by the succession of actually quoted market prices, rather than knowledge, *ab initio*, of the entire curves[8]. The model is incomplete in two respects. First, the degree of knowledge is not the outcome of an information gathering and dissemination procedure. Statistical knowledge cannot be derived from reasonable assumptions about the structure of a market in which there is assumed to be an extremely large number of traders, but in which there is no central authority or rules. It is for this reason that the degree of knowledge is introduced as a postulate[9]. The second principal defect of the model is that it has no means by which the price can be changed (SCITOVSKY 1951, p. 16). As ARROW (1959, p. 43) has said: 'Each individual participant in the economy is supposed to take prices as given and determine his choices as to purchases and sales accordingly; there is no one left over whose job it is to make a decision on price.' In fact, STIGLER, who in one place (1957) has given this model its most brilliant, illuminating, and epistemologically profound treatment, has in effect pointed out elsewhere (1941, p. 245) that a *tâtonnement* model must have rules and institutions to prevent disequilibrium transactions, and to ensure that the quoted price is varied until the initial solution price is found. The institution that is needed to establish and enforce a rule against dis-

---

7. STIGLER (1957, p. 12) has a slightly different position on this matter, but his discussion deals with normal markets and the equilibria to which they tend over time. His treatment is the same as that of the other writers in the respect that is of central importance for the issue under discussion, namely, that the 'comprehensive' knowledge of his buyers and sellers is assumed as a postulate.

8. Many economists have failed to make clear whether they were discussing perfect or statistical knowledge, partly because a terminological distinction between these two types of knowledge has not been introduced. For example, JEVONS (1957, p. 87) speaks of '...perfect knowledge of the conditions of supply and demand, and the consequent ratio of exchange...', but some of his comments that precede and follow this statement lead to one interpretation, and some lead to the other.

9. STIGLER (1957, pp. 14–15) is perfectly aware of the axiomatic nature of his assumption, and of the fact that in reality, in the absence of a central authority, the degree of knowledge bears an inverse relation to the number of traders.

equilibrium transactions, to quote and publicize the price, to collect and aggregate the traders' offers, to evaluate the state of $E(p)$, to change the price, and to set the trading price, is a central market authority.

Fourth, there is the competitive recontract model. As treated by EDGEWORTH in *Mathematical Psychics* (1881, pp. 19ff., 40–43), this is incomplete. A large number of traders are assumed to deal with each other directly, without the mediation of a central market authority, and without any market rules or conventions to control their behavior. This unregulated direct exchange would result in the emergence of a variety of simultaneous agreements at different prices (STIGLER 1957, p. 15). There are no means of securing the existence of a single price at any moment, and therefore no way of determining $D(p)$ and $S(p)$, nor consequently of determining $E(p)$. There are no information collection and dissemination procedures, no means of publicizing the terms of the agreements. As a result, D and S functions cannot describe the desires or behavior of the traders, nor therefore can the price and quantity solutions of such functions indicate the equilibrium values of the variables. Although EDGEWORTH did give brief consideration to the problem of basic conditions that would result in 'free communication', his treatment was neither complete, nor clear in its substance and objectives. It may be that EDGEWORTH thought he was making an assumption that would result in statistical knowledge when he said that the traders can be supposed to be collected at a point in space. If he meant simply that the traders are face to face, then his assumption would not in itself ensure either perfect or statistical knowledge, because there would also have to be procedures whereby the traders' offers are reported, aggregated, and the results publicized. EDGEWORTH also says (1881, p. 18) that 'free communication' would be assured if the traders were connected by telephones. This would not ensure either perfect or statistical knowledge, for there would still have to be market conventions whereby the quoted price is established and publicized. The traders would have to agree not to engage in transactions until a central authority says that they may do so. Everyone would have to communicate his individual demand or supply quantity to the central authority. The latter would have to undertake the task of aggregating the individual supply and demand quantities in order to discover the sign of $E(p)$. He would then have to go through the procedure of calling all the traders and giving them that information, or they would have to call him. A rule would have to be formulated to determine, in the event that $E(p) \neq 0$, whether price changes are initiated by the traders or by the central authority.

The missing elements in EDGEWORTH's work have been supplied by modern recontract models, but with the result that they have been converted into a variety of a different type of model, the second of the two types that are examined below. Furthermore, the remedial work has been performed at the expense of the function of the recontracting agreements made directly between the traders. Recontracting is a superfluous complication, but if it is assumed, then in order for it to work properly there must be a single price quoted at any time, the offers of the traders must be aggregated in order to discover the sign of $E(p)$, and the price must be changed to a new value if $E(p)$ is positive or negative. Those activities require that the traders report their supply and demand quantities to a central market authority, and that renders unnecessary their direct formation and breaking of contracts with each other at disequilibrium prices. This is demonstrated by NEWMAN's model (1965, pp. 85–6). He described his adjustment mechanism as 'recontract', but in fact his traders do not bother to enter into contracts with each other at disequilibrium prices. They write on tickets their individual demand or supply quantities at the announced price, and give the tickets to a price setter. He then calculates $E(p)$, and quotes a new price if $E(p) \neq 0$. This procedure on the part of a price setter is also a feature of the model developed by PATINKIN (1956, p. 37; 1965, p. 40), but he does not observe that the recontracting activity of his traders is thereby made superfluous.

The conclusions made regarding the foregoing models are that they are incomplete as competitive *tâtonnement* models, and that to make them complete it is necessary to provide them with a central market authority and the *tâtonnement* rules and procedures that it enforces. There are two ways of making the necessary modifications, and consequently there are two resulting types of models.

First, there is the *omniscient price-setter model*. The traders are not allowed to enter into direct agreements with each other. They must report their complete excess demand functions to a price setter. He then calculates and publishes the market functions and the price at which $D(p) = S(p)$, and allows trade to occur at that price. The traders cannot be allowed to change their offers after their schedules have been reported. The omniscient price setter model was first suggested by EDGEWORTH, although he presented it in the context of implying that the process illustrates how a competitive market operates under the action of impersonal forces, in the absence of the price setter. He says (1881, p. 30), regarding the way that 'perfect competition' results in the *tâtonnement* properties, that

> You might suppose each dealer to write down his *demand*, how much of an article he would take at each price, without attempting to conceal his requirements; and these data having been furnished to a sort of market-machine, the *price* to be passionlessly evaluated.

JAFFÉ showed his recognition of the sort of market machine required to calculate the *tâtonnement* equilibrium values when he described it (1967, p. 2) as 'a computer-like *intellectus angelicus*...' SCHNEIDER introduced an omniscient price setter in 1962 (p. 242), and the model was given an extensive development by NEWMAN in 1965 (p. 69 ff.). It is evident from the work of these writers that reasonable conditions that would produce the *tâtonnement* properties in a perfect-knowledge model must include a central authority and a set of rules to regulate the behavior of the traders. Furthermore, as is evident by examination of NEWMAN's model, it is sufficient for the price setter alone to be given perfect knowledge, and no need for him to inform the traders of the market demand and supply functions that he calculates. The omniscient price setter model provides the only reasonable way of securing perfect knowledge for the traders as a desired result, and that way makes it superfluous for them to have it.

The omniscient price-setter model deserves more prominence than it has had, because its properties approximate some of the features that characterize some organized markets. One class of examples is provided by stock exchanges in which specialists have buy and sell orders listed in their books, and set the price to clear the market. Again, the market for new Treasury bills is like the omniscient price setter model in the perfect-knowledge respect (SCOTT 1965, pp. 32–8, 96–7). Similarly, the London silver market was described by H. M. BRATTER (1931, pp. 362–3) as one in which the central authority is a group of four bullion firms, whose representatives meet at about 2:00 P.M. on week days and at about 11:00 A.M. on Saturday. All orders to sell or buy are placed with these brokers. They compare the orders, and the price is then fixed where it will move the greatest amount of 'at market' orders. In short, the price is determined according to demand and supply. This is called 'fixing' the price[10].

Recognition of the omniscient price setter model leads to a modification of the theory of competitive markets, because the existing analysis of stability is irrelevant for that model. This matter is so obvious that it can be treated immediately. It is first assumed that there is a single initial solution point in the omniscient price setter's market. The point must be stable, in the sense that it is definitely selected. The price setter knows the value of the initial solution price (ISP), and since he is in a *tâtonnement* market the principal rule that guides his behavior is that he must set the ISP as the trading price. Exchange occurs, and the market day ends. The price setter never follows the Walrasian pricing rule. There is no path of a quoted price; there are no convergence properties to consider. In the existing literature, it is said that an initial solution point is stable if $D'(p^*) - S'(p^*) \leq 0$ (SAMUELSON 1955, p. 263), where p^* is the ISP, but clearly this cannot be true in general, for in the omniscient price setter model the slopes of the initial market curves in the neighborhood of the ISP are irrelevant for the matter of stability. Even if $D'(p^*) - S'(p^*) > 0$, p^* is nevertheless set as the trading price.

It is now assumed that there are multiple initial solutions. In this event, some criterion in addition to the necessity of selecting an ISP must guide the price setter's behavior. There are several possible alternative guidelines, but he will never follow the Walrasian rule, and the relative slopes of the market curves cannot be of determining significance in his selection. First, he may select the solution price that is closest to the previous equilibrium price. In that case, his selection depends on initial conditions, that is, on the previous price and the positions of the initial solution points. Second, he may wish to choose, or be required to choose, the ISP that maximizes the volume of transactions. Third, he may wish to maximize the amount of money that changes hands, perhaps in order to maximize his commissions. A particular ISP may or may not satisfy more than one of these criteria. It is evident that in all three cases the price setter may

10. This example was drawn to my attention by WILLIAM JAFFÉ.

be led to pick an initial solution point which, if evaluated according to the Walrasian rule, is 'unstable'. Thus, the selection or rejection of an initial solution point is determined by the criterion that guides the price setter's selection, and not by the characteristics of $E(p)$ in the neighborhood of the point.

It can be seen that MARSHALL's perfect-knowledge model of market-day price determination is, in regard to its 'stability', like the omniscient price setter model if there is only one initial solution point. The two models differ in the case of multiple initial solution points, in that the model presented here suggests alternative objectives that the omniscient price setter might pursue, one of which would determine the point that he picks, whereas MARSHALL did not provide his traders with any such guideline. MARSHALL's oversight does not have a simple remedy, because buyers and sellers may want to pick different points, and in his model there is no central authority to adjudicate the matter. However, all the problems of his model are solved by the corrective assumptions that convert it into the omniscient price setter variety.

The second type of complete *tâtonnement* model has an *informed price setter*. Elsewhere he has been variously called the auctioneer (HENDERSON and QUANDT 1958, p. 95; NEGISHI 1962, p. 647), the secretary of the market (UZAWA 1960, p. 184), the chairman (PATINKIN 1956, p. 37; 1965, p. 40), the umpire (NEWMAN 1965, pp. 83, 85–6), the referee (QUIRK and SAPOSNIK 1968, pp. 160–1), and the price setter (BUSHAW and CLOWER 1957, p. 25). The informed price setter learns points on the D and S curves by quoting a sequence of prices, at each of which the traders report to him their individual demand and supply quantities. No trade is allowed until he finds and sets the equilibrium price[11].

Consideration of the characteristics of this model in relation to present outlook and practice makes clear that there are several changes that should be made in the treatment of competitive

---

11. In HENDERSON and QUANDT's model (1958, pp. 95, 113) the price is called out to a central authority by the traders. Disequilibrium transactions are not allowed. Any trader who is unable to contract for as much as he wishes to buy or sell can set a new price by calling it out to the price setter, who makes it public. This competitive *tâtonnement* model is no different in principle or results from one in which a central authority initiates price changes.

tâtonnement models which deal with the movement of quoted disequilibrium prices at which no trade occurs. First, many papers have been written which do not explicitly recognize that an informed price setter and *tâtonnement* rules are necessary for models of that type to be structurally complete (ARROW and HURWICZ 1958; ARROW, BLOCK, HURWICZ 1959; SOLOW 1959; NEWMAN 1959; HAHN 1961; UZAWA 1961; NEWMAN 1961; ARROW and HURWICZ 1962; TAKAYAMA and JUDGE 1964; KUGA 1965; SMITH 1965; QUIRK 1968). Subsequent models should explicitly incorporate the requisite institutions and rules.

Second, it should now be recognized that the informed price setter and the rules he must enforce are not merely useful fictions that elucidate the workings of an unregulated impersonal competitive market. The existing informed price setter models display the theory of *tâtonnement* markets in an intermediate stage. Rules and a central authority are introduced to provide for the *tâtonnement* properties, but it is still alleged that these introductions are just idealizations of the way a competitive market actually works in their absence[12]. EDGEWORTH's early expression of this view has already been observed. PATINKIN (1956, p. 37; 1965, p. 40) says that his chairman of a central registry gives 'concrete embodiment' to market forces. UZAWA (1960, p. 184) writes: 'Let us interpret the competitive exchange economy as a game in which R individuals and a fictitious player, say a Secretary of Market, play according to the following rules...'[13]. NEGISHI (1962, p. 647) says:

12. In a model of normal markets, KOOPMANS (1951, pp. 93–5) has a 'helmsman' who determines the vector of initial prices, and a set of rules according to which the other economic units in his model change prices until equilibrium is found. He regarded his model as a way of achieving the result that the thought a competitive market achieves in the absence of the helmsman and the rules (*ibid*). More recently he has either been critical of the view that impersonal market forces can generate the *tâtonnement* properties, or critical of the realism of *tâtonnement* models, and he has unquestionably taken issue with their mechanical use of the Walrasian pricing rule. He says (1957, p. 179):

The various assumptions that have been used to describe the adjustment of price or quantity in a commodity market clearly show their parentage in the laws of the physical sciences. If, for instance, the net rate of increase in price is assumed to be proportional to the excess of demand over supply, whose behavior is thereby expressed? And how is that behavior motivated?

13. It is curious that this same author neglected to provide the necessary rules and institutions in a later model (1961) in which the uniformity of price in any market is simply postulated, and also the way that the vector of prices is changed.

357

DONALD A. WALKER

In the case of the ideally well organized markets, such as the stock exchange, grain markets, and fish markets, we may *imagine*[14] for each commodity an auctioneer who, as an incarnation of the competitive force in the market, raises the price of the commodity at a rate proportional to the difference between demand and supply.

NEGISHI's treatment does not recognize that organized markets, such as those on the Chicago Board of Trade, do in fact have central authorities and market rules to regulate the traders' behavior.

The existing informed price-setter models are a step in the direction of reconciling the difference, so clearly distinguished by McNULTY (1968), between ADAM SMITH's concept of competition as a force operating in disequilibrium, and as an equilibrium state of affairs in which no competitive behavior occurs. They do provide ways of ensuring the *tâtonnement* properties, whereas there are none in the models that do not have rules and a central authority. However, the authors of the models can give no explanation of why the institutions and rules are used. If it were true that an actual 'ideally well organized market' with no central authority behaves as though there were one, the need to introduce one would not exist. Instead, it would be appropriate to give a direct account of how the *tâtonnement* properties are generated by the structural characteristics and systematic functioning of the impersonal forces of the competitive market that has no central authority. But such an account is not possible, because that type of market cannot generate the *tâtonnement* properties.

The third necessary modification is in the analysis of the stability of the informed price setter model of a competitive *tâtonnement* market. This is a major problem which goes far beyond the scope of this paper. The remaining task of this study is to indicate the reasons for the necessity of the modification. Whether the economists who constructed the price setter models thought of them as personalizing competitive forces that are actually impersonal, or realized that markets would in fact have to possess a price setter and the rules he enforces in order to generate the *tâtonnement* properties, their analyses of the stability properties of the models are in both cases in need of revision. This is because the models are dominated by the older view that the price moves under the action of impersonal forces. A

14. Emphasis added.

price setter does the work of announcing and changing the price, but he is made to follow the old Walrasian rule that was formulated independently of the notion of a price setter (PATINKIN 1956, p. 37; PATINKIN 1965, p. 40; UZAWA 1960, p. 184; NEGISHI 1962, p. 647; NEWMAN 1965, pp. 85 ff.; QUIRK and SAPOSNIK 1968, pp. 160–1). Thus the price setter is made to act in a mechanical way. He does not react intelligently to the properties that he discovers the D and S functions to possess; his experience teaches him nothing; he has no guidelines, pursues no objectives, follows no pricing rules other than the Walrasian rule. This has led to a perpetuation of the view that the stability of equilibrium is determined exclusively by the relative slopes of the D and S curves in the neighborhood of an initial solution point in the way that WALRAS described. The old pricing rule has been retained even though it produces absurd results in some cases, as when it leads to the conclusion that the quoted price would rise indefinitely, or fall towards zero, even in the face of a growing discrepancy between demand and supply. By contrast, after consideration of the behavior of an informed price setter perhaps it will be found most reasonable to assume that he will follow Walrasian pricing only as long as it leads $E(p)$ to diminish, and that in the alternative case he will adopt the rule of changing the price in the direction that diminishes the absolute magnitude of $E(p)$. Perhaps it will be considered reasonable to modify the model still further by incorporating the rules followed in real organized markets whereby limits are imposed upon the permissible magnitude of price changes on any given market day. In any event, the competitive *tâtonnement* model requires a price setter, and consequently the model needs the modifications that will result from drawing reasonable implications of his capacity for rational behavior and his degree of volitional freedom.

Indiana University   DONALD A. WALKER

REFERENCES

ARROW, K. J.: 'Towards a Theory of Price Adjustment', in M. ABRAMOVITZ, *et al.*, *The Allocation of Economic Resources*, Stanford, Stanford University Press, 1959, pp. 41–51.

ARROW, K. J, and HURWICZ, L.: 'On the Stability of the Competitive Equilibrium, I', *Econometrica*, Vol. 26 (October 1958), pp. 522–52.

ARROW, K. J., BLOCK, H. D., and HURWICZ, L.: 'On the Stability of the Competitive Equilibrium, II', *Econometrica*, Vol. 27 (January 1959), pp. 82–109.

ARROW, K. J., and HURWICZ, L.: 'Competitive Stability Under Weak Gross Substitutability', *International Economic Review*, Vol. 3 (May 1962), pp. 233–55.

BÖHM-BAWERK, E. VON: *Capital and Interest*, Vol. 2, *Positive Theory of Capital*, South Holland, Libertarian Press, 1959.

BRATTER, H. M.: 'Some Silver Fundamentals', *Journal of Political Economy*, Vol. 39, No. 3 (June 1931), pp. 321–68.

BOULDING, K.: *Economic Analysis*, Vol. 1, *Microeconomics*, 4th ed., New York, Harper and Row, 1966.

BUSHAW, D. W., and CLOWER, R. W.: *Introduction to Mathematical Economics*, Homewood, Irwin, 1957.

EDGEWORTH, F. Y.: *Mathematical Psychics*, London, C. Kegan Paul, 1881.

HAHN, F. H.: 'A Stable Adjustment Process for a Competitive Economy', *Review of Economic Studies*, Vol. 29 (October 1961), pp. 62–5.

HENDERSON, J. M., and QUANDT, R. E.: *Microeconomic Theory*, New York, McGraw-Hill, 1958.

HICKS, J. R.: *Value and Capital*, 1st ed., Oxford, Oxford University Press, 1939.

JAFFÉ, W., Ed.: *Correspondence of Léon Walras and Related Papers*, 3 vols., Amsterdam, North Holland Publishing Co., 1965.

– 'Walras' Theory of *Tâtonnement*: A Critique of Recent Interpretations', *Journal of Political Economy*, Vol. 75 (February 1967), pp. 1–19.

JEVONS, W. S.: *The Theory of Political Economy*, 5th ed., New York, Kelley and Millman, 1957.

KALDOR, N.: 'A Classificatory Note on the Determinateness of Equilibrium', *Review of Economic Studies*, Vol. 1 (February 1934), pp. 122–36.

KNIGHT, F. H.: *Risk, Uncertainty and Profit*, New York, Houghton Mifflin, 1921.

KOOPMANS, T. C.: 'Analysis of Production as an Efficient Combination of Activities', in *Activity Analysis of Production and Allocation*. New York, J. Wiley and Sons, 1951, pp. 33–97.

– *Three Essays on the State of Economic Science*, New York, McGraw-Hill, 1957.

KUGA, K.: 'Weak Gross Substitutability and the Existence of Competitive Equilibrium', *Econometrica*, Vol. 33 (July 1965), pp. 593–9.

LANGE, O., and TAYLOR, R. M.: *On the Economic Theory of Socialism*, New York, Macmillan, 1938.

MARSHALL, A.: *Principles of Economics*, 8th ed., New York, Macmillan, 1920.

McNULTY, P. J.: 'Economic Theory and the Meaning of Competition', *Quarterly Journal of Economics*, Vol. 82 (November 1968), pp. 639–56.

NEGISHI, T.: 'The Stability of a Competitive Economy: A Survey Article', *Econometrica*, Vol. 30 (October 1962), pp. 635–69.

NEWMAN, P. K.: 'Some Notes on Stability Conditions', *Review of Economic Studies*, Vol. 72 (October 1959), pp. 1–9.

– 'Approaches to Stability Analysis', *Economica*, Vol. 28 (February 1961), pp. 12–29.

NEWMAN, P.: *The Theory of Exchange*, Englewood Cliffs, Prentice-Hall, 1965.

COMPETITIVE TÂTONNEMENT EXCHANGE MARKETS

PATINKIN, D.: *Money, Interest, and Prices*, 1st ed., Evanston, Row, 1956.
- *Money, Interest, and Prices*, 2nd ed., New York, Harper and Row, 1965.
QUIRK, J., and SAPOSNIK, R.: *Introduction to General Equilibrium Theory and Welfare Economics*, New York, McGraw-Hill, 1968.
QUIRK, J.: 'Comparative Statics under Walras Law', *Review of Economic Studies*, Vol. 35 (January 1968), pp. 11–22.
REDER, M.W.: *Studies in the Theory of Welfare Economics*, New York, Columbia University Press, 1947.
RIST, C.: 'Economie optimiste et économie scientifique', *Revue de métaphysique et de morale*, Vol. 12 (July 1904), pp. 643–63.
SAMUELSON, P.A.: *Foundations of Economic Analysis*, Cambridge, Mass., Harvard University Press, 1955.
SCHNEIDER, E.: *Pricing and Equilibrium*, New York, Macmillan, 1962.
SCITOVSKY, T.: *Welfare and Competition*, Chicago, Irwin, 1951.
SCOTT, I.O., Jr.: *Government Securities Market*, New York, McGraw-Hill, 1965.
SMITH, V.L.: 'An Experimental Study of Competitive Market Behavior', *Journal of Political Economy*, Vol. 70 (April 1962), pp. 111–37.
- 'Effect of Market Organization on Competitive Equilibrium', *Quarterly Journal of Economics*, Vol. 78 (May 1964), pp. 181–201.
- 'Experimental Auction Markets and the Walrasian Hypothesis', *Journal of Political Economy*, Vol. 73 (August 1965), pp. 387–93.
SOLOW, R.: 'Competitive Valuation in a Dynamic Input-Output System', *Econometrica*, Vol. 27 (January 1959), pp. 30–53.
STIGLER, G.J.: *Production and Distribution Theories*, New York, Macmillan, 1941.
- 'Perfect Competition, Historically Contemplated', *Journal of Political Economy*, Vol. 65 (February 1957), pp. 1–16.
TAKAYAMA, T., and JUDGE, G.: 'An Intertemporal Price Equilibrium Model', *Journal of Farm Economics*, Vol. 46 (May 1964), pp. 477–84.
UZAWA, H.: 'Walras' *Tâtonnement* in the Theory of Exchange', *Review of Economic Studies*, Vol. 27 (June 1960), pp. 182–94.
- 'The Stability of Dynamic Processes', *Econometrica*, Vol. 29 (October 1961), pp. 617–31.
WALKER, D.A.: 'Marshall's Theory of Competitive Exchange', *Canadian Journal of Economics*, Vol. 2 (November 1969), pp. 590–8.
- 'Léon Walras in the Light of His Correspondence and Related Papers', *Journal of Political Economy*, Vol. 78 (July/August 1970), pp. 685–701.
WALRAS, LÉON: 'Principe d'une Théorie mathématique de l'échange', *Séances et travaux de l'Académie des Sciences morales et politiques*, Vol. 101 of the *Collection*, New Series 33rd year, January 1874, Part I, pp. 97–116. Republished in **Walras** 1883, pp. 7–25.
- 'La bourse, la spéculation et l'agiotage', *Bibliothèque Universelle*, 3rd period, Vol. 5 (March 1880), pp. 452–76, and Vol. 5 (April 1880), pp. 66–94. Republished in Walras 1936, pp. 401–45.
- *Théorie mathématique de la richesse sociale*, Lausanne, Corbaz, 1883.
- *Eléments d'économie politique pure*, Lausanne, F. Rouge, 1900.

DONALD A. WALKER

- *Etudes d'économie politique appliquée*, Lausanne, F. Rouge, 1936.
- *Elements of Pure Economics*, translated by W. Jaffé, Homewood, Irwin, 1954.

WICKSELL, K.: *Lectures on Political Economy*, Vol. 1, *General Theory*, London, Routledge and Kegan Paul, 1934.

WICKSTEED, P. H.: *The Common Sense of Political Economy*, 2 vols., London, Routledge and Kegan Paul, 1933.

SUMMARY

This study analyzes the types of competitive *tâtonnement* exchange models that have been developed, shows the necessity for further modifications of them, and draws the implications of these modifications for the direction which a revision of the analysis of the stability of the models should take. It is concluded that in order to generate the *tâtonnement* properties the models must possess a price setter, but existing models are dominated by the view that the price moves under the action of impersonal forces, and consequently employ the mechanistic Walrasian rule that was formulated independently of the notion of a price setter, whereby the rate of price change is a sign-preserving function of excess demand. It is shown that the analysis of the stability of the models needs the modifications that will result from formulating price-changing rules that are reasonable in the light of the price setter's capacity for rational behavior and his degree of volitional freedom.

ZUSAMMENFASSUNG

Der Artikel gibt einen Überblick über die bis anhin entwickelten *tâtonnement*-Tauschmodelle, zeigt die Notwendigkeit ihrer weiteren Änderung und zieht Schlussfolgerungen bezüglich der Richtung, die eine Revision der Stabilitätsanalyse dieser Modelle nehmen sollte. Der Autor gelangt zur Ansicht, dass die Modelle nur dann wirklich *tâtonnement*-Eigenschaften aufweisen, wenn ein Preissetzer eingeführt wird. Die bestehenden Modelle sind jedoch meist darauf aufgebaut, dass sich der Preis unter der Einwirkung unpersönlicher Kräfte verändert. Sie verwenden deshalb die mechanistische Walrasianische Regel, die unabhängig vom Begriff des Preissetzers formuliert ist und bei der die Rate der Preisänderung eine Funktion der Übernachfrage ist. Es wird gezeigt, dass die Stabilitätsanalyse davon profitiert, wenn Preisänderungsregeln formuliert werden, die auf vernünftigen Annahmen in bezug auf den Entscheidungsspielraum des Preissetzers und seiner Fähigkeit zu rationalem Verhalten aufbauen.

RÉSUMÉ

Le présent article donne un aperçu des modèles d'échange de tâtonnement développés, montre la nécessité de leur changement ultérieur et en tire des conclusions quant à la direction que devrait emprunter une révision de l'analyse de la stabilité de ces modèles. L'auteur prétend que les caractères de tâtonnement apparaissent dans les modèles uniquement lorsqu'on y introduit un fixateur des prix. Les modèles existants sont construits le plus souvent de telle façon que le prix change sous l'influence de forces impersonnelles. Ils utilisent ainsi la règle mécanique walrasienne qui est formulée indépendamment de la notion de fixateur des prix et qui considère le taux de variation des prix comme une fonction de la demande excédentaire. L'auteur montre que l'analyse de la stabilité se trouve renforcée lorsque les règles relatives aux variations des prix seront formulées et basées sur des hypothèses raisonnables en considération du domaine de décision et de la capacité de comportement rationnel du fixateur des prix.

Is Walras's theory of general equilibrium a normative scheme?

Donald A. Walker

I. Jaffé's Thesis

It is a commonplace of writing on the history of economic thought that the work of one or another economist is alleged to have a normative bias in the sense that values and prejudices embedded in his ideational process and philosophical outlook have crept into his work without the writer having been conscious of their influence. It is often maintained, for example, that value judgments operate in determining the selection of problems that a scientist finds interesting, or that a writer's treatment of his subject is affected by his being a member of a particular social class. The allegation made by William Jaffé regarding the work of Léon Walras was, however, of a different character, for he asserted that in developing the theory of general equilibrium in the *Eléments d'économie politique pure* Walras consciously had the objective of constructing a normative system. Jaffé maintained that although Walras's theory superficially seems to be a treatment of the economics of pure competition, in actuality it "was deliberately designed as a normative model" (1974, 14) that "would satisfy the demands of social justice without overstepping the bounds imposed by the natural exigencies of the real world" (1977d, 386), and it is therefore "through and through informed and animated by his moral convictions" (1977a, 31).[1] Walras's theory of general equilibrium, Jaffé emphasized, was constructed with "an ethico-normative purpose in mind and not, as is generally supposed, with a view to systematizing an all-encompassing theory of positive economics" (1974, 15).

This thesis was expressed very forcefully by Jaffé in his penultimate article in relation to Michio Morishima's treatment of Walras's work: "In my estimation, Morishima got off on the wrong foot . . . in supposing that 'the ultimate aim [of Walras's *Eléments*] was to construct a model, by the

---

Correspondence may be addressed to Professor Donald A. Walker, Dept. of Economics, Indiana University of Pennsylvania, Indiana PA 15705.

[1]. See also Jaffé 1977d, 371, and passim; 1980, 530–32, 537, 538, 546; 1981, 315, 334.

use of which we can examine how the capitalist system works.' That, I contend, was not the aim of the *Eléments*, either ultimate or immediate" (Jaffé 1980, 530). Instead, Walras's objective was "to portray how an imaginary system *might* work in conformity with principles of 'justice' rooted in traditional natural law philosophy. . . . The *Eléments* was intended to be and is, in all but the name, a realistic utopia" (ibid.). Walras condemned utopian schemes that totally disregard the realities of the world, but he nevertheless strove to achieve the implementation of his own ideal of social justice, one which was based upon the concepts of commutative and distributive justice which are part of the humanistic tradition that stretches back to classical antiquity (1979, 15). Walras wanted a normative system, Jaffé maintained, for use as a guide to the formulation of policies that would change the structure of the economy. It would then conform to his ideal scheme and produce in reality the beneficial consequences that he deduced in his logical experiments (1978, 574).

Jaffé argued that his thesis aids in achieving a correct understanding of the meaning of Walras's theories and in evaluating them.[2] In particular, Jaffé contended, many criticisms of them are unjustifiable because Walras was concerned with a normative scheme and not with the problems in which his critics were interested (1977d, 386). "It is because our contemporary critics of Walras, our Patinkins, our Kuennes, our Garegnanis, our Morishimas, proceed blissfully unmindful of Walras's primary aim in creating his general equilibrium model that I suspect they misunderstand it and subject it to reformulations, emendations, and corrections that are beside the point" (1980, 547). "Ever since the 1920s these misdirected criticisms have given rise to a succession of corrections, emendations, modernizations, reconstructions, and outright rejections, each more ingenious than the last, but all . . . mistaking the 'spirit' of the original" (1978, 575).

These implications of Jaffé's thesis are important issues for the history of economic thought. There is a major difference in character between the work of a scientist who strives as best as he can to achieve what he believes is objective truth—an accurate description of facts or a theoretical explanation of their behavior—and the work of someone who develops a system as a means of showing how his ideas about social justice can be distilled into rules of proper conduct, and as a way of demonstrating the desirable consequences those rules would have if they were adopted. In arguing that Walras's work was of the latter character, Jaffé made a very serious allegation about Walras as a scientist, about his theory of general equilibrium, and about the critical work of many theorists. Furthermore, my discussions

---

2. See Walker 1983a and 1983b for accounts of Jaffé's outlook on the study of the history of scientific thought and on the nature of scientific knowledge.

with many colleagues have made clear that they accept Jaffé's thesis because of his great authority and because of their predisposition, acquired during the course of studying philosophy, to believe that normative interests are important in the development of any theory. Accordingly, the purpose of the present study is to assess the validity of Jaffé's thesis, a task which entails the examination of some interesting unfamiliar parts of Walras's writings, and a re-examination of some of the familiar parts.[3]

Why, according to Jaffé, did Walras purposely conceal the normative nature of his general-equilibrium theory? The answer, Jaffé explained, is found in the circumstance that political economy was regarded with suspicion by the authorities in France in the nineteenth century. There was strict censorship during the Restoration and subsequently under Louis Philippe and Louis Napoleon, and economists had to be extremely circumspect. Consequently, when Walras decided to study economics to lay the foundation for the realization of his social ideal, he "was at first obliged by the repressive regime of the Third French Empire to give his theory the appearance of a positive theory" (Jaffé 1974, 17). In substantiation of this position Jaffé cited letters in which Auguste Walras warned his son Léon of the need to be cautious in his treatment of sensitive social issues, and through which, according to Jaffé, he instilled in Léon a "sense of *petit-bourgeois* prudence" (1965b, 231). An example of Auguste's admonitions was transmitted in a letter of 1859 prompted by Léon's authorship of a manuscript on the refutation of the economic doctrines of Proudhon:

> If you decide to publish your work, re-read it with care; don't allow anything to remain in it that would give even the slightest offense from a political point of view. Place yourself and keep yourself always on scientific ground. Arrange matters, in a word, so that if by chance anyone decides to lodge charges against you, the Imperial Prosecutor would be obliged, in order to have you condemned, to maintain that the world does not turn, that the sun is no bigger than a pumpkin, that thunder is a bar of iron forged by the Cyclops and hurled by Jupiter [A. Walras 1912, 299–300].

---

3. Most of Morishima's reply (Morishima 1980, 550–58) dealt with other issues, but he also responded briefly to Jaffé's thesis. He disagreed strongly with Jaffé, taking the position that Walras was concerned with obtaining "a first-approximation view of . . . reality," and regarding his theory "as an abstract expression of the real world rather than a moral fiction" (ibid. 551 n. 2). "It is entirely clear," Morishima maintained, "that Walras's aim in the *Eléments* is to obtain a scientific description of the real world, which is the capitalist economy in his case" (ibid. 552). In fact, however, these were merely counter-assertions by Morishima. He did not examine or controvert the evidence that Jaffé brought forward in favor of his thesis. Morishima's procedure instead was to present (ibid. 551) a few brief quotations from Walras, which Jaffé had already allowed (Jaffé 1980, 530) could be done without resolving the issue in Morishima's favor. Jaffé's thesis, by contrast, was based upon evidence that he brought forward and analyzed in several articles. His thesis has therefore yet to be evaluated.

It is understandable that Auguste would have cautioned Léon about his book on Proudhon, because it was written in France in 1859 and was not a scientific treatise but a book on "the social question," devoted to an examination of justice and property rights. In contrast, the character of the *Eléments*, written in Switzerland fourteen years later, is quite different, and Jaffé should not have alleged that the advice given by Auguste in 1859 led Léon to design it as a way of concealing a normative scheme.[4]

Intellectuals in nineteenth-century France were fully aware of the dangers of offending the political authorities. When Walras recalled conditions in 1860, a year in which he delivered a paper on taxation in Lausanne, he observed that "in those days, one was hauled into the police court and put in prison for merely inquiring into the existing institution of property. That was precisely the fate of Vacherot. But my father had made me promise not to take this risk, though I for my part should have considered myself honored by it."[5] Nevertheless, when we examine the sort of inquiry that Walras believed that the government would suppress, we find that he did not have reference to his theory of economic equilibrium, but to the politically sensitive issue of the ownership of land, for in his next sentence he went on to write: "This explains why I did no more than hint at the theory of the collective ownership of land, without enlarging upon it in my . . . *Théorie critique de l'impôt*."

The picture of Walras as a would-be reformer constrained to hide his politics by the repressive government of Louis Philippe is an exaggeration. In fact, Walras never at any time put aside a passionate and vocal interest in social reform. Consider, for example, his preface to his novel *Francis Sauveur*, published in 1858, in which he expressed himself in the following unequivocal terms. "What is this society that we are supposed to serve?" he asked rhetorically,

> And what revolting and iniquitous society is one divided into two classes of humanity: on the one side a mass of workers, despised proletarians, and on the other group of idlers, fortunate owners of the earth on which we were born? And the leaders of this unruly society, who are they? They are these same idlers who are interested in main-

---

4. Jaffé initially referred to Auguste Walras's letter as support for the contention that Léon found pure theory more congenial than the anxiety-ridden occupation of a nineteenth-century reformer. "I would like," Jaffé wrote, "to draw your attention to a single incident at that time"—the letter from Auguste to Léon—"because I believe that we will find in it the psychological reason for his great attraction to pure economic theory, even though he was passionately interested in political and practical questions" (Jaffé 1956, 214). Similarly, in 1971 the inference that Jaffé drew from the circumstances of censorship and repression was that they led Walras to put aside his earlier enthusiasm for social reform and to take refuge in purely theoretical studies (Jaffé 1971, 93).

5. Léon Walras's statement in an unmailed letter to Charles Gide dated 1906, quoted in Jaffé 1975, 812.

taining a pact according to which they receive benefits without accepting burdens, imbecile legislators whose ineptitude is equalled only by their corruption and their venality! Serve this society! We would do that by betraying it and overthrowing it, if we knew what other to construct in its place [Walras 1858, ix–x].

Similarly, Walras's concern with the censors did not prevent him from arguing in 1860 in favor of his brand of socialism (Walras 1860, viii), and he spent much of his twenties involved with normative social issues, strongly influenced by the outburst of idealistic social and political schemes that followed the insurrections of 1848. All his adult life he advocated the nationalization of land; he wrote articles on 'the social ideal' in the 1860s; he was active in the movement to establish workers cooperatives; he published his normative examination of Proudhon's ideas about property and justice; and in his *Recherche de l'idéal social*, delivered as lectures in Paris in 1867 and 1868, he once again set forth his opinions about how society and the economy should be organized (Walras 1896c).

Moreover, there may have been repression in France, but Walras was not there when he wrote and published his *Eléments*; he was in free republican Switzerland. Far from discouraging policy proposals, the authorities who appointed Walras to his position at the Académie de Lausanne in 1871 had the objective of providing for the development of social studies which could be used to aid in framing solutions to social problems, rather than leaving the field to what they regarded as the destructive and nihilistic programs of the Internationale (Walras 1871, address by Councilor of State Louis Ruchonnet, pp. 8–9). There was therefore no need for Walras to conceal an interest in social reform at the time that he wrote the *Eléments*, and he did not, revealing by the content of his speeches the improbability that he would have hidden his normative views behind the equations of an ostensibly pure theory. In his first address to a class at Lausanne, while still a visiting lecturer and therefore on probationary status, he declared his desire to inculcate in his students, with all the ardor of which he was capable, "the knowledge and love of the principles of economic science and social ethics which will definitively assure the growth of wealth and the triumph of justice" (Jaffé 1965a, vol. 1, transcript dated Dec. 16, 1870, p. 251). On the occasion of his installation as professor of economics at the Académie de Lausanne he committed himself "to the careful cultivation of the notions of economic truth and social justice in order to give birth to them in the minds of my pupils" (Walras 1871, 42). He also wrote extensively on explicitly normative topics at the same time that he was conceiving and developing his general-equilibrium theory,[6] and made a

---

6. See, for example, Walras 1896c for normative essays written during the late 1860s and subsequently.

clear distinction between his normative and positive endeavors,[7] revealing in these additional respects the improbability of Jaffé's thesis.

How did Jaffé account for Walras's adoption of a theory of general equilibrium expressed in simultaneous equations as a means of concealing his normative scheme? According to Jaffé, Walras's private jottings and correspondence indicate that he came to realize from reading Achylle-Nicholas Isnard's *Traité des richesses* and Louis Poinsot's *Eléments de statique* that he could "give a neutral aspect to his model" by using a type of equation system similar to theirs (Jaffé 1974, 17). Jaffé did not present any evidence for that contention, and it is inconsistent with the evidence that is available on the matter. Walras nowhere stated or implied that he learned from Isnard how he could hide his normative views. Walras never acknowledged receiving inspiration of any kind from Isnard's work, nor did he even mention it, except in bringing it to Jevons' attention in response to his request for titles of works on mathematical economics (Jaffé 1965a, vol. 1, letter 410, July 13, 1978, p. 570; and see Jaffé 1969, 25). Furthermore, although Jaffé's research (1909) on Isnard's work was directed at establishing that Walras drew upon it, the extent of Walras's indebtedness to Isnard is irrelevant for the issue of whether or not the reason that Walras used a system like Isnard's was that he found it a useful way of hiding the normative character of his message. When that issue is considered in the light of the direct and circumstantial evidence brought forward in the present article, it seems reasonable to conclude that if Walras adopted Isnard's economic theories and method, he did so because he thought that they were scientifically valuable.

As for Poinsot's work, it undoubtedly stimulated and reinforced Walras's conviction that only by using mathematics and by emulating the methods of the natural sciences, and particularly the model of celestial mechanics, could economics become a true science (Walras 1860, xiii; 1861, 93; Jaffé 1965a, vol. 1, letter 81, Dec. 23, 1862, p. 119). Indeed, Walras specifically indicated that his indebtedness to Poinsot was straightforwardly scientific. Walras reported, long after the event, that when he was nineteen years old, Poinsot's theory of equilibrium seemed to him so illuminating

---

7. Indeed, Jaffé was of the opinion in 1971 that Walras "confined his theoretical work to the rigorous plane of pure analysis. The very title of his major treatise, *Eléments d'économie politique pure*, announced unmistakably a study in the pure theory of economics, actually inspired by the pure theory of mechanics" (Jaffé 1971, 91). Jaffé went further to observe that Walras did not construct his pure theory for an audience that would include politicians or businessmen or humanistic scholars, but exclusively for professional economists who would be living a generation or two after his time, believing that his contemporaries could not appreciate his ideas (ibid.; see Jaffé 1965a, vol. 1, Walras's 'Notice autobiographique,' p. 12). It is unlikely that anyone with a message of social reform would aim it at such a select future audience.

and comprehensive that he read the first half in one sitting and the second in another (Jaffé 1965a, vol. 3, letter 1438, May 23, 1901, p. 148), and he still owned and admired the book in 1901 (ibid. vol. 3, letter 1495, Sept. 26, 1901, p. 161). The reason that he found it so inspirational was that he wanted to express the interrelatedness of phenomena in his economic theory, and Poinsot showed how simultaneous equation systems can perform that function.

Walras's explanation of his motivation and procedure was explicit and credible. "There is," he wrote, "a complete system of economic theory under the garb of my formulas, that is to say, a new and original conception of free competition in regard to exchange, production, and capital formation, which could not be demonstrated without mathematics, but which could be described very well outside of the mathematical form" (Jaffé 1965a, vol. 1, letter 416, Sept. 10, 1878). "The use of the mathematical language and method," Walras explained, "enabled me not only to demonstrate the laws of the establishment of equilibrium prices, but also to demonstrate the laws of the variation of those prices, and to analyze the fact of free competition and in so doing to establish it as a principle. . . . Why not . . . accept the description of the world of economic facts that conforms to the principle of free competition?" (Walras 1877, 365–66). Thus Walras maintained that free competition was a fact and that his equations and economic reasoning expressed its workings. "I felt that I had to give both [mathematical and literary treatments]," he concluded, "in order to outline, as I wished to do, a truly scientific theory of social wealth" (ibid. 366).

II. *Examination of the Evidence*

So far as I am aware, there is no place in any of Walras's writings where he stated that his theory of general equilibrium has a normative purpose, and there are many places where he stated that it does not. Furthermore, an examination of the content of Walras's theory as set forth in the *Eléments* does not establish its normative nature, and there are extensive sections in that volume in which Walras argued against the introduction of normative elements into economic theory. It could therefore be argued that on balance the evidence obtained by an analysis of Walras's general-equilibrium theory is against Jaffé's thesis. Jaffé was unwilling to draw that conclusion, however. He took the position that the textual evidence in the *Eléments* is not sufficient to establish whether Walras constructed a normative scheme or had some other purpose in mind. "On this point the *Eléments* itself is not clear" (Jaffé 1980, 531). Unable to furnish direct evidence for his thesis in Walras's exposition of general equilibrium, Jaffé instead cited other writings in which Walras discussed ethics and economics, and used certain passages in the *Eléments* as a basis for speculations that went beyond their literal meaning. The nine considerations that Jaffé brought forward in support of his thesis will now be examined.

(i) First, Jaffé placed his special interpretation upon some sections of a paper that Walras submitted for a prize offered in 1860 by the Council of State of the Vaud canton in Switzerland. Having reference to pure theoretical social science, Walras argued in his paper that the consequences of premises have an abstract and ideal character and should be criticized in the name of reason, truth, and absolute justice (see Jaffé 1975, 811 n. 8). Jaffé also offered (1980, 530 n. 6) as evidence Walras's statement that on the terrain of science we seek absolute concepts and rigorous perfection, and "it is not sufficient to have half-utility or something close to justice, it is necessary to have complete utility, and full and entire justice" (Walras 1896c, 188). Jaffé regarded these declarations as indicating that Walras thought that considerations of justice have a place in determining the content of pure theory. Walras did not, however, mean 'ideal' in the sense of 'good,' but in the sense of a pure concept, like a perfect circle, which exists only as an idea and is never perfectly exemplified in fact. This he made evident in other writings, as will be seen, and by proceeding, in his 1860 paper, to explain that pure theory is on a different plane than policy, arguing that pure theory does not dictate the details of practical applications, since on the applied level compromises have to be made and the particular characteristics of individuals have to be taken into consideration.

Furthermore, Walras did not mean that economic science contains or is based upon notions of what is just. His position on this issue and on the treatment of normative and positive economics can be made clear by presenting a representative sample of his writings. At the beginning of his career Walras distinguished positive economics and considerations of justice, and this distinction runs consistently through his entire life's work. His opinion during the early 1860s was given in the *Théorie critique de l'impôt*, in which he wrote that economic policy is the result of the application of principles of justice to the laws of economics, and in which he made clear that his statement about 'complete justice' refers to what he identified as the scientific study of justice. "Economics is an experimental science. It observes natural facts rigorously and determines their order and relationships. As for the principles of justice, they are the object of an *a priori* science; and reason, infallible reason, with the use of undebatable axioms suffices to establish ethical truths that are as incontestable as geometric theorems" (Walras 1861, 92). Once a set of norms is taken as given, Walras was arguing, the consequences of those norms in various derivative respects can be deduced. He declared that he needed a scientific theory of distribution, and socio-economic laws as rational, as evident, as productive as the laws of astronomy. Such positive laws would form a secure foundation of pure scientific knowledge, and once in possession of them, he could turn to the investigation of the practical problem of taxation, which involves the normative question of justice (ibid. 93).

Six years later in 1867—shortly before beginning the development of his theory of general equilibrium—Walras expressed his outlook by dividing the study of economics into three parts (Walras 1868; 1896c, 31). First is pure economic theory, which establishes *truth*, and which is the study of the natural laws of exchange, or the theory of social wealth. Second, there is applied economics, which deals with what is *useful*, and which is the study of the maximization of the production of wealth. This branch of economics is concerned with working out the consequences of given normative goals, as exemplified by the essays that Walras was to collect in the *Etudes d'économie politique appliquée* (Walras 1898b). Third, there is social economics, which deals with what is *just*, and which is concerned with formulating goals and assessing their consequences in the areas of property and taxation. This is the normative theory of the distribution of wealth (1896c, 30), as exemplified by the essays that he was to collect in the *Etudes d'économie sociale* (Walras 1896c).[8]

Then in 1874, in comments that introduced his theory of general equilibrium, Walras contended that practical expediency and material well-being, on the one hand, and equity and justice, on the other, are two different orders of consideration (1874b, 7; 1926, §5, p. 7).[9] It is therefore necessary, he explained, to distinguish *what is* from *what ought to be*. What ought to be, from the point of view of expediency and material well-being, is the object of applied science or art. What ought to be, from the viewpoint of equity and justice, is the object of moral science or ethics (1874b, 16–17; 1926, §15, p. 16). These distinctions are based upon the difference between natural phenomena and phenomena which result from the exercise of human will. Two further subject matters are concerned with the consequences of human decisions. First, the theory of industrial activity has to do with the production of an abundance of wealth, considering the relations between people from the point of view of material well-being. Second, the theory of property, on the other hand, is an ethical discipline which considers people in their capacity as moral beings. It has to do with

---

8. In a letter to Louis Ruchonnet, Walras repeated these ideas, enlarged upon the content of the three divisions, and gave a remarkably prescient outline of the studies that he was to undertake over the course of the next thirty years (Jaffé 1965a, vol. 1, letter 148, September 6, 1870, pp. 204–12; see also ibid., letter 403, March 11, 1878, pp. 561–62).

9. The editions of the *Eléments* cited are the earliest one in which the material appears, and the 1926 edition, which was the last. In the case of the 1926 edition, the number of the division of the text that contains the material is given in order that the passage can be located in Jaffé's translation (Walras 1954) of the 1926 edition. In this connection, it should be observed that my translations differ in detail from Jaffé's. The divisions are here called 'sections,' although Walras used that word to describe major parts of his book.

the conditions of the equitable distribution of wealth, and therefore has justice as its guiding principle (1874b, 38–44; 1926, §34–39, pp. 35–40; and see also 1879a, 15–17; 1879b, 246).

Finally, from the large body of Walras's writing on the subject, all to the same effect, a sample written in the 1890s reveals him steadfastly identifying the branch of science that deals with material well-being and the branch that deals with justice (1898b, 452–53). Economic laws and normative principles relate to different aspects of experience. Pure moral science ("science pure morale") is concerned with formulating the laws regarding facts which have their source in the exercise of human will. Pure natural science is concerned with formulating the laws regarding facts which have their origin in the play of the forces of nature (1898b, 452). Applied science, which is concerned with guiding the directions in which human will is exercised, is divided into applied ethics ("science appliquée morale") and applied natural science. Applied ethics deals with the principles of relationships between people and is pursued from the point of view of justice. Applied natural science deals with the rules of relationships between persons and things and is pursued from the viewpoint of what is useful. Applied economics, which enunciates the rules of what is useful, is an applied natural science that deals with the relationships between people, not as moral beings, but as workers undertaking tasks in accordance with their relationships with things. Thus the evidence all shows that Walras was very much aware of the distinction between normative and positive studies, and of the desirability of keeping them separate. It is also clear that he regarded economic theory as a positive study of economic behavior.

(ii) A second piece of evidence offered by Jaffé was Walras's 1868 statement that

> in regard to science, we are on the terrain of ideas, of the ideal, of perfection. No one can prevent us from defining, that is to say, from abstracting from experience, such ideas as those of social wealth; of capital and revenues; of productive services and products; of landowners, workers, and capitalists; of entrepreneurs; of the market and prices; of man in society pursuing different occupations, reasonable and free [Walras 1896c, 187, cited in Jaffé 1980, 530 n. 6].

Those observations in no way support Jaffé's thesis. Walras's statement asserts that science makes abstractions from reality and that it formulates concepts that are perfect and ideal in the sense that they are uninfluenced by extraneous complications and the idiosyncratic character of phenomena in the actual world. Once again, Walras was referring to the ideal and to perfection in the sense that characterizes the definitions of geometry or pure physics. He went on in the same passage to make a number of remarks which demonstrate not a fusion but a separation of positive and normative reasoning. On the foundation of the pure abstractions of economic science it is possible, he wrote, to establish the theory of production and distribution, a theory that demonstrates scientifically when private enterprise results in abundance and when it does not. It then becomes possible to formulate normative practical proposals as to when the state should intervene in the economy (1896c, 188).

(iii) Jaffé maintained on the basis of two considerations that Walras's theory of consumer demand embodies his normative views. One of Jaffé's contentions was that Walras's normative aim was manifested by his lack of interest in the characteristics of individual consumption, as contrasted with his concern for the relevance of the theory of demand to the conditions of market equilibrium (Jaffé 1974, 14). The absence of an area of study from a writer's work cannot be accepted as evidence of the manifestation of a normative intention in the areas that he does investigate. Jaffé's other assertion was that the purpose of Walras's theory of demand was to investigate the justice of the outcome of exchange in a competitive market (ibid. 14–15). The history of the development of Walras's theory of demand disproves that contention.

Walras labored over the theory of demand for thirteen years. At first, in his own unaided efforts, he followed a futile maze of mathematical reasoning regarding scarcity, extensive utility, intensive utility, virtual utility, effective utility, ratios of supply and demand, and a number of other purely technical considerations—a maze that had nothing to do with social reform (Walras 1860, xiv, xxxiv, xlviii–lix; Jaffé 1965a, 1:216–19, 293–94; and see Jaffé 1972, 392–97). Finally, in 1872 he asked a colleague at the Académie de Lausanne, Antoine Paul Piccard, for the answer to the problem of the derivation of the demand curve from the utility function. It is obvious from Piccard's response that Walras did not frame the problem in a normative manner, nor ask how a normative theory could be concealed within the theory of demand. Piccard provided him with a model of utility maximization and derived the demand function within it (Jaffé 1965a, vol. 1, undated transcript by Paul Piccard, pp. 309–11). Walras took over that model in its entirety and utilized it in his general-equilibrium analysis without adding normative elements to it. Subsequently he modified his theory of demand in ways that were stimulated by scientific considerations brought to his attention by other writers. His adoption of non-linear marginal-utility curves was almost certainly made in response to criticisms by Wilhelm Lexis. His discussion of the proportionality of marginal utilities under conditions of discontinuous marginal-utility curves was made in response to comments by Eugen von Böhm-Bawerk. His introduction of a second-order condition for a utility maximum was made in response to a suggestion by Ladislaus von Bortkiewicz (Jaffé 1965a, vol. 2, letter 831, April 27 and May 9, 1888, p. 248; Jaffé 1977b, 302; 1977c, 210–12).

The Walrasian theory of demand as it ultimately emerged was therefore in large part composed of the ideas of scientists other than Walras. Jaffé himself in 1972 remarked upon the circumstances of its origin in the following terms: "Does not," he asked, "the biographical narrative of Léon Walras's awesome voyage of discovery of marginal utility in terms of a differential coefficient reveal the voyage as an academic adventure, directed in large part by prevailing pedagogic winds?" (Jaffé 1972, 401). Since the same theory had been published by H. H. Gossen in Germany in 1854, and was independently discovered around 1870 by W. S. Jevons in England and Carl Menger in Austria, it was evidently the outcome of contemporary intellectual conditions, not the result of Walras's normative views.

Many other examples of Walras's work could be presented, such as his theories of interest, of bank money,[10] of production,[11] of capitalization; his treatment of business accounting and inventory; and his analysis of bimetallism and fiduciary money. An examination of them cannot fail to reveal their patently scientific and technical character. Like the theory of demand, some of them were to a considerable extent based on the ideas of other economists. It cannot accurately be maintained, therefore, that the parts of Walras's system were designed as embodiments of his normative views nor therefore that it is "through and through informed" by them.

(iv) The fourth piece of evidence that Jaffé brought forward (1980, 530-31) is the change of the wording of a passage in which Walras described his theory of capitalization. In the second edition of the *Eléments* he stated that it is a faithful expression and exact explanation of real phenomena (Walras 1889, xxii). In the third and fourth editions (1896a, xxii; 1900, xviii; 1926, xviii; 1954, 46), he described it as an abstract expression and rational explanation of real phenomena. The change to the latter wording is a manifestation of an effort to give a more careful exposition of the

---

10. In his theory of bank money, Walras analyzed (1880) the consequences of an increase in the amount of liquid assets, which are borrowed by entrepreneurs to finance the construction of new capital goods. He distinguished in this process the consequences of investment financed by new savings, investment financed through bank notes, and investment financed by an increase in the quantity of money proceeding from new gold and silver discoveries. In all this reasoning there are no normative assumptions or assertions, in contrast to those which he explicitly made in his prolific writings on monetary policy (see Walras 1898b, 3–59, 150–59; Jaffé 1965a, vol. 1, letters 473, 483, 484, 513, 570, and vol. 2, letters 618, 680, 683, 691, 731, 771, 780, 789, 1034, 1136, 1142, 1145, 1148).

11. The notion that inputs are used in productive processes is not normative, nor is the idea that they are combined in certain proportions. Was Walras's treatment of the way in which they are combined affected by his view of social justice? The answer must be that it was not. He initially assumed that their proportions were fixed, for the reason that he was ignorant of the mathematics that would have enabled him to assume that they are variable. When he made the latter assumption, it was because he finally achieved an understanding of the mathematics in which Barone presented it. In fact, the mathematical theory of marginal productivity that plays so prominent a role in Walras's theory of general equilibrium was largely a creation of Barone's (Jaffé 1964).

relationship of theory to reality, not evidence that his work is a moral fiction. This interpretation of the internal content of the passage is straightforward, and it is also supported by the viewpoint established in the *Eléments* as a whole, and by its consistency with Walras's explicit methodological position. In the first and subsequent editions of the *Eléments*, Walras explained that

> in applied geometry, for example, there are to be found only approximations of the pure ideal types defined in the science of geometry, but this does not prevent geometry from having many rich applications. Following this same method, pure economics ought to borrow from experience the concepts of exchange, of supply, of demand, of a market, of capital, of revenues, of productive services, of products. From these real phenomena, economics should abstract and define ideal types, and use them in its reasoning, not returning to reality to make its applications until the structure of the science is complete. We thus have, in an ideal market, ideal prices which have a rigorous relationship to ideal supply and demand [Walras 1874b, 32; 1926, §30, p. 30].

Walras therefore intended his entire theory to be "an abstract expression and rational explanation of real phenomena" because he believed that was the true relation of theory to reality, not because he wanted to construct a normative scheme.

(v) To lend credibility to his thesis, Jaffé formulated characterizations of French traditions in philosophy and of the age in which Walras's work was conceived, noted Auguste and Léon Walras's objective of social reform, remarked upon the characteristics of French rationalism, and concluded that the *Eléments* was designed in that tradition as "a theoretical representation of a just economy from the standpoint of 'commutative justice'" (Jaffé 1980, 532). Commutative justice refers to the ethical rightness of the results of exchanging commodities. Is it true that Walras wanted to develop a theory of exchange that embodied a scheme of social justice? Even in his earliest work he indicated that this was not appropriate. In *L'Economie politique et la justice*, written in 1860, he argued that it is possible to have a theory of value in exchange that is independent of considerations of justice (Walras 1860, 11). The theory of value in exchange and the theory of property differ, he maintained, because of their different points of view. Value in exchange is a natural fact, because it has its origin in deterministic natural forces, resulting in part from the presence of man on earth and in part from the limitation in the quantity of useful things. It should be considered to be just as independent of our psychological liberty as are the facts of mass, weight, and vegetation. Property, on the other hand, is an ethical phenomenon, because it has its origin in the free will of mankind. Mere appropriation arises because of scarcity, but property results from the ethical characteristics of ownership, which are features of the morality or immorality of the circumstances of the appropriation (ibid. 13). Thus there are two distinctly different theories dealing with different facts: the natural science of value in exchange, which is logically the first of the economic sciences, and the ethical science of property. "I would like to believe," Walras wrote,

> that M. Proudhon never thought of being astonished that mathematicians or physicists are not preoccupied with the notion of justice. It is good to be upset about rights; it is not necessary to invoke them at all points. The binomial theorem of Newton is neither just nor unjust, and the hypothesis of two electricities is not constrained by the rules of morality. Nor is the theory of value in exchange, believe it well, Monsieur Proudhon. It is a natural science and independent of justice [Walras 1860, 18–19].

That Walras adhered to that idea throughout his career has been demonstrated in the exposition of his distinction between normative and positive economics and his related tripartite division of economic studies.

(vi) Jaffé argued that the normative convictions which he believed underlie Walras's theory of equilibrium are revealed most clearly in his theorem of maximum social satisfaction (Jaffé 1977d, 371). Briefly, this is the theorem that traders can obtain the greatest possible satisfaction through trade at a single price in a purely competitive market (Walras 1874b, 99; 1877, 266–67; 1926, §22, pp. 231–32). In a Walrasian *tâtonnement* market, trade on any particular day occurs only at the price that is the solution to the supply and demand functions that have the initial asset distribution as a given parameter. Jaffé contended that Walras introduced the condition of a single price because he believed that any redistribution of aggregate asset values during the course of exchange would result in some traders benefiting at the expense of others, and he wanted to ensure that such an unjust process cannot occur. "Uniformity of competitively determined price represented for Walras not only an analytical ideal, but an ethical ideal as well, constituting an indispensable pillar of social justice" (Jaffé 1977d, 375). Jaffé concluded that "Walras's multi-equational system of general equilibrium thus appears profoundly moralistic" (ibid.).

There can be no doubt that Walras believed that a single trading price on a particular market day is desirable. He stated that thesis in his 'Théorie de la propriété,' which was avowedly devoted to normative economics. To be precise, he thought the condition of a single price is just, not because it eliminates changes in the value of a trader's assets, but because an inequitable situation would be created on a given market day if one buyer acquired a commodity for less than was paid by another, or if one seller received a higher price than another (Walras 1868; 1896c, 212). He also thought it would be unjust for changes in the value of money to occur, because otherwise, for example, a buyer might part with a smaller amount of real purchasing power than the seller subsequently finds that he has acquired. Finally, he also believed that it is just that commodities be produced and sold at as low a cost per unit as possible (ibid.). Jaffé contended that the last two arguments are in the *Eléments*, "though not in so many words" (Jaffé 1977d, 374).

What appears in the *Eléments*, however, is a theorem that in purely competitive equilibrium any commodity exchanges at a single price which equals its average cost of production, and that this produces a constrained maximum of satisfaction. Instead of mixing together science and his moral views, Walras first expressed that theorem, which he believed was an expression of a scientific truth, and then he made a normative judgment on it. This procedure is shown clearly in Walras's 'L'état et les chemins de fer,' written in 1875 (Walras 1897; 1898b, 193–236). He explained the difference between the theorem and his normative conclusion. He stated that economic theory teaches us that in pure competition the inputs in the productive process are combined in products of the kinds and in the quantities that give the greatest possible satisfaction of wants, subject to two conditions that result from competition. One is that there is a single price for each service, the price at which the supply and demand quantities are equal. The other is that the price of each output is equal to its average cost of production. These two conditions, he argued, can be reduced to the single condition that services are exchanged for each other in proportions that result from the preferences of their owners. Pure economic theory, he wrote, therefore deduces the principle that competition results in economic services being put to their most efficient use in producing want-satisfying commodities. Walras then introduced the normative judgment that this theoretical consequence of pure competition is socially desirable, so practical policies should be implemented to achieve it. It is "a condition of justice that social economics should establish," in the sense that policies should be devised to achieve it (ibid. 196–97). Applied economics should discover the cases in which competition is not possible and devise for them some other means of accomplishing the condition of justice (ibid. 197).[12]

Jaffé believed that Walras, in his discussion of the theorem of maximum satisfaction in the *Eléments*, "momentarily dropped his pure theory mask" by developing an argument in favor of pure competition "on moral grounds rather than on grounds of economic efficiency" (Jaffé 1977d, 375). The

12. For the positive theorem of maximum satisfaction, Walras referred to the *Eléments*, lessons 20, 21, and 22 (Walras 1898b, 195 n.). For the normative conclusion, he referred (ibid. 197 n.) to his 'Théorie de la propriété,' which appears in his volume on social economics (Walras 1896c).

implication that Walras framed his theorem as a means of expressing a concealed utopian scheme is an interpretation which cannot be sustained by the passage to which Jaffé refers (Walras 1877, 266–67; 1926, §22, pp. 231–32). In that passage Walras followed the same procedure as in his 'L'état et les chemins de fer.' He was careful to state that in developing the pure science of economics he had assumed competition as a fact or even as a hypothesis. It is of little significance, Walras remarked, whether it is regarded as the former or the latter, because to achieve rigor it is sufficient that a conception of pure competition can be formed. Simply because competition does not exist in all aspects of the economy does not mean it is not a useful or valid scientific assumption. In the first place, non-competitive conditions may eventually be incorporated into the equations of the model. In the second place, Walras explained, he had studied the nature, causes, and consequences of pure competition, and among those consequences he had deduced the important result that, subject to certain limits, it results in a maximum of utility. Regarding this theorem, Walras concluded with "a last observation of the greatest importance. Our demonstration of the characteristics of free competition deals with the question of material well-being, and takes no account of the question of justice." That normative question, he indicated, is open for exploration. Only after an objective statement of the theorem did Walras introduce the explicit normative judgment that it is desirable to achieve maximum utility, and formulate the proposal that all obstacles to pure competition should therefore be eliminated (Walras 1877, 268–69; 1926, §§222–23, pp. 232–34).

Could Walras have assumed that there are many prices in equilibrium in a purely competitive market if he had thought that this was a condition of social justice? The obvious answer is that he could not. Whether or not Walras approved of a single price, this market characteristic is not an axiom but a consequence of the basic institutional conditions and trading rules in a purely competitive *tâtonnement* model, as he indicated on many occasions (Walras 1874a, 6; 1898b, 197–98). Having constructed the competitive *tâtonnement* model, and having deduced among its consequences the feature of a single trading price on a given day, Walras then considered whether or not it is good. "It remains only to be known," he wrote, "if the condition of a single price is a condition of justice. This is a question which is not within the province of pure economics, and one which I treat with greatest care in the part of the science which is concerned with the distribution of wealth and in which the principles of social ethics intervene" (Jaffé 1965, vol. 2, letter 652, May 20, 1885, p. 50). Thus in his normative work Walras investigated the welfare implications of a single price, and because of the rightness that he discovered in that condition, he advocated purely competitive markets or state intervention to achieve it.

Since a single price is a consequence of purely competitive *tâtonnement* exchange, the question may be raised as to whether Walras assumed the basic postulates of pure competition as a way of introducing covert normative views. Far from substantiating Jaffé's thesis, the evidence shows that Walras had no such intention. Walras began his *Principe d'une théorie mathématique de l'échange* of 1873—his first accomplishment in economic theory, and one which expressed his methodological point of view and scientific objectives at the time that he wrote his *Eléments*—with a warning against the practice in French economics of mixing normative and positive economics together, and with a declaration that economics could be transformed into a proper science by use of the mathematical method (Walras 1874a, 5). Pure economics is the study of the necessary and natural effects of free competition in regard to production and exchange. On the other hand, applied economics is the demonstration of the conformity of these effects with the general material welfare, and consequently is the study of the application of the principle of free competition to agriculture, industry, commerce, and credit. Is it not necessary, he asked, to ascertain the results of *laisser-faire laisser-passer* in order to judge whether they are desirable?

> Let us assume that there is pure competition, pure *laisser-faire laisser-passer*, making abstraction of any consideration of expediency or of justice. I do not to any degree assume pure competition because it may be believed to be more useful or more equitable, but for the sole purpose of knowing its results [ibid.].

From that assumption, Walras continued, necessarily proceed three derivative features: commodities are produced, commodities are exchanged at determinate prices, and productive services are exchanged at determinate prices.

> These are the natural and necessary effects of free competition in regard to production and exchange. The study of these effects should be, in my opinion, pursued in a special manner, independently of any question and prior to any consequence that may result from their application [ibid. 6].

This approach to his subject was expressed by Walras repeatedly throughout his career. In a letter written in 1877 to the philosopher Charles Bernard Renouvier, for example, Walras explained:

> with respect to my pure economic theory, it studies purely and simply the facts of the determination of prices or proportions in exchange under a hypothetical regime of absolutely pure competition. It makes no conclusion either for or against that regime, and I believe that it is

necessary to remove its study from the ethical point of view. You may be sure that when I introduce that point of view, it will find the field of inquiry free from any given preconception [Jaffé 1965a, vol. 1, letter 385, Sept. 6, 1877, p. 542].

Of course, Walras did introduce the normative point of view when he turned to the formulation of economic policies, like writers that preceded and followed him. Economists as diverse in their social philosophy as Joseph Schumpeter and Oscar Lange have subscribed to general-equilibrium theory, illustrating a relation that is often found between economic theories and value judgments. A particular structure of ideas is acceptable to people with different normative beliefs because of its scientific value and its intrinsic ethical neutrality, and is then used as a foundation or justification for moral judgments and economic policies that differ in accordance with the different normative convictions of their formulators.

(vii) Jaffé alleged that Walras introduced his equations of exchange (Walras 1874b, 120–22, 142, 254, 285–87; 1926, §118, pp. 123–25; §143, p. 149; §210, p. 218; §244, pp. 254–55), which are budget constraints, as part of a utopian structure that would result in economic justice (Jaffé 1977d, 374). An implication of the equations, as Jaffé pointed out, is that traders' asset values are unchanged by trade at the equilibrium price. Jaffé believed that Walras, aware of that circumstance, introduced the equations to prevent the injustice of any trader increasing his asset values, since on a given market day that could occur only at the expense of some other trader. This was a speculation on Jaffé's part, because Walras did not remark upon any normative implications that his budget constraints might have, and an examination of them does not support Jaffé's thesis. Two considerations are relevant for judging Walras's procedure. First, by introducing the budget constraint of a trader, he was expressing a fact of economic life, not a normative condition. Second, the constancy of asset values which follows from exchange that occurs at a given price subject to a budget constraint is another fact of economic life. Walras could not have argued that the values are different after exchange if that had been the condition he preferred. Whether one likes it or not, it is simply a truism to say that a trader's money plus his stock of a commodity valued at a given price has the same total value before and after exchange at that price. Traders are able to change the value of their assets only by trading at a series of different prices, either on the same market day in a non-*tâtonnement* market, or from one day to another in a *tâtonnement* market. It is therefore clear that Walras was describing an objective feature of the exchange process.

Furthermore, he had no adverse reaction to the circumstance that one day succeeds another in a *tâtonnement* market, and that the values of the traders' assets consequently change. If Walras had wished to devise a market model in which no one changes the value of his assets, he would have had to ensure that equilibrium prices are always the same. That would have required him to introduce the absurd condition that market parameters never change, which, of course, he did not do. On the contrary, he specifically indicated that there is in actuality an endless series of market days in which the parametric constants such as "quantities possessed, utility functions, etc., vary as a function of *time*. The *fixed* equilibrium is transformed into a *variable* or *moving* equilibrium" (Walras 1900, 301; 1926, §273, p. 301).

(viii) As part of his evidence, Jaffé argued that Walras displayed a normative bias by criticizing Gossen's theorem of maximum satisfaction on the ground that it implies that the initial endowments of the traders should be pooled and then divided up in such a way as to maximize joint utility (Jaffé 1977d, 381–85). It is true that Gossen's scheme does not preserve the initial endowments, but Walras did not, contrary to Jaffé's interpretation, object to that implication of the theorem, but to two other aspects of it.[13] He argued that it is scientifically faulty because it defines an absolute maximum rather than one which is constrained by the condition of a single price at which the supply and demand quantities are equal. Gossen's theorem is wrong, Walras stated, because it does not introduce relevant market conditions (Walras 1885, 76, 78–79; 1889, 189; 1900, 169–70; 1926, §162, pp. 169–70). In contrast, Walras explained, his own theorem of maximum utility takes cognizance of the fact that free competition results in a single price, and expresses the welfare implications of that condition, defining not an absolute but a relative maximum.

Walras also saw that Gossen's theorem is not a scientific description of the welfare consequences of an actual market process, but a policy proposal, and he argued that the normative position embodied in that policy is unjustifiable because it allows different people simultaneously to trade at different prices (Walras 1900, 170; 1926, §162, p. 170). It would, Walras observed, obviously be possible to generate levels of welfare that are higher than those that result from pure competition by using non-competitive types of pricing systems, such as selling commodities at higher prices to the rich than to the poor; but what is the best system? (Jaffé 1965, vol. 2, letter 652, May 20, 1885, p. 50). Consideration of that question raises the normative issue of whether a single price, which would be provided by pure competition, is a necessary condition of justice. Walras argued that it

13. Walras did not believe that the initial endowments, that is, the distribution of wealth and income existing at any particular time, are inherently just. That is why he developed the normative discipline of social economics, in which he proposed state intervention to change endowments by nationalizing land and to provide equality of opportunity so that wealth would be obtained as a result of merit.

is, and therefore that pure competition is the best plan. "The goal that should be pursued," he wrote, "is not maximum welfare, but a welfare maximum that is *compatible with justice*" (ibid.).

Walras's second criticism of Gossen's plan was therefore frankly normative, and as such it does not constitute evidence that Walras's theory of general equilibrium was a normative scheme. As has been observed, like most economists, Walras was concerned with justice. The conditions of justice were the reason for his development of a normative branch of economic analysis and argumentation, of which his second criticism of Gossen's theorem was a part. On the basis of that normative work, however, Jaffé made an erroneous inference. As in many of his other arguments in favor of his thesis, Jaffé's treatment of Walras on Gossen's theorem contains the confusion of supposing that Walras's expressions of concern with social justice are evidence that his economic theory is normative. It is not legitimate to assert that because Walras explored and approved of the consequences of a single price he must have inserted that condition into his theory as a normative postulate. To observe that competitive markets produce a result that is compatible with a particular conception of justice is not evidence that the theory of those markets is itself a normative scheme.

(ix) Jaffé speculated that Walras's theory of *tâtonnement* was not designed, as he had originally argued, to "lend an air of empirical relevance" to the theory of general equilibrium (Jaffé 1967, 2), but to portray a "feasible desideratum rather than an empirical fact" (Jaffé 1981, 315). The evidence does not support Jaffé's contention. Walras did not assert that the *tâtonnement* process was a policy proposal that he wanted to see implemented. On the contrary, he stated that his intention was to construct an abstract account of reality, not a utopian dream, and he thought he had succeeded. His system, he wrote, is "très conforme à la réalité" (Jaffé 1965a, vol. 1, letter 453, Aug. 11, 1869, n. 3, p. 628). Similarly, in the last edition of the *Eléments* published during his life—the edition in which, according to the logic of the Jaffé thesis, Walras should have been least concerned with trying to pretend that a normative scheme was a model of real economic behavior—Walras claimed that although his theories of the determination of prices of different classes of commodities were abstract, "through the absorption by a methodical synthesis of some of them into others, we penetrate fully into reality" (Walras 1900, 172; 1926, §164, p. 172).

The *tâtonnement* process, Walras maintained, operates in both exchange and production. With regard to exchange, which includes the exchange of titles to new capital goods, Walras never deviated from the belief that real organized competitive exchange markets actually employ a *tâtonnement* process, and he stated repeatedly that the *tâtonnement* theory of exchange is a realistic model (Walras 1898, 408–9, 432; Jaffé 1965a, vol. 1, letters

256, 302; vol. 2, letters 927, 928; vol. 3, letter 1491, n. 8). "We will now see," he explained, "how the same problem of exchange of several commodities to which we have just found the scientific solution is also that which is solved empirically in real markets as a result of the mechanism of competition" (Walras 1874b, 126; 1926, §124, p. 129; and see Walras 1889, 141; 1926, §116, p. 121). "What is necessary," he asked, "to establish that the theoretical solution and the solution in the marketplace are identical? Simply that the raising and lowering of prices are a mode of solution by *tâtonnement* of the system of equations of the equality of supply and demand" (Walras 1889, 149; 1926, §125, p. 130). Again, in his discussion of new capital goods, Walras set forth a *tâtonnement* pricing model, and then observed that "the indicated *tâtonnement* is exactly that which transpires in the market for new capital goods, which is the bourse" (Walras 1900, 267; 1926, §254, p. 267).[14]

With regard to production, Walras recognized that it can be subject to disequilibrium flows. He apparently thought that such flows do not cause the equilibrating process to differ significantly from a *tâtonnement* model, but he wanted to define a pure theoretical process in which disequilibrium production is totally excluded. This was in accordance with his objective of reducing the real economic mechanism to its essential elements by eliminating all complications that he regarded as unimportant (Jaffé 1965a, vol. 2, letter 1079, October 18, 1892, pp. 509–10). The reason for his simplifying assumption was that he realized that disequilibrium production would change the parameters of the model. In that case the solutions to his equations of general equilibrium, with given parametric values for variables such as inventories and the values of firms' assets, would not be the model's true equilibrium values.

Walras habitually thought of the production *tâtonnement* model that resulted from his simplification as describing how real purely competitive markets come into a mutually determined equilibrium. Repeatedly he wrote that actual markets generate as the only trading prices those which are the solutions to a system of Walrasian equations (Walker 1970, 689–90):

> It remains only to demonstrate in regard to production as in regard to exchange, that the same problem to which we have given the theoretical solution is also that which is solved empirically in real markets by the mechanism of free competition [Walras 1877, p. 251; 1926, §206, p. 214].

> The object and . . . goal of economic theory . . . consist above all and before all in the demonstration [that] the operations on the mar-

---

14. This statement was introduced in the second edition of the *Eléments* (Walras 1889, 287), except for the last four words.

kets of raising and lowering prices, of increasing and decreasing the level of production of commodities, etc., are nothing other than the solution by *tâtonnement* of the equations of exchange, production, and capitalization [Jaffé 1965a, vol. 2, letter 927, Oct. 17, 1889, p. 364].

Walras concluded with the assertion that he had formulated a theoretical system of equations with a set of solutions, and that he had "demonstrated that the sequence of real phenomena generates in actuality the empirical solution of that system of equations. This I have done," he maintained, "successively for exchange, for production, and for capitalization" (Walras 1877, 365; 1926, §370, p. 427). Thus Walras did not design the theory of *tâtonnement* in production as a utopian scheme, but as a frictionless approximation to real production adjustments (see Walras 1874b, 49; 1926, § 41, p. 45). In no instance did he describe that *tâtonnement* process as a normative objective, and the evidence indicates that he thought that it was an abstract description of reality.[15]

III. Conclusion

The relatively permissive political climate prevailing in Switzerland at the time that Walras wrote his *Eléments* has been described. His methodological views and classification of scientific studies, which draw careful distinctions between normative and positive subject matters, have been examined. His cultivation of normative economics under that explicit title has been noted, and the related lack of a motive to construct a covertly normative general-equilibrium theory. His assertions that his theoretical works were positive and his condemnation of the intrusion of normative considerations into scientific investigation have been cited. The positive content and objectives of his theory of general equilibrium as a whole and of a number of its components have been presented.

On the basis of the evidence it must be concluded that Walras's economic theory does not carry within it a particular conception of social justice, and that his objective was to analyze the workings of the economic system. The conclusion reached here is therefore the same as the one reached by William Jaffé in his studies during the forty-year period prior to 1974.[16] The basic idea expressed by Walras's general-equilibrium theory is that

---

15. It is also true that in one place Walras formulated an iterative technique by which an economic theorist can solve the equations of equilibrium and thereby find the *tâtonnement* solution that he believed is achieved simultaneously by real interrelated markets. He described both the iterative technique and real market behavior as *tâtonnement* processes: "In considering that the tâtonnements which I thus present successively by analytical necessity in fact operate *simultaneously* in real markets, do you not have exactly in its entirety the fact of the determination of the prices of several commodities under the regime of free competition?" (Jaffé 1965a, vol. 2, letter 913, p. 345).

16. See, for example, Jaffé 1935, 192–94, 198–99; 1969, 2; 1956, 215; 1971, 91–94, 98, 104; 1972, 380–83, 401. See also notes 4 and 7 above.

markets are interrelated, which is not a normative concept. Walras's desire to analyze their interrelatedness was the reason for the character of his theory of general equilibrium, not a desire to use simultaneous equations and the idea of interrelated markets as a vehicle and veil for his moral convictions. He recognized the existence of imperfectly competitive economic behavior, and he hoped that one day it would be given a place in a general-equilibrium model, but that task was beyond him. Therefore, like dozens of theorists before and after him, in order to undertake the analysis of markets Walras made the simplifying assumption of pure competition, believing that it was a reasonable approximation to the real economy, that it was scientifically necessary because of the complexity and lack of generality of alternative assumptions, and that it resulted in a system that provided a guide to the understanding of reality. Jaffé believed that Walras purposely constructed his model as an "ideal fiction" (Jaffé 1980, p. 533). Walras, however, took a different view: "I continue to believe," he wrote, "that my conception of the equilibrium of production is not a *fiction* but an *abstraction* completely analogous to the conceptions of mechanics" (Jaffé 1965a, vol. 2, letter 1170, Nov. 10, 1893). Whether or not Walras was unconsciously influenced by his normative views in developing some parts of his theory, he did not intend it to be a normative scheme.

I am grateful to IUP for a grant that made possible the preparation of this article.

References

Jaffé, William 1935. 'Unpublished papers and letters of Léon Walras.' *Journal of Political Economy* 43 (April): 187–207. Republished, along with Jaffé's other essays on Walras cited here, in Walker 1983c.
——— 1956. 'Léon Walras et sa conception de l'économie politique.' *Annales Juridiques, Politiques, Economiques et Sociales*. Faculté de Droit d'Alger, pp. 207–21. Translated by Donald A. Walker (1983c).
——— 1964. 'New light on an old quarrel: Barone's unpublished review of Wicksteed's "Essay on the coordination of the laws of distribution" and related documents.' *Cahiers Vilfredo Pareto* 3:61–102.
———, ed. 1965a. *Correspondence of Léon Walras and related papers*, 3 vols. Amsterdam.
——— 1965b. 'Biography and economic analysis.' *Western Economic Journal* 3 (Summer): 223–32.
——— 1967. 'Walras's theory of *tâtonnement*: a critique of recent interpretations.' *Journal of Political Economy* 75 (Feb.): 1–19.
——— 1969. 'A. N. Isnard, progenitor of the Walrasian general equilibrium model.' *History of Political Economy* 1 (Spring): 19–43.
——— 1971. 'Reflections on the importance of Léon Walras.' In the P. Hennipman Festschrift edited by A. Heertje et al., *Schaarste en Welvaart* (Leiden), 87–107.
——— 1972. 'Léon Walras's role in the "marginal revolution" of the 1870s.' *History of Political Economy* 4 (Fall): 379–405.

———1974. 'Biography, a genetic ingredient of economic analysis: answer to a challenge.' Paper delivered at the Allied Social Science Associations meetings under the joint auspices of the American Economic Association and the History of Economic Society, San Francisco, December 30. Mimeographed, 29 pp.

———1975. 'Léon Walras, an economic advisor *manqué*.' *Economic Journal* 85 (Dec.): 810–23.

———1977a. 'A centenarian on a bicentenarian: Léon Walras's *Eléments* on Adam Smith's *Wealth of nations*.' *Canadian Journal of Economics* 10 (Feb.): 19–33.

———1977b. 'The Walras-Poincaré correspondence on the cardinal measurability of utility.' *Canadian Journal of Economics* 10 (May): 300–307.

———1977c. 'The birth of Léon Walras's *Eléments*.' *History of Political Economy* 9 (Summer): 198–214.

———1977d. 'The normative bias of the Walrasian model: Walras versus Gossen.' *Quarterly Journal of Economics* 91 (Aug.): 371–87.

———1978. Review of *Walras's economics: a pure theory of capital and money*, by Michio Morishima, *Economic Journal* 88 (Sept.): 574–617.

———1979. Academy of Humanities and Social Sciences. Requested self-presentation as newly inducted fellow of the Royal Society of Canada. In Royal Society of Canada, *Newsletter* 2 (Sept.): 14–15.

———1980. 'Walras's economics as others see it.' *Journal of Economic Literature* 18 (June): 528–49.

———1981. 'Another look at Léon Walras's theory of *tâtonnement*.' *History of Political Economy* 13 (Summer): 313–36.

Morishima, Michio 1980. 'W. Jaffé on Léon Walras: a comment.' *Journal of Economic Literature* 18 (June): 550–58.

Walker, Donald A. 1970. 'Léon Walras in the light of his correspondence and related papers.' *Journal of Political Economy* 78 (July-Aug.): 685–701.

———1983a. 'Biography and the study of the history of economic thought.' In Warren J. Samuels, ed., *The craft of the historian of economic thought*, vol. 1 of *Research in the history of economic thought and methodology* (Greenwich, Conn.), pp. 41–59.

———1983b. 'William Jaffé, *officier de liaison intellectuel*.' In Warren J. Samuels, ed., *The craft of the historian of economic thought*, vol. 1 of *Research in the history of economic thought and methodology* (Greenwich, Conn.), pp. 19–39.

———, ed. 1983c. *William Jaffé's essays on Walras*. Cambridge and New York.

Walras, Auguste 1912. 'Lettres inédites de et à Léon Walras,' letter to Léon Walras, Oct. 29, 1859. In *La Révolution de 1848*, 9 (Sept.-Oct.): 298–303.

Walras, Léon 1858. *Francis Sauveur*. Paris.

———1860. *L'Economie politique et la justice; Examine critique et réfutation des doctrines économiques de M. P.-J. Proudhon*. Paris.

———1861. *Théorie critique de l'impôt*. Paris.

———1868. *Recherche de l'idéal sociale. Leçons publiques faites à Paris. Première série, 1867–1868, Théorie générale de la société*. Paris. Republished in Walras 1896c: 25–171.

———1871. *Discours d'installation*. Séance académique du 20 octobre 1871, Académie de Lausanne. Lausanne.

———1874a *Principe d'une théorie mathématique de l'échange*, 1873/1874, mémoire read to the Académie des Sciences Morales et Politiques, séances of Aug. 16 and 23, 1873. Orléans.

———1874b. *Eléments d'économie politique pure*, 1st ed., 1st part. Lausanne.

———1877. *Eléments d'économie politique pure*, 1st ed., 2d part. Lausanne.
———1879. 'De la culture et de l'enseignement des sciences morales et politiques.' *Bibliothèque Universelle et Revue Suisse*, année 84, tome 3 (July): 5–32, and tome 3 (Aug.): 223–51.
———1880. 'Théorie mathématique du billet de banque.' Paper read to the Société Vaudoise des Sciences Naturelles, Nov. 19, 1879. *Bulletin de la Société Vaudoise des Sciences Naturelles* 2d ser., 16, no. 80 (May): 553–92. Republished in Walras 1898b: 339–75.
———1885. 'Un économiste inconnu: Hermann-Henri Gossen.' *Journal des Economistes*, 4th ser., 30 (April-May): 68–90. Republished in Walras 1896c, 351–74.
———1889. *Eléments d'économie politique pure*, 2d ed. Lausanne.
———1896a. *Eléments d'économie politique pure*, 3d ed. Lausanne.
———1896b. 'Théorie de la propriété.' *Revue Socialiste* 23, no. 138 (June): 668–81; and 24, no. 139 (July): 23–35. Republished in Walras 1896c: 205–39.
———1896c. *Etudes d'économie sociale*. Lausanne.
———1897. 'L'état et les chemins de fer,' (1875). *Revue du Droit Public et de la Science Politique* 7 (May-June): 417–36; and 8 (July-Aug.): 42–58. Republished in Walras 1898b: 193–236.
———1898a. 'Esquisse d'une doctrine économique et sociale.' *L'Association Catholique*, Dec. 15. Republished in Walras 1898b: 449–95.
———1898b. *Etudes d'économie politique appliquée*. Lausanne.
———1900. *Eléments d'économie politique pure*, 4th ed. Lausanne.
———1926. *Eléments d'économie politique pure*, édition définitive. Paris.
———1954. *Elements of pure economics*, definitive edition of 1926, translated by William Jaffé. Homewood, Ill.

[15]

LÉON WALRAS AND THE CAMBRIDGE CARICATURE [1]

Much of the controversy about capital theory between the two Cambridges has been presented in terms of stylised doctrinal history. Modern versions of the "classical" system, especially Sraffa (1960), are contrasted with the models of latter day neo-classicists, or neo-neo-classicists, especially Solow (1963). Unfortunately many such references to the past are based less on historical scholarship than on now well-understood polemical needs (Kuhn, 1962). To the historian of economic thought this is rather tiresome, the more so as Walras' "great name," to use Schumpeter's phrase, has been linked with other neo-classicists in an undiscriminating way (Harcourt, 1972) and the generic term "Walrasian" loosely used (Nell, 1967). I appreciate that, in establishing a new paradigm, too fine a regard for detail can be counter-productive. But a reconsideration of Walras in the light of the Cambridge caricature is due lest it becomes the orthodox view of neo-classical economics and, to steal Joan Robinson's words from their different context, "sloppy habits of thought are handed on from one generation to the next."

The neo-classical theory of capital, as criticised by Cambridge (England) holds that the marginal rate of return on capital is equal to both the rate of interest (profit) and the marginal rate of time preference: sometimes the period of production (or investment) acts as a proxy for aggregate physical capital. The rate of profit is determined, like all other prices, within the market system. The following are some recurring points of criticism:

(1) Market efficiency dominates the question of distribution.[2]

(2) The technological structure of the system is relegated to a subordinate role.[3]

(3) Capital is either explicitly homogeneous or an "unobtrusive postulate" effectively makes it so.[4]

(4) The high theme of economic progress is neglected.

My purpose in this paper is simply to examine Walras' *Eléments* in relation to these points.

[1] Paper read to the History of Economic Thought Conference at Birmingham, September 1972. I am grateful to the anonymous referees and to my colleague, Scott Moss, for helpful suggestions that have improved parts of the presentation and to William Jaffé for his friendly encouragement.

[2] "The Walrasian system claims to provide a theory of general equilibrium while it is often said that Marshall with his one-at-a-time method provides only a partial equilibrium. In fact, Walras provides only half a system for he discusses the prices of commodities without discussing the incomes of the people who trade them." Robinson, 1971, p. 67. See also Kregel, 1971, pp. 3–4.

[3] "With the Walrasian approach . . . intermediate goods often disappear from view, interdependence of the markets for 'final products' and 'factors,' in which maximising and minimising individuals are the principal actors, take the centre of the stage, and the more fundamental interdependence of production is neglected." Harcourt, 1972, p. 203. See also Nell, 1967.

[4] See for example, Pasinetti, 1969.

I. Efficiency and Distribution

Walras certainly believed that a free capital market would lead to efficient accumulation of capital. " Capital formation in a market ruled by free competition is an operation whereby the excess of income over consumption can be transformed into such types and quantities of new capital goods as are best suited to yield the greatest possible satisfaction of wants both to the individual creators of savings and to the whole body of consumers . . ." (*Eléments*, L27). This very important statement occurs in the famous chapter on the maximum utility of new capital goods which first appeared in the 1889 edition. Walras had an extremely high regard for his new theorem which, he wrote to Foxwell (C. 859),[1] formed " vraiment le couronnement de tout l'édifice de l'économique mathèmatique, comme le Théorème de la satisfaction maxima des besoins en forme la base."

The *whole* theorem comes in two parts. The first part says that, given a total value of new capital goods to be produced, then one should produce that set of capital goods which yields the largest stream of perpetual net income, *i.e.*, the set at which rates of return (or rates of net revenue) $\frac{\Pi_k}{P_k}, \frac{\Pi_{k'}}{P_{k'}}$ . . . etc., are equal to one another. The second part says that total saving is in turn determined by individual choice between present income and streams of perpetual income. (See Appendix.)

Much of the criticism levelled against the first part of the theorem was technical in nature. Walras had presented his new theorem as though rates of gross and net income could be uniform at the same time. The comments of the young Bortkiewicz were penetrating and constructive (see particularly C. 865 and C. 878) on this point which Edgeworth also seized upon. It was after these exchanges that Walras confessed " j'ai en ce moment la tête fatiguée " (C. 919).

Apart from this technical point Edgeworth complained that the whole tedious process was unnecessary. " *A priori*, it appears to me evident that as the sale of capital goods takes place in a market, there is realised that species of *maximum utility* which you have shown in your first volume to be a general property of markets. I cannot see that the symbolic restatement for the particular case of the capital market is helpful " (C. 874, see also 878). Walras was surely right to complain to Bortkiewicz that the problem of which capital goods to construct *was* a different problem from how to allocate the services of existing capital goods. Edgeworth, he wrote, " croit bonne-

---

[1] Throughout this paper the *Eléments d'économie politique pure* is referred to simply as *Eléments*. The English translation by William Jaffé, Allen and Unwin, 1954, is quoted and reference to the " lesson " only is given.

Quotations from letters are taken from Jaffé's edition of *Correspondence of Léon Walras and Related Papers*, North Holland, 1965. References are given as the letter C followed by the number assigned by Jaffé. Generally these quotations remain untranslated on the assumption that the present writer's ability in this respect is no better (and probably worse) than any reader's.

ment que je m'amuse à inventer le premier pour le plaisir de compliquer les choses" (C. 927). Edgeworth's remarks reappear, almost exactly, in the *Nature* review of 1889 but he also takes the opportunity to object to "the exuberance of algebraic foliage" and "the use of symbols in excess of the modest requirements of mathematical reasoning." (In his use of mathematics poor Walras was caught between the incomprehension of Böhm-Bawerk and the condescension of Edgeworth and Marshall). It is not too much to say that it was their reception of his capital theory that brought complete disillusionment with the English economic establishment.

On the savings side, Walras' problem was to introduce choice over time into an essentially timeless model. The possibility of dealing with this in perpetuity terms was hinted at in the second edition (when saving was related to the rate of interest in a purely empirical way) but was formally achieved only in the fourth edition (see Jaffé's translator's note h to L23). Walras' 1889 view was that "the (aggregate) amount of savings is determined by the comparison which each saver makes, at the current price of services and products, between the utility for him of 1 to be consumed immediately and the utility for him of i to be consumed *year in year out*" (Preface, my italics). As Jaffé records, Walras was reluctant to include time preference explicitly until he had hit upon the device of E, the imaginary commodity, perpetual net income. Aggregate saving could then be treated as the outcome of individual optimisation and, perhaps more importantly, on a symmetric basis with investment in new capital goods.

The empirical importance of the interest rate in savings behaviour was a different matter. Wicksell argued that family composition, for example, could be much more important (1893, p. 165, n. 2.). Formally speaking saving *is* treated in the Walrasian system as a (different) function for each household of all prices (and hence incomes) including the rate of interest.[1]

Walras and Böhm-Bawerk, unlike Walras and the English, retained a mutual respect. Walras wrote to Böhm-Bawerk in 1887 that his *Geschichte und Kritik der Kapitalzins Theorieen* was "un ouvrage qui me sera infiniment utile soit pour asseoir definitivement mes propres idées" (C. 788). Nevertheless they each acknowledged that their interest theories were entirely divergent. "In the points raised here," wrote Böhm-Bawerk in the *Positive Theory*, "I am in very thorough agreement with Walras who, like Thünen, starts from a theory of interest which, in my opinion, is essentially wrong and yet is able to arrive at many details with fine scientific feeling."

I must emphasise that, though the above exchanges could give the contrary impression, the difference between them was *not* about the essential importance of individual intertemporal optimisation; it was rather that Walras could not see how he could handle this within the context of his rates of net income and the general equilibrium system.

[1] See, for example, the discussion by Floss (1967). Even if optimisation on the savings side has to be rejected the propositions of L27 still hold.

Taking the whole efficiency theorem together, the Cambridge critics are quite right to classify Walras as one of those who stressed the optimality properties of the capital market. They are quite wrong on the other hand to count him as an apologist for the *status quo*. The best neo-classical economists have managed to be both neo-classical *and* radical by advocating property redistribution, for instance Wicksell (Gardlund, 1958) and Meade (1964).

I do not mean by this simply that Walras was a keen advocate of land nationalisation (see Correspondence, Jaffé's introduction). Explicit discussion of *laisser-faire* in the *Eléments* was rather brief but Walras said enough to make his analytical position clear. The quotations that follow indicate a clear dichotomisation between efficiency and ownership.

> " Though our description of free competition emphasises the problem of utility, it leaves the question of justice entirely to one side, since our object has been to show how a certain distribution of services gives rise to a certain distribution of products. The question of the original distribution of services remains open however. And yet, are there not economists who, not content with exaggerating the applicability of *laisser-faire, laisser-passer* to industry, *even extend it to the completely extraneous question of property*? " (L22, my italics).

" Such are the pitfalls into which science stumbles when treated as literature." Again, at the end of the very difficult L27 on the efficiency of free capital markets, he asks, " are these conditions of maximum utility just? That is for the ethical theory of the distribution of social wealth to say." Walras did not, of course, go on to work out an appropriate theoretical welfare economics. The furthest he got was to define " progress " (improvement) as implying lower *raretés* (everyone being better off).

II. Markets, Substitution and Technology

Two sorts of technology feature in the *Eléments*. A simple fixed input-coefficient technology (only one technique being available for the production of each good) is by far the more dominant. But Walras also allows that the coefficients may themselves be dependent variables requiring cost-minimising behaviour on the part of entrepreneurs. The system could then be recast so that factor services were now substitutes for one another (an infinity of techniques being available). Some of his propositions could then be restated in marginalist terms. From the standpoint of his general equilibrium system Walras would no doubt agree with Solow's pronouncement: " extreme assumptions like malleability and smooth substitutability make neo-classical capital theory easier . . . but they are not essential to it. To the extent that neo-classical capital theory can be built around the rate of return concept—including the accompanying efficiency-price frontier and the possible identification with market prices and interest rates—it can accommodate fixity of form and proportions both " (Solow, 1963).

Unfortunately Walras claimed to have gone rather further than this along the road to a now conventional marginal productivity theory of distribution. In Appendix III to the third edition and L36 of the fourth edition he not only accepted the marginal productivity doctrine but claimed precedence over Wicksteed in its discovery. His bitter comments on Wicksteed may be understood (but not excused) by the collapse of his earlier hopes that he would be his great ally in England. He had written to Perozzo (C. 925), having despaired of Marshall, Edgeworth and the rest, that " Wicksteed est beaucoup plus indépendent et sera peut-être mon homme pour l'Angleterre." Now it is certainly the case that Walras had discussed the technical coefficients as unknowns to be determined within the system and had used a set of implicit production functions for this purpose. But (except in the fourth edition) the possibility of variable coefficients had been considered only as part of the theme of economic progress. His suggestion that an explicit marginal productivity treatment of the static case had been avoided only for the convenience of readers is a little lame.

A detailed discussion of Walras' treatment of the marginal productivity theorem will be provided in the next section. For the present, it suffices to say that his favourite technology can be represented by a matrix of input coefficients linking the output of goods with factor service requirements. This seems to confirm the view that " economic thought in the Walrasian tradition emphasises the interdependence of markets, while neglecting the more fundamental interdependence of production " (Nell, 1967). Why does Walras omit intermediate inputs from his technology? The interesting thing is that Walras considered a Leontief type of technology in L20 but abandoned it in favour of primary input coefficients alone only to take up the interdependence once more in L29 when he introduced circulating capital goods and money. In the earlier lesson he had written: " Production can take place either directly or via a preliminary elaboration of raw materials; in other words it is the result either of a combination of nothing but land services, labour and capital-services or an application of these services to raw materials. It will be seen, however, that the second case is reducible to the first." He then gave a simple example of such a reduction: the primary service inputs into a raw material M are substituted for M in the appropriate price-equals-cost of production equation (*cf.* reduction to dated labour in the Sraffa system). The reduction would not be possible in cases of joint production but Walras does not consider these anyway. As long as reduction *is* possible there is no point in cluttering up the analysis of production and accumulation with intermediate goods. But by L29 things are quite different. Producers may now need to hold stocks of raw materials or finished goods for their " services of availability "; once this is allowed, such materials and goods must appear explicitly in the general equilibrium system. Thus the inter-relatedness of technology is recognised but is abstracted from up to the point at which it would make a significant difference to the results.

I would also argue that Walrasian technology completely dominates the Walrasian entrepreneur. When input coefficients are fixed the individual firm becomes pretty unimportant. The only explicit discussion of the " firm " occurs in the rather separate L41 on *Price Fixing and Monopoly*. Apart from this the entrepreneur is simply a ghost and the assumption of zero profit merely a device for bringing about output adjustment. Of course the zero profit assumption attracted criticism: the source of the difficulty was that Marshall and Edgeworth seemed to be talking about real entrepreneurs and Walras about an abstraction. " So far as profit is concerned, in the sense of profit of enterprise (bénéfice de l'enterprise) the English School fails to see that it is the correlative of possible loss, that it is subject to risk, that it depends on exceptional and not upon normal circumstances, and that theoretically it ought to be left to one side " (L40).

Incidentally, Edgeworth's comments on the relative merits of Marshall's and Walras' theories of the entrepreneur confirmed Walras in his view that Edgeworth was " un beau inféode à Marshall " (C. 925), " ce grand éléphant blanc de l'économie politique " (C. 1051). For Edgeworth had written in the *Revue d'Economie Politique*, " ce même ouvrage (Marshall's *Principles*) a rendu . . . également sans interêt ce que je me proposais de dire relativement à la situation de l'entrepreneur tel que M. Walras l'avait representé. Cet entrepreneur qui ne fait ni pertes ni gains est désormais un personnage hors de cause " (Edgeworth, 1891). The fiction of Walras' entrepreneur was simply to bring the price-equals-cost of production equations to life. All that is required, to take the capital goods case, is that changes in discounted net output are a function of $\left(\frac{\Pi_k}{i} - P_k\right)$ or income minus costs of production. In his own words " it is necessary to increase the output of those new capital goods the selling price of which is greater than their cost of production and to decrease the output of those new capital goods of which the cost of production is greater than the selling price " (L25). This nebulous concept of the entrepreneur might help to explain a puzzle that has occurred to Blaug (1968) and others. Why are capital goods produced? They are produced because households wish to trade present for future income and because they are an efficient way of achieving this end. The motives and behaviour of entrepreneurs are of no interest; all that is required of them is that output adjusts as a function of excess demand price. Walras even points out that though competition is a sufficient condition for this it is not a necessary one (L18).

Thus technology plays an absolutely central part in Walras' system;

indeed there is reason to believe that the ghostly entrepreneur was important only during the *tâtonnement*. Households are the only conscious actors; apart from them the technology and the constraints dominate.

III. Marginal Productivity of Capital

There *is* a marginal productivity theory in the substitution version of Walras' system, but it is a highly disaggregated marginal productivity theory. The price of each and every factor service will equal the value of its marginal product as well as (by implication) the marginal disutility of its offer. The theory is not fully worked out because Walras failed to inquire into the form of production function necessary for the " adding up " problem to be solved. However, he made his hostility to an aggregated theory very plain indeed.

Walras is absolutely clear that " capital " can be conceived of only at a general equilibrium set of prices, for his own treatment is explicitly heterogeneous. Two points of crucial importance stand out from the rather careful, and according to Stigler (1941) old-fashioned, distinctions of L17. The first is the stock/flow distinction. Capital goods themselves (land, persons and capital goods proper) are stocks yielding flows of services. It is the prices of the latter that are directly determined on the market. The second point is that capital goods are defined in a highly specific way: " all the remaining assets which are capital goods without being land or persons: dwelling houses in either town or country, and public buildings; business houses, factories, workshops, stores, constructions of all kinds—trees and plants of all sorts; animals—furniture, clothes, pictures, statues, carriages, jewels; machines, instruments, tools."

When it is time to introduce capital goods into the system they appear as l types of capital good with l rates of net income and l cost of production equations. As depreciation and insurance at proportionate rates (see appendix) are carried out by assumption there is no need to distinguish between capital goods of different vintages. In view of his definitions it is hardly surprising that he is highly critical of Wicksteed's more aggregated approach. He reminds us that in his own system aggregate capital is " the value, in terms of numéraire, of the different kinds of capital goods proper," whereas Wicksteed " is compelled not merely to reduce all the different varieties of personal capital to a single category and all the different varieties of capital goods to another single category but to lump these two single categories together " (Appendix III).

Walras' more detailed criticisms of Wicksteed's theory are still of interest. His principal complaints were three. (1) Capital had been aggregated in an unwarranted way (as we have just noted); (2) there was an ambiguity as to whether output was measured in physical or in value terms; (3) " rent, wages, interest, the prices of products, and the coefficients of production are all unknowns within the same problem; they must always be determined together and not independently of one another " (Appendix III). At this static level Walras was not prepared to consider as simple a case as the single capital good producing the single output.

Impeccable though it is, the approach is open to the charge of sterility. If there is a change in the *data* almost anything might happen. One important change in data is the production of new capital goods but, like Keynes, Walras seems to stop short of the point at which his new capital goods are actually used. What is there to be said *in general* about an economy that becomes richer in capital goods?

Neo-classical economists are said to use an " unobtrusive postulate " the essential function of which is to rule out reswitching. In Pasinetti's words, " as the rate of profit is consistently decreased, the techniques which successively become the most profitable ones are associated with higher and higher values of the capital goods per man . . ., the desired relationship is thereby made to emerge: ' quantity of capital ' and rate of profit are inversely related to each other " (Pasinetti, 1969). Can we find an unobtrusive postulate in Walras?

The nearest he comes to it is in a comparison (L36) between stationary states one of which is richer in capital than the other. One state (α) is unambiguously " better " (or at least not worse) than the other (β) in that there are twice as many individuals, the same quantity of land and (at least) enough extra capital to produce twice as much output. Both output per man and capital services per man will be greater in α than in β. What happens to the rate of profit? We have already seen that there is no rate of profit as such in equilibrium so we must look instead at the rate of net income (equal to the interest rate). And it does indeed happen that the rate of interest and the rate of net income fall.[1] What has been assumed to make this come out? (1) The wage rate is constant (we may take it as numéraire), (2) the prices of all goods, including capital goods, are constant, (3) the net effect of changes in the prices and amounts offered of productive services is to keep consumer incomes constant. The effect of assumptions 2 and 3 is to reduce heterogeneous output to a single good and heterogeneous capital to a single capital good. His rate of net income becomes a surrogate for a purely physical rate of return. Walras thus gets rather near to stating the conditions under which the unobtrusive postulate will hold but the problem is fairly lightly treated in two or three pages. Indeed, to use his own maxim against himself, it illustrates the dangers of " treating science as literature."

[1] Walras' rate of net income is very like what Pasinetti calls Fisher's second rate of return, *i.e.*, a perpetual rate of return in value terms. For a brief but favourable reference to Walras in Fisher see Fisher, 1930, App. 6, pp. 518–19. Walras was delighted by the relatively favourable reception of his ideas in America by Moore, Fisher and others. He thanked Fisher in 1897 for " une impartialité et une courtoisie auxquelles l'école de Marshall ne m'avait pas habitué " (C. 1327).

Even so it is a measure of his scientific intuition that his only general statement about the " rate of profit " and changing quantities of capital is hedged about by more or less appropriate restrictions.

IV. Progress

There is a strong classical flavour to Walras' discussion of " progress." Perhaps this saves him from some of the static preoccupations of neo-classicism. Walras' system, it must be remembered, is explicitly in terms of a progressive economy, *i.e.*, one in which net saving takes place. We would therefore expect some analysis of the process of capital accumulation. His limited excursions in this direction are of interest not only in their own right but also because of some critical comment from Wicksell. Wicksell had argued (1893) that Walras' treatment of the interest rate was determinate only in a progressive society. It is well-known that Wicksell came later to believe (*a*) that not only could Walras' theory be applied to a stationary state but that it was economically meaningful only in such a state and that (*b*) the theory could not, as he had previously thought, be rejected outright.[1]

> " Clearly Walras' method does not yield the *actual* rate of interest which the future reveals, but the anticipated interest on which the level of the loan rate is directly dependent at any moment of time. At this point I must withdraw an objection which I previously made against Walras, *i.e.*, that his theory of interest necessarily presupposes a progressive type of society. Walras indeed said so himself, but the truth of the matter is that it is just as applicable to the stationary state, and in fact gains thereby in rigour. The underlying assumption is that the factors of production will have the same relative values or prices in the future as they have at the present moment " (*Lectures*, p. 226, n. 1).

Wicksell then throws out a deeply interesting remark about steady-state growth.

> " Actually this is true for the stationary economy, but it does not hold for the progressive economy, unless we postulate a uniform increase in production which is strictly speaking inconceivable, as the sum of natural forces cannot be increased " (*loc. cit.*).

Compare this with an elliptical remark of Walras (L23):

> " According as the excess of income over consumption in the aggregate is greater or less than the excess of consumption over income in the aggregate, an economy is either progressive or retrogressive; but in either case the economy may still be *stationary* (my italics) if the propensities to save and the propensities to consume are assumed to be fixed over a given interval of time."

[1] For Wicksell's early objections see Wicksell (1893) and C. 1168. But in his Lecture on Cassell he wrote: " Walras constructs an extraordinarily coherent and rigorous system, which, when it is combined with the systems of Jevons and Böhm-Bawerk, both completes and is completed by them." Perhaps, after Cassell, anything seemed coherent and rigorous!

What would the growth equilibrium be like?

> "We shall be in a position, if we desire, to pass from the static to the *dynamic* point of view. In order to make this transition we need only suppose the data of the problem, viz. the quantities possessed, the utility or want curves, etc., to vary as a function of *time*. The fixed equilibrium will then be transformed into a *variable* or *moving* equilibrium; . . . (we may distinguish) a dynamic phase in which equilibrium is constantly being disturbed by changes in the data and is constantly being re-established, . . . the *new capital goods* . . . are not put to use until (this) phase. This . . . constitutes the first change in the data of our problem" (L29).

Unfortunately the "moving equilibrium" cannot be a simple steady-state because Walras, like Wicksell and like the Classics, sees land as the limiting factor. Hence his distinction between *technical* and *economic* progress.

> "It should be clearly understood that every time the production function itself undergoes a change, we have a case of *technical* progress brought about by science and that every time the coefficients of production made up of land-services decrease while those made up of capital-services increase without a change in the production function, we have a case of *economic* progress resulting from saving" (L36).

Under the assumptions used in the last section the relative price of land would rise for two reasons: first the fall in the interest rate would cause all capital values to rise and secondly the relative price of land-services themselves would rise. Walras regarded the rise in land values and rents as the chief characteristic of economic (as opposed to technical) progress; it was a great truth which "sheds as much light on social economics as in other respects, it shed on applied economics" (L36). This proposition gave a certain intellectual coherence to his views on land nationalisation.

What if these simple assumptions are not made? Then it is truly the case that very little can be said. Walras' theory is then appropriate only to capital accumulation at a single moment in time when relative prices are expected to be constant *for ever*. Once the new capital goods are available to assist in production a new set of relative prices is expected to persist *for ever* and a new set of decisions about accumulation is taken; and so on. The movement is not necessarily steady but any change is taken, for that moment, to be permanent. At each round the outcome is expected to be a new stationary state.

Perhaps this is not a very satisfactory theory. But if one rejects steady-state growth as unrealistic and if one also rejects the assumptions necessary for the unobtrusive postulate to hold, growth theory really does become rather difficult and it is hardly surprising that Walras failed to take it very far.

CONCLUSION

Some simplification of the history of economic thought is a permissible and indeed a useful tactic in debate, particularly when employed to dislodge entrenched attitudes. But such tactics may no longer be required now that the main points argued by economists in Cambridge, England against the neo-neo-classics have, one may hope, been conceded.[1] The time has therefore seemed ripe for dispassionate examination of the subtle contributions of the great neo-classical writers to capital theory without serious risk of accusation of " revisionism." From such examination, the contributions of Léon Walras emerge, I maintain, with high honours.

DAVID COLLARD

University of Bristol.

Date of receipt of final typescript: November 1972.

REFERENCES

M. Blaug, *Economic Theory in Retrospect*, 2nd Ed., Heinemann, 1968.
F. Y. Edgeworth, " The Mathematical Theory of Political Economy," *Nature*, September 1889, Vol. 40.
——, " La théorie mathématique de l'offre et de la demande et le coût de production," *Revue d'Economie Politique*, January 1891, Vol. 5, No 1, pp. 10–28.
I. Fisher, *The Theory of Interest*, Macmillan, 1930.
L. Floss, " Some Notes on Léon Walras' Theory of Capitalisation and Credit," *Metroeconomica*, Vol. 9, April 1957.
T. Gårdlund, *The Life of Knut Wicksell*, Almqvist and Wicksell 1958.
G. C. Harcourt, *Some Cambridge Controversies in the Theory of Capital*, C.U.P., 1972.
W. Jaffé (ed.), *Correspondence of Léon Walras and Related Papers*, North Holland, 1965.
J. Kregel, *Rate of Profit, Distribution and Growth: Two Views*, Macmillan, 1971.
T. S. Kuhn, *The Structure of Scientific Revolutions*, Chicago, 1962.
J. E. Meade, *Efficiency, Equality and the Ownership of Property*, Unwin, 1964.
E. Nell, " Theories of Growth and Theories of Value," *Economic Development and Cultural Change*, Vol. 16, 1967, pp. 15–26. Reprinted in *Capital and Growth*, edited by G. C. Harcourt and N. F. Laing, Penguin, 1971.
L. Pasinetti, " Switches of Technique and the 'Rate of Return' in Capital Theory," ECONOMIC JOURNAL, Vol. 79, 1969, pp. 508–31. Partly reprinted in Harcourt and Laing, *op. cit.*
J. Robinson, *Economic Heresies*, Macmillan, 1971.
P. A. Samuelson, " A Summing Up," *Quarterly Journal of Economics*, Vol. 80, 1966.
R. Solow, *Capital Theory and the Rate of Return*, North-Holland, 1963.
P. Sraffa, *Production of Commodities by means of Commodities*, Cambridge, 1960.
G. Stigler, *Production Theories*, Unwin, 1941.
L. Walras, *Elements of Pure Economics*, Trans. W. Jaffé, Allen & Unwin, 1954.
K. Wicksell, *Value, Capital and Rent*, 1893, Allen & Unwin, 1954.
——, *Lectures*, Vol. I, 1901, Routledge, 1934.

[1] By this I mean that: (*a*) Mrs. Robinson has taught everybody to be very careful indeed when talking of aggregate capital, even in parables and (*b*) the so-called neo-neo-classicals (*e.g.*, Samuelson, [1966]) have accepted the arguments of Pasinetti and others about reswitching. On the other hand, (*c*) it is not clear that distribution is better handled by an exogenous profit rate (Sraffa, [1960]) than by exogenous resource ownership (Meade [1964]) and (*d*) the disaggregated general equilibrium model remains more or less unscathed, provided the limitations imposed by its underlying assumptions are accepted and recognised.

Appendix

A summary of the *additional* equations and unknowns Walras introduced to deal with capitalisation.

(1) rates of net income are equal to each other and to the rate of interest

$$\frac{\Pi_k}{P_k} = \frac{\Pi_{k'}}{P_{k'}} \text{ etc.}, \ldots = i \qquad (l \text{ equations})$$

where $\Pi_k = p_k - P_k(u_k + v_k)$, and u and v are rates of depreciation and insurance and p is gross income per period.

Notice that we may write

$$\frac{p_k}{P_k^*} = \frac{p_{k'}}{P_{k'}^*} \text{ etc., if } P_k^* = P_k\left(1 + \frac{u_k + v_k}{i}\right)$$

see Jaffé's notes to L27, 28 and C. 865 from Bortkiewicz.

(2) prices of new capital goods are equal to their production costs

$$\sum_{j=1}^{j=n} k_j p_j = P_k \qquad (l \text{ equations})$$

where k_j is the input of service j into one unit of capital good k.

$$\left[\begin{array}{l}\text{(2a) in the variable coefficient version we have } n \text{ additional equations} \\ \text{of the following type to determine the } n \text{ coefficients.} \\ \qquad k_j = \theta(k_1, k_2, \ldots, k_{\neq j}, \ldots, k_n)\end{array}\right]$$

(3) demand for perpetual net income, saving, is a function of all prices

$$D_e p_e = F_e(p, p_e) \cdot p_e \qquad (1 \text{ equation})$$

(4) the value of new capital goods is equal to the value of net saving

$$\sum_{k=1}^{k=l} D_k P_k = D_e p_e. \qquad (1 \text{ equation})$$

In all this gives $2l + 2$ *additional* equations, together with the identity $P_e \equiv \frac{1}{i}$ to determine the l prices of capital goods, P_k, etc., the l quantities of capital goods D_k, etc., as well as D_e and $p_e \left(\text{or } \frac{1}{i}\right)$. Notice also that $D_e p_e \equiv E$ where E is the excess of income over consumption and is positive in a progressive economy.

[16]
The Wicksell Effects in Wicksell and in Modern Capital Theory

C. E. Ferguson and Donald L. Hooks

I. Introduction

THE "Cambridge Criticism" of neoclassical capital theory has stimulated an important debate over the past few years. Beginning in 1953 in its current form, the criticism has evolved into a well-defined methodological attack upon what Leontief called the "implicit theorizing" of neoclassical economics.[1] In more fashionable terminology, the criticism is directed at the "unobtrusive postulate" of neoclassical theory.[2] Essentially, this phrase is directed at the simplistic neoclassical assumptions that capital is malleable, there are infinite substitution possibilities, and capital substitution is not reversible. It is true that if these assumptions are made, the results of neoclassical capital theory hold without exception.

The Cambridge Critics also express the "unobtrusive postulate" in terms of "real" and "price" Wicksell effects. Regardless of the label attached, the criticism is theoretically sound and conceptually important.[3] Yet it has never been stated clearly. Mrs. Robinson inveighed against marginal-productivity theory and the use of "production functions," while others argued that fixed-proportions, heterogeneous-capital production functions must be used (in which

The authors are Professors of Economics at Texas A & M University and Assistant Professor of Economics at the University of Alabama.

1. The term "Cambridge Criticism" is a solipsism, having been introduced in Ferguson [1969]. The modern form of the criticism is presumably attributable to Robinson [1953]. For "implicit theorizing," see Leontief [1937]. (References are listed at the end of the article. When translations or reprints are used, the date of the original, untranslated work is given).

2. Pasinetti [1969], Garegnani [1970], and Harcourt [1969] and [1970].

3. Whether it is *actually* important, some argue, is an econometric question to which no answer has yet been given. See Brown [1969a] and Ferguson [1969]. The Cambridge Critics, on the other hand, argue that an answer is impossible on econometric grounds. See Robinson [1970a] and [1970b].

commodities are produced by means of commodities).[4] The latter approach, of course, takes one back to the classical economics of Ricardo rather than the neoclassical economics of Marshall and Clark.

The object of this essay is to determine whether the Wicksell effects of the Cambridge Critics actually appeared in the words of Wicksell. No attempt to assess the empirical importance of the criticism is made; indeed, we do not even discuss the feasibility of empirical tests.

II. Neoclassical Capital Theory

One gentle critic of neoclassical theory suggested that it is a set of parables appropriate to the Keynesian long run, in which we are all dead.[5] This is in part true; but an economy has an unlimited life span. Thus, directing attention toward economic *tendencies* rather than stark economic *reality* may be worthwhile. At least this is the view of the neoclassical theory we discuss.[6]

Taking some liberties with history, neoclassical capital theory may be dated from Böhm-Bawerk. His was the world of wine and trees, in which labor is expended in some initial time period and the product is reaped after a finite interval. Capital is the subsistence fund advanced to labor, i.e., purely circulating capital. In the simplest and logically best form of the model, labor is used in time period zero, the product is sold in time period n, and $n/2$ is the *average period of production* (or what became the "average period of investment" in Wicksell).

In this simple point input–point output model, the average-period concept may be meaningful. In less simplistic models, especially

4. Robinson [1953], [1956], [1970a], and [1970b]. For the latter view, see Sraffa [1960], Harcourt [1969], Pasinetti [1966a] and [1966b], Garegnani [1966] and [1970], Nell [1967] and [1968], and Bhaduri [1966] and [1969]. The bibliography given in Harcourt [1969] is admirably complete as of its date of publication. The chief subsequent publications are Garegnani [1970], Spaventa [1970], and Bhaduri [1970], on the one side, and Ferguson and Allen [1970] and Solow [1970] on the other.

5. Harcourt [1969].

6. The question is whether in the long run one can validly deal with the Meccano sets of Swan [1956], Meade's steel [1961] or Mrs. Robinson's "leets" [1970a], or whether the full complexity of heterogeneous "capital outfits" must always be confronted. For a statement of what we believe neoclassical theory to be, see Ferguson [1971].

models involving fixed capital goods, it is not.[7] Nonetheless, Böhm and Wicksell used the average period as a proxy for the roundaboutness of production or the capital-labor ratio. Armed with this concept they were able to "prove" the essential neoclassical results: an increase in the wage rate relative to the rate of interest leads to more roundabout techniques of production (i.e., a greater capital-labor ratio) and, therefore, to a greater output per head and a greater permanently sustainable consumption stream. The key, of course, is the inverse relation between factor proportions and relative factor prices, which in turn serves as the connecting link between commodity markets and the sphere of production.

Somewhat later Böhm's chief protagonist, J. B. Clark, was able to establish the same set of relations within the framework of a real-capital model, in which output can be written as a function of homogeneous labor and homogeneous capital inputs, say $Q = Q(L, K)$.[8] Indeed if the functional relation is homogeneous of degree one, which is the logical assumption for a competitive economy, the neoclassical theories of capital *and* distribution follow immediately.[9] Further, the neoclassical results are obtained without resort to the cumbersome and generally invalid concept of the average period of production.

III. The Wicksell Effects: A Prelude

To reiterate, the results of neoclassical capital theory imply an inverse relation between factor proportions and relative factor prices, and as a consequence, an inverse relation between the rate of interest and the permanently sustainable consumption stream available to an economy. These are the results that are challenged by the Cambridge Critics.[10] There are two main grounds of complaint, which we shall associate with the "price" and "real" Wicksell effects.

7. Wicksell himself became very skeptical of the average period concept; and it was entirely discarded by Akerman [1923] and Hayek [1931]. For a critique, see Stigler [1941]. For a futile effort to resurrect the concept, see Gaitskell [1936] and [1939]. For an excellent exposition of the difficulties encountered in period-of-production models, see Samuelson [1966a].

8. Clark [1899].

9. In its simplest form, this is the model that Samuelson calls the "J. B. Clark neoclassical fairy tale." See Samuelson [1962] and [1966b]. For a derivation of the neoclassical parables from this model, see Ferguson [1969] and the Samuelson citations.

10. Mrs. Robinson and some others, notably Pasinetti [1962], [1966b], and

Suppose there is only one commodity, Mrs. Robinson's leets. Leets and labor are used to produce leets, and the simple technical relation may be illustrated, for example, by Wicksell's famous productivity graph.[11] In such a model the neoclassical results unequivocally hold. There is no problem of capital valuation because the rate of return is the number of leets going to owners of leets divided by the number of leets used to produce leets. Similarly, the wage rate is measured in leets per hour, and the total production of leets goes to labor and owners of leets.

If the critically simplifying assumption is dropped—if, for example, labor and leets produce steel, labor and steel produce hoes, and labor and hoes produce corn—the model becomes more like those of Ricardo and Sraffa in which commodities are produced by means of commodities and labor. Leets, steel, and hoes are heterogeneous pieces of capital that enter into the production of corn. If the corn production function is to be written in the J. B. Clark form $Q = Q(L, K)$, there must be some valuation method by which to aggregate leets, steel, and hoes into "homogeneous" capital. Such methods exist, but they rely upon assumptions that one should hardly expect to be approximated in productive processes similar to that described above.[12]

Furthermore, when homogeneous capital is aggregated from heterogeneous components, the rate of interest or the rate of profit must enter the calculation. Suppose there is an exogenous increase in investment that causes the rate of interest to fall and the wage rate to rise. The *same* (existing) outfit of physical capital goods will now have a *different* value as aggregate "homogeneous" capital. This is the Wicksell effect, in which the value of capital changes but the

---

[1969], also challenge the entire marginal-productivity theory of factor-price determination and distribution. Mrs. Robinson's argument is essentially that neoclassical theory is underdetermined in the sense that the wage rate or rate of profit must be known as a *separate datum*: "... the basic fallacy on which the 'production function' is erected is the idea that the marginal product of labour determines the wage rate." Robinson [1956], p. 414, n. 1.

11. See Wicksell [1893], p. 122. The form of the graph in Wicksell [1901, p. 180] is not as appropriate, for it allows multiple solutions for the same wage/rate-of-interest ratio.

12. For some methods, see Champernowne [1953], Solow [1955], and Fisher [1965].

technique of production does not. Under certain conditions, this is sufficient to reverse the neoclassical results (in value terms).

Now suppose there are several techniques of producing corn—labor and leets can produce corn, but so can labor and steel and labor and hoes. Given a wage/rate-of-interest configuration and the corn output per head for each technique, the process of production that yields the greatest rate of profit will be selected. Under these conditions, a change in the wage/rate-of-interest ratio will have two influences: (a) the value of capital in each process will change, and (b) there may be a change in the most profitable technique. These two influences are jointly referred to as the *real* Wicksell effect. Under certain circumstances, generally called "reswitching" or "double switching" of techniques, this effect is also sufficient to reverse the conclusions of neoclassical capital theory.[13]

IV. THE WICKSELL EFFECT IN WICKSELL[14]

"Effects" are christened not by the author to whom imputed but by subsequent ones, often with material changes. For this reason this section is devoted to an examination of the Wicksell effect as it appeared largely in the following relation: *the interest rate is greater than the marginal product of capital because of the "wage absorption" of capital.*[15]

The Model and Wicksell's Assumptions

As most historians of thought have noted, Wicksell reformulated his theory of capital between the publication of *Value, Capital, and Rent* and the *Lectures on Political Economy*. Nonetheless, the change

---

13. For other discussions of a related nature, see Bhaduri [1966] and [1969], Harcourt [1969], Robinson [1956], [1970a], and [1970b], Robinson and Naqvi [1967], Samuelson and Modigliani [1966a] and [1966b], and Swan [1956].

14. Wicksell [1892], [1893], [1901], and [1923]. Most attention is devoted to Wicksell [1901]. For briefer surveys, see Blaug [1968], Lutz [1956], and Schumpeter [1954].

15. It can be shown that a necessary condition for either Wicksell effect is that the "productivity function" exhibit diminishing returns—i.e., output per head increases at a decreasing rate as the average period of production or of investment is extended. This assumption is explicitly made in all of Wicksell's works. We shall not undertake a detailed analysis of this point here. See Hooks [1970], chap. 1, for a thorough proof. Also see Dewey [1965], Hirshleifer [1967] and [1970], and Lutz [1956]. For a general appraisal of the Wicksell effect, see Osborn [1958].

was marginal. His average-period concept did make some allowance for compound interest; but the concept of capital was unchanged: "a command over useful resources, or the investment value of a process of production." Thus capital is still "circulating capital," and the rate of interest is not equal to the marginal social product of capital.

In the *Lectures* Wicksell followed the methodology of *Value, Capital, and Rent* in making comparative static analyses of stationary states in which perfect competition prevails. He used a point input–point output model in which land and labor are employed at the beginning of the process, which left capital as the value of the goods in process (maturing wine). Furthermore, Wicksell postulated an *absolute* period of production or investment rather than his earlier average-period concept.[16]

As in his earlier works, Wicksell assumed that the quantity of land, the number of workers, the value of the subsistence fund, and the wage per worker (to the firm) are given. The unknowns are the value of output per worker, the interest rate, and the investment period. Wicksell further assumed a closed economy in which the price of the product is given to both the firm and the economy.[17]

To reiterate, the firm is confronted with a given wage rate and a given, continuous productivity function relating the value of output per worker to the investment period. Then, by assumption, the firm determines its investment period so as to maximize its internal rate of return. Since in equilibrium the rate of return must equal the rate of interest, Wicksell obtained Jevons' famous formula for the rate of interest: the rate of increase in output divided by output.[18]

The Wicksell Effect

The results above apply to one firm; but they may be extended to an analysis of social capital by dropping the assumption that the

16. Wicksell [1901], pp. 172–84. Lutz attributed this asumption to Wicksell's recognition of the shortcomings of the average period approach. Lutz [1956], p. 29. Blaug suggested that Wicksell intended the model to be illustrative of the case in which no physical inputs are employed over the period of production. Blaug [1968], p. 558. The evaluation of Wicksell's thoughts regarding the role of time in production are traced out by Uhr [1960], pp. 82–84, and Frisch [1951].

17. Wicksell [1901], pp. 172–73.
18. Wicksell [1901], p. 178, and Jevons [1871].

wage rate is given. Wicksell was not entirely successful in this; to fill the void, he had to assume that the equilibrium value of social capital or the subsistence fund is equal to the value of labor services (at the *constant* firm price) plus the interest that accrues over the investment period.

On the basis of this critical assumption, Wicksell's mathematical manipulations led him to the following conclusion, which is *the* Wicksell effect in Wicksell:[19] *the marginal product of social capital is always less than the interest rate.* This definitely non-neoclassical result[20] led Wicksell to comment: "This proves that the ... theorem of von Thünen is not correct, if by 'the last portion of capital' is meant an increase in social capital."[21]

Wicksell apparently intended his mathematical exercise to constitute a proof of his 1893 discussion in *Value, Capital, and Rent* to the effect that there is an incomplete analogy between interest and wages (or rent) with respect to the application of marginal productivity theory:[22]

> ... this theory only applies to capital ... when we look at it from the point of view of the individual entrepreneur, to whom wages and rent are data, determined by the market. If we consider an increase ... in the total capital of society, then it is by no means true that the consequent increase ... in the

---

19. Wicksell [1901], pp. 178–80, esp. p. 180. Wicksell's results depend upon attaching an unequivocal sign to the first equation on p. 180. This led to a very peculiar statement. Let p and p' denote the rate of interest and its first partial derivative. Wicksell asserted that $p' < 0$, which is a puzzle. The maximization conditions require $p' = 0$, in which case Wicksell's results hold. Further, so long as he holds to the static-comparative static analysis that is conventional in capital theory, p' must equal zero. Otherwise there is a disequilibrium situation in which, presumably, capital *accumulation* drives the interest rate down. This is the only plausible circumstance under which $p' < 0$. Commenting on a different but closely related aspect of Wicksell's *Lectures*, Mrs. Robinson observed that Wicksell seemed to deal with both comparative statics and dynamic accumulation at the same time. Robinson [1956], p. 397.

20. If neoclassical properties are imputed to Arrow's "learning-by-doing" model (see Arrow [1962] and Levhari [1966]), similar results are obtained. See Ferguson [1969], pp. 296–300. For non-neoclassical interpretations, see Kaldor [1962] and Robinson [1962] and [1963].

21. Wicksell [1901], p. 180.

22. In an Åkerman-type model, Solow obtained similar, but not identical results. Solow [1962]. For a commentary, see Ferguson [1969], pp. 287–92, and Ableman [1970].

total social product would regulate the rate of interest . . . new capital competes with the old and thereby results, in the first place, in a rise of wages and rent, possibly without causing much change in the . . . magnitude of the return . . . [because the] increase in wages and rent may absorb the superfluous capital. . . .[23]

Wicksell unquestionably realized that his results were attributable to capital being measured in terms "extraneous to itself." Thus the Wicksell effect is essentially a matter of the valuation problem, a consequence of defining capital as a "sum of exchange value—whether in money or as an average of products."[24]

In concluding the discussion of Wicksell's circulating-capital model, two points should be raised. First, it has been argued that since Wicksell used the internal rate of return or *average return* as the discount factor in his aggregate analysis, he merely showed that the average productivity of investment exceeeds the marginal productivity of investment when there are diminishing returns to investment.[25]

Nevertheless, and second, if the marginal return to investment is used as the discount factor, measuring the value of capital by its present (capitalized) value does not provide a constant value measure if there are diminishing returns to investment.[26] Thus it has been argued that the Wicksell effect in Wicksell is nothing more than an explanation of why the existing stock of capital must be revalued when additions to that stock are made.[27] This is the currently accepted meaning of the *price* Wicksell effect; but it is a much broader definition than the wage absorption of capital upon which Wicksell concentrated.

23. Wicksell [1901], p. 148. Wicksell apparently failed to see that the fall in interest would free capital and thus partly offset the wage-absorption effect. On this point, see Lange [1935], p. 185.
24. Wicksell [1901], p. 149.
25. Dewey [1965], p. 66 n.
26. Dewey [1965], pp. 64–68. Also see Samuelson [1937] for a critique of the use of the internal rate of return as the maximand for the firm. He argued that the market rate of interest should be used. Lutz and Lutz [1951] provide a detailed analysis of alternative maximization criteria.
27. See Lutz [1956] and [1961].

V. The "Åkerman Problem" and the Wicksell Effect in Wicksell

Let us reemphasize that the Wicksell effect demonstrated above is *at most* a consequence of revaluing capital as factor prices change. Further, it has been shown that the fall in interest is more than offset by the increase in wages (and rents) in the circulating-capital model. However, when one introduces durable capital *goods*,[28] as Åkerman did, we shall see that the Wicksell effect may go either way.[29]

Åkerman assumed that capital consists of durable goods (machines) that are valued either at their cost of production or at the present value of their flow of services. This concept of capital corresponds to Wicksell's "capital in the wider sense," which he treated as rent goods. Furthermore, Åkerman was concerned with the cooperation of durable capital with labor in production, a problem Wicksell considered "clearly of great practical significance" but "so complex that the vast majority of economists have almost entirely passed it by as being much too difficult to be susceptible to analysis."[30]

The Model and Its Assumptions

Åkerman's model is stated here as briefly as possible, and Wicksell's mathematical reformulation is not recounted inasmuch as the Wicksell effect can be described verbally.[31] Åkerman considered a

---

28. Clark, to be sure, spoke of capital goods; but they were of subsidiary importance in his real-capital model. Clark [1899]. To Clark capital goods are heterogeneous pieces of equipment that are forever wearing out and being replaced. Indeed, he made the point that capital goods are only valuable to the extent that they are destroyed by use. *Capital*, on the other hand, is a permanent and indestructible fund which, in a stationary state, remains the same forever. It is composed of capital goods that are simultaneously created and destroyed by the production process. This line of argument led to Clark's famous reservoir-waterfall illustration and later, presumably, to Dorfman's "bathtub theorem." Dorfman [1959].

29. Åkerman [1923]. Wicksell's critique of Åkerman's book led to the demonstration of the Wicksell effect treated in this section. See Wicksell [1923]. For two modern capital models that are strikingly similar to Åkerman's, see Solow [1961b] and [1962].

30. Wicksell [1923], p. 258.

31. Lutz called Åkerman's book "one of the most laborious in economic literature." Lutz [1956], p. 35. Stigler dismissed Wicksell's reformulation as "an unusual performance," but one that "is less valuable than elegant because of

two-sector model in which labor and machines combine to produce consumption goods and labor alone produces machines. Åkerman further assumed that all labor is fully employed in the two sectors and that all capital is invested in machines (i.e., he totally ignored circulating capital). He then used general equilibrium analysis to determine the wage rate, the optimal life of machines, the value of machine service, the internal rate of return, the number of workers employed in each sector, and the output of consumption goods.[32]

In reformulating the problem, Wicksell retained most of Åkerman's assumptions; but he additionally assumed that the distribution of labor between sectors is constant. Furthermore, Wicksell's model had one fewer equations than unknowns, which required him to take the value of capital as given.[33] Wicksell then used the model to show that social capital, the life of durable capital, the value of output, and the wage rate vary directly, while the price of durable capital and the rate of interest vary inversely with social capital.[34] These are, of course, the neoclassical relations.

The Reverse Wicksell Effect

Åkerman argued that his use of durable capital enabled him to show that the marginal product of social capital was indeed equal to the rate of interest; but this result holds only if the increase in "concrete" capital is taken into account, i.e., the increase in durable capital in terms of the amount of labor invested in it. Wicksell admitted that this would be true "if only we could always . . . catch hold of this concrete capital."[35]

In his treatment of the Åkerman Problem, Wicksell showed that Åkerman's thesis was wrong "even in the form in which Åkerman

the peculiar assumptions on which it rests." Stigler [1941], p. 284. The "peculiar" assumptions to which Stigler refers are now found in many two-sector neoclassical growth models. See, for example, Solow [1962], Uzawa [1961] and [1963], and Ferguson [1968]. While the factor-intensity assumption is "peculiar," its rationale has been explained clearly by Solow [1961a].

32. Åkerman [1923].
33. Wicksell [1923], pp. 288–89. Mrs. Robinson's capital model (Robinson [1956]) is very similar except that she took the wage rate as given.
34. Wicksell [1923], p. 290. See Swan [1956], pp. 358–61, for a more detailed exposition of Åkerman's problem.
35. Wicksell [1923], p. 268. Also see Åkerman [1923], pp. 152–54, and Uhr [1960], pp. 131–32.

proposes to recast it," which amounted to subtracting the part of social capital absorbed by rising wages from the change in capital and using the remainder as the divisor in defining the marginal product of capital.[36] While this eliminates the Wicksell effect in Wicksell's model or any model using the subsistence-fund concept of capital, it does not eliminate the effect in Åkerman's model.[37] On the contrary, Wicksell found that the marginal product of social capital *exceeds* the rate of interest. This result is surprising: "I cannot enter now on the explanation of this very puzzling formula; presumably it belongs to the sphere of 'dynamic' theory...."[38]

The distinguishing characteristic of Åkerman's model is the possibility of capital-labor substitution in the consumption sector in the *final* stages of production. This makes capital losses possible, a result precluded in the point input–point output model in which capital-labor substitution is possible only for the *entire process of production*.[39] This, in essence, accounts for the possibility of a reverse Wicksell effect when durable capital is included in the model. The result, of course, may go either way; however, "except by accident, the rate of interest cannot be described as the marginal product of [social] capital in the sense that wages . . . are the marginal product of labor."[40]

VI. Wicksell, the Wicksell Effects, and the Cambridge Criticism

We have so far chiefly concentrated on the Wicksell effect in Wicksell, although we described its use by the Cambridge Critics in section III. We would argue that the Cambridge Critics have invented some theoretically valid concepts; but to impute them to Wicksell is going a bit far. Indeed the real Wicksell effect does not appear in

---

36. Wicksell [1923], p. 292. This is equivalent to substituting $dK - K(dl/l)$ for dK in the equation at the bottom of p. 183 in Wicksell [1893], thus making the marginal product of capital equal to the rate of interest. Solow pointed out that Wicksell assumed that the decision is to hold more or less in asset value, which is not the same as holding more or fewer machines. This is the basis for the Wicksell effect. See Solow [1967], p. 249.

37. Wicksell [1923], p. 292.

38. Wicksell [1923], p. 293. Osborn noted that this is not the explanation; the entire analysis is static. Osborn [1958], p. 164.

39. Metzler [1950], p. 299 n., stressed this. Swan [1956], p. 360, also noted that the direction of revaluation depends upon the relative importance of the changes in wages and interest for both durable capital and for the product.

40. Metzler [1950], p. 301.

Wicksell in any guise, and a damaging or perverse price Wicksell effect enters only tangentially in his discussion of Åkerman's problem.

Nevertheless, such effects may exist and, by whatever name, they may possibly negate the chief results of neoclassical theory. In two-sector models allowing continuous factor substitution, the real Wicksell effect must be positive although the price effect may be negative. Thus capital reversal (i.e., the movement of capital value and interest in the same direction) is possible. In fixed-proportions, heterogeneous-capital models both the price and the real effects may be negative. This corresponds to the double switching of techniques and thus implies that there may not always exist a unique inverse relation between capital intensity and the rate of interest.

A Summary of the Wicksell Effects in Wicksell

The demonstrations of the Wicksell effect involved a circulating-capital and a durable-capital model, both in value terms. It was shown that in Wicksell's circulating-capital, continuous-production model, the value of capital is higher for a higher wage rate and lower rate of interest, i.e., the price Wicksell effect is *always* positive. In the durable-capital model, however, the effect may be negative because the value of capital may be lower for higher wages and lower rates of interest. This can occur when the lower interest rate has a greater influence than the higher wage on the value of capital.[41]

Wicksell himself was only concerned with showing that the marginal product of capital is not equal to the rate of interest because of the changing valuation of existing capital. Moreover, until his investigation of Åkerman's problem, Wicksell argued that the marginal product of capital is always higher for a higher wage rate. This is necessarily true of the model in *Value, Capital, and Rent* because Wicksell did not include accrued interest in the valuation of capital. In his *Lectures* the same results are obtained, since the higher wage has a greater influence on capital value than the lower rate of interest.

When Wicksell constructed his durable-capital model, however, he found that the marginal product of durable capital may be greater than the rate of interest. This, of course, implies that the value of

---

41. For further discussion, see Robinson [1956], pp. 109–10.

capital is lower for the higher wage and lower interest rate; the price Wicksell effect is accordingly negative. This possibility is attributable to the structure of the two-sector model, in which the direction of change in the value of capital depends upon the relative influences of the changes in wages, interest, and the price of machines employed in the consumption-goods sector.

Although the price Wicksell effect may be either positive or negative, the real Wicksell effect is always positive in Wicksell's models because the productivity curves are assumed to be continuous and concave from below. It is only when this assumption is relaxed that the real Wicksell effect may be negative, giving rise to the possibility that the same capital intensity of production may correspond to more than one rate of interest.[42]

Capital Valuation and Capital Reversal

Mrs. Robinson criticized the neoclassical concept of "homogeneous capital" as a variable in a "well behaved" aggregate production function allowing continuous factor substitution. Further, she argued that when allowance is made for the more general cases of heterogeneous capital and discrete production techniques, the value of capital is not independent of distribution, since it varies with factor prices.[43]

Although the defenders of neoclassical theory hastened to revise the theory in line with these criticisms, in doing so they brought into sharper focus even more disconcerting possibilities. Champernowne, for example, produced his chain-index measure of capital, which in effect held the price Wicksell effect constant. This measure, however, is not independent of distribution, since it was necessary for Champernowne to assume that the rate of interest is given.[44]

Solow and then Fisher examined the necessary conditions for writing heterogeneous capital as a homogeneous aggregate in the production function. Unfortunately, they only dealt with variable-

---

42. Let us reiterate, however, that the *real* Wicksell effect never appears in Wicksell because Wicksell always assumed that the productivity curves are continuous and concave from below. On the other hand, the construction of his Figure 14, p. 180 of *Lectures*, violates Wicksell's mathematical assumptions concerning strict concavity.

43. Robinson [1953] and Robinson and Naqvi [1967].

44. Champernowne [1953].

proportions models, which are not the center of the Cambridge attack.⁴⁵ Samuelson next demonstrated that it is possible to obtain results consistent with the Clark parable in a fixed-proportions model.⁴⁶ It was soon pointed out, however, that Samuelson's model is a very special case in that his assumptions in fact reduce the model to one sector, i.e., a model in which labor and corn produce corn and there is no need to value capital since capital and output are identical.⁴⁷ Clearly Samuelson's model precludes negative price and real Wicksell effects. However, unfortunately for the neoclassical rebuttal, Samuelson's model reduces to a special case of the Clark parable; and, in fact, his surrogate production function reduces to the Clark neoclassical production function.⁴⁸

Reswitching of Techniques

Prior to 1965 several writers had noted the possibility of double switching or reswitching of productive techniques in fixed-proportions models. This was generally treated as a relatively uninteresting case ("perverse" or "curious" behavior) until Levhari erroneously proved the case to be erroneous.⁴⁹ Subsequently, numerous writers have dealt with the various conditions that give rise to reswitching and its implications for neoclassical theory.

A switch in technique may correspond to either a positive or a negative *real* Wicksell effect. The former implies that, for a lower rate of interest, a higher value of capital and output per man is selected (the neoclassical result). A negative real Wicksell effect, however, implies the opposite case and further demonstrates that the neoclassical results do not always hold (since a technique representing less capital intensity may be chosen at a lower rate of interest). This implies that a given technique may be profitable at more than one rate of interest and thus gives evidence that the unique inverse relation between relative factor prices and factor intensity of neoclassical theory may not hold.

Solow's emphasis on the social rate of return notwithstanding,⁵⁰

45. Solow [1955] and Fisher [1965].
46. Samuelson [1962].
47. Robinson [1962] and Pasinetti [1966a].
48. Hicks [1965] and Garegnani [1970].
49. Levhari [1965].
50. Solow [1963a] and [1970].

the major thrust of subsequent work has been to delineate the conditions under which reswitching may occur. Brown, for example, showed that if there is sufficient substitutability in production and consumption, capital-intensity uniqueness necessarily obtains.[51] Further work by Ferguson and Allen linked reswitching to changes in relative commodity price by showing that if relative price falls enough, capital-intensity uniqueness must hold.[52]

These papers raised questions concerning the importance of the Cambridge Criticism. However its validity emerged unscathed.

VII. Implications for Neoclassical Theory

At the risk of oversimplification, the chief results of the neoclassical theory of production, capital, and distribution may be briefly summarized. Assume a continuous "well behaved" variable-proportions production function in which homogeneous labor and capital are the arguments.[53] Further assume competitive factor and commodity markets and full employment of the fixed endowments of labor and capital. In equilibrium the wage and interest rates are determined by the marginal products of labor and capital respectively. Thus relative distributional shares can be uniquely determined because there is a unique inverse relation between capital intensity and relative factor prices, i.e., there is a direct relation between factor and commodity markets and the sphere of production.

As mentioned above, the first response to the critics of this simple parable was to admit heterogeneous capital goods into the model. As a result, it was found that the conditions necessary for valid aggregation of heterogeneous capital limited the generality of neoclassical theory. The next concession to the Cambridge Critics was to allow for the existence of fixed-proportions technology in recognition of the fact that relatively easy substitutability may not characterize the economy.[54] Since this generally implies heterogeneous

51. Brown [1969a] and [1969b].
52. Ferguson and Allen [1970].
53. We fully agree with Martin Bronfenbrenner's point that the assumption of homogeneous labor is as heroic as the assumption of homogeneous capital. Perhaps the Cambridge Critics have not mentioned this point because their "alternative theory" would then collapse.
54. On this score we differ markedly from Harcourt [1970] and Mrs. Robinson [1970a] and [1970b]. We are perfectly willing to accept discontinuous

capital, the Clark parable becomes even more suspect. Capital must now be measured in value terms, and this raises the problems of defining a quantity of capital and describing its behavior with respect to factor-price changes. Concomitantly, the concept of capital-intensity uniqueness must be critically examined.

As shown above, the relation between capital value and factor prices may be discussed in terms of the Wicksell effect. Generally, in a fixed-proportions, heterogeneous-capital model, the neoclassical postulate (Pasinetti's "unobtrusive postulate") that the interest rate and capital intensity are inversely related need not hold. Indeed, there seems to be no theoretical ground for assigning a positive or negative sign to the price Wicksell effect. The essential point is that the quantity of capital, and thus capital intensity, is not independent of distribution.

Even without reswitching, the fixed-proportions model allows for negative price Wicksell effects, and this alone will lead to capital reversal and thus to invalidation of the postulated generality of the relation between the rate of interest and capital intensity. Reswitching merely reinforces this result through the operation of negative real Wicksell effects. However reswitching does have additional implications for the factor-demand aspects of the theory. The possibility of reswitching implies that a unique equilibrium may not exist in the markets for capital and labor because of the possibly "perverse" behavior of the factor demand curves.[55]

We conclude by noting that the Wicksell effect in the narrow sense of Wicksell's own analysis (the price effect) provides an explanation for the operation of a neoclassical model with heterogeneous capital. Furthermore, the Wicksell effect explains the "normal" and "perverse" cases equally well. Indeed, it seems that these terms are meaningful only when the neoclassical postulate is assumed a priori.[56]

Switching and reswitching may be explained in terms of a broader definition of the Wicksell effect. It appears that Swan's

---

marginal product functions in the short run, but we are just as willing to accept leets-capital in the long run. To us, the latter seems appropriate for capital theory.

55. Garegnani [1970], pp. 424–28, and Brahmananda [1967].
56. This is presumably what gave rise to Pasinetti's reference to the "unobtrusive postulate." Pasinetti [1969].

inability to accept Mrs. Robinson's contention that the Wicksell effect is the key to the theory of distribution[57] may be attributable to the fact that she was right for the wrong reasons.[58]

REFERENCES

Ableman, Daniel J. [1970]. *An Extension of Solow's Model with Computer Simulation*. Ph.D. diss., Texas A&M University Library.

Åkerman, Gustav [1923]. *Realkapital und Kapitalzins*. 2 vols. Stockholm.

Arrow, Kenneth J. [1962]. "The Economic Implications of Learning by Doing." *Review of Economic Studies* 29: 155-73.

Bhaduri, Amit [1966]. "The Concept of the Marginal Product of Capital and the Wicksell Effect." *Oxford Economic Papers* 18: 284-88.

——— [1969]. "On the Significance of Recent Controversies on Capital Theory: A Marxian View." *Economic Journal* 79: 532-39.

——— [1970]. "A Physical Analogue of the Reswitching Problem." *Oxford Economic Papers* 23: 148-55.

Blaug, Marc [1962]. *Economic Theory in Retrospect*. Homewood, Ill.: Richard D. Irwin, Inc.

——— [1968]. *Economic Theory in Retrospect*. Revised edition.

Böhm-Bawerk, Eugen von [1888]. *Capital and Interest*. Vol. 2, *Positive Theory of Capital*. Translated by George D. Huncke. South Holland, Ill.: Libertarian Press, 1959.

Brahmananda, P. R. [1967]. "The Laws of Factor Demand Under Competitive Conditions: Double Switching in Economic Theory?" *Indian Economic Journal* 15: 43-66.

Brown, Murray [1969a]. "Substitution-Composition Effects, Capital Intensity Uniqueness and Growth." *Economic Journal* 79: 334-47.

——— [1969b]. "A Respecification of the Neoclassical Production Model in the Heterogeneous Capital Case." Mimeographed.

Champernowne, D. G. [1953]. "The Production Function and the Theory of Capital: A Comment." *Review of Economic Studies* 21: 112-35.

Clark, John Bates [1899]. *The Distribution of Wealth*. New York: Augustus M. Kelley, 1965.

Dewey, Donald J. [1965]. *Modern Capital Theory*. New York: Columbia University Press.

Dorfman, Robert [1959]. "Waiting and the Period of Production." *Quarterly Journal of Economics* 73: 351-72.

Ferguson, C. E. [1968]. "Neoclassical Theory of Technological Progress and Relative Factor Shares." *Southern Economic Journal* 34: 490-504.

——— [1969]. *The Neoclassical Theory of Production and Distribution*. Cambridge: Cambridge University Press.

——— [1971]. "Capital Theory Updated: A Comment on Mrs. Robinson's Article." *Canadian Journal of Economics*, vol. 4 (May 1971).

57. Swan [1956], p. 361, and Robinson [1956], p. 391.

58. Ferguson's participation was financed by a grant from the National Science Foundation, GS-2430. The writers have benefited from correspondence with Martin Bronfenbrenner and Geoff Harcourt. The correspondence was not based on a draft of this paper, so the usual *caveat* applies.

────── and Robert F. Allen [1970]. "Factor Prices, Commodity Prices, and Switches of Technique." *Western Economic Journal* 8: 95-109.

Fisher, Franklin M. [1965]. "Embodied Technical Change and the Existence of an Aggregate Capital Stock." *Review of Economic Studies* 32: 263-88.

Frisch, Ragnar [1951]. *Knut Wicksell: A Cornerstone in Modern Economic Theory.* Oslo: Universitetes Social-Økonomiske Institutt.

Gaitskell, H. T. N. [1936]. "Notes on the Period of Production, I." *Zeitschrift für Nationalökonomie* 7: 577-95.

────── [1939]. "Notes on the Period of Production, II." *Zeitschrift für Nationalökonomie* 9: 215-44.

Garegnani, Piero [1966]. "Switches of Techniques." *Quarterly Journal of Economics* 80: 555-65.

────── [1970]. "Heterogeneous Capital, the Production Function and the Theory of Distribution." *Review of Economic Studies* 37: 407-36.

Harcourt, G. C. [1969]. "Some Cambridge Controversies in the Theory of Capital." *Journal of Economic Literature* 7: 369-405.

────── [1970]. Review of Ferguson [1969]. *Journal of Economic Literature* 8: 809-11.

Hayek, Friedrich A. [1931]. *Prices and Production.* London: Routledge and Kegan Paul, Ltd.

────── [1941]. *The Pure Theory of Capital.* London: Macmillan and Co., Ltd.

Hicks, John R. [1965]. *Capital and Growth.* Oxford: Oxford University Press.

Hirshleifer, J. [1967]. "A Note on the Böhm-Bawerk/Wicksell Theory of Interest." *Review of Economic Studies* 34: 191-200.

────── [1970]. *Investment, Interest and Capital.* Englewood Cliffs, N. J.: Prentice-Hall, Inc.

Hooks, Donald L. [1970]. *The Wicksell Effect and Its Implications for Modern Capital Theory,* Ph.D. diss., Texas A&M University Library.

Jevons, W. Stanley [1871]. *The Theory of Political Economy.* New York: Augustus M. Kelley, 1965.

Kaldor, Nicholas [1962]. "Comment." *Review of Economic Studies* 29: 246-50.

Lange, Oskar [1935]. "The Place of Interest in the Theory of Production." *Econometrica* 3: 159-92.

Leontief, Wassily W. [1937]. "Implicit Theorizing: A Methodological Criticism of the Neo-Cambridge School." In *Essays in Economics,* pp. 58-71. New York: Oxford University Press, 1966.

Levhari, David [1965]. "A Substitution Theorem and Switches of Technique." *Quarterly Journal of Economics* 79: 98-105.

────── [1966]. "Further Implications of 'Learning by Doing.'" *Review of Economic Studies* 33: 31-38.

Lutz, Friedrich A. [1956]. *The Theory of Interest.* Translated by Claus Witlich. Chicago: Aldine Publishing Co., 1968.

────── [1961]. "The Essentials of Capital Theory." In Lutz and Hague [1961], pp. 3-17.

────── and D. C. Hague [1961]. *The Theory of Capital.* London: Macmillan and Co., Ltd.

——— and Vera Lutz [1951]. *The Theory of Investment of the Firm.* Princeton, N. J.: Princeton University Press.

Meade, James E. [1961]. *A Neo-Classical Theory of Economic Growth.* New York: Oxford University Press.

Metzler, Lloyd A. [1950]. "The Rate of Interest and the Marginal Product of Capital." *Journal of Political Economy* 58: 289-306.

Nell, Edward J. [1967]. "Wicksell's Theory of Circulation." *Journal of Political Economy* 75: 386-94.

——— [1968]. "The Social Rate of Return and the Switching Rate of Profit." Mimeographed.

Osborn, Edward [1958]. "The Wicksell Effect." *Review of Economic Studies* 25: 163-71.

Pasinetti, Luigi L. [1962]. "Rate of Profit and Income Distribution in Relation to the Rate of Economic Growth." *Review of Economic Studies* 29: 267-79.

——— [1966a]. "Changes in the Rate of Profit and Switches of Technique." *Quarterly Journal of Economics* 80: 503-17.

——— [1966b]. "New Results in an Old Framework." *Review of Economic Studies* 33: 303-6.

——— [1969]. "Switches of Technique and the 'Rate of Return' in Capital Theory." *Economic Journal* 79: 508-31.

——— [1970]. "Again on Capital Theory and Solow's 'Rate of Return.'" *Economic Journal* 80: 428-31.

Robinson, Joan [1953]. "The Production Function and the Theory of Capital." *Review of Economic Studies* 21: 81-106.

——— [1955]. "The Production Function." *Economic Journal* 65: 67-71.

——— [1956]. *The Accumulation of Capital.* London: Macmillan and Co., Ltd.

——— [1958]. "The Real Wicksell Effect." *Economic Journal* 68: 600-605.

——— [1959]. "Accumulation and the Production Function." *Economic Journal* 69: 433-42.

——— [1962]. "Comment." *Review of Economic Studies* 29: 258-66.

——— [1963]. "'Learning by Doing': A Further Note." *Review of Economic Studies* 30: 167-68.

——— [1970a]. "Capital Theory Up to Date." *Canadian Journal of Economics* 3: 309-17.

——— [1970b]. Review of Ferguson [1969]. *Economic Journal* 80: 336-39.

——— and K. A. Naqvi [1967]. "The Badly Behaved Production Function." *Quarterly Journal of Economics* 81: 579-91.

Samuelson, Paul A. [1937]. "Some Aspects of the Pure Theory of Capital." *Quarterly Journal of Economics* 51: 469-96.

——— [1962]. "Parable and Realism in Capital Theory: The Surrogate Production Function." *Review of Economic Studies* 29: 193-206.

——— [1966a]. "A Summing Up." *Quarterly Journal of Economics* 80: 568-83.

——— [1966b]. "Rejoinder: Agreements, Disagreements, Doubts, and the Case of Induced Harrod-Neutral Technical Change." *Review of Economics and Statistics* 48: 444-48.

——— and Franco Modigliani [1966a]. "The Pasinetti Paradox in Neoclassical and More General Models." *Review of Economic Studies* 33: 269-301.

—— and —— [1966b]. "Reply to Pasinetti and Robinson." *Review of Economic Studies* 33: 321-30.

Schumpeter, J. A. [1954]. *History of Economic Analysis*. New York: Oxford University Press.

Solow, Robert M. [1955]. "The Production Function and the Theory of Capital." *Review of Economic Studies* 33: 101-8.

—— [1961a]. "Note on Uzawa's Two-Sector Model of Economic Growth." *Review of Economic Studies* 29: 48-50.

—— [1961b]. "Notes Towards a Wicksellian Model of Distributive Shares." In Lutz and Hague [1961].

—— [1962]. "Substitution and Fixed Proportions in the Theory of Capital." *Review of Economic Studies* 29: 207-18.

—— [1963a]. *Capital Theory and the Rate of Return*. Amsterdam: North-Holland Publishing Co.

—— [1963b]. "Heterogeneous Capital and Smooth Production Functions: An Experimental Study." *Econometrica* 31: 623-45.

—— [1967]. "The Interest Rate and the Transition Between Techniques." In *Socialism, Capitalism, and Economic Growth*, edited by C. H. Feinstein, pp. 30-39. Cambridge: Cambridge University Press.

—— [1970]. "On the Rate of Return: Reply to Pasinetti." *Economic Journal* 80: 423-28.

Spaventa, Luigi [1970]. "Rate of Profit, Rate of Growth, and Capital Intensity in a Simple Production Model." *Oxford Economic Papers* 23: 129-47.

Sraffa, Piero [1960]. *Production of Commodities by Means of Commodities*. Cambridge: Cambridge University Press.

Stigler, George J. [1941]. *Production and Distribution Theories*. New York: The Macmillan Co.

Swan, Trevor W. [1956]. "Economic Growth and Capital Accumulation." *Economic Record* 32: 334-61.

Uhr, Carl G. [1951]. "Knut Wicksell—A Centennial Evaluation." *American Economic Review* 41: 829-60.

—— [1960]. *Economic Doctrines of Knut Wicksell*. Los Angeles: University of California Press.

Uzawa, Hirofumi [1961]. "On a Two-Sector Model of Economic Growth." *Review of Economic Studies* 29: 40-47.

—— [1963]. "On a Two-Sector Model of Economic Growth, II." *Review of Economic Studies* 30: 105-18.

Wicksell, Knut [1893]. *Value, Capital, and Rent*. Translated by S. H. Frowein. London: George Allen and Unwin, Ltd., 1954.

—— [1896]. *Finanztheoretische Untersuchungen*. Jena.

—— [1898]. *Interest and Prices*. Translated by R. F. Kahn. London: Macmillan and Co., Ltd., 1936.

—— [1901]. *Lectures on Political Economy*, vol. 1, translated by E. Classen. New York: Augustus M. Kelley, 1967.

—— [1923]. "Realkapital och Kapitalranta." *Ekonomisk Tidskrift* 25: 145-80. Translated by E. Classen and published in appendix to Wicksell [1901].

Part III
The Twentieth Century

Did the theory of market socialism answer the challenge of Ludwig von Mises? A reinterpretation of the socialist controversy

Peter Murrell

I. Introduction

In microeconomics courses, students often encounter descriptions of the interwar debate on the efficiency of resource allocation under socialism. Textbooks use that debate to motivate issues in welfare economics. The standard view of Ludwig von Mises' role in that debate is given by Samuelson:

> Around 1900 Pareto showed that an ideal socialism would have to solve the same equations as competitive capitalism. Around 1920, Ludwig von Mises, perhaps unaware of Pareto's proof, set forth the challenging view that rational economic organization was *logically* impossible in the absence of free markets. Fred Taylor of Michigan, A. P. Lerner of England and California, and Oskar Lange of Poland answered Mises with the view that socialism could conceptually solve the problems of economic organization by a decentralized process of bureaucratic trial and error [1976, 642].

The impression gained is that Mises was both wrong and lacking in scholarship in being unaware of Pareto's contribution. Although recently Mises has attracted some defenders,[1] the standard conclusion drawn from

Correspondence for the author may be sent to Dr. Peter Murrell, International Institute of Management, Platz der Luftbrücke 1-3, D-1000 Berlin 42, West Germany or Dept. of Economics, University of Maryland, College Park, MD 20742 U.S.A.

1. Since this essay was first written, Vaughn (1980) has published an important re-evaluation of the debate. Vaughn uses the works of Hayek to criticize Mises' opponents in the debate. She downplays Mises' contribution relative to that of Hayek in stating that the latter raised "more difficult issues" (1980, 537). In fact, the present article shows that Mises did raise most of the issues later presented, perhaps more clearly, by Hayek. Apart from this difference of interpretation on Mises' role, Vaughn's article and mine should be regarded as complementary contributions. Two other works have also challenged the near-consensus view of the debate. Rothbard (1976), a student of Mises, has defended Mises' views, relying mainly on quotations from Hayek and from *Human action*. Roberts (1971) has challenged the view that the opponents of Mises triumphed. In doing so, he uses some arguments similar to those of Mises, but does not defend Mises' general position. In fact, Roberts (p. 573) argues that Mises' contribution was responsible for the confusion in the debate as to the true nature of socialism.

examination of the debate is that Mises was in error. The close of the debate is usually signified by Bergson's review article (1952; first published in 1948), even though Mises declared himself triumphant in 1949.[2]

The purpose of the present article is to challenge the standard interpretation of the debate. In Section II, Mises' theory is outlined in order to describe the features of an economy which Mises thought necessary for efficient resource allocation. By claiming that these features were absent under socialism, Mises presented his challenge to socialism's proponents. The 'competitive solution,' usually regarded as the definitive response to Mises, is analyzed in Section III. The analysis shows that the competitive solution does not have those features Mises deemed necessary for efficiency.

In Section IV important differences in assumptions and emphases between Mises and his critics are identified. Those differences center on assumptions concerning changes in economic conditions and on the importance attached to an economy's ability to react to new information. These differences are also found when comparing Mises' theory and modern general equilibrium and welfare theory. As Mises' theory was usually analyzed, using the assumptions and conceptual tools of welfare economics, it is not surprising that it was misunderstood and regarded as incorrect. In contrast, the competitive solution, using the framework of modern economics, could be accepted within that framework. Thus, the debate was not resolved with victors and vanquished. The debate ended with two theories, resting on different assumptions and emphasizing different properties of economies.

The purpose of the present article is not to maintain that one cannot refute Mises' claim that socialist economies are inefficient. Mises did not make explicit all the assumptions his analysis required. His exposition was incomplete, and proofs were often either absent or sketchy. However, the proponents of the competitive solution did not criticize Mises on such grounds. They did not identify logical errors in Mises' work. Rather, they constructed an 'answer' which did not confront Mises' challenge. Thus, the theoretical debate which Mises initiated cannot be regarded as closed. Recent work in the economics of information holds the promise of addressing the issues Mises stressed. Perhaps the socialist controversy can be reopened, forty years after it was thought to have been resolved.

II. *Mises' Theory*

The debate was a theoretical one and its focus was identification of the features of capitalism which are necessary for efficiency. Mises' criticism of socialism was based on the claim that those features could not be imi-

---

2. Mises 1963, 706. The first edition of this book was published in 1949.

tated under socialism. Thus, in discussing Mises' challenge it is necessary to focus on his theory of capitalism. Acceptance of the view of the economic process contained in this theory is tantamount to rejection of the competitive solution as an answer to Mises. In presenting Mises' theory, reference will be made to both *Socialism* (1936) and *Human action* (1963, first published in 1949). The essence of Mises' argument is contained in the former, but the argument is presented more completely and clearly in the latter. Because *Human action* was published after the works that established the competitive solution, *Socialism* is used as the guide to Mises' stance during the debate. Thus, the main features of Mises' theory are established, using citations from *Socialism*. However, in some cases, interpretations of those features are justified using citations from *Human action*.

In order to function, an economy must have a means of "economic calculation" (S117, H199).[3] Economic calculation provides valuations, based on present and expected future conditions, which enable producers to choose a production point. When economic calculation fails, resources are used inefficiently. Thus, the problem of economic calculation is equivalent to the problem of economic efficiency.[4] In order to understand Mises' theory of economic calculation under capitalism, one must first state the basic assumption which underlies all his analysis.

In a stationary world, economic calculation would not be needed, and socialism could be efficient (S163). However: "In the world of reality there is no stationary state, for the conditions under which economic activity takes place are subject to perpetual alterations which it is beyond the human capacity to limit" (S196). Change is the most important environmental feature because the uncertain future produced by change is the cause of all action (H105). Thus, "the problem of economic calculation is of economic dynamics: it is no problem of economic statics" (S139). Despite Mises' emphasis on 'change,' he did not give a precise definition of the phenomenon. However, it is clear that change caused unpredictable alterations in the behavior of economic agents and that it revealed new information. In Section IV below, I comment more fully on the meaning of change and new information.

Given the importance of change, Mises did not think that the allocation

---

3. Because Mises' works are referred to frequently, a short-hand notation is used. S117 refers to p. 117 of *Socialism* (1936) and H199 to p. 199 of *Human action* (1963). The article of Mises which is usually referred to in discussions of the debate is "Economic calculation in the socialist commonwealth" (Mises 1935; first published in German in 1920). The article is almost completely embodied in *Socialism* and is therefore not referred to in these pages.

4. Mises' definition of efficiency was vague (H207). A formalization of his theory at a standard of rigor acceptable today would require a precise definition of efficiency. During the debate Mises was not explicitly criticized on this point.

of goods for present use in consumption was a crucial problem. The economic problem was one of "dissolving, extending, transforming, and limiting existing undertakings, and establishing new undertakings" (S215). Such acts would be based on "speculative" anticipations of future conditions (S205). Thus, analysis of an economic system cannot be complete without examining the way in which that system influences the relationship between expectations formation and economic outcomes.

The emphasis on expectations led Mises to attribute much importance to the entrepreneur. "Clearly any analysis of the capitalist order must take as its central point not capital nor capitalists but the entrepreneur" (S212). 'Entrepreneur' is defined functionally and does not necessarily represent a distinct person. Entrepreneurial actions are undertaken because the future is uncertain and there are differing interpretations of the basic data (H253). In taking such actions, entrepreneurs influence the employment of the factors of production (S520). This influence may be indirect, through dealings on stock or commodity markets (S139). In pursuing profits, entrepreneurs create the data, especially prices, and the conditions which guide those agents who do not focus on the future in making their decisions (S140). Therefore, entrepreneurial actions are necessary for economic calculation and "the entrepreneur fulfills a task which must be performed even in a socialist community" (S213). Thus, one must examine why Mises thought that task would be performed well under capitalism.

The majority of people have no anticipatory ability (S205). The only way to judge who has that ability is see who has previously anticipated well. The market does this judging, rewarding with profits those who succeed. Those with superior anticipatory ability then have more resources for anticipatory actions:

> The more successfully [a person] speculates the more means of production are at his disposal, the greater becomes his influence on the business of society. The less successfully he speculates the smaller becomes his property, the less becomes his influence in business. If he loses everything by speculation he disappears from the ranks of those who are called to the direction of economic affairs (S206).

This 'selective process' lies at the heart of Mises' theory. The selective process ensures that the market "tends to entrust the conduct of business affairs to those men who have succeeded in filling the most urgent wants of consumers" (H705). Thus, consumer preferences are the ultimate determinant of the selective process. Consumer sovereignty is established more effectively than when only present data affect decisions (S521).

The focus on the entrepreneurial task and the selective process follow from Mises' view of information. When new information arises, only a few will perceive the change and there will be differing appraisals of the information. Objective analysis of the meaning and significance of the data is impossible.[5] The market does not require such analysis. Differing interpretations are embodied in separate decisions. Hence, it is vital that people skilled at finding and using new information become entrepreneurs. The selective process finds those people and enables them to use their skills (S206). These entrepreneurs spread information through the price system. (S520). If no further changes in data occurred, an equilibrium would result in which entrepreneurial profits would be zero (H356). The information would be embodied in all economic decisions. Thus, the competitive market is an effective information-diffusing mechanism.

Profits not only aid the automaticity of the selective process but also encourage the ceaseless striving of entrepreneurs. This encouragement is necessary because the pain of labor is an unconditional given (S170, H131). Possibility of profit or loss also encourages entrepreneurs to make decisions with the appropriate seriousness (S217). Without such individual incentives, society would put a premium on "audacity, carelessness, and unreasonable optimism" (H709). Using modern terminology, the individual must take an appropriate attitude towards risk. Given an emphasis on change and anticipations, encouragement of such an attitude is vital for any economy.

For several reasons, Mises stresses the importance of competition, especially between entrepreneurs. First, in the absence of objective measurement of anticipatory performance, competition provides a test in the selective process. Second, competition leads to new information from diverse sources being embodied in present decisions.[6] Third, competition ensures that others will benefit from the actions of entrepreneurs (S178, H328). For if change were to cease, competition would eventually ensure that entrepreneurial profits were zero.

Mises' placed much emphasis on the need for financial markets (S139). This emphasis is not surprising, given the importance attributed to speculative acts. The following passage captures this emphasis and clarifies Mises' oft-quoted comment that socialism must result in abolition of the market:

> The entrepreneurs and capitalists establish corporations and other firms, enlarge or reduce their size, dissolve them or merge them with other enterprises; they buy and sell the shares and bonds of already existing and of new corporations; they grant, withdraw and recover credits; in short they perform all those acts the totality of which is called the

---

5. As Seligman (1971, 333) remarks, Mises' theory at this point is very similar to Hayek's (1945) theory of knowledge.

6. Mises assumed that when there is no agreement on the meaning of the information, it is better to use several interpretations rather than settling on one in a bureaucratic process.

capital and money market. It is these financial transactions of promoters and speculators that direct production into those channels in which it satisfies the most urgent wants of the consumers in the best possible way. These transactions constitute the market as such. If one eliminates them, one does not preserve any part of the market (H709).

This passage leads naturally to Mises' analysis of the relative efficiency of capitalism and socialism. Mises argued that features of an economy necessary for efficiency are present under capitalism but not under socialism. It is not the intention here to establish that Mises' theory is correct in concluding that socialism must be inefficient. Rather, it is the intention to demonstrate that the competitive solution does not refute Mises. The proponents of the competitive solution attempted to counter Mises by describing a socialist economy which, they claimed, answered his challenge. To examine their claim, one must analyze the competitive solution using Mises' theory. This is the task of the following section.

III. *The Competitive Solution*

Taylor 1964 (first published in 1929), Dickinson 1939, Lange 1964 (first published in 1938), and Lerner 1944 are usually identified as collectively giving the definitive answer to Mises. As the theory of the competitive solution is well known, a detailed summary is unnecessary. The discussion will center on those details and omissions which determine whether the competitive solution is an adequate response to Mises. In the competitive solution, economic agents behave as would the corresponding agents in a perfectly competitive economy. A Central Planning Board (CPB) imitates a Walrasian auctioneer in finding equilibrium prices. Managers of plants and of industries are to assume that prices are fixed when following two rules. The first rule is that any given output must be produced at minimum cost:

> A second rule determines the scale of output by stating that output has to be fixed so that marginal cost is equal to the price of the product. This rule is addressed to the managers of plants and thus determines the scale of output of each plant. . . . Addressed to the managers of an industry the second rule performs the function which under competition is carried out by free entry of firms into an industry or their exodus from it, i.e. it determines the output of an industry [Lange, 76–77].

These two rules and the definition of the CPB's task are the essence of the competitive solution.

The competitive solution is a static equilibrium model. Investment is taking place but is determined by present conditions. Decisions are not influenced by expectations of future conditions. These would be fundamental flaws for Mises, who emphasized the pervasiveness of change and the need to look to the future in all actions. As economic calculation is a problem of dynamics, not statics (S139), the calculation of market-clearing prices based only on present conditions does not solve that problem. A system's ability to react to change, rather than its static equilibrium properties, is the most important determinant of efficiency. As the competitive solution is a static model, its ability to react to change cannot be evaluated without specifying details omitted by the original authors.

Mises claimed that all economic decisions necessarily rest on subjective estimates of future conditions (S205, 521). Without these estimates, today's decisions, which must affect the future, will be inappropriate. The competitive solution would be inefficient because decisions, including those on investment, are based on present price. Expectations do enter one formulation of the competitive solution. Lerner mentions briefly that investment decisions must use expected future prices rather than present prices (1944, 214–15). However, there is no mention of whose expectations are to be used nor how these expectations are to be formed. The emphases in Lerner's analysis imply that discussion of the role of expectations is not crucial in convincing a reader that the 'controlled economy' is efficient. In contrast, Mises stated that "all economic activity . . . is essentially speculation" (S205).

Mises argued that under capitalism, agents would be appropriately motivated because of the nature of property rights. In undertaking exchange, agents subject their own wealth to risk. Mises and his critics agreed that under socialism means of production would be collectively owned (S239; Lange 1964, 72). As exchange is the exchange of property rights, exchange relationships in the means of production are absent in socialism (S131–32). Goods would be transferred between managers, but this is not true exchange. Thus, the basic motivating force of capitalism is absent under socialism. A substitute incentive system for socialist managers is required (S211).

The authors of the competitive solution devoted little attention to incentive problems. Lange noted that managers are not to be guided by profit maximization but provided no alternative (1964, 75). Dickinson (1939, 213–19) concluded that "quite a small pecuniary interest" would make the socialist manager a "genuine entrepreneur." He relegated the problem of incentive design to administrative science. Lerner (1944, 84) mentioned a "delicate problem" in designing incentives, without proposing a solution. He concluded: "In private enterprise under conditions of perfect competition all these problems are solved." Mises would not have disagreed.

However, he would attribute more importance to this conclusion than Lerner.[7]

Given Mises' emphasis on "dissolving, extending, transforming, and limiting existing undertakings and establishing new undertakings" (S215), an incentive scheme for managers of whole industries is especially important. These managers would have to play the same role as capitalism's entrepreneurs. Therefore these managers must be rewarded according to their anticipatory ability. In the competitive solution there is no discussion of such rewards. There is no analysis of how the appropriate attitude towards uncertainty can be fostered. There is no selection procedure to choose industry managers on the basis of anticipatory ability. A functional equivalent of capitalism's 'selective process' is absent. Thus, the competitive solution does not meet the requirements of a system designed to function in a changing world.

As industry managers are the functional equivalent of entrepreneurs, the absence of competition among these managers is a fundamental flaw in the competitive solution. The problem is not only the danger of monopolistic behavior (Bergson 1967, 658) but also inefficient use of information. Entrepreneurial competition enables the selective process to find individuals best at using information. Without competition between industry managers, their selection is not based automatically on the preferences of consumers, as in the selective process. To say, as some authors do, that such problems will necessitate inspection of costs is to miss the point. For costs must be subjective, based on anticipations.[8] To 'measure' costs is to substitute the judgment of the central administration for that of the industry manager. This would end even the limited division of intellectual labor which is the main advantage claimed for the competitive solution (H709).

In the competitive solution, industry managers cannot trade claims on their industry. In Mises' view the existence of such trading in stock and money markets is vital to an economic system (S140, 220). These markets provide future-oriented data, above all to agents whose speciality is not anticipation. Without such markets, all prices are based on present conditions rather than perceptions of the future. However, let us go beyond the competitive solution and examine whether financial markets could function appropriately under socialism. Mises, in fact, anticipated such a suggestion. Putting aside the crucial question of the selection of market participants, these markets would still work imperfectly. Because the means of production would be collectively owned, individuals would not trade

---

7. Bergson (1967, 657–58) has also noted the absence of an explicit incentive mechanism in the competitive solution.

8. Hayek's critique of the competitive solution emphasizes the immeasurability of costs. See Vaughn 1980, 549–50 for discussion and references.

their own property. Individuals would not adopt the correct attitude to uncertainty and would not have the incentive to collect all the information necessary for formulating expectations (S217). These markets would then supply misleading data to the rest of the system. Mises recognized a solution to these problems. The state could subject all participants in these markets to all consequences of their actions. This solution would entail giving those participants property rights in the means of production. Then the economic system would be capitalist, not socialist (S220).

In conclusion, for many reasons the competitive solution is not an answer to Mises' challenge. The competitive solution is based on a static theory. Mises (1932, 138, 173) holds that the economic problem exists only because the future is uncertain. The competitive solution has no role for expectations. Yet all action is based on expectations (Mises 1932, 182, 484). There are no future-oriented markets in the competitive solution whereas Mises (1932, 484) claimed that these markets are central to economic calculation. The competitive solution does not mention incentives or selection of personnel. Mises emphasized the incentive inherent in exchange and saw the selective process as a crucial determinant of efficiency (1932, 184, 188–93, 291–92). However, the competitive solution is usually regarded as an adequate reply to Mises.[9] Section IV below discusses the reasons for such a 'resolution' of the debate. Before that discussion, it is necessary to show that the outcome of the debate was not due to the fact that the participants were unaware of the ideas of their opponents. Thus, this section will end on an historical note.

The essential details of Mises' argument were published before the works on the competitive solution. Note that the references in the preceding paragraph are from the 1932 German edition of *Socialism*. Thus, Mises' theory was sufficient to answer the competitive solution in 1932.[10] This is not surprising, because the competitive solution went little beyond the work of Barone 1935 (first published in 1908; see Lange 1964, 59). Critics of Mises often imply that he must have been unaware of Barone's work. Yet quite clearly in the 1932 edition of *Socialism* (p. 115), Mises noted Barone's contribution and commented that it did not penetrate to the core of the problem. The historical record reveals that the participants in the debate had adequate opportunity to make themselves familiar with the arguments of their opponents.

IV. Conclusion: Mises and Modern Economics

In preceding sections, no indication has been given of how most economists came to regard the competitive solution as a satisfactory answer to

---

9. See note 1 above for the major exceptions to this generalization.
10. This does not imply that Mises' theory was not stated more clearly in later works: hence, the citations to *Human action* to back up some of the interpretations made in this study. However, those citations are not essential to the general argument made here.

Mises. In this section, I give a tentative explanation of the outcome of the debate. This explanation centers on Mises' basic assumption: the ubiquity of change. Mises did not precisely state this assumption. He obviously thought that the meanings of the two concepts, 'change' and 'new information,' were self-evident. However, in order to show that the assumption on change is the distinguishing feature of Mises' analysis, it is necessary to elaborate on the meanings of these two concepts.

As shown by contingent contract theory, it is possible that information can be revealed to economic agents without any consequent change in behavior. The occurrence of a particular environmental event may lead solely to implementation of a specific contingent contract. Agents' behavior could be predicted from existing contracts (Hirshleifer & Riley 1979, 1400). The occurrence of the event need not be new information in an economic sense.[11] Thus, absence of a complete set of contingent contracts is a necessary condition for new information to arise. When this condition is satisfied, an environmental occurrence will lead to transactions not previously embodied in contracts. The change which has occurred, the environmental event, and the resultant transactions are new information to which the system must react.[12]

For new information to arise there must be imperfections: absence of a complete set of contingent contracts. However, there are fundamental reasons why such imperfections exist. Bounded rationality is a sufficient condition for the absence of some contingent contracts. Radner 1968, Meade 1970, Grossman 1977, and Williamson 1975 all argue that complete contingent markets will not exist. Thus, although Mises' theory requires the existence of imperfections, it is reasonable to assume that those imperfections will be present. Mises undoubtedly had in mind a world with such imperfections (H705).

As the competitive solution is a static equilibrium model, the problem of adjustment over time to changing conditions is not addressed. This lack of emphasis on the problem of change can be shown to be responsible for most of the deficiencies of the competitive solution, as seen in Mises' perspective. In order to show this point, let us review those deficiencies, explaining how they are related to the lack of emphasis on change. The authors of the competitive solution assumed that expectations have no value in making present decisions. This assumption is untenable if new information continuously becomes available. Absence of competition between industry managers is not a problem if there are no conflicting inter-

---

11. The fact that an environmental occurrence may change subjective probabilities is not sufficient to make that occurrence new information. Agents may have subjective probabilities of subjective probabilities and may anticipate that the latter could change. Life may be viewed simply as an information service (Hirshleifer & Riley, 1394-97).

12. However, not every environmental event leads to new information.

pretations of data. Investment decisions are then obvious and can be easily evaluated. In contrast, in a world with diverse sources of new information, competition leads to efficiences in using new information and to automatic evaluation of managers in the selective process. Financial markets are not necessary in a stationary environment. However, in a changing world, financial markets are crucial to the process of "dissolving, extending, transforming" enterprises. Monetary incentives for managers would not be necessary in a static world where costs can be easily ascertained and managerial performance easily monitored and evaluated. However, when new information continually arises, costs are subjective, because they are based on expectations. Hence, managerial performance is difficult to evaluate and incentives based on individual property rights are essential.

The preceding paragraph shows that the basic difference between Mises and his critics was the importance attached to change and new information. The competitive solution was constructed using the framework of modern welfare economics (Seligman 1971, 109). Indeed, the competitive solution is often identified as an important contribution to welfare economics (Koopmans 1957, 42). Thus, Mises' critics used assumptions and conceptual tools which were perfectly consistent with those of standard general equilibrium and welfare economics. The differences between Mises and his critics were also differences between Mises and standard postwar economic theory. In the thirty years following the debate, few economists examined the issue which Mises stressed: the use of new information.[13] In the theory of competitive equilibrium, efficiency is analyzed, given expectations and the structure of information (Radner 1968, 57). In modern welfare economics, the models of certain and uncertain worlds are formally similar (Debreu 1959, p. 98). This similarity would not exist if change were viewed as the most important characteristic of an economy.

Recent theoretical developments, arising from a new interest in information, show that Mises' theory is difficult to evaluate using standard conceptual tools. Radner 1968, 54–58, has argued that traditional general equilibrium and welfare analysis may be inapplicable if market outcomes generate usable new information. The selective process is one example of an information-generating market outcome. Hirshleifer & Riley (1979, 1414) emphasize the disequilibrium nature of information processes. They conclude that the efficiency concept presently used by economists cannot be applied to information activities.[14] Thus, it is possible to conclude:

13. The same point is made by Grossman & Stiglitz 1976, 246. Stigler 1961 is an important exception to this statement.

14. As noted (see note 4 above), Mises' definition of efficiency is also unsatisfactory. However, the important point to note is that the definition of efficiency used in the competitive solution cannot be applied to an analysis of the issues stressed by Mises. Thus, the competitive solution cannot be a satisfactory answer to Mises.

"The basic character of how we ought to view the competitive economy is altered if we take seriously imperfections of information" (Stiglitz 1977, 389).

As the competitive solution used the framework of welfare economics, economists were receptive to its conclusions. Similarly, given that Mises emphasized problems which were intractable using standard conceptual tools, it is hardly surprising that he was misunderstood and regarded as in error.[15] Let us give two examples of possible misunderstandings. First, Mises used 'entrepreneur' to refer to agents who undertook actions aimed at using new information. Standard general equilibrium theory cannot be used to analyze such actions (Malinvaud 1972, 257). Therefore, for some economists an entrepreneur is simply a manager.[16] With 'entrepreneur' used in such conflicting ways, confusion could result from a claim that socialist managers cannot play the same role as capitalist entrepreneurs. Second, the use of 'equilibrium' could cause misunderstandings. Mises did not attribute any practical importance to a general equilibrium. An equilibrium would only exist in the long run after all change ceased. Thus, Mises could correctly claim that equilibrium prices never guide actions, but he would certainly be regarded as incorrect by a neoclassical economist.

The most crucial misunderstanding was over the nature of Mises' challenge. Mises emphasized a system's ability to use new information, but standard welfare economics could not be used to evaluate this ability. Thus, if Mises' challenge was to be confronted using standard conceptual tools, the nature of that challenge would be reinterpreted. Difficulties of change and new information were forgotten and the problem was summarized as follows:

> . . . let us imagine a Board of Supermen, with unlimited logical faculties, with a complete scale of values for the different consumers' goods and present and future consumption, and detailed knowledge of production techniques. Even such a Board would be unable to evaluate rationally the means of production [Bergson 1952, 446].[17]

During the debate, economists were aware of the problems posed for their discipline by information processes. Lerner (1937, 269) in helping to establish the competitive solution concluded:

---

15. This statement is not meant to imply that none of the misunderstanding was due to lack of clarity in Mises work.

16. See Hicks 1939, 79, or Layard & Walters 1978, 220.

17. Use of Bergson's words here should not be taken to imply that Bergson regarded this interpretation as correct. He offered two interpretations, the quoted one having gained the "wider currency" (1952, 445).

The objective cost of hiring [an instrument of capital equipment] depends upon the estimated value of the future use that is sacrificed to the present when the instrument is hired since this governs the hiring fee charged. The question is then the sociological one, whether the Socialist Trust is able to estimate this future value more or less accurately than the competitive owner of the hired instrument, and here we leave pure economic theory.

Thus, the problem which Mises posed was not one which economists, at that time, were willing to study. Today economists are beginning to analyze the issues raised by assuming a changing world. Work on the economics of information is burgeoning. It is surely not coincidental that this work has led to a suggestion that the socialist controversy be reopened (Grossman & Stiglitz 1976, 252). Fifty years after Mises presented his challenge, economic theory may be ready to confront the issues he raised.

I would like to thank Alan Dyer, Allan Gruchy, Daniel Hausman, David Lamoreaux, Naomi Lamoreaux, and two anonymous referees for comments on an earlier draft of this study. Research was partially funded by the General Research Board of the University of Maryland.

References

Barone, Enrico 1935. "The ministry of production in the collectivist state" (1908). In F. A. Hayek, ed., *Collectivist economic planning*. London.
Bergson, Abram 1952. "Socialist economics." In Howard S. Ellis, ed., *A survey of contemporary economics*. Homewood, Ill.
——— 1967. "Market socialism revisited." *Journal of Political Economy* 75, no. 5 (Oct.): 655–73.
Debreu, Gerard 1959. *Theory of value: an axiomatic analysis of general equilibrium*. New Haven.
Dickinson, H. D. 1939. *The economics of socialism*. Oxford.
Grossman, Sanford J. 1977. "The existence of futures markets, noisy rational expectations and informational externalities." *Review of Economic Studies* 64 (Oct.): 431–49.
——— and Joseph E. Stiglitz 1976. "Information and competitive price systems." *American Economic Review* 66, no. 2 (May): 246–53.
Hayek, Friedrich A. 1945. "The use of knowledge in society." *American Economic Review* 35, no. 4 (Sept.): 519–30.
Hicks, John R. 1939. *Value and capital*. London.
Hirshleifer, J., and John G. Riley 1979. "The analytics of uncertainty and information: an expository survey." *Journal of Economic Literature* 17, no. 4 (Dec.): 1375–1421.
Koopmans, Tjalling C. 1957. *Three essays on the state of economic science*. New York.
Lange, Oskar 1964. "On the economic theory of socialism" (1938). In Benjamin Lippincott, ed., *On the economic theory of socialism* (New York), pp. 57–143.
Layard, P. R. G., and A. A. Walters 1978. *Microeconomic theory*. New York.

Lerner, Abba P. 1937. "Statics and dynamics in socialist economics." *Economic Journal* 47 (June): 253–70.
——— 1944. *The economics of control: principles of welfare economics*. New York.
Malinvaud, E. 1972. *Lectures on microeconomic theory*. Amsterdam.
Meade, J. E. 1970. *The theory of indicative planning*. Manchester.
Mises, Ludwig von 1935. "Economic calculation in the socialist commonwealth" (1920). In F. A. Hayek, ed., *Collectivist economic planning*. London.
——— 1932. *Die Gemeinwirtschaft*. Jena.
——— 1936. *Socialism*. New York.
——— 1963. *Human action: a treatise on economics* (1949). New Haven.
Radner, Roy 1968. "Competitive equilibrium under uncertainty." *Econometrica* 36, no. 1 (Jan.): 31–58.
Roberts, Paul Craig 1971. "Oskar Lange's theory of socialist planning." *Journal of Political Economy* 79 (June): 562–77.
Rothbard, Murray N. 1976. "Ludwig von Mises and economic calculation under socialism." In Laurence S. Moss, ed., *The economics of Ludwig von Mises* (Kansas City), pp. 67–78.
Samuelson, Paul A. 1976. *Economics*. 10th ed. New York.
Seligman, Ben B. 1971. *Main currents in modern economics: economic thought since 1870*. Chicago.
Stigler, George J. 1961. "The economics of information." *Journal of Political Economy* 69, no. 3 (June): 213–25.
Stiglitz, Joseph E. 1977. "Symposium on economics of information: introduction." *Review of Economic Studies* 44, no. 3 (Oct.): 389–92.
Taylor, Fred M. 1964. "The guidance of production in a socialist state" (1929). In Benjamin E. Lippincott, ed., *On the economic theory of socialism*. New York.
Vaughn, Karen I. 1980. "Economic calculation under socialism: the Austrian contribution." *Economic Inquiry* 18, no. 4 (Oct.): 535–54.
Williamson, Oliver E. 1975. *Markets and hierarchies: analysis and antitrust implications*. New York.

Research Programmes in Competitive Structure

by D. P. O'Brien*

Introduction

In 1933 two books on competitive structure were published. One, extracted from a Harvard PhD filed six years earlier, dealt with the workings of the competitive process[1]. Seeking not to supplant, but to supplement Marshall, this book by E. H. Chamberlin focused on an effort involving the use of a diagrammatic apparatus to highlight certain fundamental relationships between variables in the competitive process. It did not analyse real firms but nor did it attempt to pretend that such were irrelevant, and to concentrate on positions of competitive equilibrium only. It dealt with problems of arrival at equilibrium, false trading, and a whole variety of issues relevant to an actual competitive process. Supervised by Allyn Young, it drew on a wide range of references and showed evidence of the kind of thorough scholarly preparation which has always been characteristic of the best American PhDs.

The other book was an essay in the Cambridge welfare economics tradition, drawing on a very limited range of material, virtually all of it Cambridge in origin[2]. Its chief sources, apart from Marshall, were Pigou and Shove. The borrowed material was blended together by its author, Joan Robinson, with enormous self-assurance and a blazing vision to provide a major work in that welfare economics tradition. It sought to explain the prevalence of universal excess capacity working as the necessary result of a world of monopoly, to show that "exploitation" was also necessarily involved in this world, and to demonstrate, consequently, that the rationalisation schemes of the 1930s were harmful. The burden of concern was made clear in the following passage:

> "The [competitive] system of the text-books perhaps never existed, and perhaps if it did it would not have been a very admirable one. But it has some merits. A system of uncontrolled private enterprise in which wages are more plastic than profits must entail the misdirection of resources and the waste of potential wealth on an extensive scale." (Robinson, 1933, p. 291)

For an historian of economic ideas, two major puzzles arise from the impact of these books.

---

*Professor of Economics, University of Durham, Durham, UK.
I am most grateful to John Creedy for comments on an earlier draft of this article.

(1) Neither contained any theory of the firm and only one (Chamberlin) contained any theory of the competitive process — Robinson merely compared successive points of equilibrium. Yet both came to be regarded as providing the theory of the firm.

(2) The two books are significantly different both in aim and content. Yet they have come to be conflated. Although both books are now very much more cited than read, the process of conflation has been at work since their publication and long before the habit of citing them without reading them grew up[3].

This article will attempt to trace the outline of what happened, although without seeking to provide complete answers to these questions.

In order to do this it is necessary to employ some framework in the history of ideas. The framework employed here is that of Imre Lakatos — in particular his idea of competing Scientific Research Programmes (SRPs)[4]. It will be argued that the two books by Chamberlin and Robinson gave rise to two competing SRPs and that there arose, partly because of the deficiencies of the two main SRPs, a third SRP associated with the Oxford Studies in the Price Mechanism.

However, a difficulty must at once be faced. There is considerable ambiguity over the scope of some of the Lakatosian terms. For instance we find the author of a recent and splendid book on economic methodology referring to the whole of neo-classical economics as an SRP — and at the same time referring to the Chicago literature on the economics of the family as an SRP[5]. In order to avoid this ambiguity a position deriving from that of Remenyi (1979) will be taken in this paper. The idea is that each main SRP spawns a series of separate SRPs each with its own hard-core (or "demi-core") and that these SRPs interact through the main one. The three SRPs referred to above are thus sub-parts of the main neo-classical SRP.

Monopolistic Competition
The thrust of Chamberlin's work was an attempt to explain the nature of competition as it existed. It started from the position that perfect competition was *not* an ideal; it was, in fact, an abstraction, only approached in the real world by "pure" competition (with price-taking but without perfect knowledge and mobility) which was not an ideal either. For his analysis of competition, Chamberlin sought to blend elements of free competition and monopoly, as characteristic of the real world, and he was particularly interested in oligopoly. A major tool in his analysis of oligopoly was the apparatus of the DD and dd curves[6] which attempted to illustrate geometrically the operation of oligopolistic reaction. He also analysed a large group case, in which interdependence could (temporarily) be ignored, but his main interest was undoubtedly oligopoly.

In seeking to explore competition as it really existed in the world, he investigated the role of price, quality variation, and advertising and selling costs, as *three* strategic variables. He paid particular attention to selling costs and, in particular, to the effects of advertising on price and on output as well as to the spill-over effects of advertising. In accordance with his overriding interests he also dealt with oligopolistic advertising[7].

He also paid a good deal of attention to product variation and differentiation — it is perhaps worth emphasising that the latter phrase is absent entirely from Joan Robinson's book. Consistently with his interest in the functioning of markets he explored the processes of market adjustment, dealing with disequilibrium trading and false trading[8]. He also dealt with questions of space, emphasising that this could, on its own, produce consumer preferences for the output of different producers[9].

In his approach, there were a number of very marked contrasts with the book by Joan Robinson which will be discussed below. For one thing Chamberlin was very far from being obsessed with his technical apparatus. He introduced Marginal Revenue without any fuss, and used both areas *and* marginal curves[10]. But perhaps the most striking point of contrast is his refusal to follow the welfare economics path. Chamberlin simply refused to draw the conclusion that his analysis showed that competition, as it existed in the world, was harmful and wasteful. Choice was an element in welfare. In addition, the distribution questions which were central to Joan Robinson were of only secondary interest to Chamberlin, and the distribution material in his thesis was omitted when the book was first published[11]. When he did turn his attention to the question of distribution, he did not follow the Robinsonian "exploitation" argument — indeed, he was to become sharply critical of it[12].

Given these contrasts it is rather ironic that, essentially on the basis of one diagram (the so-called "tangency solution") his work should have come to be identified with that of Joan Robinson — particularly as he regarded the "normal profit" outcome, as depicted in this diagram, as an extremely special case.

However, on the debit side, the book does share, in varying degrees, a number of weaknesses with that of Joan Robinson. For one thing time is omitted; it really is rather unfortunate, as Shackle has pointed out[13], that time is excluded from the analysis while the competing away of excess profits through entry requires precisely that dimension to the analysis. There is little attention paid to the role of the entrepreneur, no analysis of business decisions, and none whatever of managerial coordination. The profit concept is seriously neglected[14], and the emphasis on consumer preferences for the output of individual producers results ultimately in the destruction of the concept of industry, thereby removing the entrepreneurial frame of reference.

Imperfect Competition
The fundamental aim of Joan Robinson's book was to produce an essay in welfare economics, following the same lines as Pigou's *Economics of Welfare*[15] but making the Sraffian assumption that the world was a world of monopolies and not a world of competitors[16]. The basic approach was via the existing theory of monopoly, but it was (influentially) extended to "monopsony", and to monopoly price discrimination. In seeking to establish clearly the points of contrast between this world of monopolies and a world of (perfect) competition, the text did a great deal to clarify the very concept of perfect competition — which was attributed (without reference) to "older textbooks"[17]. This led to comparisons of monopoly and (perfect) competition with the latter given very firmly the status of an ideal, but with the equality of average revenue with *average* cost identified as the hallmark of

the determination of competitive output. The most important results of the comparison were, firstly, the fundamental welfare conclusion that "excess capacity" was all-pervasive (because the average revenue curve was tangent to the average cost curve to the left of the average cost curve's minimum point) and, secondly, the serious (though unsurprising, given the use of a monopoly model) conclusion that the supply curve had been abolished. Finally, there was a strong emphasis on "exploitation" and a major conclusion, which has escaped almost all later commentary, was that even when firms were earning only "normal profits" the universality of exploitation meant that what was "normal" was higher than it otherwise would be and thus the *macro*-distribution of income was biased against labour[18].

Of course, this was using partial equilibrium analysis for general equilibrium conclusions. The geometrical analysis of distribution stopped short of exploring the implications for product-exhaustion, and the whole analysis depended, as critics were quick to point out, upon positing one exploiting entrepreneur as co-terminus with the firm, an entrepreneur, moreover, who had no marginal product. Thus the "firm" was the unit of control controlled by one entrepreneur[19].

The profit concept itself was left vague, though profit maximisation was seen as a necessary assumption, and entrepreneurial motivation of a more general kind was neglected.

Technically the work displayed considerable boldness in the austerity of its approach, providing a marked contrast with most preceding literature. There was no time, technology was fixed, and various arbitrary uniformities were imposed in order to obtain the desired results. Empirical material — a staple of most books in this field during the period — was banished even though casual ("ivory tower") empiricism was freely employed if the argument seemed to require it. There were no recognisable firms; matters such as average cost and fixed cost, which seemed important to business men, were dismissed; and the enlightened business man was supposed to use marginal values[20]. A particular geometric technique was employed with virtuosity (and awe-inspiring confidence) and virtually squeezed dry (although unfortunately, a number of the results were in fact not proved). Analysis proceeded on the basis of positing that each individual producer was faced with a downward sloping average revenue curve which bore some unspecified relationship to the downward sloping demand curve facing the industry as a whole. Enormous stress was laid upon the concept of Marginal Revenue which was described as a "Pole" at which a number of intellectual explorers had finally arrived after prolonged struggles[21].

In the course of the argument Joan Robinson invented the geometry of, *and* pointed out the economic significance of, the kinked demand curve[22], and it is a remarkable commentary upon the lack of first-hand acquaintance with this book that this "invention" has been attributed to Sweezy, *six* years after the publication of the book[23].

Because the analysis was, despite the author's advertised intention, based upon monopoly, virtually everything of interest concerning monopolistic competition was ignored, including the origin of market positions (although this was hardly irrelevant given that monopoly and competition were to be compared), and the role of selling costs (advertising received less than half a dozen casual mentions in the entire book).

There was also a serious ambiguity throughout the book over the applicability of its conclusions. On the one hand there were a number of passages warning, rather in the spirit of Pigou, against the drawing of *simpliste* conclusions[24]; on the other hand there were a number of extremely strong conclusions about the waste and misallocation inherent in the world as analysed by Joan Robinson, and she felt free to arrive at clear conclusions concerning the harm done by the rationalisation schemes of the 1930s[25]. This ambiguity effectively remained characteristic of its author who could on the one hand describe the work, in later years, as "scholastic" while still implying — as late as 1969 — that its apparatus could be used to explain excess capacity working in the 1930s depression[26].

The Background to Monopolistic Competition

Chamberlin has explained clearly enough that his work was intended to be a supplement to, rather than an attack upon, the work of Marshall[27]. However, he drew upon a wide range of sources, having studied the work of important theorists like Pareto and Edgeworth[28]. He was also influenced, there is little doubt, by the concerns of American institutionalists and their use of phenomena such as selling costs as the basis for a criticism of economic theory[29]. In part, then, the Chamberlin SRP can be seen as defensive of the main neo-classical SRP, in contrast to the work of Joan Robinson. There was also the strong American tradition of empirical work in economics, which had much more force than corresponding work in the United Kingdom.

The overwhelming impression left by Chamberlin's book is that of very broad reading, from writers like Cournot on the one hand to the patent literature on the other, taking in along the way the business literature including that on price determination within business[30]. Amongst American economists the most important influences were J. M. Clarke and Chamberlin's supervisor for his 1927 thesis, Allyn Young. Almost as important as the positive influences on Chamberlin, in understanding the differences between the two SRPs, are those factors which had nothing whatever to do with his work. For it is important to emphasise that Chamberlin's thesis was not influenced by either Sraffa's 1926 article[31] or the "increasing returns controversy" which subsequently took place in the *Economic Journal*[32]. Nor did it have anything to do with the 1930s depression which, like these other two matters, influenced Joan Robinson. His work was, to some extent, spurred on by the Taussig-Pigou controversy over railway rates; and it is highly significant that Chamberlin did not accept the welfare conclusions drawn by Pigou[33]. Thus while Joan Robinson's work is part of the Cambridge welfare tradition, Chamberlin *started* by rejecting it.

The Background to Imperfect Competition

The origins of Joan Robinson's analysis undoubtedly lie in the Cambridge welfare economics tradition, especially in the work of Marshall (who had begun the habit of using partial equilibrium apparatus to attack general equilibrium problems)[34] and Pigou. Although the references to Marshall in *Imperfect Competition* are almost invariably negative, there were extensive debts. Indeed, the whole apparatus used was, mathematically speaking, only a trivial variant on that used by Marshall himself[35].

A somewhat cool attitude was also expressed towards Pigou, despite very substantial debts to the *Economics of Welfare*[36]. (This is in marked contrast to the generous attitude displayed by Pigou in an article published shortly after Joan Robinson's book[37].) There were also very extensive debts to G. F. Shove especially to his (unpublished) treatment of distribution in his lectures[38]. The distribution material also borrowed quite noticeably from the work of Hicks[39]. Acknowledgement was also due to Yntema (who had already obtained the most influential result in the book — price discrimination equilibrium[40] — although without influence of his own because he was "misguided" enough to use calculus instead of geometry) and to Harrod whose major creative efforts had been marred by mistakes which have resulted in his receiving much less credit than is due[41].

There were two other influences which should be mentioned. The first was a condescending attitude towards businessmen, one which manifested itself much more clearly in the work of writers associated with this SRP[42]. The second was a particular methodological position which might have attracted a good deal more comment had it ever been spelt out. This methodological position was, in summary, that economic conclusions arrived at from reasonable assumptions which had *some* (apparent) correspondence in the real world were necessarily true, so that testing was not only an irrelevance, it was almost an impertinence[43].

Development of the Chamberlinian SRP
The initial reception by reviewers of Chamberlin's book was rather more favourable, it is probably fair to say, than the reception afforded to the book by Joan Robinson[44]. However, reviewers — notably Harrod, who devoted much of his review to the question of oligopoly — pointed to weaknesses in the book which were subsequently to be ignored, for the most part, in the development of the SRP — a parallel, as will be seen with the case of Robinson's book.

In the development of the Chamberlinian SRP Chamberlin himself played a large personal role — much larger than did Joan Robinson in the development of her SRP. A significant element in this role was work in the negative heuristic rather than the positive one. For Chamberlin devoted a good deal of energy to an attempt to distance his work from that of Joan Robinson and her associates. He disagreed entirely with her emphasis on marginal revenue, regarding it not as a "Pole" but simply as the first derivative of the revenue function[45]. He did not regard the "tangency solution" as having the central importance accorded to it by Joan Robinson. In a world of differentiated products it was hardly likely that all firms would be pushed to a position of tangency[46]. He refused to accept that entry into an industry necessarily increased the elasticity of the average revenue curve facing the existing firms[47], and he mounted a valiant, and ultimately successful, attack upon the strange contention of Kaldor that in a world of "perfect divisibility" there would be no economies or diseconomies of scale[48]. He also criticised, again successfully, Kaldor's equally puzzling contention that production costs could not be distinguished from selling costs[49]. He emphasised, again and again, that he and Joan Robinson were in fact dealing with different competitive situations. She had settled for product homogeneity, with all preferences being in the minds of consumers — it is easy to see how this led to the view that consumers were "irrational". For

Chamberlin, however, product heterogeneity was of central importance precisely because product variation was a competitive weapon[50]. The idea of "irrational" consumers was in any case fully in accord with the Cambridge welfare approach; and this was something from which Chamberlin dissociated his own work[51]. He insisted on the meaningless nature of comparisons of actual competitive situations with perfect competition[52] (and insisted also upon retaining the distinction between pure and perfect competition)[53]. He was thus very critical of the Lerner index[54], and provided cogent criticism of the Robinsonian "exploitation" argument, pointing to the strategic nature of the assumption about a single entrepreneur in control of a single firm (who was thus in a position to "exploit")[55]. Above all, comparisons with perfect competition were meaningless because they resulted in the retention of a mistaken frame of reference. What was required for an understanding of competition was a Gestalt switch[56]. He was offering a full theory of competition, not of imperfections from a perfect ideal, and wanted to encompass a world with selling costs, where products were not homogeneous but variable in the competitive process, and where the existence of space (largely excluded from his rival's work) necessarily gave people preferences[57].

Unfortunately this raised some difficulties for him. The emphasis upon diversity necessitated, as he came increasingly to realise, the abandonment of the "industry"[58]. But the assumption, which he had made at one point, of the uniformity of firms, had no meaning if there was no industry; and it was therefore necessary to emphasise that such an assumption was merely a temporary, expository, expedient[59]. Chamberlin also emphasised, quite correctly, that he had made a serious attempt to analyse the problem of oligopoly, while Joan Robinson had merely side-stepped the matter[60]; at the same time, again, the very concept of oligopoly becomes much more difficult to handle if there is no industry to be oligopolistic.

Chamberlin's main work on his research programme was thus, after 1933, within the negative heuristic. His work within the positive heuristic was rather less productive. He did not return to topics which he had broached in the thesis, especially the problem of the allocation of overheads and of multiproduct firms[61]. Moreover his abandonment of the industry concept resulted in its replacement by a cross-elasticity approach with which he was clearly never completely satisfied[62].

But the positive development of the SRP was taken over by other economists, sometimes to great effect. An important writer was A. J. Nichol who had, himself, some claims to priority in this field[63]. Nichol's most important contribution was an attempt to develop a probabilistic version of the Chamberlinian model in order to deal with the uncertainty facing the entrepreneur[64]. Another important follower was Robert Triffin. It was Triffin who was influential in propagating a cross-elasticity approach, sketching (but no more) how Chamberlin's apparatus might be interpreted in a general equilibrium context[65]. There was also Hans Brems who developed an ingenious diagrammatic treatment of product variation[66]. Chamberlin's attack on the "perfect divisibility" thesis attracted support from Whitin and Peston, and from Leibenstein[67]. His resistance to the "exploitation" argument received support from Bloom[68]. Copeland, who had preceded him on the question of product differentiation, returned to the matter in the light of

Chamberlin's analysis[69] and a number of writers made use of his apparatus in the context of retailing[70]. These included Henry Smith who hovered, at times uncertainly, between the Chamberlinian and Robinsonian SRPs[71].

Chamberlin's analysis was extended to questions of tax incidence, the multiproduct firm, and the theory of international trade[72]. The kinked demand curve, since hardly anyone recognised Joan Robinson's priority[73] undoubtedly developed from the Chamberlinian DD and dd curves, particularly as Sweezy showed evidence of concern with the Chamberlinian SRP elsewhere[74].

Not all the developments were theoretical. His work received a favourable verdict from those concerned with industrial policy[75], while there was also some empirical work on cost curves notably by Joel Dean[76]. However, by far the most important empirical work was done by Bain, himself the most important of Chamberlin's followers[77]. In fact on the basis of elements derived from the work of Chamberlin and of J. M. Clarke, Bain virtually created his own SRP, developing the theory of limit-pricing.

But Chamberlin's importance was mainly theoretical. Fellner offered an oligopoly analysis which owed not a little to Chamberlin[78] and several writers attempted to replace the simple profit maximisation criterion — an interesting parallel with developments under the Robinsonian SRP[79]. One writer (Enke) also showed that with product and selling cost variation, output variation might have a subsidiary role to play in profit maximisation under certain circumstances[80]. Machlup attempted to develop further the basis of market classification in Chamberlin's work and later defended his theoretical approach as a whole in a series of famous controversies[81].

His analysis received at least mention, if not accurate incorporation, in a number of textbooks from the late 1930s onwards so that his work, like that of Joan Robinson, passed this Kuhnian test of scientific recognition[82]. However, there remained one persistent source of criticism — Chicago. The position of the Chicago writers was that while Chamberlin was an original (Stigler in particular recognised this) he was wrong[83]. There were serious elements of incoherence in his work, notably the attempt to postulate uniformity in a world in which not only were products not homogeneous but there were no industries and everything competed with everything else; and any *predictions* obtained from his theories were trivially different from those obtained through the application of a price-taking model, or a monopoly model, depending on particular circumstances. (That this seems more like retrodiction than prediction did not disturb Chicago apparently.) But, whether favourable (the majority) or not, economists rarely felt able to ignore Chamberlin's work, the one (odd) exception being in the literature on location[84]. His research programme proved powerful and persuasive.

Development of the Robinsonian SRP
The initial reception by reviewers of Joan Robinson's book was somewhat mixed[85]. Several noted that the reach exceeded the grasp; Shove in particular was critical of its ungenerous attitude towards predecessors and precursors[86], and a highly penetrating review by A. J. Nichol pointed to the unnecessary use of a fragile geometric technique, the drawing of conclusions about general equilibrium problems

from partial equilibrium analysis, and the failure to treat competition between enterprises to any serious extent at all[87]. Nonetheless, the SRP soon attracted adherents — often these were critical of detail, as is the way with much of SRP development which falls into the Kuhnian category of "normal science", but they shared the same demi-core and aims as the original work. Kaldor was particularly prominent, although in retrospect he seems to have added little of substance to the original[88]. Another English adherent was Coase[89] — surprisingly in view of the later fame of his 1937 article which drew attention to the need for a proper theory of the firm[90]. However, Hicks, the leading English theorist, remained less than whole-hearted in his endorsement of the new material[91]. But Kahn, who had supervised the original thesis and whose technical assistance is evident at a number of points in it[92], pursued the "excess capacity" question by exploring the concept of "ideal output"[93]. Kahn also explored the question of irrational consumer preferences which lay at the heart of Joan Robinson's assumption of downward sloping average revenue curves for individual producers[94]. She had no product variable — indeed, it would seem, product homogeneity[95] — yet consumers were assumed to regard the output of different producers as imperfect substitutes. Harrod, who had himself very considerable claims to pioneering here, also helped to develop the SRP[96]. An important adherent was Abba P. Lerner, who corrected the mistake in Robinson's book concerning the equality of price with average cost as a welfare criterion, showing that what was critical was equality with *marginal* cost, and developing the well-known Lerner index of monopoly[97]. This matter was also taken up by K. W. Rothschild[98]. Such a concern led directly to questions of distribution, attracting the Marxist economist Michael Kalecki who became associated with Joan Robinson[99]. Joan Robinson herself returned to the question of distribution in a separate article of 1934[100].

An interesting adhesion to the SRP came from the United States, probably inspired largely by that part of the American Institutionalist programme associated with Veblen. The most well-known name here is that of J. K. Galbraith who was particularly attracted by the implications of a world of monopolies and by the importance attached to irrational consumer preferences[101]. Another manifestation of this link with institutionalism was associated with the work of A. R. Burns, and others, who believed that competition was facing extinction[102]. The attitude of *moral* censure taken towards monopoly found an echo in these writers and also in the work of a theorist of a different stamp, Tibor Scitovsky[103]. Other American adherents were W. H. Nicholls[104], who seems in turn to have influenced Patinkin[105], and Seymour Harris who, considering the needs of wartime production, raised the possibility that it might be necessary to restrict consumer choice in order to increase production through doing away with "excess capacity"[106].

The welfare basis of the programme remained strong in other ways. Given that consumers were irrational, it was natural to treat advertising as waste. Meade, as a disciple of the programme and propagator of its message, suggested curbs on advertising[107]. However, as this part of the SRP was developed it needed to borrow from the Chamberlinian SRP which had treated these selling costs while Robinson's original book had not[108].

Since the welfare programme involved comparison with (perfect) competition, in order to show the waste inherent in normal (imperfect) competition there was scope for further clarification of the perfectly competitive ideal; in addition to the work of Lerner noted above, Joan Robinson herself paid attention to the matter in 1934[109].

As the SRP developed there was, as often seems to be the case, some undermining of its original purpose through refinement. In particular, the simple profit maximisation approach was refined in an attempt to make the motivation of the producer, who had a choice of income and leisure, on all fours with the utility maximising consumer[110]. But this, of course, greatly weakened the simple welfare conclusions relating to equilibrium positions in the original book. The average revenue curve itself also became a casualty in time, as a result of attempting to deal with some of the problems which had been glossed over in its original formulation[111]. However, the industry concept survived — consistently with the Robinsonian assumption of product homogeneity.

Most of the work on the Robinsonian SRP was of a theoretical nature. There was very little empirical work — in marked contrast to the development of the Chamberlin SRP. One author (Saxton) attempted to test the theory of the firm which he believed himself to find in *Imperfect Competition*[112]. Having found that price rigidity was the order of the day and that the firms were in no very obvious way either marginalists or short-run maximisers, he concluded, nonetheless, that the analysis was broadly correct in its *description* of business behaviour[113]. Since it was not a description of business behaviour and since the evidence did not support this conclusion, this was all rather remarkable. Another writer (Broster) attempted an interesting exercise in the development of prescriptive rules for the maximising firm, and concluded that the results of following these rules would accord with the Robinsonian analysis[114]. But these were fairly isolated exceptions. There was really little serious attempt to gather empirical material and sweeping empirical generalisations were employed as required[115].

As Kuhn has shown, the role of textbooks is important[116]. Here Joan Robinson had some early success. Although the full-scale textbook treatment based on her analysis did not appear until the 1940s and, more particularly, the 1950s[117] a number of writers in the 1930s incorporated references to her work and some followed, albeit cautiously, the geometrical analysis and even, occasionally, a few of the welfare conclusions[118].

The Rise of a Rival SRP — Oxford Studies in the Price Mechanism
The Oxford SRP arose from three diverse impulses. First, there was considerable hostility to the Cambridge welfare conclusions and to the sweeping generalisations drawn from positing a U-shaped cost curve[119]. Secondly, there was the individual creative role of Harrod which should not be underestimated[120]. In this connection, Harrod's belief in the possibility of an *inductive* methodology should not be forgotten[121]. In the event, however, the methodology adopted by the Oxford Studies was to show some evidence of naivety[122], thus making it difficult for economists to be confident in this "anthropological" method of economic investigation. Nevertheless the work of Hall and Hitch made a contribution which could not be ignored[123].

Thirdly, there was felt to be a need for a theory of the *firm,* something which was clearly lacking in both the Robinsonian and Chamberlinian SRPs. Thus the Full Cost principle should be seen as a decision process. The focus was upon the firm. At the same time the firm took its decisions within the context of the industry; it thus became necessary to resuscitate the Marshallian concept of industry, something which was not unwelcome since a desire to resurrect Marshall's work in this area was part of the Oxford SRP[124].

The Oxford publications in the late 1940s and early 1950s aroused a wave of predictably critical comment from those associated with the Cambridge work of the 1930s[125]. The most important attempts to advance the SRP, apart from the work of P. W. S. Andrews himself, which occasioned the comment, were undertaken by Farrell, Wiles, and H. R. Edwards[126], while work in the negative heuristic was undertaken by Wilson (to great effect) and by Elizabeth Brunner[128] (who provided an exemplarily clear expository survey — in an Italian journal). Thus the initial impetus did result in an SRP, with work in both the positive and negative heuristic. At the same time it was probably not widely influential and was judged by many economists to be degenerating from the outset. The reason for this is not, however the widely touted difficulty over the size of the mark-up on Full Cost. It is rather that the SRP, like Marshall himself, mixed up together certainty and uncertainty, statics and dynamics, industry and firm in a way which was reminiscent of Marshall's *Industry and Trade;* and many economists had by that time become persuaded of the benefits of a partial equilibrium static approach.

SRP Intersections
Although three SRPs have been distinguished, there is no doubt that there were intersections between them in the work of subsequent writers. The major intersections were between the Chamberlinian and Robinsonian SRPs; but there were also intersections involving Robinson and Oxford, and Chamberlin and Oxford.

(i) *Robinson and Oxford*
Intersections in this category were predictably few, but two are nonetheless noteworthy. Firstly, there was an attempt, by Hicks, to fuse profit maximisation with Harrod's insistence, as part of the Oxford programme, that short-run profits were not maximised because of the fear of entry[129]. The result, a weighted average over the long run, was both creative and sensible. The second notable contribution came from Wiles. Perceiving, correctly, that the Cambridge literature was in fact about welfare economics, he attempted to use the Oxford apparatus to deal with welfare questions in a full book-length study[130]. However, understandably in view of the hostility elsewhere amongst the Oxford writers to the Cambridge welfare approach, this seems to have produced little imitation.

(ii) *Chamberlin and Oxford*
The intersections between these two research programmes were rather more important. First, it should be noted, there was the kinked demand curve put forward by Hall and Hitch, with acknowledgement to Chamberlin's DD and dd curves[131]. Secondly, Hall and Hitch also drew to some extent on Cassels; and he had worked in

the Chamberlinian SRP[132]. Thirdly, Chamberlin himself was not at all hostile to the Full Cost approach, regarding it as a valuable supplement in throwing light on the process of business decisions which involved average rather than marginal values[133]. It thus accorded perfectly with his opposition to Joan Robinson's emphasis on marginal revenue. Bain's theory of limit pricing was easy enough to interpret in Full Cost terms, while providing a theory of the mark-up which did not depend upon uneasy calculations of elasticity. Fellner, whose oligopoly analysis owed a good deal to Chamberlin, provided an interpretation of Full Cost as reflecting decisions seeking a safety margin in the presence of uncertainty where revenue and cost functions were liable to shift[134], and J. F. Due, in seeking to apply the Chamberlinian apparatus to retail price determination, ended up with a Full Cost procedure[135]. But it does seem to be the case that, at least for a long time, the overtures came from the Chamberlinian side and were not reciprocated.

(iii) *Robinson and Chamberlin*
The habit of treating the work of these two writers as in all "essential" respects identical began at an early stage after the publication of their books. A number of writers simply lumped them together and this became the tradition in British teaching. Boulding also habitually conflated their work and other textbooks followed his example[136]. Sometimes this reflected a simple failure to discern the existence of two SRPs, as Chamberlin himself lamented[137]; more rarely it reflected hostility to both SRPs together[138]. One important writer, Triffin, seems to have exhibited an attitude almost schizophrenic, in *distinguishing* Robinson and Chamberlin and then attempting (unsuccessfully) to exhibit their *parallelism* through tables of corresponding passages[139].

None of these can be regarded as intersections of SRPs. However, there was a fairly common tendency to use the Robinson book as a geometrical supplement to that of Chamberlin and this did produce a genuine intersection. In particular, writers working in (or textbooks borrowing from) the Chamberlinian SRP borrowed from Robinson on the matter of price discrimination and that of monopsony[140]. There were also some writers who borrowed eclectically from both authors without attempting to reconcile the different approaches[141].

On the other side, the adherents of the Cambridge welfare programme gradually realised that the gap in their literature concerning advertising had to be filled and Henry Smith, concerned to find empirical counterparts of the theoretical constructs but impressed by the welfare conclusions, continued to hover uncertainly between the two SRPs[142]. Lerner, by contrast, was a clear adherent of the Cambridge programme; but he also moved into the Chamberlinian SRP and (with Singer) made a notable contribution to the literature on location which was neglected by Robinson[143]. An interesting case was provided by Norris who attempted to construct a theory of demand as a counterpart to the Chamberlinian rewriting of the theory of supply but ended up by swallowing wholesale the Cambridge welfare conclusions[144]. Most of the *genuine* intersections seem, in summary, to have arisen in the work of American economists; the English adherents of the Cambridge welfare programme by and large insisted that there was no difference between the two SRPs[145].

Conclusion
This article has traced the rise and development of two separate research programmes, the one (Chamberlin's) being essentially positive, the other (Robinson's) being normative. The first writer wished to persuade economists to think about competition in a different way from that which had become increasingly the orthodoxy in the 1920s — to make a Gestalt switch; the other wished to persuade economists that the freely competitive system was a myth and the actual competitive system involved significant welfare losses compared with a perfectly competitive "ideal". What is remarkable about these two research programmes is not only the extent to which, at least on this side of the Atlantic, they have been confused, but also their very considerable success compared with either the Oxford research programme, or with that of Stackelberg which, despite a theoretical adroitness which seems superior to that of both the main writers considered here, attracted remarkably little attention[146]. The same applies to the work of Zeuthen[147]. The reliance upon geometrical technique by Robinson and Chamberlin, however, increased the accessibility of their books and resulted in a debate in which everybody could join, from those of an institutionalist bent like J. K. Galbraith to theorists like Tibor Scitovsky. There is no doubt that the majority of economists judged one or other of these SRPs to be progressive, in the Lakatosian sense, and that these judgements have been proved correct to some extent. On the one hand Chamberlin's work has led to excellent work on industrial structure — it would hardly be an exaggeration to say that the whole Structure, Conduct and Performance literature stems from his work and that of J. M. Clarke; on the other hand a continued interest in the welfare implications of consumers having (possibly "irrational") preferences is evidence of the vitality of the Robinsonian research programme[148].

Of course, neither SRP offered a theory of the firm and we are still without one although the important work by Williamson in this field has produced a significant advance[149]. But neither Chamberlin nor Robinson can be blamed for not providing what they did not set out to provide.

However they *did* attempt to cope with the problem of oligopoly; Chamberlin by analysing it, and Joan Robinson by offering a way of ignoring it. It is in this area that the major failure of both SRPs is to be found. It may well be that Hicks was correct when, in 1939, he hinted that economic theory might not be able to deal with this problem[150]. But even in the 1930s other writers made valiant attempts to tackle oligopoly, especially Nichol[151]; and in 1950 a symposium on monopolistic competition returned again and again to the question of oligopoly[152]. Chamberlin failed to deal with it, not so much, as has been suggested, because of a lack of specified relationship between his DD and dd curves[153] but because, as Triffin pointed out long ago, reaction curves of the DD type have no meaning in a situation of interdependence — we encounter an unbreakable logical circle[154]. However, it was Chamberlin who made the serious attempt to deal with the problem of oligopoly, and for this, at least, he deserves credit. That he did not succeed, and that his successors did not succeed, either in dealing with this matter or in solving tricky matters like market share, should not lead us to underestimate the importance of these two SRPs as episodes in the 20th century history of economics.

Notes

1. Chamberlin (1933).
2. J. V. Robinson (1933).
3. See Robson (1983) on the question of such citation especially p. 24 n.3.
4. The best account of Lakatos's theory of the history of science is to be found in Lakotos and Musgrave (1970). See also O'Brien (1976).
5. Blaug (1980) pp. 160, 237, 241, 264. Blaug is, of course, perfectly well aware of this dual nature of the SRP concept.
6. Chamberlin (1933) pp. 91-2.
7. Chamberlin (1933) pp. 71-4, 118-23, 127-46, 151-9, 167-72.
8. Chamberlin (1933) pp. 26-9, 56-70. See also Chamberlin (1957) p. 231.
9. Chamberlin (1933) pp. 260-65.
10. Chamberlin (1933) pp. 13, 74-8, 84, 172.
11. Chamberlin (1933) pp. 94, 104-9, 161-6, 214-5.
12. For example, Chamberlin (1933) pp. 182-4, 216-8.
13. Chamberlin (1933) p. 139; Shackle (1967) p. 59. Shackle's comment relates to Joan Robinson but the comment is also applicable to Chamberlin.
14. Chamberlin (1933) pp. 173, 247; see also Chamberlin (1957) pp. 44-5, 49-50; Triffin (1941) pp. 162-4.
15. Pigou (1932) especially Chs. 14-17 and App. III.
16. Sraffa (1926).
17. Robinson (1933) e.g. pp. 3-4, 88, 91, 230.
18. Robinson (1933) pp. 85-91, 97-9, 143-54, 169, 206, 253-4, 269, 281-304, 312, 319-20.
19. Robinson (1933) pp. 231, 241, 248, 268; Chamberlin (1933) p. 216.
20. Robinson (1933) pp. 16-19, 21-3, 48, 50, 56, 71, 76-82, 231.
21. Robinson (1933) pp. vi-vii, 18, 28, 30-32, 37, 63, 65-6.
22. Robinson (1933) pp. 38, 81.
23. Sweezy (1939).
24. Robinson (1933) pp. 284-5, 310-14, 317, 327.
25. Robinson (1933) pp. 307, 324-5.
26. Robinson (1953) p. 579; (1969) p. vi.
27. Chamberlin (1961) reprinted in (1933) pp. 292-3, 308-18.
28. See especially Chamberlin (1933) pp. 38-9, 221-9.
29. See, e.g. Abramson (1931) and Chamberlin (1933) p. 60.
30. Chamberlin (1933) pp. 57-62, 305-7.
31. Sraffa (1926).
32. Chamberlin (1933) p. 310 and references therein.
33. Chamberlin (1933) pp. 293-296.
34. Whitaker (1975) Vol. 2, p. 186.
35. Robinson (1933) pp. 20, 54n, 89, 124-5, 128, 336.
36. Robinson (1933) pp. 136, 143-4, 149, 159-65, 166n, 181, 187n, 190, 203, 205, 282, 286. Despite p. v of the "Preface", a reader of the text who did not know Pigou's work would not appreciate the extent of the debt.
37. Pigou (1933) p. 108: "This note attempts only the subordinate task of improving, on a rather bleak ice-wall, a staircase which has already been made and ascended."
38. Robinson (1933) pp. 105-14 (and n), 127, 133, 294-5.
39. Robinson (1933) pp. 261n, 262n.
40. Robinson (1933) pp. vi, 26n, 182n, 205n.
41. Robinson (1933) p. 26n; Harrod (1930), (1931); on Harrod's contribution (and his slips) see Shackle (1967) ch. 4.
42. Robinson (1933) pp. 72-3; the most marked example is Kahn (1952) pp. 126, 127.

43. Stewart (1979) gives an excellent account of this general methodological position (pp. 121-6). See also n. 74 below. In the development of the particular theoretical positions advanced by a number of Cambridge writers, procedures were used which give rise to serious doubts about their validity. On this see Leontief (1937).
44. See Harrod (1933), Edwards (1933), Copeland (1934), White (1936). See also Wallace (1936), (1937) and Triffin (1941) pp. 17, 19n.
45. Chamberlin (1933) pp. 191-218 especially p. 203n; Chamberlin (1957) pp. vii, 64, 274-6, 307-12.
46. Chamberlin (1933) pp. 195, 302; (1957) pp. 56-7, 144.
47. Chamberlin (1933) pp. 196-8, 282-9.
48. Chamberlin (1933) pp. 198-9, 230-59 (especially 247-8); (1957) pp. 45, 169-212; Kaldor (1935).
49. Chamberlin (1933) p. 277.
50. Chamberlin (1933) pp. 200-209, 302-3n; (1957) pp. 26-30, 105-137, 141, 311.
51. Chamberlin (1933) pp. 206, 296; (1957) pp. viii, 92-3, 97-100, 294-5.
52. Chamberlin (1957) pp. 50, 72-3, 309.
53. Chamberlin (1957) p. 18.
54. Chamberlin (1933) pp. 212, 215n; (1957) pp. 82-3, 100-101. On the Lerner index see the discussion of the Robinsonian SRP on pp. 36-8 and n. 97.
55. Chamberlin (1933) pp. 215-18, 245; (1957) pp. viii, 99, 309.
56. Chamberlin (1933) pp. 204-5; (1957) pp. 26-30.
57. Chamberlin (1957) pp. viii, 26-30, 44, 56-7, 75-6, 97-101, 144-8.
58. Chamberlin (1933) pp. 312-3n; (1957) pp. viii, 94-5. Se also Blaug (1978) p. 415.
59. Chamberlin (1933) pp. 210, 246-7n.
60. Chamberlin (1933) p. 309; (1957) pp. viii, 285.
61. Chamberlin (1933) pp. 304-5; (1957) p. 20. His work in the negative heuristic also included a valiant defence against Chicago criticisms — (1957) pp. 296-305.
62. Chamberlin (1957) pp. 78, 84-91. See also Weintraub (1942), (1955); Bishop (1952), (1953); Fellner (1953).
63. Nichol (1930).
64. Nichol (1941), (1943); see also his (1934), (1934-5), (1935), (1942).
65. Triffin (1941).
66. Brems (1947-8), (1951).
67. Whitin and Peston (1954); Leibenstein (1955).
68. Bloom (1941).
69. Copeland (1940).
70. Curtis (1938); Cassady (1939); Due (1941); Grether (1939), (1941).
71. Smith (1935a), (1935b), (1937).
72. Fagan and Jastram (1939), Fagan (1942); Clemens (1951-2); Marsh (1942).
73. See above n. 23.
74. Sweezy (1937); Hall and Hitch (1951) acknowledged the connection between their (1939) kinked curve and Chamberlin (p. 122).
75. See, e.g., Mason (1939), Mund (1942).
76. Dean (1942).
77. Bain (1941), (1942), (1949), (1950), (1952), (1964).
78. Fellner (1949).
79. Higgins (1939); Lynch (1940). See discussion on pp. 36-8 on the Robinsonian SRP.
80. Enke (1941).
81. Machlup (1937), (1939), (1946), (1947), (1967).
82. See, e.g., Garver and Hansen (1937); Bye (1941); Meyers (1937), (1939); Taussig (1939). Indeed it is interesting that even a book which was criticised for omitting much of interest that had appeared in the 1920s and 1930s still included material relating to monopolistic competition (Haley, 1941). But, as Chamberlin sadly noted, what appeared was often "something quite foreign to the theory, at least as I understand it" (1957 p. 92). This reflected the tendency of textbooks to treat the

Chamberlinian and Robinsonian SRPs as, for their purposes, equivalent, and then to try to fuse their results, drawing on Robinson's geometry. On Kuhn see n. 116 below.
83. The most important Chicago critique is Stigler (1949). Other references will be found in Chamberlin's response to Chicago (1957) pp. 296-306.
84. Ackley (1942); see, however, Smithies (1941).
85. See in particular Edwards (1933), Shove (1933b), Kaldor (1934b), Nichol (1934a).
86. Shove (1933b); see also Shove (1933a).
87. Nichol (1934a).
88. In particular Kaldor (1934a), (1935), (1938), (1950-51).
89. See Coase (1934-35) and (1937-38).
90. See Coase (1937).
91. Hicks (1935), (1939a).
92. See in particular the result in Robinson (1933) pp. 31-2 which is unproven and necessarily derives from a proof supplied by Kahn at a later point (pp. 40-1n).
93. Kahn (1935).
94. Kahn (1935). This was taken up by Galbraith (1938); see also Scitovsky (1944-5).
95. Robinson (1933) p. 17; Robinson (1934-5) p. 112.
96. Harrod's contributions are illuminatingly discussed by Chamberlin in his (1957) pp. 280-95.
97. Lerner (1933-34).
98. Rothschild (1942), (1943).
99. Kalecki (1942a), (1942b). See also Kalecki (1939-40).
100. Robinson (1934).
101. Galbraith (1936), (1938), Dennison and Galbraith (1938).
102. Burns (1936), (1937a), (1937b).
103. Scitovsky (1941).
104. Nicholls (1941), (1943).
105. Patinkin (1947).
106. Harris (1941).
107. Meade (1936) pp. 95-205.
108. Kaldor (1950-51) (written in 1943); Meade (1936); J. V. Robinson (1953) p. 586.
109. Robinson (1934-5).
110. Scitovsky (1943). See also Nordquist (1965) and Leibenstein (1979).
111. Robinson (1953) p. 585.
112. Saxton (1942).
113. Saxton (1942) p. 108. See also Tress (1943).
114. Broster (1938).
115. See in particular the sweeping generalisations about entrepreneurial motives and decision processes in Robinson (1953) especially pp. 582, 586-7. It is rather ironic that adherents of the Cambridge SRP felt no need to do empirical work themselves, while treating with disdain empirical results which appeared to undermine the Cambridge conclusions. See especially Kahn (1952). But this results from the Cambridge methodological position noted above (n. 43).
116. Kuhn (1962) ch. 2.
117. See in particular Stigler (1947), Stonier and Hague (1953), Ryan (1958), Boulding (1948), Speight (1960), Weintraub (1949). The textbooks generally treated the work of Robinson and Chamberlin as equivalent.
118. See, e.g., Roll (1937) which glances at the matter, and Benham and Lutz (1941) which is an American version of Benham's 1938 textbook.
119. See especially Wilson (1952), a major critical essay, especially p. 42, and Brunner (1952) I, pp. 515-16.
120. See especially Harrod (1939); see also Lee (1981).
121. See Harrod (1956) and Phelps Brown (1980) pp. 28-9.

Competitive Structure 45

122. In particular there is evidence of *naiveté* about the role of cartels and a rather surprising failure to realise that most oligopolistic price competition takes place through discounts.
123. Hall and Hitch (1951).
124. This is made clear in Andrews (1951).
125. E. A. G. Robinson (1950), (1951); Kahn (1952).
126. Andrews (1949); Farrell (1951), (1952), (1954); Wiles (1950), (1956).
127. Wilson (1952).
128. Brunner (1952).
129. Harrod (1952b), Hicks (1954).
130. Wiles (1956).
131. See n. 74 above.
132. Hall and Hitch (1951) p. 120 acknowledged Cassel's (1937) "aggressive" and "non-aggressive" price policy in their distinction between stability and instability.
133. Chamberlin (1957) pp. 271-79.
134. Fellner (1948).
135. Due (1941).
136. Boulding (1942), (1952). Chamberlin displayed some understandable exasperation at this.
137. See n. 82 above.
138. Friedman (1953).
139. Triffin (1941) pp. 19-41.
140. Grether (1939) p. 225; Fagan and Jastram (1939); Taussig (1939) I, p. 205n; Meyers (1937) e.g. p. 55n; Meyers (1941) e.g. pp. 39-41; Bain (1952) pp. 412-414.
141. For example Curtis (1938) who used Chamberlin's apparatus to reap Cambridge welfare conclusions — that resale price maintenance led to the "tangency solution" implying "excess capacity".
142. This is particularly evident in Smith's (1937) see, e.g., p. 126.
143. Lerner and Singer (1937).
144. Norris (1941).
145. Kaldor (1938), J. V. Robinson (1953).
146. Stackelberg (1934). See, however, Hicks (1935); Leontief (1936); Fellner (1949) pp. 98-119, 233-9. The association between Stackelberg's work and National Socialism in Germany may have hindered his acceptance — c.f. Fetter (1937) though this does not deal directly with Stackelberg.
147. See Edwards (1931) for a hostile reception of Zeuthen (1930) from an industrial economist.
148. For continued interest see, e.g., Berry (1969), Gabszewicz (1983).
149. See Williamson (1977) for a highly perceptive survey.
150. Hicks (1939b) p. 85. It is, however, worth remembering Edgeworth's tart comment (when contemplating this possibility) about "chaos congenial to their mentality" referring to "descriptive" economists — Edgeworth (1925) p. 139.
151. Nichol (1934b), (1935).
152. *American Economic Review,* Suppt. 40 (1950), pp. 23-104.
153. Archibald (1961) p. 166.
154. Triffin (1941) pp. 68-70.

Bibliography
Abramson, A. V., "Advertising and Economic Theory: A Criticism", *American Economic Review,* Vol. 21, 1931, pp. 685-90.
Ackley, G., "Spatial Competition in a Discontinuous Market", *Quarterly Journal of Economics,* Vol. 56, 1942, pp. 212-30.
Andrews, P. W. S., *Manufacturing Business,* London, Macmillan, 1949.
Archibald, G. C., "Chamberlin *versus* Chicago", *Review of Economic Studies,* Vol. 29, 1961, pp. 2-28, reprinted in C. K. Rowley, *Readings in Industrial Economics,* Vol. I, London, Macmillan, 1972.
Bain, J. S., "The Profit Rate as a Measure of Monopoly Power", *Quarterly Journal of Economics,* Vol. 55, 1941, pp. 271-93.

Bain, J. S., "Market Classifications in Modern Price Theory", *Quarterly Journal of Economics,* Vol. 56, 1942, pp. 560-574.
Bain, J. S., "A Note on Pricing in Monopoly and Oligopoly", *American Economic Review,* Vol. 39, 1949, pp. 448-464.
Bain, J. S., "Workable Competition in Oligopoly: Theoretical Considerations and Some Empirical Evidence", *American Economic Review,* Vol. 40, 1950, pp. 35-47.
Bain, J. S., *Price Theory,* New York, John Wiley, 1952.
Bain, J. S., "The Theory of Monopolistic Competition after Thirty Years: The Impact on Industrial Organisation", *American Economic Review Supplement,* Vol. 54, 1964, pp. 28-32.
Benham, F. and Lutz, F., *Economics,* New York, Pitman, 1941.
Berry, R. A., "A Note on Welfare Comparisons between Monopoly and Pure Competition", *Manchester School,* Vol. 37, 1969, pp. 39-57.
Bishop, R. L., "Elasticities, Cross Elasticities and Market Relationships", *American Economic Review,* Vol. 42, 1952, pp. 779-803.
Bishop, R. L., "Reply" (to W. J. Fellner and E. H. Chamberlin on Cross Elasticities), *American Economic Review,* Vol. 43, 1953, pp. 916-924.
Blaug, M., *Economic Theory in Retrospect,* 3rd edition, Cambridge, Cambridge University Press, 1978.
Blaug, M., *The Methodology of Economics,* Cambridge, Cambridge University Press, 1980.
Bloom, G. F., "A Reconsideration of the Theory of Exploitation", *Quarterly Journal of Economics,* Vol. 55, 1941, pp. 413-442.
Boulding, K. E., "The Theory of the Firm in the Last Ten Years", *American Economic Review,* Vol. 32, 1942, pp. 791-802.
Boulding, K. E., *Economic Analysis,* revised edition, London, Hamish Hamilton, 1948.
Boulding, K. E., "Implications for General Economics of More Realistic Theories of the Firm", *American Economic Review,* Vol. 42, 1952, pp. 38-44.
Brems, H., "The Interdependence of Quality Variations, Selling Effort and Price", *Quarterly Journal of Economics,* Vol. 62, 1947-8, pp. 418-440.
Brems, H., *Product Equilibrium under Monopolistic Competition,* Cambridge, Massachusetts, Harvard University Press, 1951.
Broster, E. J., *Cost, Demand and Net Revenue Analysis,* London, Gee, 1938.
Brunner, E., "Competition and the Theory of the Firm, Parts I, II", *Economia Internazionale,* Vol. 5, 1952, pp. 509-22, pp. 727-44.
Burns, A. R., *The Decline of Competition,* New York, McGraw Hill, 1936.
Burns, A. R., "The Organisation of Industry and the Theory of Prices", *Journal of Political Economy,* Vol. 45, 1937, pp. 662-680.
Burns, A. R., "Review of: Arthur Fletcher Lucas *Industrial Reconstruction and the Control of Competition: The British Experiments*", *Journal of Political Economy,* Vol. 45, 1937, pp. 826-828.
Bye, R. T., *Principles of Economics,* 4th edition, New York, F. S. Crofts, 1941.
Cassady, R., "Maintenance of Resale Prices by Manufacturers", *Quarterly Journal of Economics,* Vol. 53, 1939, pp. 454-464.
Cassells, J. M., "Excess Capacity and Monopolistic Competition", *Quarterly Journal of Economics,* Vol. 51, 1937, pp. 426-443.
Cassells, J. M., "Monopolistic Competition and Economic Realism", *Canadian Journal of Economics and Political Science,* Vol. 3, 1937, pp. 376-393.
Chamberlin, E. H., *The Theory of Monopolistic Competition,* 1933, 8th edition, Cambridge, Massachusetts, Harvard University Press, 1962.
Chamberlin, E. H., *Towards a More General Theory of Value,* New York, Oxford University Press, 1957.
Chamberlin, E. H., "The Origin and Early Development of Monopolistic Competition Theory", *Quarterly Journal of Economics,* Vol. 75, 1961, pp. 515-543.
Clemens, E. W., "Price Discrimination and the Multiple-Product Firm", *Review of Economic Studies,* Vol. 19, 1951-52, pp. 1-11.
Coase, R. H., "The Problem of Duopoly Reconsidered", *Review of Economic Studies,* Vol. 2, 1934-35, pp. 137-43.

Competitive Structure 47

Coase, R. H., "The Nature of the Firm", *Economica*, N. S., Vol. 4, 1937, pp. 386-405.
Coase, R. H., "Some Notes on Monopoly Price", *Review of Economic Studies*, Vol. 5, 1937-38, pp. 17-31.
Copeland, M. A., "The Theory of Monopolistic Competition", (review of E. H. Chamberlin *The Theory of Monopolistic Competition), Journal of Political Economy*, Vol. 42, 1934, pp. 531-536.
Copeland, M. A., "Competing Products and Monopolistic Competition", *Quarterly Journal of Economics*, Vol. 55, 1940, pp. 1-35.
Curtis, C. A., "Resale Price Maintenance", *Canadian Journal of Economics and Political Science*, Vol. 4, 1938, pp. 350-361.
Dean, J., "Department-Store Cost Functions", pp. 222-254 in Lange, O., McIntyre, F. and Yntema, T. O. (Eds.), *Studies in Mathematical Economics and Econometrics in Memory of Henry Schultz*, Chicago, University of Chicago Press, 1942.
Dennison, H. S. and Galbraith, J. K., *Modern Competition and Business Policy*, New York, Oxford University Press, 1938.
Due, J. F., "A Theory of Retail Price Determination", *Southern Economic Journal*, Vol. 7, 1941, pp. 380-397.
Edgeworth, F. Y., "The Pure Theory of Monopoly", in *Papers Relating to Political Economy*, London, Macmillan, for the Royal Economic Society, Vol. I, 1925, pp. 111-142.
Edwards, C. D., Review of: F. Zeuthen, *Problems of Monopoly and Economic Warfare, American Economic Review*, Vol. 21, 1931, pp. 701-704.
Edwards, C. D., Review of *The Theory of Monopolistic Competition*, by E. H. Chamberlin and of *The Economics of Imperfect Competition*, by J. V. Robinson, *American Economic Review*, Vol. 23, 1933, pp. 683-686.
Enke, S., "Profit Maximisation under Monopolistic Competition", *American Economic Review*, Vol. 31, 1941, pp. 317-326.
Fagan, E., "Tax Shifting in the Market Period", *American Economic Review*, Vol. 32, 1942, pp. 72-86.
Fagan, E. and Jastram, R. W., "Tax Shifting in the Short Run", *Quarterly Journal of Economics*, Vol. 53, 1939, pp. 562-589.
Farrell, M. J., "The Case Against the Imperfect Competition Theories", *Economic Journal*, Vol. 61, 1951, pp. 423-426.
Farrell, M. J., "Deductive Systems and Empirical Generalisations in the Theory of the Firm", *Oxford Economic Papers*, Vol. 4, 1952, pp. 45-49.
Farrell, M. J., "An Application of Activity Analysis to the Theory of the Firm", *Econometrica*, Vol. 22, 1954, pp. 291-302.
Fellner, W., "Average Cost Pricing and the Theory of Uncertainty", *Journal of Political Economy*, Vol. 56, 1948, pp. 249-252.
Fellner, W. J., *Competition Among the Few*, (1949), reprinted, New York, A. M. Kelley, 1960.
Fellner, W. J., "Elasticities, Cross Elasticities and Market Relationships: Comment", *American Economic Review*, Vol. 43, 1953, pp. 898-910.
Fetter, F. A., "Planning for Totalitarian Monopoly", *Journal of Political Economy*, Vol. 45, 1937, pp. 95-110.
Friedman, M., *Essays in Positive Economics*, Chicago, University of Chicago Press, 1953.
Gabszewicz, J. J., "Blue and Red Cars, or Blue Cars Only? A Note on Product Variety", *Economica*, N. S., Vol. 50, 1983, pp. 203-6.
Galbraith, J. K., "Monopoly Power and Price Rigidities", *Quarterly Journal of Economics*, Vol. 50, 1936, pp. 456-475.
Galbraith, J. K., "Rational and Irrational Consumer Preference", *Economic Journal*, Vol. 48, 1938, pp. 336-342.
Garver, F. B. and Hansen, A., *Principles of Economics*, revised edition, Boston, Ginn, 1937.
Grether, E. T., *Price Control under Fair Trade Legislation*, New York, Oxford University Press, 1939.
Grether, E. T., Review of Jules Backman, *Government Price Fixing*, New York, Pitman, 1938, in *Journal of Political Economy*, Vol. 49, 1941, pp. 633-634.
Haley, B. F., Review of Haney, L. H., *Value and Distribution: Some Leading Principles of Economic Science*, New York, D. Appleton Century Co., 1939, in *Journal of Political Economy*, Vol. 49, 1941, pp. 919-923.

Hall, R. L. and Hitch, C. J., "Price Theory and Business Behaviour", (1939) reprinted in T. Wilson and P. W. S. Andrews (Eds.), *Oxford Studies in the Price Mechanism,* Oxford, Clarendon, 1951.

Harris, S. E., *The Economics of American Defense,* New York, Norton, 1941.

Harrod, R. F., "Notes on Supply", *Economic Journal,* Vol. 40, 1930, pp. 232-41.

Harrod, R. F., "The Law of Decreasing Costs", *Economic Journal,* Vol. 41, 1931, pp. 566-76.

Harrod, R. F., Review of E. H. Chamberlin, *The Theory of Monopolistic Competition, Economic Journal,* Vol. 43, 1933, pp. 661-666.

Harrod, R. F., "Price and Cost in Entrepreneurs' Policy", *Oxford Economic Papers,* No. 2, 1939, pp. 1-11.

Harrod, R. F., *Economic Essays,* London, Macmillan, 1952.

Harrod, R. F., *Foundations of Inductive Logic,* London, Macmillan, 1956.

Hicks, J. R., "Annual Survey of Economic Theory: The Theory of Monopoly", *Econometrica,* Vol. 3, 1935, pp. 1-20.

Hicks, J. R., Review of H. von Stackleberg, *Marktform und Gleichgewicht, Economic Journal,* Vol. 45, 1935, pp. 334-336.

Hicks, J. R., "The Foundations of Welfare Economics", *Economic Journal,* Vol. 49, 1939, pp. 696-712.

Hicks, J. R., *Value and Capital,* (1939), 2nd edition, Oxford, Clarendon, 1946.

Hicks, J. R., "The Process of Imperfect Competition", *Oxford Economic Papers,* Vol. 6, 1954, pp. 41-54.

Higgins, B., "Elements of Indeterminancy in the Theory of Non-Perfect Competition", *American Economic Review,* Vol. 29, 1939, pp. 464-479.

Kahn, R. F., "Some Notes on Ideal Output", *Economic Journal,* Vol. 45, 1935, pp. 1-35.

Kahn, R. F., "Oxford Studies in the Price Mechanism", *Economic Journal,* Vol. 62, 1952, pp. 119-130.

Kaldor, N., "The Equilibrium of the Firm", *Economic Journal,* Vol. 44, 1934, pp. 60-76.

Kaldor, N., "Mrs. Robinson's Economics of Imperfect Competition", *Economica,* N.S., Vol. 1, 1934, pp. 338-341.

Kaldor, N., "Market Imperfection and Excess Capacity", *Economica,* N.S., Vol. 2, 1935, pp. 33-50.

Kaldor, N., "Professor Chamberlin on Monopolistic and Imperfect Competition", *Quarterly Journal of Economics,* Vol. 52, 1938, pp. 513-29.

Kaldor, N., "The Economic Aspects of Advertising", *Review of Economic Studies,* Vol. 18, 1950-51, pp. 1-27.

Kalecki, M., "The Supply Curve of an Industry under Perfect Competition", *Review of Economic Studies,* Vol. 7, 1939-40, pp. 91-112.

Kalecki, M., "Mr. Whitman on the Concept of 'Degree of Monopoly' — A Comment", *Economic Journal,* Vol. 52, 1942, pp. 121-7.

Kalecki, M., "A Theory of Profits", *Economic Journal,* Vol. 52, 1942, pp. 258-67.

Kuhn, T. S., *The Structure of Scientific Revolutions,* (1962), 2nd edition, Chicago, University of Chicago Press, 1970.

Lakatos, I. and Musgrave, A., *Criticism and the Growth of Knowledge,* London, Cambridge University Press, 1970.

Lee, F. S., "The Oxford Challenge to Marshallian Supply and Demand: the History of the Oxford Economists' Research Group", *Oxford Economic Papers,* Vol. 33, 1981, pp. 339-351.

Leibenstein, H., "The Proportionality Controversy and the Theory of Production", *Quarterly Journal of Economics,* Vol. 69, 1955, pp. 619-625.

Leibenstein, H., "A Branch of Economics is Missing: Micro-Micro Theory", *Journal of Economic Literature,* Vol. 17, 1979, pp. 477-502.

Leontief, W., "Stackelberg on Monopolistic Competition", *Journal of Political Economy,* Vol. 44, 1936, pp. 554-559.

Leontief, W., "Implicit Theorising: A Methodological Criticism of the Neo-Cambridge School", *Quarterly Journal of Economics,* Vol. 51, 1937, pp. 337-351.

Lerner, A. P., "The Concept of Monopoly and the Measurement of Monopoly Power", *Review of Economic Studies,* Vol. 1, 1933-34, pp. 157-175.

Competitive Structure 49

Lerner, A. P. and Singer, H. W., "Some Notes on Duopoly and Spatial Competition", *Journal of Political Economy*, Vol. 45, 1937, pp. 145-186.

Lynch, E. S., "A Note on Mr. Higgins' 'Indeterminancy in Non-Perfect Competition'" (with reply to B. Higgins), *American Economic Review*, Vol. 30, 1940, pp. 347-350.

Machlup, F., "Monopoly and Competition: A Classification of Market Positions", *American Economic Review*, Vol. 27, 1937, pp. 445-451.

Machlup, F., "Evaluation of the Practical Significance of the Theory of Monopolistic Competition", *American Economic Review*, Vol. 29, 1939, pp. 227-236.

Machlup, F., "Marginal Analysis and Empirical Research", *American Economic Review*, Vol. 36, 1946, pp. 519-54.

Machlup, F., "Rejoinder to an Antimarginalist", *American Economic Review*, Vol. 37, 1947, pp. 148-154.

Machlup, F., "Theories of the Firm: Marginalist, Behavioural, Managerial", *American Economic Review*, Vol. 57, 1967, pp. 1-33.

Marsh, D. B., "The Scope of the Theory of International Trade under Monopolistic Competition", *Quarterly Journal of Economics*, Vol. 56, 1942, pp. 475-486.

Mason, E. S., "Price and Production Policies of Large-Scale Enterprise", *American Economic Review*, Supp. Vol. 29, 1939, pp. 61-74.

Meade, J. E., *An Introduction to Economic Analysis and Policy*, Oxford, Clarendon, 1936.

Meyers, A. L., *Elements of Modern Economics*, New York, Prentice Hall, 1937.

Meyers, A. L., *Modern Economic Problems*, New York, Prentice Hall, 1939.

Mund, V. A., "Monopolistic Competition Theory and Public Price Policy", *American Economic Review*, Vol. 32, 1942, pp. 727-743.

Nichol, A. J., *Partial Monopoly and Price Leadership*, Philadelphia, 1930.

Nichol, A. J., Review of J. V. Robinson, *Economics of Imperfect Competition*, *Journal of Political Economy*, Vol. 42, 1934, pp. 257-259.

Nichol, A. J., "Professor Chamberlin's Theory of Limited Competition", *Quarterly Journal of Economics*, Vol. 48, 1934, pp. 317-337.

Nichol, A. J., "The Influence of Marginal Buyers on Monopolistic Competition", *Quarterly Journal of Economics*, Vol. 49, 1934-35, pp. 121-135.

Nichol, A. J., "Edgeworth's Theory of Duopoly Price", *Economic Journal*, Vol. 45, 1935, pp. 51-66.

Nichol, A. J., "Probability Analysis in the Theory of Demand, Net Revenue and Price", *Journal of Political Economy*, Vol. 49, 1941, pp. 637-661.

Nichol, A. J., "Monopoly Supply and Monopsony Demand", *Journal of Political Economy*, Vol. 50, 1942, pp. 861-879.

Nichol, A. J., "Production and the Probabilities of Cost", *Quarterly Journal of Economics*, Vol. 57, 1943, pp. 69-89.

Nicholls, W. H., *Imperfect Competition within Agricultural Industries*, Ames, Iowa, Iowa State College Press, 1941.

Nicholls, W. H., "Social Biases and Recent Theories of Competition", *Quarterly Journal of Economics*, Vol. 58, 1943, pp. 1-26.

Nordquist, G. L., "The Breakup of the Maximisation Principle", *Quarterly Review of Economics and Business*, Vol. 5, 1965, pp. 33-46, reprinted in David R. Kamerschen (Ed.), *Readings in Microeconomics*, Cleveland, Ohio, World Publishing Co., 1967, pp. 278-295.

Norris, R. T., *The Theory of Consumer Demand*, New Haven, Connecticut, Yale University Press, 1941.

Patinkin, D., "Multiple-Plant Firms, Cartels, and Imperfect Competition", *Quarterly Journal of Economics*, Vol. 61, 1947, pp. 173-205.

Phelps Brown, H., "Sir Roy Harrod: A Biographical Memoir", *Economic Journal*, Vol. 90, 1980, pp. 1-33.

Pigou, A. C., *The Economics of Welfare* (1932), 4th edition, reprinted, London, Macmillan, 1946.

Pigou, A. C., "A Note on Imperfect Competition", *Economic Journal*, Vol. 43, 1933, pp. 108-112.

Remenyi, J. V., "Core Demi-core Interaction — Toward a General Theory of Disciplinary and Sub-disciplinary Growth", *History of Political Economy*, Vol. 10, 1979, pp. 30-63.

Robinson, E. A. G., "The Pricing of Manufactured Products" (a review of P. W. S. Andrews, *Manufacturing Business), Economic Journal,* Vol. 60, 1950, pp. 771-780.
Robinson, E. A. G., "The Pricing of Manufactured Products and the Case Against Imperfect Competition: A Rejoinder", *Economic Journal,* Vol. 61, 1951, pp. 429-433.
Robinson, J. V., *The Economics of Imperfect Competition,* (1933), reprinted, London, Macmillan, 1948.
Robinson, J. V., "Euler's Theorem and the Problem of Distribution", *Economic Journal,* Vol. 44, 1934, pp. 398-414.
Robinson, J. V., "What is Perfect Competition?", *Quarterly Journal of Economics,* Vol. 49, 1934-35, pp. 104-120.
Robinson, J. V., "Imperfect Competition Revisited", *Economic Journal,* Vol. 63, 1953, pp. 579-93.
Robinson, J. V., Preface to *Economics of Imperfect Competition,* 2nd edition, London, Macmillan, 1969.
Robson, J. M., "Which Bentham was Mill's Bentham?", *The Bentham Newsletter,* No. 7, 1983, pp. 15-26.
Roll, E., *Elements of Economic Theory,* London, Oxford University Press, 1937.
Rothschild, K. W., "The Degree of Monopoly", *Economica,* NS., Vol. 9, 1942, pp. 24-39.
Rothschild, K. W., "A Further Note on the Degree of Monopoly", *Economica,* NS, Vol. 10, 1943, pp. 69-70.
Ryan, W. L., *Price Theory,* London, Macmillan, 1958.
Saxton, C., *The Economics of Price Determination,* London, Oxford University Press, 1942.
Scitovsky, T., "Prices under Monopoly and Competition", *Journal of Political Economy,* Vol. 49, 1941, pp. 663-685.
Scitovsky, T., "A Note on Profit Maximisation and its Implications", *Review of Economic Studies,* Vol. 11, 1943, pp. 57-60.
Scitovsky, T., "Some Consequences of the Habit of Judging Quality by Price", *Review of Economic Studies,* Vol. 12, 1944-45, pp. 100-105.
Shackle, G. L. S., *The Years of High Theory,* Cambridge, Cambridge University Press, 1967.
Shove, G. F., "The Imperfection of the Market: A Further Note", *Economic Journal,* Vol. 43, 1933, pp. 113-24.
Shove, G. F., "Review of J. V. Robinson, *The Economics of Imperfect Competition",* Economic Journal,* Vol. 43, 1933, pp. 657-661.
Smith, H., "Discontinuous Demand Curves and Monopolistic Competition: A Special Case", *Quarterly Journal of Economics,* Vol. 49, 1935, pp. 542-550.
Smith, H., "The Imputation of Advertising Costs", *Economic Journal,* Vol. 45, 1935, pp. 682-699.
Smith, H., *Retail Distribution: A Critical Analysis,* London, Oxford University Press, 1937.
Smithies, A., "Optimum Location in Spatial Competition", *Journal of Political Economy,* Vol. 49, 1941, pp. 423-439.
Speight, H., *Economics: The Science of Prices and Incomes,* London, Methuen, 1960.
Sraffa, P., "The Laws of Returns under Competitive Conditions", *Economic Journal,* Vol. 36, 1926, pp. 535-50.
Stackelberg, H. v., *Marktform und Gleichgewicht,* Vienna and Berlin, Springer, 1934.
Stewart, I. M. T., *Reasoning and Method in Economics,* London, McGraw Hill, 1979.
Stigler, G. J., *The Theory of Price,* New York, Macmillan, 1946.
Stigler, G. J., "Monopolistic Competition in Retrospect", pp. 12-24 in *Five Lectures in Economic Problems,* London, Longman, 1949.
Stonier, A. W. and Hague, D. C., *A Textbook of Economic Theory,* London, Longman, 1953.
Sweezy, P., "On the Definition of Monopoly", *Quarterly Journal of Economics,* Vol. 51, 1937, pp. 362-3.
Sweezy, P., "Demand under Conditions of Oligopoly", *Journal of Political Economy,* Vol. 47, 1939, pp. 568-73.
Taussig, F. W., *Principles of Economics,* 4th edition, New York, Macmillan, 1939.

Competitive Structure 51

Tress, R. C., Review of C. Clive Saxton, *The Economics of Price Determination, Economic Journal*, Vol. 53, 1943, pp. 119-20.

Triffin, R., *Monopolistic Competition and General Equilibrium Theory*, Cambridge, Massachusetts, Harvard University Press, 1941.

Wallace, D. H., "Monopoly Prices and Depression", pp. 346-356 in *Explorations in Economics: Notes and Essays Contributed in Honor of F. W. Taussig*, New York, McGraw Hill, 1936.

Wallace, D. H., "Monopolistic Competition at Work: A Review" (of Arthur Robert Burns, *The Decline of Competition), Quarterly Journal of Economics*, Vol. 51, 1937, pp. 374-387.

Weintraub, S., "The Classification of Market Positions: Comment", *Quarterly Journal of Economics*, Vol. 56, 1942, pp. 666-677.

Weintraub, S., *Price Theory*, New York, Pitman, 1949.

Weintraub, S., "Revised Doctrines of Competition", *American Economic Review*, Vol. 45, 1955, pp. 463-479.

Whitaker, J. K., *The Early Economic Writings of Alfred Marshall*, 2 vols., New York, Free Press, 1975.

White, H. G., "A Review of Monopolistic and Imperfect Competition Theories", *American Economic Review*, Vol. 26, 1936, pp. 637-649.

Whitin, T. M. and Peston, M. H., "Random Variations, Risk and Returns to Scale", *Quarterly Journal of Economics*, Vol. 68, 1954, pp. 603-612.

Wiles, P., "Empirical Research and Marginal Analysis", *Economic Journal*, Vol. 60, 1950, pp. 515-30.

Wiles, P., *Price, Cost and Output*, Oxford, Blackwell, 1956.

Williamson, O. E., "Firms and Markets" in S. Weintraub (Ed.), *Modern Economic Thought*, Pittsburgh, University of Pennsylvania Press, 1977.

Wilson, T., "The Inadequacy of the Theory of the Firm as a Branch of Welfare Economics", *Oxford Economic Papers*, Vol. 4, 1952, pp. 18-44.

Zeuthen, F., *Problems of Monopoly and Economic Warfare*, London, Routledge, 1930.

Hayek's Ricardo effect: a second look

Laurence S. Moss and Karen I. Vaughn

I. Introduction

In this article we review a long-standing controversy in twentieth-century economic thought: the debate over Hayek's Ricardo effect. Hayek developed his interpretation of the Ricardo effect in the context of his theory of business cycles primarily in the late 1930s and early 1940s. At that time Hayek's use of the familiar proposition was held up to close scrutiny by many talented critics, including Nicholas Kaldor, H. D. Dickinson, and R. G. Hawtry, all of whom, according to Hayek, failed to understand what he was saying.[1] In each case Hayek countered their criticism with a restatement of his proposition which in turn failed to satisfy the critics.[2] Indeed, this apparent miscommunication was still taking place as late as 1969 when Hayek wrote his last piece on the Ricardo effect in answer to a criticism leveled by Sir John Hicks.

Correspondence may be addressed to Professor Moss, Dept. of Economics, Babson College, Babson Park (Wellesley) MA 02157-0901; or to Professor Vaughn, Dept. of Economics, George Mason University, 4400 University Drive, Fairfax VA 22030.

1. A partial list of English language writers includes, in chronological order, Nicholas Kaldor, 'Capital intensity and the trade cycle,' *Economica*, Feb. 1939, 40–66, reprinted in idem, *Essays on economic stability and growth* (Glencoe, Ill., 120–47; Tom Wilson, 'Capital theory and the trade cycle,' *Review of Economic Studies* 7 (1938–40): 169–79; H. D. Dickinson, Review of Hayek's *Freedom and the economic system*, in *Economica*, Nov. 1940, 435–37; R. G. Hawtrey, 'The trade cycle and capital intensity,' *Economica*, Feb. 1940, 1–22; Hugh Townshend, Review of Hayek's *Profits, interest and investment*, in *Economic Journal*, March 1940, 99–103; Nicholas Kaldor, 'Professor Hayek and the concertina effect,' *Economica*, Nov. 1942, 359–82, reprinted in idem, *Essays on economic stability*, 148–76; Sho-Chieh Tsiang, *Variations of real wages and profit margins in relation to the trade cycle* (London, 1947), reprinted, W. Germany, 1970; Sho-Chieh Tsiang, 'Rehabilitation of time dimension of investment in macrodynamic analysis,' *Economica*, Aug. 1949, 204–17; William J. Baumol, 'Income effect, substitution effect, Ricardo effect' *Economics*, Feb. 1950, 69–80; Friedrick Lutz and Vera Lutz, *The theory of investment of the firm* (Princeton, 1951), 137–42; R. G. Hawtrey, *Capital and employment* (1937; London, 1952), 248–255; John Hicks, 'The Hayek story,' in idem *Critical essays in monetary theory* (Oxford, 1967), 203–15; Mark Blaug, *Economic theory in retrospect* (Homewood, Ill., 1968), 543–48; Walter Adolf Johr, 'Note on Professor Hayek's "True theory of unemployment,"' *Kyklos* 30 (1977): 713–723; and David H. Howard, Review of Hayek, *Denationalisation of money*, *Journal of Monetary Economics* 3 (1977): 483–85.

2. Hayek adopted the name 'Ricardo effect' toward the end of the 1930s, but the effect itself is discussed in some detail in the following references: F. A. Hayek, *Prices and production* (London, 1935), 69–100 and 148–57; idem, *Profits, interest and investment* (London, 1939), 3–71; idem, 'A comment,' *Economica*, Nov. 1942, 383–85; idem, 'Three elucidations of the Ricardo effect,' *Journal of Political Economy*, 1969, 274–85.

The purpose of our article is to discover whether in this debate it was Hayek who was out of step with the profession or the profession that was out of step with Hayek. We shall argue that the reason that Hayek's argument seemed so elusive to his contemporary colleagues (and some later critics) was that his method of analysis was foreign to their way of thinking. While English economists in the 1930s (especially after Keynes published the *General theory*) were concerned primarily with the static problem of balancing income and expenditure flows at acceptable levels of employment, Hayek was attempting to develop a dynamic theory of business cycles that involved tracing out the path of adjustment of the capital stock of an economy from one equilibrium state to another. This problem of describing the transitional process only became the subject of serious professional attention long after the debate over the Ricardo effect was concluded.[3]

In the course of our exposition, we will demonstrate that Hayek's Ricardo effect was not, in Blaug's words, "only another instance of the vice of neoclassical economics: the hasty application of static theorems to the real world."[4] Indeed, we shall argue that this is the *last* accusation one could logically hurl at Hayek's analysis. The very reason why Hayek encountered so much difficulty in communicating his message was precisely that he was not presenting an exercise in comparative statics but was rather hypothesizing a particular adjustment process where the final equilibrium state depended upon the particular path of adjustment followed in the economy.

In recent years the founders of the 'new classical economics' have praised the broad outlines of Hayek's approach to the business cycle. Robert Lucas pointed out that as early as 1929 Hayek articulated what remains today the single most important theoretical question in business cycle research. Hayek asked, How can cyclical phenomena be incorporated "into the system of economic equilibrium theory?"[5] Lucas goes on to regret the unfortunate Keynesian diversion of research effort from a thoroughgoing theory of the business cycle to what, in Lucas's words, is the "simpler question of the determination of output at a point in time."[6] It is well known that Hayek also regretted the unfortunate "Keynesian diversion" and resisted the redirection of research away from what he considered to be one of the most important macroeconomic questions: how production

---

3. E. Burmeister, *Capital theory and dynamics* (Cambridge, 1980).
4. Blaug, 548.
5. F. A. Hayek, *Monetary theory and the trade cycle* (London, 1933), 33 n. The German edition of Hayek's essay appeared in 1929. Cf. Robert E. Lucas, Jr., 'Understanding business cycles,' in K. Brunner and A. Meltzer, *Stabilization of the domestic and international economy* (Amsterdam, 1977), reprinted in R. Lucas, Jr., *Studies in business cycle theory* (Cambridge, Mass., 1981), 215.
6. Lucas, 215.

structures adjust to the underlying demand conditions and savings patterns of the community. It was this concern that made him wary of an economic theory that made it appear possible to push an economy into a perpetual state of boom.[7] He feared that instead of perpetual boom, inflationist policies would only result in short-term, illusory gains followed by a collapse with all of its undesirable macroeconomic effects.

Hayek's approach (much like the modern approach of Lucas and others) was to derive macroeconomic consequences from an analysis of the self-interested behavior of market participants. This was a continuation of the Misesian research program of reducing aggregative relationships to statements about individual action in markets.[8] Hayek's particular analytic structure combined elements of a Wicksellian cumulative expansion that included Cantillon effects with an 'Austrian' description of production as consisting of a succession of stages that had to be synchronized and coordinated with each other through appropriate price signals.[9] This framework allowed Hayek to argue that changes in the quantity of money would have non-neutral effects on individual prices and on the allocation of resources. All this led Hayek to admit the stimulative impact of Keynesian monetary policies but severely criticize the Keynesian claim that unemployment could be permanently cured by government-engineered expansions of aggregate demand. If governments try such engineering, they will be thwarted by the Ricardo effect.

We have organized our discussion as follows. In Section II we identify two uses of the Ricardo effect in Ricardo's *Principles*, each of which bears a certain similarity to the mechanism Hayek finally developed. In Section III, we trace the intellectual roots of Hayek's theory to the 'reverse movement' problem in the trade cycle theory of Ludwig von Mises. Mises' theory was itself a variant of the 'cumulative process' analysis first presented by K. Wicksell at the turn of the century. In Section IV, we summarize Hayek's main concern during the 1930s, that economic development required voluntary savings on the part of the economy and that government-created booms would prove to be self-defeating. The Ricardo effect served as the trigger that would bring on the crisis. In Section V we review the substance of the Hayek-Kaldor debate over the micro-

---

7. See for example the selected passages from Hayek's writings in F. A. Hayek and S. Shenoy, *A tiger by the tail* (London, 1972); idem, *Full employment at any price?* (London, 1975).

8. On the Misesian 'research program' see L. S. Moss and K. I. Vaughn, 'Ludwig von Mises and the Austrian tradition,' paper read at the 1980 meeting of the American Economic Association in Denver, MS; and L. S. Moss, 'The monetary economics of Ludwig von Mises,' in idem, *The economics of Ludwig von Mises: toward a critical reappraisal* (Kansas City, Mo., 1974), 13–49.

9. G. O'Driscoll, *Economics as a coordination problem* (Kansas City, Mo., 1977), pp. xv–xxi, 1–11, and 153–55.

foundations of the Ricardo effect. This debate was especially important to the development of Hayek's theory. It was by responding to Kaldor's formidable criticisms of that mechanism that Hayek finally realized why the comparative static approach based on perfect information was totally out of step with the type of phenomena Hayek was trying to model.

II. Ricardo's Ricardo Effect

As a proposition in comparative statics, the Ricardo effect compares two equilibrium states of the economy—before and after a change in relative factor prices has induced a switch in production techniques. As part of a dynamic theory, the Ricardo effect examines the path by which an economy reestablishes equilibrium after a disequilibrating shock to the system occurs. Both uses of the Ricardo effect appear in Ricardo's *Principles*, and both uses influenced Hayek in naming his own composite mechanism of relative price changes after the work of his English predecessor.[10] It may be helpful to explain the Ricardo effect as it appeared in Ricardo's *Principles* so as to better appreciate the way in which the mechanism functions in Hayek's trade cycle theory.

Comparative static statement

In his famous first chapter "On Value" in the *Principles*, Ricardo explained why the labor theory of relative commodity prices breaks down in a capital-using economy. It breaks down because of different durabilities of capital or, as Ricardo noted elsewhere, the varying role of time in the production of commodities.[11] More specifically, Ricardo demonstrated why a sudden across-the-board rise in wages must raise the prices of commodities manufactured with labor-saving machinery by a lesser amount than that same wage increase will raise the prices of commodities produced without any machinery at all. His analysis proceeded in two steps.

First, at the 'firm level,' the manager finds himself indifferent between two techniques of production, Technique A and Technique B, each capable of producing a given volume of output at the same identical cost. Technique A, consists of a $5,000 machine lasting one year and capable of performing 100 man-years of work. Technique B, consists of directly hir-

---

10. See David Ricardo, *On the principles of political economy and taxation*, in *The works and correspondence of David Ricardo* (Cambridge, 1951) 1:39–43, and 386–397. Hayek cited both places in Ricardo's *Principles* as the location of what he (Hayek) termed the 'Ricardo effect' (see Hayek, 'The Ricardo effect' in idem, *Individualism and economic order* (London, 1949) 220. O'Driscoll, a recent commentator, emphasized the dynamic Wicksellian nature of Hayek's analysis 'The specialization gap and the Ricardo effect: comment on Ferguson,' *History of Political Economy* 7.2 (1975): 268—but did not emphasize the close connection between the argument of Ricardo's machinery chapter and Hayek's Ricardo effect mechanism; cf. O'Driscoll, *Economics as a coordination problem*, 92–128.

11. David Ricardo, Letter to McCulloch, 13 June 1820; cf. P. Sraffa, Introduction to Ricardo, *Principles*, p. xlv.

ing 100 man-years of labor to do the work unaided by any machinery at all. At a supposed wage of $50 per man-year, both techniques cost $5,000. Ricardo explained that it is obviously a "matter of indifference" to the manager which of the two techniques is used.[12]

The second step of Ricardo's argument requires that we upset this state of indifference by supposing wages unexpectedly rise from $50 per man-year to $55 per man-year—a 10 percent rise in wages. Technique B, the labor-intensive technique, will now cost $5,500. The machine-intensive technique, Technique A, will also increase in price, but not by as much. The price of the machine cannot increase to $5,500 because if it was formerly profitable to sell those machines at $5,000 (the price of the machine prior to the rise in the price of labor), then each machine had to have contained *less than* 100 man-years of labor to allow for profits to the machine makers. As a general rule, a machine must contain less labor than it displaces, and so a rise in wages will raise its price by *less than* 10 percent.[13] Faced with a cheaper way of getting the work done, the manager will substitute the machine method for the direct-labor method of production.

Now moving from the firm level of analysis to the economic system as a whole, Ricardo was quite explicit about the role competition plays in keeping machine producers from increasing the prices of their machines by the full 10 percent. Such an effort would elevate profits among machine manufacturers above the going rate established by the productivity of marginal investments in agriculture.[14] This would create a situation in which an "unusual quantity of capital" would flow into machinery manufacture expanding the supply of machines and forcing their prices down.[15] Competitive forces would therefore drive the price of machines down again.

A corollary of Ricardo's argument is that the substitution of machinery for labor causes the prices of commodities produced with machines to decline relative to the prices of commodities produced entirely with direct labor. In other words the adoption of labor-saving machinery by capitalist-managers, in an effort to maximize profits, eventually results in a decline in specific consumer-goods prices.[16] Thus, we can summarize the conclu-

12. Ricardo, *Principles*, 40.
13. Ibid.
14. On Ricardo's so-called 'agricultural theory of profit' see P. Sraffa, Introduction to Ricardo, *Principles*, pp. xxx–xxxvii. For an application of that theory to how it 'regulates' the overall market rates on competing investments and a summary of the recent doctrinal debate surrounding that application, see L. S. Moss, 'Professor Hollander and Ricardian economics,' *Eastern Economical Journal* 5 (Dec. 1979): 503.
15. Ricardo, *Principles*, 41. Our discussion is entirely consistent with S. Hollander's claim that Ricardo's "intention" was to show that a once-and-for-all rise in wages would not raise the level of prices, but only alter relative commodity prices; cf. L. Moss, 'Professor Hollander and Ricardian economics,' 503–6.
16. Ibid. 37–38.

sions of the comparative static version of Ricardo's Ricardo effect as follows:

(i) A rise in wages will encourage managers to substitute machine-intensive for labor-intensive methods of production; and
(ii) In the new equilibrium position, the prices of consumer goods made with (labor-saving) machinery will decline relative to the prices of other commodities.[17]

The Ricardo effect in a dynamic context

Hayek refers to a second place in Ricardo's *Principles* to support his use of the Ricardo effect: Chapter 31 "On Machinery." In that now famous chapter, Ricardo addressed the problem of whether the introduction of a new technology could ever make workers worse off. Added only in the third edition, his surprising conclusion was that under certain circumstances, the introduction of a technological innovation could reduce the real wages of labor and lead to unemployment in the short run.[18] He argued that if the introduction of the new technology is sudden and there is no growth in the economy, the fact that labor will have to be diverted from the production of consumer goods to the production of capital will lead to a reduction in the real wage of labor and to reduced employment.[19] That is, during the transition period while new capital goods are being produced, less food can be produced with the same total resources as one had before. Hence in the next time period, workers find that there is less for them to buy with their money, reducing their real wages, and they find that some of the labor that was previously employed has now become 'redundant' because of the increased productivity of the new machinery. Here we have the germ of the idea that later appears in the Austrian theory of the boom—that capital-intensive methods of production cannot be instantly installed; rather, a costly transition period must be financed and this financing requires real savings on the part of the community. It was an idea, however, that Ricardo himself did not explore further.

After raising this extremely interesting problem about the process by

---

17. Although Ricardo did not specifically discuss the economic impact of a sudden decline in the wages of labor, we can infer from his comparative-static framework that a once-and-for-all decline in wages will encourage managers to substitute labor-intensive or direct methods of production (Technique B) for labor-saving (i.e., capital-intensive) methods of production (Technique A). Also, the decline in wages will bring about a decline in the prices of consumer goods made without machinery relative to the prices of consumer goods manufactured with the aid of machinery. This is the form of Ricardo's comparative-static theorem that most closely resembles the one Hayek tried to develop—see the text.

18. On the details of Ricardo's controversial chapter, see P. Sraffa. Introduction. pp. lvii–lx; and S. Hollander, 'The development of Ricardo's position on machinery,' *History of Political Economy* 3.1 (1971): 105–35.

19. Ricardo, *Principles*, 390.

which new capital goods are financed, Ricardo assured his readers that the practical significance of his example of an innovation crisis was slight. These conditions could occur only in an economy without net investment, and even then it would only be during the temporary transition period that the workers would experience distress.[20] As a practical matter, sudden switches from "circulating to fixed capital" occur concurrently with capital accumulation. This meant that there is typically enough real community savings available to sustain the flow of consumer goods while some labor is being diverted to constructing capital goods. In the context of capital accumulation all that happens is wages rise less quickly than they otherwise would. The financing of the new capital goods does not require that wages fall absolutely. Thus, with net investment, the introduction of new technology during the process of accumulation improves the economic welfare of the workers. The worker's wage is lower than it would otherwise be, but higher than it was in the past.

Hayek's version

As recently as 1969 Hayek articulated his Ricardo effect theorem that "an increase in the demand for consumer goods will lead (in conditions of full employment) to a decrease in the demand for the kind of investment goods appropriate only to more highly capital intensive modes of production."[21] Hayek demonstrated that the Ricardo effect can be presented as a theorem in comparative statics by comparing two equilibrium positions identical in all respects except one—the ratio of product-to-factor prices is higher in one than in the other.[22] But as the rest of his 1969 restatement made clear, Hayek's Ricardo effect was employed to do a great deal more than simply compare the logic of choice under varying patterns of relative prices. The raison d'être of the mechanism was to explain why the end of the boom phase of the trade cycle nearly always consists of a depression.

Much as Ricardo had used his proposition to draw out the possible disequilibrium consequences of the attempt to introduce a new technology before adequate savings are available, Hayek used the Ricardo effect as an important component of a dynamic theory of the trade cycle to elucidate the implications of a disequilibrium phenomenon. Drawing on the comparative static proposition in Ricardo's chapter I, Hayek employed the notion that changing real factor prices induce entrepreneurs to switch from labor-saving methods of production back to labor-intensive methods, thereby ending the boom. But what is it that caused the factor prices to change in the first place? As early as 1931 Hayek elaborated that success-

20. Ibid. 395.
21. F. A. Hayek, 'Three elucidations of the Ricardo effect,' 275–77. See also Hayek, *Profits, interest and investment*, 3–72.
22. Hayek, 'Three elucidations,' 275–76.

fully switching from a labor-intensive to a labor-saving technology requires that there be a diversion of national product from consumption to investment so as to "finance the transition." According to Hayek it was "voluntary savings" that provided this "diversion" and nothing else could do as well. An inflationary process seldom succeeds, because it relies on "forced savings" rather than voluntary savings, and forced saving is rarely if ever adequate. As we shall explain below the inadequacy of forced savings manifests itself in a change in factor prices ultimately inducing the switch back to labor-intensive methods of production and the crises.

Hayek referred his readers to *both* chapters in Ricardo's writings to support his analysis. Several commentators compare Hayek's mechanism to Ricardo's first version and fail to emphasize the close connection between the argument of Ricardo's chapter "On Machinery" and the central problem of Hayek's theory.[23] In addition to the influence of Ricardo's *Principles* on Hayek, we must also consider the impact of a particular unresolved problem in the so-called Austrian theory of the business cycle on Hayek's thinking about economic problems.

III. *The Reverse Movement Problem*

During the 1920s Ludwig von Mises' 'circulation-credit' theory of the business cycle (now commonly called the 'Austrian' theory) was widely regarded as the most important of the contributions of the younger generation of Austrian writers to modern, neoclassical economics.[24] Mises took issue with the phenomenon Wicksell described in his *Interest and prices* of a steady and evenly accelerating increase in prices so long as the market rate of interest is held below the natural rate and the quantity of money steadily increased.[25] According to Mises the injection of new money into the economy has to raise certain prices ahead of others as entrepreneurs try to construct more capital-intensive investment projects. When new money enters the economy through the loan market, after a period of economic expansion consumer-goods prices will rise ahead of wages, and this will encourage entrepreneurs to substitute labor-intensive for capital-intensive techniques of production. This will discourage the sales of capital

---

23. Except for this omission, see G. P. O'Driscoll's useful critique of Ferguson's remarks about Hayek's version of the Ricardo effect in 'The specialization gap and the Ricardo effect.' Hayek refers to both of Ricardo's versions in 'The Ricardo effect,' *Economica* 34 (May 1942): 127–152 n. 3. One major difference between the two versions has to do with Ricardo's suggestion that technological changes induce the substitution of machines for labor, while Hayek's analysis is restricted to a choice of techniques that is induced by a change in factor prices.

24. G. Haberler, *Prosperity and depression* (Geneva: League of Nations, 1941), 33–35; H. S. Ellis *German monetary theory 1905–1933* (Cambridge, Mass., 1934), 335–74.

25. Knut Wicksell, *Interest and prices* (1898; London, 1936), 102–21.

goods and bring about an economic crisis. The process of capital-goods construction cannot go on indefinitely. Mises insisted that a 'reverse movement' must inevitably set in, ending the boom and ushering in the crisis even if entrepreneurial expectations were to remain optimistic and even if the operation of the international gold exchange standard did not produce contractionary pressures on the banking system.[26] Mises' discussion of the reverse movement problem was incredibly terse:

> This is one of the ways in which the equilibrium of the loan market is reestablished after it has been disturbed by the intervention of the banks. The increased productive activity that sets in when the banks start the policy of granting loans at less than the natural rate of interest at first causes the prices of production goods to rise while the prices of consumption goods, although they rise also, do so only in a moderate degree, viz., only insofar as they are raised by the rise in wages. Thus the tendency towards a fall in the rate of interest on loans that originates in the policy of the banks is at first strengthened. But soon a counter-movement sets in: the prices of consumption goods rise, those of production goods fall. That is, the rate of interest on loans rises again, it again approaches the natural rate.[27]

While this analysis set forth a broad outline of a theory of the trade cycle, it left several theoretical questions unanswered. The most important from the Austrian point of view were these: What was the market mechanism that could bring about the counter-movement? How can one explain how each entrepreneur pursuing his own interest can be led to make decisions which, when reconciled with the decisions of other managers, produce the end of the boom and the subsequent crisis? In other words, what are the microeconomic foundations for the "spontaneous *disorder*" that seems to characterize the business cycle?

Shortly after Hayek arrived in London, he was invited to deliver the special university lectures at the London School of Economics (1930–1931). Hayek used this occasion to elaborate on the Mises account of the boom and crisis in a way that made more explicit use of the Austrian description of production as a succession of stages through which resources must pass toward their ultimate destination of becoming consumer goods. This course would enable him to explain, he believed, why a credit-financed boom would necessarily have to end in crisis. The published version of his lectures, *Prices and production* (1931) immediately attracted the interest and commmentary of most of the leading economists of his

---

26. L. v. Mises, *Theory of money and credit* (1912; London, 1934), 362–63. Cf. John S. Mill, *Principles of Political economy with some of their applications to social polity,* 2 vols. (Toronto, 1965), 2:528 n.

27. Mises, ibid.

day and led to his appointment to the prestigious Tooke chair at the London School.[28]

Hayek analyzed the reverse-movement problem in Lecture 3. According to Hayek, a credit-induced boom leads entrepreneurs to bid resources away from consumer-goods industries without any compensating voluntary savings on the part of consumers. This resulting relative decrease in the supply of final goods and services at a time when wage incomes are rising due to the newly created money causes final goods prices to rise faster than the price of labor. There is a consequent decline in the real wage of labor (where real wage means the ratio of product price to per-unit labor cost). This is most pronounced in the stage of production nearest to the consumer and leads to a surge in profits on short-term investment projects. This surge encourages entrepreneurs to turn away from machine-intensive methods of production in favor of more labor-intensive methods, thereby discouraging sales of capital goods.[29] Entrepreneurs, determined to complete their endangered long-term capital projects, turn to the banks for more bank credit, and a tug of war begins. Producers seek new bank loans, the banking system accommodates the new loan demand by creating new money, product prices rise ahead of wage costs. In each market period the process repeats itself, with product prices always rising ahead of wages.[30] Hayek argued that any attempt to reduce the flow of bank credit will bring this

28. According to Abba Lerner, "I had just learned about the average period of production from Professor Friedrich von Hayek's first course at the London School of Economics on capital theory [1931–32]. At the time, a group of my fellow students (who were avid discussants of economic theory in the third year undergraduate study room) were very excited about my essay and its three-dimensional diagram. We persuaded the editor of the *Clare Market Review,* the LSE student magazine to print it in the magazine." Lerner, shortly before his death, revised the exposition under the title 'Paleo-Austrian capital theory,' and it has been published posthumously in A. Lerner, *Selected economic writings of Abba P. Lerner,* ed. D. Colander (New York, 1983), 563–83. Other responses to the main argument of *Prices and production* include John R. Hicks, 'Equilibrium and the trade cycle,' *Zeitschrift für Nationalökonomie* 4 (June 1933), reprinted in *Economic Journal* 18 (Oct. 1980): 523–34; Hans Neisser, 'Monetary expansion and the structure of production,' *Social Research* 1 (Nov. 1934): 434–57; and E. F. M. Durbin, *Purchasing power and trade depression: a critique of underconsumption theories* (London, 1933; revised 1934); R. G. Hawtrey, *Capital and employment* (London, 1952), 220–55. Last, but by no means least, was Piero Sraffa's stinging review, 'Dr. Hayek on money and capital,' *Economic Journal,* March 1932, 42–53. Also cf. Hayek's response, 'Money and capital: a reply,' *Economic Journal,* June 1932, 236–49, followed by Sraffa's 'Rejoinder,' ibid. 249–51. The Sraffa-Hayek debate has only in recent years inspired discussion; see M. Desai, 'The task of monetary theory: the Hayek-Sraffa debate in modern perspective' (working paper at Institut des Sciences Economiques in Belgium); M. Milgate, 'On the origin of the notion of "Intertemporal Equilibrium,"' *Economica* 46 (Feb. 1979): 1–10; and L. M. Lachmann, 'Austrian economics under fire: the Hayek-Sraffa duel in retrospect' (MS, 18 pp.).

29. See F. A. Hayek. 'The paradox of savings,' in idem, *Profits, interests and investment* (New York, 1939), 199–263. See C. Menger's discussion of the various 'orders' of production in his *Principles of economics* (Glencoe, Ill., 1950), 149–74. Cf. Hayek, *Prices and production,* 32–50; and J. R. Hicks, *Capital and time* (Oxford, 1973), 3–26.

30. Hayek always emphasized that the appropriate measure of real wages was the nominal wage divided by the price of the immediate product that labor helped produce. To

process of competing errors to a halt, turning the boom into a bust and leading to a readjustment of the capital-goods industry to a new equilibrium consistent with real patterns of consumer demand.[31]

In his 1969 restatement of the Ricardo effect, Hayek objected to Hicks's description of the mechanism presented in *Prices and production* as being predicated on wages "lagging" behind consumer-goods prices.[32] Hayek argued that his explanation did not depend upon a lag, if that meant that one incorrect market value is somehow trying to catch up with a correct value with which it must be in harmony. Rather, *both* product prices and wages are incorrect in the sense of being inconsistent with the underlying objective conditions of supply and demand for consumer goods. The fact that consumer expenditures are ultimately used to pay for intermediate goods creates the objective conditions in the market that generate a particular price sequence. As he argued in 1939 and 1942, when capital creation is financed through expanding bank credit, the signals that communicate the objective conditions to entrepreneurs are distorted, and incorrect investment decisions are made. The incorrect decisions are corrected by way of a crisis.

In essence, the Ricardo effect as Hayek described it occurred in the context of a process of genuine macroeconomic disequilibrium in which a crisis could not be averted. The crisis, he argued, was a necessary consequence of a boom brought about by money creation and characterized by a constant incompatibility between relative prices and the growing structure of real capital.

IV. *The Inevitability of the Crisis*

The first major point Hayek was making during his lectures and in several articles he published in the years immediately following *Prices and production* was simply that any real growth in the capital stock takes time and requires voluntary net savings. There is no way for an expansion of the money supply in the form of bank credit to short-circuit the process of economic growth. His second major point was more difficult. He argued that forced savings can only distort the mix of capital and consumer goods, by generating false relative price signals. These false signals throw the economy into a genuine macroeconomic disequilibrium that cannot be sustained over time. Eventually, the underlying consumer preferences will

---

distinguish this concept of the real wage from the usual nominal wage divided by the price index, Hayek spoke of the "own-wage" of labor. We have glossed this distinction in the text, since none of our conclusions is affected by it. See Hayek, 'The Ricardo effect' in idem, *Individualism and economic order*, 251–53.

31. F. A. Hayek, *Prices and production*, 90–94. On the tug-of-war thesis, see Murray N. Rothbard, *America's great depression* (Princeton; 1963), 17–21.

32. F. A. Hayek, 'Three elucidations,' 278–79. Curiously, Hayek had earlier described his theory as involving "lags"; see idem, *Prices and production*, 146.

reassert themselves. All that credit can do is to encourage competition between consumers and producers for the same pool of scarce resources, leading ultimately to a state of affairs in which producers switch from capital-intensive to labor-intensive methods of production. This switch, when carried out by a large number of managers, will choke off investment and bring on a full-scale crisis. But was either the switch or the crisis inevitable? Hayek argued that they are, but most of his early critics disagreed.[33]

Suppose the inflation caused by an expansion of bank credit could only last for, say, twenty-two months, but that a larger (i.e., 'more roundabout' or 'deeper') capital structure could be erected in less time. Wouldn't that mean that even when the eventual halt to credit expansion came, the economy would be richer with a larger per capita capital stock that could potentially produce enough income to generate the savings to maintain itself without collapse? If this scenario were possible—say, under conditions of less than full employment of resources—it would seem that a deliberate policy of credit creation could bootstrap the economy into a permanently larger flow of consumer goods without suffering the consequences of a disruptive crisis.[34]

At one place Hayek did agree that under certain restricted conditions a credit expansion could occur that did not end in collapse with a misplaced collection of capital goods. He warned, however, that the conditions were so stringent that they were unlikely to have much empirical relevance. This happy state of affairs could only occur in a 'progressive economy' where credit expansion did not lead to increased prices, but only managed to keep price levels constant as output grew. In this case, where voluntary saving was already high and the proportion of capital formation financed by forced saving was very low, it was just possible that a crisis could be averted if the credit expansion had been gradual and the contraction equally gradual. However, even in this case, he argued, forced saving did not actually increase the capital stock that can be accumulated in the long run, but only speeded up the process of creating it, since once the credit expansion stopped, "for a time the current voluntary savings will be used to take over, as it were, the capital created by means of forced saving; and current savings would then have to serve, not to make further new investment possible, but merely to maintain capital which has been formed in

---

33. Apparently, consumers must change their *flow* of savings in order to build up a *stock* of capital. Once the stock is built up (i.e., completed), savings can be reduced. H. Neiser, 'Monetary expansion,' 439–42, and also P. Sraffa, 'Dr. Hayek on money and capital,' 46–48. Cf. Haberler, *Prosperity and depression*, 54–56. Cf. L. Lachmann, *Capital and its structure* (London, 1956), 100–127.

34. Hayek, 'The present state and immediate prospects of the study of industrial fluctuating,' trans. from the German, 'Der Stand und die nächste . . . .," in Hayek, *Profits, interest and investment*, 180.

anticipation of these savings."³⁵ Under these circumstances, there would still be a relative price change for real wages and real cost of capital that would trigger a switch of techniques. But in this case, the switch would not lead to a crisis. Thus, as a theoretical matter, the crisis need not inevitably follow the boom. The likelihood of such a set of events, however, was extremely limited. As Hayek explained, this was not a scenario upon which to build one's plans for smooth economic growth, since the conditions under which it might obtain were extremely restrictive. As a practical matter, credit expansions followed by economic crises were the norm, not the exception.

In Hayek's early book, *Monetary theory and the trade cycle*, he presented a theory of trade cycles that made them endogenous to a monetary economy.³⁶ Cyclical fluctuations were simply the consequences of information problems inherent in an economic system that relied on credit banking. In *Prices and production* he described a process of economic growth that consisted of a time-consuming transition from one full-employment equilibrium to another. Business cycles were a consequence of attempting to finance this transition process by an expansion of the money supply via bank credit creation. In both these books, Hayek was well on his way to working out a macroeconomic theory that incorporated money and time into a theory of growth from one equilibrium state to another.

However, after the publication of Keynes' *General theory*, the rules of the game changed and professional attention shifted from the problem of economic growth as a transition process from one equilibrium to another, to the problem of the determination of flows of income and expenditure at a moment in time. The limelight shifted from Hayek to Keynes.

In 1939 Hayek produced a restatement of his view of the trade cycle more in line with these contemporary trends. Instead of starting from a position of full-employment equilibrium as he had before, he tried to meet Keynes and his followers on their own ground by making standard Keynesian assumptions of unemployment, rigid wages and interest rates, immobile labor, in order to show how the economic system would nevertheless still find itself unable to sustain a boom.³⁷ It was here that he first used the term the 'Ricardo effect' to underline the venerable pedigree of the mech-

---

35. Ibid.
36. Hayek, *Monetary theory*, 147.
37. This claim was asserted by Mises in 1912 and restated toward the end of the 1930s by Hayek. See esp. *Profits, interest and investment* where Hayek states: "What I am concerned with is to show how [the rate of profit] would act if the rate of interest failed to act at all" (6–7). At another place in his essay Hayek concludes, "We might get the trade cycle even without changes in the rate of interest" (64). Cf. O'Driscoll, *Economics as a coordination problem*, 94–96.

anism that figured so prominently in his attempt to give a microeconomic account of how individual maximizing decisions on the part of entrepreneurs will lead to the switch of techniques that brings about an economic crisis. In 1939, then, the debate over the Austrian theory of the business cycle focussed explicitly on the choice-theoretic foundations of the turning point in business cycles.

V. *Microfoundations of the Ricardo Effect*

Let us suppose along with Hayek that during the boom, consumer-product prices do rise ahead of wages, and hence real wages fall. Is this alteration in relative prices by itself sufficient to produce a crisis? As we have shown, Hayek believed that the price effect would induce entrepreneurs to substitute labor-intensive for labor-saving methods of production. Although each entrepreneur makes the decision to alter investment priorities independently of other entrepreneurs, the aggregative effect of their decisions is to produce a decline in net investment (that is, a decline in the sales of capital goods) and the onset of the crisis. By 1939 Hayek was arguing that the crisis will begin even if the monetary authorities stand ready to continue to supply bank credit at less than the natural rate.[38] Indeed, one important corollary of Hayek's Ricardo effect was to show that while a commodity standard (that is, a gold standard) might by itself be sufficient to arrest a boom, it was by no means necessary. A boom would end because of the incentives created by changes in the relationship among wages, prices, and profits.

In order to appreciate the choice-theoretic foundations of Hayek's Ricardo effect, it will be helpful to think of entrepreneurs as managing a number of on-line investment projects. In fact, the firm itself may be construed as a "portfolio of investment projects" rather than, as in standard Marshallian terms, an organization that produces a single product.[39] Now each investment project can be identified with a particular product and calculable rate of return. The entrepreneurs are assumed to reshuffle the amount of liquid capital available to them so as to maximize the present value of the firm: they calculate the rate of return on each separate project and then allocate money capital among the projects so as to equalize returns at the margin.[40]

---

38. Hayek, *Profits, interest and investment*, 64.
39. Members of the Austrian school were never endorsers of the Marshallian firm/industry distinction. See M. Rothbard, *Man, economy and the state*, 2 vols. (Princeton, 1962), 1:304–8). The modern 'management view' of the firm (similar to the Austrian view) sees the firm as a bundle of investment projects, see B. Henderson. *Henderson on corporate strategy* (Cambridge, Mass., 1972), 145–66. In the example taken from Hayek (to be discussed below) Hayek speaks of three "firms" rather than three investment projects within a single firm. This modification allows us to clarify our exposition considerably.
40. See Tsiang, *Variations of real wages*, 133–34. F. A. Hayek, 'The Ricardo effect.'

In his 1939, 1942, and 1969 expositions of the Ricardo effect mechanism, Hayek started his analysis (much as Ricardo did) with the firm in "long-period investment equilibrium" earning the same rate of return on the investments in each different project. In some projects capital turns over rapidly (bakery products), while in other projects (selling rare books) funds are typically tied up for years on end. Offsetting these 'waiting periods' of varying lengths are the actual returns on the different projects which differ in absolute amounts so as to yield an identical internal rate of return among all projects. The internal rate of return (I) is equal to the product of the rate of turnover (T) and the profit margin (M). In equilibrium then, $M = I/T$ for all projects.[41]

Now, let us disturb this equilibrium situation by permitting a sudden unexpected rise in product prices (relative to wages) and we discover that the rate of return on quick-turnover projects will have risen relative to the returns on slow-turnover projects. Entrepreneurs would obviously attempt to shift their money capital to quick-turnover projects in which the returns are now relatively greatest. These quick-turnover projects are necessarily more labor-intensive, and hence the demand for capital investment relative to labor will fall. Now it is absolutely vital to keep in mind the following arithmetic facts in order to appreciate the controversy surrounding Hayek's mechanism: (i) the internal return on quick-turnover projects has indeed risen relative to slower-turnover projects but (ii) all rates of return are necessarily higher than they were prior to the rise in product prices.[42]

The second of the two facts led T. Wilson, Nicholas Kaldor, and the majority of Hayek's critics after 1940 to accuse Hayek's theory of being

---

227. Hayek's firm-manager tries to maximize the "internal rate of return on investments"; see Lutz and Lutz, 16–26. For a general critique of using the internal rate of return as an index of investment success see Hirshleifer, *Investment, interest and capital* (Princeton, 1970), 51–56, and K. E. Boulding, 'The theory of a single investment,' *Quarterly Journal of Economics* 49 (May 1935).

41. According to Hayek, "the per annum net percentage return on the whole capital of a firm (or on any part of it for which we find it necessary to compute separately), net of 'wages of management' and of risk premium, we shall designate as the 'internal rate of return.'" Initially, the internal rate of return is equal on all projects. Hayek explained: "If we call the internal rate of return I, the rate of turnover T, and the profit margin M, the relationship will be presented by $I = TM$ or $M = I/T$. If . . . the internal rate is 6 percent, [then] the profit margin of a firm turning over its capital six times a year will have to be 1 percent, while a firm turning over its capital only once in two years will have to earn 12 percent on all sales, and a firm turning over its capital only once in every ten years will have to earn a profit of 60 percent" (Hayek, 'Ricardo effect,' 227).

42. "For the three [investments] which we have just considered by way of illustration, the first (with an annual rate of turnover $T = 6$) will find its profit margin increased from 1 to 6 percent; the second [with $T = \frac{1}{2}$] from [12] to [17] percent; and the third (with $T = \frac{1}{10}$) from 60 to 65 percent. Multiplying these profit margins by the corresponding rates of turnover, we obtain the new internal rates of return of $6 \times 6 = 36$ percent for the first, $[\frac{1}{2} \times 17 = 8.5]$ percent for the second, and $\frac{1}{10} \times 65 = 6.5$ percent for the third [investment activity]" (Hayek, 'Ricardo effect,' 227).

logically inconsistent.⁴³ According to Hayek's critics the rational firm-manager would not simply switch from one kind of project to another, but would try to invest more in each and every project. If before the rise in product prices all returns were equal to the firm's cost of capital, then in the next equilibrium position the scale of the firm must increase because the firm will invest in all its investment projects until each internal rate of return falls back down to equal the cost of capital.⁴⁴ The cost of capital remains fixed throughout the analysis because Hayek has assumed that during the boom the banking authorities are making loanable funds freely available at a rate of interest below the natural rate.

According to Kaldor:

> [Hayek committed the same fallacy as those who argue that] a rise in demand for a commodity will cause a rise in its price, and the rise in price causes a restriction in demand (because less is bought at a higher price than a lower price), the increase in demand will lead to a reduction in the amount bought. No doubt the rise in price will make the increase in purchases (following upon the increase in demand) less than it would have been if the price had not risen. But it cannot make it less than before, since the price has only risen because the amount bought has gone up. In the same way, the reduction in capital intensity will make the rise in investment expenditure less than it would have been if capital intensity had remained constant. But it cannot eliminate it altogether because capital intensity would not have fallen if investment expenditure had not risen.⁴⁵

In short, Kaldor claimed that Hayek had assumed a situation in which the substitution effect outweighed the scale effect, a situation which a comparative static analysis of the Ricardo effect mechanism demonstrated to be impossible.

Hayek responded to Kaldor's criticism by claiming that it missed the point. Kaldor along with other critics seemed unable to understand his mechanism for two basic reasons: (i) their stubborn attachment to the 'perfect competition' model of market structure even when the descriptive realism of that model was at odds with the particular market under study and (ii) their insistence on evaluating his Ricardo effect mechanism solely within a comparative statics framework.

Consider the first charge. If the loanable-funds market were perfect in that the cost of capital facing the firm were to remain constant regardless of the absolute volume of funds the firm wished to borrow, then the rational manager would indeed expand the size of the firm in all directions

---

43. Kaldor, 'Professor Hayek and the concertina effect,' *Economica*, Nov. 1942. Reprinted in Kaldor, *Essays on economic stability and growth* (London, 1960), 2:148–76.

44. Ibid. See also Wilson, 'Capital theory and the trade cycle,' 177; Hawtrey, *Capital and employment*, 240–45; and Tsiang, *Variations of real wages*, 141–44.

45. Kaldor, ibid.

as Kaldor insisted he would. But, Hayek argued, the market for loanable funds is not and cannot be modeled as 'perfect' under these conditions. Under any real conditions, the cost of capital facing the firm could not remain equal to the external market rate of interest while the firm expanded in size; there is a "limit beyond which [the firm-owner] can raise capital only at higher costs."[46] Loans to the same borrower will never represent the "same commodity" in the sense in which the term is used in theory of competition. Bankers will not lend infinite amounts of bank credit to any single borrower at a uniform rate because they will perceive an increased risk associated with a higher debt-to-equity ratio.[47] But are the bankers' perceptions based on an understanding of the real underlying conditions that prevail in the market or are their perceptions based instead on the imperfect and incomplete information available to the creditors at the time the applications for the loans are received?

Hayek later clarified this point. He admitted that creditors "misjudge" the credit-worthiness of borrowers because they fail to take into consideration the favorable impact inflation will have on the firm's revenues. In the long run, increasing product prices might imply that the credit-worthiness of a firm has increased and therefore should justify increased loans at no additional risk premium. But long before creditors perceive that this sort of long-run equilibrium adjustment has occurred, the Ricardo effect will have already asserted itself. Hayek's argument then rested on the assumption that increasing product prices increased the firm's demand for loanable funds more quickly than the banks could subjectively reevaluate the credit-worthiness of the firm itself. Under these circumstances, the firm is constrained by the upward sloping portion of the supply curve of credit which acts as a brake on the firm's expansion.[48] Hence, with incomplete knowledge the scale effect cannot outweigh the substitution effect as Kaldor maintained. In this way Hayek readily admitted what several of his critics had pointed out: the upward sloping supply of credit to the firm acted as a kind of rationing device to constrain the growth of the firm. The manager adjusts by investing his limited capital in short-term (that is, labor-intensive) investment projects.

Hayek's resort to this kind of credit rationing was by no means *ad hoc*. The credit rationing was a rational response to the informational lags that occur during a period of accelerating inflation. The assessment of the credit-worthiness of the firm in one period imposes a "finance constraint" on the amount it can borrow (at the old interest rate) in the next period.[49]

---

46. Hayek, 'Ricardo effect,' 237.
47. Ibid. 236. Cf. M. Kalecki, 'The principle of increasing risk,' *Economica*, Nov. 1937.
48. Hayek, 'Ricardo effect,' 235–37.
49. Cf. M. Kohn, 'In defense of the finance constraint,' *Economic Inquiry* 19 (181): 177–95.

Consider, now, the merits of Hayek's charge that his critics misunderstood his theory because of their preoccupation with perfectly competitive equilibrium conditions and comparative statics. According to Hayek, even if the supply of credit were infinitely elastic to the economy as a whole, the Ricardo effect would still occur because of the finance constraints encountered along the path of business expansion. However, one cannot see that point simply by comparing two equilibrium states. Such a comparison, Hayek argued, would disguise precisely the mechanism he was interested in discussing. As he put it:

> The situation which we consider . . . is indeed the classical instance of a cumulative process. . . . the perfectly elastic supply of credit at a rate of interest lower than the internal rate of all or most of the firms will be the cause of continuous changes of prices and money incomes where each change makes further changes necessary. There is no point in saying with respect to such a situation that "in equilibrium there must" exist such and such a relationship, because it necessarily follows from the assumptions that the relationship between at least some prices must be out of equilibrium.[50]

This disequilibrium is a situation in which the different price-determining tendencies in the economy are inconsistent with one another and lead to perpetual change. Hayek tried to explicate his problem by resorting to an imaginative analogy: "The question is rather similar to that whether, by pouring a liquid fast enough into one side of a vessel, we can raise the level at that side above that of the rest to any extent we desire." Of course, we cannot, since this depends upon the viscosity of the liquid itself. Hence, "the speed at which an increase of incomes leads to an increase in the demand for consumers' goods limits the extent to which, by spending more money on factors of production, we can raise their prices relative to those of the products."[51] In the end, real wages will have to fall, if for no other reason than the unavailability of consumer goods to meet the demand; and hence it is inevitable that the Ricardo effect will be triggered.

To throw Hayek's problem into relief, consider the subsequent Hicksian construct of the 'progressive economy.'[52] In a progressive economy the managers expect the demand for their products to be rising. Based on this expectation they proceed to invest and expand the scales of their firms. They do this over a market period long enough for the net investment that takes place to generate exactly enough extra income and new savings for

---

50. Hayek, 'Ricardo effect,' 239.
51. Ibid. 241. Cf. idem, 'Three elucidations,' 281.
52. J. R. Hicks, *Capital and growth* (Oxford, 1956), 90–93. This is not to be confused with Hayek's use of the term 'progressive economy,' referred to earlier in this article.

savings and investment to remain equal to each other. In Hicks's progressive economy, investment generates income without delay—the period of construction of capital goods is assumed to be zero.[53] In the new equilibrium position, managers find out that they have constructed exactly the quantity and variety of capital goods they wished to have at the beginning of the market period. Thus, the economy started out in stock equilibrium and ended up in stock equilibrium. In addition, the flow of net investment during the market period was exactly matched by a flow of net savings. Flow and stock equilibrium occur together in the progressive economy. The boom, to return to Hayek's terminology, has proceeded smoothly and without the slightest possibility of ending in crisis.

Now clearly this construction of a progressive economy rules out the Mises-Hayek crisis phenomenon as a matter of definition. If all plans are coordinated at the beginning of the market period and also at the end, then where is the "cluster of business errors" that constitutes the crisis? In this sense, Hayek was quite correct when he objected to Kaldor's use of comparative static methodology. The methodology of comparing isolated equilibrium states rules out precisely the phenomenon of the crisis.

Suppose on the other hand, that Hayek's entrepreneurs only *believe* they are in a progressive state. The lowering of the interest rate suggests that consumers have provided a larger amount of real savings and the managers eagerly begin the task of constructing the new equipment.[54] But the entrepreneurs have only been deceived into thinking the flow of new voluntary savings is larger than it really is because (as we know) it is only the money supply that is increasing. Now the flow of actual net savings is brought exactly into balance with the flow of actual net investment through the familiar forced-saving mechanism. Still, at the end of the period the actors come to realize that their stocks of capital goods are inappropriate to satisfy consumer demand. In old-fashioned terminology, there is too much fixed capital and not enough circulating capital—a realization brought on by Hayek's Ricardo effect mechanism. In summary, we have stock equilibrium at the beginning of the market period, flow equilibrium within the period, and stock *dis*equilibrium at the end.

Hayek's point is that precisely because the entrepreneurs are mistaken about the true real savings of the consumers, a time must come when they have evidence of their mistakes and take steps to correct them. A comparative static analysis of the economy at two points in times, where the capital structure at T_2 is larger than at T_1 compares two equilibrium situations. Hayek preferred a market period approach over a comparative static analysis because it enabled him to identify the sequence of events by which

---

53. Ibid. 91.
54. Hayek, *Monetary theory and the trade cycle*; and cf. Rothbard, *America's great depression*, 16–17.

the entrepreneurs come to realize that the equilibrium toward which they are all heading is no longer economic. They come to that conclusion because the underlying structure of production makes the simultaneous realization of their business plans impossible. This information is transmitted to the entrepreneurs through the price system by way of the internal rates of return on investment projects. Hayek's objection to applying comparative statics to this problem of dynamical change and adjustment seems to us remarkably cogent. The problem is not to learn about maladjustments by comparing states of equilibrium but rather to ask if the conditions prevailing at T_1 make the transition to T_2 at all possible. Kaldor's approach indeed assumed away the very problem that Hayek's theory was designed to analyze, the problem of the transition an economy undergoes in moving from one coordinated capital structure to another. The revival in the 1970s of interest in modeling this transition process gives Hayek's favorite mechanism a decidedly modern ring.[55]

VI. Conclusion

By emphasizing the inapplicability of the perfectly competitive model especially in the supply of loanable funds, and by insisting on the disequilibrium nature of the cumulative process, Hayek was speaking a different language from his peers in the 1930s, 1940s and, surprisingly, in the late 1960s as well. Hayek challenged the relevance and appropriateness of comparative static analysis to an expanding economy. His struggle to free himself from the precepts of comparative static analysis constitutes, in our view, the elusive element in his thinking and explains why so much miscommunication occurred. Hayek's most formidable opponent, Kaldor, seemed unable to structure the problem except in comparative static terms, and this we believe is what prompted Hayek to focus on their methodological differences.

It is gratifying that by the 1970s Hayek's favorite problem of the process of adjustment from one coordinated state of equilibrium to another was finally recognized and tackled by some of the finest minds in the profession, including one of Hayek's own critics—Hicks.[56] While the particular solution and the methods of analysis Hayek proposed may be controversial, there is now no longer any question that the problem Hayek raised about the feasibility of reaching one equilibrium based on the conditions

---

55. Hicks, *Capital and time*, 47–80. See also E. Burmeister, *Capital theory and dynamics*. See, however, Lachmann's 'A reconsideration of the Austrian theory of industrial fluctuations,' *Economica* 7 (May, 1940); in idem, *Capital expectations and the market process* (Kansas City, 1977), 267–86.

56. Hicks, *Capital and time*, 81–150. Hicks like Hayek harks back to Ricardo's machinery chapter for doctrinal precedent. See Hicks.

prevailing prior to reaching that equilibrium is an important one. The issues Hayek raised during the 1930s have their counterpart in the modern debates about the structural limits placed on short-run macroeconomic policy. This, of course, remains a central concern of the 'new classical economists,' some of whom have recognized Hayek as a pioneer investigator.[57] We have taken a second look at Hayek's Ricardo effect in order to illuminate certain novel elements in Hayek's thinking and their relevance to contemporary economic theorizing.

---

57. Hayek did not reach the same conclusion as certain radical exponents of the "new Classical economics." For one thing, Hayek would not agree that a fully announced set of policy changes will have no effect on real macroeconomic variables as has been maintained by T. Sargent and N. Wallace in '"Rational expectations," the optimal monetary instrument and the optimal money supply rule,' *Journal of Political Economy* 83 (April 1975): 241–54. Hayek argued that Keynesian stimulative policies would have short-run beneficial effects. Hayek disagreed with Keynes when Hayek insisted these beneficial effects would be at the expense of long-run disruptions.

[20]
Friedman on the Quantity Theory and Keynesian Economics

Don Patinkin
The Hebrew University of Jerusalem

The article is based on textual evidence from the quantity-theory and Keynesian literature. It shows, first, that the conceptual framework of a portfolio demand for money that Friedman denotes as the "quantity theory" is actually that of Keynesian economics. Conversely, Friedman detracts from the true quantity theory by stating that its formal short-run analysis assumes real output constant, while only prices change. Friedman also incorrectly characterizes Keynesian economics in terms of absolute price rigidity. He does this by overlooking the systematic analysis by Keynes and the Keynesians of the role of downward wage flexibility during unemployment, and of the "inflationary gap" during full employment. Otherwise Friedman's interpretation of Keynes is the standard textbook one of an economy in a "liquidity-trap" unemployment equilibrium. The author restates his alternative interpretation of Keynesian economics in terms of unemployment *dis*equilibrium.

> "When *I* use a word," Humpty Dumpty said, in rather a scornful tone, "it means just what I choose it to mean—neither more nor less."
> "The question is," said Alice, "whether you *can* make words mean so many different things."
> "The question is," said Humpty Dumpty, "which is to be master—that's all." [LEWIS CARROLL, *Through the Looking Glass*]

Milton Friedman's recent article on "A Theoretical Framework for Monetary Analysis" (Friedman 1970a) has two concerns. The first and—from the viewpoint of the space devoted to it—major one is the chapter in the

---

I am indebted to my colleagues Yoram Ben-Porath, Yoel Haitovsky, Giora Hanoch, Ephraim Kleiman, and Josef May, and to Stanley Fischer of the University of Chicago, for helpful criticisms of early drafts of this paper.

history of monetary doctrine which deals with the nature of—and interrelationships between—the quantity theory and Keynesian monetary theory. The second concern is to present an analytical framework to analyze the dynamics of monetary adjustment. In this paper I shall concentrate primarily on the doctrinal aspects of Friedman's paper. For this reason I shall not discuss Friedman's subsequent paper (1971), which—with one exception (see n. 9 below)—does not deal with these aspects.

Clearly, questions about the history of economic doctrine are empirical questions which can be answered only on the basis of evidence cited from the relevant literature. Indeed, the "elementary canons of scholarship call for [such] documentation" (Friedman 1970b, p. 318). My criticism of Friedman is, accordingly, that on many occasions he has not provided such evidence; that, indeed, on some occasions he has ignored the detailed evidence which has been adduced against the views he expresses; and that on still other occasions he has indulged in casual empiricism in the attempt to support his doctrinal interpretations. These criticisms will be documented in what follows.

I. Friedman on the Quantity Theory: The Doctrinal-History Aspects

In the paper under discussion, Friedman once again (see Friedman 1956, 1968) presents a theory of money whose central feature is a demand function for money, where this demand is treated "as part of capital or wealth theory, concerned with the composition of the balance sheet or portfolio of assets" (Friedman 1970a, p. 202). Accordingly, his demand function depends on wealth and the alternative rates of return on money and other assets (1970a pp. 202–05).

If Friedman had simply presented this as a conceptual framework to be used for monetary analysis, then few would have disagreed with him. On the contrary, most of us would have enjoyed the systematic clarity of the exposition; would have considered the suggested influence on the demand for money of the division between human and nonhuman wealth (which Friedman carries over from his well-known work on the consumption function) to be a fruitful one, well worth exploring; and would also have benefited from the insightful presentation of the rate of change of the price level as one of the alternative rates of return which affect the demand for money. For though this last factor has been referred to in both the quantity-theory and Keynesian literature (Fisher 1922, p. 63; Brown 1939, p. 34), it was not systematically integrated into our thinking until the work of Friedman and his associates, particularly Cagan (1956).

But, as indicated in my introductory remarks, Friedman is not concerned solely with substantive analytical matters but has a major concern with the doctrinal-history aspects of monetary theory. Once again, few would have disagreed if Friedman had described his conceptual framework as being a particular instance of the Keynesian liquidity-preference theory, while noting the specific contributions indicated in the preceding paragraph. This, however, is not Friedman's way. Instead he tells us that "the general theoretical framework that underlies" his empirical studies—and which has been referred to at the beginning of this section—is that of "the quantity theory of money" (Friedman 1970a, p. 193). Accordingly, he presents this framework as the sequel to a fairly detailed presentation, first of Fisher's transactions equation, $MV = PT$ (which Friedman describes as being primarily concerned with "the mechanical aspects of the payments process");[1] then of the income form of this equation, $MV = Py$; and finally of the Cambridge cash-balance equation, $M = kPy$ (with which Friedman claims the closest affinity) (1970a, pp. 194–202).

What, then, does this leave as Keynes's contribution to his theoretical framework? Friedman's answer to this question is expressed in the following passage:

> J. M. Keynes's liquidity preference analysis (discussed further in section 5, below) reinforced the shift of emphasis from the transactions version of the quantity equation to the cash-balances version—a shift of emphasis from mechanical aspects of the payments process to the qualities of money as an asset.[2] Keynes's analysis, though strictly in the Cambridge cash-balances tradition, was much more explicit in stressing the role of money as one among many assets, and of interest rates as the relevant cost of holding money. [1970a, p. 202]

In his subsequent discussion of the demand function for money in section 5—entitled "The Keynesian Challenge to the Quantity Theory"—Friedman goes on to say:

> Keynes's basic challenge to the reigning theory [was in his proposition that the] demand function for money has a particular empirical form—corresponding to absolute liquidity preference —that makes velocity highly unstable much of the time, so that changes in the quantity of money would, in the main, simply produce changes in V in the opposite direction. [P. 206]

Thus the picture which Friedman attempts to create is clear: namely, the conceptual framework he uses for monetary analysis is that of the quantity theory; its basic difference from the Keynesian theory lies in the

---

[1] As a general characterization, this is somewhat unfair; for, as I have shown elsewhere, Fisher's analysis of the effects of a monetary change is actually far less mechanical than that of the Cambridge School (Patinkin 1965, pp. 166–67).

[2] From much the same viewpoint, one could say that Newton's theory reinforced the shift from Ptolemaic to Copernican astronomy.

fact that the latter assumed the demand function for money to become highly (infinitely) interest elastic. As against this picture, I would like to present the following one: the conceptual framework which Friedman uses to analyze the demand for money is that of the Keynesian theory of liquidity preference—with Friedman's addendum that empirically this demand does not become highly (infinitely) elastic, and is indeed relatively inelastic. And, as important as are the policy implications of this addendum, we should not let it wag the theory.

It is obviously no criticism of Friedman—nor does it derogate from his stature as a monetary economist—to say that his analytical framework is Keynesian. All that is being criticized is Friedman's persistent refusal to recognize this is so.

Let me also say that to accept the Keynesian conceptual framework for the analysis of the demand for money does not imply that one must reject the quantity-theory conclusions about the long-run impact of monetary changes on the economy. This is a proposition which has been emphasized for many years in the literature (Modigliani 1944, sec. 14; Patinkin 1949, pp. 23–26; 1954; 1965, chaps. 10–11). But the converse of this proposition is also true: namely, that there is no need for modern-day quantity theorists to attempt to reinterpret the history of monetary doctrine so as to minimize the Keynesian nature of their analytical framework.

As I have shown elsewhere (Patinkin 1969a, pp. 58–61), there are two (related) justifications for the usual practice of treating the Keynesian theory as a distinct one, and not simply as a variation of the Cambridge cash-balance theory. The first is the different relationship of these two theories to one of the central distinctions of economic analysis—that between stocks and flows. In particular, Keynesian liquidity-preference theory is concerned with the optimal relationship between the stock of money and the stocks of other assets, whereas the quantity theory (including the Cambridge school) was primarily concerned with the direct relationship between the stock of money and the flow of spending on goods and services. Furthermore, the quantity-theory discussion of this relationship either did not make the distinction between stocks and flows—or at least was imprecise about it. This stands in sharp contrast with the Keynesian analysis of the effect of monetary changes in terms of initial balance-sheet adjustments among assets which generate changes in their relative yields, which in turn ultimately affect the flows of expenditures and receipts. Similarly, quantity theorists paid little, if any, attention to the effects on the rate of interest and other variables of shifts in the tastes of individuals as to the form in which they wish to hold their assets.

The second justification lies in the different treatment by these two theories of what continues to be[3] one of the central issues of monetary

---

[3] As attested particularly by the extensive empirical literature of the past fifteen

economics—the influence of the rate of interest on the demand for money. For, though quantity theorists did frequently recognize this influence,[4] they did not fully integrate it into their thinking. Most revealingly, they failed to do so in their empirical work—which, by its very nature, confronted them with a concrete situation in which they were called upon to list the major theoretical variables which might explain the data, even if some of the variables might subsequently be rejected as statistically unimportant. It is therefore significant that the first empirical study (to the best of my knowledge) which explicitly deals with the influence of interest on the demand for money is the 1939 Keynesian-inspired study by A. J. Brown.[5]

These hallmarks of the Keynesian liquidity-preference theory also characterize Friedman's exposition. It should be said that Friedman has taken some account of criticisms and has in recent years partly acknowledged this intellectual indebtedness. Thus in his 1956 essay Friedman presented his analytical framework as one that "conveys the flavor" of the Chicago quantity-theory tradition of Simons, Mints, Knight, and Viner—and did not even mention Keynes or the liquidity-preference theory (Friedman 1956, pp. 3–4). In contrast, in his 1968 and 1970 essays he does not mention either the Chicago School or its individual members—and he describes his framework as "a reformulation of the quantity theory that has been strongly affected by the Keynesian analysis of liquidity preference" (Friedman 1968, p. 439b).

At the same time, Friedman has not yet faced up to the implications of the fact[6] that whatever the similarities in policy proposals (and there are significant differences here too [Patinkin 1969a, p. 47]), the theoretical framework of the Chicago School of the 1930s and 1940s—a major center of the quantity theory at the time—differed fundamentally from his. In particular, the Chicago School—as exemplified especially by Henry Simons—was basically not interested in the demand function for money (Simons never even mentioned this concept!) and carried out its analysis instead in terms of Fisher's $MV = PT$ equation. Furthermore (and in marked contrast with Friedman) the basic assumption of the Chicago School analysis was that the velocity of circulation is unstable. Correspondingly, it considered sharp changes in this velocity to be a major source of instability in the economy.

Similarly, Friedman has not changed his basic contention that his con-

---

years; see the convenient summary in Laidler (1970, chap. 8), noting especially the questions relating to the rate of interest listed on p. 89.

[4] For specific references to the writings of Walras, Wicksell, the much-neglected Karl Schlesinger, Fisher, and the Cambridge School (Marshall, Pigou, and especially Lavington), see Patinkin (1965, p. 372 and supplementary notes C, D).

[5] For supporting documentation and fuller discussion of this and the preceding paragraph, see Patinkin (1969a, sec. 4).

For a more systematic and detailed treatment of the questions at issue here, see my paper on "Keynesian Monetary Theory and the Cambridge School" (1972b).

[6] Demonstrated in Patinkin (1969a, secs. 2, 3).

ceptual framework is that of the quantity theory. Indeed, his 1970 essay includes a further misinterpretation of the nature of this theory. In particular, in his discussion of the transactions approach to the quantity theory, Friedman makes the familiar distinction between the Fisherine equation $MV = PT$ and the "income form of the quantity equation," $MV = Py$, where y is real national income and V accordingly represents the income velocity of circulation. He then goes on to say:

> Clearly, the transactions and income versions of the quantity theory involve very different conceptions of the role of money. For the transactions version, the most important thing about money is that it is transferred. For the income version, the most important thing is that it is held. This difference is even more obvious from the Cambridge cash-balances version of the quantity equation. Indeed, the income version can perhaps best be regarded as a way station between the Fisher and the Cambridge versions. [1970a, p. 200]

No evidence is given in support of this assertion about the nature of the income version of the transactions approach—which, if true, would obviously increase the possible relevance of Friedman's interpretation of the quantity theory in terms of the individual's demand to hold money as a component of a portfolio of assets. This is not the occasion to undertake a full-scale study of the development of the income-velocity form of the quantity theory. Let me only say that a brief examination of the interwar quantity-theory literature shows that the income-velocity approach was used as a variant of the transactions approach—and involved no more emphasis on the *holding* of money (as contrasted with its being *transferred*) than did the latter. The reasons for using income velocity were either considerations of data availability or the feeling that the volume of final output and/or the price level of this output were more meaningful economic variables than the gross volume of transactions and/or its price level (to use modern terms, more strategic variables). To the extent that the income-velocity approach constituted a "way station," it was one on the road between the Fisherine quantity theory and the Keynesian income-expenditure approach. It was not one on the road to the Cambridge cash-balance approach.[7]

I have so far criticized Friedman for claiming too much for the quantity theory; let me now indicate one direction in which he has claimed too little. This occurs in the context of his identification of the quantity theory with the short-run assumption that real income is constant, while

---

[7] This paragraph is based on Robertson (1948, pp. 33, 38), Angell (1933, pp. 43–46), Warburton (1945, p. 161), and Chandler (1940, pp. 71–72; 1953, p. 543). I hope on some future occasion to deal more fully with this question, as well as the general question of the relations between the three forms of the quantity theory.

only the price level changes (for details, see the next section). Here Friedman states:

> There is nothing in the logic of the quantity theory that specifies the dynamic path of adjustment, nothing that requires the whole adjustment to take place through P rather than through k or y. It was widely recognized that the adjustment during what Fisher, for example, called 'transition periods' would in practice be partly in k and in y as well as in P. *Yet this recognition was not incorporated in formal theoretical analysis.* [Friedman 1970a, p. 208; italics added]

The facts of the case, however, are quite different. Thus Fisher's analysis of the "transition period"—which was assumed to last ten years on the average, and during which both the level of real output and the velocity of circulation were changing—assigned a critical role to the difference between the money and real rates of interest. In this way Fisher integrated his analysis of the "transition period" into his formal theoretical analysis of the distinction between these two rates of interest—a distinction that was a basic component of his theoretical framework even before he turned to monetary problems. It might also be noted that Fisher wrote incomparably more on his monetary proposals for mitigating the cyclical problems of the "transition period" than on the long-run proportionality of prices to money. This concentration on short-run analysis was even more true of the policy-oriented Chicago quantity-theory school of the 1930s and 1940s: indeed, Simons and Mints showed little, if any, interest in the long-run aspects of the quantity theory. Again, representatives of the Cambridge School such as Lavington, Pigou, and Robertson wrote entire monographs on the problems of the "trade cycle" and of "industrial fluctuations"—and devoted substantial parts of these monographs to the analysis of the role of money in these fluctuations. Needless to say, this role was also a primary concern of Wicksell and Hawtrey. Thus, far from being a question dealt with in "asides," the systematic analysis of the short-run variations in output and velocity generated by monetary changes was a major concern of the pre-Keynesian quantity theorists.[8]

In order to avoid any possible misunderstanding, I wish to emphasize that Friedman in his own application of his "modern quantity theory" obviously assigns a central role to the short-run effects of changes in the quantity of money on k and y; what I am criticizing here, however, is

---

[8] See Fisher (1896; 1907; 1922, chap. 4). For a detailed description of Fisher's voluminous writings on his policy proposals (the main one of which was to stabilize the price level), see Reeve (1943, chap. 11). On the Chicago School, see Patinkin (1969a, secs. 2, 3). This question is discussed in greater detail in my paper "On the Short-Run Non-Neutrality of Money in the Quantity Theory" (Patinkin 1972a).

Friedman's contention that the traditional quantity theorists themselves did not recognize this role in their "formal theoretical analysis."

II. Friedman on the Quantity Theory: Some Analytical Issues

In the preceding section I have dealt with the history of doctrine. In the present section I shall turn briefly to analytical issues and again criticize Friedman for claiming too little: namely, for not presenting the long-run quantity theory in the most general way that one can, once one has decided to reformulate it. To a large extent, what is involved here is a question of tastes. My own are for introducing explicitly into the mathematical model the assumptions of the text—particularly when this yields (without much inconvenience) a more general model.

Friedman's presentation of the "simple quantity theory" is in terms of the following general equilibrium model which, "in Keynes's spirit, . . . refers to a short period in which the capital stock can be regarded as fixed" (1970a, p. 218):

$$f(y, r) + g(r) = y, \tag{1}$$

$$l(y, r) = \frac{M_0}{P}, \tag{2}$$

where y is real national income, r is the rate of interest, and M_0 is the fixed quantity of money; and where the left-hand side of (1) consists respectively of the consumption and investment functions, while the left-hand side of (2) consists of the demand function for money—all expressed in real terms (Friedman 1970a, pp. 217–18).

This is a system of two equations in three variables: y, P, and r. Hence, continues Friedman,

> there is a missing equation. Some one of these variables must be determined by relationships outside this system. . . . The simple quantity theory adds the equation
>
> $$y = y_0; \tag{3}$$
>
> that is real income is determined outside the system. In effect, it appends to this system the Walrasian equations of general equilibrium, regards them as independent of those equations defining the aggregates, and as giving the value of [y], and thereby reduces this system to one of [two] equations determining [two] unknowns.

Equation (3) then permits "a sequential solution" of system (1)–(2). In particular, substituting from (3) into (1), we can solve for $r = r_0$. Substitution of this value into (2) then yields the "classical quantity equation"

$$M_0 = Pl(y_0, r_0) = P \frac{l(y_0, r_0)}{y_0} y_0 = \frac{P y_0}{V}, \qquad (4)$$

which then determines P (Friedman 1970a, pp. 219–20).

Instead of initially creating a problem of a "missing equation" which is then solved by determining y "outside the system," I would prefer including in the model from the very beginning that part of the "Walrasian equations of general equilibrium" needed to determine y endogenously. This preference is reinforced by the fact that all that need be added to the model for this purpose are the production function and the excess-demand equation in the labor market. For the assumption of wage and price flexibility (which, in the context of the quantity theory, is in any event being made) assures that the equilibrium level of employment will be achieved in the labor market. And since the capital stock is fixed, the production function then determines the equilibrium level of real output, y, corresponding to this level of employment. Indeed, this procedure has been the standard one in the literature since Modigliani (1944).

Again, in view of the crucial role that Friedman assigns to the real-balance effect in assuring the long-run equilibrium of the system (Friedman 1970a, pp. 206, 215), I would prefer introducing this effect explicitly into the commodity-demand functions. This would also seem to provide an expression of Friedman's view that

> the key insight of the quantity-theory approach is that such a discrepancy [that is, between the nominal quantity of money demanded and supplied] will be manifested primarily in attempted spending. [1970a, p. 225]

It will not come as a surprise to the reader that these modifications yield a model which I have developed at length elsewhere (Patinkin 1954; 1965, chaps. 9–10). The long-run proportionality of P to M specified by the quantity theory holds true in this model even though it cannot, in Friedman's terms, be "solved sequentially" (or, to use the more usual term, it cannot be dichotomized), so as to reduce it to one equation (that for money) in one variable (the price level). Thus this model requires us to abandon the traditional single-equation form of the quantity theory which Friedman apparently prefers. On the other hand, the model has what is for me the more than compensating advantage of demonstrating that the long-run validity of the quantity theory does not (as it was at one time thought—and as might mistakenly be inferred from Friedman's presentation) depend on the restrictive assumption that the system can be dichotomized in the foregoing manner (Patinkin 1965, p. 175).

III. Friedman on Keynesian Economics

A Keynesian, according to Friedman, is one who makes the above system (1)–(2) determinate in the short run by adding the equation

$$P = P_0 \qquad (5)$$

instead of equation (3), $y = y_0$ (Friedman 1970a, pp. 206, 219–20). Thus, the contrast that Friedman tries to draw is between the quantity theorists —who assume real income constant and prices flexible, and indeed changing in direct proportion to changes in the money supply, and the Keynesians— who make the opposite assumptions about real income and prices.[9]

Let me first of all point out that this description of the quantity theory is misleading. For, though Friedman presents both of the foregoing positions as referring to the short run (Friedman 1970a, pp. 206, 222), quantity theorists did not actually assume real income to remain constant— and the price level to change proportionately with the quantity of money— except in the long run. In the short run (as shown at the end of Section I above) they believed that a (say) decrease in the quantity of money would decrease both the velocity of circulation and the level of real output as well as the price level. Thus part of what Friedman presents as a difference between Keynes and the quantity theory is really a difference between these "runs."

Let me also say that presentations of the Keynesian theory of unemployment usually begin with an analysis based on the assumption of absolute wage and price rigidity. However, the basic question here at issue is whether these presentations have gone on to generalize the theory to the case of wage and price flexibility.

The clear implication of Friedman's interpretation (1970a, esp. pp. 206, 209–11) is that Keynesian economics provided no such generalization. But Friedman achieves this interpretation only by overlooking the chapter in the *General Theory* devoted to—and indeed, entitled—"Changes in Money Wages,"[10] by overlooking those portions of interpretations of

---

[9] In Friedman 1971 (p. 324, n. 1) this interpretation of Keynes is slightly modified— but not in a way that really affects the following criticism.

[10] I have long considered this chapter to be the apex of Keynes's analysis (Patinkin 1951, p. 283, n. 38). In support of this interpretation let me cite its opening paragraphs: "It would have been an advantage if the effects of a change in money-wages could have been discussed in an earlier chapter. For the Classical Theory has been accustomed to rest the supposedly self-adjusting character of the economic system on an assumed fluidity of money-wages; and, when there is rigidity, to lay on this rigidity the blame of maladjustment. It was not possible, however, to discuss this matter fully until our own theory had been developed. For the consequences of a change in money-wages are complicated. A reduction in money-wages is quite capable in certain circumstances of affording a stimulus to output, as the classical theory supposes. My difference from this theory is primarily a difference of analysis; so that it could not be set forth clearly until the reader was acquainted with my own methods" (Keynes 1936, p. 257; see also pp. 231–34).

Keynes that he does cite in which the implications of wage and price flexibility are analyzed within the Keynesian system (for example, Tobin 1947, pp. 585–86;[11] Patinkin 1948, 1951, sec. 14; Leijonhufvud 1968, pp. 319 ff., 340 ff.),[12] and, finally, by overlooking entirely the classic interpretation of Keynes by Modigliani, which has provided the basis for so many textbook expositions. Indeed, in this interpretation the case of downward wage and price flexibility that depresses the rate of interest until it ultimately pushes the economy into the "liquidity trap" is even singled out for designation as "the Keynesian case" (Modigliani 1944, sec. 16[A]).[13]

More specifically, in chap. 19 of the *General Theory,* Keynes analyzes in detail the ways in which a decrease in the wage rate caused by the

---

[11] Again, the opening paragraph of this article—entitled "Money Wage Rates and Employment"—indicates the perspective from which the writer approaches the question: "What is the effect of a general change in money wage rates on aggregate employment and output? To this question, crucial both for theory and for policy, the answers of economists are as unsatisfactory as they are divergent. A decade of Keynesian economics has not solved the problem, but it has made clearer the assumptions concerning economic behavior on which the answer depends. In this field, perhaps even more than in other aspects of the *General Theory,* Keynes' contribution lies in clarifying the theoretical issues at stake rather than in providing an ultimate solution" (Tobin 1947, p. 572).

[12] In presenting his interpretation of Keynes, Friedman expresses his indebtedness to Leijonhufvud's book (Friedman 1970a, p. 207, n. 7). One might therefore note Leijonhufvud's view that "the most common interpretation is perhaps that, once having adopted the assumption of 'wage-rigidity' and built his model on this assumption, Keynes had little further interest in questions relating to money price flexibility. That this is a superficial explanation is apparent both from our discussion in Chapter II and from the fact that Keynes devoted a large portion of the latter half of the *General Theory* to these problems" (Leijonhufvud 1968, p. 332). One might also note that Leijonhufvud (1968, p. 332, n. 1) supports this view with a reference to my 1951 article, which as just noted, is also referred to by Friedman.

[13] For reasons elsewhere presented (Patinkin 1965, chap. 14, sec. 3), I do not agree with this identification of Keynesian economics with the "liquidity trap"—an identification which has also been followed by Friedman (1970a, pp. 206, 212 ff.) This point is further discussed in the next section.

Friedman (1970a, p. 206) identifies Keynesian economics with price rigidity as well as the "liquidity trap." Actually, however, the "liquidity trap" assumes its critical role in Keynesian economics only in the case of price flexibility.

For examples of Keynesian macroeconomic-textbook analyses of wage and price flexibility under conditions of unemployment, see Klein (1947, pp. 87–90), Dillard (1948, chap. 9), Hansen (1949, pp. 122–29), McKenna (1955, chap. 12), Dernburg and McDougall (1960, pp. 144–47), Siegel (1960, pp. 225–31), Ackley (1961, pp. 191–98, 377–93), and Shapiro (1966, pp. 477–87). These discussions refer not only to the indirect effect of a wage decrease on the demand for commodities via the rate of interest but also to the direct (Pigou or real-balance) effect. Needless to say, my own discussions of these problems have included both of these effects of wage and price flexibility—and have interpreted the difference between Keynesian and classical economics within this context (see the next section). I might, however, note that I have also analyzed the case of absolute wage and price rigidity and have—for this case—drawn the contrast between Keynes and the classics in terms of the "reversal of roles" of y and p with respect to the question as to which is constant and which is variable (Patinkin 1965, chap. 13, sec. 4, esp. p. 331).

pressure of unemployment might be expected to increase the level of employment. He argues that the main way is by the reduction in interest caused by the increase in the real quantity of money thus generated—and the consequent increase in investment. After discussing the limitations of this mechanism he concludes:

> There is, therefore, no ground for the belief that a flexible wage policy is capable of maintaining a state of continuous full employment;—any more than for the belief that an open-market monetary policy is capable, unaided, of achieving this result. The economic system cannot be made self-adjusting along these lines. [Keynes 1936, p. 267]

Thus wage rigidities in this chapter are not an *assumption* of the analysis but the *policy conclusion* which Keynes reaches after investigating the results to be expected from wage flexibility.

Let me note that Friedman does state that Keynes qualified his assumption of price rigidity by

> assuming it to apply only to conditions of underemployment. At 'full' employment, he shifted to the quantity-theory model and asserted that all adjustment would be in price—he designated this a situation of 'true inflation.' However, Keynes paid no more than lip service to this possibility, and his disciples have done the same; so it does not misrepresent the body of his analysis largely to neglect the qualification. [Friedman 1970a, pp. 209–10]

Surely, "lip service" is hardly the term to use to describe the detailed analysis of full employment—and the consequent upward wage and price movement—which Keynes provides in the *General Theory* (1936, pp. 295–306; see also pp. 118–19, 171–74, 239–41, 289–91, 328). Indeed, despite the fact that he wrote during a period of mass unemployment, Keynes warns of the danger that wages will begin to rise with increasing unemployment even before full employment is reached (1936, p. 301). Furthermore, the upward flexibility of the wage rate under conditions of full employment is one that is basic to Modigliani's interpretation of Keynes (1944, pp. 189, 201–2)—and indeed to the standard textbook expositions of Keynesian economics. For obvious reasons, the case of full employment has concerned Keynesian economics much more since World War II than before. But to write today and "neglect as a qualification" the extensive Keynesian literature (particularly during World War II) on the inflationary gap—and the upward price movements it generates—is indeed to misrepresent the nature of this analysis.[14]

---

[14] On Keynes's own contributions to this literature, see Klein (1947, chap. 6). Friedman (1970a, p. 211, n. 11) claims to find support for his interpretation in Holzman

FRIEDMAN ON QUANTITY THEORY

I think I can best summarize Keynes's own view of the role of price—and output—variations in his system by citing the paragraph with which he ends chapter 20 ("The Employment Function") of the *General Theory:*

> There is, perhaps, something a little perplexing in the apparent asymmetry between Inflation and Deflation. For whilst a deflation of effective demand below the level required for full employment will diminish employment as well as prices, an inflation of it above this level will merely affect prices. This asymmetry is, however, merely a reflection of the fact that, whilst labour is always in a position to refuse to work on a scale involving a real wage which is less than the marginal disutility of that amount of employment, it is not in a position to insist on being offered work on a scale involving a real wage which is not greater than the marginal disutility of that amount of employment. [Keynes 1936, p. 291]

Returning to the case of unemployment, let me now examine the evidence Friedman adduces in support of his interpretation of the role of price and wage rigidity in the Keynesian system. In this context Friedman writes:

> Keynes embodied this assumption [of wage rigidity] in his formal model by expressing all variables in wage units, so that his formal analysis—aside from a few passing references to a situation of 'true' inflation—dealt with 'real' magnitudes, not 'nominal' magnitudes (Keynes 1936, pp. 119, 301, 303). [Friedman 1970*a*, p. 209][15]

This passage reflects two basic and related misunderstandings. First, to "express all variables in wage units"—that is, to deflate nominal quantities by the wage rate—is surely not to assume that this unit is constant! This is clear from such passages in the *General Theory* as the following:

> Consumption is obviously much more a function of (in some sense) *real* income than of money income. . . . a man's real income will rise and fall . . . with the amount of his income measured in wage-units. . . . As a first approximation, therefore, we can reasonably assume that if the wage-unit changes, the expenditure

---

and Bronfenbrenner's survey article (1963) in which (contends Friedman) "theories of inflation stemming from the Keynesian approach stress institutional, not monetary, factors." This contention is hardly consistent with Holzman and Bronfenbrenner's discussion (under the heading of "Demand Inflation") of "Keynesian inflation theory" in terms of the inflationary gap of the "Keynesian cross" diagram (1963, p. 53)—or with their detailed description of the literature which subsequently developed on this question (1963, pp. 55–59).

[15] The references to the *General Theory* provided here by Friedman are not to passages dealing primarily with the procedure of measuring variables in terms of wage units, but to the allegedly "few passing references to a situation of . . . inflation."

on consumption corresponding to a given level of employment will, like prices, change in the same proportion. [Keynes 1936, p. 91; italics in original]

In a similar vein we find:

> Unless we measure liquidity-preference in terms of wage-units rather than that of money (which is convenient in some contexts), similar results [that is, the increased demand for nominal transactions balances] follow if the increased employment ensuing on a fall in the rate of interest leads to an increase in wages, *i.e.*, to an increase in the money value of the wage-unit. [1936, p. 172; see also pp. 248–49]

As a final example, let me cite the following:

> But if the quantity of money is virtually fixed, it is evident that its quantity in terms of wage-units can be indefinitely increased by a sufficient reduction in money wages. [1936, p. 266]

And to those passages can be added all those cited above in which Keynes discusses the effect of full employment—and the approach thereto—on the wage unit.

Similarly, to express a model in "real magnitudes" does not mean to assume that wages and prices are rigid or exogenously determined. It is, instead, simply to assume that there is no money illusion in the system (Patinkin 1954, 1965). Indeed, for this reason I would consider as a priori implausible any model which is *not* expressed in "real magnitudes."[16] Furthermore, this absence of money illusion is a necessary condition for the validity of the quantity theory. Thus, both of the quantity-theory models discussed in the preceding section—Friedman's as well as my own—are concerned solely with real variables, including real money balances. But since the nominal quantity of money is given, there is an inverse one-to-one correspondence between the level of these balances and the price level.

The major piece of additional evidence which Friedman brings in support of his interpretation of Keynesian economics is the following:

> A striking illustration [of the treatment of the price level as an institutional datum] is provided in a recent Cowles Foundation Monograph, edited by Donald Hester and James Tobin, on *Financial Markets and Economic Activity* (Hester and Tobin 1967). A key essay in that book presents a comparative static analysis of the general equilibrium adjustment of stocks of assets. Yet the distinction between nominal and real magnitudes

---

[16] Correspondingly, my criticism of Goldfeld (1966) on this issue would be exactly the opposite of Friedman's. Thus, compare my criticism of Arena (1963) in Patinkin (1965, p. 660) with Friedman's (1970a, p. 211, n. 11) criticism of Goldfeld.

is not even discussed. The entire analysis is valid only on the implicit assumption that nominal prices of goods and services are completely rigid, although interest rates and real magnitudes are flexible. [Friedman 1970a, p. 211][17]

Of the five articles which Friedman cites in support of this interpretation of the Keynesian literature (1970a, p. 211, n. 11), three are not relevant to the question at issue, one is relevant but not for the reason adduced by Friedman,[18] and only one is validly cited.

In particular, the three articles by Tobin and Brainard (1967), Brainard (1967), and Gramley and Chase (1965), all explicity restrict themselves to an analysis of the nature of the stock (or balance-sheet, or asset-portfolio-composition) equilibrium achieved under the assumption that the situation in the market for the flow of current output is taken as given; correspondingly, the assumption of this analysis is not (as Friedman would have us believe) that prices are rigid while real income varies, but that—at the stage of the analysis being presented—both prices *and the flow of current income* are assumed to be held constant.[19] In the illuminating words of

---

[17] In the footnote attached to this passage, Friedman cites—as an example documenting his last sentence—Tobin and Brainard's assumption "that central banks can determine the ratio of currency (or high-powered money) to total wealth including real assets"—and he contends that "if prices are flexible, the central bank can determine only nominal magnitudes, not such a real ratio." In this contention, however, Friedman is not correct. For as I have shown elsewhere, even if prices are flexible, an open-market operation by the central bank will affect the rate of interest—and hence the optimum ratio of money balances to total wealth. The reason the equilibrium rate of interest is affected in such a case—as contrasted with the case in which the quantity of money changes as a result of deficit financing—is that an open-market operation causes a change in the relative quantities of financial assets (measured in real terms) in the equilibrium portfolios of individuals. Now, a change in the price level affects the real value of nominal financial assets in an equiproportionate manner and hence cannot effect such relative changes. Correspondingly, equilibrium can be restored in this case only by variations in the relative rates of return on the various assets so as to make individuals willing to hold them in their changed proportions. The price movement which simultaneously takes place does indeed dampen the extent of the changes in the equilibrium rate(s) of interest, but, for the reasons just explained, it cannot eliminate them entirely. This argument also holds for shifts in liquidity preference as well as for the introduction of financial intermediaries or of new types of financial assets. For further details, see Patinkin (1961, pp. 109–16; 1965, chap. 10, secs. 3–4, chap. 12, secs. 4–6).

[18] I am referring here to Friedman's criticism of Goldfeld (1966); see n. 16 above. What Friedman does not, however, point out—and what is the relevant point—is that Goldfeld's study does not include the price level as an endogenous variable (Goldfeld 1966, p. 136). It should, however, be noted that one of the directions in which Goldfeld indicates that this model might be refined is that "the wage-price nexus might be introduced. This would bring in supply considerations and make the price level endogenous" (1966, p. 197). This point will be further discussed at the end of this section.

[19] See Tobin and Brainard (1967, pp. 59–60), Brainard (1967, pp. 98–100), Gramley and Chase (1965, pp. 221–22). Note also the inclusion of Y as an exogenous variable in Brainard and Tobin (1968, p. 102), in addition to the assumption of a given commodity price level (1968, p. 105). The holding of both Y and p constant at this stage

Brainard, the concern of these articles can be described as being "analogous to exploring the vertical displacements of the 'LM' curve which result from monetary actions" (Brainard 1967, p. 99).

On the other hand, a valid criticism can be made of Brainard and Tobin (1968). For though most of this article is devoted to the kind of analysis described in the preceding paragraph, it does contain a section which provides for the endogenous determination of income but not of prices (pp. 112–13). And if it is this section that Friedman has in mind (he provides no specific page references), then he has a point—but only a point. For Brainard and Tobin themselves describe this section as a "primitive extension of the model" (1968, p. 112). A more basic extension—to include the production function and labor market—is not provided; and, as will be shown in the following discussion, it is these which play a vital role in the determination of absolute wages and prices in the Keynesian system.

I definitely agree that Tobin and his colleagues are to be criticized for not having made such an extension in these articles—for one of the primary tasks of monetary theory is indeed to explain the determination of the wage and price levels.[20] But a far more important question in the present context is whether those Keynesian discussions that do extend the analysis to the labor market assumed (as Friedman contends they did) that the wage and price levels are exogenously determined.

I have already cited the contrary evidence of the analysis of the effects of wage and price flexibility in the theoretical discussions of Keynes and the Keynesians (see above). But, as before, it seems to me that the best way to answer such questions is to examine the empirical writings of the economists involved. In particular, let us see how Keynesian economists treated the wage and price level in their econometric models of the economy as a whole, for the methodology of model building requires the specification of the variables as endogenous or exogenous.

Of particular interest in this context is the work of Lawrence R. Klein, both because of its relative earliness and because of its being explicitly

---

of his analysis is most clear from the methodological discussion in Tobin (1969, pp. 15–16); see also Tobin's listing of the exogenous variables in the various models he presents here (1969, pp. 21, 24, 28). As will, however, be shown in the next paragraph, these last two articles are subject to criticism on the point at issue.

[20] However, to maintain a proper perspective on this criticism one should remember that this, after all, is the same Tobin whom Friedman himself (1970a, p. 206, n. 5) cites as being one of the first to point out the key role of the real-balance effect generated by a downward price movement in assuring the existence of a long-run equilibrium position. A characteristic of Friedman's present exposition which may partially explain his losing sight of this aspect of Tobin's work is the fact that Friedman never explicitly refers to the role of the movement of the price level in this equilibrating process; thus see Friedman (1970a, pp. 206 bottom, 215).

It is also the same Tobin who—in one of his few analyses of a model with a production function and labor market—explains that the "equilibrium absolute price level" is determined at that level "that provides the appropriate amount of real wealth in liquid form" (Tobin 1955, p. 107).

motivated by the desire to provide an empirical expression of the Keynesian system. The first large model (for the United States, 1921–41) constructed by Klein (in the late 1940s) does provide some support for Friedman's contention. For in analyzing the market as a whole, Klein assumes that—because of the lack of competition—"instead of taking price as the adjustment variable here, we take output" (Klein 1950, p. 102; see also pp. 50–57, 85). Nevertheless, the adjustment equation which Klein actually presents is one in which the change in the price level also appears as a variable (1950, p. 102). Furthermore, Klein explicitly treats this price level as an endogenous variable of the system as a whole (1950, p. 105).

In his subsequent work—in the early 1950s—Klein himself criticized the preceding model for giving "inadequate treatment to prices and wages, both absolute and real" and noted that "the postwar inflation showed this deficiency in a striking manner" (Klein and Goldberger 1955, p. 2). Correspondingly, in the model which they proceeded to construct (for the United States, 1929–52) Klein and Goldberger presented a "labor market adjustment equation" which is

> the strategic equation for determining the level of absolute wages and prices in the system. . . .
>
> The main reasoning behind this equation is that of the law of supply and demand. Money wage rates move in response to excess supply or excess demand on the labor market. High unemployment represents high excess supply, and low unemployment below customary frictional levels represents excess demand. [1955, p. 18]

Another relevant factor is the rate of change of prices, for workers take this into account when they bargain for money wages. Thus, the rate of change of the wage rate depends on the volume of unemployment and the rate of change of the price level; and the volume of unemployment, in turn, is essentially determined as the difference between the number of people in the labor force and the input of labor as endogenously determined by the production function. Needless to say, both the wage rate and the price level are endogenous variables of this model. (Klein and Goldberger 1955, pp. 17, 34–35, 37, 41, 52.)

This theory of wage determination has characterized all of Klein's later work. In the revised version of the Klein-Goldberger model, much the same wage-adjustment equation is associated with the Phillips curve (Klein 1966, p. 239). In the subsequent Wharton model there is a further elaboration on the wage equation, as well as the introduction of a mark-up equation (which also reflects the demand situation in the market) to explain the movements of the price level (Evans, Klein, and Schink 1967, pp. 33–36). And this is carried over to the Brookings Model as well (Duesenberry, Klein, et al. 1965, pp. 284–85, 311). Thus in all of these models the wage rate and price level continue to be treated as endogenous variables.

That this is true not only of Klein's work can be seen most easily from the tabular survey of macroeconometric models prepared by Nerlove (1966). Of the twenty-five models there described (including the preceding four) the great majority provide for the endogenous determination of the wage and price levels.

I can most easily summarize the findings of this section by noting that they show how misleading is Friedman's contention that

> initially, the set of forces determining prices was treated [by Keynesian economics] as not being incorporated in any formal body of economic analysis. More recently, the developments symbolized by the 'Phillips curve' reflect attempts to bring the determination of prices back into the body of economic analysis, to establish a link between real magnitudes and the rate at which prices change from their initial historically determined level (Phillips 1958). [Friedman 1970a, p. 220]

First of all, an economic analysis of wage movements was already provided by the *General Theory*. Indeed, the Phillips-curve theory itself is foreshadowed in chapters 19 and 21 of this book. Second, even before the flourishing of the Phillips curve, Keynesian econometric models generally treated the wage rate and price level as endogenous variables of the system. And this has continued to be the case.

One final observation should be made. It has already been indicated in this section that Keynesian economics is concerned with disequilibrium states, with the principal market in disequilibrium being that for labor. Correspondingly, in the Keynesian system—and particularly in the econometric expressions thereof—there is no equilibrium equation for the labor market but rather a dynamic wage-adjustment equation determining the rate of change of the nominal wage rate in response to the state of excess supply in this market. And, as we have seen, it is this equation which plays a vital role in the endogenous determination of nominal wages and prices.

It is, therefore, not surprising that an equilibrium model, without a labor market—and this is the nature of Friedman's model—does not reveal the nature of the endogenous dynamic process by which the time paths of the nominal wage rate and price level have been analyzed in the Keynesian literature.

IV. Concluding Remarks

The standard interpretation of Keynesian economics as developed by Hicks, Modigliani, and Hansen presents as its central message—and basic differentia from classical economics—the possible existence of a position of "unemployment equilibrium." Correspondingly—in order to explain how the level of unemployment remains unchanged in such a position—this interpretation assigns a crucial role to the "liquidity trap." For it is this "trap" that keeps constant the rate of interest, hence the level of aggregate demand, and hence the levels of output and employment in the economy.

Friedman follows this standard textbook interpretation in presenting the "trap"—or, to use (as Friedman does) Keynes's term, the case of "absolute liquidity preference"—as part of "Keynes's basic challenge to the reigning theory" (Friedman 1970a, pp. 206, 212 ff.).[21] All this, it might be noted, is in contrast with Keynes's own statement that "whilst this limiting case might become practically important in the future," he knew "of no example of it hitherto" (1936, p. 207).[22]

An alternative interpretation that I have elsewhere developed[23]—and of which I have made use in the preceding section—presents Keynesian economics as the economics of unemployment *dis*equilibrium. More specifically, the fundamental issue raised by Keynesian economics is the stability of the dynamic system: its ability to return automatically to full-employment equilibrium within a reasonable time (say, a year) if it is subjected to the customary shocks and disturbances of a peacetime economy. In this context Keynesian economics contends that as a result of high interest elasticity of the demand for money and low interest elasticity of investment, on the one hand, and distribution and expectation effects, on the other, the automatic adjustment process of the market—even when aided by a monetary policy that pushes the rate on interest down—is unlikely to converge either smoothly or rapidly to the full-employment equilibrium position. And since this interpretation thus frees Keynesian economics from the confines of an equilibrium system, it also frees it from any logical dependence on the existence of a "liquidity trap."

In brief, even if monetary policy could be depended upon to ultimately restore the economy to full employment, there would still remain the

---

[21] Once again (see n. 12 above) Friedman (1970a, p. 207, n. 7) cites "Leijonhufvud's penetrating analysis" in support of his (Friedman's) view—even though Leijonhufvud's actual position is exactly the opposite! Thus Leijonhufvud writes: "The 'Liquidity Trap' notion is anti-Keynesian not only in that Keynes explicitly rejected the idea that the money-demand function would be perfectly interest-elastic within any range that we would possibly be interested in, but also in its neglect of the downward shift of the entire schedule that, in a continuing state of depression, 'at long last . . . will doubtless come by itself.' Cf. *Treatise, loc. cit.*" (1968, p. 202, n. 26). Similarly, on pp. 160–61 Leijonhufvud rejects interpretations of Keynes that are based on the "liquidity trap."

[22] This contrast—as well as the passage from Keynes just cited in the text—is further discussed in Patinkin (1965, pp. 349, 352–54, esp. n. 29). This passage is also referred to by Friedman (1970a, p. 215).

[23] The following three paragraphs draw freely on the discussions in Patinkin (1948 and 1951, sec. 14; 1965, chap. 14 and suppl. n. K:3).

crucial question of the length of time it would need. There would still remain the very real possibility that it would necessitate subjecting the economy to an intolerably long period of dynamic adjustment: a period during which wages, prices, and interest would continue to fall, and—what is most important—a period during which varying numbers of workers would continue to suffer from involuntary unemployment. Though I am not aware that he expressed himself in this way, this is the essence of Keynes's position. This is all that need be established in order to justify his fundamental policy conclusion that the "self-adjusting quality of the economic system"—even when reinforced by central-bank policy—is not enough, and that resort must also be had to fiscal policy.

Thus this interpretation takes the debate on the degree of government intervention necessary for a practicable full-employment policy—which is the basic policy debate between Keynes and the classics—out of the realm of those questions that can be decided by a priori considerations of internal consistency and logical validity, and into the realm of those questions that can be decided only by empirical considerations of the actual magnitudes of the relevant economic parameters.

Friedman can undoubtedly point to passages in his article which agree with this last sentence (for example, 1970a, p. 234). The trouble is that there are many more passages in which he presents quite a different interpretation of the relations between Keynes and the classics. It is these other passages which constitute the major part of his article—and to which, accordingly, my own has been devoted.

I would like to conclude this paper with one observation of an analytical nature on the dynamic equations which Friedman presents in his paper (1970a, p. 224). These, unfortunately, are not the structural equations that one might have expected from Friedman's opening statement that the purpose of this paper is to present the theoretical framework implicit in his and Anna Schwartz's book on *A Monetary History of the United States* (1963b).[24] Instead, they are essentially reduced-form equations. The coefficients of these equations are undoubtedly dependent on the elasticities of the structural equations, as well as on their respective speed-of-adjustment parameters. But since Friedman does not specify the nature of this dependence, his dynamic equations do not enable us to investigate what is, after all, one of the basic questions at issue: namely, the way in which—in a given policy context—different assumptions about

---

[24] Nor, correspondingly, does Friedman's present discussion provide any additional details about the admittedly "tentative" dynamic analysis which he sketched in Friedman and Meiselman (1963, pp. 217–22) and Friedman and Schwartz (1963a, sec. 3). The main point of this analysis is that monetary changes initially generate portfolio-composition (balance-sheet) adjustments, and hence changes in the prices (and hence rates of return) of the assets (including consumer durables) held in the portfolio; these, in turn, generate changes in the demands for commodity flows and hence in their prices and/or output.

the various elasticities of demand and dynamic parameters affect the respective time paths of price and output in the system.

References

Ackley, Gardner. *Macroeconomic Theory.* New York: Macmillan, 1961.
Angell, James. "Money, Prices and Production: Some Fundamental Concepts." *Q.J.E.* (November 1933), pp. 39–76.
Arena, John J. "The Wealth Effect and Consumption: A Statistical Inquiry." *Yale Econ. Essays,* no. 2 (1963), pp. 251–303.
Brainard, William. "Financial Intermediaries and a Theory of Monetary Control." In *Financial Markets and Economic Activity,* edited by Donald Hester and James Tobin. Cowles Found. Monograph, no. 21. New York: Wiley, 1967.
Brainard, William, and Tobin, James. "Pitfalls in Financial Model Building." *A.E.R.* (May 1968), pp. 99–122.
Brown, A. J. "Interest, Prices, and the Demand Schedule for Idle Money." *Oxford Econ. Papers* 2 (May 1939): 46–69. Reprinted in *Oxford Studies in the Price Mechanism,* edited by T. Wilson and P. W. S. Andrews. London: Oxford Univ. Press, 1951.
Cagan, Phillip. "The Monetary Dynamics of Hyperinflation." In *Studies in the Quantity Theory of Money,* edited by Milton Friedman. Chicago: Univ. Chicago Press, 1956.
Chandler, Lester V. *An Introduction to Monetary Theory.* New York: Harper, 1940.
———. *The Economics of Money and Banking.* 2d ed. New York: Harper, 1953.
Dernburg, Thomas, and McDougall, Duncan. *Macro-Economics.* New York: McGraw-Hill, 1960.
Dillard, Dudley. *The Economics of John Maynard Keynes.* New York: Prentice-Hall, 1948.
Duesenberry, James; Fromm, Gary; Klein, Lawrence R.; and Kuh, Edwin. *The Brookings Quarterly Econometric Model of the United States.* Chicago: Rand McNally, 1965.
Evans, Michael; Klein, Lawrence; and Schink, George. *The Wharton Econometric Forecasting Model.* Wharton School of Finance and Commerce Studies in Quantitative Economics, no. 2. Philadelphia: Univ. Pennsylvania Press, 1967.
Fisher, Irving. *Appreciation and Interest.* New York: Macmillan, 1896. Reprint. New York: Kelley, 1961.
———. *The Rate of Interest.* New York: Macmillan, 1907.
———. *The Purchasing Power of Money.* 2d rev. ed. 1922. Reprint. New York: Kelley, 1963.
Friedman, Milton. "The Quantity Theory of Money—a Restatement." In *Studies in the Quantity Theory of Money,* edited by Milton Friedman. Chicago: Univ. Chicago Press, 1956.
———. "Money: Quantity Theory." In *International Encyclopedia of the Social Sciences.* Vol. 10. New York: Macmillan and Free Press, 1968.
———. "A Theoretical Framework for Monetary Analysis." *J.P.E.* 78 (March/April 1970): 193–238. (*a*)
———. "Comment on Tobin." *Q.J.E.* (May 1970): 318–27. (*b*)
———. "A Monetary Theory of Nominal Income." *J.P.E.* 79 (March/April 1971): 323–337.
Friedman, Milton, and Meiselman, David. "The Relative Stability of Monetary

Velocity and the Investment Multiplier in the United States, 1897–1958." In *Stabilization Policies,* Commission on Money and Credit. Englewood Cliffs, N.J.: Prentice-Hall, 1963.

Friedman, Milton, and Schwartz, Anna. "Money and Business Cycles." *Rev. Econ. and Statis.* (suppl.; February 1963), pp. 32–64. Reprinted in Friedman, Milton. *The Optimum Quantity of Money and Other Essays.* Chicago: Aldine, 1969. (*a*)

———. *A Monetary History of the United States, 1867–1960.* Princeton, N.J.: Princeton Univ. Press (for Nat. Bur. Econ. Res.), 1963. (*b*)

Goldfeld, Stephen M. *Commercial Bank Behavior and Economic Activity.* Amsterdam: North-Holland, 1966.

Gramley, Lyle, and Chase, S. B., Jr. "Time Deposits in Monetary Analysis." *Federal Reserve Bull.* 51 (October 1965): 1380–1406. Reprinted in *Targets and Indicators of Monetary Policy,* edited by Karl Brunner. San Francisco: Chandler, 1969.

Hansen, Alvin. *Monetary Theory and Fiscal Policy.* New York: McGraw-Hill, 1949.

Hester, Donald, and Tobin, James, eds. *Financial Markets and Economic Activity.* Cowles Found. Monograph, no. 21. New York: Wiley, 1967.

Holzman, Franklyn, and Bronfenbrenner, Martin. "Survey of Inflation Theory." *A.E.R.* (September 1963), pp. 593–661. Reprinted in *Surveys of Economic Theory.* Vol. 1. *Money, Interest, and Welfare.* American Econ. Assoc. London: Macmillan, 1968.

Keynes, J. M. *The General Theory of Employment, Interest and Money.* New York: Harcourt Brace, 1936.

Klein, Lawrence R. *The Keynesian Revolution.* New York: Macmillan, 1947. 2d ed. New York: Macmillan, 1966.

———. *Economic Fluctuations in the United States, 1921–1941.* Cowles Commission Monograph, no. 11. New York: Wiley, 1950.

Klein, L. R., and Goldberger, A. S. *An Econometric Model of the United States.* Amsterdam: North-Holland, 1955.

Laidler, David. *The Demand for Money: Theories and Evidence.* Scranton, Pa.: Internat. Textbook, 1970.

Leijonhufvud, Axel. *On Keynesian Economics and the Economics of Keynes.* London: Oxford Univ. Press, 1968.

McKenna, Joseph P. *Aggregate Economic Analysis.* New York: Holt, Rinehart & Winston, 1955.

Modigliani, Franco. "Liquidity Preference and the Theory of Interest and Money." *Econometrica* 12 (January 1944): 45–88. Reprinted in *Readings in Monetary Theory,* edited by F. A. Lutz and L. W. Mints. Homewood, Ill.: Irwin, 1951.

Nerlove, Marc. "A Tabular Survey of Macro-Econometric Models." *Internat. Econ. Rev.* (May 1966), pp. 127–75.

Patinkin, Don. "Price Flexibility and Full Employment." *A.E.R.* (September 1948), pp. 543–64.

———. "The Indeterminacy of Absolute Prices in Classical Economic Theory." *Econometrica* (January 1949), pp. 1–27.

———. "Price Flexibility and Full Employment." In *Readings in Monetary Theory,* edited by F. A. Lutz and L. W. Mints. Homewood, Ill.: Irwin, 1951. (Revised version of Patinkin 1948.)

———. "Keynesian Economics and the Quantity Theory." In *Post-Keynesian*

Economics, edited by Kenneth Kurihara. New Brunswick, N.J.: Rutgers Univ. Press, 1954.
———. "Financial Intermediaries and the Logical Structure of Monetary Theory." *A.E.R.* (March 1961), pp. 95–116.
———. *Money, Interest, and Prices*. 2d ed. New York: Harper & Row, 1965.
———. "The Chicago Tradition, the Quantity Theory, and Friedman." *J. Money, Credit and Banking* 1 (February 1969): 46–70. (*a*)
———. "Money and Wealth: A Review Article." *J. Econ. Literature* (December 1969), pp. 1140–60. (*b*)
———. "On the Short-Run Non-Neutrality of Money in the Quantity Theory." *Banca Nazionale Lavoro Q. Rev.* (March 1972), pp. 3–22. (*a*)
———. "Keynesian Monetary Theory and the Cambridge School." In *Issues in Monetary Economics*, edited by Harry G. Johnson and A. R. Nobay. Proceedings of the Money Study Group Conference, Bournemouth, February 1972. Oxford Univ. Press, 1972. [This paper also appears, without appendix, in *Banca Nazionale Lavoro Q. Rev.* (June 1972).] (*b*)
Phillips, A. W. "The Relation between Unemployment and the Rate of Change of Money and Wage Rates in the United Kingdom, 1861–1957." *Economica* (November 1958), pp. 283–99.
Reeve, Joseph E. *Monetary Reform Movements*. Washington: American Council on Public Affairs, 1943.
Robertson, D. H. *Money*. 4th ed. London: Pitman, 1948.
Shapiro, Edward. *Macroeconomic Analysis*. New York: Harcourt Brace, 1966.
Siegel, Barry. *Aggregate Economics and Public Policy*. Homewood, Ill.: Irwin, 1960.
Tobin, James. "Money Wage Rates and Employment." In *The New Economics*, edited by Seymour Harris. New York: Knopf, 1947.
———. "A Dynamic Aggregative Model." *J.P.E.* 63 (April 1955): 103–15.
———. "A General Equilibrium Approach to Monetary Theory." *J. Money, Credit and Banking* (February 1969), pp. 15–29.
Tobin, James, and Brainard, William. "Financial Intermediaries and the Effectiveness of Monetary Controls." In *Financial Markets and Economic Activity*, edited by Donald Hester and James Tobin. Cowles Found. Monograph, no. 21. New York: Wiley, 1967.
Warburton, Clark. "The Volume of Money and the Price Level between the World Wars." *J.P.E.* 53 (June 1945): 150–63. Reprinted in *Depression, Inflation, and Monetary Policy: Selected Papers, 1945–1953*. Baltimore: Johns Hopkins, n.d.

DAVID HUME AND MONETARISM*

Thomas Mayer

> Of the twelve characteristics of modern monetarism, five are explicit in Hume's writings: the quantity theory, the Chicago transmission process, private sector stability, the vertical Phillips curve, which Hume originated, and preference for free markets. Two others, irrelevance of allocative detail and focus on the price level as a unit, are implicit. Preference for reduced-form models fits Hume's theory of causation. Preference for stable money growth fits the whole tenor of Hume's discussion. Two propositions on targets and indicators were irrelevant in Hume's day, but Hume rejected the monetarists' strong opposition to inflation.

As current economic theories change, so should our evaluation of previous economists. This paper, therefore, suggests that David Hume's reputation, which has declined since the nineteenth century, should now be rising again because in 1752, long before Ricardo, he anticipated modern monetarism on an amazing number of issues.[1] To see how Hume did this, one must first set out the characteristics of monetarism. Elsewhere [Mayer, 1975] I characterized it by twelve interrelated propositions and characteristics.[2] They are as follows:

A. Core Propositions and Characteristics:

1. Changes in the money stock lead to predictable changes in money income, and these changes in the money stock are the predominant variable determining money income. This is the quantity theory.

2. A specific approach to the transmission process, which focuses on the money stock rather than on interest rates, and on a relatively large number of channels.

---

* The author is indebted for helpful comments to Peter Berman, Robert Blewett, Phillip Cagan, Dietrich Fausten, Gillian Garcia, Robert Hetzel, Thomas Humphrey, David Laidler, Charles Lieberman, Raymond Lombra, Will Mason, Hans Palmer, Don Patinkin, T. Y. Shen, and Alan Stockman. Earlier versions of this paper were presented at a seminar at UCLA and at the 1978 Western Economic Association meetings.

1. For Hume's position in economics see Feilbogen [1890], pp. 699–700; Johnson [1937], p. 163; Vickers [1968], p. 218; O'Brien [1975], pp. 7, 17; and Arkin [1956], p. 217. With respect to monetary theory von Hayek [1976, p. 23] wrote that "Richard Cantillion and David Hume began the development of modern monetary theory," while Friedman [1975, pp. 176–77], in discussing the rediscovery of money in the last twenty-five years, wrote: "We have advanced beyond Hume in two respects only: first, we now have a more secure grasp on the quantitative magnitudes involved; second, we have gone one derivative beyond Hume." The latter is due to the fact that whereas Hume could take stable prices as a norm, nowadays we must focus on the change in the inflation rate.

2. This list does not include the monetarist theory of the balance of payments, since it is not clear whether or not it is part of monetarism per se. (See Laidler [1978], and Fausten [1978].) Moreover, it is also open to dispute whether Hume should be considered its ancestor. (See Fausten [1979], Frenkel [1976], Keleher [1978], and Parkin [1977].) The rational expectations approach is also excluded from the list, since many monetarists do not accept it.

3. Belief in the inherent stability of the private sector.

B. Method:

4. Irrelevance of allocative detail for the explanation of short-run changes in money income, and belief in a fluid capital market.

5. Focus on the price level as a unit rather than on individual prices, in the sense of not attributing inflation to supply pressures in those sectors in which relative prices are rising.

6. Reliance on small, rather than large, econometric models.

C. Monetary Policy:

7. Use of the reserve base or related measures as the indicator of monetary policy.

8. Use of the money stock as the target of monetary policy.

9. Acceptance of a stable money growth rate rule, or a similar rule.

D. General Macro Policy:

10. Rejection of an unemployment-inflation tradeoff.

11. Relatively greater concern about inflation than about unemployment.

12. Support of free markets rather than government intervention.

Most of these propositions can be traced to a general tendency of monetarists to emphasize the long run much more than Keynesians do. (See Fellner [1977], Gordon [1976], pp. 55–57, and Modigliani [1977], p. 20.)

One difficulty that arises in trying to find these, or any other current ideas in an earlier writer, is that it is so easy to read them into his work by focusing on isolated passages and obiter dicta. But as Patinkin [1972, p. 139] has remarked: "isolated passages do not a theory make." To show that this is not a problem with Hume's monetarism, after discussing whether Hume had each of these propositions, I reverse field and take up the points that were central to Hume, to see whether they are important components of modern monetarism as well. Another seeming difficulty is that modern monetarism should be seen in the context of a reaction to Keynesianism. But Hume too was reacting to the mercantilists who shared a number of ideas with Keynes.

The Quantity Theory and Interest Rate Theory

Hume certainly could not claim to be the *originator* of the quantity theory in the sense of being the first to attribute inflation to an increase in the quantity of money; in 1694 Brisco had already written out an equation of exchange, though omitting velocity

[Schumpeter, 1954, p. 314]. Moreover, Hume has been accused by von Hayek [1935, p. 9] of plagiarizing from Cantillion, and by Marx and Engels of plagiarizing from Vanderlint [Sekine, 1973, p. 274]. But other economists have defended Hume against these charges. (See Humphrey [1932], p. 237, Sekine [1973], pp. 274-75, and Stadlin [1954], pp. 24-25.) Schumpeter [1954, p. 316] credited Hume with being the first to show "clearly and explicitly" that, on an abstract level, there is no unique quantity of nominal money that a country needs. He thus understood the distinction, so much emphasized by modern monetarists, between the real and the nominal quantity of money. Hegeland [1951, p. 34] described Hume's discussion as the "most elucidating account" of the essence of the original quantity theory. And O'Brien [1975, p. 144] attributed to Hume, Cantillion, and Harris the first published "clear formulation" of the quantity theory. Here is Hume's own exposition [1955, pp. 33, 41, and 48]:

If we consider any one kingdom by itself, it is evident, that the greater or less plenty of money is of no consequence; since the prices of commodities are always proportioned to the plenty of money.... It is a maxim almost self-evident, that the prices of everything depend on the proportion between commodities and money, and that any considerable alteration on either has the same effect, either of heightening or lowering the price.... All augmentation [of gold and silver] has no other effect than to heighten the price of labor and commodities....

Hume recognized that the money stock and prices need not always move proportionately. Transactions could vary. "It is the proportion between the circulating money, and the commodities in the market, which determines the prices" [Hume, 1955, p. 43]. Hume was much less explicit about velocity. He surely learned about it by reading Locke, who had a highly developed analysis of velocity, including its relation to the interest rate [Leigh, 1974]. Perhaps Hume was less explicit about velocity because, at the time, the "quickness of circulation" was included in the concept of the quantity of money [Blaugh, 1968, p. 20; and Stadlin, 1954, p. 30.][3]

-----

3. Hume did make a few references to velocity. In one [p. 42] he wrote that coin "locked up in chests . . . is the same thing with regard to prices as if they were annihilated." In addition, he recognized the importance of money substitutes, writing:

"Banks, funds and paper credit . . . render paper equivalent to money, circulate it throughout the whole state, make it supply the place of gold and silver, raise proportionably the price of labor and commodities.... Public securities are with us become a kind of money, and pass as readily at the current price as gold or silver" [Hume, 1955, pp. 67-68].

Hume then went on to say that these money substitutes lower the cost of holding working-capital, and hence, by reducing cost of production, lower prices [p. 93]. This is a strange argument. One possible explanation is that Hume here forgot his own theory that prices are determined by the quantity of money. The second possibility is that he was thinking of relative prices. The former interpretation seems somewhat more plausible.

An important characteristic of Hume's quantity theory is that, instead of stating it only as a truistic, comparative statics proposition as Locke did, Hume presented it as a causal theory of price determination. Blaugh [1968, p. 20] and Hegeland [1951, p. 168] attributed this to confusion, but monetarists are more likely to praise Hume for it. Another characteristic of Hume's quantity theory is that, like present day international monetarism, it applies to the whole world rather than to any single country, since a country's money stock is not exogenous, but is determined by the specie-flow mechanism [Keleher, 1978]. Hence, for a single country causation can run from prices to money, as well as from money to prices. Hume's emphasis on the interrelation of monetary economics and the balance of payments theory became an important strand of thought in British monetary analysis until the 1930s.

Like modern quantity theorists, Hume had a real theory of the interest rate. A high stock of money does not mean a low interest rate:

Lowness of interest is generally ascribed to plenty of money. But money, however plentiful, has no other effect, *if fixed*, than to raise the price of labour. Interest in BATAVIA and JAMAICA is at 10 *percent*, in Portugal at 6; though these places, as we may learn from the price of everything, abound more in gold and silver than either LONDON or AMSTERDAM [Hume, 1955, p. 47].

Compare this to Friedman's 1968 [pp. 6–7] statement:

... high and rising nominal interest rates have been associated with rapid growth in the quantity of money, as in Brazil or Chile or in the United States in recent years, and ... low and falling interest rates have been associated with slow growth in the quantity of money, as in Switzerland now, or in the United States from 1929 to 1933.

The only differences are that Hume, unlike Friedman, did not have the "Fisher effect" available, and also talked about a high stock of money instead of a high growth rate.

Hume believed that an increase in the money stock may sometimes lower the interest rate temporarily, depending upon where the money is injected. If it is concentrated in a few hands, then it will initially be offered on the loan market, and thus lower the rate of interest *temporarily*. But this is not so if the additional money enters the economy gradually and is widely spread among many people. Even then, however, like in our growth models, it can have *some* long-run effect on the rate of interest by temporarily stimulating output, which raises the stock of accumulated savings, and thus lowers interest rates. (See Lowe [1954], p. 125.)

The Transmission Process

The modern monetarist transmission process has several characteristics. According to its critics, one is its use of a "black box," despite the fact that Brunner and Meltzer [1976a] give a detailed and complex analysis of the transmission process. Other characteristics are that it is formulated in terms of money rather than interest rates, and that money directly affects consumption as well as "investment." Finally, the Brunner-Meltzer version has a relative price and a wealth interpretation of the transmission process.

The seeming "black box" approach of the Chicago school fits well into Hume's theory of causation, which is a salient contribution to philosophy. He treated cause and effect as being fundamentally nothing but correlation; if event A always occurs in connection with—and before—event B, then A is the cause of B (see Blake, Ducasse, and Madden [1960], Ch. 4).[4] In his own discussion of the specie flow mechanism, Hume explicitly used "black box" reasoning, writing [p. 77]:

> ... Money always finds its way back again by a hundred canals, of which we have not notion or suspicion.... For above a thousand years, the money of EUROPE has been flowing to ROME, by an open and sensible current; but it has been emptied by many secret and insensible canals.

In his treatment of the quantity theory, Hume also did not discuss the transmission channels in any detail. There is only a single passage in which he pointed out that money can affect prices only by changing aggregate demand [Sekine, 1973, pp. 275–76], though Patinkin [1965, p. 530] has suggested that Hume may simply not have bothered to state what was obvious.

Moreover, he focused on changes in the money stock, and not on the resulting changes in interest rates, since in his model a rise in the money stock need not lower the interest rate even temporarily, except for the "growth model" effect previously mentioned. Hume's discussion of the difference between the effects of concentrated and widely dispersed increases in the money supply also shows that Hume agreed with modern monetarists that a change in the money supply can affect consumption as well as investment. Admittedly, Hume did not have the sophisticated relative price and wealth analysis of

---

4. This did not prevent Hume from sometimes describing the causal chain involved. And indeed, Hume's theory may require correlation between variables that are finely detailed. But in his own discussion of the quantity theory, he showed no concern about using a black box.

Brunner and Meltzer, but in any case this analysis is by no means accepted by all modern monetarists. There is also some debate as to whether it is actually monetarist [see Brunner and Meltzer, 1976b; and Dornbusch, 1976, pp. 123–24].

STABILITY OF THE PRIVATE SECTOR

Hume's discussion of the stability of the private sector dealt with whether mercantilist policies are needed to preserve a country's supply of specie; to this Hume's answer was clear. Though he was not the first to point out that the supply of specie could, and should, be left to look after itself, he was by far the most influential proponent of this view in his day.

Unemployment was a serious problem in Hume's day, though it may well have been more regional and structural than cyclical. Mercantilist writers advocated full employment policies, arguing, for example, that a worker has a right to a job [Furniss, 1920, Chs. 3 and 4]. But not so Hume. Although at least at one point he implied that involuntary unemployment existed [see Vickers, 1957, p. 230; and O'Brien, 1975, p. 163], he had very little to say about it. Moreover, he believed that prices are highly flexible, which goes a long way to ensure the stability of the private sector:

Nor is it probable, that the diminution of circulating money was ever sensibly felt by the people, or ever did them any prejudice. The sinking of the prices of all commodities would *immediately* replace it, by giving England the advantage in its commerce with the neighboring kingdoms [Hume, 1955, p. 73, emphasis added].

Stability of the private sector not only implies the absence of severe unemployment, but also that the private sector does not itself generate inflation. Unless there is a large increase in the world supply of specie or paper money, this condition is implicit in Hume's quantity theory. And further, in his discussion of taxes Hume [p. 87] argued that sales taxes cannot start a cost-push, thus supporting the monetarist rejection of cost-push inflation.[5]

THREE METHODOLOGICAL PROPOSITIONS

The first proposition is that one should deemphasize allocative

---

5. However, in listing the disadvantages of "exhorbitant" taxes [p. 85], Hume mentioned that they raise wages. *Perhaps* the explanation of the apparent contradiction is that "exhorbitant" taxes have to be passed on, since the worker can lower his living standard only to a limited extent.

details in macroeconomics. Aggregate demand is determined "from the top down" by the stock of money, rather than built up by adding up demands in various sectors. The second is that one should think of the price level as a single unit. Hume did not discuss these two propositions explicitly, but this is more or less true of modern monetarists, too. Both of them are definitely implied in Hume's espousal of the quantity theory.[6]

Then there is the monetarist's preference for small reduced-form models. Obviously, Hume did not discuss econometric techniques, but one of the issues involved here is the "black box" argument. On this issue, Hume was on the side of the monetarists.

Monetary Policy

The next three monetarist propositions would have had little meaning for Hume, since monetary policy, in the current sense of the term, did not exist in his day. For Hume the quantity of money was determined by the specie flow mechanism, and the issue was whether it should be allowed to operate freely or whether the government should aim for a positive balance of trade. Hence, the question of what the targets and indicators of monetary policy should be was totally meaningless for Hume.

The next monetarist proposition is adherence to a monetary rule. Hume obviously could not advocate a policy of stable money growth, but he did share some of the underlying conceptions that dispose monetarists to favor it. He showed a great deal of skepticism regarding the efficiency of discretionary policy in his criticism of mercantilism, and his discussions of deficit spending and paper money. After pointing out the advantage of paper money, he nonetheless opposed it because of its inherent riskiness [Hume, 1955, p. 68 n]. He did not mention the possibility that the government might issue paper money and maintain its soundness.

Moreover, Hume, unlike modern monetarists, did not have to advocate a stable money growth rule to eliminate discretionary policy; the specie flow mechanism operates with even less discretion than does a money growth rate rule.[7]

---

6. Furthermore, Hume assumed that prices are highly flexible. If so, then price behavior in a particular industry has little effect on the overall price level; if steel prices rise because of increased monopoly, other prices are forced down due to the decline in real balances.

7. Friedman [1962, pp. 221–22] argued that if it were feasible, an automatic commodity standard would be an "excellent solution."

General Macro Policy

Monetarists believe that an increased money growth rate raises employment for only a quite limited time, and after that just raises prices. This point was discovered by Hume, who "perhaps for the first time in economics" [Taylor, 1965, p. 77] drew a sharp distinction between the short run and the long run when he wrote:

Though the high price of commodities be a necessary consequence of the encrease of gold and silver, yet it follows not immediately upon that encrease; but some time is required before the money circulates through the whole state, and makes its effect be felt on all ranks of people. At first, no alteration is perceived; by degrees the price rises, first of one commodity, then of another; till the whole at last reaches a just proportion with the new quantity of specie which is in the kingdom. In my opinion, it is only in this interval or intermediate situation, between the acquisition of money and rise of prices, that the encreasing quantity of gold and silver is favourable to industry.... Here are a set of manufacturers or merchants .... who have received returns of gold and silver for goods which they sent to CADIZ. They are thereby enabled to employ more workmen than formerly, who never dream of demanding higher wages, but are glad of employment for such good paymasters. If workmen become scarce, the manufacturer gives higher wages, but at first requires an encrease of labor.... it is easy to trace the money in its progress through the whole commonwealth; where we shall find, that it must first quicken the diligence of every individual, before it encreases the price of labor [Hume, 1955, pp. 37–38].

It would therefore be fitting to call the prominent principle in current literature that an increased money growth rate raises output only temporarily the "Hume effect," to honor one of the greatest minds who ever wrote on economics, even though Hume did not discuss workers being temporarily fooled by inflation, and did not allow for the development of inflationary expectations.

The next monetarist characteristic is relatively greater concern about inflation than about unemployment and deflation. Hume was *not* a monetarist in this respect. He did not mention any losses resulting from inflation, and in this respect is similar to the mercantilists [Stadlin, 1954, p. 26]. In part, this may be due to the fact that, since he did not allow for the development of inflationary expectations, he did not appreciate that the temporary rise in output resulting from an increased money growth rate has to be paid for eventually. Another part of the explanation may be that Hume, like the mercantilists, did not treat full employment output as a given. Dealing as he was with an underdeveloped economy, he believed that there was a potential for rapid economic growth through stimulating production for the market rather than only for personal consumption (see Rotwein's introduction in Hume [1955], pp. LXI–LXVI). An increase in the money supply, by helping to monetize the economy, was therefore, desirable. Hence, he wrote:

> The good policy of the magistrate consists only in keeping ... money, if possible still encreasing; because, by that means, he keeps alive a spirit of industry in the nation, and encreases the stock of labour .... A nation whose money decreases, is actually, at that time, weaker and more miserable than another nation, which possesses no more money, but is on an encreasing hand [Hume, 1955, pp. 39-40].

The final monetarist proposition is the superiority of the free market over government intervention. In the contemporaneous context Hume, with his criticism of mercantilism, is obviously in the monetarist camp on this score, even though Viner warned us that "in Hume's economic writings the laissez-faire doctrine is to be found only by implication if at all" [Viner, 1937, p. 99]. An example of Hume's distrust of government intervention is his rejection of the "Keynesian" argument of some of his contemporaries that a large public debt is harmless because "we owe it to ourselves." In Hume's view:

> The practice, therefore, of contracting debt will almost infallibly be abused, in every government. It would scarcely be more imprudent to give a prodigal son a credit in every banker's shop in London, than to impower a statesman to draw bills, in this manner, upon posterity [Hume, 1955, p. 92].

An underlying hallmark of monetarism is emphasis on the long run. This too, was shared by Hume. According to Keynes [1936, p. 343 n.]:

> Hume began the practice amongst economists of stressing the importance of the equilibrium position as compared with the ever-shifting transition towards it, though he was still enough of a mercantilist not to overlook the fact that it is in the transition that we actually have our being.

In addition Hume, like modern monetarists, emphasized empirical testing. While of course he did not run regressions, he did—like Friedman and Schwartz—make much use of that other great source of empirical tests, history. Hume, after all, was the author of a massive and pioneering history of England. His writings are replete with references to the experience of both classical civilization and contemporary Europe. Moreover, like monetarists and unlike many Keynesians, he showed sympathy for businessmen whom he compared favorably to professionals [Hume, 1955, pp. 53-54]. Finally, on a much more detailed level, Hume [1955, p. 36] advocated 100 percent reserve banking.

Nonmonetarist Aspects of Hume's Thought

Hume also held some views that are not monetarist. The most important one—explained by the time he lived in—was his great emphasis on economic development through monetizing the economy and his preference for rising prices. Hume also treated government debt as a close substitute for money, even calling it [p. 95] "a kind of paper credit" that tends to replace gold and silver in large transactions and to raise prices.

Moreover, Hume believed that, in moderation, taxation is desirable, since it stimulates effort.[8] In addition, Hume remained a mild protectionist [O'Brien, 1975, p. 36], and was concerned with increasing the strength and power of the British state relative to other states.[9]

Finally, Hume was a person who always saw both sides of any issue, and tried to make as good a case as he could for his opponents. He was too much of a skeptic to take unequivocal positions. [See Feilbogen, 1890, pp. 709–12.] This is hardly a salient characteristic of modern monetarism.

THE ROLE OF MODERN MONETARISTS' PROPOSITIONS IN HUME'S THOUGHT

Were Hume's monetarist ideas significant components of his thought, or mere casual asides? The quantity theory was obviously central to Hume's economics. In the transmission process, the Chicago monetarist's deemphasis of the channels of causation fits well into a dominating aspect of Hume's thought, his theory of causation. The focus on the money stock rather than the interest rate, as well as the proposition that money affects not only investment, but also consumption, are both required by Hume's theory of interest, which is an important component of his economics. The stability of the private sector received little explicit discussion by Hume, but that very fact suggests by implication that it was an important proposition for him. Hume was a man of wide social sympathy, and had he thought that unemployment was an important problem, he would, in all probability, have discussed it at length.

The next two monetarist propositions, the unimportance of allocative detail, and the treatment of the price level as a whole are not discussed by Hume, and can be read into his work only by implication.

---

8. See O'Brien [1975], p. 242. Many of his contemporaries went much farther than Hume and considered high taxes on workers to be desirable since this forces them to work harder. Hume, on the other hand, tempered his advocacy of taxes. He considered it a useful attribute of a tax that there was a natural limit beyond which it could not be expanded [Humphrey 1932, p. 286].

9. Johnson [1937, p. 177] argued that "although Hume's essays postulated that the happiness of individuals should be the purpose of policy, the greatness of the state should always be regarded as an even more important goal." But this may be an overstatement.

But then the same is true of most modern monetarist writings. Moreover, these propositions, despite being implicit, were important for Hume, since they are necessary implications of the quantity theory. But a preference for reduced-form models is relevant only in a very indirect way, since it relates to Hume's theory of causation.

The monetarist views of policy targets and indicators were, of course, not applicable in Hume's time, but on the issue of a monetary rule we have Hume's strong distrust of government intervention and his specie-flow mechanism, both of which were far from being mere asides. The absence of a long-run tradeoff between unemployment and inflation was also central to Hume because, if such a tradeoff exists, it weakens the specie-flow mechanism and the quantity theory, since prices then do not rise in proportion to the increase in the quantity of money. Mercantilist policies of reducing unemployment by improving the balance of trade might then succeed.

Another way to see whether monetarism played a significant, and not just a peripheral, role in Hume's thought is to reverse field, and ask whether the three basic themes running through Hume's monetary analysis are also important for modern monetarists. They are the quantity theory of money, the specie-flow mechanism, and the benefits of increased monetization of the economy. The first of these is obviously central to modern monetarism; the second is connected with certain propositions about the international distribution of (convertible) money that are basic to a close relative of modern monetarism, the monetary theory of the balance of payments. Only the third one, increased monetization—no longer a relevant issue in developed countries—is not part of modern monetarism.[10]

Stepping outside the confines of monetary theory, we meet two other ideas that were of great importance to Hume, and fit in well with modern monetarism. They are his distrust of government intervention and his theory of causation.

Conclusions

This paper discussed Hume's positions on twelve propositions of modern monetarism. On five of them he was explicitly in the monetarist camp. They are the following: the quantity theory, the Chicago school's transmission process, the stability of the private sector, the temporary effect of inflation on output, and a preference

---

10. The degree of monetization is, however, of great concern to one prominent economist who is, at least partially, a monetarist. See Shaw [1973].

for private market process. Two other monetarist propositions, the irrelevance of allocative detail and the focus on the price level as a unit rather than on individual prices, are clearly implied by the quantity theory, and hence Hume was implicitly a monetarist on these two issues also. Moreover, the use of a reduced-form model instead of a structural model fits in well with Hume's theory of causation. Further, while Hume did not advocate a stable money growth rate rule, such a rule follows naturally in the spirit of his writings, much better than a Keynesian belief in discretionary policy does. Two other characteristics of monetarism, using a reserve base measure as the monetary policy indicator and using the money stock as the target of monetary policy, were not relevant issues in Hume's day. The only monetarist characteristic Hume rejected is the monetarist's strong opposition to inflation.

UNIVERSITY OF CALIFORNIA, DAVIS

REFERENCES

Arkin, Marcus, "The Economic Writings of David Hume: A Reassessment," *South African Journal of Economics*, XXIV (1956), 204–20.
Blaugh, M., *Economic Theory in Retrospect* (Homewood, IL: Irwin, 1968).
Blake, Ralph, Curt Ducasse, and Edward Madden, *Theories of Scientific Method, The Renaissance Through the Nineteenth Century* (Seattle: University of Washington Press, 1960).
Brunner, Karl, and Allan Meltzer, "An Aggregative Theory for a Closed Economy," in Jerome Stein, ed., *Monetarism* (Amsterdam: North-Holland Publishing Co., 1976a), pp. 69–113.
——, "Reply—Monetarism: The Principal Issues, Areas of Agreement and the Work Remaining," in Jerome Stein, ed., *Monetarism* (Amsterdam: North-Holland Publishing Co., 1976b) pp. 150–82.
Dornbusch, Rudiger, "Comments" in Jerome Stein, ed., *Monetarism* (Amsterdam: North-Holland Publishing Co., 1976), pp. 104–25.
Fausten, Dietrich, "Beyond the Analytics of the Monetary Approach to the Balance of Payments: Methodology, Innovation and Monetarism," unpublished manuscript, 1978.
——, "On the Humean Origins of the Contemporary Monetary Approach to the Balance of Payments," this *Journal*, XCIII (Nov. 1979), 655–74.
Feilbogen, Sigmund, "Smith und Hume," *Zeitschrift fur die Gesamte Staatswissenschaft*, XLVI (1890), 695–716.
Fellner, William, "Schools of Thought in the Mainstream of American Economics," *Acta Oekonomica*, XVIII (1977), 247–62.
Frenkel, Jacob, "Adjustment Mechanisms and the Monetary Approach to the Balance of Payments: A Doctrinal Perspective," in E. Claasen and P. Salin, eds., *Recent Issues in International Monetary Economics* (Amsterdam: North-Holland Publishing Co., 1976), pp. 29–48.
Friedman, Milton, "Should There Be an Independent Monetary Authority?" in Leland Yeager, *In Search of a Monetary Constitution* (Cambridge, MA: Harvard University Press, 1962), pp. 219–43.
——, "The Role of Monetary Policy," *American Economic Review*, LVIII (1968), 1–17.
——, "25 Years After the Rediscovery of Money: What Have We Learned?: Discussion," *American Economic Review*, LXV (May 1975), 176–79.

Furniss, Edgar, *The Position of Labor in a System of Nationalism* (Boston: Houghton Mifflin, 1920).

Gordon, Robert J., "Comments," in Jerome Stein, *Monetarism* (Amsterdam: North-Holland Publishing Co., 1976), pp. 52–66.

Hegeland, Hugo, *The Quantity Theory of Money* (Gotenborg, Sweden: Elanders Boktryckeri, 1951).

Hume, David, *Writings on Economics*, E. Rotwein, ed. (London: Nelson, 1955).

Humphrey, Don, "David Hume: Economist," Ph.D. thesis, University of California, Berkeley, 1932.

Johnson, E. A. J., *Predecessors of Adam Smith* (London: P. S. King and Son, 1937).

Keleher, Robert, "Of Money and Prices: Some Historical Perspectives," unpublished manuscript, 1978.

Keynes, John Maynard, *The General Theory of Employment, Interest and Money* (New York: Harcourt-Brace, 1936).

Laidler, David, "Mayer on Monetarism: Comments from a Britist Point of View," in Thomas Mayer *et al.*, *The Structure of Monetarism* (New York: W. W. Norton, 1978), pp. 133–144.

Leigh, Arthur, "John Locke and the Quantity Theory of Money," *History of Political Economy*, VI (1974), 200–19.

Lowe, J. M., "The Rate of Interest: British Monetary Opinion in the Eighteenth Century," *Manchester School*, XXII (May 1954), 115–38.

Mayer, Thomas, "The Structure of Monetarism," *Kredit und Kapital*, VIII (1975), 191–215, and 293–313; reprinted in T. Mayer *et al.*, *The Structure of Monetarism* (New York: W. W. Norton, 1978).

Modigliani, Franco, "The Monetarist Controversy, or Should We Forsake Stabilization Policies?" Federal Reserve Bank of San Francisco, *Economic Review, Supplement* (Spring 1977).

O'Brien, D. P., *The Classical Economists* (Oxford: Clarendon Press, 1975).

Parkin, Michael, "A 'Monetarist' Analysis of the Generation and Transmission of World Inflation: 1958–71," American Economic Association, *Papers and Proceedings*, LXVII (1977), 104–71.

Patinkin, Don, *Money, Interest and Prices* (New York: Harper and Row, 1965).

———, "Keynesian Monetary Theory and the Cambridge School," Banca Nazionale del Lavoro, *Quarterly Review* (June 1972), 138–58.

Schumpeter, Joseph, *A History of Economic Analysis* (New York: Oxford University Press, 1954).

Sekine, Thomas, "The Discovery of International Monetary Equilibrium by Vanderlint, Cantillion, Gervais and Hume," *Economia Internazionale*, XXVI (May 1973), 262–82.

Shaw, Edward, *Financial Deepening in Economic Development* (New York: Oxford University Press, 1973).

Stadlin, Alois, *Die Entwicklung der Quantitatstheorie* (Winterthur, Germany: P. G. Keller, 1954).

Taylor, W. L., *Francis Hutcheson and David Hume as Predecessors of Adam Smith* (Durham, NC: Duke University Press, 1965).

Vickers, Douglas, "Method and Analysis in David Hume's Economic Essays," *Economica*, XXIV (Aug. 1957), 225–34.

———, *Studies in the Theory of Money 1690–1776* (New York: Augustus Kelley, 1968).

Viner, Jacob, *Studies in the Theory of International Trade* (New York: Harper and Row, 1937).

von Hayek, Friedrich, *Prices and Production* (London: George Routledge and Sons, 1935).

———, "Choice in Currency," Institute of Economic Affairs, London, Occasional Paper #48, 1976.

Name Index

Agassi, J. 150
Akerman, G. 276, 277
Andrews, P. W. S. 315
Antonelli, G. B. 149
Arrow, K. J. 212, 218, 224
Auspitz, R. 149

Bailey 12
Bain, J. S. 312, 316
Baumol, W. J. 87–103
Becher, J. J. 14
Becker 88
Bergson, A. 192, 197
Bharadwaj, K. 19, 20, 159
Black, R. 146, 155
Blake, R. 375
Blaug, M. 145, 146, 150, 261, 329, 374, 375
Block, H. D. 212, 224
Bloom, G. F. 311
Bloor, D. 146, 147
Böhm-Bawerk, E. von 218, 258, 270
Boland, L. 156
Bos, H. 150
Boisguillebert 14
Boulding, K. 217
Bowley, M. 145
Brainard, W. 363, 364
Bratter, H. M. 221
Brems, H. 311
Brown, A. J. 350, 353
Brown, M. 282
Brunner, E. 315
Brunner, K. 375, 377
Bukharin, N. 146
Burdett, F. 112
Burns, A. R. 313
Bushaw, D. W. 223

Cagan, P. 350
Cannon, S. 149
Chamberlain, J. 171
Chamberlin, E. H. 305, 306, 307, 309, 310, 311, 312, 316
Chase 363
Checkland, S. 157

Chipman 64, 72, 73
Clark, J. B. 16, 270
Clarke, J. M. 317
Clower, R. 158, 223
Coase, R. H. 313
Coats, A. 146, 155
Collard, D. 256–67
Copeland, A. 16, 17, 205, 209
Crowe, M. 151

Debreu, G. 301
Dennis, K. 155
Dickinson, H. D. 296, 297, 328
Dobb, M. 126
Dornbusch, R. 377
Ducasse, C. 375
Due, J. F. 316
Duesenberry, J. 365
Dupuit, J. 156, 201–4, 205

Eatwell, 19, 30
Edgeworth, F. Y. 16, 148, 219, 220, 221, 224, 257, 258, 261
Edwards, J. R. 315
Ekelund, R. B. Jr 189–204

Farrell, M. J. 315
Feilbogen, S. 381
Fellner, W. J. 316, 373
Ferguson, C. E. 268–87
Fetter, F. 59, 60
Fisher, I. 149, 280, 350
Foxwell, H. S. 176
Friedman, M. 210, 349–69
Furniss, E. 377

Galbraith, J. K. 313, 317
Gardlund, T. 259
Garegnani, P. 19, 20, 21, 157
Georgescu-Reogen, N. 157
Goldberger, A. S. 365
Goodwin, C. 146, 155
Gordon, D. F. 3–13
Gramley 363
Gramm, W. P. 205–11
Grampp, W. D. 104–25

Grossman, H. 126, 300, 303

Hahn, F. H. 212, 224
Hall, R. L. 314, 315
Hankins, T. 151
Harcourt, G. C. 256
Harman, P. N. 149, 150, 151
Harris, S. 313
Harrod, R. F. 314
Hawtry, R. G. 328
Hayek, F. 328–48, 374
Hébert, R. F. 189–204
Heckscher, E. F. 14
Hegeland, H. 374, 375
Heidelberger 150
Henderson, J. M. 223
Hicks, J. R. 158, 214, 313, 315, 328
Hirschleifer, J. 301
Hitch, C. J. 314, 315
Hodgskin 7
Hollander, J. 72
Hollander, S. 19, 20, 31
Hooks, D. L. 268–87
Howey, R. S. 155
Hume, D. 15, 115, 116, 121, 122, 372–83
Humphrey, D. 374
Hurwicz, L. 212, 224
Huskisson, W. 116, 117, 118, 124
Hutchison, T. W. 164–88

Jaffé, W. 7, 213, 214, 215, 221, 231–53, 258
Jahnke, H. 150
Jevons, W. S. 16, 145, 146, 147, 153, 154, 166, 167, 168–73
Judge 224

Kahn, R. 150, 313
Kaldor, N. 212, 313, 328, 342, 343, 347
Kalecki, M. 313
Kauder, E. 146, 155
Keleher, R. 374
Keynes, J. M. 89, 359–60, 362, 367, 380
Klein, L. R. 364, 365
Kline, M. 151
Koopmans, T. C. 213, 301
Knight, F. 16, 17, 18, 149, 217, 218
Kuga, K. 224
Kuhn, T. 147, 157, 256, 314

Lange, O. 296, 297
Latsis, S. 156
Laundhardt, W. 149
Leigh, A. 374
Lerner, A. P. 296, 297, 302, 313, 316

Levine, D. 160
Lieben, R. 149
Lowe, A. 149, 374
Lucas, R. 156, 329

Madden, E. 375
Malinvaud, E. 302
Malthus, T. R. 12, 28, 29, 69, 110–11
Marshall, A. 67, 157, 159, 160, 173, 177–88, 205, 209, 210, 215, 216, 223, 261
Marx, K. 6, 129
Mayer, T. 372–84
McCulloch, J. R. 4, 5, 12, 59, 81, 82, 95, 108–9
MacNulty, P. J. 14–18, 225
Meade, J. E. 259, 300, 313
Meek, R. 24, 26
Meltzer, A. 375, 377
Menger, C. 154, 155
Meyerson, E. 150
Mill, James 4, 5, 6, 12, 59–86, 87–103
Mill, John S. 16, 59, 85, 86, 164, 165, 205, 209
Minard, J. 193–200
Mirowski, P. 145–63
Mises, L. von 291–303, 335, 336
Modigliani, F. 352, 357, 359, 373
Moskzkowska, N. 126
Moss, L. S. 328–48
Murrell, P. 291–304

Navier, H. 190–3
Negishi, T. 212, 223, 224, 225, 226
Nell, E. 256, 260
Nerlove, M. 366
Newman, P. K. 221, 223, 224, 226
Nichol, A. J. 311, 312
Nicholls, W. H. 313

O'Brien, P. 109, 305–27, 374, 377, 381
Okishio, N. 135
Ong, N-P. 38–58
Otte, N. 150

Pareto, V. 148, 153
Parijs, P. van 126–41
Pasinetti, L. L. 263
Patinkin, D. 220, 223, 224, 226, 313, 349–71, 373, 375
Peach, T. 19–37
Phillips, A. W. 366
Picard, A. P. 241
Place, F. 114, 115
Poinsot, L. 236
Popper, K. 146

Quandt, R. E. 223

Quirk, J. 223, 224, 226

Radner, R. 300, 301
Ricardo, 4, 5, 8, 9, 10, 12, 15, 19–37, 38–58, 59, 60, 66, 68–72, 75–80, 85, 88, 109–10, 116, 117, 121, 205
Riley, J. G. 201
Rist, C. 215
Robbins, Lord 67, 77, 83
Robinson, J. 126, 256, 268, 271, 280, 305, 307, 308, 309, 312–14, 316

Samuelson, P. 149, 154, 156, 212, 214, 291
Saposnik, R. 223, 226
Say, J. B. 75, 87–103
Schneider, E. 216
Schrödinger 151
Schumpeter, J. A. 14, 16, 374
Schwartz, A. 368
Scitovsky, T. 218, 313
Scott, I. O. 221
Sebba, G. 149
Sekine, T. 374, 375
Seligman, B. B. 301
Senior 113
Shackle, G. L. S. 158
Shaikh, A. 126, 135, 136
Shehab, F. 181
Sidgwick, H. 175, 176
Smith, A. 3, 6, 11, 12, 14–17, 44, 100, 111–12, 217
Smith, H. 316
Solow, R. 224, 256, 260, 280, 281
Sorokin, P. 158
Sowell, T. 88, 95, 97, 101
Spence, M. 62, 96
Spengler, J. J. 88, 97, 101
Sraffa, P. 19, 20, 21, 22, 23, 24, 30, 36, 38, 44, 52, 54, 67, 76, 159, 256
Stadlin, A. 374, 379
Stark, W. 146
Steuart, Sir J. 24
Stigler, G. J. 3, 4, 14, 16, 17, 18, 206, 217, 218, 262
Stiglitz, J. E. 303

Streissler, E. 155
Sweezy, P. M. 126

Takayama, T. 224
Taylor, F. M. 296
Taylor, R. M. 213
Taylor, W. L. 379
Theobald, D. W. 150
Thoben, H. 149
Thompson, G. L. 6
Thweatt, W. O. 59–88
Tobin, J. 359, 363, 364
Torrens, R. 59, 60, 63, 64, 66, 84, 85, 113–14
Toynbee, A. 173, 174
Tucker, G. S. L. 147
Turgot 15

Uzawa, H. 212, 224, 226

Vaughn, K. I. 328–48
Vickers, D. 377
Vinr, J. 60, 61
Volterra, V. 149

Walker, D. A. 212–30, 231–55
Walras, L. 147, 148, 153, 154, 155, 213, 214, 215, 226, 231–55, 256–65
Weintraub, E. R. 156
Weisskopf, N. 149
Wicksell, K. 213, 258, 264, 268–82
Wicksteed, P. H. 215, 216, 262
Wiles, P. 315
Williamson, O. E. 300
Wilson, T. 242
Winch, D. 101
Wong, S. 156
Woodfall, W. 112

Young, A. 107

Zeuthen, F. 317